Contents

PREFACE *xv*

1 INTRODUCTION   **1**

    1.1   Basic Concepts   1

    1.2   Structured Layers of a Computer System   4

          1.2.1   Hardware Layer, 5
          1.2.2   Software Layer, 13
          1.2.3   User Layer, 19

    1.3   Programming Design Techniques   20

          1.3.1   Top-down Programming, 21
          1.3.2   Bottom-up Programming, 24
          1.3.3   Middle-out Programming, 24

    1.4   Exercises   24

2 FOUNDATIONS   **26**

    2.1   Number Systems   26

          2.1.1   Unsigned Integer Representation, 27
          2.1.2   Conversion from One Base to Another, 29
          2.1.3   Unsigned Integer Arithmetic, 33
          2.1.4   Signed Integer Representation, 40
          2.1.5   Two's Complement Representation, 45

2.2   Boolean Logic   48

    2.2.1   *Basics, 48*
    2.2.2   *Boolean Algebra, 49*
    2.2.3   *Boolean Functions and Circuits, 57*
    2.2.4   *Truth Tables, 58*
    2.2.5   *Boolean Representations and Operator Precedence, 60*
    2.2.6   *Normal Forms for Expressions and Minimization, 62*
    2.2.7   *Karnaugh Maps, 65*
    2.2.8   *Summary of Boolean Logic, 73*

2.3   Gates—Implementation   74

    2.3.1   *Circuit Characteristics, 75*
    2.3.2   *Bipolar Technology, 76*
    2.3.3   *Unipolar Technology, 80*
    2.3.4   *Gallium Arsenide Technology, 83*
    2.3.5   *Integrated Circuits and IC Packaging, 83*

2.4   Logic Circuits—Implementation   86

    2.4.1   *Clocks and Timing Cycles, 86*
    2.4.2   *Combinational Circuits, 89*
    2.4.3   *Sequential Circuits, 93*

2.5   Exercises   102

3   PRINCIPAL COMPONENTS OF A COMPUTER SYSTEM   *106*

    3.1   Main Memory Organization   106

        3.1.1   *Unit of Storage, 106*
        3.1.2   *Smallest Addressable Unit, 106*
        3.1.3   *Memory Capacity, 108*
        3.1.4   *Address Space and Bus, 108*
        3.1.5   *Data Bus, 108*
        3.1.6   *Words, 109*
        3.1.7   *Longwords, 111*
        3.1.8   *Alignment, 111*
        3.1.9   *Character Representation, 112*
        3.1.10   *Memory Types, 115*

    3.2   CPU   115

        3.2.1   *General-register Architecture, 115*
        3.2.2   *Accumulator Architecture, 121*

    3.3   Secondary Storage   122

        3.3.1   *Sequential Access Storage Devices, 123*
       3.3.2   *Direct-access Storage Devices, 126*

3.4   I/O Device Interaction   130
        3.4.1   Device Controllers, 130
        3.4.2   Device Drivers, 133

3.5   Computer Communications   133

        3.5.1   Networks, 134
        3.5.2   Multiprocessing, 135

3.6   Exercises   138

4   SIM68 COMPUTER   **140**

4.1   Main Memory Organization   140

        4.1.1   Data Information, 140

4.2   CPU   141

        4.2.1   Data Registers, 141
        4.2.2   Address Registers, 142
        4.2.3   Program Counter Register, 142
        4.2.4   Status Register, 142

4.3   SIM68 Machine Language   143

        4.3.1   Operand Addressing, 143
        4.3.2   Instructions, 145
        4.3.3   Instruction Set Summary, 170
        *4.3.4   Coding and Executing SIM68 Machine Language
                 Programs, 170*

4.4   SIM68 Assembly Language   180

        4.4.1   Basic Concepts of an Assembler, 180
        4.4.2   Source Module, 180
        4.4.3   ASM68 Instructions, 186
        4.4.4   ASM68 Directives, 188
        4.4.5   Example, 192

4.5   Exercises   193

5   SYSTEM COMPONENT IMPLEMENTATION   **199**

5.1   Building Blocks   199

        5.1.1   Encoders and Decoders, 199
        5.1.2   Multiplexers and Demultiplexers, 202
        5.1.3   Tristate Buffers, 205

5.2   Main Memory   206

        5.2.1   Static RAM, 208
        5.2.2   Dynamic RAM, 208

5.3   General-Purpose Computation Unit   210

    5.3.1   ALU, 211
    5.3.2   ALU Status Lines, 217
    5.3.3   Shift/Rotate Unit, 220
    5.3.4   CPU Control Design, 220

5.4   Additional Architecture Terminology   238

    5.4.1   Von Neumann Architecture, 238
    5.4.2   Harvard Architecture, 238
    5.4.3   Functional Unit, 238
    5.4.4   Pipelining, 238
    5.4.5   Cache, 239

5.5   General CPU Designs   239

    5.5.1   Single-register Designs, 240
    5.5.2   Multiple-register Designs, 241
    5.5.3   General-purpose Register Designs, 242

5.6   SIM68 CPU Detail Design   245

    5.6.1   Timing and Sequencing, 247
    5.6.2   CPU Design, 249
    5.6.3   Microprogrammed Implementation, 277

5.7   Illustrative Architectures   286

    5.7.1   MC68000—16/32-Bit Architecture, 286
    5.7.2   MC68020 and MC68030 Modern CISC Architectures, 286
    5.7.3   MC68040—CISC Architecture, RISC Engine, 287
    5.7.4   MC88100—Modern RISC Architecture, 287

5.8   Exercises   290

6   ADDRESSING SCHEMES AND THE MC68000   **292**

6.1   Addressing Modes   292

    6.1.1   Immediate Addressing Schemes, 293
    6.1.2   Register Addressing Schemes, 294
    6.1.3   Memory Addressing Schemes, 295
    6.1.4   Use of Addressing Modes, 301
    6.1.5   Why So Many Modes?, 302

6.2   MC68000 Computer   303

6.3   Main Memory Organization   304

    6.3.1   Data Information, 304

6.4   CPU   304

    6.4.1   Data Registers, 304
    6.4.2   Address Registers, 304

        6.4.3   Program Counter Register, 305
        6.4.4   Status Register, 305

  6.5   MC68000 Machine Language   308

        6.5.1   Instructions, 308
        6.5.2   MC68000 Addressing Modes, 308
        6.5.3   Coding of Machine Language Instructions, 310

  6.6   MC68020/030/040 Addressing Modes   314

  6.7   RISC Addressing Modes   316

  6.8   Exercises   317

7   ASSEMBLY LANGUAGE FOR THE MC68000   319

  7.1   Basic Concepts   319

        7.1.1   Symbols, 320
        7.1.2   Opcodes, 320
        7.1.3   Operands, 321
        7.1.4   Register Notation, 324
        7.1.5   Mode Specification and Operand Notation, 325

  7.2   Categories of Addressing Modes   333

  7.3   Directives and Constants   335

        7.3.1   Run-time Constants, 335
        7.3.2   Assembly-time Constants, 336
        7.3.3   ORG and END Directives, 337
        7.3.4   INCLUDE Directive, 338
        7.3.5   LIST and NOLIST Directives, 338
        7.3.6   CNOP Directive, 338

  7.4   Position-dependent versus Position-independent Code   339

  7.5   Instructions   342

        7.5.1   Binary Integer Arithmetic, 343
        7.5.2   Moving of Data, 367
        7.5.3   Branching and Looping, 382
        7.5.4   Logical and Bit Operations, 387
        7.5.5   Decimal Arithmetic, 415
        7.5.6   Real Number Arithmetic, 420

  7.6   Exercises   432

8   SUBROUTINES AND MACROS   437

  8.1   Subroutines   437

        8.1.1   What Is a Stack?, 440
        8.1.2   Calling Subroutines, 441

8.1.3   *Returning from Subroutines, 443*
8.1.4   *Passing Parameters, 446*
8.1.5   *Recursive Routines, 449*
8.1.6   *Subroutines in a High-level Language Environment, 454*

8.2   Modules, and Internal and External Subroutines   461

8.2.1   *Internal Subroutines, 461*
8.2.2   *External Subroutines, 461*
8.2.3   *Standard Parameter Convention, 468*

8.3   Subroutine Libraries   468

8.3.1   *Static versus Dynamically Linked Libraries, 469*

8.4   Macros   470

8.5   Conditional Assembly   477

8.6   Exercises   481

9   EXCEPTIONS   *483*

9.1   Internal Exceptions   489

9.1.1   *Trace Exception, 489*
9.1.2   *Divide by Zero Exception, 489*
9.1.3   *Privileged Instruction Exception, 491*
9.1.4   *Unimplemented and Illegal Instruction Exceptions, 491*
9.1.5   *Trap Exceptions, 495*
9.1.6   *Check Instruction, 496*
9.1.7   *Address Error, 497*

9.2   External Exceptions   497

9.2.1   *Reset, 497*
9.2.2   *Interrupts, 498*
9.2.3   *Bus Error, 501*

9.3   Nested Exceptions   504

9.4   Exception Processing in the MC68010/20/30   505

9.4.1   *MC68010, 505*
9.4.2   *MC68020, 505*
9.4.3   *MC68030, 506*

9.5   Exercises   506

10   COMMUNICATING WITH THE OUTSIDE WORLD   *508*

10.1   I/O Modules   509

10.1.1   *Internal Interface, 510*
10.1.2   *External Interface, 510*
10.1.3   *Programmers Interface, 512*

10.2   Methods of I/O   515

    10.2.1   Programmed I/O, 515
    10.2.2   Interrupt-driven I/O, 515
    10.2.3   Direct Memory Access (DMA), 518

10.3   Memory Hierarchy   523

    10.3.1   Caches, 523
    10.3.2   Virtual Memory, 525

10.4   Multiprocessor Systems   532

    10.4.1   Design Considerations, 532
    10.4.2   TAS Instruction, 533

10.5   ECB   533

    10.5.1   Principal Components of the ACIA, 534
    10.5.2   I/O Programming the ACIA, 540
    10.5.3   Principal Components of PI/T, 546
    10.5.4   Timer, 556

10.6   Exercises   566

11   *Computer Networking*   *567*

11.1   Historical Perspective on Computing   567

11.2   Advantages and Disadvantages of Computer Networks   572

11.3   Network Terminology and Configurations   574

11.4   ISO/OSI Reference Model   579

    11.4.1   ISO/OSI Model Introduction, 579
    11.4.2   Layer 1—Physical Layer, 582
    11.4.3   Layer 2—Data Link Layer, 584
    11.4.4   Layer 3—Network Layer, 588
    11.4.5   Layer 4—Transport Layer, 591
    11.4.6   Layer 5—Session Layer, 592
    11.4.7   Layer 6—Presentation Layer, 593
    11.4.8   Layer 7—Application Layer, 601

11.5   Design Considerations   604

    11.5.1   Subnet Design, 604
    11.5.2   LAN Design, 607

11.6   Example Network Protocols—Internet   608

    11.6.1   LAN Standards, 608
    11.6.2   MAN Standards, 611
    11.6.3   TCP/IP Internetworking, 612
    *11.6.4   Sample Applications: Telnet, FTP, SMTP,
           and NNTP, 620*

11.7   ISDN and WAN   631

      11.7.1   ISDN Services, 632
      11.7.2   Channel Access and Reference Points, 633
      11.7.3   Numbers and Addressing, 635
      11.7.4   Standards and ISDN, 635
      11.7.5   Summary, 636

11.8   Networking Summary   637

11.9   Exercises   638

APPENDIX A   SOFTWARE FOR THE TEXT   640

APPENDIX B   SIM68 AND ASM68. THE MC68000
SUBSET SIMULATOR AND ASSEMBLER   641

    B.1   Load Files from Textual Machine Language Files   641

    B.2   Load Files from ASM68, the SIM68 Assembler   643

    B.3   Loading Your Load File Into Simulator   644

    B.4   Using SIM68   644

      B.4.1   Setting the Program Counter, 644
      B.4.2   Running Your Program, 644
      B.4.3   Trace, 644
      B.4.4   Register Modify, 645
      B.4.5   Viewing the Effects of Your Program, 645
      B.4.6   Help and Exit, 646

APPENDIX C   SIM68K AND XSIM68K:
THE MC68000 SIMULATORS   647

    C.1   The SIM68K Environment   647

      C.1.1   Viewing Commands, 648
      C.1.2   Modify Commands, 649
      C.1.3   Register Modify, 649
      C.1.4   Block Fill, 650
      C.1.5   Program Control, 650
      C.1.6   Load/Store, 652
      C.1.7   EXIT, 652

    C.2   Using SIM68K   653

    C.3   TRAP #14 I/O Functions   653

    C.4   XSIM68K   654

    C.5   Explanation of Terms Used   657

APPENDIX D ASM68K. THE MC68000 ASSEMBLER   658

D.1   Invoking Assembler   658

D.2   Fields   659

    D.2.1   Comments, 659
    D.2.2   Label Field, 659
    D.2.3   Opcode Field, 660
    D.2.4   Operand Field, 660
    D.2.5   Comment Field, 662

D.3   Directives   663

    D.3.1   Assembly Control Directives, 663
    D.3.2   Symbol Definition Directives, 663
    D.3.3   Data Definition Directives, 664
    D.3.4   Listing Control Directives, 664
    D.3.5   Conditional Assembly Directives, 664
    D.3.6   Macro Directives, 665
    D.3.7   General Directives, 667

D.4   Relocatable Assembler   667

    D.4.1   Additional Directives, 667
    D.4.2   Linker, 668

APPENDIX E ASCII CODES   670

APPENDIX F SAMPLE ROUTINES   672

F.1   Introduction and Assembler Equates   672

    F.1.1   Read a Character, 672
    F.1.2   Read a String, 672
    F.1.3   Wait on Space Bar, 673
    F.1.4   Write a Character, 674
    F.1.5   Write End-of-Line Character, 674
    F.1.6   Write a String, 674
    F.1.7   Clear Screen, 675
    F.1.8   Skip to End-of-Line, 675
    F.1.9   Convert to Lower Case, 675
    F.1.10   Convert to Upper Case, 676
    F.1.11   Convert Ascii Hex to Integer, 677
    F.1.12   Convert Integer to Ascii Hex, 678
    F.1.13   Convert Integer to Ascii Binary, 679
    F.1.14   Convert Integer to Ascii Decimal, 679
    F.1.15   Convert Binary to Text, 681

F.1.16 Convert Decimal to Integer, 681
F.1.17 Convert Integer to Decimal, 683
F.1.18 Memory Allocate, 684
F.1.19 Print Elements in a Linked List, 685

INDEX   **689**

Preface

BASIC RATIONALE

In the past, the subjects of **computer organization** and **assembly language programming** have been taught as separate entities. This decision has been justified based on the observation that the computer science discipline *itself* has evolved rapidly from hardware and beyond. Thus, it was natural that during the 1970s and early 1980s computer scientists were expected to be thoroughly familiar with the internal organization of a computer and be proficient assembly language programmers. As computer science continues to grow, a wealth of new material has appeared in high-level software developments. Current trends in this arena may be found in window management software, computer aided software engineering tools, and networked applications. This abundance of new material clearly places pressure on the computer science curriculum with the result that the lower levels are squeezed. Often this results in material at the lower levels being dropped from the curriculum. This is quite appropriate, to a point. We believe, however, that some introduction to both the areas of computer organization and assembly language programming are *essential* to all computer science students. Computer organization enables computer scientists to talk intelligently about computers with engineers and appreciate the limitations imposed by conventional computers; likewise, assembly language programming is necessary for computer scientists to visualize the relationship between higher-level programming and the computer.

With these observations in mind, we have composed a single text that provides a thorough, yet brief, introduction to both computer organization *and* assembly language programming. In doing this, our goal was to effectively reduce two separate courses into one. We have attempted to harmonize the two topics by using a particular architecture, the MC68000, as a model for the hardware aspects of the text as well as the programming component. We note at the outset that to provide a hardware realization of the MC68000 is quite beyond the scope of this introductory text. Instead, a subset referred to as SIM68 is used to demonstrate how a computer might be designed using register-level components, and this subset is also used to introduce MC68000 assembly language programming. Although this coupling is not perfect, it does provide students with the necessary insight that we seek. In achieving this goal, the task of teaching a combined course can become difficult; these issues are addressed in later paragraphs. In writing this *introductory* textbook we have attempted to address the following issues:

1. *Suitability for classroom use and self-instruction.* An introductory text in any subject is primarily intended for novices; therefore, it must be their first, not last, book on the subject. As a first book, it must present the topics in a complete and "detailed" fashion; issues that may seem "trivial" to the experts are not so to novices. This obviously should *not* be accomplished at the expense of an accurate and thorough treatment of the subject.

With such an approach the book becomes lengthy, but the responsibility of the instructor is to *navigate* the student through the book; therefore, he or she may cover what seems appropriate. In addition, computer science is no longer a bag of tricks; it has evolved into a highly technological *science*. Therefore, instruction should not terminate with the end of class. We hope that this text will help the student clarify and understand the answers to the "trivial" issues that may not be presented during classroom time.

2. *Study of computer organization.* The principal difficulty associated with many textbooks using the title *Computer Organization* is that they are not targeted at an introductory level. There are many texts suitable for students with a broad knowledge of the area. These texts implicitly assume that students are familiar with arithmetic in different bases, the concepts of bytes, bits and word alignment, and the principal components of a computer. Often, however, this is not the case. Typically students at an early stage have had only high-level programming experience, or less! It is to these students that this course is directed. Another problem with current computer organization texts is that although machine code and assembly language programming are introduced, it is in a highly artificial context. Texts frequently assume that the material will be covered elsewhere (i.e., in an assembly language programming course) and cover the concepts far too quickly for students without experience to grasp.

This book discusses computer organization at several levels thereby permitting different issues to be offered to different people. In particular, note the following topics that are presented:

a. *Gate level.* For students that have had previous exposure to introductory engineering the text discusses several transistor technologies used today. The purpose is to demonstrate that the mechanism underlying modern computers may be traced from the most abstract level down to the materials level. There was some deliberation whether the text should include an introduction to VLSI techniques; however, even though this material is quite interesting, it will add no essential detail to concepts already presented.

b. *Register level.* Although the gate level is provided, it is expected that in general the starting point for this course from the computer organization text perspective will be at the register level. In this text, as with several others, we introduce the building blocks of the computer. We have organized the material so that students with no experience in this arena should be able to follow the presentation without difficulty. We have included sufficient material for students to design new register level components using those provided as building blocks.

c. *System level.* It is at the system level that we have merged the components of computer organization and assembly programming. As we shall see shortly, SIM68 is introduced as an abstract model for assembly programming. However, in the sections where computer organization is discussed, we show how portions of such an abstract computer could be realized using *only* the components discussed in earlier sections. We use SIM68 as an example to design a simple central processing unit (CPU). During this phase, we further introduce the notion of clocked sequential control and microprogramming. Because students will already be familiar with SIM68, there is a greater appreciation of the material covered.

d. *Network level.* We have extended the computer organization into networked computers with a discussion of the devices used to connect computers and some broader issues of networking in general. We have used the ISO/OSI model to explain the difficulties that must be overcome when networking computers; we have also provided an example network application using Internet. We consider this to be the highest level of computer organization.

3. *Study of assembly language programming.* A similar criticism may be leveled at most texts on assembly language programming as was discussed for computer organization. That is, they assume a greater breath of knowledge than the students possess. Specifically texts will frequently discuss device control and interrupts in later chapters without describing the relationship between these components and the rest of the system (i.e., they assume a computer organization course). There was also an emphasis during the 1980s on explaining how high-level programs are supported at the assembly language level using frames, modules, and so on. Although this is useful to some degree, the current trend toward simpler instruction sets (i.e., the RISC architectures) suggests that such support is unnecessary at the processor level. With these comments in mind, we note the following topics covered in assembly language programming:

a. *Computer system basics.* The material presented early in the text is common to both computer organization and assembly programming. In these sections we have attempted to explain how to manipulate numbers in different bases; an overview of a computer system, how data, code, and instructions are represented in a computer, and notions such as a **byte** of storage and **word alignment** are some of the subjects presented. The material is expressly written to be easily understood by novices.

b. *Simple programmers model—SIM68.* Assembly language programming is introduced using a simple subset of the Motorola MC68000 instruction set known as SIM68. The programmer's model contains sufficient detail to permit students to write programs using the SIM68, which may be demonstrated using the SIM68 simulator freely available from the authors. Through use of SIM68, many of the concepts associated with both machine code organization and assembly language programming may be discussed without the complexities inherent in the full MC68000 model. In addition to the programming aspect of SIM68, the computer architecture sections use the same instruction set to demonstrate how, using components already defined, SIM68 could be realized in hardware. This coupling provides additional interest for both computer organization and assembly language programming.

c. *Programming on the MC68000.* Once SIM68 has been introduced, it becomes an easy transition to move to the MC68000. Students have already had exposure to different addressing modes and instruction types via SIM68. The MC68000 is simply an extension of these concepts (albeit a large extension). Later in the text we also introduce the notion of subroutines, the frame concept, and exception processing. The latter issue clearly ties into computer organization.

d. *Controlling devices.* An excellent demonstration of reasons why we have coupled computer organization and assembly language programming may be observed in the sections on device control. We present these devices from the programmers perspective; however, the diagrams of the devices and a notion of how they could be implemented will be carried by the students from the organization section.

This book is the outgrowth of four years of class notes and lectures, and has been designed primarily for a course in computer science to address the more elementary issues in *computer architecture* as described by Peter Denning et al. in "Computing as a Discipline," *Communications of the ACM,* vol. 32, no. 1, January 1989, pp. 9–23. The text does not break new ground; it does, however, permit the entire lower-level material in architecture and assembler programming to be taught from a single text, in either one or two semesters depending on the material covered.

ORGANIZATION OF THIS BOOK

Chapter 1 serves as an introduction to the topics that are covered in the later chapters of the book. First we identify, by means of examples, the issues involved in computer organization. We then proceed to present the basic foundation of computer system material as the three "onions" that correspond to the **hardware, software,** and **user** views. It is the combination of these views around which the remaining text is based.

Chapter 2 contains the "foundations" for the remaining chapters and includes the following sections:

1. *Number systems.* A thorough discussion is given, including addition, subtraction, multiplication, and division in different bases and one's complement, two's complement, and sign-magnitude representations.

2. *Boolean logic.* This section includes boolean algebra, operator representations, normal forms, and expression simplification using Karnaugh maps.

3. *Gate implementation.* This provides information regarding how gates are implemented in different technologies and includes the characteristics of different technologies and packing methods.

4. *Clocks and timing issues.* This introduces the notion of a clock and why one is necessary.

5. *Combinational and sequential circuits.* This section includes all the components used later in the hardware design of SIM68.

The material covered in Chapter 2 will be determined by the student's previous exposure. In the interest of completeness, however, we have included everything that we think is necessary to teach the remaining material.

Chapter 3 discusses the principal components of a computer system. It is written so that it may be taught without reference to the hardware considerations discussed in Chapter 2.

Chapter 4 describes the programmer's view of SIM68 and introduces the student to machine language programming and assembly language programming using a very simple instruction set. This material, along with the fundamentals, provides the necessary motivation for the next chapter.

Chapter 5 describes the register-level building blocks used in computers including registers, encoders, decoders, multiplexers, memory, and arithmetic and logic units. The chapter then proceeds to demonstrate how SIM68 might be constructed from these components while introducing the student to register description languages, clocked sequence logic, and microprogramming. The chapter concludes with a discussion of the MC68000, MC68010, MC68020, MC68030, MC68040, and MC88100 (RISC) processors and is intended to be used for supplemental (or "advanced") reading.

Chapter 6 introduces addressing modes as a general issue and then introduces the MC68000 from the programmer's perspective. We have attempted to first explain addressing modes without specific mention of MC68000. It is hoped that this "preview" of addressing and a discussion of why addressing modes are useful will allow an easier grasp of the plethora of addressing modes provided by the MC68000. After discussing the MC68000 we conclude the chapter by examining the more advanced addressing modes as found in the MC68020, MC68030, MC68040, and RISC architectures. This material is intended as an "advanced" section. Again this chapter is written so that architecture is not a required component.

Chapters 7 to 9 contain a full treatment of the various instructions, modes, and operand sizes of the MC68000. Chapter 7 presents the majority of the instructions and is most detailed. The chapter introduces instructions as follows: binary integer arithmetic, moving data around, branching and looping, logical and bit operations, and decimal arithmetic. In Chapter 8 we extensively discuss subroutines, the frame concept for high-level programming support, introduce the concepts of static and dynamic libraries, and explain macroprocessing. Chapter 9 discusses exception processing including internal and external interrupts. These chapters contain the bulk of the assembly language component of the text. As with earlier chapters, we also include some "advanced" topics related to the MC68020, MC68030, MC68040, and RISC processors as appropriate.

Chapter 10 contains device control and memory management. We provide a detailed explanation of a simple serial port controller, a parallel port controller, and a timer. These explanations include code examples. Also discussed are component-level diagrams of more complex DMA devices including disk-drive and Ethernet controllers. Through these demonstrations and discussions, we hope that the student will at least be able to understand the concepts of device drivers and device control, which they might encounter in later courses (e.g., operating systems). The section on virtual memory, although not really an external "device" is included as an "advanced" topic.

Chapter 11 contains an introduction to computer networks. The authors view this area, in particular, as an extension of single-system computer organizations. Included in this chapter is a brief history of computers and how networks fit into this history; a simple taxonomy for networks; an introduction to the ISO/OSI model; an example using the Internet; and how computer networks are reaching into the domestic environment via ISDN.

It should be clear from the previous paragraphs that this text provides both an introduction to computer organization and to assembly language programming. By appropriate use of this text, an instructor may cover either one, the other, or both of these components depending on curriculum requirements and how familiar this material is to the student. We believe that this (re)integration of these subjects will satisfy CIS requirements without taking the time that completely separate courses would require.

USING THIS BOOK AS A TEXTBOOK

This book has been used for the last four years as the main text in a three-credit semester course, Introduction to Computer Organization, at the Department of Computer and Information Sciences at the University of Florida. The students enrolled in this class are both graduate and undergraduate students in Engineering, Liberal Arts and Sciences, as well as Business students. The course is meant for those who have acquired respectable programming skills, knowledge of at least one modern high-level language (preferably Pascal or C). Exposure to courses such as Data Structures and Operating Systems would help to a certain degree, but, they are not prerequisites.

It is our experience that it is very difficult for an instructor to cover the entire book in class. Instead, we prefer to present the most important topics in class and assign other parts of the book as background reading. Certain sections can be omitted altogether. The issue of what may be considered an important topic depends both on the background of the students and what the instructor thinks is important. In our case we rapidly cover the material in Chapters 1 and 2 with the exception of some boolean algebra, gates, and minimization. We then cover Chapters 3 and 4 completely. At this point there is plenty of additional material that may be assigned if required. Also, the students are now in a position to begin writing programs using SIM68. We always assign one machine code program. After Chapter 4 we cover Chapters 6 to 8. This block represents the MC68000 component and allows us to assign successively more complex programs. We then cover Chapter 5, which overlaps with their assignments. Finally we discuss the computer connected to the outside world with Chapters 9 to 11. Again Chapters 9 and 10 allow us to assign simple device control exercises, and Chapter 11 is covered in class.

Because we believe that the students learn programming by writing assembly programs, we give three to four programming assignments during the semester. Each of these assignments deals with some aspect related to the course. The early assignments are directed toward table manipulation and simple arithmetic operations; the later assignments are "real projects" such as writing portions of a SIM68 assembler in MC68000 code. This provides the students with a link between the hardware (computer organization) and the software (assembly language programming). We make use of Motorola's single-board computers in a lab; however, we have a complete portable software environment (described in Appendix F) that allows students to write, assemble, and "run" (via simulation) MC68000 programs on many platforms including the IBM PC, the Unix environment, and the Amiga. This environment is available at no cost from the authors.

ACKNOWLEDGMENTS

Many people have been helpful and supportive during the period we have been writing this text. First, we would like to thank the following for their technical assistance: Andy Wilcox, for keeping things running smoothly(!); Steve Croll, for his assistance in writing the MC68000 assembler and several program segments; Wayne Wolfe, for developing the MC68000 simulator; Laura Allen, for including a disassembler and breakpoint support into the simulator; Tom Hain, for his work on the SIM68 hardware design; Debra Livadas and Joseph Vice for their excellent preliminary editing; and the many other consultants for their input. We would next like to thank our wives Debra and Kathleen who have given support and understanding throughout, have made many useful suggestions, and have stimulated extensive discussions about topics throughout the text. We would also like to thank the following reviewers for their thoughtful comments: James F. Peters III, University of Arkansas; Ron McCarty, Behrend College; Charles T. Zahn, Pace University; and John McCabe, Manhattan College. Finally, we would like to thank our many students (who used the first, as well as subsequent, drafts of this text) for their help in identifying areas of the book that needed more clarification and for their support.

1

Introduction

Consider for a moment the possibility that your senses are restricted to reading and writing numbers. Assume also that you have a perfect memory (for numbers, after all what else is there?). Finally imagine that you possess the rudiments of mathematics (to add, subtract, multiply, and divide). Your entire life is dictated by a sequence of instructions that reside in your memory and by the numbers that you receive from the outside. Your one saving grace within this closed world is that you're fast, very fast by human standards. This is the world of computers. This environment may seem somewhat claustrophobic; however, as we shall see in subsequent chapters within this simple model there is a richness undreamt of.

In this text we cover this world in some depth, starting with the building blocks of computers: working with numbers; storing them in memory; and manipulating them using instructions. We examine in detail both an idealized model of a computer, in which efficiency and aesthetics coexist unencumbered, and a practical microcomputer, the MC68000, which although far from perfect, is cheap, readily available, and in common use everywhere. This book is intended to provide the details of typical computer organizations, the concepts of microcomputer language programming, and a practically oriented introduction to the MC68000 microcomputer.

1.1 BASIC CONCEPTS

Our goal in this section is to present some basic concepts and terminology related to computer systems.

There are many reasons why one would choose to use a computer system. One major reason is the ability to solve problems whose range varies from the trivial, such as adding two numbers, to the extremely complicated, such as computing the travel path of the space shuttle. Almost everyone is aware that in loose terms a computer is a collection of complex electronic components connected together by wires; for the present we will simply call this physical arrangement the **hardware**. In general this hardware remains idle *unless* it is instructed by a human being to perform a task or set of tasks. As a trivial example consider that you just purchased an ordinary calculator; the calculator remains idle unless you take some action. Given that we have a problem that we wish solved, the question becomes how do we use our calculator (hardware) to achieve a solution? For example, suppose we have the problem that we wish to know the result of adding the number 235 to the number 192. How should we proceed?

The solution seems obvious. Enter the number 235, press the "+" button, enter the number 192, press the "=" and there's the answer. Easy! Although this sounds perfect, it is actually flawed, and considering it in detail provides us with an insight into the broader task of programming computers. The first step in solving our problem is to define an **algorithm** to solve the problem. An algorithm[1] is defined as an ordered sequence of steps that terminates in a finite time, with each step satisfying the following properties:

1. Each step runs only for a finite time. By this we mean that none of the steps are questions that might never be answered (e.g., "find the largest prime number").
2. Each step is computable. By this we mean that steps must have well defined answers (nothing about the nature of the universe).
3. Each step is nonparadoxical. We do not allow steps that would cause paradoxes in the algorithm.[2]

Notice that if one or more of the steps is not guaranteed to terminate, we call the sequence an **effective procedure**. These may also be useful but will not be considered in this text.

Algorithms may be applied to anything, not just numbers. The recipe in a cookbook is an algorithm to produce tasty food; the instruction manual to fix a car contains algorithms for repairing different automotive failures. In fact we use algorithms all the time without consciously thinking about them. Notice that the steps are intended for a person; in the case that the instructions (or algorithm) were intended to be performed by a computer, we would call the sequence a **computer program** (or program for short). Another point to notice is that algorithms may involve decision making (i.e., following one of several different paths) provided that none of the preceding conditions are violated. We now formalize our original plans into a clear concise algorithm that is presented in Table 1.1.

TABLE 1.1

```
[1].  Depress the key labeled by a "2" on the keyboard;
[2].  Depress the key labeled by a "3" on the keyboard;
[3].  Depress the key labeled by a "5" on the keyboard;
[4].  Depress the key labeled by a "+" on the keyboard;
[5].  Depress the key labeled by a "1" on the keyboard;
[6].  Depress the key labeled by a "9" on the keyboard;
[7].  Depress the key labeled by a "2" on the keyboard;
[8].  Depress the key labeled by a "=" on the keyboard;
```

Notice that we have defined our algorithm in a stylized form of English. The language that we use is known as a **pseudocode**. There are many different pseudocodes we could have chosen. The advantage with the preceding one is that given the appropriate calculator and the previous instructions, any one could **execute** the algorithm and obtain the

---

[1] Programming techniques to develop algorithms are discussed in the last section of this chapter.

[2] For example, statements of the form "this statement is false" is a paradox. If the statement is true, then it tells us it is false; conversely, if the statement is false, we can infer from it that it is true.

correct solution. Notice that the *order* in which the steps must be executed is of crucial importance; for example, exchanging steps 2 and 4 would lead to an erroneous result.

Although this has clarified the process, there is still an error in the algorithm. Suppose the calculator was not turned on! Pressing the buttons would have achieved nothing; thus, we say the algorithm was not *robust*. One could argue that it was implied that the calculator was initially "on";[3] *however*, the fact is that when the user executes an algorithm he or she should never be concerned with "implications" of an algorithm or even the "intent" of the person who defined the algorithm. This is particularly true if the set of instructions is a program and is to be executed by the computer. Computers execute exactly the set of instructions that is presented; nothing is ever assumed or can be implied. Given this a robust algorithm is given in Table 1.2.

TABLE 1.2

```
[ 1].  Turn the calculator on;
[ 2].  Depress the key labeled by a "2" on the keyboard;
[ 3].  Depress the key labeled by a "3" on the keyboard;
[ 4].  Depress the key labeled by a "5" on the keyboard;
[ 5].  Depress the key labeled by a "+" on the keyboard;
[ 6].  Depress the key labeled by a "1" on the keyboard;
[ 7].  Depress the key labeled by a "9" on the keyboard;
[ 8].  Depress the key labeled by a "2" on the keyboard;
[ 9].  Depress the key labeled by a "=" on the keyboard;
[10].  Switch the calculator off;
```

Although the pseudocode is ideal for people it makes no sense to the calculator. The language of the calculator is defined by those keys on its keypad ([on],[off],0,1,2,3,4,5,6,7,8,9,+,-,*, and %). As far as the calculator is concerned the program is

```
[on] 2 3 5 + 1 9 2 = [off]
```

We call the instructions that are recognized by the machine (in this case the calculator) the **machine language instructions** (or **machine code**), and a program written in them a **machine language program**. Notice also that the machine code is very different from that which is easily understandable by the user. When we examine computers in more detail in the following sections we will see that machine-level programs are even more complex than the preceding ones; thus, the translation between pseudocode and machine level language is a multistaged affair. Clearly it is very important that during the different translations from user pseudocode to a machine language program, the original intention of the user is the one solved by the computer. Although this may seem obvious, it is often not the case!

Summarizing the previous discussion, we can formally say that a **computer program** is a plan (algorithm) that may be understood by a computer, which specifies a sequence of actions to be taken and the order in which they should take place.

---

[3] This would amount to a **precondition**, that is, a condition that must be satisfied before our actions. We also have the notion of a **postcondition**, that is, a condition that *must* be true after our actions.

Returning to our previous example we can see that our program consists of just one operation or instruction, the addition of two integers. In mathematical language the operation is denoted by the operator "+," which appears "in between" the operands (i.e., $235+192$) and is referred to as the **infix** notation. Computers almost universally require **prefix** notation whereby the operator, referred to as the **opcode**, precedes the operands. Actually, the hardware on examination of the opcode decides the number of operands required for execution of the instruction. As in mathematics, there exist **binary** operations that require two operands to perform the operation (as in the case of addition) as well as **unary** operations that require only one operand (as in the case of negation[4]). Notice that for the operation of addition to occur the **values** of the operands must be known. These values are referred to as the **data**.

The discussion in the last paragraph suggests that a computer program can be viewed as a collection of **instructions** and **data**.

1.2 STRUCTURED LAYERS OF A COMPUTER SYSTEM

The reader should have noticed that the calculator example suggests that the execution of the task of adding two numbers requires three basic components: the **hardware** component (the calculator and possibly a power supply); the **software** component (the program); and the **user** component. The collection of these three components is what is referred to as a **computer system**. In addition, as the title of this book, *Computer Organization and the MC68000*, suggests, those different components are in some sense of the word "ordered."

In many respects one may consider the overall structure of a computer system as an onion. The analogy with an onion is used because each aspect of the system may be considered as a succession of layers that when peeled off reveals a new layer of greater detail. The exterior layer is the user's layer, the middle layer is the software layer, and the innermost layer is the hardware layer. Figure 1.1 illustrates this conceptual view of a computer system in terms of its three principal components: hardware, software, and user.

Closer examination of Figure 1.1 reveals that we have separated the exterior layer, the user layer, into three areas that are labeled system view 1, system view 2, and system view 3, respectively. The reason for this is that a single system offers each *class* of user a particular view of the system depending on his or her needs. As an example a user operating an electronic bank teller may not even be aware that he or she is using a computer system. To another user the system may offer banking services to process payrolls and provide financial forecasting, whereas to another user the same system may be a word processor and office automation system, and to yet another user the system may control a robot assembly plant *all at the same time*.

Notice that these are different views of the same system. Thus each class of user has his or her own view of the hardware and software layer. To gain a more complete picture of the system, all aspects need to be considered; however, it is not necessary that all the views be understood to perform useful work on a computer; in fact, often in real life we interact with different computer system views without even realizing it. Again, the automated teller is an excellent example. This is very important because a thorough under-

---

[4] Subtraction (−) is a binary operator with the same symbol as negation; however, the use of a single symbol for two operations should not cause confusion.

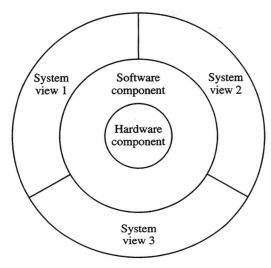

Figure 1.1   The computer system onion. Conceptual view of a computer system.

standing of each view would require many thousands of pages of text and would leave computers with very restricted uses (as was the case when they were first developed). The intention here is rather to introduce the reader to the *terminology* used in many different computer system environments and to provide a *conceptual framework* to understand the remainder of the text better.

Although an onion is usually peeled from the exterior layer to the interior, in the discussion that follows we will consider first the hardware layer, then the layer that provides the interface between the two extreme layers, user and hardware, the software layer and finally the user layer.

1.2.1 Hardware Layer

The hardware components are tangible physical objects; the primary components (the central processor, main memory, and secondary devices such as disk drives, tape drives, and terminals, all to be explained later) are a combination of mechanical and electrical components enclosed in a variety of different containers. For example the "computer" may be a small cabinet that contains printed circuit cards on which the central processor and main memory reside. Secondary devices such as disk drives and tapes (which act as repositories for data) may be either in the cabinet or in separate cabinets connected by cables. The user interfaces such as display terminals would typically be placed on the user's desk and connected via some communication media to the computer. To make a comparison with a human being, the hardware is the physical side of a person. The central processor and memory are the brain, the primary senses are the input/output (I/O) devices, whereas the legs and arms are devices controlled by the brain. Even though these components will be discussed in more detail in subsequent chapters, their principal characteristics and functions will be discussed briefly in the following sections.

Primary storage.   **Primary** or **main storage (memory)** is a large storage area where all programs are **loaded** before they are executed. In other words, in order for a program to be executed, it must be resident in main memory. You may think of the main

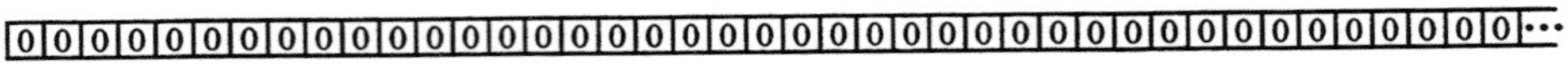

Figure 1.2   First portion of main memory.

memory as an ordered sequence of squares[5] and where each square contains a **bit** of information. A bit of information is represented by either a zero (0) or a one (1). Figure 1.2 illustrates the first portion of main memory.

We will see later that all instructions as well as data are stored in main memory as a *sequence* of bits that are referred to as **bit strings**. In addition we will see that the hardware can distinguish between two different instructions according to the bit pattern of the binary string that forms the instruction. The previous remark suggests that hardware can understand *only* one language that is known as **machine language**.

The **alphabet** of a machine language consists of only two characters, 0 and 1, and its vocabulary consists of a set of "words" each of which is represented by a string of bits. The machine language is closely "tied-up" with the hardware in such a way that the latter can understand the "words" (instructions) spoken to it; therefore, each computer's manufacturer develops its own predefined vocabulary compatible with the system's hardware. In other words, despite the fact that all machine languages are defined over the same alphabet, each computer "speaks" only the manufacturer's predefined language.

The previous discussion indicates that the programmer *should* be familiar with the machine language supported by the computer system at his or her disposal to be able to communicate with it.

Even though we examine main memory in Chapter 3, we should note here that memories can be either **volatile** or **nonvolatile**. The former term indicates that when the power is turned off, all information that has been stored in it is lost. At the other extreme nonvolatile memories retain the information stored in them at all times. Given the relatively expensive outlay of capital, nonvolatile main memories are seldom employed.

I/O devices.   As was indicated in the previous section, for a program to be executed, it should be loaded into main memory first. To accomplish this "transfer" of data we need an **input** device. Such devices are the **keyboard** of a terminal and a **card reader**.[6] Assume now that our program has been loaded via a keyboard and has been executed. Moreover, let's assume that the function of our program was to add two numbers. Clearly, we would like to know the result. Hence, the result must be displayed and, therefore, there is the need for an **output** device. Such devices are the **screen** of a terminal, a **printer**, a **card puncher**, a **plotter**, and so on. What we have seen is that there is the need for input and output devices. In general, the term **Input/Output device** (or simply **I/O device**) describes a hardware component that plays the dual role of an input and an output device such as a terminal.

Secondary storage.   The preceding discussion suggests that with the existence of the hardware components of main memory and an I/O device, we are able to send information and retrieve information from the main memory. As we have seen, however, mem-

---

[5] Several million and sometimes more than a billion in number.

[6] Devices such as a **joystick**, **mouse**, and a **light pen** are special input devices referred to as **locator** devices.

ories are volatile; therefore, if the power is momentarily interrupted or for that matter is turned off, all stored information is lost, and, therefore, so is our program! Hence, there is the need for a nonvolatile medium where programs that are not being executed as well as all data can be stored when not in use. Examples of these are **magnetic tapes, magnetic disks, floppy disks,** and **magneto-optical disks.** These devices are also used to store programs as well as data and are collectively referred to as **secondary storage** devices to differentiate them from primary storage.

Although secondary storage is extensively discussed in Chapter 3, we should note here that its use permits one to get the most out of the use of main memory; its cost is considerably less than that of primary storage; and it permits the storage of massive amounts of information. Finally, programs and data (all represented again as a sequence of bits) are organized in secondary storage as **files.**

To get an intuitive understanding, as an example you may think that a magnetic tape[7] is like a cassette tape. You may assume that a **file** is a recorded song. To listen to one of your favorite songs "Computers Are Wonderful" you first should **mount** the cassette that contains the song into the tape deck. The next step would be to **search** for this song (file); after this process has been completed, you should transfer the contents of the file to your amplifier where the song (program) can be **executed,** and you would, therefore, be able to listen to it. The process of transferring the recorded information into the amplifier is known as **reading** the data. On the other hand, the process of **writing** data is similar to the recording of a song. After you listen to the song, stop and dismount the cassette, notice that the songs (files) are permanently recorded and the information is not lost; the information will remain there unless you rerecord (rewrite) over it.

Controller.   In the computer world the reading as well as the process of writing data is done by executing a program that is referred to as an **I/O program.** To get a feeling for such a program, consider the example given earlier. Recall that after the appropriate cassette has been mounted to search for your favorite song, you should issue a set of **input** instructions by depressing the appropriate keys on the cassette deck. Assuming that you are as well organized as a computer, to find that song you will have a *look-up* table where the title of each song can be found with its *address* within this tape (i.e., counter number 800) alongside it. The next step that you would perform is to inspect the value in the counter.[8] If it is less than 800, you will depress the *forward* key; if its value is greater than 800, you will depress the *backward* key. When the value is equal to 800, the next step is to depress the *play* key.

The preceding discussion contains the algorithm that is required to read data from a secondary device by a computer. The computer will perform all the tasks (find the address of the song from its own look-up table, and locate and read the song) as a response to a command by the user such as

Play the song "Computers Are Wonderful"

---

[7] The reader should be aware that magnetic tapes are not the most useful secondary medium, but they serve as a good example in the presentation of the concepts that we would like to convey at this point.

[8] We assume that at the time that the cassette is mounted, it is rewound to its physical beginning, and the deck counter is set to address 0.

Then the computer as a response to your command will execute the *input program* given in Table 1.3. The natural question is who will *interpret* and therefore execute the I/0 commands of steps 2 and 3. The answer is a special hardware component known as the **device controller**. In analogy with the cassette example, the controller performs the tasks that you were performing when you were depressing the appropriate keys.

TABLE 1.3

```
[1]  Find address of file "Computers are Wonderful" from the look-up
table.
[2]  If address is less than 800 fast forward to 800.
[3]  If address is greater than 800 rewind to 800.
[4]  Read data.
```

Summarizing the previous discussion, we refer to a program that performs *reads* and *writes* between primary and secondary storage as an **I/O program** and its instructions as **I/O commands**. Moreover, the controller is that hardware component that responds to the I/O commands and locates the appropriate data in the secondary storage.

Central processing unit.   We have seen that to execute a machine language program the program must be resident in main memory. Moreover, a component is needed that interprets and executes the machine language instructions of the program and supervises the transfer of data between primary and secondary memory. That component is the **Central Processing Unit (CPU)**.

Hence, the CPU contains the electronics necessary to execute the machine language instructions and control the transfer of data between main and secondary memory. Typically, CPUs are capable of executing anywhere from 1 million to 50 *million instructions per second* (**MIPS**) at the present level of technology. CPUs are discussed extensively in Chapter 3.

Different architectures.   In the previous section we presented the main components of a computer and the function of each. **Computer architecture** is a term used to describe the way in which these components are connected and the manner in which they communicate. Two of these architectures are presented in this section.

IBM 360/370 system.   Figure 1.3 illustrates the hardware components employed by the IBM 360/370 system. Notice the existence of two more hardware components that were not discussed in the previous section but are used by this architecture: **cache memory** and **channel**. A brief explanation of the need for these components and the way that they communicate is outlined subsequently.

Channel.   As noted earlier, the CPU is operating at electronic speeds on the order of microseconds.[9] At the other extreme, secondary memory devices are operating in electromechanical speeds on the order of milliseconds. The reason for slow speeds of electromechanical devices (disks) is that when a request for transmission of data is issued, the first

---

[9] Recall $1 \mu s = 10^{-6} s$ and $1 ms = 10^{-3}$ s.

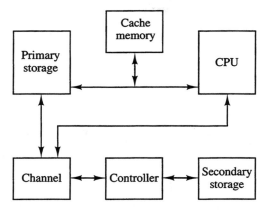

Figure 1.3 Hardware components of IBM 360/370 computer system.

step is to locate the "target" data in the secondary storage device. Thus the read/write head of the drive must be *moved* in such way that it is positioned over the physical beginning of the "target" data.[10] That "movement" requires not only the aid of electronic signals but also the aid of mechanical parts. It is these parts that cause the delays. To see the magnitude of these delays, note that a moderate estimate of the time required to complete a data transfer from the time that the request was issued is 25 ms. Assuming a CPU capable of executing 2 MIPS, then with the data transfer of 25 ms, the CPU is capable of executing $2,000,000 \times 0.025$ or $50,000$ instructions, which obviously would be equivalent to $0.025 \times 50,000,000$ or $1,250,000$ instructions for a computer capable of executing 50 MIPS. Thus if the task of managing and supervising the transfer of data was assigned to the CPU, it would be idle most of the time waiting for the completion of the transfer.

To relieve the CPU of this duty, one uses the **channel**. The channel is another type of processor with its own instruction set (I/O commands), instruction counter, and control logic. When a request for a physical data transfer is issued, the CPU loads the channel's instruction counter with the beginning address of the I/O program discussed earlier that has been loaded in the main memory known as the **channel program**. It then signals the channel to start executing this program. The CPU is now relieved of the data transfer task and is therefore free to perform other tasks.

Cache memory.   Because only one device can access main memory at a time, the channel interrupts the CPU, in midexecution if necessary, whenever it needs a new instruction, or whenever it is ready to transmit data between main and secondary storage. This often results in a bottleneck. To alleviate this many CPUs execute instructions not from main memory but instead from a very fast memory, **cache memory**, where the instructions that the CPU is to execute have been loaded ahead of time. With this enhancement the channel interrupts the CPU only occasionally. It should be noted here that only relatively small cache memories are used because of their high costs.

Selector, byte multiplexor, and block multiplexor channels.   Assume that an I/O request is issued to write data onto the disk. Here is the pseudocode of the required channel program.

---

[10] Consider the case of a CD player, and assume that we would like to listen to the third song. The "arm" that the pick-up has been attached to must be moved over the appropriate track.

```
Perform a "seek" to the appropriate track;
Find the proper position within the track;
Write the data onto the track from memory address;
```

In the preceding pseudoalgorithm, the term "seek" requires two steps; the first step is to perform a seek to find the required track (cylinder[11]), and the second is to activate the write head (of the appropriate track). The first step is a mechanical movement, and this requires, as we have seen, an average of 25 *ms*. Therefore, the channel cannot execute the second channel command until the "seek" operation has been completed; therefore, the channel remains idle between the two channel commands. Given that the "seek" can only be completed by the controller,[12] this means that the channel will remain idle for a period before it resumes execution with the next channel command. Hence, use of the channel may be increased by attaching to it more than one device; so, when one device is busy and not using the channel, a new physical I/O operation may be initiated on another device attached to the channel. To be able to implement such channel multiprogramming one needs special types of channels. The following paragraphs are discussions of three popular channel types.

A **selector channel** can be connected to up to 256 different devices, but only one device can be selected at a time. In other words a device is selected, and the physical I/O operation completed; then, another device is selected, and the process is repeated. These channels are therefore usually used with high-speed devices.

A **byte multiplexor channel** may also be connected to as many as 256 different devices. The byte multiplexor interleaves the transmission of bytes (eight bit strings) from the different devices to which it is connected. Notice that unlike the selector channel, this channel does not need to wait for the physical I/O to be completed in a device. Because it interleaves bytes, the byte multiplexor channel must be connected to slow-speed devices such as terminals and printers.

Finally, a **block multiplexor channel** resembles a byte multiplexor in that the channel does not need to wait for a channel program to be completed; therefore, it can execute multiple channel programs. Unlike the byte multiplexor, this channel interleaves the transmission of blocks (integral number of bytes) from the different devices to which it is connected, and, therefore, these devices must operate at high speeds.

A channel program issues commands to read or write data, to locate data physically in the external storage, and so on. Because each secondary device has its own characteristics, however, there is a need for another component that interprets and executes those channel commands subject to the device that it "controls"—in other words, a component that is directly connected to a channel at one end and to a secondary device at the other end. This provides the interface between the standard I/O software interface of the channel and the device-dependent characteristics. This component is referred to as the **device controller** that was discussed in an earlier section. Because the channel provides a standard I/O interface, each channel can be connected to more than one controller, whereas each controller can be connected to several secondary storage devices provided that they are of the same type. Figure 1.4 illustrates the previously discussed points.

---

[11] Secondary devices are discussed in Chapter 3.
[12] Controllers are discussed in the following section.

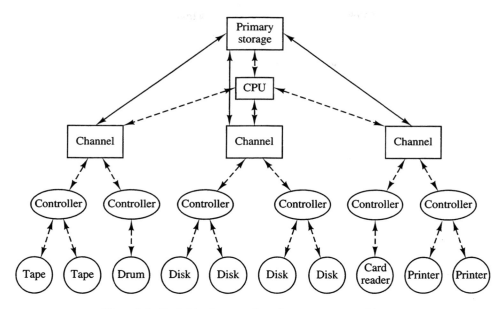

Figure 1.4   Typical hardware configuration.   IBM 360/370 architecture.

MC68000 System.   Another popular architecture is the **single bus** architecture, such as is used in many MC68000 machines with the **Versa Module Europe (VME)** bus and is presented in Figure 1.5.

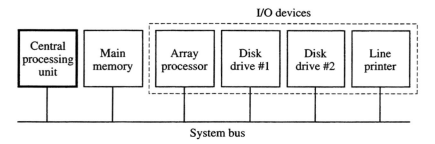

Figure 1.5   Organization of single bus system.

The bus is a collection of wires that run in parallel and is known as the **backplane**. The bus possesses enough lines (wires) to permit addressing, data, and control information to be passed along it. The bus is used by one device at a time, with one device designated as the **bus master**. This device may coordinate communications with other devices that act as **bus slaves**. Typically the CPU is the bus master, although this need not be the case. The principal idea behind the bus is that any of the devices connected to the bus may communicate with any of the other devices provided that one of them takes the responsibility as bus master and the other as bus slave.

Clearly the advantages of this system are the relative ease with which different devices communicate with one another. The disadvantage is that all the devices are competing for one resource (namely the bus), which invites the possibility of a bottleneck. In particular, notice that main memory is connected onto the bus; thus all instructions and data must go through the bus, which may limit the effective performance of the system. As with the IBM systems, caches may be used to alleviate this problem.

Inner layers of hardware. Earlier we said that the computer only understands machine language instructions. This image of a computer may be regarded as the highest layer of the hardware view (i.e., what the computer is). In this section we consider the computer in terms of its hardware layers (Figure 1.6).

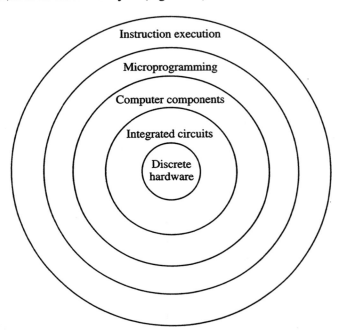

Figure 1.6   Physical view.

Again starting at the innermost layer, we may view the computer as a collection of discrete electronic components. We shall be considering these components in more detail in Chapter 2; however, we will briefly mention them here. The primary discrete component is the **transistor**. Recall from the hardware section that we think of computers as acting on binary numbers (1 or 0) only; in fact these binary numbers are actually two different voltage levels in an electrical circuit at the transistor layer (typically 0 V and +5 V). A transistor has the desirable property that, when operated properly, it may be used to switch between these two voltages using little current, and at very high speeds. For example, typical Schottky transistors operate (i.e., switch voltage levels) in 10 ns.[13] Thus it can manipulate our binary numbers easily. Another important consideration of transistors is that they may be made extremely small and may be packed together. For example, a modern transistor takes up only $5 \times 10^{-6} \text{cm}^2$.

Although the transistor is the building block of digital computers, they are not a convenient layer to use because of their limited function. At the next layer we see that a few

---

[13] Recall 1 ns $= 10^{-9}$ s.

transistors may be grouped together to form **gates**. A gate provides the user with some *logical* function in which the computer may be thought of as acting only in binary (1 and 0 only). For example, a gate may be used to perform the logical **or** (denoted by the symbol ∨) of two inputs (i.e., given two inputs that may be either 0 or 1, the output will be a 1 if either of the inputs is 1 and 0 otherwise), or the logical **and** (denoted by the symbol ∧) of two inputs (i.e., given two inputs that may be either 0 or 1, the output will be 1 if both the inputs are 1, and 0 otherwise) or the **negation** (denoted by the symbol ⁻ above the input) of an input (i.e., given an input that may be either 0 or 1, the output is 1 if the input is 0, and 0 otherwise). A more detailed introduction to computer (i.e., binary boolean) logic is given in Chapter 2.

Using gates, we may form more complex (and useful) components, these are called **integrated circuits** (so called because they integrate many gates to build one component). There are many scales of integrated circuit varying from small-scale integration (SSI, comprising 1–10 gates) used for individual **logic gates**; medium-scale integration (MSI, comprising 10–100 gates) used for complete logic functions such as **adders, shift registers** etc.; large-scale integration (LSI, comprising 100–100,000 gates) used for complete components in a computer system, for example an **arithmetic logic unit**, which performs simple arithmetic operations on binary numbers or an **instruction sequencer**, which allows different instructions to be executed depending on the results from previous operations; and very large scale integration (VLSI, comprising 100,000+ gates) used for complete **microprocessors** and other functional units. Although the reader will probably feel bewildered by all these terms, they are explained in Chapter 2 and are used only to illustrate how computers are constructed from standard building blocks. Notice that as the scale becomes larger, the size becomes greater, and the manufacturing process becomes more complex.

As we saw in the previous section, the primary components of a computer are the central processor, memory, and devices. Each of these is a **component** in the computer and is usually constructed out of either medium- or large-scale integrated circuits "glued" together by small-scale integrated circuits.

As we said earlier the larger components become more complex to manufacture; this includes the design, testing, and fabrication. In particular very large components (for example the central processor) become extremely difficult to design without error. For this reason (and others to be explained in Chapter 5) it is often the case that the central processor is *itself* composed of several microprogrammable components. The central processor would consist of different arithmetic and logic units, very high-speed storage, and sequencing controllers. The use of such a model permits the manufacturer to *program* the central processor. Such a device is said to be **microprogrammable**. The advantages in using microprogramming are the ability to change the central processors instruction set and correct errors in the instruction design easily, a reduction in the design costs, and flexibility when extending the instruction set.

At the highest layer the user sees an instruction set presented by the central processor to the "outside world."

1.2.2 Software Layer

The software components are sequences of instructions that the central processor interprets and acts on. These instructions may be used to perform arithmetic on data in the central processor or may be used to control one of the secondary devices. Thus the software in the computer system is a collection of different programs that may or may not be currently in use. The hardware may therefore be thought of as executing programs that are encoded in such a way that the hardware is able to interpret them. Unlike the hardware that is tangible, software is difficult to see. At best we can see the human readable printout of a program written for a computer. To extend the analogy between a computer system and a human being, the software is everything that has been learned. In the same way that memory and learning are associated with the brain, so software is associated with the computer's main memory and secondary storage devices.

Hence, by the term **software**, we mean the collection of all programs and data. In this section, some examples of software programs are presented. At the outset one distinguishes the class of **user** or **application programs**. Those are programs that are written by users. Then there is the collection of all programs that is required to assist in the *execution* of user programs such as **assemblers, compilers, loaders**, and so on. Chief among the latter programs is the **operating system**, which is a large and complex software product whose function is to manage all the resources of the computer.

Looking at the logical overview of a computer system (i.e, in terms of what a computer system is logically composed of) there are five identifiable layers, as shown in Figure 1.7.

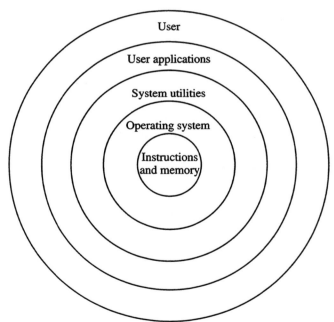

Figure 1.7   Logical view.

At the lowest layer, the computer hardware offers the programmer a number of **machine language instructions, memory space** and an assortment of different **devices** to control. All of these terms should be familiar from the hardware introduction previously.

This machine-level environment is very difficult to work with; devices are complex to control properly and are often not sharable between more than one user at a time (consider what would happen if several people attempted to use a printer at the same time). In addition, to permit several people to make use of the computer system simultaneously to support these functions, a computer system uses a program known as the **operating system** (or control program, monitor, executive, etc.). There are many different operating systems ranging from quite simple control programs to extremely complex operating systems that manage many users and resources (including multiple central processors) simultaneously. The operating system is responsible for coordinating and controlling all of the systems **resources** and scheduling when different programs should run, and when they should wait. In fact the operating system is so complex that it deserves a view of its own, which we shall see later. Because of the complexity of an operating system, it is typical to find one or more people whose job is to keep the operating system running smoothly; this task is performed by **system administrators**.

With an operating system installed, we now see a computer system that allows the user to access files, request resources, submit programs for execution, and generally present us with an easy to work with environment. We are still not able to do very much, however. For example, to create a text file requires an **editor**. An editor is a program that allows you to create, modify, and save text files (a text file is one that may be displayed on the terminal). Once a program has been entered via the editor the user will probably wish to run it. Before a program may be run, however, it must first be converted into the machine instructions that the hardware may execute. The transformation is accomplished by an **assembler**.[14] Assemblers take text programs written in low-level human-readable[15] programming languages and convert them into machine-readable format. Both of these utilities (the editor and the assembler) are examples of utilities that are essential when working with computer systems; as such they are known as **system utilities**; typical utilities are compilers, assemblers, editors, linkers, loaders, mail handlers, and so on.

Now that we have an operating system and system utilities to support us, the computer system is almost complete. Clearly, different systems will have different requirements; for example, a banking institution will possess many programs related to finance, whereas an engineering company may possess computer aided design packages. Many of these programs are also very large, perhaps costing tens of thousands of dollars and will consume a large portion of the computer's resources. These are the **application programs** and in large systems will be maintained by staff in much the same manner as the operating system.

Finally we may view the computer system as a whole, the hardware executing the programs, the operating system maintaining the resources and tasks, the system utilities offering useful functions, application programs tailored to the systems environment, and finally the **user**, able to make use of this environment. As we shall see later, however, the user's *view* of the system is not necessarily all of these facilities; in fact, there are several different user views common in computer systems.

Layers of operating system. The operating system is a single coherent program that is responsible for managing all the **resources** and **tasks** in the system. By resources we are referring to memory, the physical devices (such as disk drives, tape units, printers, terminals, etc.), and logical devices (i.e., offering services not supported by hardware). By tasks (also known as **processes**) we refer to any self-contained segment of code executed on the system that performs some useful action. Typically a program is composed of one or more tasks. These include the operating system utilities, applications programs, and user programs. The operating system therefore provides a **virtual machine** to the user

---

[14] Other tools exist for taking higher-level programs and either generating assembler programs (known as **compilers**) or executing them directly on the hardware (known as **interpreters**).

[15] As sequences of characters coded into 7 or 8 bits.

that makes it easy to create processes, access files and other resourses, and communicate between processes. From the user's perception then, the operating system is defined by a set of functions that fall into six main classes: **process management, file system management, file management, interprocess communication, time management,** and **miscellaneous.** These functions are invoked by a process when it requires some activity to be performed. Examples of typical operating system functions are shown in Table 1.4. Each function requires several arguments that would indicate details of the request (not provided below).

TABLE 1.4   Typical functions that are supported by an operating system

Operating system's functions	
Function	Explanation
procgen(...)	Create a new process.
execute(...)	Replace a processes core image with a new image.
wait(...)	Wait for a process to terminate.
exit(...)	Terminate a process and return some exit status.
getid(...)	Get the current process identification number.
link(...)	Create a new directory entry in the file system.
unlink(...)	Remove a directory entry from the file system.
mount(...)	Add a secondary storage device to the file system.
unmount(...)	Remove a secondary storage device from the file system.
sync(...)	Force all outstanding data to be written to a device.
changedir(...)	Change the current working directory.
create(...)	Create a new file.
open(...)	Open a file for reading, writing, or both.
close(...)	Close an open file.
read(...)	Read data from a file into a memory buffer.
write(...)	Write data from a memory buffer to a file.
seek(...)	Move the current access point in a file to a particular location.
status(...)	Return the status of a file.
dup(...)	Copy the information regarding an open file to a file so it can be shared by several processes.
getsmem(...)	Get a shared memory region.
relsmem(...)	Release a shared memory region.
pipe(...)	Create a communication path between two processes.
time(...)	Return the time in seconds since some predefined epoch.
stime(...)	Set the elapsed time since the epoch.
utime(...)	Set the time a file was last accessed.
signal(...)	Send a communication signal from one process to another.
kill(...)	Kill another process.
alarm(...)	Schedule the operating system to send an alarm signal to this process in the future.
chmod(...)	Change the file permissions (i.e., who can access it) of a particular file.
getid(...)	Get the current user identification.
chown(...)	Change which user "owns" a particular file.
pause(...)	Suspend the current process for some period.

In addition to the set of operating system functions there are a number of support utilities for the user. These are written using the preceding operating system functions and typically permit the user to view the files they possess, create and delete files, view directories, print files, and so on. They may be considered part of the operating "system," although they are, in fact, applications.

The *interface* to the operating system, therefore, is organized through a set of functions, whereas the operating system itself is organized in layers. The core of this layered model is shown in Figure 1.8. The core provides many different services. At the innermost layer (known as the **kernel**), the operating system provides three services: the **first-level interrupt handler**, the **semaphore mechanism**, and the **dispatcher**.

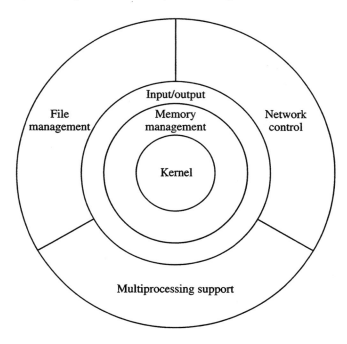

Figure 1.8   Operating system view.

The first-level interrupt handler is responsible for processing each interrupt as it is issued by the user or generated by an outside device. For example, a user's process (or task) may request from the operating system a block of data from a file. This request would take the form of setting up the request and generating an interrupt (or supervisor request). The interrupt would cause the process to be suspended and the first-level interrupt handler to be initiated. The handler would then look at the request and place it in a device request list. When the device had completed the read it would generate an external interrupt. The first-level interrupt handler would again be initiated and would permit the process to continue. The enquiring reader may wonder why the user's process is prevented from accessing the device directly. There are several answers: First, users are typically not interested in knowing where a file physically resides, they are interested in a particular piece of text *within* a file, and the conversion from this relative location within a file to its actual location on a disk is complex and therefore best left to the operating system. Second, the operating system is able to schedule all the different users' disk requests efficiently, thus speeding up the system throughput. Third, the operating system can check that the user is authorized to make the file access.

The semaphore mechanism is used to permit process communication and synchronization. Communication between two processes often requires that exclusively one process has access to some data region for a short while to permit some action to occur.

During this time other processes are excluded from this region. This requirement is known as **mutual exclusion** between competing processes. To see why this is necessary consider the case of an airline reservation system. Two travel agents wish to reserve a seat for a particular flight. A typical scenario for some agent would be:

```
If (Seat_Id_Free(id))
    THEN Reserve_Seat(id)
```

This simple program segment would work if there was only one process using the code. However in an environment in which there are several processes that wish to reserve a seat, the following might happen:

```
agent 1:   If (Seat_Id_Free(27))
                                    -- seat 27 free
agent 2:   If (Seat_Id_Free(27))
                                    -- seat 27 free
agent 1:         THEN Reserve_Seat(27)
                                    -- seat now marked as no longer
                                       free
agent 2:         THEN Reserve_Seat(27)
                                    -- oops - double booked
```

What happened? Clearly we want exclusive access to the data pertaining to seat 27 while we check (and optionally reserve) it. This mechanism for exclusive access is provided by the operating system as a tool that many other operating system and user functions may use.

Finally in the operating system kernel is the dispatcher. The dispatcher is responsible for checking that each process gets a certain time quantum of activity on the central processor. Once the time quantum has expired, the process is suspended by the dispatcher and another process permitted to execute. This mechanism prevents processes from "hogging" the central processor or from getting stuck in infinite loops. Clearly the dispatcher is a process, so one may wonder who dispatches the dispatcher! The answer is that a hardware clock is responsible for generating a periodic interrupt that suspends the current process in favor of the dispatcher.

The next layer of the operating system contains the memory management processes. These routines along with hardware support are responsible for mapping a virtual memory (that the user "sees") to the physical memory available in the computer. The concept of virtual address translation is discussed in Chapter 10, and so no further discussion will be made here. From a user's perspective, the operating system provides functions that allow for the allocation and deallocation of main memory and optionally permits different processes to share memory (useful for interprocess communication).

The I/O routines are responsible for taking user requests and issuing the appropriate commands to the device in question. These devices are typically interrupt driven and thus when the device has completed the command issued to it, it will interrupt the processor. These interrupts are also passed to the I/O routines that in turn update the status of the process that originally requested the I/O access.

At the outermost layer of the operating system is file support, multiprocessing support, and network control. The file support was discussed previously. The way in which a user views the file structure, and an individual file, is a design issue that is supported by the file manager. This is responsible for the creation and deletion of files, and for maintaining file system consistency. For example, a user process may request the file manager that file *xxxxx* be opened; the file manager will then locate the file on disk, check authorization and access privileges, and open the file. The multiprocessing support provides services for access to different processors on a multiprocessor machine. These machines have a set of system calls that enables several processes to share data and synchronize execution. Another facet of communications that now plays an important role is that of networking several computers together. Frequently it is now the case that network functions are integrated into the operating system—for example, remote procedure calls to other systems and so on.

1.2.3 User Layer

We have already seen that a computer system is capable of maintaining many different programs; this capability makes it possible for a computer to present several different views to different users. Although one user may be interested in using the computer for business operations, with software programs to maintain a company's payroll, another user may have a different set of programs that offers office automation. For example, the programs might allow them to write letters, send memos and mail to other users, prepare presentations, and so on. This ability of a computer system to offer many different facilities depending on the software is one of the great strengths of a computer in that it is a flexible tool whose uses are only limited by the imagination. To stretch the analogy with humans a final time, a person may be a spouse, a parent, an office clerk, and an athlete, depending on the situation.

As mentioned previously the view of a computer system presented to a user may vary depending on the application. Consider the case of an automatic bank teller. You insert your bank card into the slot, request a finance transaction, and receive your card back. In fact a bank teller is part of a computer system. One would be extremely surprised if one were waiting in line and noticed the person in front entering a computer program at the teller! This is because the user view of the system has been carefully restricted so that only a few operations are available. In general there are four scenarios: the **dedicated view**, the **multiple applications view**, the **application administration view**, and the **systems administration view**. We now look briefly at each of these views.

The single application view is very popular in the business sector. Frequently the system has a single specific function. The terminals may be specially designed if warranted, and the application program may run continuously. Typical environments are banks, travel agencies, gas stations, stores, and so on. It is often the case that the user is completely unaware that he or she is even interacting with a computer system.

Another typical environment particularly in small business is the limited application environment. The user's environment is carefully restricted so that he or she has access to only a limited number of utilities. For example, an office environment may permit composing letters, running a spreadsheet, sending mail to colleges, and accessing a calendar or appointment system. The user selects one of these from a menu and uses it; however, the full capability of the system is carefully hidden.

Another environment used in large businesses is the application administration environment. Consider the case of the bank again. A typical banking program will be a major portion of the computer environment. This program will require the attention of a team of

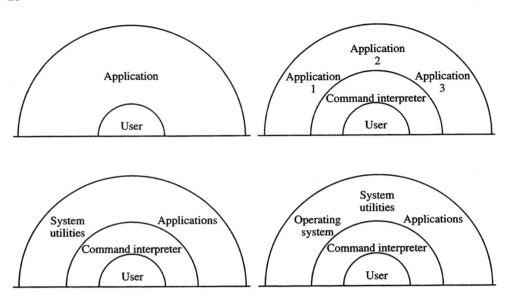

Figure 1.9   Different user views.

administrators to oversee that everything runs smoothly. This team will clearly require access to the different subprograms and files that make up the system. They will need a selection of different utilities (editors, etc.) to perform their task. This team does not need access to the system support side of the operation, however.

The final view of the system is that given to the systems administrator. Typically the systems administrator is able to "see" the entire system. Thus the systems administrator has access to the files used by the different application utilities and is able to use all of the operating system resources. This is essential so that he or she is able to monitor and correct system problems as they arise. It also shows one of the problems in computer systems. The systems administrator is frequently in a position that is open to abuse. There have been occasional cases of systems programmers and administrators using their privileges to their own advantages.

1.3 PROGRAMMING DESIGN TECHNIQUES

Although this text is primarily concerned with the internal workings of a computer system, there is also an emphasis on assembly language programming. Because of this emphasis, it is important that effective programming design techniques are introduced.

There are essentially three design strategies: **top-down design, bottom-up design,** and **middle-out design.** Each of these strategies has distinctive features that make it more or less appropriate according to the situation. Although these different strategies are collectively labeled as "modern" programming design techniques, in fact they have been used for many years and were informally used by successful programmers who found that applying these ideas led to more manageable code. More recently these ideas have been formalized and several highly stylized models have been developed that, when followed, assist the user in designing and managing large software projects. Although many of these tools are worthy of note, they are too cumbersome for practical use in the smaller problems that are addressed by this text. We also note that the design strategies outlined subsequently are appropriate for solving tasks that require a few hundred lines of code. They will not be used for very short code segments (e.g., describing the individual operation of a single instruction).

1.3.1 Top-down Programming

Top-down programming is perhaps the most widely used programming style. The essence of top-down programming is the successive decomposition of the original problem that focuses on flow of control.

The first step is to study the problem we are attempting to solve and break it into a small number (3–10) of independent modules. A **module** is defined as a block of code that has a well-defined function. Each module should be selected such that it performs some meaningful task that may be easily grasped by the coder. It is important at this stage to think carefully about the data that will be communicated between modules. Often there are several ways of breaking a problem; however, some may require only a small amount of data to be shared by two adjacent modules, whereas another may require much data to be shared. In general, passing fewer parameters to a module increases the probability that they will be used correctly. Also, limiting the data transferred between modules restricts the extent that a module can affect other portions of the final program. Thus when writing modules it is preferable to select a problem perspective that limits data transfer. Another point about a module is that it should provide well-defined individual functions, so that one may say "Oh yes, module ... does ... specific task." Extending this argument we see that a well-constructed module should consist of a collection of **abstract data types** (or data structures) and a set **operators** on these types that perform specific tasks. An example module might be to provide a queue mechanism. The data structures would include those that are internal to the module (e.g., internal implementation of the queue) and those that are visible to other modules (e.g., a new *data type* called queue). The operators on the visible structures would then be the functions init_queue(), push(), pop(), empty(), and full(). This design strategy is called **modular programming**. The advantages are that it greatly simplifies the task of debugging programs, and it permits changes to a module to remain transparent to the remainder of the program. Also, a well-designed module may be used in several different programs, thus saving programming costs. Although the topic of modular programming is an interesting one, it is unfortunately beyond the scope of this text.

Once the top level of the design has been completed, the process is repeated using the modules from the previous expansion. At this stage it is important that when a module is broken into submodules, it makes use of only the information (data) available in the module directly above it. The design process is repeated until such time as all of the modules are detailed enough to be coded in the selected programming language and are small enough to be understood in a single sitting. It is recommended that the code derived from a single module should be less than 30 lines. The following text outlines the advantages of top-down design:

- The design procedure is consistent with usual planning. That is, given a complex task, one usually starts by breaking it down into subtasks and attempting to solve each of these separately.
- The difficult decisions may be postponed during the design process until such time as it becomes apparent how they should be handled.

- By designing the program in a top down manner it should be possible to change a single module (at any of the levels) and only have this affect the lower levels directly below it. The remainder of the program is unaltered.

Balanced against these advantages are the following disadvantages:

- Occasionally by deferring decisions on a particularly complex issue, the user may complete a top-down design without solving several "knotty" problems. Thus when the coding is attempted, the user discovers that some modules are extremely difficult (if not impossible) to code. This forces the user to start again with these particular problems in mind.
- In a large program there are frequently so many layers that it becomes difficult to see where a particular module fits into the grand scheme. This situation often suggests that the problem should be strongly compartmentalized at a high level to make lower levels manageable.

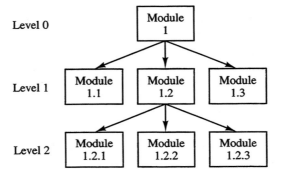

Example.   Consider the case of solving $x = \sqrt{a}$. The top level might simply be considered as solving the root of x problem.

Thinking more about the problem, we realize that first we must input the data (in this case x), we then need to compute the root, and finally output the result (i.e., y). Thus the second level of the design might be as follows:

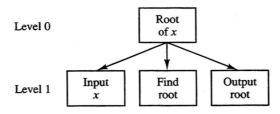

Assuming that the input and output routines are not difficult to write, the next stage is to decompose the problem of finding the root. Because $x = \sqrt{a}$ is the root of the equation $x^2 = a$ which may be rewritten as $x^2 - a = 0$, $x = \sqrt{a}$ is a zero of the function

$$f(x) = x^2 - a \tag{1.1}$$

Then we also have the formula

$$f'(x) = 2x \tag{1.2}$$

Using our knowledge of the Newton approximation method, we recall that for a given function on x, denoted $f(x)$, and its derivative $f'(x)$ we may repeatedly apply the following formula to compute the zeros of the function $f(x) = 0$ using successively more accurate values of x until an acceptable solution is found. This technique will yield a good approximation to the solution for well behaved functions provided the initial guess is reasonable. In particular, this technique works well for the $\sqrt{x}$ problem.

$$x_{n+1} = x_n - \frac{f(x_n)}{f'(x_n)} \tag{1.3}$$

$$= x_n - \left(\frac{x_n^2 - a}{2x_n} \right) \tag{1.4}$$

$$= \frac{2x_n^2 - x_n^2 - a}{2x_n} \tag{1.5}$$

$$= \frac{2x_n^2 + a}{2x_n} \tag{1.6}$$

Thus the algorithm begins with a guess (e.g., $\sqrt{x} = x$) and loops around computing a more accurate value of x until the difference between successive iterations is negligible. We see that one iteration of the algorithm requires that given an initial value x_n we first compute $f(x_n)$ and $f'(x_n)$ using equations 1.1 and 1.2, then use these in equation 1.6 to find a new value for x. With this in mind the new design might be as follows:

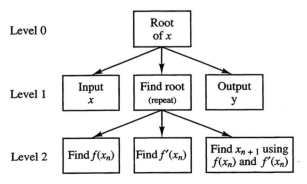

This process of refining the model would be repeated until such time as all the modules were easy to program. The design process would then be finished, and coding could begin. A top-down programming approach is well suited to complex programming tasks. This is because it permits an effective division of the program into subprograms, which may be written almost independently. In the case of a program written by many authors this is an important and desirable characteristic. With this in mind, we note that most modern high-level programming languages have been designed to facilitate a top-down design, and this is the design method of choice.

1.3.2 Bottom-up Programming

In contrast to top-down design, with bottom-up design, the user makes a quick appraisal of the situation and identifies the most complex aspects of the problem. The user then starts work on these isolated areas with the intention of providing a detailed specification on how these areas might best be coded. Once the difficult areas have been completely defined, the remainder of the specification is tailored to join these pieces together. The advantages with bottom-up design are as follows:

- The design procedure is clearly best suited to a situation in which the user knows in advance that there are a few critical code areas that will influence the rest of the design. If these are addressed early, design of the remainder of the program should be simplified.
- By coding immediately, the design for a low-level module has been fixed, and its user is in a position to test out and verify that particular problem areas are going to work.

The principal disadvantage in bottom-up design is that in a problem in which there are no areas of localized complexity, it is an inferior overall strategy to top-down design.

1.3.3 Middle-out Programming

It is often the case in large programs that both top-down and bottom-up design are desirable. In this case, a mixture of the two known as middle-out design is used. By using the data inputs and required outputs as guidelines an approximate design is developed; this is then used to isolate areas that require immediate attention; the design for these is then solidified (using bottom-up design), and this knowledge is used to proceed with a more effective top-down design.

1.4 EXERCISES

1. Name the basic components of a computer system.
2. Briefly describe the hardware layer.
3. Briefly describe the software layer.
4. Briefly describe the user layer.
5. What "language" does the computer understand? What is the alphabet used in this language? Is this language transportable between all computers?
6. Describe primary storage. Why is it used?
7. What are I/O devices? How is data stored in secondary storage? What are the advantages and disadvantages of different I/O device? (Name two.)
8. What is the controller? How does it work? Why is it used?

9. What is the difference between volatile memory and nonvolatile memory?
10. What is a channel on the IBM 360/370? Why is it used? What are the advantages and disadvantages?
11. What kind of devices would be connected to a byte multiplexor channel? Give examples.
12. What kind of devices would be connected to a block multiplexor channel? Give examples.
13. Describe the VME bus architecture. What are the advantages and disadvantages of using such an architecture?
14. Name three components in a VME architecture that can act as bus master. Describe the reasons why the component must act as bus master.
15. What is a transistor? What are the properties of the transistor that makes it useful in a computer?
16. What is a gate? What is an integrated circuit? How do they differ?
17. Define and contrast SSI, MSI, LSI, VLSI. State a use for each.
18. What does the term *microprogrammable* mean? What are the advantages in using microprogramming?
19. Define the term *software* and give four examples.
20. What is the purpose of an operating system?
21. Define the functions of the outer layers of the operating system.
22. Define the functions of the kernel.
23. Define first-level interrupt handler, semaphore mechanism, and dispatcher.
24. Why is it advantageous to have the computer present different views to different users?
25. List and briefly describe the different user views.
26. Briefly describe the following programming design strategies: top-down, middle-out, and bottom-up.

ADDITIONAL READING

BENNETT, J. M. *68000 Assembly Language Programming—A Structured Approach.* Englewood Cliffs, N.J.: Prentice Hall, 1987.

DALE, N., LILLY, S. C. *Pascal Plus Data Structures, Algorithms, and Advanced Programming*, 2nd ed. Lexington, Mass.: D. C. Heath, 1988.

DEITEL, H. M. *An Introduction to Operating Systems.* Reading, Mass.: Addison-Wesley, 1984.

HOROWITZ, E., SAHNI, S. *Fundamentals of Data Structures.* Computer Science Press, 1977.

KAIN, R. Y. *Computer Architecture: Software and Hardware*, vol. 1 and 2. Englewood Cliffs, N.J.: Prentice Hall, 1989.

KRUSE, R. L. *Data Structures and Program Design.* Englewood Cliffs, N.J.: Prentice Hall, 1984.

MANO, M. M. *Computer Engineering Hardware Design.* Englewood Cliffs, N.J.: Prentice Hall, 1988.

MOTOROLA. *M68000 8-/16-/32-Bit Microprocessors User's Manual*, 6th ed. Englewood Cliffs, N.J.: Prentice Hall, 1989.

TANENBAUM, A. S. *Operating Systems Design and Implementation.* Englewood Cliffs, N.J.: Prentice Hall, 1987.

2

Foundations

In this chapter we introduce several topics that are considered important to the understanding of digital computers. We hope that this combined approach will remove the "magic" from computers. Once the reader appreciates how computer components are composed, it is easier to understand how computers operate and consequently easier to operate them. The chapter is divided into four sections: **number systems, boolean logic, gate implementation**, and **logic implementation**. The reader is not required to cover every section (those that may be skipped are marked with an asterisk); however, the optional sections serve to provide a complete picture of computers.

2.1 NUMBER SYSTEMS

Whenever we think of "numbers," immediately we think in terms of the **decimal** number system, because it is the basis of our education in numbers and calculations from early childhood. Naturally, then, humans employ the decimal number system to which they are accustomed to communicate with the computer. On the other hand, computers universally employ the **binary** number system. Moreover because "numbers" internally are stored in binary, to aid in their interpretation we use the **hexadecimal** number system. Although the reader may have encountered these number systems before, we will briefly discuss them below for the sake of completeness.

Before we begin, it should be emphasized that the discussion here will be limited to **integers** or the **fixed-point** numbers. Recall that a real number such as 103.23 consists of an **integral** part, "103," and a **fractional** part, "23"; in addition, these two parts are separated by the decimal point ".". Because the decimal point is the natural separator of those two parts and the decimal point can be in any place among the digits,[1] we usually refer to these numbers as **floating-point** numbers, as opposed to **fixed-point** numbers in which the decimal point is to the immediate right of the *rightmost* digit (i.e., in 7. and 10323.). In the latter case the position of the decimal point is fixed[2] and therefore omitted.

There is one more point that must be mentioned. It is important for one to distinguish between two classes of integers, the **unsigned** and **signed** integers. In the latter class, one

---

[1] As an example consider the numbers 1032.3 and 1.0323.

[2] If we let I denote the set of integers and R the set of real numbers then I denotes the set of fixed-point numbers, whereas the set $(R - I)$ denotes the set of floating-point numbers.

has to differentiate between positive and negative integers, whereas in the for
integers are considered unsigned. The reason for this is that their internal rep
well as the rules of arithmetic is fundamentally different. We examine each o

2.1.1 Unsigned Integer Representation

The number systems (decimal, binary, hexadecimal) that we referred to earlier belong to
the class of **positional** number systems. Each such system is characterized by its **base** or
radix r; r is an unsigned integer greater than 1 and defines the number of different **symbols**
or **digits** available within this system $\Delta_r = \{\delta_1, \delta_2, \delta_3, \ldots, \delta_r\}$. For example, if the radix r
= 10, we speak of the decimal system, and the number of digits in this system is equal to
10, which are denoted by $\Delta_{10} = \{0, 1, 2, 3, 4, 5, 6, 7, 8, 9\}$. If $r = 2$, we speak of the binary
number system, where the number of digits is equal to 2, and they are denoted
by $\Delta_2 = \{0, 1\}$. Finally, if $r = 16$, we speak of the hexadecimal number system,
where the number of digits is equal to 16, and they are denoted by $\Delta_{16} =$
$\{0, 1, 2, 3, 4, 5, 6, 7, 8, 9, A, B, C, D, E, F\}$.

A number in any positional system of radix r is an *ordered* sequence of digits

$$\alpha_{n-1}\alpha_{n-2}\ldots\alpha_1\alpha_0 \tag{2.1}$$

with $\alpha_i \varepsilon \Delta_r$ for each $i = 0, 1, \ldots, n-1$ and where the position of each digit determines the
value of the integer. In particular the value[3] of the integer is computed via the following
general formula:

$$\alpha_{n-1} \cdot r^{n-1} + \alpha_{n-2} \cdot r^{n-2} + \ldots + \alpha_2 \cdot r^2 + \alpha_1 \cdot r^1 + \alpha_0 \cdot r^0 \tag{2.2}$$

or via the equivalent, more compact expression

$$\sum_{k=0}^{n-1} \alpha_k \cdot r^k \tag{2.3}$$

In the following paragraphs a brief discussion of the three number systems is presented.

Decimal number system. In a *decimal* integer such as 423, the position of each
digit determines the value of the integer. Thus, the value of 423 is computed as

$$4 \cdot 10^2 + 2 \cdot 10^1 + 3 \cdot 10^0$$

In general, for a n-digit decimal integer

$$d_{n-1}d_{n-2}\ldots d_1d_0 \tag{2.4}$$

where d denotes any decimal digit, the *value* of the integer is computed as

$$d_{n-1} \cdot 10^{n-1} + d_{n-2} \cdot 10^{n-2} + \ldots + d_2 \cdot 10^2 + d_1 \cdot 10^1 + d_0 \cdot 10^0 \tag{2.5}$$

Binary number system. Analogously to decimal integers, any unsigned *binary* integer is a sequence of the binary digits 0 and 1 arranged in such an order that the position of
each bit implies its value in the integer. For example, the value of the binary integer 11001
is computed as follows:

---

[3] Computed always in base 10.

$$1 \cdot 2^4 + 1 \cdot 2^3 + 0 \cdot 2^2 + 0 \cdot 2^1 + 1 \cdot 2^0 = 16 + 8 + 0 + 0 + 1 = 25$$

In general, for an n-digit binary integer

$$b_{n-1} b_{n-2} \ldots \ldots b_1 b_0 \tag{2.6}$$

where b denotes any binary digit, the *value* of the integer is computed as

$$b_{n-1} \cdot 2^{n-1} + b_{n-2} \cdot 2^{n-2} + \ldots \ldots + b_2 \cdot 2^2 + b_1 \cdot 2^1 + b_0 \cdot 2^0 \tag{2.7}$$

Binary numbers are therefore known as base 2 numbers. To avoid misinterpretation, they are often written with a subscript "2" or equivalently in this text are preceded by the percent sign "%." In other words the binary number "11001" can be represented in one of the following two forms

$$(11001)_2, \text{ or } \%11001$$

In this book we will employ the latter notation.

Hexadecimal number system. In this positional number system the radix is equal to 16 and

$$\Delta_{16} = \{0, 1, 2, 3, 4, 5, 6, 7, 8, 9, A, B, C, D, E, F\}$$

The first ten symbols have their usual meaning; the remaining six, A through F, represent the values ten through fifteen when used as hexadecimal digits. The choice of base 16 is based on the fact that $2^4 = 16$; therefore, each hex digit is equivalent to one 4-bit binary number. Table 2.1 illustrates this correspondence.

TABLE 2.1

Hex digit	Decimal value	Binary code
0	0	0000
1	1	0001
2	2	0010
3	3	0011
4	4	0100
5	5	0101
6	6	0110
7	7	0111
8	8	1000
9	9	1001
A	10	1010
B	11	1011
C	12	1100
D	13	1101
E	14	1110
F	15	1111

Calculation of the value of a hexadecimal number is again quite straightforward. The number is expanded analogous to the other bases discussed to the powers of 16. For example, the value of the hexadecimal number AC23 is given by

$$A \cdot 16^3 + C \cdot 16^2 + 2 \cdot 16^1 + 3 \cdot 16^0 = 10 \cdot 4096 + 12 \cdot 256 + 2 \cdot 16 + 3 \cdot 16^0 = 44067$$

In general, for an n-digit hexadecimal integer

$$h_{n-1}h_{n-2}\ldots\ldots h_1 h_0 \qquad\qquad (2.8)$$

where h denotes any hex digit, the *value* of the integer is computed as

$$h_{n-1} \cdot 16^{n-1} + h_{n-2} \cdot 16^{n-2} + \ldots\ldots + h_2 \cdot 16^2 + h_1 \cdot 16^1 + h_0 \cdot 16^0 \qquad (2.9)$$

To avoid misinterpretation, hexadecimal numbers are often written with a subscript "16" or equivalently are preceded by the dollar sign "$." In other words, the hex number "8539" can be represented in one of the following two forms:

$$(8539)_{16}, \text{ or } \$8539$$

In this book we will employ the latter notation.

2.1.2 Conversion from One Base to Another

What we have seen is that the basis of our daily use of numbers has its roots in the decimal number system. On the other hand, computers use the binary number system. The binary number system is too cumbersome to work with, however. Therefore, to aid in the interpretation of the binary numbers we use the hexadecimal system. The conversion, therefore, from one base to another is of fundamental importance to the student, and consequently general procedures are required that permit one to convert a number from one base to another. These procedures are discussed in the following sections.

Conversion from base r to decimal.   This conversion has previously been discussed. Namely, if one is given a number in any base r, to convert this number to its decimal representation, the number must be expanded in the powers of the base r. As an example consider the **octal**[4] (base 8) number 437. Its equivalent decimal representation can be found via the equation

$$4 \cdot 8^2 + 3 \cdot 8^1 + 7 \cdot 8^0 = 4 \cdot 64 + 3 \cdot 8 + 7 = 287$$

Conversion from decimal to base r.   Let p_0 be a decimal number and assume for simplicity that we wish to evaluate its corresponding binary representation, that is, we would like to determine the binary digits α_k for $k = 0, 1, 2, \ldots, n-1$ where

$$p_0 = \%\alpha_{n-1}\alpha_{n-2}\ldots\ldots \alpha_1\alpha_0 \qquad\qquad (2.10)$$

The preceding equation suggests that

$$p_0 = \alpha_{n-1} \cdot r^{n-1} + \alpha_{n-2} \cdot r^{n-2} + \ldots\ldots + \alpha_2 \cdot r^2 + \alpha_1 \cdot r^1 + \alpha_0 \cdot r^0 \qquad (2.11)$$

---

[4] In this case $\Delta_8 = \{0, 1, 2, 3, 4, 5, 6, 7\}$.

or via the more compact but equivalent expression

$$p_0 = \sum_{k=0}^{n-1} \alpha_k \cdot r^k$$

(2.12)

The preceding equation can be rewritten as

$$p_0 = r \cdot \left(\sum_{k=1}^{n-1} \alpha_k \cdot r^{k-1} \right) + \alpha_0$$

(2.13)

If we let p_1 denote the expression inside the parentheses in the preceding equation, that is,

$$p_1 = \sum_{k=1}^{n-1} \alpha_k \cdot r^{k-1}$$

(2.14)

we have

$$p_0 = r \cdot p_1 + \alpha_0$$

Again p_1 can be rewritten as

$$p_1 = r \cdot \left(\sum_{k=2}^{n-1} \alpha_k \cdot r^{k-1} \right) + \alpha_1$$

(2.15)

If we repeat the same sequence of the preceding steps by letting p_2 denote the expression inside the parentheses in the previous equation, that is,

$$p_2 = \sum_{k=2}^{n-1} \alpha_k \cdot r^{k-1}$$

(2.16)

we have

$$p_1 = r \cdot p_2 + \alpha_1$$

Also, p_2 can be rewritten as

$$p_2 = r \cdot \left(\sum_{k=3}^{n-1} \alpha_k \cdot r^{k-1} \right) + \alpha_2$$

(2.17)

Inductively, then, we obtain a sequence of decimal integers $\{ p_i \}_{i=0}^{n-1}$ with

$$p_i = \sum_{k=i}^{n-1} \alpha_k \cdot r^{k-1}$$

(2.18)

More important, however, the terms of this sequence are related via the set of n equations

$$p_0 = r \cdot p_1 + \alpha_0$$

$$p_1 = r \cdot p_2 + \alpha_1$$

$$p_2 = r \cdot p_3 + \alpha_2$$

$$p_3 = r \cdot p_4 + \alpha_3$$

$$\cdots \cdots \cdots \cdots \cdots \cdots \cdots$$

$$\cdots \cdots \cdots \cdots \cdots \cdots \cdots$$

$$p_{n-2} = r \cdot p_{n-1} + \alpha_{n-2}$$

$$p_{n-1} = r \cdot 0 + \alpha_{n-1}$$

The preceding derivations indicate that the conversion algorithm is very simple and is given in Table 2.2.

TABLE 2.2 The convert algorithm

```
Algorithm Convert_from_Decimal_to_Radix_r(p₀,r);
```

[1]. $n \leftarrow 0$;

[2]. $p_{n+1} \leftarrow$ Integer_Quotient $\left(\dfrac{p_n}{r}\right)$;

        $\alpha_n \leftarrow$ Remainder $\left(\dfrac{p_n}{r}\right)$;

[3].   if $(p_{n+1} \neq 0)$ then
                                {n ← n+1;
                                 go to [2]};

[4].   Write('Result = $(\alpha_{n-1}\alpha_{n-2}\ldots\ldots\alpha_1\alpha_0)_r$,');

[5].   Exit.

The algorithm is straightforward. Initially (step 2) the number p_0 is divided by the base; the quotient of the division is recorded as p_1 and the remainder α_0. If the quotient p_1 is not zero, the process is repeated (step 3) by dividing now p_1 by r; again the quotient of this division is recorded as p_2, whereas the remainder is recorded as α_1. On the other hand if p_n is equal to zero, the conversion is completed and the number is formed as the sequence of the remainders is derived (step 4).

Example

Consider the task of converting the decimal number 23 to its equivalent binary representation. In this case $p_0 = 23$ and $r = 2$. The successive divisions are displayed subsequently.

$$p_0 = r \cdot p_1 + \alpha_0 \;\rightarrow\; 23 = 2 \cdot 11 + 1$$

$$p_1 = r \cdot p_2 + \alpha_1 \;\rightarrow\; 11 = 2 \cdot 5 + 1$$

$$p_2 = r \cdot p_3 + \alpha_2 \;\rightarrow\; 5 = 2 \cdot 2 + 1$$

$$p_3 = r \cdot p_4 + \alpha_3 \;\rightarrow\; 2 = 2 \cdot 1 + 0$$

$$p_4 = r \cdot p_5 + \alpha_4 \;\rightarrow\; 1 = 2 \cdot 0 + 1$$

Hence,

$$23 = p_0 = \%\alpha_4\alpha_3\alpha_2\alpha_1\alpha_0 = \%10111$$

The algorithm outlined previously could be illustrated for convenience sake in tabular form, as Figure 2.1 indicates.

Conversion from (to) hexadecimal to (from) binary.   Because the internal representation of the integers (and as we will see shortly that of the characters) is in binary form, one is faced with the task of working in the binary system. Unfortunately, as mentioned earlier, the binary system is simply too cumbersome to work with easily as the following simple example indicates.

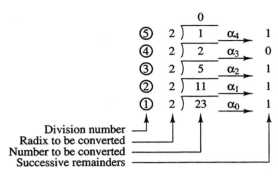

Division number ⎯⎯⎯

Radix to be converted ⎯⎯⎯

Number to be converted ⎯⎯⎯

Successive remainders ⎯⎯⎯

Figure 2.1 Tabular illustration of the successive division algorithm.

Suppose that we would like to decide whether or not the following two binary strings numbers are the same.

%110110010001010110010110111111011, %110110010001010110110110111111011

The mechanism for this determination is straightforward; the 2-bit strings must be examined in a bit-by-bit fashion; if the comparison of any 2 bits is different, the strings are different. The reader can easily see the cumbersome task at hand. Imagine now the effort that is required if we were to compare two bit strings of length 160 bits! Therefore, the notation is simplified by employing the representation in the hexadecimal system.

Because the bases of the hexadecimal and binary systems are related by the equation $16 = 2^4$, conversions between the two systems do not require use of the general procedures described earlier. Instead, the following two rules are almost always used:

1. To convert from hexadecimal to binary, we replace each hexadecimal digit with its equivalent 4-bit binary representation.
2. To convert from binary to hexadecimal, we replace every 4 consecutive binary digits by their equivalent hexadecimal digit, starting from the right-hand digit and adding zeros on the left, if necessary.

The following examples demonstrate these rules. The reader should verify that the results obtained are equivalent to those that would be obtained using the general procedures described earlier. Note that spaces are used after each set of 4 binary digits to facilitate reading.

Binary	0001 0010	0100 0000	1111 1101 1011	1110 0010 0100 1010
Hexadecimal	1 2	4 0	F D B	E 2 4 A

Thus

$$10010_2 = 12_{16},\ 1000000_2 = 40_{16}$$

$$1110001001001010_2 = E24A_{16},\ \text{and}\ 111111011011_2 = FDB_{16}$$

Returning to the comparison of the two original bit strings one should be able to determine that the strings in hex notation are written as

$$\$D91596FB,\ \$D915B6FB$$

respectively, and the comparison from this point is much easier.

At this point we should emphasize (again) that internal representation of integers as well as other data is always in binary string form; hexadecimal representation is employed *only* to make internal representations more readable and therefore easier to work with.

General case.   The task at hand is to convert *directly*[5] from a base r_1 to a base r_2. It should be relatively easy to see that the algorithm developed for converting a decimal number to any base r can be extended to that of converting from any base r_1 to any other base r_2. The only modification is that the successive divisions must be performed in the number system of the base that is to be converted *from*, that is, in base r_1. The remainders that are obtained must be converted into the number system of the base that we are interested to convert *to*.

As an example, Figure 2.2 illustrates the steps that are required to convert directly from the number $25 to its equivalent representation in binary (a) and the conversion of the number %100101 to its equivalent hex representation (b).

$25 = %?
$25 = $12 • $2 + $1
$12 = $9 • $2 + $0
$9 = $4 • $2 + $1
$4 = $2 • $2 + $0
$2 = $1 • $2 + $0
$1 = $0 • $2 + $1
$25 = %100101

%100101 = $?
%100101= %10 • $10000 + %101
%10   = %0 • $10000 + %10
%100101 = $25

(i)   (ii)

Figure 2.2   Converting hex number $25 to binary (a) and binary number %100101 to hex (b) by performing successive divisions. Notice that operations are performed in *old* base.

Notice that in (a) we have $r_1 = 16$ and $r_2 = 2$; therefore, all operations are performed in base 16. On the other hand the roles of the number systems are reversed where $r_1 = 2$ and $r_2 = 16$; therefore, the operations are performed in the binary system, and the remainders %101 and %10 are converted to their hex representations $5 and $2, respectively.

2.1.3 Unsigned Integer Arithmetic

The arithmetic involving integers in any radix r is very similar to that involving decimal numbers and is briefly discussed subsequently.

Addition

Addition of two decimal integers.   Recall that the addition operation on the set of the unsigned decimal integers is a **closed** operation in the sense that the addition of two decimal integers α and β, where the first term of the sum α is called the **augend**, whereas the second term β is called the **addend**, yields an unsigned integer γ. Moreover, the algorithm

---

[5] One could always perform this conversion *indirectly* via an intermediate conversion to a number in the decimal system.

for performing the addition is very simple. We first write the addend immediately below the augmend in such a way so that their rightmost digits are aligned in the same column.[6] For example for $\alpha = 5632$ and $\beta = 493$ the numbers are aligned as follows

$$5632$$
$$493$$

One proceeds by adding the digits appearing in the same columns starting from the rightmost vertical column and proceeding to the leftmost. The rules for adding two decimal digits are given in Table 2.3.

TABLE 2.3 Addition of two decimal digits: addend is represented in first vertical column, augmend is represented in first horizontal column, and c represents carry that is equal to 1 in all cases

+	0	1	2	3	4	5	6	7	8	9
0	0	1	2	3	4	5	6	7	8	9
1	1	2	3	4	5	6	7	8	9	0+c
2	2	3	4	5	6	7	8	9	0+c	1+c
3	3	4	5	6	7	8	9	0+c	1+c	2+c
4	4	5	6	7	8	9	0+c	1+c	2+c	3+c
5	5	6	7	8	9	0+c	1+c	2+c	3+c	4+c
6	6	7	8	9	0+c	1+c	2+c	3+c	4+c	5+c
7	7	8	9	0+c	1+c	2+c	3+c	4+c	5+c	6+c
8	8	9	0+c	1+c	2+c	3+c	4+c	5+c	6+c	7+c
9	9	0+c	1+c	2+c	3+c	4+c	5+c	6+c	7+c	8+c

When the addition of two digits in a particular vertical column generates a **carry** ($c = 1$), the carry is inserted as an extra digit at the "top" of the column that lies immediately to the left of the current column. The process is repeated until the digits in each of the "columns" have been operated on. As an example, Figure 2.3 illustrates the four steps that are required for the addition of the two decimal numbers 5632 and 493.

```
           1        1 1       1
 5 6 3 2   5 6 3 2  5 6 3 2   5 6 3 2
   4 9 3     4 9 3    4 9 3     4 9 3
 6 1 2 5       2 5    1 2 5   6 1 2 5

 Step 1    Step 2   Step 3    Step 4
```

Figure 2.3 Four steps required for addition of two decimal integers 5632 and 493. Digits on column where addition occurs at each step appear in bold.

Addition of binary numbers. Consider the very simple task of forming the sum $\alpha + \beta$ where α and β represent two binary numbers. The process of adding the two numbers proceeds exactly as in the case of decimal numbers in "columnwise" fashion, but the addition of the binary digits is done according to the rules illustrated in Table 2.4.

---

[6] This alignment forces the coefficients of the same powers of 10 to be aligned in the same vertical column.

TABLE 2.4 Addition of two binary digits:
Addend is represented in the first vertical column,
augmend is represented in first horizontal column,
and carry c is equal to %1

+	0	1
0	0	1
1	1	0+c

Example

Consider the task of adding the two binary numbers %111010 and %11011. Figure 2.4 indicates the sequence of seven steps required for its solution.

Therefore, %111010 + %11011 = %1010101.

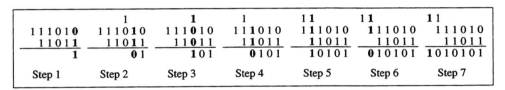

Step 1	Step 2	Step 3	Step 4	Step 5	Step 6	Step 7

Figure 2.4   Seven steps required for addition of two binary integers %111010 and %11011. Digits on column where addition occurs at each step appear in bold.

Addition of hexadecimal numbers.   Now consider how the sum $\alpha + \beta$ is formed where α and β represent two hexadecimal numbers. The process of adding the two numbers proceeds exactly as in the case of decimal numbers in "columnwise" fashion; but, the addition of hexadecimal digits is followed according to the rules illustrated in Table 2.5.

TABLE 2.5   Addition of two hexadecimal digits: Addend is represented in first vertical column, augmend is represented in first horizontal column, and c represents the carry that is equal to $1 in all cases"

+	0	1	2	3	4	5	6	7	8	9	A	B	C	D	E	F
0	0	1	2	3	4	5	6	7	8	9	A	B	C	D	E	F
1	1	2	3	4	5	6	7	8	9	A	B	C	D	E	F	0+c
2	2	3	4	5	6	7	8	9	A	B	C	D	E	F	0+c	1+c
3	3	4	5	6	7	8	9	A	B	C	D	E	F	0+c	1+c	2+c
4	4	5	6	7	8	9	A	B	C	D	E	F	0+c	1+c	2+c	3+c
5	5	6	7	8	9	A	B	C	D	E	F	0+c	1+c	2+c	3+c	4+c
6	6	7	8	9	A	B	C	D	E	F	0+c	1+c	2+c	3+c	4+c	5+c
7	7	8	9	A	B	C	D	E	F	0+c	1+c	2+c	3+c	4+c	5+c	6+c
8	8	9	A	B	C	D	E	F	0+c	1+c	2+c	3+c	4+c	5+c	6+c	7+c
9	9	A	B	C	D	E	F	0+c	1+c	2+c	3+c	4+c	5+c	6+c	7+c	8+c
A	A	B	C	D	E	F	0+c	1+c	2+c	3+c	4+c	5+c	6+c	7+c	8+c	9+c
B	B	C	D	E	F	0+c	1+c	2+c	3+c	4+c	5+c	6+c	7+c	8+c	9+c	A+c
C	C	D	E	F	0+c	1+c	2+c	3+c	4+c	5+c	6+c	7+c	8+c	9+c	A+c	B+c
D	D	E	F	0+c	1+c	2+c	3+c	4+c	5+c	6+c	7+c	8+c	9+c	A+c	B+c	C+c
E	E	F	0+c	1+c	2+c	3+c	4+c	5+c	6+c	7+c	8+c	9+c	A+c	B+c	C+c	D+c
F	F	0+c	1+c	2+c	3+c	4+c	5+c	6+c	7+c	8+c	9+c	A+c	B+c	C+c	D+c	E+c

Example

Consider the task of adding the two hex numbers $FB1963 and $DB1FA. Figure 2.5 indicates the sequence of seven steps required for the completion of this task. Therefore, $FB1963 + $DB1FA = $108CB5D.

	1	1		1	11	1
FB1963	FB1963	FB1963	FB1963	FB1963	FB1963	FB1963
DB1FA	DB1FA	DB1FA	DB1FA	DB1FA	DB1FA	DB1FA
D	**5**D	**B**5D	**C**B5D	**8**CB5D	**0**8CB5D	**1**08CB5D
Step 1	Step 2	Step 3	Step 4	Step 5	Step 6	Step 7

Figure 2.5 Seven steps required for addition of two hexadecimal integers $FB1963 and $DB1FA. Digits on column where addition occurs at each step appear in bold.

Subtraction

Subtraction of two decimal integers   Unfortunately, the subtraction operation on the set of unsigned decimal integers is *not* a closed operation, in the sense that subtraction of two decimal integers $\alpha - \beta$, where the first term of the difference α is called the **minuend** and the second term β is called the **subtrahend**, does not necessarily yield an unsigned integer γ. Therefore, when dealing with unsigned integers, we will define this operation only in the case in which the subtrahend is less than or equal to[7] the minuend. The algorithm for performing subtraction is similar to the algorithm employed for addition, in that we first write the subtrahend immediately below the minuend in such a way so that their rightmost digits are aligned in the same vertical column.[8] For the subtraction of example for $\alpha = 5632$ and $\beta = 493$ the digits are aligned as follows:

$$5632$$
$$493$$

One proceeds by subtracting the digits appearing in the same vertical column starting from the rightmost column and proceeding to the leftmost. The rules of subtracting two decimal digits are given in Table 2.6. When a subtraction of two digits generates a **borrow** $(b = 1)$, the borrow is inserted as an extra digit at the "top" of the column that lies to the immediate left of the current column and is subtracted from the topmost digit before the operation of subtraction in this column can be be performed. This process is repeated until the digits in each of the "columns" have been operated on.

Example

Consider the task of subtracting the two decimal numbers 5632 and 493. Figure 2.6 indicates the sequence of four steps required for its solution.

1	11	1	
5632	5632	5632	5632
493	493	493	493
9	**3**9	**1**39	**5**139
Step 1	Step 2	Step 3	Step 4

Figure 2.6 Four steps required for subtraction of the two decimal integers 5632 and 493. Digits on column where subtraction occurs at each step appear in bold.

---

[7] Under the natural ordering.

[8] This alignment forces the coefficients of the same powers of 10 to be aligned in the same vertical column.

TABLE 2.6 Subtraction of two decimal digits: Minuend is represented in first vertical column, subtrahend is represented in first horizontal column, and *b* represents borrow that is equal to 1 in all cases

-	0	1	2	3	4	5	6	7	8	9
0	0	9-b	8-b	7-b	6-b	5-b	4-b	3-b	2-b	1-b
1	1	0	9-b	8-b	7-b	6-b	5-b	4-b	3-b	2-b
2	2	1	0	9-b	8-b	7-b	6-b	5-b	4-b	3-b
3	3	2	1	0	9-b	8-b	7-b	6-b	5-b	4-b
4	4	3	2	1	0	9-b	8-b	7-b	6-b	5-b
5	5	4	3	2	1	0	9-b	8-b	7-b	6-b
6	6	5	4	3	2	1	0	9-b	8-b	7-b
7	7	6	5	4	3	2	1	0	9-b	8-b
8	8	7	6	5	4	3	2	1	0	9-b
9	9	8	7	6	5	4	3	2	1	0

Subtraction of binary numbers.   Consider the formation of forming the difference $\alpha - \beta$ where α and β represent two binary numbers. The process of subtracting these two binary numbers proceeds exactly as in the case of decimal numbers in "columnwise" fashion, but subtraction of the binary digits is performed according to the rules illustrated in Table 2.7.

TABLE 2.7 Subtraction of two binary digits: Minuend is represented in first vertical column, subtrahend is represented in first horizontal column, and borrow *b* is equal to %1

-	0	1
0	0	1-b
1	1	0

Example

The six-step process of subtracting the binary number %11110 from the binary number %111011 is illustrated in Figure 2.7. Therefore, %111011 − %11110 = %11101.

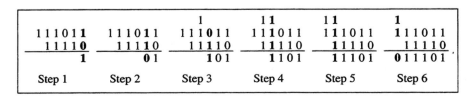

Figure 2.7   Six steps required for subtraction of two binary integers %111011 and %11110. Digits on column where subtraction occurs at each step appear in bold.

Subtraction of hexadecimal numbers.   Here we will calculate the difference $\alpha - \beta$ where α and β represent two hex numbers. The process of subtracting these two numbers proceeds exactly as in the case of decimal numbers in "columnwise" fashion, but subtraction of the hex digits is performed according to the rules illustrated in Table 2.8.

TABLE 2.8 Subtraction of two hex digits: Minuend is represented in first vertical column, subtrahend is represented in first horizontal column, and b represents the borrow's hex value, which is equal to $1

–	0	1	2	3	4	5	6	7	8	9	A	B	C	D	E	F
0	0	F–b	E–b	D–b	C–b	B–b	A–b	9–b	8–b	7–b	6–b	5–b	4–b	3–b	2–b	1–b
1	1	0	F–b	E–b	D–b	C–b	B–b	A–b	9–b	8–b	7–b	6–b	5–b	4–b	3–b	2–b
2	2	1	0	F–b	E–b	D–b	C–b	B–b	A–b	9–b	8–b	7–b	6–b	5–b	4–b	3–b
3	3	2	1	0	F–b	E–b	D–b	C–b	B–b	A–b	9–b	8–b	7–b	6–b	5–b	4–b
4	4	3	2	1	0	F–b	E–b	D–b	C–b	B–b	A–b	9–b	8–b	7–b	6–b	5–b
5	5	4	3	2	1	0	F–b	E–b	D–b	C–b	B–b	A–b	9–b	8–b	7–b	6–b
6	6	5	4	3	2	1	0	F–b	E–b	D–b	C–b	B–b	A–b	9–b	8–b	7–b
7	7	6	5	4	3	2	1	0	F–b	E–b	D–b	C–b	B–b	A–b	9–b	8–b
8	8	7	6	5	4	3	2	1	0	F–b	E–b	D–b	C–b	B–b	A–b	9–b
9	9	8	7	6	5	4	3	2	1	0	F–b	E–b	D–b	C–b	B–b	A–b
A	A	9	8	7	6	5	4	3	2	1	0	F–b	E–b	D–b	C–b	B–b
B	B	A	9	8	7	6	5	4	3	2	1	0	F–b	E–b	D–b	C–b
C	C	B	A	9	8	7	6	5	4	3	2	1	0	F–b	E–b	D–b
D	D	C	B	A	9	8	7	6	5	4	3	2	1	0	F–b	E–b
E	E	D	C	B	A	9	8	7	6	5	4	3	2	1	0	F–b
F	F	E	D	C	B	A	9	8	7	6	5	4	3	2	1	0

Example

Consider the task of subtracting the two hex numbers $FB1963 and $2B1FA. Figure 2.8 indicates the sequence of steps required for solution of the problem. Therefore, $FB1963 – $2B1FA = $F86769.

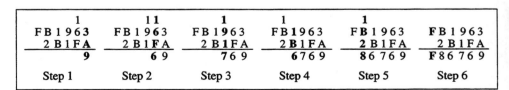

Figure 2.8   Six steps required for subtraction of two hexadecimal integers $FB1963 and

$2B1FA. Digits on column where subtraction occurs at each step appear in bold.

Multiplication

Multiplication of binary numbers.   The multiplication of binary numbers parallels that of multiplication of decimal numbers with only one fundamental exception. Namely, multiplication of two binary digits will never generate a carry as Table 2.9 indicates.

TABLE 2.9 Multiplication of two binary digits: Multiplicand represented in first vertical column, and multiplier is represented in first horizontal column

x	0	1
0	0	0
1	0	1

Example

Figure 2.9 illustrates the method of multiplication by multiplying the binary numbers %1110001101 and %10110.

Therefore the product of the two binary numbers %1110001101 and %10110 yields the binary number %100111000011110.

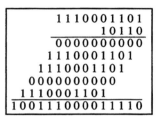

Figure 2.9 Six steps (five multiplications and one addition) required for multiplication of two binary integers %1110001101 and %10110.

Multiplication of hexadecimal numbers.   The multiplication of hexadecimal numbers parallels that of multiplication of decimal numbers with the only exception being that the operation between digits should occur in the hexadecimal number system. Table 2.10 illustrates these rules.

TABLE 2.10 Multiplication of two hex digits: Multiplicand is represented in first vertical column, multiplier is represented in first horizontal column, and, in an expression of the form $r+c$, hex integer c represents carry's hex value

*	0	1	2	3	4	5	6	7	8	9	A	B	C	D	E	F
0	0	0	0	0	0	0	0	0	0	0	0	0	0	0	0	0
1	0	1	2	3	4	5	6	7	8	9	A	B	C	D	E	F
2	0	2	4	6	8	A	C	E	0+1	2+1	4+1	6+1	8+1	A+1	C+1	E+1
3	0	3	6	9	C	F	2+1	5+1	8+1	B+1	E+1	1+2	4+2	7+2	A+2	D+2
4	0	4	8	C	0+1	4+1	8+1	C+1	0+2	4+2	8+2	C+2	0+3	4+3	8+3	C+3
5	0	5	A	F	4+1	9+1	E+1	3+2	8+2	D+2	2+3	7+3	C+3	1+4	6+4	B+4
6	0	6	C	2+1	8+1	E+1	4+2	A+2	0+3	6+3	C+3	2+4	8+4	E+4	4+5	A+5
7	0	7	E	5+1	C+1	3+2	A+2	1+3	8+3	F+3	6+4	D+4	4+5	B+5	2+6	9+6
8	0	8	0+1	8+1	0+2	8+2	0+3	8+3	0+4	8+4	0+5	8+5	0+6	8+6	0+7	8+7
9	0	9	2+1	B+1	4+2	D+2	6+3	F+3	8+4	1+5	A+5	3+6	C+6	5+7	E+7	7+8
A	0	A	4+1	E+1	8+2	2+3	C+3	6+4	0+5	A+5	4+6	E+6	8+7	2+8	C+8	6+9
B	0	B	6+1	1+2	C+2	7+3	2+4	D+4	8+5	3+6	E+6	9+7	4+8	F+8	A+9	5+A
C	0	C	8+1	4+2	0+3	C+3	8+4	4+5	0+6	C+6	8+7	4+8	0+9	C+9	8+A	4+B
D	0	D	A+1	7+2	4+3	1+4	E+4	B+5	8+6	5+7	2+8	F+8	C+9	9+A	6+B	3+C
E	0	E	C+1	A+2	8+3	6+4	4+5	2+6	0+7	E+7	C+8	A+9	8+A	6+B	4+C	2+D
F	0	F	E+1	D+2	C+3	B+4	A+5	9+6	8+7	7+8	6+9	5+A	4+B	3+C	2+D	1+E

Division

Division of binary numbers. This operation parallels that of decimal division, and an example is presented subsequently. It is worth noting that this operation provides us with both a **quotient** and a **remainder**.

Example

Figure 2.10 illustrates the division of the binary number %1010111 by the binary number %10. Therefore, the quotient is equal to %101011, and the remainder is equal to %1.

```
 1010111    |10
-10          1
 -------
  010111
 -00         0
 -------
   10111
  -10        1
 -------
    0111
   -00       0
 -------
     111
    -10      1
 -------
      11
     -10     1
 -------
       1
Remainder ↑  ↑ Quotient
```

Figure 2.10 Dividing binary integer %1010111 by %10. Digits of dividend where division occurs at each step appear in bold.

2.1.4 Signed Integer Representation

Consider the situation in which the numbers that we would like to represent are signed numbers. Until now we were able to represent such numbers in the decimal system by denoting their sign the via the symbols "+" and "–". Again, however, computers employ a different representation internally. In this section we will present the three most common representations.

Sign-magnitude representation. Recall that each integer is characterized by its magnitude and its sign. For example, the decimal numbers +423 and –423 have the same magnitude 423 but opposite signs. The Sign-Magnitude method takes advantage of this observation and uses the following technique. Given any n-digit number in radix r with magnitude

$$\alpha_{n-1}\alpha_{n-2}\ldots\ldots\alpha_1\alpha_0 \tag{2.10}$$

the number is represented by an $n+1$-digit number

$$b_n\alpha_{n-1}\alpha_{n-2}\ldots\ldots\alpha_1\alpha_0 \tag{2.11}$$

where the appended digit b_n is a *binary* digit that reflects the sign of the number. By convention the value of b_n is equal to 0 if the number is positive or 0; otherwise, its value is equal to 1. For example, the two binary numbers %10011 and %00011 represent the decimal numbers –3 and 3, respectively.

In general, given the sign-magnitude representation of an $n+1$-digit number in radix r as in equation 2.11, the value of the integer can be computed via the equation

$$(1-2\cdot b_n)\cdot\left(\alpha_{n-1}\cdot r^{n-1}+\alpha_{n-2}\cdot r^{n-2}+\ldots\ldots+\alpha_2\cdot r^2+\alpha_1\cdot r^1+\alpha_0\cdot r^0\right) \quad (2.12)$$

or via the more compact, equivalent expression

$$(1-2\cdot b_n)\cdot\sum_{k=0}^{n-1}\alpha_k\cdot r^k \quad (2.13)$$

Before the other two representations are discussed, we will present some necessary terminology and definitions.

Diminished radix-complement.   Consider a n-digit integer γ in radix r. That is

$$\gamma=\alpha_{n-1}\alpha_{n-2}\ldots\ldots\alpha_1\alpha_0 \quad (2.23)$$

The *diminished radix-complement* (*true-complement*, *[r–1]'s complement*) of the integer γ denoted by $\overline{\gamma}$ is defined via the equation

$$\overline{\gamma}=(r^n-1)-\gamma \quad (2.24)$$

As an example consider the decimal integer $\gamma=3421$. Then the diminished radix-complement of this number is given by

$$\overline{\gamma}=10^4-3421-1=6578$$

Despite the fact that the preceding calculations are straightforward, we are ready to develop a method that will permit one to calculate the diminished radix-complement by avoiding all exponentiations. Let

$$\gamma=\alpha_{n-1}\alpha_{n-2}\ldots\ldots\alpha_1\alpha_0 \quad (2.25)$$

and

$$\overline{\gamma}=\overline{\alpha}_{n-1}\overline{\alpha}_{n-2}\ldots\ldots\overline{\alpha}_1\overline{\alpha}_0 \quad (2.26)$$

Then according to equation 2.24, we should have

$$\gamma+\overline{\gamma}=r^n-1 \quad (2.27)$$

The left side of the preceding equation is equal to

$$(\alpha_{n-1}+\overline{\alpha}_{n-1})\cdot r^{n-1}+(\alpha_{n-2}+\overline{\alpha}_{n-2})\cdot r^{n-2}+\ldots\ldots\ldots$$
$$+(\alpha_1+\overline{\alpha}_1)\cdot r^1+(\alpha_0+\overline{\alpha}_0)\cdot r^0 \quad (2.28)$$

and in compact form

$$\gamma+\overline{\gamma}=\sum_{k=0}^{n-1}(\alpha_k+\overline{\alpha}_k)\cdot r^k \quad (2.29)$$

Equation 2.27 in view of equation 2.29 can be rewritten as

$$\sum_{k=0}^{n-1}(\alpha_k+\overline{\alpha}_k)\cdot r^k=r^n-1 \quad (2.30)$$

Considering the geometric sum $\sum_{k=0}^{n-1}r^k$ we obtain

$$\sum_{k=0}^{n-1}r^k=\frac{r^n-1}{r-1}$$

Multiplying both sides of the preceding equation by $(r-1)$, we obtain

$$(r-1) \cdot \sum_{k=0}^{n-1} r^k = r^n - 1$$

or

$$\left(\sum_{k=0}^{n-1} (r-1) \cdot r^k \right) = r^n - 1$$

Combining equations 2.27 and 2.29 we obtain

$$\sum_{k=0}^{n-1} (\alpha_k + \overline{\alpha}_k) \cdot r^k = \sum_{k=0}^{n-1} (r-1) \cdot r^k$$

The preceding equation yields the set of the following n equations

$$(\alpha_k + \overline{\alpha}_k) = (r-1) \text{ for } k = 0, 1, \ldots, n-1$$

Rewriting the preceding equations we obtain

$$\overline{\alpha}_k = (r-1) - \alpha_k \text{ for } k = 0, 1, \ldots, n-1$$

Hence, the preceding calculations illustrate the following general rule:

> *To calculate the diminished radix-complement representation of an integer, each of its digits is subtracted from $(r-1)$.*

Radix-complement.   Consider a n-digit integer γ in radix r. That is

$$\gamma = \alpha_{n-1} \alpha_{n-2} \ldots \ldots \alpha_1 \alpha_0 \tag{2.31}$$

The *radix-complement (radix-minus-one, r's complement)* of the integer γ denoted by $\overline{\overline{\gamma}}$ is defined via the equation

$$\overline{\overline{\gamma}} = r^n - \gamma \tag{2.32}$$

As an example consider again the decimal integer $\gamma = 3421$. Then the radix-complement of this number is given by

$$\overline{\overline{\gamma}} = 10^4 - 3421 = 6579$$

Despite the fact that the preceding calculations are straightforward, a method similar to the one in the previous section that will permit one to calculate the radix-complement by avoiding all exponentiations is developed subsequently. Let (as before)

$$\gamma = \alpha_{n-1} \alpha_{n-2} \ldots \ldots \alpha_1 \alpha_0 \tag{2.33}$$

and

$$\overline{\overline{\gamma}} = \overline{\overline{\alpha}}_{n-1} \overline{\overline{\alpha}}_{n-2} \ldots \ldots \overline{\overline{\alpha}}_1 \overline{\overline{\alpha}}_0 \tag{2.34}$$

Then according to equation 2.32 we should have

$$\gamma + \overline{\overline{\gamma}} = r^n \tag{2.35}$$

Following the same steps as earlier we arrive at the following equation:

$$\sum_{k=0}^{n-1} (\alpha_k + \overline{\overline{\alpha}}_k) \cdot r^k = \sum_{k=1}^{n-1} (r-1) \cdot r^k + r \tag{2.36}$$

The preceding equation yields the set of the following n equations:

$$(\alpha_k + \overline{\overline{\alpha}}_k) = (r - 1) \text{ for } k = 1, \ldots, n-1$$

and

$$(\alpha_0 + \overline{\overline{\alpha}}_0) = r$$

Rewriting the preceding equations we obtain

$$\overline{\overline{\alpha}}_k = (r-1) - \alpha_k = \overline{\alpha}_k \text{ for } k = 1, \ldots, n-1$$

and

$$\overline{\overline{\alpha}}_0 = r - \alpha_0 = \overline{\alpha}_0 + 1$$

Hence, the preceding calculations illustrate the following general rule:

To calculate the radix-complement representation of an integer, each of its digits is subtracted from $(r-1)$, and the integer 1 is added to the result.

One's complement representation.   Earlier it was stated that the internal representation of integers is in binary form. Because the radix r is equal to two, the one's complement representation is an extension of the diminished radix-complement notion discussed earlier. In particular if a number is positive, then its representation is the *same* as in the sign-magnitude method; otherwise, its representation is the same as that of the diminished radix-complement of its absolute value.

As an example consider the decimal number 18. Because this number is positive and if we assume an 8-bit binary integer, in one's complement its representation is

$$18 \;\rightarrow\; \%00010010$$

where the leftmost bit represents the sign of the integer, and the seven rightmost bits represent the magnitude of the number.

In the case in which the decimal number was -18, then the one's complement representation of this number would coincide with that of $\overline{\gamma}$ where $\gamma = \%00010010$, and according to our previous discussions

$$\overline{\gamma} = \%100000000 - \%00010010 - \%00000001 = \%11101101$$

Finally we could use the general property developed earlier in which each digit should be subtracted from $r - 1$. In this case $r - 1 = 1$; hence, if the binary digit is equal to 0, the result of its subtraction from 1 is 1; however, if the binary digit is 1, the result of its subtraction from 1 is 0. Therefore, in the binary system the one's complement representation of a negative integer is calculated by first figuring the sign-magnitude form of its absolute value; then we replace each 0 bit with 1 and each 1 bit with 0. This process is referred to as the process of **complementing** each bit, and this is because the complement of the 0 bit denoted by $\overline{0}$ is the 1 bit, whereas the complement of the 1 bit, denoted by $\overline{1}$, is the 0 bit.

Summarizing the preceding discussion we can see that the one's complement representation of the decimal integer -18 can be calculated via

$$\overline{\gamma} = \%\overline{00010010} = \%11101101$$

Two's complement representation.   As the one's complement representation is an extension of the diminished radix-complement, the two's complement representation is an extension of the radix-complement notion discussed earlier. If the number is positive or zero, its representation is the *same* as in the sign-magnitude method; otherwise, its representation is the same as that of the radix-complement of its absolute value.

As an example consider the decimal number 18. Because this number is positive and if we assume an 8-bit binary integer, its two's complement representation is

$$18 \;\rightarrow\; \%00010010$$

where the leftmost bit represents the sign of the integer and the seven rightmost bits represent the magnitude of the number.

If the decimal number was -18, then the two's complement representation of this number would coincide with that of $\overline{\overline{\gamma}}$ where $\gamma = \%00010010$; and according to our previous discussions

$$\overline{\overline{\gamma}} = \%100000000 - \%00010010 = \%11101110$$

Finally we could use the general property developed earlier whereby each digit should be subtracted from $r-1$ and then adding 1 to the result. In this case because $r-1=1$, the same argument that was made in the case of one's complement applies here. Namely, subtracting a digit from 1 is equivalent to complementing that digit. Hence, the conversion of a negative integer is a three step process: find the sign-magnitude representation of the absolute value of the number; complement each bit, and then add $\%1$ to the result.

Summarizing the preceding discussion, we can see that the two's complement representation of the decimal number -18 can be found via

$$\overline{\overline{\gamma}} = \overline{\%00010010} + \%1 = \%11101110$$

Brief comparison of three representations.   We have seen that there are three possible ways to represent a signed integer internally in binary: sign-magnitude representation, one's complement representation, and two's complement representation. Unfortunately, computers allocate a fixed number of bits where an integer can be stored. For simplicity, let's assume that this fixed number is 4 bits. Then the decimal numbers as well as their binary equivalent representations are given in Table 2.11.

On closer examination of Table 2.11 the following points can be observed.

- In any one of the preceding representations, the number of *different* bit strings that can be formed is equal to $2^4 = 16$. In general, there are 2^m different bit strings that can be formed in a storage area m-bits wide.
- The sign-magnitude and one's complement forms, despite their simplicity, admit two representations for the decimal number zero. The third representation removes that shortcoming by assigning a unique code to that decimal number; therefore, a code is freed that can be used to represent a decimal integer (-8) that was not represented under neither of the first two methods.
- As we will see shortly, the two's complement representation has the distinct advantage over the one's complement representation in that calculating the result of arithmetic operations is easier. Hence, most of the machines use the two's complement representation as opposed to the other two.

TABLE 2.11   Decimal integers and their binary representations

Decimal integer	Sign-magnitude representation	One's complement representation	Two's complement representation
−8	−	−	1000
−7	1111	1000	1001
−6	1110	1001	1010
−5	1101	1010	1011
−4	1100	1011	1100
−3	1011	1100	1101
−2	1010	1101	1110
−1	1001	1110	1111
−0	1000	1111	−
+0	0000	0000	0000
+1	0001	0001	0001
+2	0010	0010	0010
+3	0011	0011	0011
+4	0100	0100	0100
+5	0101	0101	0101
+6	0110	0110	0110
+7	0111	0111	0111

2.1.5 Two's Complement Representation

As was stated earlier, signed integer arithmetic is simplified greatly by using the two's complement representation. In this section we will illustrate the reasons, but first we should look at certain issues pertaining to the two's complement more closely.

Closer look at the two's complement representation   First, it is important to realize that the range of signed integers that can be represented internally depends entirely on the number of bits that is allocated for their storage. In particular if we assume that with m-bits of storage allocated, the smallest number that can be represented is -2^{m-1}, whereas the largest is $2^{m-1} - 1$.

Second, the value of signed integer d represented by the m-bit string

$$b_{m-1}b_{m-2}b_{m-3}\ldots\ldots b_1 b_0$$

can be found via the equation

$$d = (-b_{m-1} \cdot 2^{m-1}) + \sum_{i=0}^{m-2} b_i \cdot 2^i$$

Finally, notice that the m-bit string %10000000.0 represents the smallest signed decimal integer that can be stored (-2^{m-1}); moreover, it is the only integer that has no radix-complement and is not the radix-complement of any m-bit representation. In other words, the two's complement system is not closed under negation.

Addition.   Recall that addition of signed decimal integers, given that we are accustomed to it, is a simple matter. For example, consider the following four addition operations:

$$(a)\ 7 + (-1) = 6,\ (b)\ 5 + (1) = 6,\ (c)\ (-1) + (-8) = -9,\ (d)\ 5 + 6 = 11$$

Despite the fact that the calculations are simple, the underlying algorithm involves several tests relative to the sign of the operands. As an illustration, consider additions a and b. Notice that in the former case we examine the signs of the operands, and we find that they are different. In the next step we compare the absolute values of those operands. Because the magnitude of the first operand is larger than that of the second, we conclude that the result is positive, and its magnitude is equal to the difference between the magnitude of the first and second operand. In the case of addition c, we first examine the signs of the operands. We decide that the result is a negative number (because both integers are negative); therefore, the magnitude of the result is equal to the sum of the magnitudes of the operands.

With the use of either the sign-magnitude or the one's complement representation, one should perform similar tests to arrive at the result. With the use of two's complement representation, all these tests become unnecessary. In particular, in the latter case the two integers are added as though they were representing unsigned integers, and no consideration is placed on their sign. Figure 2.11 illustrates these concepts by assuming a 4-bit-wide storage area.

Figure 2.11   Four addition examples. Examples a and d yield overflow. Carries into and out of sign bit position as well as discarded digit appear inside boxes.

The reader should have observed that in all cases 1 bit is discarded. Some will arrive at the *erroneous* conclusion that if the discarded bit is 1, then an error has occurred, whereas if the discarded bit is 0 no harm is done. To see this, consider examples a and d in Figure 2.11. In the former case despite the fact that the discarded bit is 1, the answer is as expected (6); therefore, no error has occurred. In the latter case, while the discarded digit is 0, the result (-5) is different from the expected (11); therefore, an error has occurred. As a matter of fact, an error occurs only when the result of the operation is an integer that is outside the range of integers that can be stored. Such a situation is referred to as an **overflow**. The rule of determining an overflow is the following:

If the carry into the sign bit position is different from the carry out of the sign bit position, an overflow has occurred.

With this simple rule at hand we can immediately conclude that additions c and d in Figure 2.11 result in an overflow.

Subtraction.   Consider the following simple task: subtract y from x; that is, calculate $x - y$. With the aid of mathematics, one can see that the last expression can be rewritten as $x + (-y)$. The last equation indicates that when a subtraction is to be performed, one just negates the subtrahend and then performs addition. Hence, assuming now two's complement representation, to subtract %1011 from %1111 one negates the subtrahend and then performs addition. It should be clear that to negate an integer that is represented in two's complement, we simply calculate the radix complement of that number.[9] Figure 2.12 illustrates the two steps that are required to subtract two integers assuming again a 4-bit-wide area.

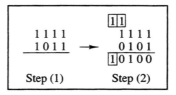

Figure 2.12 One subtraction example. In step 1, radix complement of subtrahend is calculated, which is added to minuend in step 2.

Multiplication.   As in decimal operations, the product of two binary m-digit integers yields a binary integer whose number of digits exceeds m. The number of digits required to represent the product never exceeds $(2m - 1)$, however. To see this, notice that the product of two (bounded) integers becomes *maximal* whenever both factors are maximal. Assuming two's complement representation, the product becomes maximal whenever both signed integers are equal to -2^{m-1}, and in that case the product is equal to 2^{2m-2}, which requires exactly $2m - 1$ bits of storage. Henceforth, the product of two m-bit signed integers is represented in $2m$ bits of storage. Notice that the product of two m-bit signed integers could yield *more* than $2m$ bits, but the leftmost bits are truncated to bring the product to size, and the result (despite this truncation) is *always* accurate.

Figure 2.13 illustrates the steps that are required to multiply the two 4-bit signed integers %1101 and %0110. Notice that before the multiplication is to be performed, the 4-bit multiplicand %1101 is expanded to 8-bits by propagating its sign bit to the left. The resulting representation %11111101 does not affect either the sign or the magnitude of the multiplicand. After the expansion of the multiplicand is performed, the multiplication takes place as though the two bit strings were representing unsigned integers. After the multiplication has been completed the leftmost 3 bits of the product are discarded, and the rightmost 8 bits represent the result.

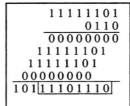

Figure 2.13 Multiplication of two 4-bit-wide signed integers (−3 and +6). Multiplicand is expanded to $2 \cdot 4 = 8$ bits. Multiplication is performed as though integers were unsigned; 11-bit result is truncated to left in such way so it is represented by 8 rightmost bits (enclosed in rectangle).

---

[9] Notice that an overflow will occur if we attempt to negate the number %1000.

2.2 BOOLEAN LOGIC

As we have seen, computers work only with 1's and 0's (i.e., in binary or base 2 arithmetic). In this section we introduce the mathematical foundations used by computers to perform binary computation. An understanding of **boolean logic** helps students see how the logic circuits of a computer (i.e., logic gates) may be modeled by simple mathematical functions. For now, we define a **logical circuit** as a black box that has several inputs (which may take on the values 0 or 1) and a number of outputs (which may also be 0 or 1). The mathematical tools developed in this section of algebraic expression manipulation, normal form representation, truth tables, and Karnaugh maps will be necessary to understand the design of the central processor components to be described in later sections.

2.2.1 Basics

We start our discussions by presenting some definitions. Let S be a set of objects, that is,

$$S = \{\, a, b, c, d, \dots \,\}$$

A **variable** x on the set S, is a symbol (x) used to represent any element of the set S and we write $x \in S$. In our specific example $x \in S$ indicates that x may take any value on the set S, that is, $x = a$ or $x = b$ and so on. In the following text, the variables will be denoted by the lowercase italic characters and may be subscripted. For example, x, y, and v_1 will denote variables.

If $x \in S$ and x takes only one value in the set S, say $x = a$, then the variable is said to be a **constant** variable or simply constant.

Let S and T be two sets. A **unary operator** f defined on S is a mapping from S to T, a **binary operator** g defined on $S*S$ is a mapping from S to T. If $S = T$ then the operator is said to be **closed**. As an example, if $S = T = \Re$, where $\Re$ denotes the set of real numbers, then the negation operator defined by $f(r) = -r$ is closed on $\Re$ because the negative of any real number is a real number. On the other hand, if we consider the same operation defined on the set of natural numbers $\{1, 2, 3, 4, 5, \dots\}$ it is easy to see that the operation is not closed.

Notice that the operator f defined previously is a **unary** operator because it operates on a single number (argument). On the other hand, the addition "+" and the subtraction "−" operators defined on the set of real numbers are examples of **binary** operators because each of these mappings operates on a two-tuple (x, y). For example $+(5,7)=5+7=12$ and $-(5,7)=5-7=-2$.

An operator, **op** defined on a set S, is **commutative** if the following property holds:

$$x \,\textbf{op}\, y = y \,\textbf{op}\, x \qquad \text{for each pair } x, y \in S$$

As an example, the + operator defined on the set of real numbers is commutative because $x + y = y + x$ for each pair x, y of real numbers. On the other hand, the subtraction operator − defined on the same set is not commutative, because $2 - 3 \neq 3 - 2$.

An operator, **op** defined on S, is **associative** if the following property holds:

$$(x \,\textbf{op}\, y) \,\textbf{op}\, z = x \,\textbf{op}\, (y \,\textbf{op}\, z) \text{ for each } x, y, z \in S$$

Thus again in ordinary arithmetic, the + operator is associative. That is $(x + y) + z = x + (y + x)$. As a counterexample, think of the case of integer division. For example: $(40/4)/2 = 5$, whereas $40/(4/2) = 20$.

An operator, $\mathbf{op_1}$, **distributes** over another operator $\mathbf{op_2}$ if the following property holds:

$$x\ \mathbf{op_1}\ (y\ \mathbf{op_2}\ z) = (x\ \mathbf{op_1}\ y)\ \mathbf{op_2}\ (x\ \mathbf{op_1}\ z)\ \text{for each}\ x, y, z \in S$$

As an example, in ordinary arithmetic the $*$ operator distributes over the $+$ operator. Thus $x * (y + z) = (x * y) + (x * z)$. However, notice that in ordinary arithmetic, $+$ does not distribute over $*$. To see this notice that $3 + (2 * 5) = 13$ whereas $(3 + 2) * (3 + 5) = 40$.

2.2.2 Boolean Algebra

Mathematically speaking, a **boolean algebra** B is a four-tuple defined by $B = \{\mathbf{B}, \wedge, \vee, \overline{}\}$ where $\mathbf{B}$ is a set that includes variables and two distinguished elements, 0 and 1; $\wedge$ and $\vee$ are two closed operators defined on $\mathbf{B}$ and referred to as the wedge (meet) and vee (join) operators, respectively; and, $\overline{}$ is a closed unary operator on $\mathbf{B}$ referred to as the complementation operator. Finally, we require rules for the composition of variables and operators. These are the **postulates** or **axioms** of the system. The axioms that are listed in Table 2.12 must be satisfied for all x, y, and $z \in B$.

TABLE 2.12 Axioms required to define a boolean algebra

Name	$\wedge$ version	$\vee$ version
Axiom 1	$x \wedge 1 = x$	$x \vee 0 = x$
Axiom 2 (commutative)	$x \wedge y = y \wedge x$	$x \vee y = y \vee x$
Axiom 3 (distributive)	$x \wedge (y \vee z) = (x \wedge y) \vee (x \wedge z)$	$x \vee (y \wedge z) = (x \vee y) \wedge (x \vee z)$
Axiom 4	$x \wedge \overline{x} = 0$	$x \vee \overline{x} = 1$
Axiom 5	$\overline{0} = 1$	$\overline{0} = 1$

The interpretation of the two binary operators $(\wedge, \vee)$ will be made clear in the next section. The crucial feature of boolean algebra, and the one that makes it of interest to us, is that it expressly deals with statements that are either true/false (or 1/0, on/off, or in other words binary statements). It will be seen that the algebra is **sound** in the sense that all statements that deal in only true/false are representable, and that all conclusions derived by the operators are correct. Conversely, the system is **complete** in the sense that all logical statements in the system may be derived from the basic axioms. Thus boolean algebra is the perfect tool to use when describing binary computers, because everything that may be computed by a computer is representable in boolean logic.

Operator interpretation.   The interpretation of the operators (although precisely defined by the axioms in Table 2.12) requires an explanation. Each operator may be defined by a "black box" with one or more inputs and a single output. A unary operator has a single input. A binary operator has two inputs. The input(s) and output must be the constants 1 or 0. Given this, the operator may be uniquely identified by the output generated for all input sequences.

Consider the black box view of a unary operator with input x and output o as shown in Figure 2.14.

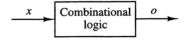

Figure 2.14 Unary operator.

With a unary operator there are only $2^1 = 2$ possible input states, that is, 0 and 1. For each of these possible input states the output may be either a 0 or 1. Thus looking at the number of possible sets of output states for the given input states, we see there are $2^{2^1} = 4$ different groups. Table 2.13 gives all the possible output states for each input state.

TABLE 2.13 Possible outputs for unary operator

x	$S1$	$S2$	$S3$	$S4$
0	0	0	1	1
1	0	1	0	1

Notice that state **S1** corresponds to "always 0," whereas state **S4** corresponds to "always 1." State **S2** represents x, that is, the output is the same as the input, and state **S3** represents the inverse of the input, that is, when the input is 1 the output is 0 and vice versa. Of the four possibilities, state **S3** is the only one of interest as an operator, because states **S1** and **S4** are already defined by the constants 0 and 1, and state **S2** does nothing! The usual name for **S3** is **not**, and it corresponds to the $^-$ in algebraic expressions. Thus $\bar{x}$ is the inverse of x. If x is 1, then $\bar{x}$ is 0, and, conversely, if x is 0, then $\bar{x}$ is 1.

One powerful visual tool for the representation of operators is the **truth table**. In a truth table, the values of the inputs are listed in consecutive columns, followed by the corresponding output formed by each input row. The truth table is a convenient method of defining an operator because it specifies precisely the output for every input combination. Additional uses for truth tables are discussed in Section 2.3.3. The truth table for the **not** operator is given in Table 2.14.

TABLE 2.14
The **not** operator

not

x	$\bar{x}$
0	1
1	0

The other operator type specified in boolean algebra is the two-input operator (or binary) operator. A black-box diagram representing binary operators is given in Figure 2.15.

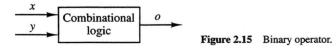

Figure 2.15   Binary operator.

The operators $\wedge$ and $\vee$ are both binary operators. We notice that in a binary system with only two possible inputs, there are exactly 2^2 different input states (i.e., 00, 01, 10, 11). For each of these states the output may be either 0 or 1. Thus the number of different sets of output states for all possible input values is given by $2^{2^2} = 16$. Table 2.15 gives the output for the differing input values of x and y.

TABLE 2.15 Possible outputs for binary operator

x	y	$S1$	$S2$	$S3$	$S4$	$S5$	$S6$	$S7$	$S8$	$S9$	$S10$	$S11$	$S12$	$S13$	$S14$	$S15$	$S16$
0	0	0	0	0	0	0	0	0	0	1	1	1	1	1	1	1	1
0	1	0	0	0	0	1	1	1	1	0	0	0	0	1	1	1	1
1	0	0	0	1	1	0	0	1	1	0	0	1	1	0	0	1	1
1	1	0	1	0	1	0	1	0	1	0	1	0	1	0	1	0	1

Thus, given a stateless black box with only two inputs, it must generate an output equivalent to one of the preceding state columns. Again notice that state **S1** is "always 0" and state **S16** is "always 1." The operators $\wedge$ and $\vee$ must correspond to one of these 16 states. In fact, we define the $\wedge$ operator as state **S2**, and the $\vee$ operator as state **S8**. *These operators are given the more usual terms* **and** *and* **or** *and are defined by the truth tables given in Table 2.16.*

TABLE 2.16 The and and or operators

and

x	y	x∧y
0	0	0
0	1	0
1	0	0
1	1	1

or

x	y	x∨y
0	0	0
0	1	1
1	0	1
1	1	1

One may wonder why the algebra is defined in terms of these two operators. The answer is that they possess similar meanings in logic as their spoken counterparts. Thus we have a high degree of familiarity with them. The two operators correspond to **and** and **or** by the following definitions:

If x is true and *y is true, then x $\wedge$ y is true. Otherwise, x $\wedge$ y is false.*

Similarly,

If x is true or *y is true (or both are true), then x $\vee$ y is true. Otherwise, x $\vee$ y is false.*

Hence, our **and** and **or** operators possess simple intuitive properties. We note here that given the operators $\wedge$, $\vee$, and $^-$ along with the rules of composition defined in Table 2.12 we are able to generate all the other binary operators that appear in Table 2.15. In Table 2.17 we list the three operators presented so far in four different representations. The first is the name of the operator, the second is the mathematical symbol, the third is the truth table definition (or function definition), and the last is the diagrammatic symbol used in engineering circuit diagrams.[10]

TABLE 2.17 Representations of algebraic operators

Name	Symbol	Truth table	Diagram symbol
not	$-$	$\begin{array}{c\|c} x & \bar{x} \\ \hline 0 & 1 \\ 1 & 0 \end{array}$	
and	$\wedge$	$\begin{array}{cc\|c} x & y & x \wedge y \\ \hline 0 & 0 & 0 \\ 0 & 1 & 0 \\ 1 & 0 & 0 \\ 1 & 1 & 1 \end{array}$	
or	$\vee$	$\begin{array}{cc\|c} x & y & x \vee y \\ \hline 0 & 0 & 0 \\ 0 & 1 & 1 \\ 1 & 0 & 1 \\ 1 & 1 & 1 \end{array}$	

Recall from the previous section that the standard algebra consisting of only two elements (0 and 1) has 16 binary operators. We shall see in Section 2.3 that we are able to construct **circuits** using **semiconductor components** that behave in an analogous fashion to some of the boolean operators defined earlier. We shall use two voltages levels +5 V and 0 V to represent the logical values 0 and 1, respectively, and **gates** (formed from transistors) to realize the different operators. The **circuit symbols** for the most common operators are given in the final column of Table 2.17. These circuit symbols may be connected together to form circuits that correspond to particular boolean expressions[11] and may be realized using transistors. Thus, in the following discussions, the reader is encouraged to remember that the "abstract" manipulations we perform in boolean algebra will be useful later when we design components. Another set of operators including **nand** and **nor** that are also useful in terms of their interpretation at the transistor level are defined in Table 2.18. Notice that the **nand** and **nor** operators have a small circle on their outputs; this symbol corresponds to *negation* and is used in circuit diagrams on either the input or output of a component to indicate signal negation.

TABLE 2.18 Additional symbols used in computer applications

Name	Symbol	Truth table	Diagram symbol
nand	$\oslash$	$\begin{array}{cc\|c} x & y & x \ y \\ \hline 0 & 0 & 1 \\ 0 & 1 & 1 \\ 1 & 0 & 1 \\ 1 & 1 & 0 \end{array}$	
nor	$\ovee$	$\begin{array}{cc\|c} x & y & x \ y \\ \hline 0 & 0 & 1 \\ 0 & 1 & 0 \\ 1 & 0 & 0 \\ 1 & 1 & 0 \end{array}$	
xor	$\oplus$	$\begin{array}{cc\|c} y & x & x \oplus y \\ \hline 0 & 0 & 0 \\ 0 & 1 & 1 \\ 1 & 0 & 1 \\ 1 & 1 & 0 \end{array}$	
co-in	$\otimes$	$\begin{array}{cc\|c} x & y & x \otimes y \\ \hline 0 & 0 & 1 \\ 0 & 1 & 0 \\ 1 & 0 & 0 \\ 1 & 1 & 1 \end{array}$	No symbol

Notice that according to the definition of a boolean algebra, we know that $\wedge$ and $\vee$ are commutative and distributive. In fact they are also both associative as we shall show shortly.

---

[10] Symbols as defined in IEEE 91-1973 Standard.
[11] The precise definition of a boolean expression will be given shortly, for now the intuitive interpretation will suffice.

Axioms and theorem construction

The axioms of Table 2.12 may be used to construct several basic theorems that enable us to manipulate boolean strings. A summary of the original axioms and some basic theorems are listed in Table 2.19.

TABLE 2.19   Axioms and basic theorems of boolean algebra

Name	**and** version	**or** version
Axiom 1	$x \wedge 1 = x$	$x \vee 0 = x$
Axiom 2 (commutative)	$x \wedge y = y \wedge x$	$x \vee y = y \vee x$
Axiom 3 (distributive)	$x \wedge (y \vee z) = (x \wedge y) \vee (x \wedge z)$	$x \vee (y \wedge z) = (x \vee y) \wedge (x \vee z)$
Axiom 4	$x \wedge \overline{x} = 0$	$x \vee \overline{x} = 1$
Axiom 5	$\overline{0} = 1$	$\overline{0} = 1$
Theorem 1	$x \wedge x = x$	$x \vee x = x$
Theorem 2	$x \wedge 0 = 0$	$x \vee 1 = 1$
Theorem 3 (involution)	$\overline{(\overline{x})} = x$	as **and** version
Theorem 4 (absorption)	$x \wedge (x \vee y) = x$	$x \vee (x \wedge y) = x$
Theorem 5 (unique complement)	If $x \vee y = 1$ and $x \wedge y = 0$ then $y = \overline{x}$	as **and** version
Theorem 6	If $x \wedge y = z \wedge y$ and $x \wedge \overline{y} = z \wedge \overline{y}$ then $x = z$	If $x \vee y = z \vee y$ and $x \vee \overline{y} = z \vee \overline{y}$ then $x = z$
Theorem 7 (associative)	$x \wedge (y \wedge z) = (x \wedge y) \wedge z$	$x \vee (y \vee z) = (x \vee y) \vee z$
Theorem 8 (DeMorgan)	$\overline{(x \wedge y)} = \overline{x} \vee \overline{y}$	$\overline{(x \vee y)} = \overline{x} \wedge \overline{y}$

To show how the axioms may be used to derive new theorems, we shall now prove the **and** version of each of theorems 1 to 8 in Table 2.19.

Theorem 1

$$x \wedge x = (x \wedge x) \vee 0 \qquad \text{(Axiom 1)}$$

$$= (x \wedge x) \vee (x \wedge \overline{x}) \qquad \text{(Axiom 4)}$$

$$= x \wedge (x \vee \overline{x}) \qquad \text{(Axiom 3)}$$

$$= x \wedge 1 \qquad \text{(Axiom 4)}$$

$$= x \qquad \text{(Axiom 1)}$$

Theorem 2

$$x \wedge 0 = (x \wedge 0) \vee 0 \qquad \text{(Axiom 1)}$$

$$= (x \wedge 0) \vee (x \wedge \overline{x}) \qquad \text{(Axiom 4)}$$

$$= x \wedge (0 \vee \overline{x}) \qquad \text{(Axiom 3)}$$

$$= x \wedge \overline{x} \qquad \text{(Axiom 1)}$$

$$= 0 \qquad \text{(Axiom 4)}$$

Theorem 3. Theorem 3 is known as involution. It states that complementing a complemented expression yields the original expression. Theorem 3 may be proved by the following reasoning. Assume that x is true; then by axiom 4 (**and** version) $\bar{x}$ is false. Conversely, assume that x is false; then by axiom 4 (**or** version) $\bar{x}$ is true. Thus, the complement is defined for x and similarly for $\bar{x}$. Thus we notice that x and $\bar{\bar{x}}$ will always have the same logical value, that is, $x = \bar{\bar{x}}$.

Theorem 4. Theorem 4 is known as absorption. It states that if x is true, and x or y is true, then we know that x is true, that is, we can absorb the more restrictive disjunctive clause.

$$x \wedge (x \vee y) = (x \vee 0) \wedge (x \vee y) \qquad \text{(Axiom 1)}$$

$$= x \vee (0 \wedge y) \qquad \text{(Axiom 3)}$$

$$= x \vee 0 \qquad \text{(Theorem 2)}$$

$$= x \qquad \text{(Axiom 1)}$$

Theorem 5. Theorem 5 is known as the uniqueness of the complement. It states in effect that if the disjunction of two terms is 0 and their conjunction is 1, the two terms are complements. We will show that $y = y \vee \bar{x}$ using the hypothesis $x \vee y = 1$, and that $\bar{x} = y \vee \bar{x}$ using the hypothesis $x \wedge y = 0$. Thus the theorem is shown true assuming both hypothesis.

$$\text{a. } \quad y = y \vee 0 \qquad \text{(Axiom 1)}$$

$$= y \vee (x \wedge \bar{x}) \qquad \text{(Axiom 4)}$$

$$= (y \vee x) \wedge (y \vee \bar{x}) \qquad \text{(Axiom 3)}$$

$$= (x \vee y) \wedge (y \vee \bar{x}) \qquad \text{(Axiom 2)}$$

$$= 1 \wedge (y \vee \bar{x}) \qquad \text{(Hypothesis)}$$

$$= (y \vee \bar{x}) \wedge 1 \qquad \text{(Axiom 2)}$$

$$= y \vee \bar{x} \qquad \text{(Axiom 1)}$$

b. The second half is left as an exercise (see exercise 27) at the end of this chapter.

Theorem 6. Theorem 6 may be thought of as a useful enhancement of theorem 5.

$$x = x \wedge 1 \qquad \text{(Axiom 1)}$$

$$= x \wedge (y \vee \bar{y}) \qquad \text{(Axiom 4)}$$

$$= (x \wedge y) \vee (x \wedge \bar{y}) \qquad \text{(Axiom 3)}$$

$$= (z \wedge y) \vee (z \wedge \bar{y}) \qquad \text{(Hypothesis)}$$

$$= z \wedge (y \vee \bar{y}) \qquad \text{(Axiom 3)}$$

$$= z \wedge 1 \qquad \text{(Axiom 4)}$$

$$= z \qquad \text{(Axiom 1)}$$

Theorem 7.   Theorem 7 is a proof of the associative property discussed previously. Note that the following two theorems are slightly more complex than the previous ones, and are included to demonstrate manipulation and composition of algebraic expressions. Theorem 7 will be proved in two parts. In part a of the derivation we shall show

$$(x \wedge (y \wedge z)) \vee x = x = ((x \wedge y) \wedge z) \vee x$$

Then in part b we shall show

$$(x \wedge (y \wedge z)) \vee \overline{x} = \overline{x} \vee (y \wedge z) = ((x \vee y) \vee z) \wedge \overline{x}$$

Finally we will use theorem 6, with the replacement of variables x by $(x \vee (y \vee z))$, y by x, and z by $((x \vee y) \vee z)$ to prove the theorem.

a. $x \wedge (y \wedge z) \vee x = x \vee (x \wedge (y \wedge z))$ (Axiom 2)

$= x$ (Theorem 4)

$((x \wedge y) \wedge z) \vee x = x \vee ((x \wedge y) \wedge z)$ (Axiom 2)

$= (x \vee (x \wedge y)) \wedge (x \vee z)$ (Axiom 3)

$= x \wedge (x \text{ or } z)$ (Theorem 4)

$= x$ (Theorem 4)

b. $(x \wedge (y \wedge z)) \vee \overline{x} = \overline{x} \vee (x \wedge (y \wedge z))$ (Axiom 2)

$= (\overline{x} \vee x) \wedge (\overline{x} \vee (y \wedge z))$ (Axiom 3)

$= 1 \vee (\overline{x} \vee (y \wedge z))$ (Axiom 4)

$= \overline{x} \vee (y \wedge z)$ (Axiom 1)

The second half is left as an exercise (see exercise 28) at the end of this chapter.

Theorem 8.   Theorem 8 is known as DeMorgan's theorem, and is frequently used to move negations into and out of expressions. To prove theorem 8 we will make use of the uniqueness of complement (theorem 5) and associativity (theorem 7). The uniqueness complement will be shown in two parts. In part a we show $(x \wedge y) \vee (\overline{x} \vee \overline{y}) = 1$. In part b we show $(x \wedge y) \wedge (\overline{x} \vee \overline{y}) = 0$. Thus showing that $(x \wedge y)$ and $(\overline{x} \vee \overline{y})$ are complements, proving the original equality.

a. $(x \wedge y) \vee (\overline{x} \vee \overline{y}) = (\overline{x} \vee \overline{y}) \vee (x \text{ and } y)$ (Axiom 2)

$= ((\overline{x} \vee \overline{y}) \vee x) \wedge ((\overline{x} \vee \overline{y}) \vee y)$ (Axiom 3)

$= (x \vee (\overline{x} \vee \overline{y})) \wedge ((\overline{x} \vee \overline{y}) \vee y)$ (Axiom 2)

$= ((x \vee \overline{x}) \vee y) \wedge (\overline{x} \vee (y \vee \overline{y}))$ (Theorem 7)

$= (1 \vee \overline{y}) \wedge (\overline{x} \vee 1)$ (Axiom 4)

$= 1 \wedge 1$ (Axiom 2)

$= 1$ (Axiom 2)

b. The second half is left as an exercise (see exercise 29) at the end of this chapter.

Algebraic simplification of boolean expressions. Using the previously defined theorems we are able to perform algebraic simplification on arbitrary expressions. Recall that we have available the following "tools" at our disposal: Distributing terms (axiom 3), factoring terms (axiom 3), combining terms (theorem 1), eliminating terms (theorems 2 and 6), and eliminating literals (axiom 1). Additionally, as we have seen in several of the theorems, it is sometimes necessary to add redundant terms in order to permit further simplification of a particular expression. We now demonstrate the use of these tools with a more complex example.

Example

Simplify the following expression:

$$(\bar{a} \wedge \bar{c}) \vee (a \wedge (\bar{c} \vee (\bar{c} \wedge \bar{d}))) \vee (a \wedge \bar{d} \wedge (c \vee (\bar{b} \vee (\bar{b} \wedge c))))$$

Although there are many ways of performing the simplification the following demonstrates a cross-section of the techniques available:

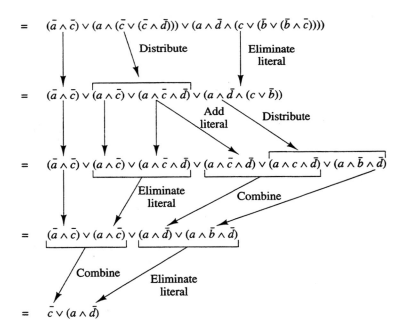

Boolean expressions and functions. So far the boolean algebra has been constructed using only derivations from the basic axioms. To permit a more expressive form for the algebra, we define the notion of a boolean function.

A **literal** is the appearance of a variable or its complement in an expression. Thus, the expression

$$x \wedge y \vee (x \wedge \bar{z})$$

consists of four literals but only three variables.

A **boolean expression** is an expression using literals $s_1, s_2, \cdots, s_n$ constructed with the operators $\wedge$ or $\vee$ and $^-$ as follows.

All literals are boolean expressions. If α and β are boolean expressions, then so too are $\alpha \wedge \beta$, $\alpha \vee \beta$ and $\bar{\alpha}$. Given a boolean algebra **B** and a boolean expression τ with literals $u_1, \ldots, u_n$, we can determine a boolean function as follows.

A **boolean function** on the symbols $s_1, s_2, \ldots, s_n$ where each s may take the value in **B** is formally defined as a mapping from $\mathbf{B}^n$ to **B**. The function is defined by evaluating the expression τ for each of the input combinations. Thus, the expression $x \vee (y \wedge z)$ determines the following function, $f(x, y, z)$, with respect to boolean algebra.

$$f(0,0,0)=0$$

$$f(0,0,1)=0$$

$$f(0,1,0)=0$$

$$f(0,1,1)=1$$

$$f(1,0,0)=1$$

$$f(1,0,1)=1$$

$$f(1,1,0)=1$$

$$f(1,1,1)=1$$

Thus given a function in three variables

$$f(x,y,z)=x \vee (y \wedge z) \wedge \bar{x}$$

then we say that f is a function of x, y and z. At this point it is useful to explain what boolean algebras we are interested in. We wish to consider a **combinational** device with n inputs $(I_1, I_2, \cdots, I_n)$, and one or more outputs $(O_{1_2}, \ldots, O_m)$. Thus we are interested in the algebra **Q** of all boolean functions f of $I_1, \ldots, I_n$. An easy counting argument indicates that there are 2^{2^n} such functions, thus **Q** consists of 2^{2^n} elements. $\wedge$, $\vee$, and $^-$ are defined in **Q** in the natural way:

$$(f \wedge g)(I_1, \ldots, I_n) = f(I_1, \ldots, I_n) \wedge g(I_1, \ldots, I_n)$$

$$(f \vee g)(I_1, \ldots, I_n) = f(I_1, \ldots, I_n) \vee g(I_1, \ldots, I_n)$$

$$(\bar{f})(I_1, \ldots, I_n) = \overline{f(I_1, \ldots, I_n)}$$

In general we will use a relaxed notation when specifying a function by omitting the function parameters as these are obvious from the expression. Notice that there are different expressions that define the same boolean function. For example, the expressions $(\bar{x} \wedge y) \vee (x \wedge y)$ and $(x \wedge y) \vee (\bar{x} \wedge y)$ both define the same function. We say two expressions are **equivalent** if they define the same function. The concept of equivalent expressions is important in digital computers as we shall see later.

Notice that for a particular list of variables (literals) a function is unique in the sense that the value of the function is defined for each n-tuple from **B** (i.e., a particular assignment of 1's and 0's). Notice also that for a particular n-tuple of elements from **B** the value of the function will be either 1 or 0.

2.2.3 Boolean Functions and Circuits

We are now in a position to make the connection between boolean functions and logic circuits. A boolean function with n variables may be represented by a circuit with n inputs and a single output. The circuit is constructed by connecting together the circuit symbols corresponding to the boolean function. For example, the function $f(x, y) = x \wedge y$ would be represented by the single circuit symbol together with a specification of the inputs. This is shown in Figure 2.16(a). We include the circuit in a box to indicate that the function is a "black box," which takes n inputs and has a single output. A more complex example is given in Figure 2.16(b). In this figure the function $f(u, v, w, x) = (u \wedge v) \vee ((u \wedge v \wedge w) \otimes x)$ is represented. We may generate the circuit diagram directly from the function as follows. The inputs to the circuit correspond to the variables of the function. We construct the dia- . gram by mapping the innermost terms in the expression to the corresponding circuit symbols. The output of these are then connected together using the appropriate circuit symbols in accordance with the next terms in the boolean expression. This sequence is repeated until the complete expression is represented. The output from the final circuit symbol corresponds to the function. Notice that we may use the input lines and the outputs of a circuit symbol as input to any number of other circuit symbols (this is know as the **fan-out**). Notice also that in the case that several outputs are required, each output will be represented by a separate function.

2.2.4 Truth Tables

We have already introduced the notion of a truth table. You may recall that the **and** and **or** operators were initially described by the output values for the input combinations. In this section we formally describe truth tables and how they may be used to map logic functions.

The truth table is a simple graphic tool that can be used to great effect to determine the output states of a general boolean system. In short, the truth table lists the desired

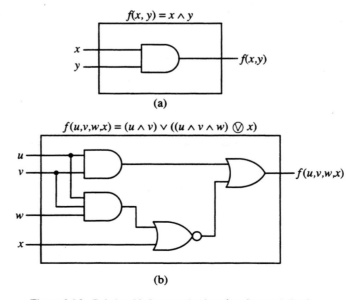

(a)

(b)

Figure 2.16   Relationship between boolean functions and circuits.
(a) Circuit realization for **and** function, $f(x, y) = x \wedge y$.
(b) More complex function $f(u, v, w, x) = (u \wedge v) \vee ((u \wedge v \wedge w) \otimes x)$.

output function for all possible input combinations. For an expression with n inputs, the truth table will possess 2^n rows. The columns of the table may be used to show the logical state of some subexpression of the original expression. Consider the previous function described in truth table form (Table 2.20).

TABLE 2.20   Three-variable truth table

x	y	z	Result
0	0	0	0
0	0	1	0
0	1	0	0
0	1	1	1
1	0	0	1
1	0	1	1
1	1	0	1
1	1	1	1

Notice that the first three columns in each row in the table corresponds to a single assignment of 1's and 0's to the function, with the first column corresponding to the first function variable, the second column corresponding to the second function variable, and so on.

One problem that frequently occurs in circuit design is how to establish the function corresponding to a particular boolean expression. The use of truth tables is one simple technique to achieve this goal. For example, consider the following expression:

$$(x \wedge y \vee z) \vee (\overline{x} \wedge z)$$

This determines the value of the following function:

$$f(x, y, z) = (x \wedge y \vee z) \vee (\overline{x} \wedge z) \tag{2.38}$$

Clearly f is a *function* of x, y, z. The problem is, how do we determine the output given the input states? One possible approach might be to attempt to simplify the expression. As we have seen, however, it may become quite complex. Another approach would be to attempt to ascertain the value of the function for random inputs states. This rather ad hoc technique becomes unwieldy for complex expressions. A more systematic approach to solve the problem is to write out the truth table for each of the subexpressions in the function (using temporary symbols to denote each subexpression). If the subexpression is compound (i.e., contains subexpressions) the procedure is applied to the nested subexpressions. We then combine the subexpressions to obtain more complex expressions, finally leading to the solution. Notice that we may use the truth tables defined for the boolean operators to determine the results for the subexpressions. In Table 2.21 we list the truth table with subexpressions for the previous function.

Notice that the truth assignment for each subexpression of the equation is listed in the truth table as a step toward the conclusion.

Notice also that we may use truth tables to establish if two expressions are the same. We simply determine the truth table for each expression and compare them. If the outputs are the same for the same inputs (comparably ordered), then the expressions define the same function, that is, the expressions are equivalent.

TABLE 2.21 Truth table for equation 2.38

x	y	z	$t_1 = x \wedge y$	$t_2 = t_1 \vee z$	$t_3 = \overline{x}$	$t_4 = z \wedge t_3$	$f = t_2 \vee t_4$
0	0	0	0	0	1	0	0
0	0	1	0	1	1	1	1
0	1	0	0	0	1	0	0
0	1	1	0	1	1	1	1
1	0	0	0	0	0	0	0
1	0	1	0	1	0	0	1
1	1	0	1	1	0	0	1
1	1	1	1	1	0	0	1

Don't-care conditions. It is frequently the case in digital circuits that we are uninterested in the output for particular input combinations. Consider the digital circuit in Figure 2.17 in which the boxes contain some arbitrary logic circuit. Stage **A** consists of three functions that have common variables, $x, y,$ and z. The functions are $a(x, y, z)$, $b(x, y, z)$, and $c(x, y, z)$. Stage **B** consists of one function f whose inputs are the outputs of stage **A**, that is, a, b, and c.

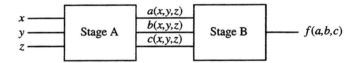

Figure 2.17 Two-stage logic circuit.

It may be the case that there are certain input combinations to stage **B** that will never occur. For example, the sequence $a = 1, b = 1, c = 0$ may never be generated for all input combinations of x, y, and z. In this event, we are uninterested in the output of stage **B** for this input sequence. In other words it may be a 0 or a 1; we simply don't care! In this event, we place an x in the output column of the truth table to signify that the output may be either 0 or 1. Notice that technically the truth table of stage **B** no longer represents a single function (why?).

2.2.5 Boolean Representations and Operator Precedence

It is unfortunately the case that the study of boolean logic spans several fields, notably Mathematics, Engineering, and Language processing—unfortunate in the sense that each field uses its own set of symbols to represent the operators. So far we have presented only the symbols used in Mathematics ($\wedge$, $\vee$, $\overline{}$). Within the engineering world, however, these symbols are inconvenient (for historical typographical reasons); thus, a different set of symbols is used. The "." is used to represent the $\wedge$, the "+" is used to represent the $\vee$, and often the "'" (placed to the right of the term in question) is used to represent the $\overline{}$. The different representations are summarized in Table 2.22.

TABLE 2.22 Alternative terminology for boolean operators

Operator	Math	Engineering
and	$\wedge$	.
or	$\vee$	+
not	$-$	,

Thus the following expressions are equivalent:

$$a \wedge (b \vee c)$$

$$a . (b+c)$$

a **and** (b **or** c)

In general we will use the symbol set that is most appropriate for the topic in question. Thus while discussing algebra (as we have been doing so far), we will use the mathematical terminology. As we become more involved in logic design from the viewpoint of engineering (as will shortly be the case), however, we will make use of the engineering terminology. Note that the differences in no way affect the expressive power of boolean algebra.

In addition, to make expressions compact (and thus easy to read), a precedence is defined for the operators, which permits parentheses to be dropped in many cases. Consider the following cases:

$$x \wedge y \vee z$$

This could either be

$$(x \wedge y) \vee z$$

or

$$x \wedge (y \vee z)$$

Without a convention, the removal of brackets would cause ambiguity. Thus the convention adopted is one of **operator precedence**. When evaluating an expression, the precedence (or binding) for boolean operators is as given in Table 2.23.

TABLE 2.23   Operator precedence

Operator	Precedence
()	Highest
not	
and	
or	Lowest

Using this convention, one may determine expressions that would otherwise be ambiguous. The rule for evaluating expressions is to evaluate those terms that have the highest precedence first. Clearly then from Table 2.23, expressions inside brackets have to be evaluated before the remainder of the expression may be determined. Notice that operator precedence corresponds to those used in arithmetic (**not** is analogous to unary minus, **or** is analogous to addition, and **and** is analogous to multiplication). Of course brackets are still required when particular groupings that violate precedence are required. As an example consider the following expression:

$$a \wedge b \wedge (c \vee d) \vee e$$

The way to interpret the value of this statement is to work from the lowest to the highest precedence as follows: (1) determine the value of $c \vee d$; (2) determine the value of this result $\wedge b$; (3) determine the value of this result $\wedge a$, and finally; (4) determine the value of this result $\vee e$.

Within engineering, a further textual simplification is performed, that is the removal of the "$\cdot$". This may be done without introducing ambiguity. Thus the terms $x. y$ and xy are equivalent. Notice that there is no conflict between boolean algebra expressions and arithmetic expressions, which use the same symbols, by virtue of the context in which they are used.

Using truth tables or algebraic constructs you are invited to verify that the following expressions are all unambiguous and describe the same function:

$$f(a, b, c) = a\,b\,\overline{c} + a\,(\,c + c\,)$$

$$f(a, b, c) = a\,c\,(\,a + b\,) + a\,b$$

$$f(a, b, c) = a\,(\,a\,b + a\,c\,)$$

2.2.6 Normal Forms for Expressions and Minimization

As we have seen from the previous section, we may use truth tables to assist in the comparison of boolean expressions. Another operation suggested by truth tables is the standard representation of boolean expressions. For a particular truth table, we define a **minterm** as an expression formed by taking the product (i.e., ".") of the literals in a single row (i.e., each variable appears exactly once in the minterm, in either its complemented or uncomplemented form). Because each literal appears once; a minterm of an expression with n literals will itself have n literals. Thus each minterm corresponds to an assignment to the variables that would make the function true (1). The function corresponding to the entire truth table may now be conveniently represented as the sum (i.e., +) of all those minterms for that the function is true (1). Using Table 2.21 as an example, a typical minterm would be $\overline{x}\,\overline{y}\,\overline{z}$, which results in the function value false (0). A minterm that would make the function true (1) would be $\overline{x}\,\overline{y}\,z$. Clearly for the n variables, there are 2^n different minterms, each unique. Thus the function represented in the table may be expressed as the following sum of minterms:

$$f(x, y, z) = \overline{x}\,\overline{y}z + \overline{x}yz + x\overline{y}z + xy\overline{z} + xyz$$

A function represented in this fashion is known as a **minterm expansion**, which is also known as the **Sum of Products** or **Disjunctive Normal Form** (DNF).

Notice that the minterm expansion may be quite lengthy and may be simplified by using the expression simplification techniques presented earlier. Notice also that a minterm expansion may be immediately realized using an **and** gate for each minterm, with the outputs from these gates as inputs to a single **or** gate. The minterm expansion circuit realization for Table 2.21 is given in Figure 2.18. Finally notice that because there is a 1-to-1 mapping between truth table rows and minterms, the minterm expansion for a particular function is unique up to rearrangement of terms.

Because each minterm corresponds to a row in the truth table, we may represent the term by its row number in the table (i.e., the numeric representation of the input literals expressed in decimal). For example, the minterm $x\overline{y}z$ corresponds to row 101 in binary or 5 in decimal. Thus we indicate this minterm as m_5 where the m notation is short for minterm. Thus the minterm expansion for f earlier is the logical sum of m_1, m_3, m_5, m_6, and m_7. This follows from observing that the function f equals 1 when *any* of the

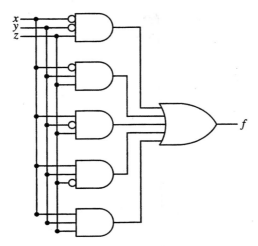

Figure 2.18   Circuit realization of Table 2.21.

minterms are 1. Notice also that to reflect the truth table correctly, the minterm expansion must contain **all** of the minterms that cause the function to be 1. The function may therefore be written as follows:

$$f(x, y, z) = m_1 + m_3 + m_5 + m_6 + m_7$$

Using the Σ sign for summation this yields the compact representation below:

$$f(x, y, z) = \sum m(1, 3, 5, 6, 7)$$

As is often the case in boolean logic, there is a dual to the minterm. We define the sum of all the complemented literals in a particular row of the truth table as its **maxterm**. Notice also that the maxterm for a particular row is the **complement** of the minterm. This is clear from the **principle of duality**, which states that we may obtain the **dual** of a boolean function by replacing all the **and**'s with **or**'s, the **or**'s with **and**'s, 1's with 0's and 0's with 1's. Variables and their complements are left unchanged. Given that two functions are equal, their duals will also be equal. This property may be seen by inspecting Figure 2.19,[12] which shows the Principal of Duality clearly. We indicate maxterms using a subscripted M. Thus M_1 represents $x + y + \overline{z}$. Notice that again for a function with n variables, there are 2^n maxterms. So, using examples from Table 2.21, a typical maxterm would be M_0 $(x + y + z)$, whereas a maxterm that makes function 0 would be M_4 $(\overline{x} + y + z)$. The relationship between the truth table and minterm/maxterm is depicted in Table 2.24.

TABLE 2.24   Maxterm and minterms for 2 variable function

Expression		Row no.		Minterm	Maxterm
		Binary	Decimal		
$\overline{x}$	$\overline{y}$	00	0	$m_0 = \overline{x}\,\overline{y}$	$M_0 = x + y$
$\overline{x}$	y	01	1	$m_1 = \overline{x}y$	$M_1 = x + \overline{y}$
x	$\overline{y}$	10	2	$m_2 = x\overline{y}$	$M_2 = \overline{x} + y$
x	y	11	3	$m_3 = xy$	$M_3 = \overline{x} + \overline{y}$

---

[12] The reader is invited to experiment with a few simple examples to see that the Principle of Duality holds.

In the same way that the minterm is used to specify the sum of those variable assignments that make the function 1, the maxterms are used to specify the product of those literal assignments that makes the function 0. This follows by observing that the function will be 0 only if *every* maxterm is 0. Thus any expression may be specified using the **maxterm expansion** also known as the **product of sums** or **conjunctive normal form (CNF)**. Thus, the f of Table 2.20 may be written as the product of the maxterms not used in the minterm expansion, as follows:

$$f(x, y, z) = M_0 \, M_2 \, M_4$$

Using the Π notation for product this yields the following compact representation:

$$f(x, y, z) = \prod M(0, 2, 4)$$

To see this relationship more clearly consider the following example:

$$f(a, b, c) = \sum m(1, 3, 4)$$

thus the complement of f, that is, $\overline{f}$ is given by

$$\overline{f}(a, b, c) = \sum m(0, 2, 5, 6, 7)$$

$$= m_0 + m_2 + m_5 + m_6 + m_7$$

$$= \overline{x} \, \overline{y} \, \overline{z} + \overline{x} \, y \, \overline{z} + \cdots$$

$$f(a, b, c) = \overline{\overline{x} \, \overline{y} \, \overline{z} + \overline{x} \, y \, \overline{z} + \cdots} \qquad \text{(Complement)}$$

$$f(a, b, c) = \overline{(\overline{x} \, \overline{y} \, \overline{z})} \; \overline{(\overline{x} \, y \, z)} \cdots \qquad \text{(DeMorgan)}$$

$$= (\overline{x} + \overline{y} + \overline{z})(x + \overline{y} + z) \cdots \qquad \text{(DeMorgan)}$$

$$= M_0 \, M_2 \, M_5 \, M_6 \, M_7$$

Notice that none of the equivalent terms used to construct the minterm expansion are used to construct the maxterm expansion and visa versa (i.e., if m_x is used in the minterm expansion for f, then M_x will not be used in the maxterm expansion). This property makes it easy to switch between the two expressions. For example,

$$f(x, y) = xy + \overline{x} \, \overline{y}$$

$$= \sum m(0, 3)$$

$$= \prod M(1, 2)$$

In the event that a general expression is to be converted to its minterm expansion, either use the truth table or these following steps:

1. The expression is expanded to a sum of products form using algebraic manipulation.
2. For each term, perform the following step: For each variable x missing, the expression $(x + \overline{x})$ is **anded** with the term (because $x + \overline{x} = 1$ and $x \cdot 1 = x$).
3. The expression is again expanded into the sum of products and duplicate terms removed.

As an example consider the following:

$$f(a,b,c,d)=a\,b+a\,(\overline{b}\,d+c\,d)$$

$$=a\,b+a\,\overline{b}\,d+a\,c\,d \qquad\qquad\text{(Expand)}$$

$$=a\,b\,(c+\overline{c})(d+\overline{d})+a\,\overline{b}\,(c+\overline{c})\,d+a\,(b+\overline{b})\,c\,d \quad\text{(Complete)}$$

$$=\begin{array}{l}a\,b\,c\,d+a\,b\,c\,\overline{d}+a\,b\,\overline{c}\,d+a\,b\,\overline{c}\,\overline{d}+\\[2pt]a\,\overline{b}\,c\,d+a\,\overline{b}\,\overline{c}\,d+a\,b\,c\,d+a\,\overline{b}\,c\,d\end{array} \qquad\text{(Expand)}$$

$$=\sum m(9,11,12,13,14,15)$$

As one might expect, in the event that the maxterms are required, the missing literals are included by oring $x\cdot\overline{x}$ with the term and expanding to a product of sums form.

As we have seen in several examples, there are many different expressions that give rise to the same function. Clearly some of these are more complex than others. When dealing with computer design, we shall see that there is a direct mapping between the logical operators ("$\cdot$",$+$,$^-$) and their electronic counterparts. Thus reducing the complexity of a boolean expression used to describe an electronic circuit will result in a reduction in the number of electronic components. This saving will result in reduced costs and possibly faster components. Thus, circuit minimization is an important concept in digital logic design.

Formally, then, given two DNF expressions e_1 and e_2, we say that e_1 is simpler than e_2 if and only if e_1 has fewer (or equal) literals than e_2 and e_1 has fewer (or equal) disjunctions than e_2, with at least one of the inequalities strict. For example, b is simpler than $\overline{a}b+ab$ because it has fewer literals (1 as opposed to 4) and has fewer disjunctions (0 as opposed to 1).

2.2.7 Karnaugh Maps

Another useful pictorial representation of a function is the **Karnaugh map**. We noted previously that a truth table may be used to represent a function, providing an easy way to establish the equivalence of two expressions. It does little to help the user ascertain the minimal expressions for a function, however. In fact, as we have seen in the previous section, the 1's of the truth table may be used to establish the DNF for the function, which is typically more complex than the minimal expression. In another representation, the Karnaugh map may be used to visually examine functions of two to six variables. Properties of the Karnaugh map permit the user to rapidly identify minimal expressions without the complexity of manipulating expressions (as discussed previously). A Karnaugh map of n variables is a rectangle divided into n cells. Each cell in the map corresponds to the value of the function evaluated for a particular tuple from B^n (i.e., each cell corresponds to a fundamental conjunction, or row, in the truth table). A Karnaugh map has the property that, for all cells in the map, any two adjacent cells differ by the complementation of exactly one literal in the fundamental conjunction. We will now consider the organization of maps with successively more variables.

Two-variable maps.   A Karnaugh map representation for a two-variable function is shown in Figure 2.19(a). With two variables, there are $2^2=4$ cells, each cell representing a single tuple from the truth table. The first **column** corresponds to tuples that contain $\bar{a}$ (recall that each variable occurs exactly once in either its uncomplemented or complemented form). The second column corresponds to tuples that contain a. Notice that the disjunction of these two columns contains all the tuples in the truth table. In a similar fashion, the first **row** contains all tuples that contain $\bar{b}$, whereas the second row contains all tuples that contain b. The Karnaugh map, therefore, is able to represent all boolean expressions in two variables as depicted in Figure 2.19(b). Notice that, as with the minterms and maxterms, we may assign a number to each cell that corresponds to the truth table row number as shown in Figure 2.19(c).

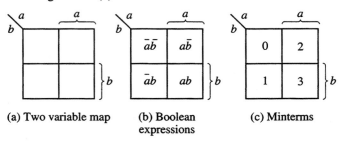

(a) Two variable map   (b) Boolean expressions   (c) Minterms

Figure 2.19   Two-variable Karnaugh map.

The Karnaugh map is used to represent a particular function f in either a disjunctive form or a conjunctive form. We shall consider mainly the disjunctive form, leaving the conjunctive form for later. To represent f on the map, we use the minterm expansion, placing a 1 in each cell of the map for which the corresponding minterm is present in the function, and leaving spaces elsewhere.

To represent the function, it is clearly necessary to define an expression that encompasses exactly those cells that are marked. We mark cells that have defined clauses with closed loops around the cells in question. Thus it is easy to identify those minterms that we have yet to include. For example, the simple function given in the truth table of Figure 2.20(b) may be represented by the minterm expansion $f = \bar{a}b$. Thus we place a single 1 in the corresponding cell of the Karnaugh map as shown in Figure 2.20(a). In this example we have completed the definition of the function. We now proceed to the simplification phase. In this simple example, there is no opportunity for simplification; thus we would circle the single term $f = \bar{a}b$ on the Karnaugh map as shown in Figure 2.20(c). Because there are no other marked cells which are uncircled, the circled cells completely define the original function. Consider the Karnaugh Map for the following minterm expansion:

$$f(a, b) = \bar{a}\,\bar{b} + \bar{a}b + a\bar{b}$$

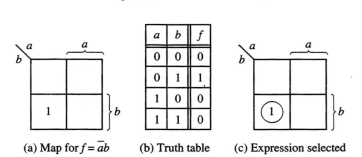

(a) Map for $f = \bar{a}b$ (b) Truth table   (c) Expression selected

Figure 2.20   Karnaugh map for two variables.

Because there are three minterms, there will be three 1's in the map, as shown in Figure 2.21(a). To simplify the original expression we note that any two marked cells adjacent to one another represent a minterm in which both a single literal *and its complement* are present in the function. Thus, by combining the terms, we are able to simplify the expression, replacing the original two minterms with one minterm of lesser length. We mark this simplification on the Karnaugh map with a circle enclosing the two adjacent cells as shown for the two terms in Figure 2.21(a). This circle corresponds to the simplification of $\overline{a}b + \overline{a}\,\overline{b}$ to $\overline{a}$. Notice that so far not all of the marked cells have been circled; therefore, the function has yet to be completely defined. One possibility to complete the definition would be to circle the remaining term ($a\overline{b}$). Because there are no more uncircled terms the simplification is complete yielding the final expression $f = \overline{a} + a\overline{b}$ as shown by Figure 2.21(a).

Recalling that our original goal was expression minimization one might ask whether some other expression is simpler. The answer is yes. Consider Figure 2.21(b); the term $\overline{b}$ corresponds to the two top cells, both of which are marked. In other words, the function is 1 whenever b is false (i.e., $\overline{b}$ is true). Because the minimization we are performing will result in a DNF expression, cells may be used as often as required to generate different terms (as is the case with the cell corresponding to $\overline{a}\,\overline{b}$). Thus, a simpler expression for the function would be $f = \overline{a} + \overline{b}$. In fact, as can be seen from the Karnaugh map, this expression is minimal.

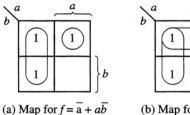

(a) Map for $f = \overline{a} + a\overline{b}$ (b) Map for $f = \overline{a} + \overline{b}$

Figure 2.21   Karnaugh map function minimization.

Three-variable maps.   We may extend these concepts to simplify functions of three variables. With three variables, there will be $2^3 = 8$ cells arranged as shown in Figure 2.22(a). Again the cells are organized so that adjacent cells differ by exactly one literal. The rightmost four cells correspond to terms with the literal a, whereas the leftmost four cells correspond to terms with the literal $\overline{a}$. To use another example, the top four cells correspond to terms with $\overline{c}$, and the bottom four cells correspond to terms with c. Figure 2.22(b) shows the boolean expressions represented by each of the cells in the Karnaugh map. Again, if we wish, we may reference each cell according to the truth table row number as shown in Figure 2.22(c). For an example of working with three variables, consider the following minterm expansion:

$$f = \overline{a}\,\overline{b}\,\overline{c} + \overline{a}b\overline{c} + \overline{a}bc + ab\overline{c} + abc$$

Drawing the Karnaugh map, we would mark the cells as shown in Figure 2.23(a). Again the map may be used to locate a pair of adjacent cells as shown in Figure 2.23(a) by the simplification of $\overline{a}\,\overline{b}\,\overline{c} + \overline{a}b\overline{c}$ to $\overline{a}\,\overline{c}$ (to see this, notice that $\overline{c}$ selects the top row, whereas $\overline{a}$ selects the four leftmost cells; thus the conjunction of these will be two cells circled). This is certainly a significant saving on the original expression.

Notice also that with three variables, there is an opportunity for removing two literals from a group of related terms. Using Karnaugh maps, this corresponds to a block of four

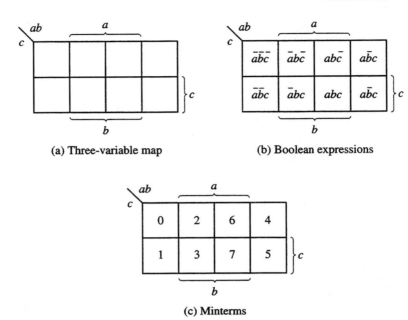

(a) Three-variable map

(b) Boolean expressions

(c) Minterms

Figure 2.22   Three-variable Karnaugh map.

adjacent cells or a line of four adjacent cells. Thus looking at Figure 2.23(a), the block of four marked cells in the center may be circled corresponding to the single term b. Clearly, selecting a single group of four is preferable to selecting two groups of two, just as selecting a single group of two is preferable to selecting two groups of one. Equally, there is no point in selecting a group that is completely included in a group or combination of groups, because it is redundant. Because all the marked terms are now circled, we have the final (minimal) expression for the function given by

$$f = b + \overline{a}\,\overline{c}$$

The circuit realization for this expression is given in Figure 2.23(b).

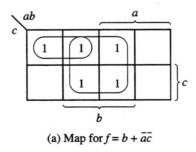

(a) Map for $f = b + \overline{a}\overline{c}$

(b) Circuit realization

Figure 2.23   Expression minimization using three-variable Karnaugh map.

To show another example consider the following minterm expansion:

$$f = \overline{a}\,\overline{b}\,\overline{c} + \overline{a}\,\overline{b}c + \overline{a}b\overline{c} + \overline{a}bc + ab\overline{c} + abc$$

with the Karnaugh map shown in Figure 2.24. We are able to simplify the expression using the two four-cell blocks to the following minimal expression:

$$f = \overline{a} + b$$

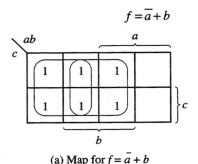

(a) Map for $f = \overline{a} + b$

Figure 2.24   Karnaugh map in three variables.

As we mentioned previously, the Karnaugh map may be thought of as wrapping around in both the horizontal and vertical directions. Thus as a final example, consider the case of the following function expressed in the short minterm m form (which we will now use for brevity):

$$f = \sum m(0, 1, 2, 4, 5, 6)$$

We see from looking at the Karnaugh map in Figure 2.25, that a line of four cells corresponding to $\overline{c}$ and a block of four cells corresponding to $\overline{b}$ may be selected to completely define f. Thus we identify the minimal expression:

$$f = \overline{b} + \overline{c}$$

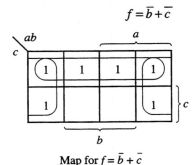

Map for $f = \overline{b} + \overline{c}$

Figure 2.25   Expression minimization using three-variable Karnaugh map.

Four-variable maps.   By now you should be starting to feel familiar with Karnaugh maps. The extension to four variables is accomplished by an additional eight cells forming a square as shown in Figure 2.26(a). Again the full sixteen minterms from the truth table are represented as shown in Figure 2.26(b), with the corresponding row numbers as shown in Figure 2.26(c). With the increased number of variables, there exists the possibility of grouping together eight cells, leaving a single literal (either complemented or uncomplemented). On the map, this grouping will resemble a $2 * 4$ rectangle, which may wrap around sides. Notice also that a block of four cells may now occupy the corner four cells yet represent a single two-literal term.

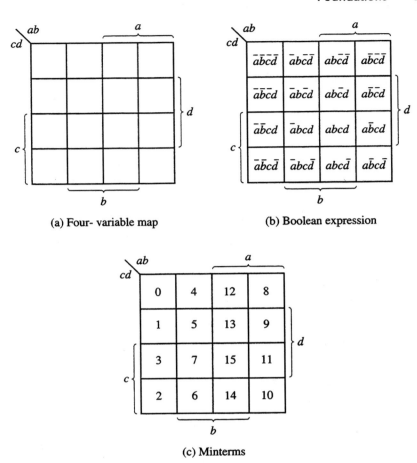

(a) Four- variable map

(b) Boolean expression

(c) Minterms

Figure 2.26   Four-variable Karnaugh map.

Use of the four-variable map should be clear from the following examples. Consider the function defined by the minterm expansion:

$$f = \sum m(0, 1, 4, 5, 8, 9, 10, 12, 13, 14)$$

By drawing the Karnaugh map as shown in Figure 2.27, we are able to see immediately that we are able to represent eight of the minterms using only $\bar{c}$; the other two terms could be included by the additional term $ac\bar{d}$; however, we notice that $a\bar{d}$ will also covers these cases and requires one fewer literal. Thus, the resulting minimal expression will be

$$f = \bar{c} + a\bar{d}$$

As a final example using the four-variable map, consider the function represented by the following minterm expression:

$$f = \sum m(1, 3, 5, 7, 8, 10, 11)$$

Using the Karnaugh map given in Figure 2.28, we immediately recognize the four-cell block corresponding to $\bar{a}d$. The other three terms are best represented as two groups of two corresponding to $a\bar{b}c$ and $a\bar{b}\bar{d}$. These observations yield the following minimal expression:

$$f = \bar{a}d + a\bar{b}c + a\bar{b}\,\bar{d}$$

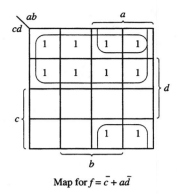

Map for $f = \bar{c} + a\bar{d}$

Figure 2.27 Expression minimization using four-variable Karnaugh map.

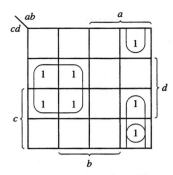

Map for $f = \bar{a}d + a\bar{b}c + a\bar{b}\bar{d}$

Figure 2.28 Expression minimization using four-variable Karnaugh map.

Five- and six-variable maps.   Because minimization on five- and six-variable maps requires visualization in three dimensions and is not well represented on paper, little time will be spent on them. For those with a special interest, however, we provide the following information.

The five-variable Karnaugh map requires thirty-two cells and may be thought of as two four-variable maps stacked on top of each other as shown in Figure 2.29(a). The top plane corresponds to the those minterms that contain the uncomplemented a, whereas the bottom plane corresponds to those minterms that contain the complement of a (i.e., $\bar{a}$). Unlike with previous maps, it is now necessary to recognize relationships between terms on two planes. To assist with this, it is helpful to draw the two planes together by using a diagonal line to separate the top and bottom as shown in Figure 2.29(b). Thus a block of two could now be a marked cell above and below the diagonal in the same box. Similarly, a block of four could be two cells on the top plane with two adjacent cells in the bottom plane as shown in Figure 2.29(b).

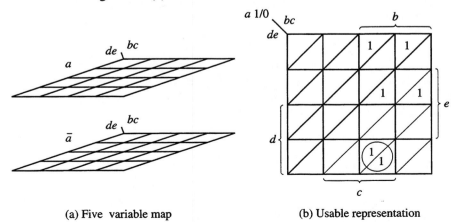

(a) Five variable map   (b) Usable representation

Figure 2.29 Representation of five-variable Karnaugh map.

The six-variable Karnaugh map requires sixty-four cells and represents an extension of the ideas used to construct the five-variable map. The basic principle is indicated in

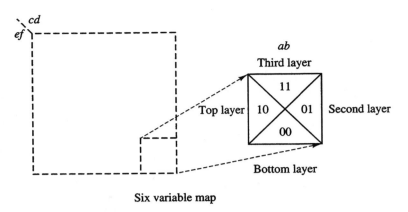

Six variable map

Figure 2.30   Representation of six-variable Karnaugh map.

Figure 2.30 in which each box now represents four cells. The cells are arranged such that again terms in adjacent layers (i.e., layers two and three) may be combined. The task of minimizing expressions with more than six variables is best left to numerical techniques.[13]

Use of Karnaugh maps for maxterm functions.   As we mentioned at the beginning of the section on Karnaugh maps, we may also use the Karnaugh map to represent maxterms. In this event, each cell represents the **sum** of the literals in question. Thus the user marks with a 0 on the map those cells for which the function is false. To simplify the maxterm expansion, the user again identifies groups of cells that can be simplified. For example, $(a+b+c+d)$ and $(a+b+c+\overline{d})$ may be simplified to $(a+b+c)$, which on the map corresponds to a circle of two cells.

To make the concept concrete, consider the following minterm expansion:

$$f = \sum m(0, 3, 4, 7, 8, 10, 11, 12, 14, 15)$$

Recall from Section 2.2.5 that the corresponding maxterm expansion for this would be the following:

$$f = \prod M(1, 2, 5, 6, 9, 13)$$

corresponding to those occasions that the function is 0. Marking these with a 0 on a Karnaugh map results in a map similar to Figure 2.31(a). We notice immediately that the function f may, therefore, be represented by the conjunction of the following expressions $(c+\overline{d})$ and $(a+\overline{c}+d)$, as given by the following equation:

$$f = (c+\overline{d})(a+\overline{c}+d)$$

The circuit realization for this product of sums expression is shown in Figure 2.31(b).

Don't-care conditions.   As was demonstrated during the section on truth tables, expression simplification opportunity is greater when "don't-care" conditions exist

---

[13] For numerical solutions to boolean expression simplification see suggested reading texts at the end of this chapter.

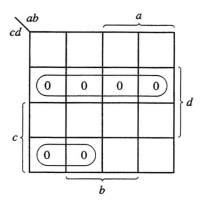

(a) Map for $\bar{f} = \bar{c}d + \bar{a}c\bar{d}$ or $f = (c + \bar{d})(a + \bar{c} + d)$

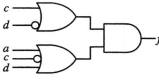

(a) Circuit realization

Figure 2.31 Expression minimization for product of sums Karnaugh map.

(i.e., when we don't care about the function result for a particular assignment of literals). This simplification is easily realized in Karnaugh maps. As with the truth table, an X is placed in the cell corresponding to the don't-care values. The map is then used as previously, except that any cell containing an X may be treated as a 1 *if a simplification would result*; otherwise, it is considered a space.

To see don't-care conditions in use, consider Figure 2.32(a). The initial minterm expansion is given by the following:

$$f = \sum m(1, 2, 5, 8, 12, 13)$$

Using the map to simplify the expression we are left with the following:

$$f = \overline{abd} + \overline{a}\,\overline{c}d + b\overline{c}d + \overline{b}\,\overline{c}\,\overline{d},$$

which is still rather complex. Had there been some don't-care conditions, for example as in Figure 2.32(b), the expression may have been further reduced to yield

$$f = \overline{b}\,\overline{d} + \overline{c}d$$

2.2.8 Summary of Boolean Logic

In the preceding paragraphs, the reader has been introduced to the mathematical theory supporting *all* computer operations including logical decisions in the CPU. Notice that given an arbitrarily complex function with any number of inputs, we can construct the logic expression using the operators **not** and **or**. The reader is also invited to prove (by constructing the three previous operators) that any expression may be realized using either the **nand** or **nor** operators. It should be clear from reading the text that we have introduced three distinct representations of expressions, as algebraic equations, as

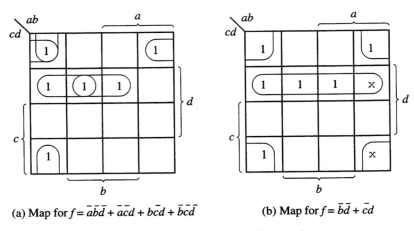

(a) Map for $f = \bar{a}\bar{b}\bar{d} + \bar{a}cd + b\bar{c}d + \bar{b}c\bar{d}$ (b) Map for $f = \bar{b}\bar{d} + \bar{c}d$

Figure 2.32 Don't-care conditions in Karnaugh maps.

truth tables, and as Karnaugh maps. Each of these representations offers particular advantages, depending on the requirements. Truth tables are ideal for establishing the values of the function given particular input combinations. This in turn leads to the normal form representations (DNF, CNF), which permit expression simplification by either algebra or Karnaugh maps. It is important to recognize the appropriate representation for a particular problem and to apply it efficiently and correctly.

2.3 GATES — IMPLEMENTATION

So far we have looked at only the theoretical realization of gates. Before seeing how they are used, we first consider the electrical foundations used by computers to perform digital computation and how the gates are implemented. An understanding of the **hardware** is useful to see how these mathematical functions may be realized using electronic engineering. We will look at the two primary classes of logic, bipolar and unipolar. Within these classes are different families that are distinguished by the following characteristics: gate construction technique used, basic gates used, and operating characteristics. In view of the scope of this text, we shall only very briefly introduce the transistor level and discuss features of the different families.

The physical medium on which transistors (and hence gates) is based, is the **semiconductor**. A semiconductor is a material somewhere between a conductor (such as copper) and an insulator (such as glass). It is impossible within this text to discuss in any detail the mechanism by which semiconductors operate. In general terms, however, a semiconductor is composed from extremely pure insulators (group IV in the periodic table of the elements) impregnated (or **doped**) with very small quantities of either group III or V elements. Some elements in these groups possess the property that when implanted in the crystalline structure of a group IV material require very little energy to permit the flow of electrical current through the resulting semiconductor. Semiconductors that are made using group III elements are known as *p*-type semiconductors, whereas those that use group V are known as *n*-type semiconductors. These semiconductors may be joined together in such a way that there is electrical continuity between the different types. As we shall see, the resulting components have particular electrical characteristics that permit them to be used to form gates. In computers, the two semiconductors used are silicon and germanium. These are impregnated with either gallium (group III), phosphorus, or arsenic (group V). As we shall see, most of the currently popular integrated circuits are made using silicon.

2.3.1 Circuit Characteristics

As you saw earlier, digital computers are constructed from the composition of simple logic gates. Thus, the differences between technologies and families lie not in their logical function, but in several considerations that characterize gates. The principle characteristics of the different semi-conductor technologies and families are **performance**, **power dissipation**, **circuit density**, and **cost**. We discuss each of these subsequently.

Performance.   The performance of a gate is the time taken by the gate to respond to input signals. This delay varies depending on the technology used and the family. Typically, the manufacturer will specify the response time for the device, and, if necessary, the refresh time (some devices have to pause for a short while after operation although their initial response time might be very fast).

Power dissipation.   All electrical circuits use power; however, the amount of power used by a circuit varies greatly depending on the technology and family. Although the power requirement for a single gate is small, we must remember that the number of gates will be large. While supplying the power is sometimes a problem, the principle difficulty comes from ensuring the proper dissipation of heat generated by the gate. Clearly, the more power a gate requires to operate it, the more heat it generates. When many gates are packed together, the heat generation becomes an important consideration.

Circuit density.   The number of gates that may be packed together per unit area is known as the circuit density. As one might expect, higher densities permit more functions to be placed on a chip and are, therefore, desirable when manufacturing integrated circuits. Again, different technologies and families possess widely different circuit densities.

Cost.   The cost of a particular technology is another important consideration. Cost is determined by the manufacturing complexity and the volume of the product.

2.3.2 Bipolar Technology

The term bipolar refers to the fact that both *n*-type and *p*-type semiconductors are used in the fabrication of the transistors. There are many different component families using bipolar technology. The different families present essentially the same logic gates to the users. The difference between the families is the way in which the gates are constructed. The different construction techniques imply that each family has different characteristics. The primary families are **resistor transistor logic (RTL)**, **diode transistor logic (DTL)**, **transistor transistor logic (TTL)**, **input injection logic (IIL)**, and **emitter coupled logic (ECL)**. Of these, by far and away the most popular is TTL logic. In the following section, we introduce the primary active components used in computers, transistors, and diodes; then we discuss each of the bipolar families and their characteristics.

Building Blocks

Diodes.   As shown in Figure 2.33(b), a diode is composed of a single *p-n* junction and is given the symbol as in Figure 2.33(a). In fact, a diode is usually fabricated by growing (or evaporating) a thin layer of *p*-type material onto an *n*-type substrate. Metal contacts

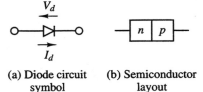

(a) Diode circuit   (b) Semiconductor
      symbol   layout

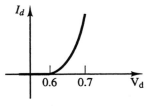

(c) Electrical characteristis

Figure 2.33 Semiconductor diode: (a) symbol, (b) semiconductor model, and (c) electrical characteristics.

are then attached to both the substrate and the p-type layer to connect the diode to the outside world. Notice that from the electrical characteristics given in Figure 2.33(c), the diode will only permit current to flow if the voltage V_d is positive and greater than about 0.7 volts. Under these conditions, the diode is said to be **forward biased** and will conduct electricity. Notice also from Figure 2.33(c) that the voltage across the diode does not increase much above 0.7 V. Thus we may say that there is a voltage drop of about 0.7 V across a forward biased diode. If the voltage across the diode is less than 0.7, the junction is said to be **reverse biased**, and will not conduct electricity ($I_d = 0$).

Transistors. A transistor is a somewhat more complex device than a diode. Notice, however, that from Figure 2.34(b) the transistor may be thought of as two diodes joined back to back. In fact, as with the diode, the junctions between the different semiconductor regions are created by layering p-type and n-type semiconductors on an n-type substrate. Notice that connections are labeled the **base**, the **emitter**, and the **collector** of the transistor. Notice also that the transistor is depicted as completely symmetrical; in fact, there is some difference between the emitter-base junction and the base-collector junction. This difference is determined only by the doping densities of these different regions. A diagram for the transistor (with a base resistor and a load resistor) is shown in Figure 2.34(a). Another point to notice is that transistors may be one to two types, npn transistors or pnp transistors. The difference lies in the layering of the semiconductor material. In the case of npn transistors, current flows into the base and collector using positive voltages measured from the emitter. In the case of pnp transistors, current flows out of the base and emitter with negative voltages measured from the emitter.

To understand the operation of transistors in computers, it is necessary to consider their operational characteristics. This is best demonstrated by implementing an inverter using an npn transistor. The electrical characteristics are shown in Figure 2.34(c). Figure 2.34(a) shows the circuit diagram for an npn transistor (with two external resistors) in a common emitter configuration. A transistor may function either as an amplifier or as a switch. Clearly, for operation in a digital computer, we are interested in the transistor's operation as a switch. Notice, from Figure 2.34(c.i), that the base-emitter junction behaves much like a diode, whereas, from Figure 2.34(c.ii), the collector-emitter junction behaves like a current source whose value is determined by the current flowing into the base (I_b).

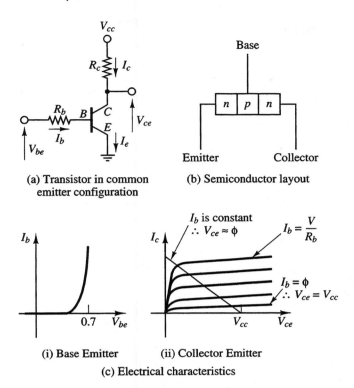

(a) Transistor in common emitter configuration

(b) Semiconductor layout

(i) Base Emitter   (ii) Collector Emitter

(c) Electrical characteristics

Figure 2.34   Transistor: (a) circuit diagram, (b) semiconductor layout, and (c) electrical characteristics.

Thus for a particular value of I_b, determined by V_{be} and R_b, I_c remains constant. Provided that the voltage V_{be} is less than 0.7 V, the base/emitter junction (acting like a diode) will be reverse biased and will not conduct electricity. In this state, according to Figure 2.34(c.ii), the collector-emitter junction behaves like an open circuit; thus, V_{ce} will be approximately V_{cc} V. As soon as V_{be} becomes greater than about 0.7 V the base-emitter junction becomes forward biased and conducts electricity. The base current I_b is therefore equal to $(V_{be}—0.7)/R_b$. Thus, the base current changes from 0 A to a constant determined by V_{be} and R_b. Looking again at Figure 2.34(c.ii) we notice that the characteristics of the collector-emitter junction are determined by the base current, with the circuit acting as a current source dependent on I_b. Thus, once we have set the forward bias base current I_b by a resistor, the voltage V_{ce} will be determined by the supply current I_e and the resistor R_c. By setting the appropriate value of V_b, we can ensure that whenever the base-emitter is forward biased, the voltage of V_{ce} will be about 0 V. Thus, the transistor operates as a switch, in that when the base voltage is low (input 0 V or logic level 0), the transistor output is high (output 5 V or logic level 1), and when the base voltage is high (input 5 V or logic level 1), the transistor output is low (output 0 V or logic level 0); thus, we have an **inverter**.

Early families—RTL and DTL.   Using the simple model of a transistor presented earlier, we briefly discuss the implementation of the early logic circuits. One of the advantages in these circuits is that it is easy to see how the gates are implemented. The first logic family is RTL. Using only resistors and transistors, we are able to construct a **nor** gate as shown in Figure 2.35.

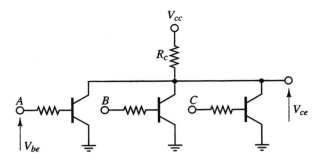

Figure 2.35 RTL implementation for three-input NOR gate.

Notice that when any of the inputs are high, the respective transistor will be forward biased, the output V_{ce} will be 0 and the output low. Only when all of the inputs are low will V_{ce} be at the same voltage as V_{cc}; thus, the output will be high. The truth table therefore corresponds to the **nor** gate. Recall from the section on logic circuits that all logic gates may be constructed from **nor** gates only.

Another early family of gates was the family of diode transistor logic gates, or DTL. By the judicious use of diodes, it is possible to make a multiple input **nand** gate as is shown in Figure 2.36. The inputs A, B and C act as an **and** gate in that if any of the inputs is low, the point P will be at 0.7 V. In this state, the output is open circuit and thus high. Conversely, if A, B, and C are all high, the point P will be at nearly 5 V. The diodes $D1$, $D2$, and $D3$ will drop the voltage so that V_{be} will be forward biased. In this state, the transistor is on and the output will be low.

Popular family — TTL.   TTL is the most widely used form of integrated circuit logic. In Figure 2.37 we show the circuit diagram for a TTL **nand** gate. Notice that a multiple emitter transistor is used in much the same way that the diodes were used in DTL. If any of the inputs are low, the transistor is turned on (because the base-emitter is forward biased). With T_1 turned on, the input to T_2 is low; thus, the input to T_4 is high, and the input to T_3 is low. With T_3 off and T_4 on, the output is high. Conversely, if all inputs are high, then T_1 is off

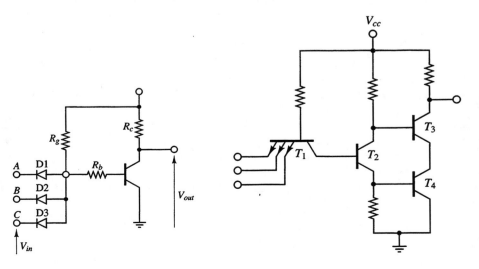

Figure 2.36 Three-input DTL NAND gate.

Figure 2.37 TTL **nand** gates.

(because the base-emitter is now reverse-biased). With T_1 on, T_2 is now forward-biased and, therefore, T_3 is on, and T_4 is off (because the emitter of T_4 is at least 1.4 V above ground).

In the Tables 2.25 and 2.26, we list the different members of the TTL family with the characteristics of each. Notice that the propagation delay for gate to respond to changes in its input is given in nanoseconds (*ns*). The maximum number of cycles per second (i.e., logic level changes per second) for this component is given in Hertz (Hz) and is the reciprocal of the propagation delay. Thus standard TTL gates can switch at a maximum of 100 MHz. In addition, we show a very small sample of the different standard TTL gates that may be purchased. These gates are packaged in dual inline packages (DIP's) and have the code number 74*nn* when *nn* is a two-digit number (or 74*nnn* when *nnn* is a three-digit number). In fact, there are many hundreds of different standard gates.

TABLE 2.25   Characteristics of TTL family

Name	Abbreviation	Propagation delay (ns)	Power dissipation (mW)
Standard TTL	TTL	10	10
Low-power TTL	LTTL	33	1
High-speed TTL	HTTL	6	22
Schottky TTL	STTL	3	19
Low-power Schottky TTL	LSTTL	9.5	2

TABLE 2.26   Sample of common TTL gates

Code number	Description
7404	6 Single-input inverters
7400	4 Two-input **nand** gates
7410	3 Three-input **nand** gates
7420	2 Four-input **nand** gates
7430	1 Eight-input **nand** gate

Special application families—IIL and ECL.   The other families that use bipolar junction technology are IIL and ECL. Both of these families are newer than TTL logic; however, for reasons that will become obvious shortly, they have not enjoyed the same popularity as TTL.

IIL is the newest logic member of the bipolar technologies. The characteristics are high gate density. Because of the gate density, IIL is used mainly for MSI and LSI applications and is not available in SSI packages. IIL is similar to RTL logic; however, the RTL resistors are replaced by transistors, and the individual transistors used for each RTL input are replaced by a single multicollector transistor. Unlike the other logic families, IIL gates may not be analyzed alone; interconnection to other gates is essential for the circuit to make sense. For this reason, we will not discuss IIL further.

The other transistor type using bipolar technology is ECL. Unlike all of the other logics, the transistors in ECL are not saturated when switched on. This feat is achieved by using several transistors to provide a differential amplifier on the inputs, followed by an internal voltage and temperature bias network, followed finally by emitter follower output drivers. For this reason, the gates are able to switch much faster than all of the other gates. Thus, ECL is used in high-speed logic applications. As one might expect, the tradeoff is that the noise immunity is low, and the power dissipation is high.

We conclude this section on bipolar transistors by summarizing the characteristics of each of the technologies in Table 2.27.

TABLE 2.27   Comparison of bipolar junction technologies

Name	Propagation delay range (ns)	Power dissipation (mW)	Noise margin (v)	Transistor count
RTL	25	12	0.4	3
DTL	30	12	1.0	2
TTL	3-33	1-22	0.4	3-6
IIL	1-20	n/a	n/a	3-4
ECL	1	25	0.3	8

2.3.3 Unipolar Technology

As was mentioned at the start of this section, the unipolar technology makes use of only one type of carrier. These transistor families make use of field effects within the semiconductor, consequently the transistors are known as **field effect transistors (FETs)**. For digital computers, the unipolar technology is known as **metal-oxide semiconductor (MOS)** technology. Again, substrates of semiconductor are doped with impurities to form a circuit that behaves in much the same fashion as the bipolar junction transistor. As with bipolar circuits, there are two basic structures for the MOS transistor as shown in Figure 2.38.

Like the bipolar transistor, the MOS transistor has three contacts with the outside world: a source, a gate, and a drain. The circuit symbol for the MOSFET is given Figure 2.39. A voltage applied to the gate (similar to the base in bipolar transistors) is used to control the current flow from the source to the drain, using an n-channel MOSFET for an example. When the gate-source voltage is zero, the region between the source and drain acts as an insulator, and no current flows between the source and the drain. Conversely, when the gate-source voltage is positive, the channel region becomes an n-channel, permitting current to flow between the source and drain. Using positive logic, we specify that logic level 1 will turn the transistor on, and logic level 0 will turn the transistor off.

Building blocks.   The building blocks for MOS gates are an inverter, **nand** gates and **nor** gates. These gates are shown in Figure 2.40. Recall from the discussion on bipolar junction transistors that problems exist in fabricating resistors in semiconductor devices. For this reason, it is desirable to use only FETs to form the gates. Thus, a MOSFET is used to provide the necessary resistance.

PMOS, NMOS, and HMOS.   Clearly, from Figure 2.40, it is the case that an entire family of basic logic gates may be constructed using only n-channel or only p-channel MOS logic. For this reason, there exist NMOS IC's and PMOS IC's. Although these are becoming more popular, they are still less common than a combination of the two

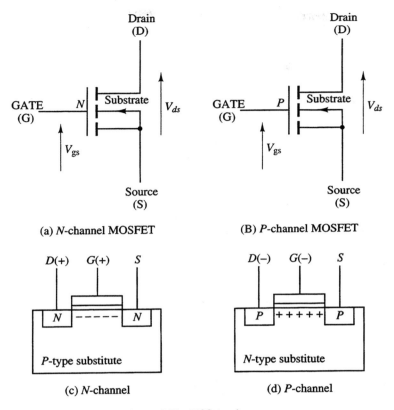

(a) *N*-channel MOSFET   (B) *P*-channel MOSFET

(c) *N*-channel   (d) *P*-channel

Figure 2.38   MOS transistors.

known as complementary metal-oxide semiconductor (CMOS), to be discussed shortly. Comparing NMOS and PMOS, we note that NMOS is significantly faster and consequently more common. As NMOS design and fabrication techniques have improved there has been a progression of families starting with HMOS (high-quality NMOS) and subsequently followed by HMOS II. Characteristics of these different families are outlined in Table 2.28.

Popular family—CMOS.   Notice that *n*-channel MOS logic is on (i.e., conducts) when the gate-source is positive, and *p*-channel MOS logic is on when the gate-source is negative. Both types are off when the voltage is zero. This feature may be used to an advantage by using both *n*-channel and *p*-channel transistors to construct the basic logic gates. This is accomplished by fabricating both logics on the same surface (or **substrate**) and gives rise to a popular MOS type known as CMOS. In Figure 2.41, the diagrams for the three basic gates are shown.

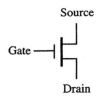

Figure 2.39   Circuit symbol for MOSFETs.

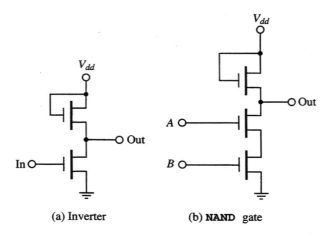

(a) Inverter   (b) **NAND** gate

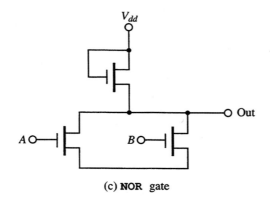

(c) **NOR** gate

Figure 2.40 *n*-channel MOS logic **not**, **nand**, and **nor** gates.

To see the advantage of using both *n*-channel and *p*-channel MOSFETs, consider the operation on the inverter. When V_{in} is on (high), gate G_1 will be positive with respect to its source (because it is an *n*-channel FET). G_1 is therefore on. Conversely, G_2 is negative with respect to its source (because it is a *p*-channel FET). G_2 is therefore off. Thus, the voltage V_{out} will be off (low). When the input V_{in} is off (low) the opposite occurs, that is, V_{out} is on (high). Thus, during either logic state (on or off), only one of the FETs is turned on; the other is always off. The effect of this is a significant reduction in the power used by the gate. In fact, CMOS circuits dissipate about only 10 nW; this is significantly lower than the power requirements of the bipolar logic circuits.

TABLE 2.28   MOSFET technology

Name	Propagation delay range (ns)	Power dissipation (mW)	Noise margin (V)	Transistor count
NMOS	4–14	10	N/A	2–4
HMOS	1	10	N/A	2–4
HMOS II	0.4	N/A	2–4	
CMOS	25	10	N/A	2–4

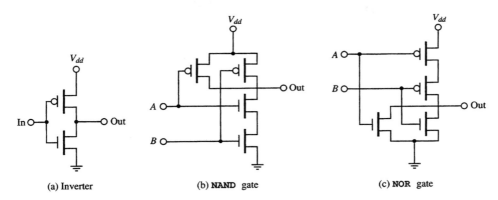

(a) Inverter   (b) NAND gate   (c) NOR gate

Figure 2.41   CMOS logic **not**, **nand**, and **nor** gates.

Note from Table 2.27 that the noise margin for CMOS is about 40% of the supply voltage. With a supply voltage of 3 V to 18 V, this permits considerable noise immunity if required. Because of the low-power requirements and flexible voltage supply, CMOS has become popular, particularly in high gate-density applications (e.g., microprocessors, etc.)

2.3.4 Gallium Arsenide Technology

As mentioned at the start of Section 2.2, the other primary semiconductor used in the fabrication of integrated circuits is a gallium arsenide (GaAs) composite. Because of certain physical properties (notably electron mobility), GaAs has speed characteristics inherently superior to silicon-based devices. In fact, GaAs devices have been used for several years in microwave applications (e.g., signal processing, etc.) and are occasionally used for digital applications when speed is critical. GaAs-based transistor oscillators are now able to reach more than 70 GHz. Based on the physical characteristics, it is reasonable to predict a speed factor of at least 2 over silicon, assuming other factors equal. Unlike silicon FETs in which both p-channel and n-channel are used, GaAs FETs (called metal semiconductor FETs [**MESFETs**]) use only the n-channel. As with the unipolar technology, there are several different structures (e.g., enhanced MESFET or EMESFET and depleted MESFET or DMESFET) and gate realizations based around GaAs. The main problems associated with using GaAs are in production, poor reliability, and the exacting tolerances that are required. Presently, GaAs technology trails behind silicon with GaAs ICs still primarily in the range of MSI and LSI (although VSLI is becoming possible).

Despite the difficulties associated with developing GaAs ICs, it seems certain that the lure of increased performance will inevitably draw manufacturers to using it. In particular, GaAs ICs are an attractive option for supercomputers where the higher costs and lower circuit densities are an acceptable trade off.

2.3.5 Integrated Circuits and IC Packaging

The extremely fast-switching speeds of semiconductor devices accounts for only half the success that the technology enjoys. The other half is the small size occupied by each gate and the ability to place many such gates on a single chip connected together to form a func-

tional unit. Consider the problems associated with wiring together 1,000,000 discrete transistors (a typical value required to build a modern CPU). Apart from the reliability issues,
the circuit would be extraordinarily unwieldy, akin perhaps to the digital computers of the
1950s, and significantly different to the 1^2 cm required using IC packaging! As we have
already mentioned, IC packages may be classified as SSI, MSI, LSI, and VLSI according to
Table 2.29.

TABLE 2.29   IC Package Densities

Name	Abbrev.	Approx. number of gates per chip
Small-scale integration	SSI	3–30
Medium-scale integration	MSI	30–300
Large-scale integration	LSI	300–3000
Very large-scale integration	VLSI	>3000

In Section 2.4 and Chapter 5, we will introduce a variety of different circuits ranging
from SSI to VLSI. Before discussing them, we briefly define a few terms used in conjunction with ICs. The actual integrated circuit consists of several gates on the same substrate
connected together according to the desired logical function. During production, several
ICs are made on a common sheet of substrate known as a wafer, as shown in Figure 2.42.

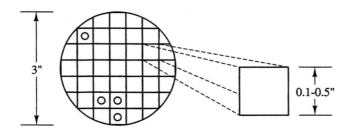

3"

0.1-0.5"

Figure 2.42   IC wafer. Notice that a
single wafer is cut to produce many
separate ICs. Chips with defects are
marked and discarded after cutting.

(a) Integrated circuit wafer   (b) Single IC chip

Each IC on the wafer is then tested and the defective ICs marked. The wafer is then
cut, and the good ICs are mounted in packages so that they may be placed on a printed circuit board. There are several popular packaging techniques that depend on the number of
pins required by the component. In general, the more complex the chip, the greater the
number of pins required to use it. Figure 2.43 shows the **Dual-In-Line (DIL)** Package used
for SSI components. Notice that the chip is set in a ceramic block. The pins are numbered
1 to 14 in the order shown in Figure 2.43. An alignment notch is used to ensure that the IC
is inserted correctly on the board.

Because of the initial costs associated with packaging an IC in the first place, it is typical for chip manufactures to bundle together several similar SSI circuits on the same chip.
We show by way of an example a couple of TTL 7400 series packages in Figures 2.44 and
2.45. Note that we have yet to introduce the operation of the JK flip-flop that is described
in Section 2.4.3; we have presented the diagram to demonstrate the packaging only.

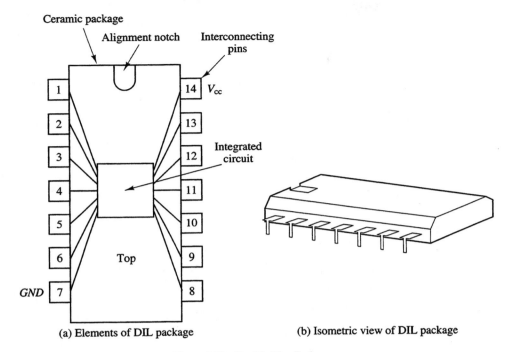

(a) Elements of DIL package   (b) Isometric view of DIL package

Figure 2.43   Dual-In-Line Package.

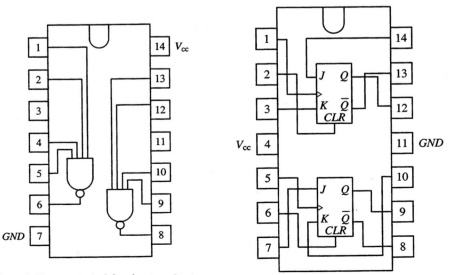

Figure 2.44   SN7420 dual four-input **nand** gate.

Figure 2.45   SN7473 dual JK flip-flop.

2.4 LOGIC CIRCUITS — IMPLEMENTATION

In this section, we discuss how the logical circuits described in Section 2.2 and realized in Section 2.3 may be connected together. By connecting gates together, we are able to construct more complex components. These in turn may again be connected together, eventually leading to a complete functional unit (such as an arithmetic and logic unit). We then show how these functional units may be combined with the appropriate combinational logic and control to form the CPU. The CPU is then connected to other system components via buses and I/O channels to form the computer hardware component.

Logical circuits may be classified into two major categories: **combinational logic** circuits and **sequential logic** circuits. Given that a circuit has some number of inputs, and outputs, the difference between the categories is as follows. In combinational logic, the outputs depend only on the current values of the inputs. Thus, the circuit may be said to be **stateless** (in that no state information is maintained). Conversely, the output from a sequential logic circuit depends not only on the current input but also on the history of the circuit. Sequential circuits are therefore said to be **state dependent**.

For an analogy with combinational versus sequential logic consider the case of determining the route to a store in an unfamiliar town. Because you do not know the route, you have two inputs, your current location and the destination location, and, an output, the route between the current location and destination. The black box is a map of the town, paper, a pen, and you. You then sit down and carefully write a route between source and destination. This corresponds to combinational logic. Notice that no prior knowledge of the situation was required. Conversely, consider the case of determining a route between a location and a destination in a familiar town. Again, the inputs are the same, and the black box may have some similar components (map, paper, pen, you). The sequence of operations is completely different, however. You now draw on your *past experience* to determine the best route, that is, you remember information from the past that will help you in this operation. You may know of a "back way" to the store. During the course of determining the route, it may be the case that you discover a better route than you last remember; this being the case, you will remember this new information so that next time you have the problem, the *state* of the "black box" has changed. This corresponds to sequential logic.

2.4.1 Clocks and Timing Cycles

In this section, we introduce some problems introduced when we realize the logical expressions described in Section 2.2 using physical components. In particular we notice that delays in physical circuit response influences the fundamental design of combinational and sequential circuits, necessitating the use of central clock to coordinate system activity. We now discuss these concepts in detail.

Delays in digital circuits.   It should be clear from the Section 2.3 that even the fastest electronic component takes some small time to respond to an input transition. It should also be clear that the response will be continuous, in the sense that although gates are in a binary state of 0 or 1, they must move continuously between the two levels. Consider the simple **not** gate depicted in Figure 2.46. Assume that the input is logic 0, before our analysis. A change in the input to a logic 1 will occur as a continuous rise in the signal level over the interval t_0 to t_1 as shown in the top graph plotting input voltage versus time. At some point during this interval, the gate will start to respond to the transition, switching the output to logic 0. This will again take some small interval, as shown in the bottom

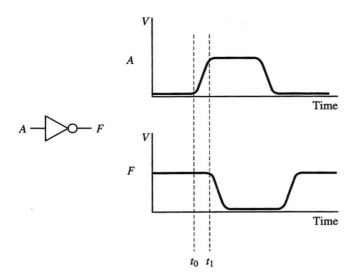

Figure 2.46   Propagation delay through a **not** gate.

graph. This delay between input and output is called the **gate propagation delay** and has important ramifications in the design of digital circuits.

Typically the time for the signal level to change from a logic 0 to 1 (and vice versa) is much shorter than the gate propagation delay. Thus we may consider a gate as responding to instantaneous changes in the signal level after a short delay. To see this, consider the logic circuit depicted in Figure 2.47 which consists of a **not** gate connected to an **and** gate. On the graphs we now represent the changes between the logic levels as occurring instantaneously. Thus, a change in the input A from logic 0 to 1 at time t_0 will cause the output B to change from logic 1 to 0 slightly later at time t_1 because of gate propagation delay. Now consider the effect of this slight delay on the output F.

Clearly, in the context of boolean logic, the expression $F = A \wedge \overline{A}$ is always logic 0. Looking at the bottom diagram in Figure 2.47, however, we see that because of the delay encountered in the gate, both inputs to the **and** gate will be momentarily logic 1. Thus the output from the **and** gate will also be momentarily logic 1. This is clearly an erroneous situation.

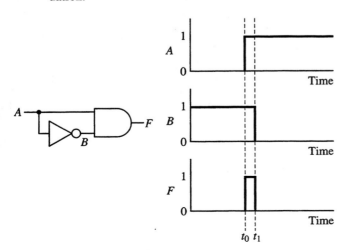

Figure 2.47   Undesired logic conditions caused by the delay of a **not** gate.

You might wonder if perhaps this momentary anomaly might be ignored; however, the problem may easily be exacerbated. Consider the case of Figure 2.48 in which we have replaced the **not** gate with some (arbitrarily) complex logic circuit that is *equivalent* to the **not** gate. Again the output will be erroneous but may now remain in this state for a considerable time.

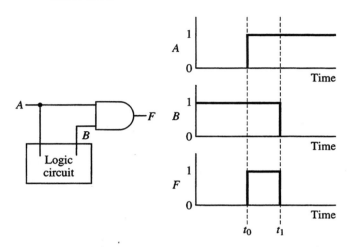

Figure 2.48   Propagation delay in digital circuits.

In fact the problem is essentially one of timing. In essence we are only interested in "looking" at the outputs from a particular combinational circuit when it has settled to its logically correct value. We are not interested in any momentary (or **transient**) responses. Thus, if we wait sufficiently long enough, the output will indicate the correct result. In fact, as we shall see later, the timing problem is complicated still further by sequential circuits (which possess memory of a previous state). One way in which we may ensure that timing errors do not affect the desired operation of the circuit is by the use of a common clock as described next.

Clocks to regulate circuit activities.

A **clock** in the context of computer components is a hardware device that produces a regular rectangular wave as shown in Figure 2.49. Often a single clock is used within a CPU to control the activity of all the different components; for this reason the clock is sometimes called the **system clock** or **CPU clock**. Within computers, this clock is usually a quartz crystal that oscillates under electrical stimulation at a very high frequency. The periodicity of the oscillation is extremely regular and is used to control circuitry generating the clock pulses.

The time between a rising edge (0 to 1 transition) and the following falling edge (1 to 0 transition) is called the **mark interval**, whereas the time between a falling edge and the following rising edge is called the **space interval**. The ratio of the two is called the **mark-**

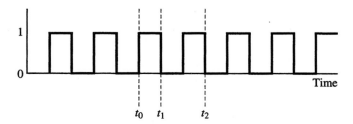

Figure 2.49   Computer clock.

space ratio and need not be 1. Finally, the time between two successive rising edges is called the **clock cycle time** and is measured in Hertz (1 Hz = 1 cycle per second). Typically, a CPU will have a system clock with a cycle time of many MHz (millions of cycles per second). Notice that the cycle time of the system will not be the same as the **instruction execution rate**. This is because each computer instruction will take several clock cycles to execute.

To see how the clock is used to regulate the system, we require that all the activity associated with a single state change in the computer occur within a single clock cycle. Thus if there is a complex combinational logic circuit which takes several inputs (defined by the current state of the computer) and it generates a new state (defined by its outputs), we require that all of the inputs to the combinational logic are quiescent and that the circuit has had time to respond to the inputs. An edge of the clock is then used to load (or **latch**) the new outputs into the sequential circuit, which in turn modifies the state of the computer. The following edge is then used to place the new state information as inputs to combinational circuits, thus presenting the combinational circuits with new inputs. Clearly for this synchronized activity to occur, it is necessary that the cycle time be longer than the time for the combinational circuit to settle. Given this solution, erroneous output caused by propagation delays within the combinational circuit will be ignored. In the context of computers, an "activity" is a sequence of combinational logic gates and may be thought of as either a simple instruction (e.g., take the one's complement of a register) or it may be a portion of a more complex instruction (e.g., load a register from memory) and is given the name **microinstruction** to distinguish it from the CPU **macroinstructions**. Typically, CPUs are designed for working at the micro instruction level. Additional details may be found on timing and microinstructions in Chapter 5 when we discuss the SIM68 hardware design. Notice that because of the many different paths that may be taken through a circuit we have to use the worst-case path thorough the logic as the minimum clock cycle time. Notice also that we do not suggest that a particular activity must be performed in one cycle (e.g., multipling two integers together), provided it may be subdivided into several less complex stages, each of which may be performed within a cycle (also known as a **t-state**), with any pertinent state information saved between the stages.

With this model for instruction execution we see that the computer may be viewed as a network of combinational circuit elements with inputs from the outside world and several sequential logic circuits that maintain the current state of the computer. To ensure that all data values change predictably, a common clock is used to drive the sequential circuit elements. Thus the inputs along with the current state precisely define the outputs from the system and the next state that the computer will be in. This is depicted in Figure 2.50.

2.4.2 Combinational Circuits

With boolean algebra discussed in Section 2.2 and gate realizations discussed in Section 2.3, we are now in a position to introduce some combinational circuits. Unlike the algebra section that was purely abstract, we will discuss combinational logic in the context of digital computers. Thus, we will be considering logic circuits that have a useful interpretation when applied to digital computers. We have already seen the circuit symbols representing the primitive gates (**and, or, not,** etc.). By connecting these symbols together using lines (i.e., connections at the gate level), we are able to generate a graphic representation of a logic circuit. From these basic building blocks, we introduce increasingly more complex logical constructs that will eventually lead to the primitive arithmetic operations that are used by digital computers.

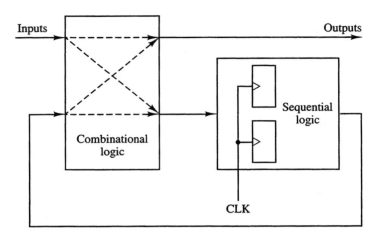

Figure 2.50 Decomposition of logic circuit into two components; the combinational logic and (clocked) sequential logic.

Half adder. The first step toward an arithmetic unit is the construction of a 1-bit binary adder. Recall from Section 2.1 that whenever two numbers are added together, the sum has the same number of digits plus an optional carry. A logical circuit that takes two single-bit numbers (x and y) and adds them to yield a sum bit (s) and carry bit (c) is known as a **half adder**. The black-box diagram for a half adder is given in Figure 2.51.

Thus, we seek logical expressions for functions that represent the 1-bit sum and optional carry of two single-bit numbers. We may then realize these expressions using gates to implement the required function. Figure 2.52 shows this concept.

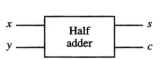

$$\begin{array}{r} + \quad x \\ y \\ \hline c \quad s \end{array} \qquad \begin{array}{l} x = 1/0 \\ y = 1/0 \\ c = 1/0 \\ s = 1/0 \end{array}$$

Figure 2.51 Half adder.

Figure 2.52 Binary addition of two 1-bit numbers.

Because there are two inputs, each function must be identified by considering the four resulting cases. Clearly if x and y are both 0, the sum and carry will both be 0. If either the x or the y (but not both) is 1, the sum will be 1, and the carry 0. If both the x and the y are 1, then the sum will be 0, and the carry will be 1. Using truth tables, we have the table as given in Table 2.30.

TABLE 2.30 Truth table for half adder

x	y	s	c
0	0	0	0
0	1	1	0
1	0	1	0
1	1	0	1

This may be written as an expression:

$$s = x\,\bar{y} + \bar{x}\,y$$

$$= x \oplus y$$

$$c = x\,y$$

These logical functions are realized in their circuit component forms in Figure 2.53. Notice that if we knew in advance the hardware technology to be used (e.g., TTL), we could optimize the expressions (and hence the circuit) to minimize the number of gates provided by that technology.

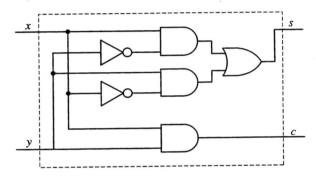

Figure 2.53   Circuit realization of a half adder.

Full adder.   Recall again from Section 2.1 the sequence of operations necessary to add two binary numbers. We start by adding the least significant bits x_1 and y_1; this generates a sum s_1 and carry c_1. The carry, c_1, is then added together with the next two inputs x_2 and y_2. This generates a sum s_2 and carry c_2, and so on. We have already seen how a half adder may be used to start the arithmetic. The next logic circuit is therefore an adder that takes as input x, y, and c_i a carry in, and generates a sum s and carry out c_o. This circuit is known as a **full adder**. A black-box diagram for the full adder is given in Figure 2.54.

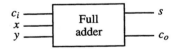

Figure 2.54   Full adder.

Because there are now three inputs to the circuit, the truth table is a little more complex. This is given in Table 2.31.

TABLE 2.31   Truth table for full adder

c_i	x	y	s	c_o
0	0	0	0	0
0	0	1	1	0
0	1	0	1	0
0	1	1	0	1
1	0	0	1	0
1	0	1	0	1
1	1	0	0	1
1	1	1	1	1

Using this one possible expression for each logic function is

$$s = x \oplus y \oplus c_i$$

$$c_o = x\,y + x\,c_i + y\,c_i$$

We may also think of the circuit as two cascaded half adders. That is, we add x to y, yielding s_1 and c_1. Then we add s_1 from this to c_i, yielding s_2 and c_2. The only point we have to be careful about is c_0. The carry out is set when either c_1 is set or when c_2 is set. With this in mind, a circuit realization of the full adder is given in Figure 2.55.

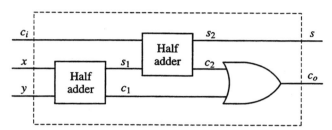

Figure 2.55 Circuit realization of full adder.

Eight-bit parallel cascade adder. Using the half and full adders described previously, we see that it is an easy matter to develop an adder that operates on two bit-strings. Formally, we want to be able to take a pair of two's complement integers held in registers X and Y, add them together, and place the result in the third register F, as shown in Figure 2.56.

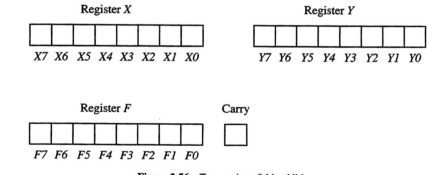

Figure 2.56 Two-register 8-bit addition.

Logically, the problem may be solved by using a half adder to compute the least significant bit of the result, and full adders for the remaining bits. Thus, the formula is as described subsequently.

$$f_0 = x_0 + y_0$$

$$f_1 = x_1 + y_1 + c_0$$

$$f_2 = x_2 + y_2 + c_1$$

$$\cdots$$

Where c_0 is the carry-out from the half adder, c_1 is the carry-out from the first full adder, and so on. Figure 2.57 depicts a 4-bit adder using only full adders. Notice that the carry-in to the low bit is always 0, thus giving the correct result.

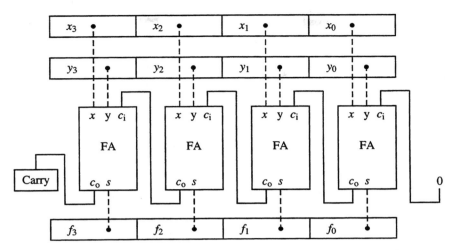

Figure 2.57   Four-bit cascade adder.

2.4.3 Sequential Circuits

The second major category of circuit logic is sequential circuits. Recall that a sequential circuit is one in which the outputs depend on both the input and the current state of the circuit (which depends on previous operations). Notice that in the previous circuits the output was always a function of the input only (i.e., the result from the 8-bit adder depends only on the two integers to be added). In contrast, the following circuits retain state information that permits the output to vary given the same input.

Flip-flops.   Perhaps the simplest class of sequential circuit is the flip-flop. The characteristics of the flip-flop are that: (1) flip-flops assume one of two stable output states; (2) they have a pair of complementary outputs Q and $\bar{Q}$; and (3) they have one or more inputs that may be used to change the output states. There are four main types of flip-flop: the **SR flip-flop**, the **D-type flip-flop**, the **T-type flip-flop**, and the **JK-flip-flop**. In the following section, we consider the construction of an SR flip-flop, starting with the basic flip-flop and improving it to handle race and timing problems that occur. We then present the other flip-flops in their final form (i.e., without the intermediate steps). The intention of this section is to convince the reader by using simple logic gates and an external clock (discussed previously), we are able to develop building blocks for CPU registers and other state dependent components.

SR Flip-Flop.   The set-reset flip-flop has the characteristic that the outputs will remain set according to the last high input. Thus, if the last high input was set (S), the output will be Q high and $\bar{Q}$ low, whereas if the last high input was reset (R) the output will be Q low and $\bar{Q}$ high. To see this, consider Figure 2.58. Assume that both set and reset are low to start with. We have one of two possible stable states: either Q high and $\bar{Q}$ low, in which case the inputs to the R **nor** gate are 0 and 0 giving an output of $Q = 1$, and the inputs to the S gate are 0 and 1 giving an output of $\bar{Q} = 0$; alternatively, the opposite state occurs (i.e., Q low and $\bar{Q}$ high) by similar reasoning.

From this state, consider the case in which the S state is momentarily high (e.g., pulse). If Q was high then the S **nor** gate output ($\overline{Q}$) is low; thus, both inputs to the R **nor** gate are 0, giving an output of Q high. Conversely if Q was low, then the S NOR output ($\overline{Q}$) is low; thus, both inputs to the R NOR gate are 0 giving an output of Q high. Notice that the values of Q and $\overline{Q}$ will not change, even if S returns to 0.

In the same way that the S input sets the Q output, the R input resets the Q output. Thus, after a pulse to the R input, Q will be low and $\overline{Q}$ will be high. One might wonder what happens if both the R and S inputs are high *at the same time*. The answer is that the state of the flip-flop is undetermined with the outputs oscillating between high and low. Clearly such behavior is undesirable in a computer.

The functional diagram for the SR flip-flop is given subsequently. The inputs are the set and reset lines. The outputs are Q and its complement $\overline{Q}$.

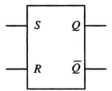

Figure 2.58   Basic SR flip-flop.

In the same way that we represent combinational logic circuits by using truth tables and logical expressions, so too can we represent sequential logic circuits. The difference lies in that with sequential circuits it is necessary to include state information in the expression. The truth table for the SR flip-flop is given in Table 2.32.

TABLE 2.32   Truth table for SR flip-flop

S(t)	R(t)	Q(t)	Q(t + ε)	$\overline{Q}$ (t + ε)
0	0	0	0	1
0	0	1	1	0
0	1	0	0	1
0	1	1	0	1
1	0	0	1	0
1	0	1	1	0
1	1	0	—	—
1	1	1	—	—

Notice that when both R and S are high, the outputs for Q and $\overline{Q}$ are undefined. The expression for the *SR* flip-flop is as follows:

$$Q^+ = S + (\overline{R} \, Q)$$

where Q^+ represents the value of Q in the state following the current state. You may be convinced of this fact by writing the truth table for the preceding expression and comparing it with the previous truth table.

To realize the SR flip-flop, we require 2 two-input **nor** gates as shown in Figure 2.59.

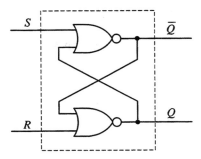

Figure 2.59   Gate realization of SR flip-flop.

Clocked SR Flip-Flop.   The SR flip-flop as presented earlier is **asynchronous**. That is, as soon as one of the inputs changes, a short time later (ε) the outputs will change. This change will clearly depend on the gate propagation delay. Asynchronous operation is undesirable in complex circuits because we are unable to determine exactly when the output states have reached a stable state, and it is easy for such circuits to become involved in a **race condition**. That is, the sequence of events in the logic is determined by the gate delays; thus, it is impossible to ensure that the outputs of several logic sequences will occur simultaneously if they are to be used as inputs to a common gate. One way in which these timing problems may be controlled is by the use of a system clock as shown in Figure 2.60 as discussed in Section 2.4.1. We ensure that the output from sequential circuits changes only after a clock pulse is received. Looking again at the SR flip-flop we see that by using two **and** gates connected to the R and S inputs, we are able to prevent any changes in the output, unless the clock is high.

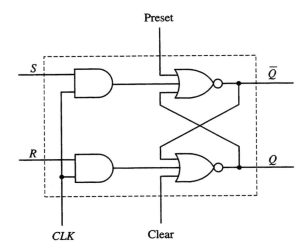

Figure 2.60   Gate realization of clocked SR flip-flop.

Master-Slave SR Flip-Flop.   Although the clocked SR flip-flop is an improvement on the basic SR flip-flop, there are still problems when it is used in digital circuits. Notice that the R and S inputs have to be valid during the entire time that the clock pulse is high. If the pulse were to extend beyond the time allocated by the gates that are driving the flip-flop, the values clocked into the SR flip-flop may be incorrect. Thus, we see that the clocked SR flip-flop is still dependent on timing for correct operation. To prevent this problem, we desire flip-flops that respond only to *transitions* in the clock. In particular, it is desirable to clock the input to the flip-flop on the rising (falling) edge of the clock pulse and then clock the new output on the falling (rising) edge of the clock. In this way, the output from any gate will be available to the next input stage on the next clock pulse, regardless of the time taken by individual components. With these concepts in mind, we show the master-slave SR flip-flop in Figure 2.61. Notice that we are able to use two clocked SR flip-flops and a **not** gate to achieve our goals. To see how the master-slave flip-flop operates, consider the legal values on the R and S inputs and a single positive clock pulse. As soon as the the clock becomes high, the data into the master slave flip-flop will cause Q and $\bar{Q}$ to be set appropriately in the first clocked flip-flop. Because the second flip-flop has been disabled these changes will not be transferred to the next stage. After some short time, the clock pulse will fall, causing the second flip-flop to become active. Provided the pulse width is greater than the operation time for the first flip-flop, the results from Q and $\bar{Q}$ will be available to change the second flip-flop appropriately. This will cause the new output to become available shortly after the fall of the clock pulse. Notice that provided the other circuits are also clocked on pulse edges, the timing again does not matter. Any changes in the outputs Q and $\bar{Q}$ for the master-slave flip-flop will not have an effect on subsequent clocked gates, until the next clock pulse.

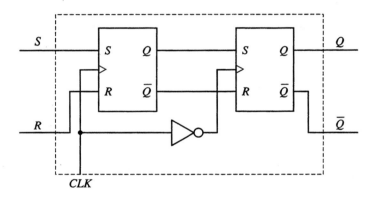

Figure 2.61   Realization of master-slave RS flip-flop.

D-type Flip-Flop.   The delay (D) flip-flop has a single input D and a pair of complementary outputs Q and $\bar{Q}$. The action of the D-type flip-flop is simple; the output of the flip-flop at the next clock pulse will be the input at the current clock pulse. Thus, the D-type flip-flop offers a one clock delay in a sequential logic circuit. The circuit diagram for a D-type flip-flop is given in Figure 2.62.

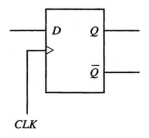

Figure 2.62   D-type flip-flop.

The flip-flop may be represented by the truth table given in Table 2.33 and the following logical expression:

TABLE 2.33 Clocked
D-type flip-flop

D	Q	Q^+	$\overline{Q^+}$
0	0	0	1
0	1	0	1
1	0	1	0
1	1	1	0

$$Q^+ = D$$

It should be obvious that the D-type flip-flop may be constructed from an SR flip-flop with the single input connected directly to the R and its complement (via a **not** gate) to the S inputs of the SR flip-flop as shown in Figure 2.63.

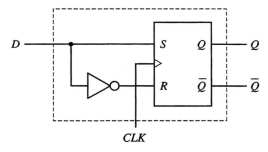

CLK   **Figure 2.63**   Clocked D-type flip-flop.

T-type Flip-Flop.   The Trigger (T) flip-flop performs another simple function. The output is toggled from its previous state every time that the T input is pulsed. Thus, the T flip-flop acts like a toggle switch. The circuit diagram is given in Figure 2.64, along with the truth table in Table 2.34 and the logical expression.

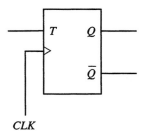

CLK   **Figure 2.64**   T-type flip-flop.

TABLE 2.34 T-type
flip-flop

T	Q	Q^+	$\overline{Q^+}$
0	0	0	1
0	1	1	0
1	0	1	0
1	1	0	1

$$Q^+ = \overline{T}\, Q + T\, \overline{Q}$$

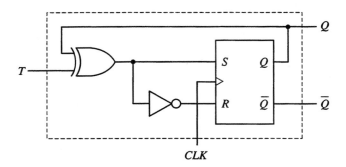

CLK

Figure 2.65(a) Clocked T-type flip-flop.

JK Flip-Flop. Recall from the discussion about the SR flip-flop that the output is undetermined for the case in which both the S and R inputs are 1. To provide a sequential circuit that does not have this property, the SR flip-flop may be modified so that when both inputs are 1 the flip-flop behaves like the T flip-flop (i.e., it toggles the Q and $\overline{Q}$ outputs). This modified flip-flop is known as the JK flip-flop. The J and the K inputs correspond to the S and R inputs on the SR flip-flop. The circuit diagram for the JK flip-flop is given in Figure 2.65(b).

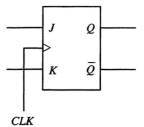

CLK

Figure 2.65(b) Clocked JK flip-flop.

The truth table (Table 2.35) and logical expression of the circuit are given subsequently.

TABLE 2.35 Clocked JK
flip-flop

J	K	Q	Q^+	$\overline{Q^+}$
0	0	0	0	1
0	0	1	1	0
0	1	0	0	1
0	1	1	0	1
1	0	0	1	0
1	0	1	1	0
1	1	0	1	0
1	1	1	0	1

$$Q^+ = Q\,\overline{K} + \overline{Q}\,J$$

The circuit may be realized by the modification of an SR flip-flop using two **and** gates as shown in Figure 2.66.

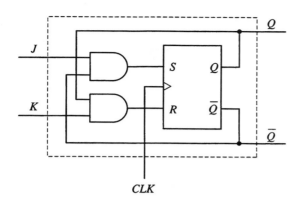

Figure 2.66   JK flip-flop.

Registers.   In the same way that combinational logic circuits may be used to create arithmetic units such as the adder, sequential logic circuits may be used to construct
storage and data movement circuits such as registers. In the following section, we show
two examples of sequential logic circuits constructed from flip-flops and some combinational logic, the serial shift register and the parallel shift register.

Parallel Load Register.   Each bit of the humble register, which the programmer becomes so familiar with, may be constructed from nothing more than a single master-
slave D-type flip-flop as shown in Figure 2.67. To control when data is to be loaded into
the flip-flop, we **and** an additional line, the **enable line**, with the clock. If the enable is low,
a change in the input will have no effect; only when the enable is high will the input be
latched in.

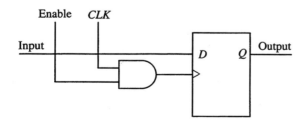

Figure 2.67   Single bit of loadable
register.

This procedure may easily be extended to form an n-bit register, as is shown for the
case of four in Figure 2.68. To affect the parallel load, we need only to connect the outputs
from one register to the inputs of another via a set of lines as shown. Again, the registers
are composed from D-type flip-flops; they are arranged so that a single clock pulse will
transfer data from register A to register B. Such a parallel load register may be used to load
data to or from an arithmetic logic unit.

Serial Shift Registers.   A serial shift register may be composed from D-type flip-
flops connected in series as shown in Figure 2.69. For each clock pulse, the serial shift register takes the data in the shift register and moves each bit (determined by the Q values of
the D-type flip-flops) to the right one place, loading a new value into the leftmost flip-flop.
Notice that by connecting each of the input values to external logic, it would be possible to
load a bit string into the register, shift it several times, and then read the result from the

(a) Four-bit parallel load register

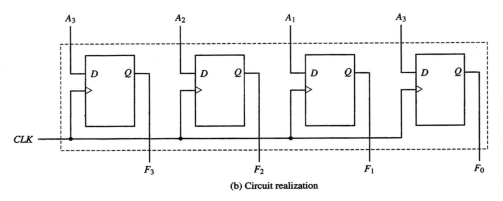

(b) Circuit realization

Figure 2.68   Diagram and circuit realization of four-bit register.

register. Thus, we see that the arithmetic shift function (see Chapter 5), for example, may be implemented quite easily.

As an example of a sequential circuit consider how a combination right shift/parallel load register might be realized. Using such a register we could parallel load a value and then shift it right several bit positions. The circuit required to achieve this for a single bit is shown in Figure 2.70. Notice that the SR line may be used to select either an external input A_{x-1} (i.e., parallel load) or the previous Q output F_x (i.e., right shift).

In a similar manner we can implement a combination left shift/parallel load register as is shown in Figure 2.71.

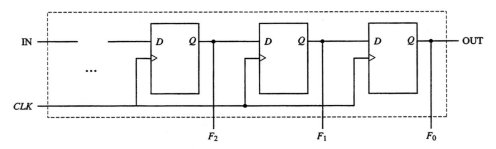

Figure 2.69   Four-bit serial shift right register.

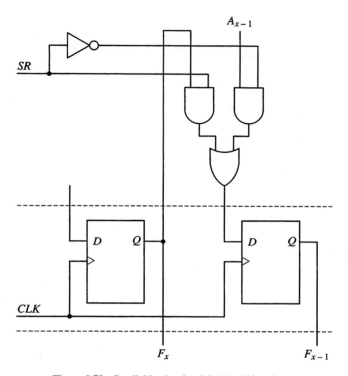

Figure 2.70   Parallel load and serial right-shift register.

Thus to conclude this chapter we show the implementation of a parallel load register with left-shift and right-shift capability in Figure 2.72. Notice the three control lines LS, LOAD, and RS to select either a left shift, a parallel load, or a right shift. Clearly only one of these lines will be high at any given time.

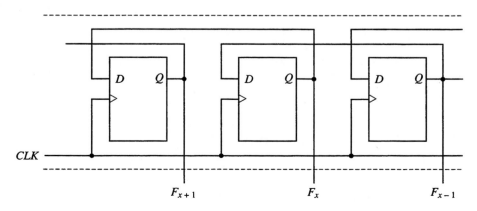

Figure 2.71   Serial left-shift register.

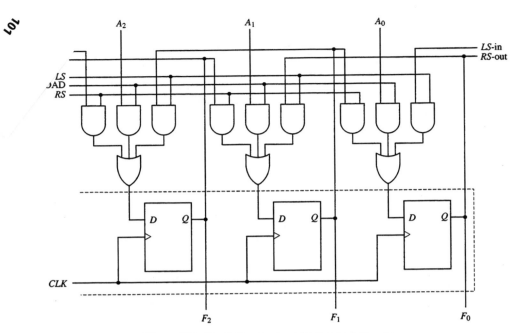

Figure 2.72   Parallel load and serial left-right shift register.

2.5 EXERCISES

1. Convert the unsigned decimal integer 727 to the following bases:
   a) base 2, b) base 3, c) base 12, d) base 16

2. Convert the unsigned decimal integer 62 to the following bases:
   a) base 2, b) base 3, c) base 7, d) base 16

3. Convert the unsigned decimal integer 223427 to the following bases:
   a) base 2, b) base 8, c) base 16, d) base 20

4. Convert the unsigned integer 356 (base 7) to the following bases:
   a) base 4, b) base 13, c) base 16

5. Convert the unsigned integer 126 (base 9) to the following bases:
   a) base 2, b) base 8, c) base 16

6. Convert the unsigned integer 23210 (base 4) to the following bases:
   a) base 2, b) base 10, c) base 15

7. Convert the following unsigned integers to base 2, base 8, base 10, and base 16:
   a) 1111011110_2, b) 124_8, c) 273_{10}, d) $FCD1_{16}$, e) 1010_3, f) 2563_9

8. Convert the following unsigned integers to base 2, base 8, base 10, and base 16:
   a) 110111011110_2, b) 472_8, c) 11101_{10}, d) $45BE_{16}$, e) $F001_{16}$, f) $AB81_{14}$

9. Convert the following unsigned integers to base 2, base 8, base 10, and base 16:
   a) 110011101101_2, b) 7771_8, c) 127_{10}, d) $ABCD_{16}$,.e) 7347_{16}, f) 8352_{32}

10. Compute the following by using unsigned integer arithmetic (leave in the appropriate base):
    a) %110101 + %001110, b) %100001 − %1111,
    c) %10001 * %1001, d) %011001 / %111,
    e) $1F10 + $F12F2, f) $FF9F2C4 − $A932F,
    g) $11 * $2B34, h) $ABC/$D

11. Compute the following by using unsigned integer arithmetic (leave in the appropriate base):
    a) %110110 + %100110, b) %110011 − %111,
    c) %01011 * %1111, d) %1111101/%11001,
    e) $1210 + $FF2, f) $AF27 − $F9EA,
    g) $33 * $AF6A, h) $94D/$8

12. Compute the following by using unsigned integer arithmetic (leave in the appropriate base):
    a) %111111 + %101010, b) %001001 − %001,
    c) %10001 * %0101, d) %101001/%101,
    e) $D93F + $11AE2, f) $24C02 − $9C3F2,
    g) $42 * $186E, h) $CDE/$2

13. Show the sign-magnitude, one's complement, and two's complement representation of the following signed decimal numbers. (The answers should be in binary; assume an 8-bit representation.)
    a) 100, b) 22, c) 111, d) −81, e) −27, f) −111

14. Show the sign-magnitude, one's complement, and two's complement representation of the following signed decimal numbers. (The answers should be in binary; assume an 8-bit representation.)
    a) 114, b) 32, c) 121, d) −81, e) −27, f) −111

15. Show the sign-magnitude, one's complement, and two's complement representation of the following signed decimal numbers. (The answers should be in binary; assume an 8-bit representation.)
    a) 120, b) 18, c) 210, d) −61, e) −47, f) −101

16. Show the sign-magnitude, one's complement, and two's complement representation of the following signed decimal numbers. (The answers should be in binary; assume an 8-bit representation.)
    a) 89, b) 123, c) 99, d) −1, e) −53, f) −99

17. Calculate the following using two's complement arithmetic. Assume an 8-bit (binary) representation. Be sure to state if overflow occurs.
    a) 11001001 + 00001100, b) 10000000 − 00000011,
    c) 00111001 + 01111001, d) 00010001 − 00101001,
    e) 00000111 + 00111010, f) 11111111 − 11110010

18. Calculate the following using two's complement arithmetic. Assume an 8-bit (binary) representation. Be sure to state if overflow occurs.
    a) 11101001 + 01001100, b) 10110010 − 00101011,
    c) 00111101 + 10111101, d) 01011001 − 00011111,
    e) 10000111 + 00011101, f) 11110111 − 11111001

19. Calculate the following using two's complement arithmetic. Assume an 8-bit (binary) representation. Be sure to state if overflow occurs.
    a) 11111001 + 10001100, b) 10110001 − 00100011,
    c) 10111001 + 01111101, d) 11010001 − 10010101,
    e) 00000111 + 10011111, f) 01111111 − 11000000

20. Calculate the following using two's complement arithmetic. Assume an 8-bit (binary) representation. Be sure to state if overflow occurs.
    a) 11011101 + 11001100, b) 01111000 − 00110011,
    c) 00111101 + 10111101, d) 10010001 − 00110101,
    e) 10000111 + 10011101, f) 11000111 − 10011001

21. Find the 15's complement and the 16's complement for the following (16-bit wide) signed integers:
    a) $0045, b) $F402, c) $DB2A, d) $203C, e) $6989, f) $12A3

22. Find the 15's complement and the 16's complement for the following (16-bit wide) numbers:
    a) $0B45, b) $C578, c) $DA2F, d) $01D0, e) $FF34

23. Find the 15's complement and the 16's complement for the following (16-bit wide) numbers:
    a) $F045, b) $F112, c) $0F32, d) $BA12, e) $1ABC

24. Find the 15's complement and the 16's complement for the following (16-bit wide) numbers:
    a) $F37D, b) $F562, c) $1F3A, d) $4E40, e) $00E4

25. Prove part b of theorem 5 in Table 2.18.

26. Prove part b of theorem 7 in Table 2.18.

27. Prove part b of theorem 8 in Table 2.18.

28. Give the truth tables of the following functions:
    a) Exclusive **or** of two variables,
    b) **nand** for three variables,
    c) $((x \vee y) \wedge x)$,
    d) $x \wedge y \wedge z \vee x \wedge y \vee z$,
    e) $\bar{x} \wedge y \wedge \bar{z} \vee y \wedge \bar{z} \vee \bar{x} \wedge y \vee \bar{z}$,
    f) $\bar{x} \wedge (y \vee \bar{z}) \vee y \wedge \bar{z} \vee x \wedge (x \vee y)$

29. Give the Karnaugh map of the following functions:
    a) $f = xyz + xy + z + yz$,
    b) $f = \bar{x}yz + x\bar{y}\bar{z} + x\bar{y}z + \bar{x}y\bar{z} + xy\bar{z}$,
    c) $f = \bar{z} + xyz + \bar{y}z + xz$,
    d) $f = \bar{x}\bar{y}\bar{z} + x\bar{y}z + xyz + \bar{x}y\bar{z} + \bar{x}yz$,
    e) $f = \bar{a}\,\bar{b}c\bar{d} + bd + ac\bar{d} + a + d$,
    f) $f = \bar{a}e + a\bar{b}c + e + c\bar{e}$

30. For the preceding give the function minimizations.

31. Give the Karnaugh map and minimization of the following minterm expressions:
    a) $f = \sum m(0,1,3,5)$,
    b) $f = \sum m(3,5,6,10)$,
    c) $f = \sum m(0,2,4,5,7,8,10,14,15)$,
    d) $f = \sum m(0,1,4,5,9,10.11.13)$,
    e) $f = \sum m(1,3,5,7,9,10,11)$

32. What is the property of semiconductors that makes them useful in the building of transistors?

33. What is the difference in construction of a diode and a transistor?

34. What are the major characteristics of semiconductors? Describe each.

35. What is the difference between a *pnp* and *npn* transistor?

36. CMOS is by far the most popular family of logic gates; give three reasons why this logic is so popular in silicon-based devices.

37. Why is there a significant savings in power consumption with CMOS. (Be specific; don't just quote the book.)

38. If the response time for a CMOS device is hindered only by the capacitance during switching, how can the speed be improved without changing circuit design. (*Hint*: You can change the capacitance, but how and for what reasons.)

39. Logic circuits are in two major families; what are the major differences between them?

40. What are the dangers and disadvantages of digital circuits, considering they have small time delays in response to inputs?

41. What is the purpose of the system clock in digital computers?

42. Draw the circuit that will perform an addition of three two bit registers with a carry. You need not draw the internal circuitry of full and half adders.

43. There are four flip-flops described in the text; give the advantages of each. What purpose is each one best suited for?

44. Draw the circuit that will allow for a 0-, 1-, or 2-bit shift in either direction. The circuit must complete the shift in one clock cycle.

45. Draw the circuit that will allow a rotation of 0, 1, or 2 bits to the left (only) in one clock cycle.

46. The output of an **odd parity generator** is one if, and only if, the number of 1's on its input lines is odd. Build a four-input odd parity generator. (*Hint*: consider the **nor** gate.)

47. An *n*-bit **comparator** has two *n*-bit inputs, the output is a 1 if the inputs are equal and 0 otherwise. Build a 4-bit comparator.

48. Design the logic at either end of a left-right shifter to permit the user to specify the following operations: arithmetic shift left-right, rotate left-right, pass through.

49. Draw the logic diagram for a 32-bit adders, assuming that you already have 4-bit adders at your disposal.

ADDITIONAL READING

BOOTH, T. L. *Digital Networks and Computer Systems.* 2nd ed. Englewood Cliffs, N.J.: Prentice Hall, 1980.

MANO, M. M. *Digital Logic and Computer Design.* Englewood Cliffs, N.J.: Prentice Hall, 1973.

MENDELSON, E. *Boolean Algebra and Switching Circuits.* New York: McGraw-Hill, 1970.

ROTH, C. H. *Fundamentals of Logic Design.* 2nd ed. St. Paul, Minn.: West Publishing, 1979.

SLOAN, M. E., *Computer Hardware and Organization.* Chicago: Science Research Associates, 1983.

WAKERLY, J. F. *Digital Design Principles and Practices.* Englewood Cliffs, N.J.: Prentice Hall, 1990.

WIATROWSKI, C. A., and House, C. H. *Logic Circuits and Microcomputer Systems.* New York: McGraw Hill, 1980.

3

Principal Components of a Computer System

3.1 MAIN MEMORY ORGANIZATION

3.1.1 Unit of Storage

As mentioned earlier, the *main (primary, real) memory* is a large storage area where both *data* and *instructions* are stored. Moreover, according to our discussions in the previous chapter, all information must be stored as strings of 1's and 0's, or equivalently as a sequence of binary digits *bits* where a bit is 0 or 1. Therefore, the unit of storage is the bit.

3.1.2 Smallest Addressable Unit

Main memory consists of a very large number of bits; however, the bit positions themselves are *seldomly* directly individually accessible or **addressable.** Despite the fact that the fundamental unit of storage in main memory is the bit, the smallest addressable or accessible unit in almost all computers is *not* the bit; instead, the smallest addressable unit is a consecutive "collection" of bits usually 8 bits long that is referred to a **byte,** and the memory is referred to as **byte addressable.**[1] It is important to notice the quotation marks around the word collection; the reason is that not every collection of 8 bits forms a byte. The rule for the formation of bytes is that the first byte is the collection of the first 8 bits of main memory; the second byte is the collection of the next 8 bits, and so on. Figure 3.1 illustrates a byte.

7	6	5	4	3	2	1	0
0	1	0	1	1	1	0	1

Figure 3.1 Byte and its contents.

Even though the individual bits of a byte are not addressable, we refer to the leftmost bit as bit 7 and to the rightmost as bit 0,[2] and this numbering will be employed throughout the text. Bit 7 is also referred to as the **most significant bit** or **high-order bit,**

---

[1] Few memories are **word addressable.** Words are discussed in a following section.

[2] In certain memory organizations as in IBM 360/370 the bit numbering is exactly the reverse of the one just presented.

whereas bit number 0 is referred to as the **least significant bit** or **low-order bit** of the byte. Moreover a collection of k consecutive bits that contains the high-order bit is called a collection of k *high-order bits;* however, if the collection contains the low-order bit, it is called a collection of k *low-order bits.*

Each byte is accessed via its **address.** The addressing scheme in most organizations is as follows.[3] Bytes are addressed (numbered) consecutively so that the very first byte is byte 0, the second byte 1, and so on. Figure 3.2 illustrates the "grouping" of the bits into bytes and the first 24 bytes together with their addresses in main memory.

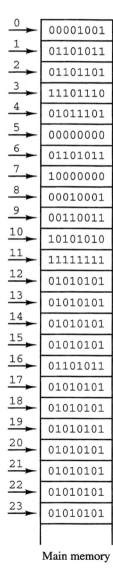

Main memory

Figure 3.2   First 24 bytes of main memory organization.

---

[3] For an exception see the section on aligned versus nonaligned data.

3.1.3 Memory Capacity

One of the principal characteristics of main memories is their **capacity**, which is defined as the number of bytes that can be accessed, or equivalently, stored. A collection of $1,024$ bytes is referred to as a kilobyte (Kb); a collection of 1024 kilobytes is referred to as a megabyte (Mb); and a collection of 1024 megabytes is referred to as a gigabyte (Gb). These are approximately equal to one thousand, one million, and one billion bytes, respectively.

3.1.4 Address Space and Bus

Given the fact that the cost of memories has been drastically reduced in recent years, one would be tempted to conclude that a computer system provides us with an unlimited amount of memory. Unfortunately, that conclusion is erroneous. This is because the CPU can access only a certain amount of memory at any time, and this area is referred to as the CPU's **address space**. This limitation is imposed by the hardware mechanism employed for the CPU to access memory, and this mechanism is conceptually very simple. The CPU puts the memory address that should be accessed on the **address bus**; the address bus consists of a collection of n wires, where the number n is called the **width** of the bus. The address bus can be thought of as being attached to the CPU at one end and to main memory at the other end. Figure 3.3 illustrates these concepts.

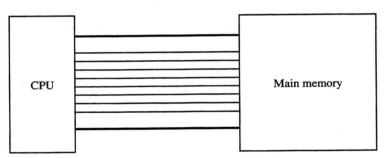

Figure 3.3   Address bus of 8-bit width.

Because each "wire" can carry a single bit of information, what is transferred via the address bus is an unsigned n-bit binary integer; as we have seen, the smallest n-bit binary integer is %000000000...0, whereas the largest is %111111111...1. Equivalently in the decimal system, the smallest is the number 0, whereas the largest is equal to $2^n - 1$. In the example of Figure 3.3, the 8-bit bus indicates that the largest memory address is %11111111 or in decimal notation 255. Therefore, the CPU's address space consists of 256 bytes.

The preceding discussion suggests that Figure 3.2 is somewhat misleading. The addresses were presented in their decimal representation; however, in reality the addresses should always be represented as unsigned binary integers and for the sake of readability as unsigned hexadecimal integers.

3.1.5 Data Bus

The principal reason that one would like to access memory is either to access or to store information. For example, consider the situation of Figure 3.3 and assume that the CPU needs to access the data at location $FD. That address is placed in the address bus, the corresponding memory location is accessed, and the contents of that location $42 must be "shipped" to the CPU. For this data to be transferred, another bus referred to as the **data bus** is employed where the data are placed and eventually are made available to the CPU. Figure 3.4 illustrates these concepts assuming a data bus with an 8-bits width.

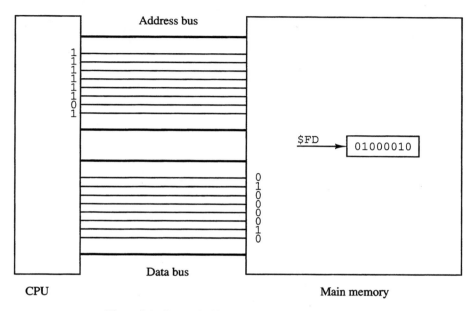

Figure 3.4   Data and address buses. Width of each is 8 bits.

3.1.6 Words

Even though the byte is the smallest addressable unit, most computers permit the access of memory areas larger than a byte. Most computers will permit the access of **words**; a word is a "collection" of two consecutive bytes or equivalently of 16 consecutive bits as illustrated in Figure 3.5.

The first memory word comprises bytes 0 and number 1; the second word comprises bytes 2 and 3, and so on. The leftmost byte of a word is referred to as the *most significant byte* of the word, whereas the rightmost byte is referred to as the *least significant byte* of the word. Observe that bytes with *lower* memory addresses (further to the left) correspond to *higher* significance in the word.

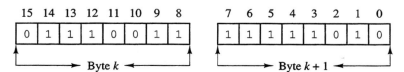

Figure 3.5   Word and its contents.

Again words are accessed via their addresses; the address of a word is defined as being equal to the address of its high-order byte. Notice that according to our earlier discussion word addresses *must* be **even** addresses. Memory addresses that are divisible by 2 are known as **word boundaries**; certain memory organizations do require that words be **aligned** at word boundaries. Assuming this requirement, Figure 3.6 illustrates the first 12 words of the main memory together with their addresses.

Although the individual bits of a word are not addressable, we do refer to the leftmost bit as bit 15 and to the rightmost as bit 0. Bit 15 is also referred to as the *most significant bit* or *high-order bit*, whereas bit 0 is referred to as the *least significant bit* or *low-order bit* of the word. If a collection of k consecutive bits contains the high-order bit, it is called a collection of k *high-order bits;* however, if the collection contains the low-order bit, it is then called a collection of k *low-order bits.*

Addr (a)	Byte
0	00001001
1	01101011
2	01101101
3	11101110
4	01011101
5	00000000
6	01101011
7	10000000
8	00010001
9	00110011
10	10101010
11	11111111
12	01010101
13	01010101
14	01010101
15	01010101
16	01101011
17	01010101
18	01010101
19	01010101
20	01010101
21	01010101
22	01010101
23	01010101

Addr (b)	Word	
0	00001001	01101011
2	01101101	11101110
4	01011101	00000000
6	01101011	10000000
8	00010001	00110011
10	10101010	11111111
12	01010101	01010101
14	01010101	01010101
16	01101011	01010101
18	01010101	01010101
20	01010101	01010101
22	01010101	01010101

(a)   (b)

Main memory

Figure 3.6 First 24 bytes (a) and first 12 words (b) of main memory organization.

3.1.7 Longwords

In addition to bytes and words, most computer systems permit the access of *longwords*. A longword is a "collection" of two consecutive words or 4 consecutive bytes or equivalently of 32 consecutive bits as illustrated in Figure 3.7.

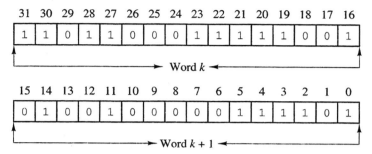

Figure 3.7   Longword and its contents.

The first longword consists of bytes 0 through 3; the second longword consists of bytes 2 through 5, and so on. Moreover, the leftmost byte (word) is referred to as the *most significant byte (word)* of the longword, whereas its rightmost byte (word) is referred to as the *least significant byte (word)* of the longword. Longwords are again accessed via their addresses; the address of a longword is defined to be equal to the address of its high-order byte (word). Moreover, we define as **longword boundary** to be an address that is a word boundary in the context of our earlier definition of the word boundary. In other words, longword boundaries are addresses that are divisible by 2.[4] Certain memory organizations do require that longwords be **aligned** at longword boundaries. Assuming this requirement, Figure 3.8 illustrates the longwords with addresses 0, 2 and 6, respectively.

Even though the individual bits of a longword are not addressable, we do refer to the leftmost bit as bit 31 and to the rightmost as bit 0. Bit 31 is also referred to as the *most significant bit* or *high-order bit*, whereas bit 0 is referred to as the *least significant bit* or *low-order bit* of the byte. Moreover, a collection of k consecutive bits that contains the high-order bit is called a collection of k *high-order bits*, whereas if the collection contains the low-order bit, it is called the collection of k *low-order bits*. The leftmost word (byte) is referred to as the *most significant word (byte);* and, the rightmost word (byte) is referred to as the *least significant word (byte)* of the longword.

3.1.8 Alignment

We have noted repeatedly that the memory organizations that we have concentrated on have their bytes numbered in the natural way and consecutively; also the data must be aligned. That is, if a word must be accessed from memory and the supplied address is not a word boundary, an exception[5] will occur. On the other hand, you should note that there are

---

[4] The terminology and alignments of the data varies from manufacturer to manufacturer. For example, in the system IBM 360/370 and its terminology one may access *bytes, halfwords, words* and *doublewords*. Bytes should be aligned at byte boundaries, halfwords at halfword boundaries (addresses divisible by 2), words at word boundaries (addresses divisible by 4), and doublewords at doubleword boundaries (addresses divisible by 8).

[5] Exceptions are discussed formally in Chapter 9. For the time being we agree that an exception indicates an error.

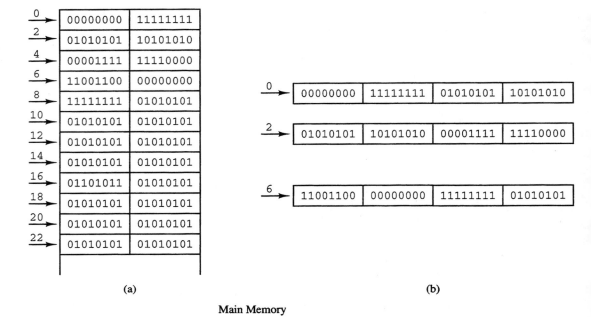

(a)   (b)

Main Memory

Figure 3.8   First 12 words (a) and three longwords with addresses 0, 2, and 6 (b) of main memory organization.

memory organizations that do not adhere to most of the features presented so far. As an example, we will briefly discuss the Intel 8086 family whose memory organization is illustrated in Figure 3.9.

First, one should notice that the bytes are not numbered according to their physical arrangement. Second, words are not required to be aligned. In other words, one could address as well words 0 and 1. Word 0 consists of bytes 0 and 1, whereas word 1 consists of bytes 1 and 2. Although words at odd addresses can be accessed, their access requires two memory accesses. In particular, first word 0 and then word 2 will be accessed to form word 1. Note that a programmer that is interested in optimizing the performance of his or her program should avoid employing nonaligned words in such an environment.

3.1.9 Character Representation

Readers who have written programs in high-level languages will recall that there is a facility that permits one to *read* (from the keyboard) and to *write* (on the screen of a **cathode ray tube (CRT)** and also on paper via a printer) alphabetical characters. The reader should obviously wonder how alphabetical as well as other characters such as ";" and "!" can be stored and manipulated by a computer given that the internal representation is in binary. All characters are represented internally as bit strings. In particular, there are two widely used representations, called **character codes**, that will be discussed briefly.

EBCDIC representation.   **Extended binary coded decimal interchange code (EBCDIC)** representation allows each character to be represented as an 8-bit code. For example, the EBCDIC representation of the character A is %11000001 or equivalently $C1, whereas the representation of the lowercase character a is %10000001 or equivalently $81. Summarizing, each character has a byte representation; therefore, under this coding scheme, up to $2^8 = 256$ characters can be represented.

ASCII representation. **American standard code for information interchange** (ASCII) representation allows each character to be represented as a 7-bit code. For example, the ASCII representation of the character A is %1000001 or equivalently $41, whereas the representation of the lowercase character a is %1100001 or equivalently $61. With this coding scheme, a total of $2^7 = 128$ characters can be represented.

There is one remark to be made here. Computers allocate 1 byte per character. Given that the length of a byte is 8 bits and that the ASCII codes are 7 bits in length, the character code is stored right-justified within the byte. The *free* bit in each such byte as we will see later is used for another specific purpose.

Collating sequence.   The assignment of codes to characters is not arbitrary. The reason is, as we will see later, that sometimes there is a need to compare two characters or two character strings. A **character string** is a string of characters, the number of which is referred to as the **length** of the string. For example, consider the two strings A and C of length one. We already know that the latter string is *greater* than the former, because uppercase (as well as the lowercase) alphabetical characters themselves are in a specific order known as the **lexicographical** ordering. Because the hardware should arrive at the same result anyway and each code can be interpreted by the computer as an unsigned

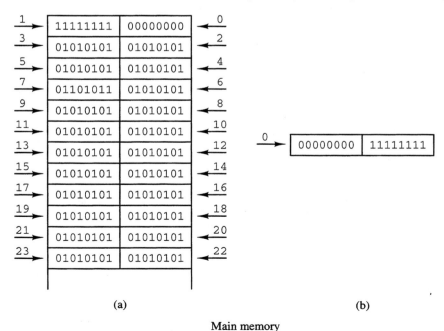

(a)   (b)

Main memory

Figure 3.9   First 24 bytes (a) and word with address 0 (b) of main memory organization of 8086 Intel family.

binary integer,[6] the codes are assigned so that their unsigned integer representation preserves their ordering. You should have noticed that lexicographical ordering is defined over the alphabetical characters. Computers employ a larger character set and, therefore, impose a predetermined ordering referred to as the **collating sequence** of the code on the character set that they support. The collating sequences corresponding to the two coding schemes are *different*, however. Therefore, one should be aware of the coding scheme employed by the machine, because the results of such comparisons could be different according to the coding scheme. From the examples that were presented earlier, one can see that A ≤ a in an ASCII machine, whereas A ≥ a in an EBCDIC machine. A partial list of codes is given in Table 3.1, and the entire ASCII set is presented in Appendix E.

TABLE 3.1 EBCDIC and ASCII codes for selected characters; All code entries are in hexadecimal

Character	EBCDIC	ASCII
	8-bit code	7-bit code
<	4C	3C
&	50	26
/	61	2F
a	81	61
b	82	62
w	A6	77
A	C1	41
B	C2	42
W	E6	57

Before we conclude this section, the reader should be aware of the fact that when one types 0 on a keyboard, the code (EBCDIC or ASCII) for this character is actually what is transmitted to main memory. If the application program were to treat this character as either an unsigned or signed integer (one that will participate in arithmetic operations), then the application program should convert it to its *numeric* (2's complement) representation, before the operations are performed. In other words, an expression such as "0018" has a different internal representation as a character string than as a signed integer as illustrated in Figure 3.10.

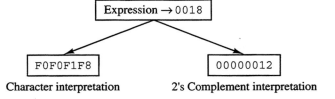

Character interpretation   2's Complement interpretation

Figure 3.10 Two possible internal representations of the expression "0018" depending on the interpretation. EBCDIC character code is assumed.

---

[6] This is what computers do. Only humans in the strict sense differentiate between characters and numbers.

Conversely, if one were given the longword $\$F0F0F1F8$, it could be interpreted either as representing the 2's complement representation of the decimal integer $-252, 644, 872$ or as representing the character string "0018." A third possible interpretation is that this longword represents an instruction, if in fact there is such an instruction! The reader should be aware of these differing interpretations of a binary sequence.

3.1.10 Memory Types

Before we close the discussion on main memory organization, one should note that there is more than one "type" of memory. A brief discussion will follow.

The main memories discussed so far permit one to access every memory location and also to read or write in each of these locations. Hence, a memory of this type is referred to as **random access memory** (RAM) because of the former property or **read write memory** (RWM) in view of the latter property.

A memory that permits one to only *read* from it is referred to as a **read-only memory** (ROM). Read-only memories that can be programmed[7] (to write on them) are referred to as **programmable read-only memories** (PROM). Certain ROMs permit one to erase[8] them and then rewrite on them. These are referred to as either **erasable programmable read-only memory** (EPROM) or **electrically erasable programmable read-only memory** (EEPROM). The difference between the last two types of memories depends on the fact that the former is erased via its exposure to ultraviolet light, whereas the latter is erased electrically. It must be stated that the difference between PROMs and EPROMs is that the former are write once, whereas the latter are write many times. Finally, a new type of memory the **electrically alterable programmable read-only memory** (EAPROM) permits one to selectively erase and rewrite certain memory locations, as opposed to both EPROM and EEPROM families in which the erasure is global.

It is important to notice that *all* types of ROMs are nonvolatile, because the information on them is retained at all times.

3.2 CPU

The CPU is both the "heart" and the "brain" of a computer. It consists of several electronic components that both interpret and execute machine language instructions, control the transfer of data and instructions from and to main memory and from main to secondary memory, and conversely. Furthermore, it is responsible for detecting various types of errors.

As in the case of memory organizations, there are several different processor architectures. The major architectures are **general-register** and **accumulator**.[9] Each will be discussed in turn; we will begin with the general-register architecture.

3.2.1 General-register Architecture

Before the principal components of the CPU are discussed, a short discussion of the **machine language instructions** follows.

---

[7] Via a calculator type computer referred to as a PROM programmer.

[8] By "erase" we mean that every bit location takes a certain fixed bit value, usually 1.

[9] Another less popular architecture, the **Stack** machine, is not discussed here.

Instructions. Recall that the execution of a machine language **program** is performed by the electronic components of the CPU. Moreover, we know that a machine language program consists of a sequence of instructions and data.

As should be expected, a machine language instruction is only a string of bits. For example, the following 32-bit binary string

1001 0010 0000 0011 1011 1011 1000 0001

represents an IBM 360/370 instruction; execution of this instruction causes the byte %10000001 to be copied in the memory location specified by the instruction. In particular, the preceding instruction can be viewed as a collection of three substrings, as Figure 3.11 indicates.

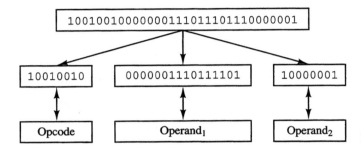

Figure 3.11   Instruction subviews.

Closer examination of Figure 3.11 reveals that with a "pencil-and-paper" approach, we must *break down* the preceding instruction into three principal fields: the **opcode** field, the **operand₁** field, and the **operand₂** field. The significance of each field follows.

The value of the opcode field indicates first and foremost the operation to be performed. The opcode $92, shown in the preceding example, indicates that a byte must be copied. In addition, the opcode value indicates the number of operands required for successful execution of the instruction. In the preceding example, two **operands** are required; therefore, the instruction is referred to as a **two-operand** instruction. At this point we should note that not all instructions require two operands. The operation of negating an integer requires just one operand. In general, therefore, an **m-operand** instruction is one that requires m operands.

Furthermore, the opcode indicates the **mode** under which each operand should be accessed as well as the *nature* of each operand. The opcode $92 indicates that the first operand **operand₁** represents a memory address that must be calculated according to the **base-displacement** mode,[10] whereas the second operand represents data. In general, instructions that contain data in an operand field are referred to as **immediate (quick)** instructions. To emphasize this point further, an instruction similar to the one in Figure 3.11 with an opcode of $D2 could be employed to move a byte from one memory location to another. In this case, both operands should represent the appropriate memory addresses.

Registers. The execution of a machine language program that consists of instructions and data is performed by the electronic components of the CPU. Assume for simplicity that there are only four machine language instructions: a stop instruction, an add instruction, and two move instructions.

The purpose of the stop instruction, as its name suggests, is to halt execution of the

---

[10] Modes are discussed extensively in Chapter 6.

program. Execution of the add instruction causes the contents of a memory location to be added to the contents of a specified data register. The first move copies a word from an indicated memory location to an indicated data register, whereas the second one copies a word from an indicated data register to an indicated memory location. We will present the principal components of the CPU as well as their function by *tracing* the execution of a simple machine language program.

To this end, assume that the program will perform the task of adding the two signed integers x and y and store the result in memory location z. Assume that the program has been coded and has been **loaded** starting at memory location 000000[11] and that execution of a program is initiated by depressing a start button. A possible pseudocode for this program is given in Table 3.2.

TABLE 3.2   Adding two integers

```
[1].    move   the contents of memory location x to data register 0.
[2].    add    the contents of memory location y to data register 0.
[3].    move   the contents of data register 0 to memory location z.
[4].    stop
```

The first question that naturally arises is how can the CPU differentiate between instructions and data? More important, how does the CPU know which instruction to execute? The answer is very simple. A register is dedicated whose only function is to store the *memory address* of the *next* instruction to be executed. That particular register is referred to as the **program (location) counter.** According to our assumption, the program has been loaded starting at location 000000; therefore, the first instruction to be executed is the one at that location. The only function of the start button is to set the contents of the program counter to 000000. Hence, the mechanism for the determination of the next instruction to be executed by the CPU is straightforward; the program counter **points** to the memory location where the next instruction has been stored.

Returning to our simple program, we have established that the "next" instruction to be executed is the one at location 000000. What kind of instruction must be executed— a move, an add, or by assuming a larger instruction set, what other instruction? It should be clear that the CPU does not know what the instruction *is*. The only way that the CPU can determine what is the next instruction is by *interpreting (decoding)* the instruction explained earlier via the pencil-and-paper approach. Therefore, the CPU is furnished with its own **instruction interpreter.**

Because this instruction is located in main memory, however, the instruction must be **transferred (fetched, loaded)** from its memory location to the CPU for the interpreter to be able to interpret it. The CPU is furnished with another register where this instruction can be loaded, and it is referred to as the **instruction register.** The interpreter can now access the instruction and consequently decode it.

The reader should be wondering what is the exact mechanism under which the next instruction or, for that matter, data are transferred from main memory to the CPU. We will indicate this mechanism subsequently for the execution of the first instruction—the one at location 000000. The instruction at this location should be copied into the instruction

---

[11] Not usually the case.

register. The first step consists of copying the memory address where the data are to be accessed into a designated register referred to as the **memory address register** (MAR). The contents of this register are loaded onto the address bus; the corresponding memory location is accessed; the contents (data) of this location are put onto the data bus; finally the data are loaded (via the data bus) into a specially designated register referred to as the **memory buffer register** (MBR). The CPU may now use the data any time it needs, via the MBR. The sequence of events is almost the same in the case in which one needs to perform a **store** operation. In particular, the memory address of where the data are to be stored is loaded into the MAR; the data are loaded (by the CPU) into the MBR; and the data are transferred via the data bus into the appropriate memory location. The preceding discussion indicates that the address bus is *unidirectional*, whereas the data bus is *bidirectional*.

Assuming that the first instruction has been loaded into the instruction register and has been executed, the question now is how can the next instruction be accessed? Again the answer is very simple. The CPU knows that the next instruction to be executed is the instruction that resides immediately after the instruction that was just completed;[12] consequently, it increments the contents of its program counter by an amount equal to the length of the instruction just completed and the process is repeated.

Summarizing the preceding discussion, we have seen that the CPU is furnished with its own special memory elements known as registers. Despite the fact that their number, nature, and size (in terms of bits) depends on the individual manufacturer, we will distinguish between the following types of registers:

- Arithmetic operations are invariably performed on a set of registers that are referred to as **data registers**. Moreover, if the data represent fixed-point numbers, the data register is referred to as a **fixed-point register**; however, if the data represent a floating-point number, a different data register is used for this purpose, and it is referred to as a **floating-point register**.

- Furthermore, certain manufacturers provide registers that serve as *pointers* to memory addresses. In other words, their contents represent memory addresses, and these registers are referred to as **address registers**.

- Several special registers are dedicated as scratchpads for the CPU and are referred to as **working registers** but these registers are invisible to the programmer because he or she cannot access them.

- There is one **program counter register** that is used as a pointer to the next instruction.

- There is one **instruction interpreter register** that is used to decode the current instruction.

- There is one **memory address register** that contains the memory address that should be accessed.

- The purpose of the **memory buffer register** is to contain data that has just been fetched from memory or data that are to be stored in memory.

- Finally, there is one more register that is employed to record *status* information, and it is referred to appropriately as the **status register**.

Figure 3.12 illustrates a CPU that employs eight data registers, eight address registers, a program counter register, an instruction register, an instruction interpreter, a status register, a set of working registers, a memory buffer register, and memory address register.

---

[12] Unless the completed instruction was a *branch* instruction, which is discussed in the next section.

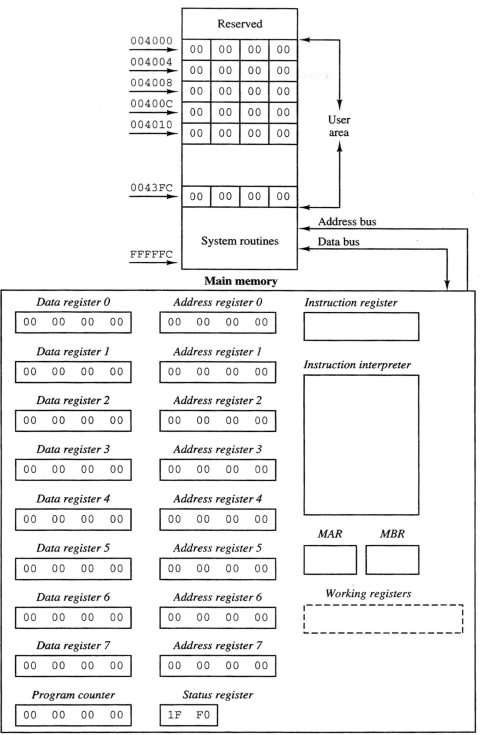

Figure 3.12 Principal components of CPU.

Instruction execution cycle.   What we have seen in the previous section is that the execution of each instruction follows a predetermined cycle of events. These events are summarized in terms of a flowchart in Figure 3.13. A brief explanation of these events follows for the case in which the instruction that is ready to be executed is the instruction: add a word from the memory location x to the contents of data register r.

In step 1, the contents of the program counter are loaded into the memory address register; the address bus is activated, and the contents of the memory location pointed to by the MAR are placed into the data bus and are loaded into the memory buffer register (step 2). The contents of the MBR, which indicate the instruction to be executed, are loaded into the instruction register (step 3). The instruction interpreter decodes the instruction in step 4 and realizes that this is an add instruction. The address x is extracted from the instruction and is placed into the MAR (step 5). The address bus is activated; the contents of memory location x are accessed and placed into the data bus; the contents are eventually placed into the MBR (step 6). The contents of register r are transferred into one of the

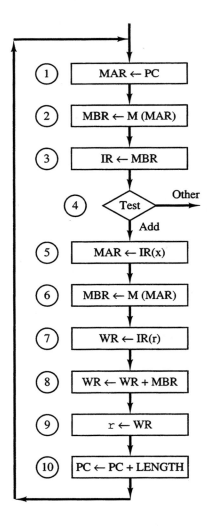

Figure 3.13   Steps required for execution of add instruction.

available working registers WR (step 7); the contents of the MBR are added to the contents of this working register (step 8). The final result is loaded back into data register r in step 9. The length of the instruction just executed is added to the contents of the program counter; therefore, the program counter points to the next instruction to be executed, and the process is repeated.

3.2.2 Accumulator Architecture

The first processors developed were furnished with only *one* register that was referred to as the **accumulator**. Therefore, all operations had to be performed on this single register. In this case, as one would expect, most of the instructions required only one operand, because all movement of data took place through the accumulator. As an example, the counterpart pseudoalgorithm of the one in Table 3.2 that adds two integers is illustrated in Table 3.3.

TABLE 3.3   Adding two integers

```
[1].   move the contents of memory location x to accumulator.
[2].   add  the contents of memory location y to accumulator.
[3].   move to memory location z from accumulator.
[4].   stop
```

Notice that the destination in statements 1 and 2 as well as the source in statement 3, is *implicitly* defined to be the accumulator. This processor architecture leads to shorter instructions than the instructions required in general-register machines and also to a considerable monetary savings. These programs are much more difficult to code and are more inefficient given the considerably greater number of moves to memory of the intermediate results required to free and prepare the accumulator for the next desired operation.

To make both points clearer, consider the following example. Memory locations x, y, z, and w contain four integers of values X, Y, Z, and W, respectively. We would like to calculate the expression $A = ((X + Y) \cdot (Z + W))$ and store the result A in memory location a. The pseudoalgorithms that perform this task in a general-register machine versus in an accumulator machine are given in Tables 3.4 and 3.5, respectively. It is easy to see that an extra move instruction is required in the second case.

TABLE 3.4   Adding two integers in a general-register machine

```
[1].   move the contents of memory location x to data register 0.
[2].   add  the contents of memory location y to data register 0.
[3].   move the contents of memory location z to data register 1.
[4].   add  the contents of memory location w to data register 1.
[5].   mult the contents of data register 0 by the contents of data
register 1.
[6].   move the contents of data register 1 to memory location a.
[7].   stop
```

TABLE 3.5 Adding two integers in an accumulator machine

```
[1].  move the contents of memory location x.
[2].  add  the contents of memory location y.
[3].  move to memory location c.
[4].  move the contents of memory location z.
[5].  add  the contents of memory location w.
[6].  mult by the contents of memory location c.
[7].  move to memory location a.
[8].  stop
```

3.3 SECONDARY STORAGE

As with main memory, **secondary (backing) storage**, is another large storage area where both data and instructions are stored. In terms of utility, the differences between primary and secondary storage are the relative capacity and access times of the storage media. Whereas main memory capacity is typically 1 Mbyte to 100 Mbytes (depending on the computer system), secondary storage is typically 20 Mbytes to 20 Gbytes. Conversely, although the **access time** (i.e., the time taken by the CPU to access a word of data) for main memory is only 50 ns, the access time for a secondary storage device may be over 20 ms.[13] Recall also from Chapter 1 that secondary storage devices are *always* nonvolatile. Thus data stored in secondary storage will remain after a loss of power. Although there do exist nonvolatile main memories, this is not usually the case. Finally, whereas main memory is entirely electronic (no moving parts), secondary storage devices are usually electromechanical, with spinning tapes or disks and moving detectors. Thus we may characterize primary storage as being a high-speed, medium-capacity, volatile storage medium, whereas secondary storage is a lower-speed, large-capacity, nonvolatile medium. Again, as mentioned in Chapter 1, examples of secondary storage devices are **magnetic disks, magnetic tapes, electro-optical disks, optical disks**, and **magnetic drums**.[14]

Storage systems may be described as either **online** or **offline**. Data that are online are immediately available for use by a program. Online storage devices include magnetic disks, electro-optical disks, optical disks, and drums. Data that are offline are stored on media that must be mounted (usually by an operator) before they may be used. Offline storage devices include magnetic tapes and cartridges; however, they may include removable disk packs. In a large system such as banking, all active data (e.g., current account information) is maintained online. Similarly all inactive data (e.g., closed accounts, last year's transactions, etc.) is offline, stored on tapes in a vault until needed.

Devices can be classified as either **sequential access storage devices** (SASD) or **direct access storage devices** (DASD). The difference lies in the fact that when a specific record of a file is accessed with the former devices, the access of *all* predecessor records is *always* required, whereas the latter permits a record to be accessed directly.[15] The remainder of

---

[13] Although this is much slower than main memory, we note that secondary storage devices transfer data in fixed-size blocks; thus, the principal delay comes from starting the transfer. Once started, the transfer rate to or from a secondary storage device is comparable with main memory.

[14] Punch cards could also be considered as storage media, although they are now obsolete.

[15] Depending on the file structure.

this section will focus on the characterists of particular storage devices and the difference among them will become clearer.

3.3.1 Sequential Access Storage Devices

In this category we find the magnetic tape. In the following discussion we will describe the characteristics of a 1/2-in unit; however, the same principles apply to all tape-like devices (e.g., 1/4-in and 8-mm cartridge tapes, etc.).

General characteristics.   A magnetic tape is a continuous plastic strip of mylar with a ferrous oxide coating. Tape lengths range from 200 to 6400 ft but are typically 2400 ft, whereas their width is approximately 1/2 in.

The physical beginning and end of a tape is marked by two metallic strips called *load point mark* and *end of reel* mark. These markers are electronically detected by photocells in the drive mechanism enabling one to read and write on the tape only in between these two markers. The tape itself is divided into nine[16] horizontal lines called *tracks* along its length. Data are written onto the tape character by character. If data are recorded in ASCII[17] format, each character requires 7 bits to be represented. For example, the character A has the representation shown in Figure 3.14. This byte always is represented in parallel, that is, the 8 bits will be recorded in eight parallel tracks. This leaves one track free that is used to record the *vertical parity bit*.

0	1	0	0	0	0	0	1

Figure 3.14   ASCII representation of character A. Most significant bit is leftmost one.

Before the function of the vertical parity bit is explained, one should note that because of the anticipated frequent use of the tape, the edges of the tape physically deteriorate, so the most significant bit (bit 7) of the byte is stored toward the middle of the tape to protect it. Table 3.6 illustrates this.

TABLE 3.6   Nine-Track Tape (EBCDIC code)

Track number	Bit number	Tape
0	3	0
1	1	0
2	7	1
3	6	1
4	5	1
5	VPB	1
6	4	1
7	0	1
8	2	0

---

[16] There are also seven track tapes.

[17] Data could also be stored in EBCDIC format.

Vertical and longitudinal parity check. The vertical parity bit is set to either 0 or 1 and is used for error checking. The mechanism in setting the parity bit is quite straightforward. When a byte (character) is to be written onto the tape, the number of 1's in the byte is counted, and the vertical parity is set to either 0 or 1 according to the parity convention. For **even** mode parity, the total number of 1's in the 9 tracks must be even. In Table 3.6, the vertical parity bit has been set to 1, which assumes that the even parity mode was used.

In several cases, another parity check is performed to ensure that the block is written correctly. To do this, an extra byte is allocated at the end of each block. Each bit of that byte is called the *longitudinal parity bit,* and each such bit is set to 0 or 1 to indicate the parity of the set of all bits of the block along the track to which this parity bit corresponds. Assuming that the parity mode is even, if the total number of 1's along track 3 is an even number, then the longitudinal parity bit is set to 0. Notice that if both checks for parity, vertical and longitudinal, are used, the probability for an error to escape detection is very close to 0. In addition, the read head is positioned "after" the write head so that a parity check can be made immediately after each byte and block has been written as Figure 3.15 illustrates. This method is known as *write verification.*

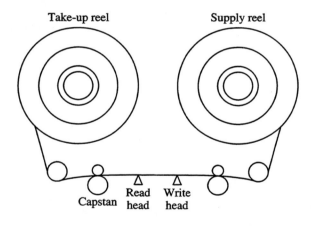

Take-up reel   Supply reel

Read   Write
Capstan   head   head

Forward direction   **Figure 3.15**   Tape drive.

If now, during a read, the number of 1's in a byte turns out to be odd, then the controller (whose responsibility it is to check parity) calls an interrupt routine. This routine instructs the controller to reread the physical record several times. If at a reread the byte in question is read with no error (which could very well happen either because of noise or accumulated dust on the tape) then the process continues; otherwise, an error is indicated.

Density, capacity, and use. Tapes are also characterized by their *density.* Density is defined as the number of characters that can be recorded in an inch of tape and is measured in *bytes per inch* (bpi). Typical tapes are available with a density of 1600 or 6120 bpi. If the length and density of the tape is known, then the *capacity* of the tape can be found. The capacity of the tape is defined as the number of bytes (characters) that can be stored in the entire tape. In other words, if the density of the tape is D bpi, and L indicates the length of the tape in inches, then the capacity of the tape is given by

$$C = L \cdot D \text{ bytes}$$

For a typical tape of density 1600 bpi[18] and length equal to 2400 ft, the capacity of the tape can be found by

$$C = 2400 \cdot 12 \cdot 1600 \, \text{bytes} = 44 \, \text{Mb}$$

Unfortunately, the entire tape cannot be used in the sense that not all available storage can be used to store the user's data. The reason is the following. For reasons that will be explained later, the unit of transfer between main memory and secondary storage is the *block*. A block is a collection of bytes, the number of which depends on the particular environment. For a block to be transmitted, as the result of a `read` or `write` request, the tape must already be mounted onto a tape drive. For the drive to be able to read or write from the tape correctly, the tape must move at a constant speed over the read/write (R/W) head, typically on the order of 10 ft/s, a speed that is attained via the *Capstan* a small wheel that pulls the tape across the R/W heads (Figure 3.15). For the tape to reach this speed (because initially it was idle), a certain time must elapse. In that period, the portion of the tape that passes through the R/W head cannot be written[19] onto or read correctly. Hence, each block must be preceded and followed by an unused portion of the tape that allows the tape to accelerate to a normal R/W speed and decelerate to a stop, respectively. The unused portion of the tape is called an *interblock gap (IBG)*. Figure 3.16 illustrates this concept.

IBG	BLOCK	IBG	BLOCK	IBG

Figure 3.16   Each physical block is surrounded by two interblock gaps.

Hence, the *utilization U* of the tape is a function of both the *block size (BS)* and *interblock size (GS)*. Namely, *U* is given by:

$$U = \frac{BS}{BS + GS}$$

Advantages and disadvantages of magnetic tape.   It is clear that if a file resides on a tape, then the records of that file must be processed sequentially. That is, to access a record, all preceding blocks must be accessed. Hence, by their nature, tape drives are sequential devices, and the only file structure that is allowed in a tape is a physical sequential structure. Moreover, a record cannot be updated in place. The direct result is that the entire file must be rewritten. Nevertheless, the low cost of magnetic tape makes it an attractive way to store data rather than on a more expensive direct-access device. Magnetic tape is also the most efficient way of transferring data from one computer system to another, the only requirement being that the systems must be compatible, regardless of manufacturers. In addition, they are compact and portable, facilitating off line storage.

Other tape devices.   The 1/2-in tape unit is now being replaced by newer and more compact formats. In particular a 1/4-in data cartridge format, 600 ft in length, with a density of 15,000 bpi is one popular media (for a capacity of 80 Mb). Another is the 8-mm cartridge format, which uses videotape format and a density of 43,200 bpi to offer a capacity of 2 Gb.

---

[18] Tapes of density 6120 bpi are also popular.

[19] To prevent accidental writing on a magnetic-tape reel a small plastic ring, called the *file-protection ring*, is placed on the reel. Therefore, to be able to write the ring must be removed first. We note that some systems require the reverse process.

3.3.2 Direct-access Storage Devices

In this category we find several devices such as the **magnetic disks**, CD-ROM,[20] **electro-optical disks**, and **write once read many (WORM) disks**. As with our earlier discussion of sequential devices, in this section we will consider the characteristics of a particular disk, the magnetic disk, to introduce the important concepts and characteristics. You should remember, however, that the same arguments apply to other disk media.

General characteristics.   As shown in the previous section, tape drives are sequential devices. Disks, on the other hand, support both sequential accesses and random accesses. Recall that random access means that a record can be accessed directly (via an address) without having to access all preceding records. It is for this reason that magnetic disks are called *direct-access storage devices (DASD)*. Basically, a disk, or a disk pack is a collection of platters. The platters, all of equal size, are permanently mounted in their center on a spindle. Each surface of a platter consists of a collection of concentric rings called *tracks*. Tracks are numbered in sequence usually with the track closest to the outside edge numbered as track 0 (Figure 3.17). Data are encoded on each track in a serial representation (Figure 3.18).

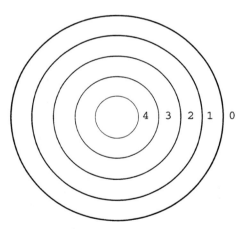

Figure 3.17   Platter with five tracks.

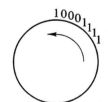

Figure 3.18   Encoded (EBCDIC) representation of character 1.

The *capacity of a track (TC)* is defined as the number of bytes that can nominally be stored on the track. Despite the fact that the circumference of the tracks toward the center of the platter is less than those further from the center, all tracks normally[21] have the same capacity, because the *bit density* of the tracks toward the center is greater than those nearer the periphery.

A *cylinder* is the set of all tracks with the same number in a pack, that is, the tracks from each platter. The cylinder number is the common number of all tracks that define it. For example, cylinder 8 is the set of all tracks bearing the track 8. To address a specific

---

[20] CD-ROM optical disks are read only, which prevents their modification.

[21] Systems do exist in which all tracks do not have the same capacity.

track of the disk, two parameters are needed. First, the number of the cylinder must be specified; second, the relative number of the track within the cylinder must be indicated. The track at the topmost surface is usually referred to as track 0, the one in the next recording surface is referred to as track 1, and so on, as shown in Figure 3.19.

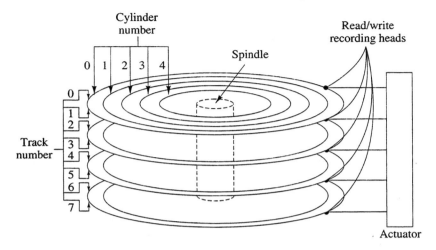

Figure 3.19   Disk with five cylinders and eight tracks per cylinder.

Disk capacity.   The *disk capacity (DC)* is defined as the number of bytes that can be stored on it. In particular, if the number of cylinders is represented by *NC*, the number of tracks per cylinder is represented by *TPC*, and the capacity of each track is denoted by *TC*, then

$$DC = NC \cdot TPC \cdot TC \text{ bytes}$$

The IBM 3350[22] disk has 555[23] cylinders, thirty-nine tracks per cylinder, and a capacity of 19,256 bytes per track. Hence, the capacity of the disk is

$$DC = 555 \cdot 39 \cdot 19256 \text{ bytes} = 397 \text{ Mb}$$

Seek and latency time.   To either read or write from a disk, the disk must be mounted on a disk drive. The disk drive causes the disk to rotate continuously at a constant speed about its *spindle*. The IBM 3350 disk performs one revolution every 16.7 ms. In addition, the disk drive has an *actuator*[24] mounted to it. A set of arms of equal length are mounted to the actuator, and at the end of each arm is a set of R/W heads. There are as many R/W heads as there are tracks per cylinder or equivalently as the number of recording surfaces. The R/W heads float on a cushion of air over the spinning platters. The distance between the R/W heads and the platters is referred to as the *head flying distance*, and it is usually on the order of 100 millionths of an inch.

---

[22] In the *native* mode. The IBM 3350 is capable of emulating either a set of two IBM 3330 disk packs or just one 3330 disk pack in the other two modes.

[23] And five alternative tracks.

[24] Some disks are supplied with two *independent* actuators, independent in the sense that their movements are independent. For example, the IBM 3370 disk has two actuators, the first of which can service only tracks 0 through 5, whereas the second can service only tracks 6 through 11 of the 12 tracks in each cylinder.

To service a request in a certain block residing on a certain track of a specified cylinder, the actuator has to move (under the disk controller's control) from the current cylinder to the requested one. The time elapsed is referred to as *seek time*. The R/W head corresponding to the requested track must be activated because only one R/W head can be active at a time. The time required to activate a R/W head is called *head switching time*. Moreover, an additional delay may occur. Namely, one must wait until the beginning of the requested physical block is positioned immediately below the R/W head before the block can be accessed. This rotational delay is called the *latency time*.

Fixed-head versus movable-head disks.   Observe that if the seek time was not present, then the effective data transfer rate soars to approximately 196,078 bytes/s. The seek time can be eliminated if the disk drive is equipped with an actuator, which provides a R/W head per track, per cylinder.[25] In that case, no seek is required. Such disks are called *fixed-head* disks as opposed to the ones that were introduced in the beginning of this section, which are called *movable-head* disks. It should be clear that fixed-head disks are much more expensive than movable disks given the additional complexity of the controller's circuitry and many heads.

Fixed disks, on the other hand, are magnetic disks in which the recording media is not removable. Conversely, disks in which the recording media is removable are called *removable* disks.

Disk architecture.   Recall that in a direct-access device a block can be accessed directly (randomly) via its address. These devices are classified into two categories: *sector addressable devices* and *block addressable devices*. The difference lies in the addressing scheme employed. Each of these categories will be examined subsequently.

Sector versus Block Addressable Devices.   In sector addressable devices, each track is divided into a fixed number of *sectors*, each one of which has the same fixed capacity. This process, of dividing each track into sectors can be carried out either by the manufacturer, in which case one speaks about *hard sectoring,* or by the disk controller, subject to user's defined requirements, in which case one speaks about *soft sectoring*. In either case, a sector is the smallest addressable unit. The physical boundaries of a sector are detectable by its physical beginning and its capacity is known to the disk drive, in the case of hard sectoring, or via special markers that are written on the disk surface by software during the formatting process, in the case of soft sectoring.

Because the sector size is predefined, a record of small length will generate unused storage at the end of the sector, whereas a record of length longer than the sector size will require more than one sector to be stored. Both of these phenomena will be present in the case of variable length records.

In the case of block addressable devices the size of the block, as well as the blocking factor, is user defined. This means that the number of blocks can vary from track to track. Most of the IBM-manufactured devices are block addressable devices. Two different block formats are supported; *count data* format and *count-key data* format. Further discussion of these devices is beyond the scope of this text.

---

[25] Certain disk packs come with fixed read/write heads over only a subset of the set of the available cylinders. As an example, the IBM 3344 disk pack has 560 cylinders, and there is a feature in which the actuator assembly provides fixed read/write heads only for the first two cylinders.

Floppy disks.   Another popular storage medium, particularly with personal computer users, is the **floppy disk**. A floppy disk is a single 5¼-in disk enclosed in a square fiber-lined sleeve for protection. The disk is constructed from mylar on a thin polycarbonate substrate. Floppy disks may be easily flexed usually without damage (although this is not recommended!), hence, their name. Like hard disks, floppy disks may be either hard or soft sectored. Floppy disks are a low-capacity, low-cost media. Typical capacities range from 360 Kb (recorded on both sides) to 1.4 Mb and may cost only a few dollars each. Clearly with such an inexpensive technology, data transfer rates are also much lower than for hard disk units. A newer generation of floppy disks is only 3½-in in diameter and are packaged in hard plastic cases. These offer increased capacity and are easily transported.

Optical disks.   Another storage media that has been gaining popularity during the past ten years is optical storage. The principal advantage of optical storage over magnetic media is storage density. Optical disks typically have a much greater capacity than magnetic disks because of the precision with which the laser is directed onto the disk and the smaller size of an optical bit. High precision permits the tracks to be placed more closely together while small bits permit a greater number to be packed into a given area. Three classes of optical disk are currently available: **CD-ROM**, **WORM**, and **magneto-optical** (MO).

CD-ROMS.   CD-ROM is the oldest and most familiar optical storage medium. It is based on standards developed by Phillips and Sony Corporation in the early 1980s. The standard is similar to that used for the 5¼-in **compact disk** (**CD**) media with each CD capable of storing 600 Mb. Because the media and CD-ROMs use the same technology as CDs the devices are inexpensive and have become the most popular optical storage media to date. The major problem with CD-ROMs is that they are read only. That is, the data are impressed onto the disk when it is manufactured and may not be altered. This clearly prevents CD-ROM from being used as "normal" secondary storage; however, there are still applications in which they may be used. In particular, CD-ROMs have become popular for storing works such as encyclopedias, books, stock reports, publications, and citation indexes, which are useful to many personal computer users. Also, they have become popular as the preferred distribution media for operating system software.

Worms.   Another optical storage device gaining popularity is the **write once read many** (WORM). As the name suggests, data may be written onto a WORM; but, once written, it may not be changed. Thus the user may write only once to each bit position. Although this characteristic again prevents it from being used an a general-purpose secondary-storage device, it is useful for storing customer data that is not updated often. Updates in these cases would be handled by reading the file into main memory, updating it, and writing out a new file onto the WORM in a different location. The reason for WORM's unusual property is that a bit is marked on the disk by creating a pit (or bubble) in the recording layer using a laser. The state of a bit (i.e., 1 or 0) may be detected by using the laser at low power and detecting the reflectivity of the received signal. Thus, once a bit is set, it may not be reset! The worm may be thought of as the secondary storage equivalent of the EPROM. WORM disks come in a variety of different formats with capacities ranging from 300 Mb to 6 Gb. The most popular sizes are 5¼-in, 12-in, and 14-in disks.

Magneto-optical disks.   The newest optical storage media is a class known as **magneto-optical** (**MO**) disk storage. These make use of both a laser and local magnetic field to store the magnetic polarity of a bit. To write a bit of data the appropriate portion of the disk is heated while a local magnetic field is applied to specify the bit value. Once the bit has cooled the magnetic orientation is fixed in the recording layer. The bit value may be read using a low-power laser by measuring the Kerr rotation[26] of the reflected signal. Currently MO disks are more than twice as slow at writing data as magnetic disks; however, their large storage capacity and read/write capability makes them a strong contender. Again, disk capacities are in the range of 300 Mb to over 1 Gb, with disk sizes of 5¼-in and 12-in.

3.4 I/O DEVICE INTERACTION

3.4.1 Device Controllers

An **I/O device controller** permits the computer to communicate with its external environment as was discussed in Chapter 1 and is illustrated in Figure 1.3. The external environment includes all physical devices that are connected to the system. Each I/O controller is actually a specialized control unit and contains its own counters, simple instruction processing facilities, command registers that are used to specify the I/O operation, and status registers that are used to indicate the status of previous I/O requests. Each I/O controller is an intelligent unit—intelligent in the sense that it is able to interpret I/O requests and operate asynchronously (i.e., without direct synchronization) from the CPU. For a typical personal computer the external environment includes **disk drive controllers, asynchronous communications controllers**, a **graphics controller**, and **network controllers**. Each of these components is discussed subsequently.

Disk-drive controllers.   A disk controller is responsible for transferring data to and from a disk drive. Recall that a disk drive is a secondary storage device containing anywhere from 10 Mb to a gigabyte. In the following discussion we do not differentiate between the different disk types (magnetic, optical, floppy, etc.) because they are all controlled in a similar manner. Note also that a single controller may control two or four disk drives simultaneously as is illustrated in Figure 1.4. To issue a read or write request to the controller, the user specifies, in memory,[27] the sequence of actions that are required of the controller. The user then issues a `startio` instruction to the controller,[28] giving the memory location of the I/O instruction sequence. The controller then reads this sequence of instructions and attempts to satisfy them as shown in Figure 3.20. A typical instruction in pseudocode form might be

```
read the block from disk unit #1, cylinder #20, sector #4
into main memory starting from location $1000
```

(recall that a disk is a block-oriented device; therefore, only blocks of data may be read or written). The actual request would be encoded as a control command (one or more bytes) followed by the arguments (one or more). This data structure is called a **device control**

---

[26] The polarization of light in the presence of a magnetic field.

[27] In the case of memory mapped I/O, the request is placed in the "memory locations" corresponding to the device.

[28] In the case of memory mapped I/O, this may be implied by the action of writing the instruction into the appropriate location.

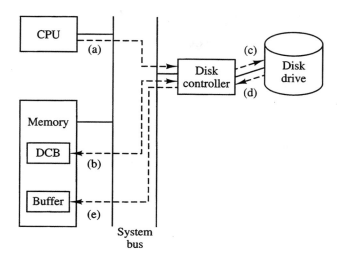

Figure 3.20 Typical I/O sequence: (a) CPU issues a start I/O request to the disk controller unit; (b) controller reads DCB from memory (which we assume is read request); (c) controller positions disk drive and starts read; (d) controller reads data off disk and starts DMA transfer to buffer specified in DCB; (e) data transferred to buffer.

block (DCB) and may be quite complex. Once the controller has been initiated by the CPU (via a `startio` command or writing to a control register in the controller) it interprets the instruction portion of the DCB; sends the necessary control signals to the actuator motor to position it to the correct location; waits for the disk to rotate to the correct position; and starts reading the data off the disk. Meanwhile, CPU is free to continue working on other tasks. As the data are read from the disk, the controller checks it and writes it directly into the appropriate memory location. This task is handled by the controller employing **direct memory access** (DMA). A device capable of DMA transfer is one that is able to use the system bus in the same manner as the CPU; that is, the controller acts as a bus master. Once the controller has completed its instructions, it reports back to the CPU by setting its status register and issuing an interrupt. The CPU, when interrupted, examines the status register to determine the outcome of its request. A write request would take place in a similar fashion. We note in conclusion that many DMA devices permit DCBs to be chained together so the controller may handle a sequence of I/O requests.

Asynchronous communications controller.   Bit serial asynchronous communication is used for low- to medium-speed data transfer. Typical applications include nongraphic terminals, keyboards, mice, modems, printers, plotters, and other character-oriented devices. With **serial** communications data are transmitted to the device along a single wire, one bit at a time.[29] The term **asynchronous** means that the receiver and sender are not synchronized by a common clock; this is discussed in detail in Chapter 10. Notice that although each bit is sent separately, the controller communicates entire characters (bytes) only. Unlike block oriented devices, for a serial controller we need only to specify the transfer of one character at a time.[30] Once one understands how data is transferred to and from a disk controller, it is a simple matter to understand other device types. In the case of serial communications, the user will specify as part of the I/O instruction, the character to

---

[29] Some printers are driven by a parallel interface. In this case each character is sent using eight wires, all bits being sent simultaneously (i.e., in parallel). From the perspective device control these are similar to asynchronous drivers and will not be considered further.

[30] Some controllers permit the user to specify a sequence of bytes to be read or written.

be read or written. Again, when the device has completed receiving or sending the character, it sets a status register and interrupts the CPU. A more detailed description of serial communications is presented in Chapter 10. Unlike disk controllers that initiate both read and writes, serial controllers respond to incoming data without the CPU necessarily having issued a read instruction. We therefore may require that I/O interrupt handlers buffer incoming data in memory until the CPU is ready for it.

Graphics controller.   In many personal computer systems the user interacts with a **graphics terminal**. A graphics terminal is able to display pictures as well as text, and may be either monochrome or color. The resolution of a graphics terminal is defined by the number of individual picture elements (or **pixels**) that it is able to display. Thus a typical display might be 280*480 pixels, that is, 280 rows by 480 columns yielding a total of 13, 440 pixels. In the case of monochrome the picture is displayed using a number of **gray scales** which correspond to the different shades of gray (i.e., intensity levels) that each pixel may take. The least number is 2 "shades" requiring 1 bit of storage per pixel, yielding black (0) and white (1). The next value would be 4 shades, requiring 2 bits per pixel: black (%00), dark gray (%01), light gray (%10), and white (%11). In the case of color, each pixel's shade is determined by "blending" the intensity values for the three primary colors, red, green, and blue (often called **RGB**). Notice that this may require as much as 3 bytes per pixel (1 byte, giving 256 intensity levels, for each primary color). One way that color displays may save on memory requirements while still providing many colors is by use of a **color table**. Each pixel contains an index value into a table of colors that is set by the user. Thus a single byte per pixel could be used to access a **palette** of 256 different colors out of a possible 2^{24}. Although inferior to the previous method, this does save storage and is most popular.

Network controller.   Another device found in many computers is the network controller. Example networks are Ethernet and Token Ring.[31] A network controller allows for the transfer of data between the computer and other computers via a network. Again, to the user, the procedure that allows the transfer of the data from one computer to another computer across a network is much like that for transferring data to disk. For example, to issue a write request to the controller the user specifies, in memory,[32] the sequence of actions that are required of the controller. The user then issues a `startio` instruction to the controller,[33] giving the memory location of the I/O instruction sequence. The controller then reads this sequence of instructions and attempts to satisfy them. A typical instruction might be

```
write to node #1234, a block of memory starting at
location $1000 and extending for $100 bytes
```

Again, the actual request would be encoded as a DCB including the command and all required arguments. The controller interprets the instruction portion of the DCB; it then sends the necessary control signals to the network to complete the data transfer. Again, a network controller is a DMA device that can operate independently from the CPU. Once the controller has completed its instructions it reports back to the CPU by setting an appropriate

---

[31] See Chapter 11—Computer Networking.

[32] In the case of memory-mapped I/O, the request is placed in the "memory locations" corresponding to the device.

[33] In the case of memory-mapped I/O, this may be implied by the action of writing the instruction into its appropriate location.

status register and issuing an interrupt. The CPU, when interrupted, examines the status register to determine the outcome of its request. As with serial and parallel controllers, the incoming data may not have been explicitly requested by the CPU; in this case, the controller must buffer the data in memory until the CPU is ready to examine it. A more detailed examination of a particular network controller is presented in Chapter 10.

3.4.2 Device Drivers

With the exception of graphics controllers, all the preceding controllers provide a similar service, i.e., reading and writing data. With this in mind, designers of operating systems usually attempt to provide a clean interface between the operating system and the I/O controllers. This interface is called the **device driver** for each particular device type. It is through this device driver that users (e.g., applications programs) access the device. Using the Unix[34] operating system as an example, a character device-driver interface (to be used for serial and parallel I/O) would consist of data structures and a set of assembly language routines[35] as described subsequently.

```
chprobe(...)
```
 – a routine called at system startup to establish if device ch is actually attached to the system, and to notify the operating system of its memory requirements.

```
chattach(...)
```
 – a routine to initialize the device and driver data structures.

```
chpoll(...)
```
 – a routine called by the operating system when it polls each device.

```
chintr(...)
```
 – an interrupt routine invoked by the operating system whenever this device interrupts the processor.

```
chopen(...)
```
 – a routine called each time an application opens this device for I/O.

```
chclose(...)
```
 – a routine called each time an application closes this device.

```
chread(...)
```
 – a routine called each time an application wishes to read from this device.

```
chwrite(...)
```
 – a routine called each time an application wants to write data to this device.

```
chioctl(...)
```
 – a routine called by the application to perform miscellaneous device control functions.

The first four routines are used by the operating system, whereas the last five routines are employed by the user and correspond to those functions listed in Table 1.4. You should also be aware of the fact that these routines are appropriate for all device classes; thus, an application is not required to know the details of the underlying device itself.[36]

3.5 COMPUTER COMMUNICATIONS

Communicating with other computers is another principal component of the system; this interaction may be either **tightly coupled** or **loosely coupled**. Loosely coupled systems are

---

[34] Unix is a trademark of AT&T.

[35] C language routines in the case of Unix.

[36] The Unix system defined two classes of devices: block and character. All block devices are treated in a similar fashion, as are all character devices.

physically distributed over a region that may vary from a few hundred feet to many thousands of miles. Typically the activities on different systems will be unrelated, although in principle several systems could work together on the same problem. A loosely coupled system would be exemplified by several workstations connected to one another by a **computer network**. Such a network is supported by a combination of hardware and system software that aid processes on one system to send data to processes on another. The hardware includes I/O devices, dedicated cables and wires, and perhaps leased telephone lines. The software includes programs to transfer data between processes and utilities to provide the essential user services in a loosely coupled network. These include file transfer, remote terminal access, and mail. An overview of computer networks is provided in Chapter 11. In contrast, tightly coupled systems are in close physical proximity often sharing the same backplane (i.e., system bus). These tightly coupled systems are usually called **multiprocessor systems**; they frequently work on different parts of the same problem. Because this text is concerned with single processor organization, we will restrict our discussion of multiprocessors to this section only.

3.5.1 Networks

A **computer network** is a collection of autonomous computers able to communicate with one another. The term *autonomous* means that each computer is able to initiate communications; thus, we exclude "dumb" terminals from the network. The term *communicate* means that for two computers "on the network" we are able to pass data from one to the other. As we mentioned earlier, the actual network (as distinct from the computers) is composed of a combination of hardware and software. From a logical perspective, we are able to separate the computers from the network. We use the term **hosts** when referring to the computers that use the network. These hosts are connected together by a **subnet**, which is a collection of interconnected **interface message processors** (IMPs). An IMP is either a general purpose or special purpose computer that is dedicated to forwarding messages that originated from a source host toward its intended destination. IMPs are connected to one another through dedicated lines, leased telephone lines, or some other physical media (e.g., microwave link, CATV cable, or fiber link). A link between two IMPs is called a **hop**, indicating that one "hops" from one node to the next. These principle elements are shown in Figure 3.21.

The reader may be wondering why we earlier called this only a *logical view* of the system. The reason is that host computers may also perform the activities of an IMP. Thus a typical workstation may be a host from the user's perspective, and act as an IMP by forwarding messages for other hosts in the subnet. In addition, with improvements in technology, it is possible to have IMP functionality on an expansion card that plugs into the host like other I/O devices. Examples of this are network communication cards such as the Ethernet card, which may be purchased for workstations.

Services offered on a computer network vary greatly; however, the following features are always found:

1. File transfer between hosts.
2. Remote terminal access to other hosts.
3. Mail between users.
4. Remote disk mounting.

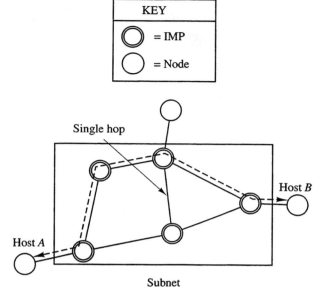

Figure 3.21 Principal elements of a computer network.

Additional details on networking including its history, its hardware and software organization, and how typical applications are implemented is provided in Chapter 11.

3.5.2 Multiprocessing

A **multiprocessor system** is one in which several CPUs are **closely coupled** to one another. Closely coupled implies that the processors are in close proximity, may pass data between one another with little delay, and share access to other devices. For example, in a bus system we may connect several processors to a common bus. In general, a multiprocessor system may be considered as multiple CPUs, memories, and I/O devices connected together by some interconnection network as shown in Figure 3.22.

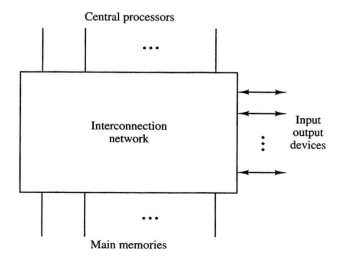

Figure 3.22 Overview of a multiprocessor system.

There are two principal classes of multiprocessors: **shared memory** and **message passing**. In the former case, these processors share either some or all of their address space with other processors. This may be accomplished through either a common bus or a switch system. In the latter class, communication is performed through channels supported in the hardware. First we will discuss shared memory systems.

In a common bus configuration, a multiprocessor would be organized as shown in Figure 3.23. Notice that the increase in hardware is quite minimal. Apart from the extra processors and perhaps a couple of extra control lines on the bus (to the CPUs to compete fairly for access to the bus), there are little modifications required. Note also, however, that the bandwidth of the bus must now be much higher to support the extra traffic.

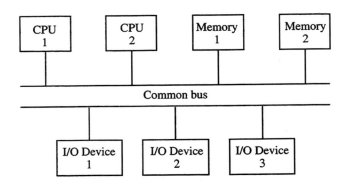

Figure 3.23   Common bus multiprocessor system.

An example of a system in which the interconnection network is through a switch is C.mmp[37] as shown in Figure 3.24. In this system each processor (originally a DEC PDP-11) has its own bus. One special device on the bus is the *D*-map, which interfaces the bus to a memory switch. The memory switch selects one of 16 banks of memory. A path through the memory switch is selected for each memory access. This switch is able to accommodate all 16 processor requests simultaneously.

In another multiprocessor system we permit each processor to have its own local storage and I/O devices. Again, units are connected together using either a switch or a bus. The advantages to these organizations are that processors are not required to share memory and bus bandwidth *except* for interprocess communication. An example of this organization is the BBN Butterfly[38] as shown in Figure 3.25.

The other principle approach to multiprocessing is message passing. In this paradigm, communication between processors is made via communication procedures at the machine level and a naming convention to reach the destination machines. Examples of message-passing multiprocessors are the Connection Machine[39] and the Transputer.[40] These systems are architecturally complex and are considered beyond the scope of this text. A typical message passing architecture is shown in Figure 3.26.

---

[37] A multiprocessor system designed at Carnegie-Mellon University in 1971.

[38] Developed by BBN Inc. The Butterfly is a parallel processor system based on the MC68020 processor, expandable to 256 processors.

[39] Developed by Thinking Machines Inc. The CM1 and CM2 use many special purpose processor slices each with local memory. The processors are connected in a cube that is expandable to 65,536 processors.

[40] Developed by SGS Thompson Inc. Transputers are full 32-bit special-purpose processors, each with four connection links. The user may configure the links dynamically.

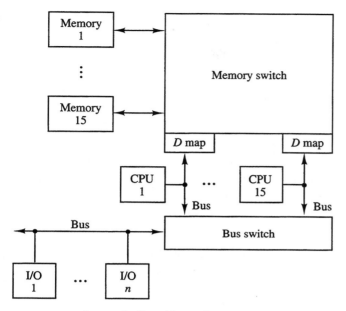

Figure 3.24   Organization of C.mmp.

In concluding this section, we will mention that other improvements can be made to a computer system to obtain additional performance. One popular method is **vector processing**, in which hardware support is added to permit the CPU to operate on vectors (i.e., arrays of values) instead of scalars. Other options use several different technologies when constructing the CPU; another cools the computer down to very low temperatures. These techniques are typically applied to supercomputers, where the demand for thousands of billions of floating-point calculations per second would justify the expense.

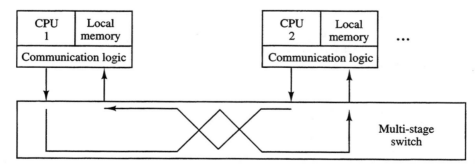

Figure 3.25   Architecture of BBN Butterfly.

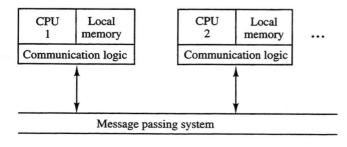

Figure 3.26   Typical message-passing architecture.

:ISES

hat is the smallest addressable unit in main memory? What is the rule for the formation of
s unit? How is this unit accessed?

...iat are the other addressable units in memory? Define them. What are word boundaries?

3. Define kilobyte, megabyte, and gigabyte.

4. Describe the operations of the address bus and data bus.

5. What is the significance of a word boundary as opposed to a byte boundary?

6. Can the word $ABC1 be stored at location $01EB? Can the preceding word be stored at location
$01EF? Is there any location, between the preceding addresses, that a word can be stored?

7. If a word can be stored at a given address, can a byte be stored there? A longword? Explain.

8. If a byte is stored at address $1000, can a word be stored adjacent to it? If the byte is stored at
address $1001, does this change your answer? If so, for what reason?

9. Describe the differences between the EBCDIC and ASCII character representations. What is
meant by a collating sequence?

10. What are the three principal fields of a machine instruction? Explain the purpose of each field.

11. Explain the purpose of the program counter (PC) and how it operates.

12. What are the different types of registers? Explain the purpose of each.

13. Explain how an instruction is retrieved, interpreted, and executed in a computer.

14. Discuss three different secondary storage devices.

15. Explain the difference between direct-access storage and sequential access storage. Which
would you recommend for backing up the archives of a bank's old account information. Why?

16. The IBM 3420/8 tape drive has the following characteristics: density = 1600 bpi, IBG length =
0.6 in, V = 200 in/s, and rewind V = 800 in/s. A file of 20,000 fixed-length records must be
stored on a brand new tape of length 2400 ft. The size of each logical record is 170 bytes.
Physical records are 1024 bytes in size.
   a. Find the capacity of the tape.
   b. Find the Utilization.
   c. Assuming that the tape drive is ready to write the first block (at the physical beginning of
   the tape), find the minimum time to write the file onto the tape and to rewind the tape.

17. A file with 20,700 fixed-length logical records is loaded on a brand new IBM 3350 disk. The
file structure is physical sequential, and the first block is written at the physical beginning of
cylinder 0. Logical record length is 200 bytes and the blocking factor is 16. Assuming that no
interblock gaps are present, find the number of cylinders required to store the entire file. Find
also the time required to write the entire file onto the disk assuming that initially the read/write
head is positioned over cylinder 0.

18. The GTD and IBM 3420/8 tape drives have the following characteristics:

Tape drive	Density	IBG	Start/stop time	Read/write speed	Rewind speed
GTD	D bpi	I"	S ms	RW"/s	RS"/s
IBM 3420/8	6250 bpi	0.6"	1 ms	200"/s	640"/s

A file of 2 million fixed-length records must be stored on tape. The length of each record is 90
bytes. Blocks are to be 2048 bytes. Assuming no block overhead and unspanned records for
the GTD tape drive, develop equations that define the following:
   a. The blocking factor.
   b. The minimum expected time to write the file onto tape and rewind the tape assuming the
   R/W head is ready to write the first block.

    c. Evaluate all equations that were derived in parts a and b using the device characteristics of the IBM 3420/8 tape drive.

19. The DEC RM03 disk drive has the following characteristics: 832 cyl/disk, 5 tracks/cyl, 32 sectors/track, 512 bytes/sector, IBG 114 bytes/sector, 8 ms/(one cylinder seek), average seek time 30 ms, and latency of 8.3 ms. Answer the following questions by stating all your assumptions:
    a. What is the storage capacity of the disk?
    b. Suppose that enough sectors are to be written to fill 20 consecutive cylinders. What is the minimum expected time needed to perform this operation?
    c. Suppose all data blocks that were written in part (iii) are to be read in reverse order. Estimate the time to perform this operation.

20. A new disk drive has the following characteristics: C cyl/disk, 1 track/cyl, S sectors/track, D bytes/sector, IBG G bytes/sector, M ms/(one cylinder seek), average seek time A ms, and average latency of L ms. Suppose that the operating system allows block sizes to be defined in terms of an integral number of sectors. For example, a block of $2 \cdot D$ bytes would be stored in two consecutive sectors, each sector containing D bytes. K blocks are to be written in order of ascending block numbers (i.e., $1, 2, 3, \ldots, K$). Each block is stored in B consecutive sectors. Assuming that all K blocks can be written on a single track, derive an equation for the expected time to read these K blocks in the order: $K, K-1, K-2, \ldots, 2, 1$. Clearly define your approach to solving this problem and state all your assumptions.

21. Your boss requests that you recommend a secondary storage media for a database system. Which media would you select. Why?

22. Given that the capacity of a disk drive is 300 Mb, how many 2400-ft tapes would be required to back it up at 1600 bpi? How many 8-mm cassettes?

23. Explain the function of a disk controller. Provide a sample DCB to transfer $1000 bytes of data to disk 1, cylinder 0, sector 39. Label the fields in your DCP and list likely commands for the command word.

24. Is the number of devices on a system equal to the number of controllers? Why?

25. Given a personal computer system with a monitor, keyboard, serial port, floppy disk, and hard disk, how many device controllers are required?

26. Explain the difference between a tightly coupled system and a loosely coupled system.

27. A user writes a program to invert a $100 * 100$ matrix (a numerically intensive task). How might they improve the performance using a multiprocessor system?

28. In a shared bus system, where is the potential bottleneck? Is this removed by using a crossbar switch? What problems are encountered instead?

ADDITIONAL READING

HAYES, J. P. *Computer Architecture and Organization*, 2nd ed. New York: McGraw-Hill, 1988.

STALLINGS, W. *Computer Organization and Architecture*, 2nd ed. New York: Macmillian, 1990.

TANENBAUM, A. S. *Structured Computer Organization*, 3rd ed. Englewood Cliffs, N.J.: Prentice Hall, 1990.

TOMEK, I. *The Foundations of Computer Architecture and Organization.* New York: W. H. Freeman and Company, 1990.

LIVADAS, P. E. *File Structures, Theory and Practice.* Englewood Cliffs, N.J.: Prentice Hall, 1990.

RELATED PUBLICATIONS

Byte Magazine. New York: McGraw-Hill.

4

SIM68 Computer

In this chapter, we will present a small hypothetical computer, the SIM68 a simple view of which is presented in Figure 4.1. The presentation consists of three parts. The first part will detail the computer's architecture; the second part will outline the SIM68's machine language, and consequently we will be able to design and run our first machine language programs. Finally, the third part will present an assembler for the SIM68 that will enable us to code and execute our first assembly language programs.

The reader should be aware that despite the fact that our machine is a hypothetical one and its capabilities are minimal, its study is of *utmost* importance, given that its study will provide one with the fundamental building blocks for upcoming discussions of the MC68000 microprocessor.

4.1 MAIN MEMORY ORGANIZATION

The smallest addressable unit is the byte, and the address bus of the SIM68 is 24 bits wide. This suggests that all memory addresses are represented by an unsigned binary integer 24 bits in length. Although the address space is large, only 16 Kb will be available to the user. In other words, user programs that are to be executed on this machine are limited to a size of 16 Kb. In particular, the user may use the continuous memory area delimited by the addresses $000000 and $003FFF. If an application program attempts to access a memory location outside this range, the program will be **terminated** by the operating system because of a **bus error**.

4.1.1 Data Information

SIM68's data bus is 16 bits wide, which determines the word size. Furthermore, SIM68's instruction set assumes only signed integer data[1] in 2's complement representation. Moreover, each such representation is assumed to be of **word** size. Finally, integers **must** be aligned at word boundaries. If an application program attempts to access a word, and the indicated memory address is not a word boundary,[2] the program will be terminated or equivalently "crash" because of an **addressability error**.

---

[1] Instructions that manipulate character data are not provided.

[2] Recall that only addresses divisible by two represent word boundaries.

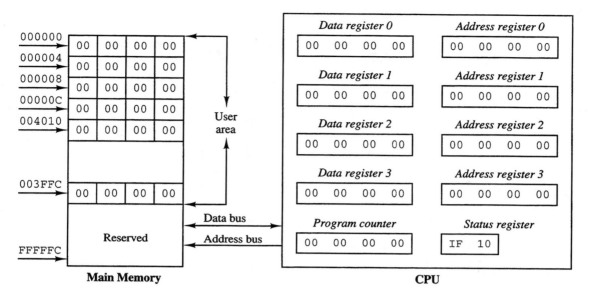

Figure 4.1   Simple view of SIM68 machine. Hexadecimal notation is employed throughout.

4.2 CPU

4.2.1 Data Registers

There are a total of four data registers; each has a width of 32 bits. The address of the first register is 0, the second 1, and so on. It should be clear that each data register address could be specified with 2 bits; in our case, we will use 3 bits to specify[3] such an address. Therefore, the address of the first register is %000, the second %001, the third %010, and the last %011.

Even though the bits of a data register are not individually addressable,[4] we can manipulate (address) only words (16 bits). If a word is to be addressed or be operated on, the word accessed is always the least significant word of the register (bits 15 through 0). The high-order word of a data register cannot be operated on *directly;* however, as we will see later, it can be accessed and then *moved* to the low-order word of the destination data register where it can be operated on. Figure 4.2 illustrates these concepts.

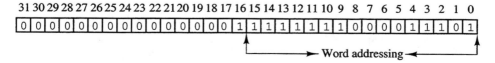

Figure 4.2   Addressing a data register.

---

[3] This allows for future expansion.

[4] SIM68 does not provide such instructions.

4.2.2 Address Registers

There are a total of four address registers; each is 32 bits wide. The address of the first register is 0, the second 1, and so on. Similar to the case of data registers, the binary address of the first register is %000, the second %001, the third %010, and the fourth %011. Even though the addresses of both data and address registers are the same, we will see shortly that all seeming ambiguities relative to the type (data or address) of register addressed are removed from some other information that should be included in the machine language instruction; therefore, the hardware is able to distinguish the type of register addressed. Furthermore, because the contents of an address register are *assumed* to represent addresses only longword operations are permitted in such a register.

At this point we should note that whenever a memory location is to be accessed (pointed to by that address register), only the low-order 24 bits will be used for the formation of that address. Figure 4.3 illustrates these concepts.

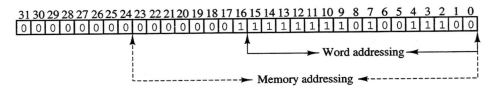

Figure 4.3   Addressing an address register.

4.2.3 Program Counter Register

There is only one program counter register that is 32 bits wide. There are two points to be made here. First, although this register is 32 bits wide, only the 24 low-order bits are used in the formation of a memory address as illustrated in Figure 4.4. In addition, *only* longword operations are permitted in this register.

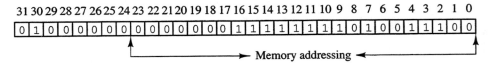

Figure 4.4   Memory addressing mechanism via program counter. Recall that program counter points to next instruction.

4.2.4 Status Register

There is only one status register; it is 16 bits wide. Despite the fact that this register is 16 bits wide, only the five least significant bits are available for inspection by the user, as illustrated in Figure 4.5. The value of each of these bits has special significance to the programmer, and a special terminology is associated with each bit.

- Bit 4 is referred to as the **extend** (X) bit.
- Bit 3 is referred to as the **negative** (N) bit.
- Bit 2 is referred to as the **zero** (Z) bit.

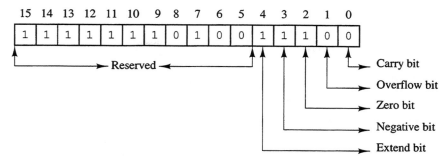

Figure 4.5   Status-register bit assignment.

- Bit 1 is referred to as the **overflow** (V) bit.
- Bit 0 is referred to as the **carry** (C) bit.

These five low-order bits of the status register are collectively referred to as the **condition code**; the low-order byte of this (conceptual) register is simply referred to as the **condition code register** (CCR).

4.3 SIM68 MACHINE LANGUAGE

4.3.1 Operand Addressing

Consider the simple operation of addition. In particular let's assume that we would like to add the two integers denoted by x and y. The mathematical notation for this operation would be $z = x + y$. The mathematical language interpretation of the previous expression is the following. Add the number denoted by x to the one denoted by y and represent the result by z. On the other hand, the computer language interpretation is the following. Add the number at address x to the one at address y and store the result at address z. Unfortunately, the previous interpretation indicates that for this operation to be possible, a three-operand instruction is needed. SIM68's machine language does not provide one. As we will see, SIM68 provides a two-operand addition instruction. Hence, in the SIM68 "lingo" one could say add the number at address x to the one at address y. The question that naturally arises is where is the result stored? The answer is very simple; the result **replaces** one of the addends. The previous answer raises a new question. Which of the addends should be replaced? The answer again depends on which of the operands has been specified as the **source** and which has been specified as the **destination**. The rule for most of the two operand instructions is the following: The result *replaces* the destination, and the source remains *unchanged.* For example, if x had been specified as the source (and therefore y as the destination), then the contents of y would be replaced by the result of the addition $x+y$ after the instruction has been executed.

Earlier we noted that the computer language interpretation of $x+y$ was to add the integer with address x to the one with address y. Recall that it is the function of the *instruction interpreter* to interpret the instruction. It is easy to see that the interpreter is now faced with a new task. What do these addresses represent? Memory locations or register addresses? In the latter case, there is one more question to be asked. Does the register address refer to a data register or to an address register? In short, the question is equivalent to what is the **mode** of addressing.

SIM68 supports three modes of addressing—modes 0, 1, and 5. In the case of the first two modes, the interpreter realizes that the address specified is a **register address.** If the mode is 0, the register is a **data** register, whereas if the mode is 1, the addressed register is an **address** register. On the other hand, if the mode is 5, then the interpreter assumes that a **memory** location is addressed; the address of the memory location that is to be accessed is referred to as the **effective address.**

The question now is how these two pieces of information (mode and address) can be specified in machine language. The answer lies in the fact that if an address is to be specified, then one must specify the **mode** and the **address** (register and memory), depending on the mode. The mode requires three bits to be specified; if it is equal to 0 or 1, three additional bits are required for the specification of the register address. In the case in which the address is a memory address (mode 5), the effective addresses are always 24 bits long. One would expect that in this case, the effective address would be specified in a machine language instruction with as many bits. The designers realized that if each memory address was to be specified via the 24 required bits, however, then the length of the machine language instruction would be too long; therefore, the size of the machine language program would be unreasonably large. In addition, if the address was *explicitly* defined as part of the machine language instruction, accessing a different location would require recoding of the instruction. Therefore, the effective address *is not* specified in the machine language instruction; instead the **address** of an address register is specified that *contains* either the *entire* effective address or *part* of the effective address.[5] This way the number of bits required for the specification of the effective address is reduced, and the addressing mechanism becomes more flexible.

These six bits (mode and register address) are collectively referred to as the **mode specification** (MS). The first three bits indicate the mode, whereas the remaining three indicate the address of a register operand or the address of an address register that contains part of the effective address of a memory operand.

Summarizing, SIM68 supports three possible modes of addressing. Mode 0 is referred to as **data register direct addressing**, because the contents of a data register are to be accessed. Mode 1 is referred to as **address register direct addressing** because the contents of an address register are to be accessed. Finally, mode 5 is referred to as **address register indirect addressing with displacement** because the effective address of the memory location that is to be accessed is formed *indirectly* from the contents of an address register. These addressing modes will be revisited in the following paragraphs and will be discussed in much more detail. Table 4.1 indicates the three possible mode specifications.

TABLE 4.1   Summary of addressing modes supported by SIM68; dn and an represent data and address register n, respectively

Addressing modes	Mode specification	
	mode	register
Data register direct addressing	0	dn
Address register direct addressing	1	an
Address register indirect addressing with displacement	5	an

---

[5] The exact mechanism (which depends on the mode) will be explained shortly.

4.3.2 Instructions

There are ten possible operations that one can perform with the machine language instructions supported by SIM68. Briefly, these instructions are Add, Subtract, Multiply, Divide, Compare, Move, Branch, Swap, Dump, and Stop. The first six instructions are two-operand instructions, the next two are one-operand instructions, and the last two are zero-operand instructions. Considering the fact that certain instructions permit a different mode of addressing of an operand, we will see that the total number of machine language instructions supported by SIM68 is 28. The instructions have variable length (from one to three words) and can be classified according to the format of their first word, which will be referred to as the **format** of the instruction. We may distinguish a total of seven formats (F1 through F7). These are illustrated in Table 4.2 together with their length.

TABLE 4.2   Machine language formats (according to the first word),
bit assignments, and length (in words) of the instructions supported by SIM68

Format	Bit assignment				Length
F1	OP_4	dRn_3	om_3	sMS_6	1
F2	OP_4	ddn_3	OP_1 om_2	sMS_6	1
F3	OP_4	ddn_3	OP_3	sMS_6	1
F4	OP_2 om_2	ddn_3	dmd_3	sMS_6	1, 2, 3
F5	OP_4	$Cond_4$	$Displacement_8$		1, 2
F6	OP_{12}			V_4	1
F7	OP_{13}			dn_3	1

Even though these formats will be discussed in detail in the following paragraphs, we present a synopsis of the fields as well as their significance of the instructions in Table 4.2.

- OP_n denotes an n-bit opcode.
- MS_6 denotes the 6-bit mode specification. sMS_6 denotes the mode specification of the source operand, whereas dMS_6 denotes the mode specification of the destination operand.
- dn_3, an_3, and rn_3 represent the 3-bit address of data register n, address register n, or either a data or address register n respectively. When the register is preceded by a d, this indicates a destination operand; if it is preceded by an s, a source operand is denoted. For example, a field labeled by ddn_3 indicates that this 3-bit field contains the address of a data register, which is the destination operand of this instruction.
- V_4 denotes a 4-bit (vector) address.
- $Displacement_8$ denotes an 8-bit signed integer.

- om_2 and om_3 denote a 2- and a 3-bit **operation mode** field, respectively.
- $Cond_4$ denotes a 4-bit code known as the **condition**.
- dmd_3 denotes the 3-bit mode of the destination operand.

Binary integer arithmetic. The SIM68's instruction set provides instructions that will allow one to perform signed integer *addition, subtraction, multiplication,* and *division*. All these instructions, except one version of the add instruction, which permits the destination to be an address register, have the common property that both operands represent data register addresses. The last remark implies that both integers should be loaded into the appropriate registers for the instructions to be executed properly. These instructions are discussed in detail subsequently.

Addition. SIM68 provides the user with the ability to add two signed integers. Furthermore, the internal representation of the integers is assumed to be 2's complement. There are two versions of the addition instruction. In both cases the format of the instruction is the same, F1. The source register is a data register (mode 0); the destination register in the first version must be a data register, whereas in the second version it must be an address register. Hence, in either case the mode of addressing of the source operand is *data register direct*, whereas that of the destination operand is either *data* or *address register direct*.

Closer examination of the F1 format indicates that the opcode is 4 bits wide; in the case of the add instruction, this opcode is %1101. The 3-bit field om_3 *should* have the value %011, whenever the destination is an address register, whereas it *should* have the value %001, when the destination is a data register. In addition, considering that the only mode allowed for the source operand is 0, the bit assignments for each of the two versions are given in Figure 4.6.

F1	OP$_4$	dRn$_3$	om$_3$	sMS$_6$	
	1101	dAn$_3$	011	000	sDn$_3$
	1101	dDn$_3$	001	000	sDn$_3$

Figure 4.6 Bit assignments for addition instruction. dan$_3$ and ddn$_3$ represent addresses of the destination address and data register, respectively, whereas sdn$_3$ represents address of the source data register.

The source operand is a word size operand represented by the low-order word of the indicated data register; the destination operand is of word size, if the destination is a data register (its low-order word), whereas it is of longword size if the destination is an address register. In the latter case, the source word is *sign-extended* (i.e., the sign-bit is propagated sixteen times to the left) to a longword[6] before it is added to the entire contents of the destination address register. In the latter case, the source word is *sign-extended* (i.e., the sign-bit is propagated sixteen times to the left) to a longword[6] before it is added to the entire contents of the destination address register.

Before we give an example, one should note that whenever an add instruction is executed, the result is a signed number, positive, negative, or zero. Moreover, as we have already indicated, there is always the possibility of overflow. Therefore, on completion of execution of an *add to data register* (but *not* of an *add to address register* instruction), the hardware sets (the value of the bit is set to 1) or resets (the value of the bit is set to zero or

---

[6] This extension does not affect the contents of the source register.

cleared) the value of the *carry, overflow, zero, extend,* and *negative* flag bits of the *status register.* Although the SIM68 does not provide any instructions that permit *direct* access of any of these bits, the reader should be aware of this because as we shall see, an application program is capable of *indirectly* examining certain bits. The result of the operation determines the rules by which these bits are set or reset and are given subsequently.

- If a carry was generated as a result of the operation, both the **carry** and **extend** bits are *set*. Otherwise, both are *reset*.
- If the result of the operation is a negative number, the **negative** bit is *set;* otherwise, it is *reset*.
- If the result of the addition is equal to the number zero, the **zero** bit is *set* to reflect this fact; otherwise, it is *reset*.
- Finally, the **overflow** bit is *set* when an overflow has occurred; otherwise, this bit is *reset*.

With the aid of these flag bits, an application program can detect the nature of the result. In the following paragraphs, we give some examples that will illustrate the concepts discussed earlier.

Example

Consider the memory and register in Figure 4.7(a) at the instant in which the execution of a certain instruction has been completed. The contents of the location counter indicate that the instruction that must be executed next is the one at memory location $0000AA.

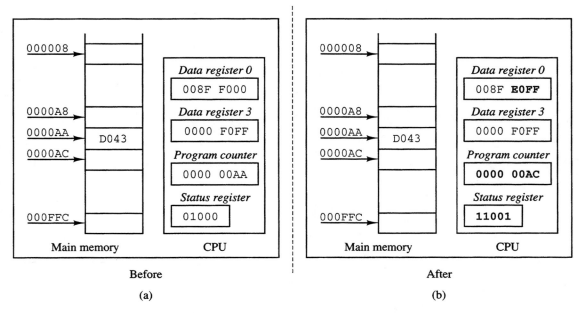

Figure 4.7 Memory and register contents immediately before (a) and after (b) execution of (add) instruction at location $0000AA. All contents are in hex except that of the condition code that are in binary.

Note that comparison of the first 4 bits of the instruction $D043 with the first 4 bits of that in Figure 4.6 indicates that this instruction is an *add* instruction and, furthermore, the format of the instruction is F1. Moreover, comparing the binary representation, %1101 000 001 000 011, of this instruction with the bit assignments of Figure 4.6, we see that the sMS_6 field indicates that the source is data register 3. Moreover, field om_3 = %001, and according to our previous discussions, this setting indicates that the destination is a data register whose address is indicated by the 3-bit field drn_3 which in this case is set to %000. Hence, after the instruction is fetched into the instruction register, the interpreter will interpret the instruction as follows.

Add the low-order word of the source register (d3) to the low order word of the destination register (d0). The result replaces the low-order word of the destination register.

Therefore, the word $F0FF will be added to the word $F000, and the result $E0FF will replace the low-order word of the destination register (d0). Both the extend and carry bits are set because a carry was generated. The negative bit is set because the 16-bit result represents a negative number. Finally, the overflow and zero bits are reset because no overflow occurred, and the result is not zero.

On the other hand, if the instruction at location $0000AA was as in the following Figure 4.8, according to our discussions of the previous example, it is simple to see that this is again an add instruction where the source is data register 3, *but* the destination register is address register 0.

In this case, the low-order word of the source data register 3, $F0FF, will be accessed and sign extended to the 32-bit longword $FFFFF0FF. The latter longword will be added to the longword contents, $008FF000, of the destination address register 0. The result $008FE0FF replaces the contents of the destination register. Finally, notice that the condition code setting is not affected by execution of this instruction.

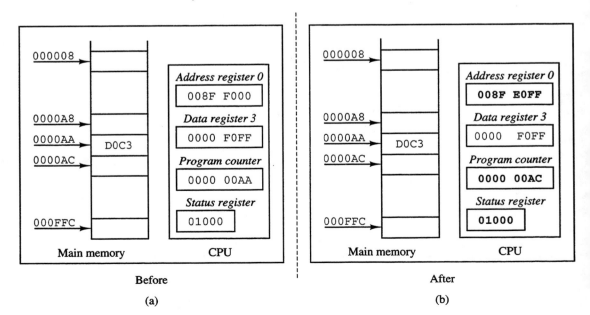

Figure 4.8   Memory and register contents immediately before (a) and after (b) execution of (add) instruction at location $0000AA. All contents are in hex except that of condition code that are in binary.

Subtraction. The subtraction instruction is very similar to that of addition. The machine language format of the instruction is F1 and the only addressing mode supported for both operands is *data register direct*. Figure 4.9 illustrates in detail the machine language format of this instruction. Notice that the opcode is %1001, that the field om_3 contains the same bit values as addition and that the only mode allowed in addressing the destination is 0.

F1

OP$_4$	dRn$_3$	om$_3$	sMS$_6$	
1001	dDn$_3$	001	000	sDn$_3$

Figure 4.9 Bit assignments for subtraction instruction. ddn_3 and sdn_3 represent addresses of destination and source data registers, respectively.

Hence, to subtract the low-order words of the two data registers 2 and 3, we should supply their addresses in the two fields ddn_3 and sdn_3. Observe that the former field represents the *destination* register, whereas the latter represents the *source* register.

Before we give an example, it should be noted that execution of this instruction causes the processor sets the condition code in almost the same fashion as in the case of the add instruction. The only difference being that the carry and extend bits are *set* if a borrow was generated; otherwise, both are *reset*.

In the following paragraphs some examples are given that will illustrate the concepts discussed earlier.

Example

Assume that the instruction to be executed is the one at location $0000AA and the memory and register contents are as in Figure 4.10(a).

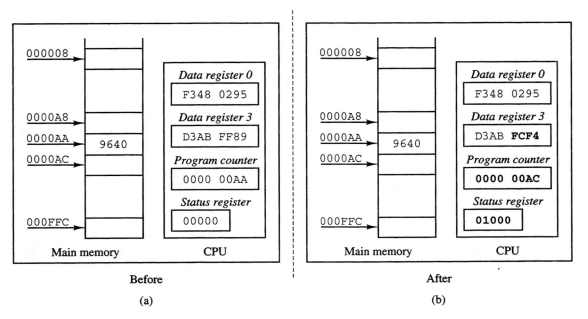

Before

(a)

After

(b)

Figure 4.10(a) Memory and register contents immediately before (a) and after (b) execution of (subtract) instruction at location $0000AA. All contents are in hex except that of condition code that are in binary.

After the instruction is fetched into the instruction register, the interpreter will interpret the instruction as follows:

Subtract the low-order word of the source register (d0) from the low-order word of the destination register (d3). The result replaces the low-order word of the destination register.

Hence, the word $0295 will be subtracted from the word $FF89 to yield the negative integer represented by the word $FCF4, which replaces the low-order word of the destination. The reader is encouraged to verify the condition code setting in this example.

Multiplication.   The multiplication instruction as well as the division instruction have the same format, F3. Here again, the only addressing mode supported for both operands is *data register direct.* Let us look a little more closely at this machine language instruction. First, we can observe that the opcode of this instruction is 7 bits wide and in particular it is equal to %1100111. The 6-bit field sMS_6 indicates the mode specification of the source operand. Because the only addressing mode permitted (for this operand) is mode 0, we can conclude that the first 3 bits of this field *should* be %000, whereas the remaining 3 bits represent the source data register address sdn_3 as is illustrated in Figure 4.11. Note that the address of the destination data register (operand) is indicated by the 3-bit-wide field marked by ddn_3.

F3

OP_4	dDn_3	OP_3	sMS_6	
1100	dDn_3	111	000	sDn_3

Figure 4.11   Bit assignments for multiplication instruction. ddn_3 and sdn_3 represent addresses of destination and source data registers, respectively.

An example is given later, but first we should note that whenever such an instruction is executed, the result is a *longword* signed integer. In other words, the multiplication of two words produces a longword result. Unlike the case of add and subtract instructions when only the lower-order word of the destination register is affected, the *entire* destination register is affected. Moreover, the hardware at the completion of execution of the multiplication instruction, adjusts the values of the *carry, overflow, zero,* and *negative* bits of the *status register* according to the following rules.

- **Carry** and **overflow** bits are *reset* regardless of the nature of the result.[7]
- If the result of the operation is a negative number, then the **negative** bit is *set;* otherwise, it is *reset.*
- If the result of the multiplication is equal to the number zero, then the **zero** bit is *set* to reflect this fact; otherwise, it is *reset.*
- Finally, the **extend** bit is not affected.

In the following paragraphs some examples are given that will illustrate the concepts discussed earlier.

Example

The instruction that is about to be executed is the one at location $0000AA, and the memory and register contents are the same as in Figure 4.12(a).

---

[7] By "result" in these rules, we mean the *longword* integer result.

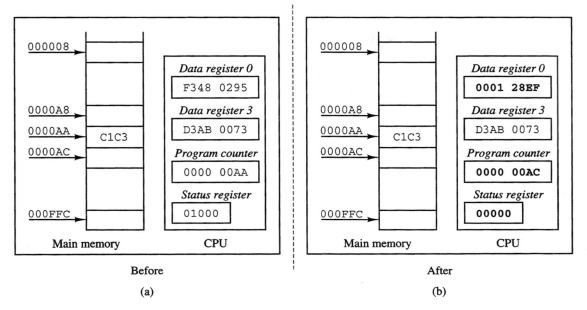

Figure 4.12   Memory and register contents immediately before (a) and after (b) execution of the instruction at location $0000AA. All contents are in hex except that of the condition code that are in binary.

After the instruction is fetched into the instruction register, the interpreter will interpret the instruction as follows:

Multiply the low-order word of the source register (d3) by the low-order word in the destination register (d0). The **longword** result replaces the contents of the entire destination register.

Therefore, the word $0295 is multiplied by the word $0073. This multiplication yields the longword result $000128EF, which replaces the longword in the destination register. The reader is encouraged to compare and verify the setting of the condition code, as a result of execution of the two multiplication instructions, as illustrated in Figures 4.12 and 4.13.

The reader should also wonder how the result of the multiplication can be accessed, because according to our previous discussions, we can only access the low-order word of a data register. Well, if the result is an integer within the bounds -2^{15} and $2^{15} - 1$, the high-order word of the destination register contains sixteen copies of the sign-bit (i.e., 16 bits of either all 0's or 1's) of the integer represented by the low-order word of that register. In this case, therefore, both the longword representation and the low-order word represent the *same* signed decimal integer, and access to the high-order word and the longword is unnecessary. At the other extreme, when the result is outside the bounds given earlier, for all practical purposes we may assume that a *word overflow* has occurred. The previous remark raises another question. Namely, how does one detect this case? The answer lies in the examination of the high-order word of the result, and we will be able to see later that SIM68 provides an instruction that will permit us to "isolate" the high-order word of any data register.

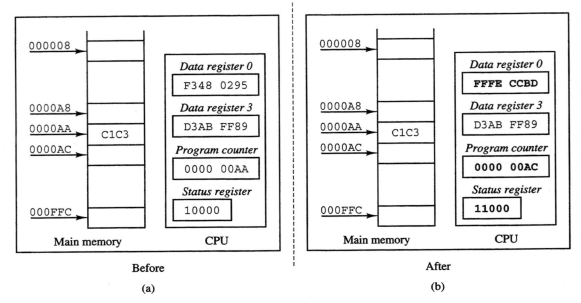

Figure 4.13 Memory and register contents immediately before (a) and after (b) execution of instruction at location $0000AA. All contents are in hex except that of condition code that are in binary.

Division.   The division instruction has the same format as the multiplication instruction, F3. Here again, the only addressing mode supported for both operands is *data register direct*. Specification of the source and destination register parallels that of multiplication. The only difference is that the opcode for this instruction is %1000111. Therefore, the machine language instruction is as it is in Figure 4.14.

The field ddn$_3$ represents the *destination* register whose *longword* contents represents the *dividend*, whereas the latter sdn$_3$ field represents the *source* register whose *low-order word* contents represent the *divisor.*

Recall that in mathematics, the division of two integers produces a real result. For example, $5/2 = 2.5$. In SIM68, however, the binary integer division of a longword dividend A by a word divisor B produces an *integer* **quotient** Q of word size and an integer **remainder** R. These four variables are related via the equation

$$A = Q \cdot B + R.$$

The values of the quotient and the remainder are determined according to the following rules:

- The quotient Q is determined according to the following equation:

$$Q = \begin{cases} \left\lfloor \dfrac{A}{B} \right\rfloor & \text{if } (A/B) \geq 0 \\ \left\lceil \dfrac{A}{B} \right\rceil & \text{if } (A/B) < 0 \end{cases}$$

F3 | OP_4 | dDn_3 | OP_3 | sMS_6 |

| 1000 | dDn_3 | 111 | 000 | sDn_3 |

Figure 4.14 Bit assignments for division instruction. ddn_3 and sdn_3 represent addresses of destination and source data registers, respectively.

Recall that $\lceil x \rceil$ denotes the ceiling function that returns the smallest integer y that is greater than the real number x. In addition, $\lfloor x \rfloor$ denotes the floor function that returns the greatest integer y that does not exceed the real number x. For example, $\lfloor 4.95 \rfloor = 4$ while $\lceil -4.95 \rceil = -4$.

- The remainder is determined according to the equation

$$R = A - Q \cdot B$$

It is important to notice that unless the division is perfect,[8] the sign of the remainder is the *same* as that of the dividend.

The calculated remainder and quotient are stored in the *high-order* and *low-order* word of the destination register, respectively. According to our discussion in the previous section, the application program is capable of retrieving both of these components. Notice that in this case, as in the case of the multiplication instruction, the *entire* destination register is affected.

It is important to notice that if the divisor is equal to zero, then processor will notify the operating system, which in turn will suspend execution of the instruction. On the other hand, the hardware can detect an overflow[9] *during* the execution of the instruction. In the latter case the overflow bit will be set; the operands will not be affected; execution will resume with the next instruction. In all other cases, the hardware, at the completion of the execution of the instruction, will set or reset the value of the *carry, overflow, zero,* and *negative* flag bits of the *status register* according to the following rules:

- **Carry** bit is reset, whereas the extend bit retains its previous value.
- If the quotient generated is a negative number, the **negative** bit is *set;* otherwise, it is *reset.*
- If the quotient generated is equal to the number zero, the **zero** bit is *set* to reflect this fact; otherwise, it is *reset.*
- Finally, the **overflow** bit is *set* when an overflow occurs. Otherwise, this bit is *reset.*

In the following paragraphs some examples are given that will illustrate the concepts discussed earlier.

Example

Suppose that the instruction to be executed is the one at location $\$0000AA$; and the memory and register contents are as in Figure 4.15(a).

---

[8] In this case the remainder is equal to zero.

[9] An overflow occurs when the quotient is either greater than $2^{15} - 1$ or less than -2^{15} in which case it requires more than 16 bits to be specified.

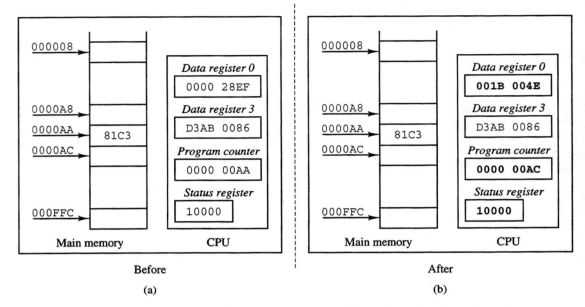

Figure 4.15 Memory and register contents immediately before (a) and after (b) execution of instruction at location $0000AA. All contents are in hex except that of condition code that are in binary.

After the instruction is fetched into the instruction register, the interpreter will interpret the instruction as follows:

Divide the longword in the destination register (d0) by the low-order word of the source register (d3). Store the quotient and the remainder of the division in the lower and upper words of the destination register, respectively.

Hence, the longword $000028EF will be divided by the word $0086. According to our earlier discussions, the operation will yield the positive quotient of word size $004E that is placed in the low-order word of the destination register, whereas the positive remainder $001B is placed and can be found in the high-order word of the destination register.

The reader should note that to access the remainder the high-order word of the destination register must be retrieved. The manner in which this can be accomplished will be discussed shortly.[10] Finally, another example is shown in Figure 4.16 which the reader is encouraged to verify.

Comparison.   The format for the comparison instruction is F2. Again, the only addressing mode supported for both operands is *data register direct*. The opcode for this instruction is %10110. Given also that the 2-bit code om_2 *should* be %01, we can conclude that the machine language instruction is as in Figure 4.17.

Execution of this instruction causes the word contained in the source register to be subtracted from the word in the destination register. The status bits are set as though the

---

[10] The curious reader could find the related discussion in the section on swapping later in this chapter.

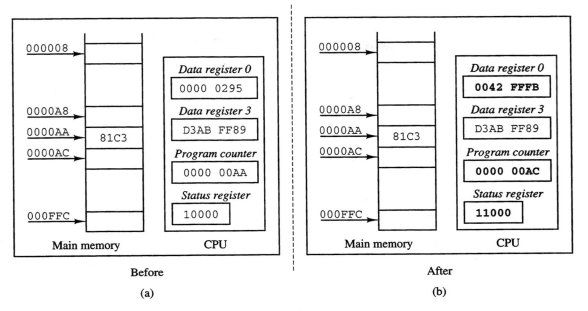

Figure 4.16   Memory and register contents immediately before (a) and after (b) execution of instruction at location $0000AA. All contents are in hex except that of condition code that are in binary.

instruction were a subtract operation.[11] The contents of *neither* of the involved registers are affected, however.[12]

On the completion of the instruction, the condition code is set according to the result of the operation. Specifically,

- **Extend** bit is not affected.
- If a borrow is generated as a result of the operation, the **carry** bit is *set.* Otherwise, it is *reset.*
- If the result of the operation is a negative number, the **negative** bit is *set;* otherwise, it is *reset.*
- If the result of the subtraction is equal to the number zero, the **zero** bit is *set* to reflect this fact; otherwise, it is *reset.*
- Finally, the **overflow** bit is *set* when an overflow occurred; otherwise, this bit is *reset.*

F2

OP_4	dDn_3	OP_1	om_2	sMS_6	
1011	dDn_3	0	01	000	sDn_3

Figure 4.17   Bit assignments for comparison instruction. ddn_3 and sdn_3 represent addresses of destination and source data registers, respectively.

---

[11] Refer to the appropriate section.

[12] The subtraction operation occurs in a working register.

Notice that if no overflow occurs and the negative bit is set, this is an indication that the contents of the destination are smaller than that of the source. At any rate, the following example illustrates the concepts discussed above.

Example

Suppose that the instruction to be executed next is the one at location $0000AA; and the memory and register contents are set as in Figure 4.18(a).

After the instruction is fetched into the instruction register, the interpreter will interpret the instruction as follows:

Subtract the low-order word of the source register (d0) from the low-order word of the destination register (d3) without affecting the contents of either register; set the condition code according to the nature of the result.

Hence, the word $28EF is subtracted from the word $08C1. The result is the word $DFD2. Because the result is a negative number, the negative bit is set, and the zero bit is reset. Furthermore, because the operation generated no overflow, the overflow bit is reset.

Swapping.   Earlier we indicated that in certain instances the high-order word of a data register must be accessed. When a data register is addressed, we have seen that the low-order word is the one that is accessed. The SIM68 instruction set, therefore, provides an instruction that *swaps* the low- and high-order words of the indicated *data* register. In other words, execution of this instruction causes the low-order word to become the high-order word and the high-order word to become the low-order word of the data register indicated.

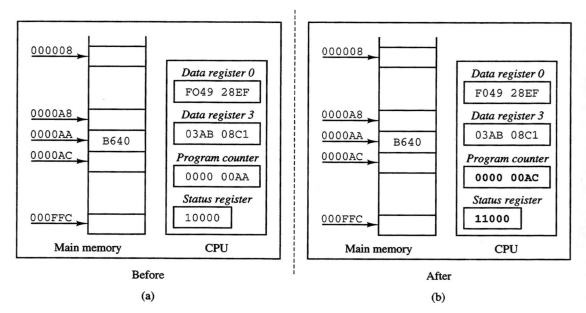

	Before				After	

Before (a)   After (b)

Figure 4.18   Memory and register contents immediately before (a) and after (b) execution of instruction at location $0000AA. All contents are in hex except that of condition code that are in binary.

The format of this instruction is F7 and its opcode is %0100100001000. Therefore, the machine language instruction is as in Figure 4.19.

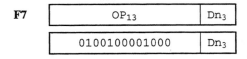

Figure 4.19 Bit assignments for the swap instruction. dn_3 represents address of data register whose words must be swapped.

Whenever such an instruction is executed, the result is assumed to be the *longword* signed integer that is obtained after the swap of the two words of the indicated data register. In addition, the hardware adjusts the value of the *carry, overflow, zero,* and *negative* flag bits of the *status register* accordingly. The rules that govern the setting and resetting of these bits are detailed as follows:

- Both the **carry** and **overflow** bits are *reset.*
- If the swap operation produced a longword that was a negative number, the **negative** bit is *set;* otherwise, it is *reset.*
- If the swap operation produced a longword that is equal to the number zero, the **zero** bit is *set* to reflect this fact; otherwise, it is *reset.*

In the following paragraphs some examples are presented that illustrate the concepts discussed earlier.

Example

Suppose that the instruction to be executed next is the one at location $0000AA; the memory and register contents are as in Figure 4.20(a).

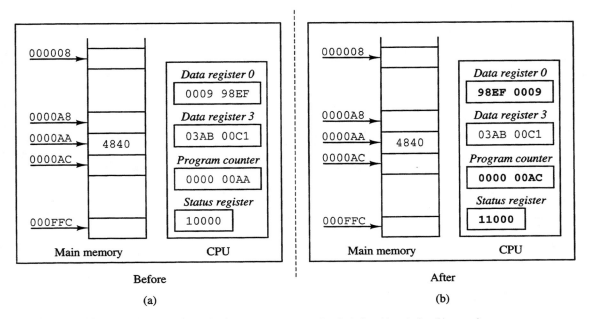

Before

(a)

After

(b)

Figure 4.20 Memory and register contents immediately before (a) and after (b) execution of instruction at location $0000AA. All contents are in hex except that of condition code that are in binary.

After the instruction is fetched into the instruction register, the interpreter will interpret the instruction as follows:

Swap the high and lower words of the indicated data register (d0).

The reader is encouraged to verify that the result of the execution of the instruction in location $0000AA in Figure 4.20 is as indicated.

Process of moving data around.   Because arithmetic on integer data occurs in the data registers and initially the data are stored in main memory, instructions are needed that will permit one to **load** the data into the designated register. Furthermore, given the limited number of registers, in several instances one would be forced to use a register without destroying the *intermediate data* that resides in the register. When this happens, the intermediate data should be **stored** in main memory, thereby freeing the register to participate in other computations. Finally, in many instances the application program must **transfer** the contents of one memory location to another or the contents of one register to another.

Summarizing, one has the need for *load* instructions that are memory to register transfers, for *store* instructions that are register-to-memory transfers, and for *copy* instructions that are memory-to-memory or register-to-register transfers. SIM68 supports all these transfers, via a machine language instruction that is referred to as a move instruction. The type (memory-to-memory, register-to-memory, memory-to-register) as well as the length of the move instruction depends solely on the specification of the source and destination modes. Anyway, the format of the first word of all the move instructions is F4, and the bit assignment is as Figure 4.21 demonstrates.

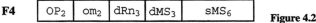

F4 $\quad$ | OP_2 | om_2 | dRn_3 | dMS_3 | sMS_6 | **Figure 4.21**   F4 format.

Moreover, as we will see shortly, this is the first instruction that we have encountered so far that will allow all three addressing modes for both operands and, therefore, all their possible combinations. Let's look a little bit more closely at this machine language instruction. First, we can observe that the opcode of this instruction is 2 bits wide, the bit code is %00, and the 2-bit field om_2 should be %11. The 6-bit field sMS_6 indicates the mode specification of the *source* operand, whereas the mode specification of the *destination* operand is indicated via the dMS_3 and the drn_3 fields. The former field indicates the *mode* of addressing of the destination, whereas the latter field indicates the corresponding *register* address.

Condition code.   The hardware, on execution of all move instructions, except those whose destination is an address register, adjusts the values of the *carry, overflow, zero,* and *negative* bits of the *status register* according to the following rules:

- Independent of the nature of the result of the operation, both the **carry** and **overflow** bits are *reset.*
- If the result of the operation is a negative number, the **negative** bit is *set;* otherwise, it is *reset.*
- If the result of the operation is equal to zero, the **zero** bit is *set* to reflect this fact; otherwise, it is *reset.*

Register-to-Register Transfers.   Here, the low-order word of the source register is moved into the destination register. Notice that there are four possible instructions generated as Figure 4.22 illustrates.

F4	OP_2	om_2	dRn_3	dmd_3	sMS_6	
	00	11	dDn_3	000	000	sDn_3
	00	11	dAn_3	001	000	sDn_3
	00	11	dDn_3	000	001	sAn_3
	00	11	dAn_3	001	001	sAn_3

Figure 4.22 Four possible register-to-register moves. The two 3-bit fields, ddn_3 and sdn_3, represent the address of a destination and source data register, respectively; the other two 3-bit fields, dan_3 and san_3, represent the address of a destination and source address register, respectively. Notice that the length of all these instructions is equal to one word.

At this point, we would like to warn the reader that when the destination is an *address* register, then the "moved" word is sign extended to a *longword*, and the latter longword is what is "moved" into the destination address register; otherwise, the word is moved into the lower-order word of the destination register. In the following paragraphs some examples are given that will illustrate the concepts discussed earlier.

Example

Imagine that the instruction that is to be executed is located at location $0000AA; and that the memory and register contents are as Figure 4.23(a) illustrates.

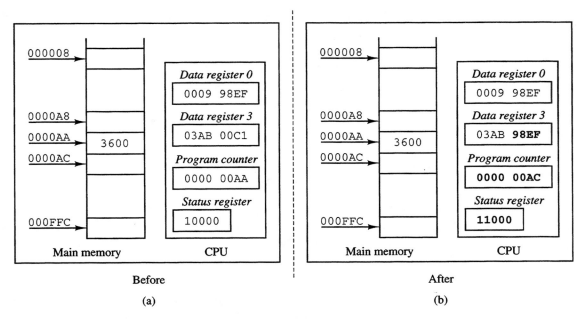

Figure 4.23 Memory and register contents immediately before (a) and after (b) execution of instruction at location $0000AA. All contents are in hex except that of condition code that are in binary.

After the instruction is fetched into the instruction register, the interpreter will interpret the instruction as follows:

Move the low-order word of the source register (D0) into the low-order word of the destination register (D3).

Therefore, the word $98EF is moved into the low-order word of data register 3 and the condition code is set to reflect the fact that the moved number is a negative number.

On the other hand, if the destination register is an address register as in the instruction in location $0000AA of Figure 4.24, the low-order word $90C1 of the source register d3 is accessed, and the word is sign extended to a longword, $FFFF90C1, which replaces the longword contents of the destination address register a3. Furthermore, notice that the condition code is not affected as a result of this move.

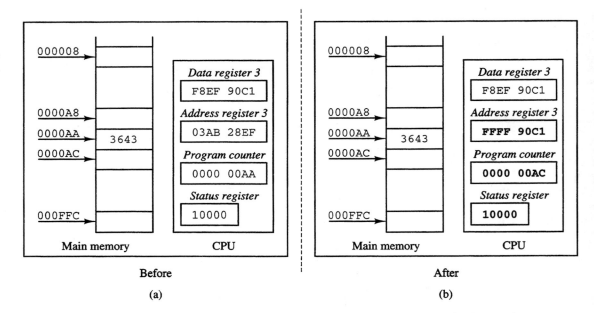

Before   After

(a)   (b)

Figure 4.24 Memory and register contents immediately before (a) and after (b) execution of instruction at location $0000AA. All contents are in hex except that of condition code that are in binary.

Register-to-Memory Transfers.   Execution of this instruction causes the low-order word of the source register to be moved into a specified memory location. The address of the memory location *should* be a word boundary. The mode of the destination operand should be 5, whereas that of the source operand should be either 0 or 1, depending on the nature of the source register. Moreover, this is the first case that we have encountered in which the length of an instruction is equal to two words; the second word of the instruction is the one that indicates the displacement value and whose role will be explained shortly. Notice that two possible instructions are generated in this case as Figure 4.25 illustrates.

Let's look a little bit more closely at these two instructions. In both cases, the destination is a memory location. Its **effective address** is calculated in the following fashion.

OP_2	om_2	dRn_3	dmd_3	sMS_6	
00	11	dAn_3	101	001	sAn_3	d-Displacement$_{16}$
00	11	dAn_3	101	000	sDn_3	d-Displacement$_{16}$

Figure 4.25 Two possible register-to-memory moves. Fields sAn_3 and sDn_3 specify address (of source) of address register and of data register, respectively. dAn_3 represents address of an address register that is employed to specify in with d_displacement$_{16}$ field effective address of conjunction destination. Notice that length of both instructions is equal to two words.

The 16-bit displacement indicated by the second word of the instruction is expanded to a *longword*. The longword so obtained is added to the contents of the indicated address register. The 24 low-order bits of the result represent the **effective address** of the destination.[13] The following examples should clarify these concepts.

Example

Consider the instant in which the memory and register contents are as in Figure 4.26(a). Therefore, the instruction that is to be executed next is the one at location $0000AA.

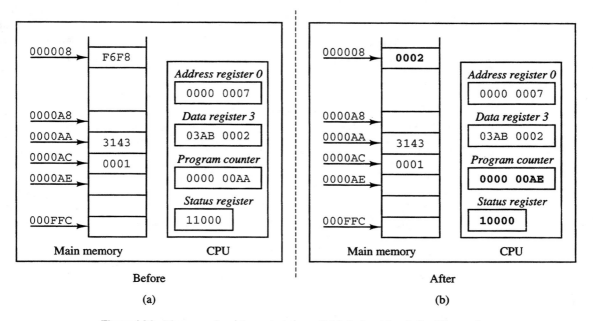

Before

(a)

After

(b)

Figure 4.26 Memory and register contents immediately before (a) and after (b) execution of instruction at location $0000AA. All contents are in hex except that of condition code that are in binary.

---

[13] All calculations occur in the working registers, and therefore the contents of the address register are not altered.

After the instruction is fetched into the instruction register, the interpreter will interpret the instruction as follows:

Move the low-order word of the source register (d3) into the memory location whose effective address, x, is computed as the sum of the contents of the specified address register 0 and the indicated displacement.

The steps involved for the calculation of the effective address x are outlined subsequently. The 16-bit displacement, $0001, specified in the instruction is accessed; and it is sign extended to the longword $00000001. The so-obtained longword is added to the longword contents of the indicated address register 0, $00000007, which yields $00000008. The 24 low-order bits of this longword is the effective address; in this case it is $000008. Finally, the low-order word, $0002, of the source data register is moved to the memory location $000008, and the condition code is set appropriately.

It is important to note here that the 16-bit displacement is interpreted as the 2's complement representation of an integer. This permits the displacement to be either negative or positive, that in turn permits one to move backward or forward in memory, respectively.

Memory-to-Register Transfers. In this scenario, the word at the source memory location (that should be a word boundary) is moved into the low-order word of the specified register. It should be clear that this case is analogous to the preceding one, in the sense that the mode of the destination should be either 0 or 1, whereas that of the source should be equal to 5. Again, as before, the displacement is indicated by the second word of the instruction, and the effective address is calculated as explained in the previous section. There are two possible instructions generated in this case as Figure 4.27 illustrates.

OP_2	om_2	dRn_3	dmd_3	sMS_6		
00	11	dAn_3	001	101	sAn_3	s-Displacement$_{16}$
00	11	dDn_3	000	101	sAn_3	s-Displacement$_{16}$

Figure 4.27 Two possible memory-to-register moves. Notice that the length of both instructions is equal to two words.

Example

Suppose that the instruction to be executed is at location $0000AA, and the memory and register contents are as in Figure 4.28(a). is fetched into the instruction register, the interpreter will interpret the instruction as follows:

Move word from memory address to the low-order word of the destination register (d3). The effective address is indicated by the 24 low-order bits of the sum of the contents of the indicated address register (address register 0) and the indicated displacement.

The steps involved for the calculation of the effective address x are outlined below. The 16-bit displacement, $0004, specified by the second word of the instruction is accessed, and it is sign-extended to the longword, $00000004. The longword so obtained is added to the longword contents of the indicated address register 0, $00000004, which yields $00000008. The 24 low-order bits of this longword is the effective address; in this case it is $000008. Finally, the word, $0000, at location $000008 is moved into the low-order word of the destination data register 3, and the condition code is set appropriately.

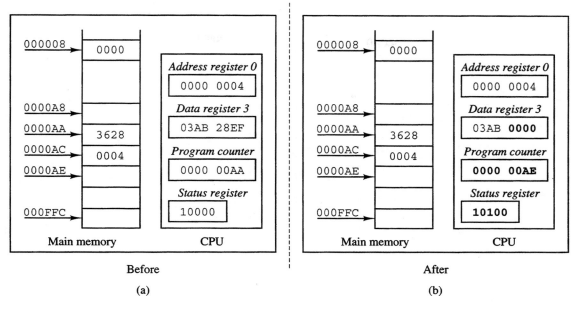

Figure 4.28   Memory and register contents immediately before (a) and after (b) execution of instruction at location $0000AA. All contents are in hex except that of condition code that are in binary.

Memory-to-Memory Transfers.   The last version of the move instructions permits one to move a word from one (source) memory location into another (destination) memory location.[14] The mode of both operands should be 5. This is the only instruction that we have examined so far that has a length equal to three words. The second word of the instruction (field $s\_Displacement_{16}$) indicates the displacement value associated with the source, whereas the third word of the instruction (field $d\_Displacement_{16}$) represents the displacement value associated with the destination. It should be clear that there is only one instruction generated in this case, as Figure 4.29 illustrates.

OP_2	om_2	dRn_3	dmd_3	sMS_6			
00	11	dAn_3	101	101	sAn_3	$s\text{-}Displacement_{16}$	$d\text{-}Displacement_{16}$

Figure 4.29   Machine language instruction that performs memory-to-memory move. Notice that length of this instruction is equal to three words.

Example

Suppose that the instruction that is to be executed is the one at location $0000AA, and the memory and register contents are as in Figure 4.30(a).

---

[14] Both locations *should* represent word boundaries.

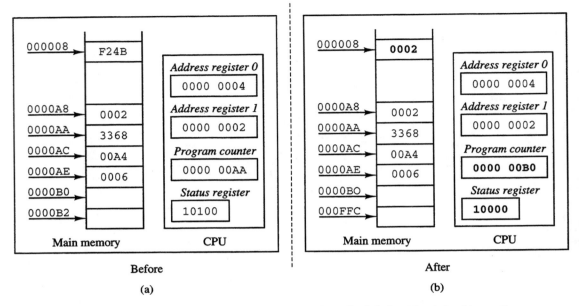

Figure 4.30 Memory and register contents immediately before (a) and after (b) execution of instruction at location $0000AA. All contents are in hex except that of condition code that are in binary.

After the instruction is fetched into the instruction register, the interpreter will interpret the instruction as follows:

Move the word from memory location x to memory location y.

Both effective addresses x and y are calculated similarly and in the same fashion as indicated in the previous section. In particular, x is equal to the 24 low-order bits of the sum of the long-word contained in address register 0, $00000004 and the sign extended to longword 16-bit s_Displacement $00A4; hence, x is equal to $0000A8. Similarly, y is equal to the 24 low-order bits of the sum of the longword contained in address register 1, $00000002 and the sign extended to longword 16-bit d_Displacement, $0006; therefore, y is equal to $000008. Hence, the word, $0002, from memory location with address $0000A8 is accessed and moved into memory location with address $000008, and the condition code is set appropriately.

Branching.   The format of the branching instructions is F5, and the bit assignments (of the first word) are shown in Figure 4.31. The 4-bit-wide opcode has the value %0110, and the length of this instruction is either one or two words. There are two classes of branching instructions: **conditional** and **unconditional**. Each one is examined in turn.

Figure 4.31 Bit assignments for branch instruction.

Unconditional Branches.   There is only one unconditional branching instruction; the field cond$_4$ is specified via the 4-bit code %0000. On execution of this instruction, the following events occur:

1. The byte-long displacement field that is assumed to represent a signed integer is examined. There are two distinct possibilities:
   a. The displacement represents a number other than zero. In this case, the instruction is referred to as a **short** branch (Fig. 4.32[a]), and the byte-displacement field is sign extended to a longword, which for simplicity will be referred to as the *intermediate* displacement.
   b. The displacement represents the number zero. In this case, the instruction is referred to as a **long** branch (Fig. 4.32[b]), and the *next* word is accessed, and its contents are assumed to represent the displacement. This word is sign extended to a longword, which for simplicity will be referred to as the *intermediate* displacement.

2. The *intermediate* displacement determined in the previous step is *added* to the *contents* of the program counter.[15] It is crucial to note that if the branch instruction were stored at address PC, the contents of the program counter (before the addition of the intermediate displacement) would be equal to PC + 2 because a word already has been accessed. Moreover, irrespective of the size of the instruction (i.e., short or long), the contents of the program counter after execution of this instruction will always be (PC + 2) + (intermediate displacement).

Note that execution of this instruction will cause the "next" instruction in line for execution to be the one indicated by the new contents of the program counter. The instruction specified by this address can be located several bytes away from the just executed branch instruction. The exact number of bytes depends, as mentioned earlier, on the specification of the displacement field. Therefore, a branching instruction can be used to *jump* forward or backward a certain number of memory locations. With a short branch, the length of the machine language instruction is equal to one, and the range of displacement, or **offset**, from the current location is between -2^7 and $2^7 - 1$ bytes. With the long branch version of the instruction, however, the range of the offset expands from -2^{15} to $2^{15} - 1$. At any rate, the bit assignment of the two versions of the machine language instruction is illustrated in Figure 4.32. In the following paragraphs some examples are given that will illustrate the concepts discussed earlier.

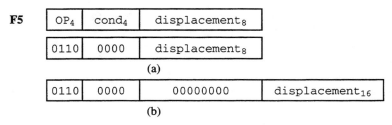

Figure 4.32   The short (a) and long (b) versions of the unconditional branch instruction.

---

[15] The expansion of a byte (or a word) to a longword is dictated by the remark made earlier that only longword operations are permitted in the program counter register.

Example

Consider the memory and register snapshot in Figure 4.33(a) at the instant in which the execution of a certain instruction has been completed. The contents of the location counter indicate that the instruction that is to be executed is the one at memory location $0000AA.

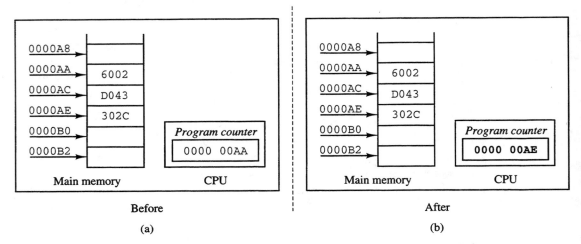

Before   After

(a)   (b)

Figure 4.33   Memory and register contents immediately before (a) and after (b) execution of instruction at location $0000AA. All contents are in hex.

After the instruction is fetched into the instruction register the interpreter will interpret the instruction as follows:

Set the contents of the location counter to the sum of its current contents and of the indicated displacement.

Specifically, after the first word is decoded, the program counter contains $0000000AC; the second byte of the instruction indicates that this is a short branch and that the displacement is equal to $0002. Hence, the program counter will be loaded with

$$\$0000000AC + \$00000002 = \$0000000AE$$

and the instruction to be executed, thereafter, will be the one at the latter location. On the other hand, examination of the first byte of the instruction at location $0000AA of Figure 4.34 indicates an unconditional branch; moreover, the second byte indicates a long branch, because its contents indicate a value of zero. Hence, the displacement is indicated by the second word of this instruction, that is, the word at location $0000AC. Therefore, the program counter is loaded with

$$\$0000000AC + \$FFFFFFFA = \$0000000A6$$

Conditional Branches.   The program will *always* make the indicated branch when using the unconditional branch instruction. In certain instances, one would need the program to branch only if a certain condition were met; otherwise, the program should continue with the next instruction. In this case, one of the *three* conditional branching instructions provided by SIM68 could be used. These instructions are discussed in the following paragraphs.

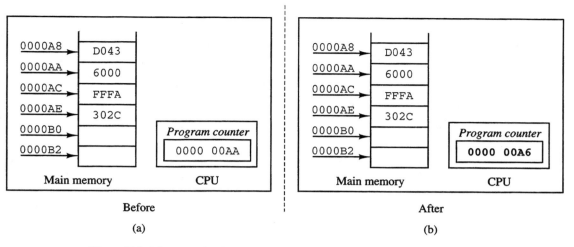

Figure 4.34   Memory and register contents immediately before (a) and after (b) execution of instruction at location $0000AA. All contents are in hex.

Branch on equal.   The opcode of this instruction is the same as that of the unconditional branch instruction. The value of the 4-bit-wide field $cond_4$ is equal to %0111. Execution of this instruction, as well as of all the conditional branch instructions, causes an examination of the status register. If the condition that is conveyed by the $cond_4$ field is met, the program branches to an address whose calculation is exactly the same as that of the unconditional branch instruction; otherwise, the next instruction is executed.

Specifically, under this instruction a branch is taken if, and only if, the value of the zero (Z) bit of the condition code register is equal to one. The bit assignment for this instruction is illustrated in Figure 4.35.

F5

OP_4	$cond_4$	$displacement_8$	
0110	0111	$displacement_8$	
0110	0111	00000000	$displacement_{16}$

Figure 4.35   The short and long versions of branch on equal instruction.

Example

Consider the memory and register snapshot in Figure 4.36(a) at the instant in which the execution of a certain instruction has been completed. The contents of the location counter will indicate that the instruction to be executed is the one at memory location $0000AA.

After the instruction is fetched into the instruction register, the interpreter will interpret the instruction as follows:

Since the condition is met, adjust the contents of the location counter.

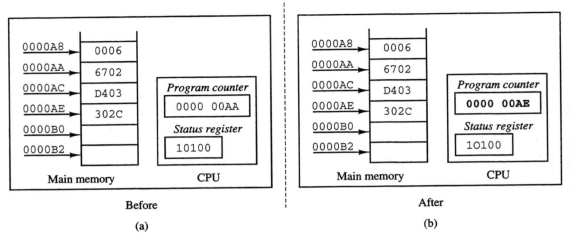

Figure 4.36 Memory and register contents immediately before (a) and after (b) execution of instruction at location $0000AA. All contents are in hex except that of condition code that are in binary.

Branch on greater than. This instruction is similar to the one just presented. The only difference between the previous instruction and this one is that its $cond_4$ field is defined to be %1110 and that a branch is taken in only two cases. Namely, the branch is taken when the Z bit is reset, and either both the N and V bits are set, or both are reset.

We mention here that the designers assumed that a conditional branch instruction as the one that we discuss here would be issued after some kind of operation such as comparison or subtraction has been performed. Therefore, the test just described involving the overflow and negative bits allows for correct comparison even when the subtraction (or comparison) gives an out-of-range result. The bit assignment of this instruction is shown in Figure 4.37.

0110	1110	displacement$_8$

Figure 4.37 Bit assignments of first word of branch on greater than instruction.

Branch on less than. The only difference between this branch instruction and the other two branching instructions presented earlier is that its $cond_4$ field is defined as %1101 and, therefore, a branch is taken only if either the N-bit is set *and* the V bit is reset or the N bit is reset *and* the V bit is set. The bit assignment of this instruction is shown in Figure 4.38.

0110	1101	displacement$_8$

Figure 4.38 Bit assignments of first word of branch on less than instruction.

Stopping and Dumping. The opcode for this instruction is %010011100100 and its format is F6. The 4-bit address V_4 *should* be %0000. Therefore, the machine language instruction is as illustrated in Figure 4.39.

F6	OP$_{12}$	V$_4$
	010011100100	0000

Figure 4.39 Bit assignments for four instructions of type F6 supported by SIM68.

This machine language instruction[16] represents *four* distinct instructions (!); each of these instructions is determined by the contents of the low-order word of data register 0 and is examined individually in the following sections.

Stop.   If the contents of the low-order word of data register 0 represent the integer 3, then this designates a stop instruction. In other words, execution of the program is terminated.

Register and Memory Dumps.   Debugging a program requires inspection of the intermediately computed values. SIM68 provides such a facility that permits the user to inspect, at the time of his or her choosing, the contents of the registers, of main memory, or both. Whichever contents are requested will be conveyed to the processor via the contents of data register 0. Each of these three cases is discussed subsequently.

First, execution of this instruction *while* the contents of the low order word of data register 0 represent the signed integer 2 causes the current contents of all registers to be output (in hex). This operation is referred to as a register dump. Table 4.3 provides an example of a register dump. Notice that three pieces of information are conveyed to the user via a register dump.

TABLE 4.3   Example of a register dump

```
USER DUMP at      0000 0022

REGISTER DUMP

d0    D6AB 0002      a0    0000 0014
d1    4932 0037      a1    21D5 DD36
d2    3048 0000      a2    5AA0 D0A7
d3    0B38 0001      a3    5411 5E8B

STATUS: 0000000000000000
```

Specifically, examination of Table 4.3 indicates that the memory location of the instruction that caused this *particular* dump is provided via the

```
             USER DUMP at      0000 0022
```

statement; in this example the dump was caused by the instance of the instruction at memory location $0000 0022. Moreover, the longword contents of each of the four data registers labeled d0 through d3 (as well as of each of the four address registers labeled a0 through a3) are displayed alongside them (in hex). Furthermore, the contents of the status register, which is labeled as STATUS, are displayed in binary.

Second, execution of this instruction while the contents of the low-order word of data register 0 represent the signed integer 1 causes the current contents of main memory to be output. That is referred to as a memory dump. As Table 4.4 illustrates, the dump displays the memory location of the instruction that caused this dump as well as the memory locations (left column) alongside their longword (right column) contents.

---

[16] Actually this is a software trap instruction. Traps are discussed in Chapter 9.

TABLE 4.4 Example of a memory dump

USER DUMP at	0000 0026

MEMORY DUMP

000000-	9040 3040
000004-	3428 0028
000008-	3628 002A
00000C-	3228 002C
000010-	D041 D0C3
000014-	D0C3 9443
000018-	6EF2 3200
00001C-	9040 D043
000020-	D043 4E40
000024-	9043 4E40
000028-	000A 0001
00002C-	000A 0009
000030-	0008 0007
000034-	0006 0005
000038-	0004 0003
00003C-	0002 0001
000040-	514D 8BFA

It is worth noting that one can see the instructions in the memory dump (locations $000022 and $000026) that caused the register and memory dumps of Tables 4.3 and 4.4, respectively.

Finally, one can request a register and a memory dump to be provided at the same time by executing this instruction while the contents of the low-order word of data register 0 represent the integer 0.

4.3.3 Instruction Set Summary

The instructions supported by SIM68, together with their associated bit assignments, are presented in Figure 4.40. We should emphasize that if the displacement$_8$ field of any branch instruction represents the decimal signed integer zero, the length of the instruction should be equal to two words, and the second word will represent the 16-bit displacement. Moreover, whether an instruction is interpreted as a stop instruction or a dump instruction depends entirely on the contents of data register 0 at the instant the instruction is executed.

4.3.4 Coding and Executing SIM68 Machine Language Programs

This section describes the procedure required to code and execute a SIM68 machine language program. The three basic steps required are the following:

1. Code the SIM68 machine language program.
2. Generate the object module.

Add	1101	dDn_3	001000	sDn_3
	1101	dAn_3	011000	sDn_3

Subtract	1001	dDn_3	001000	sDn_3

Multiply	1100	dDn_3	111000	sDn_3

Divide	1000	dDn_3	111000	sDn_3

Compare	1011	dDn_3	001000	sDn_3

Swap	0100100001000	dDn_3

Move (register to register)

0011	dDn_3	000000	sDn_3
0011	dAn_3	001000	sDn_3
0011	dDn_3	000001	sAn_3
0011	dAn_3	001001	sAn_3

Move (register to memory)

0011	An_3	101001	sAn_3
$Displacement_{16}$			

0011	An_3	101000	sDn_3
$Displacement_{16}$			

Move (memory to register)

0011	dAn_3	001101	sAn_3
$Displacement_{16}$			

0011	dDn_3	000101	An_3
$Displacement_{16}$			

Move (memory to memory)

0011	An_3	101101	An_3
$s\text{-}Displacement_{16}$			
$d\text{-}Displacement_{16}$			

Branch (unconditional)	01100000	$Displacement_8$
Branch on equal	01100111	$Displacement_8$
Branch on greater	01101110	$Displacement_8$
Branch on less	01101101	$Displacement_8$

Stop, dump	010011100100	0000

Figure 4.40   SIM68's instruction set.

3. Use the object module as the input file to the loader so that the object code can be loaded and run.

We will examine all these concepts one at a time in the following paragraphs.

Coding a SIM68 machine language program. The first decision that one should make is where should the program be loaded in main memory. In other words, what will be the location in memory where the first instruction will be loaded? This address is known as the **loading origin** of the program.

As soon as this decision is made and given our earlier discussions, it should be clear that the next instruction that will be executed will be the one that follows the first instruction in memory.[17] Therefore, it is important to **separate** the data from the instructions.[18] There are several different ways to "separate" the instruction and data areas, and Figure 4.41 illustrates two of these methods.

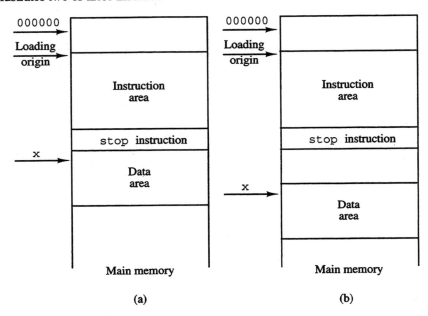

Figure 4.41   Instruction and data areas.

In Figure 4.41(a) the data area is adjacent to the instruction area, whereas in Figure 4.41(b) it is not. Irrespective of the technique employed, however, note first that the *last* instruction in the instruction area **must** be the `stop` instruction,[19] and second that the addresses x and loading origin should represent word boundaries. If the `stop` instruction is omitted, the program will proceed to execute the "instruction" at the next location. In other words, the data at location x in Figure 4.41(a) will be interpreted as an instruction (!), and the result will be disastrous. Finally, if the address x does not represent a word boundary,[20] execution will be suspended when the first memory (register) to register (memory) `move` instruction is used.

---

[17] Assuming that the first instruction is not a branch instruction.

[18] So data would not be erroneously interpreted as instructions.

[19] Strictly speaking the `stop` instruction *should* be the last instruction to be executed.

[20] Recall that all data in SIM68 must be aligned at word boundaries. As a matter of fact, instructions should be too. Given that the length of any instruction is an integral multiple of a word, however, this alignment is assured unless trivial mistakes are made.

SIM68 machine language code.   In this section we will present the general method of coding a SIM68 machine language program. To illustrate this technique, we will write (code) a program that performs a very simple task. This program will add two given signed integers X and Y and will store the result at location Z. In addition, we will present two versions of this program. In version I, we will assume the format of Figure 4.41(a) and the loading origin at $000000. In version II, we will assume the technique of Figure 4.41(b) with the loading origin at $000400 and the data area at location $000520.

Version I.   Considering our earlier assumptions, the machine language program will have the format illustrated in Figure 4.42.

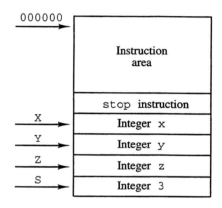

Figure 4.42   SIM68 machine language program format.

Now we are ready to give the pseudocode required to perform this task. The add instruction provided by the SIM68 requires both operands to be in data registers; therefore, both integers should be loaded from memory locations X and Y into the two data registers 0 and 1, respectively; the contents of those two registers must be added, and the result of the addition must be stored in memory location Z. The pseudocode, using the logic developed earlier, is given in Table 4.5.

TABLE 4.5

```
[1]. load  first integer from memory location X to data register 0.
[2]. load  second integer from memory location Y to data register 1.
[3]. add   contents of data register 1 to contents of data register 0.
[4]. store result (contained in data register 0) to memory location Z.
[5]. load  the integer 3 to data register 0.
[6]. stop
```

The next step is to **map** the pseudocode given earlier to a set of SIM68 machine language instructions. According to our earlier discussions, the pseudoinstruction of step 1 of Table 4.5 should be mapped to a memory to register move instruction. According to Figure 4.40, we can see that dr_3 should be %000, whereas any of the address registers can be selected to serve as a_3. Let's set a_3 equal to %000. First and foremost we need to set the contents of our indirect address register to represent the integer zero. To accomplish this task, we will need to issue *two* instructions. Namely, we will issue a subtract instruction that will cause the lower-order word of the data register to represent the integer 0; then, we will issue a move instruction that will cause the low-order word of the data register 1 to be copied (with the appropriate propagation of its sign bit) into the address register 0. These two instructions of the program are illustrated in Table 4.6(a).

TABLE 4.6(a)   Notice that locations are given in hex, whereas their contents are in binary

location	code
000000	1001 001 001000 001
000002	0011 000 001000 001

Because the address register contains $000000, the effective address that should be calculated (X) should be equal to the one indicated by the $displacement_{16}$ field. At this point, however, we *do not* know the effective address X. The reason is that this location *depends* entirely on the number and length of the instructions in the instruction area. Therefore, we should *wait* before the contents of the displacement field are indicated. So far, with the pencil-and-paper approach, we have partially coded three of the required instructions as is illustrated in Table 4.6(b).

TABLE 4.6(b)

location	code	
000000	1001 001 001000 001	
000002	0011 000 001000 001	
000004	0011 000 000101 000 ??????????????	(X)

Because the length of the last coded instruction is equal to two words, the contents of the location counter should be equal to $000004 + $000004 = $0000008. Furthermore, the pseudoinstruction of step 2 is again a move instruction; therefore, the machine language for this instruction is the same as the one that we just previously coded with two exceptions. First, the destination register should now be data register 1; second, the displacement field should represent the effective address Y. For the same reasons as before, we do not know yet the address Y; therefore, we will delay the bit assignment in the displacement field as is shown in Table 4.6(c).

TABLE 4.6(c)

location	code	
000000	1001 001 001000 001	
000002	0011 000 001000 001	
000004	0011 000 000101 000 ??????????????	(X)
000008	0011 001 000101 000 ??????????????	(Y)

The location counter now contains $00000C and the coding of the add instruction required in step 3 is straightforward. Hence, we have derived the code that appears in Table 4.6(d).

TABLE 4.6(d)

location	code	
000000	1001 001 001000 001	
000002	0011 000 001000 001	
000004	0011 000 000101 000 ?????????????????	(X)
000008	0011 001 000101 000 ?????????????????	(Y)
00000C	1101 000 001000 001	

The contents of the location counter are updated to $00000E, and the next pseudo-instruction in step 4 is a register to memory move instruction. Again, because the effective address Z is not known at this time, we will postpone the bit assignment in the displacement field of this instruction. Moreover, because the coding of the pseudoinstruction of step 4 parallels that of steps 2 and 3 and given that the coding of the stop instruction is straightforward, we will proceed to code all these pseudoinstructions. Therefore, we obtain the code that is illustrated in Table 4.6(e).

TABLE 4.6(e)

location	code	
000000	1001 001 001000 001	
000002	0011 000 001000 001	
000004	0011 000 000101 000 ?????????????????	(X)
000008	0011 001 000101 000 ?????????????????	(Y)
00000C	1101 000 001000 001	
00000E	0011 000 101000 000 ?????????????????	(Z)
000012	0011 000 000101 000 ?????????????????	(S)
000016	0100111001000000	

At this point, the program counterpoints to (contains) $000018; therefore, we can conclude that X = $000018, Y = $00001A, Z = $00001C, and S = $00001E. Hence, we will perform a second **pass** over the code derived in Table 4.6(e). We set the displacement fields unassigned during the first pass in such a way so that they reflect the appropriate effective addresses. Finally, if we assume that x = 11 and y = −1, the complete code is given in Table 4.7.

We remark that the 16-bit assignment at location $00001C corresponding to operand Z is required to allocate storage space that is eventually employed to store the result. The value reflected from its initial contents is irrelevant, because these contents will be "written over" by the result.

TABLE 4.7 Object code for Version I; Notice that the locations are given in hex, whereas their contents are in binary

```
location                          code
--------        -------------------------------------
000000          1001 001 001000 001
000002          0011 000 001000 001
000004          0011 000 000101 000 0000000000011000
000008          0011 001 000101 000 0000000000011010
00000C          1101 000 001000 001
00000E          0011 000 101000 000 0000000000011100
000012          0011 000 000101 000 0000000000011110
000016          0100111001000000
000018          0000000000001011
00001A          1111111111111111
00001C          0000000000000000
00001E          0000000000000011
```

We can therefore summarize the strategy for coding a SIM68 machine language program as follows:

1. Derive a pseudoalgorithm, as in Table 4.5, that performs the task required.
2. Map each statement of the pseudocode to machine language instruction(s). In some instances the entire instruction can be coded such as the instruction that performs the function of step 3. In other instances, when a required piece of information is needed, but is not available at this time, we defer the bit assignments for later. This way all the required instructions can be coded, and the result of the **first pass** is obtained, which is illustrated in Table 4.6(e). After this pass is completed, a second pass is performed over the file of Table 4.6(e), and the information that had not been filled in during the first pass is filled in now. The result of the **second pass** is illustrated in Table 4.7.

Version II.   As is clear, the algorithm presented in Table 4.5 is still valid. The only difference is that the addresses X, Y, Z, and S are independent of the size of the instruction area; therefore, the values that they represent can be placed in the displacement of the field of the corresponding instruction during the first pass. The reader is encouraged to verify that the machine language code for this case will be as illustrated in Table 4.8.

Object module and loader.   Now we know that for our program to be executed, the program should be loaded into main memory and run. Both of these tasks are the function of a software component known as the **loader**. A loader expects a file as input, the **object module**, which contains the following:

1. The machine language program that has been coded.
2. Directions (to the loader) about where the program should be loaded (in memory) as well as from which location the execution of the program should begin.

TABLE 4.8 Object code for Version II; Notice that locations as well as their contents are given in hex

location	code
000400	9241
000402	3041
000404	3028 0520
000408	3228 0522
00040C	D041
00040E	3140 0524
000412	3028 0526
000416	4E40
000520	000B
000522	FFFF
000524	0000
000526	0003

The object module is a collection of records, the **object records**,[21] each of which consists of three fields as illustrated in Figure 4.43. The first field is a 24-bit field referred to as the *location*. The second field, known as the *byte count*, is a 4-bit field, and the third field is a 15-byte field referred to as the *object code* field.

Location	Byte count	Object Code

Figure 4.43 Object record.

The location field indicates where the loader must store the very first byte that appears in the object code field of this record; in addition, the loader will store the remaining bytes of the object code field consecutively in main memory. The purpose of the byte count field is to indicate the total number of bytes in the object code field of this object record. As an example, a possible object module for the machine language program of Table 4.7 is given in Table 4.9.

TABLE 4.9 Object module for code in Table 4.7

| 000000 | E | 92413041302800183228001
6D041 |
|--------|---|--------------------------|
| 00000E | E | 3140001C3028001E4E40000BFFFF |
| 00001C | 4 | 00000003 |

Finally, an object module for the version II program is given in Table 4.10.

TABLE 4.10 Object module for code in Table 4.8

| 000400 | E | 92413041302805203228052
2D041 |
|--------|---|--------------------------|
| 00040E | A | 31400524302805264E40 |
| 000520 | 8 | 000BFFFF00000003 |

---

[21] The object records for the SIM68 loader are presented here.

Second example.   Assume that we would like to write a program that calculates the sum of ten given signed integers. For simplicity, assume that the magnitude of the given integers is sufficiently small so that the possibility of overflow can be excluded. Moreover, assume that the result is to remain in data register 1, that the loading origin is at $000000, and that the data area is adjacent to the instruction area. An algorithm that performs this task is given in Table 4.11.

TABLE 4.11

```
[1].    sum ←0;
[2].    number_of_integers ← 10;
[3].    sum ← sum + "next"_integer;
[4].    number_of_integers ← number_of_integers-1;
[5].    if (number_of_integers>0) go to step [3];
[6].    exit;
```

Let's see in detail how the machine language program is constructed. First, notice that steps 1 and 2 are very simple; namely, we dedicate data register 0 to accumulate the sum and data register 2 to "hold" the number of integers. The next step 3 is the one that needs some attention. We need to establish how the "next" integer will be determined. In terms of machine language, the question is how the address of the "next" integer can be computed. To answer this question, notice that if we store these ten integers *consecutively* in main memory, the address of the "next" integer is larger by two than the address of its predecessor. Consequently, if we know the address of the *first* integer of the set, we can find the address of the *second* by adding two to it, and so on. It is only now that one can appreciate the convenience provided to the programmer by addressing mode 5. Specifically, when the effective address of the first integer is specified, we will use address register 0 as the register that will contain the indirect address. Initially, the contents of this register is set to 0, and the displacement field of the move instruction is set to reflect the effective address of the first integer of this set. Notice that if we add 2 to the contents of that address register, the new effective address would be 2 larger than the previous; therefore, it will point to the "next" integer.

With the above discussion in mind the pseudocode of Table 4.11 can be rewritten (with some necessary housekeeping) as in Table 4.12.

TABLE 4.12

```
[1].    Zero out d0   (so sum=0).
[2].    Move d0 into a0 (so the a0=0).
[3].    Move into d2 the number_of_integers.
[4].    Move increment/decrement into d3   (so d3=1).
[5].    Move "next"_integer into d1.
[6].    Add d1 to d0 (so sum is accumulated in d0).
[7].    Increment a0 by the contents of d3 twice.
[8].    Decrement d2 by the contents of d3 (so the number_of_integers
        is reduced by one).
[9].    If the contents of d2 is not equal to zero (so there are more
        numbers to add) go to 5.
```

[10]. Move RESULT from d0 into d1.
[11]. Zero out d0.
[12]. Increment d0 by the contents of d3 twice (so a register dump
      can be issued).
[13]. Dump registers.
[14]. Increment d0 by the contents of d3 (so a stop instruction may
      be issued).
[15]. Stop.

The complete SIM68 code is given in Table 4.13.

TABLE 4.13

000000	1001 000 001000 000	; Zero out d0
000002	0011 000 001000 000	; Move d0 into a0
000004	0011 010 000101 000 0000000000101000	; Move into d2 # of ints to add
000008	0011 011 000101 000 0000000000101010	; Move inc/dec ctr into d3
00000C	0011 001 000101 000 0000000000101100	; LOOP: Move next int into d1
000010	1101 000 001000 001	; Add integer to the current sum
000012	1101 000 011000 011	; Increment a0
000014	1101 000 011000 011	; Increment a0
000016	1001 010 001000 011	; Decrement number counter (d2)
000018	0110 1110 11110010	; BGT LOOP
00001A	0011 001 000000 000	; Move RESULT into d1
00001C	1001 000 001000 000	; Zero out d0
00001E	1101 000 001000 011	; increment d0
000020	1101 000 001000 011	; increment d0
000022	010011100100 0000	; Trap #2 (dump registers)
000024	1101 000 001000 011	; increment d0
000026	010011100100 0000	; Trap #3 (exit)
000028	0000 0000 0000 1010	; NUMBER OF INTEGERS (10)
00002A	0000 0000 0000 0001	; INCREMENT AMOUNT (1)
00002C	0000 0000 0000 1010	; INTEGER #1
00002E	0000 0000 0000 1001	; INTEGER #2
000030	0000 0000 0000 1000	; INTEGER #3
000032	0000 0000 0000 0111	; INTEGER #4
000034	0000 0000 0000 0110	; INTEGER #5
000036	0000 0000 0000 0101	; INTEGER #6
000038	0000 0000 0000 0100	; INTEGER #7
00003A	0000 0000 0000 0011	; INTEGER #8
00003C	0000 0000 0000 0010	; INTEGER #9
00003E	0000 0000 0000 0001	; INTEGER #10

4.4 SIM68 ASSEMBLY LANGUAGE

Already the reader should have noticed that the task of coding a machine language program is quite cumbersome. Therefore, a tool is needed that will permit a simpler coding of an application program. Hence, a new language is developed that will facilitate this type of coding. For example, we have seen that to add the contents of data register 0 to the contents of data register 1, the following machine language instruction must be coded.

1	1	0	1	0	0	1	0	0	1	0	0	0	0	0	0

A much simpler approach would be to code the following.

```
add        d0,d1
```

and let a program, called the **assembler,** translate the preceding instruction and **generate** the desired code. Closer examination of the preceding assembly language instruction indicates that this instruction consists of two fields. The first field (add) is referred to as the **opcode** field, whereas the second field (d0, d1) is referred to as the **operand** field. The former field contains the **mnemonic** for the opcode for this instruction, whereas the latter field contains the **operands.** Notice that the operand field has two operands (as was expected because the add instruction is a two-operand instruction); the first indicates the data register 0, whereas the second indicates the data register 1. In the case of a two-operand instruction, the assembler[22] always assumes that the first operand (d0) is the **source** and that the second operand (d1) is the **destination.** One should now wonder how the address specification is conveyed to the assembler. Well, the address specification is implied by the syntax that is employed in defining the operands. For example, the assembler assumes a *data register direct* addressing whenever a register is listed as dn, whereas it assumes a *address register direct* whenever a register is specified via an.[23]

4.4.1 Basic Concepts of an Assembler

Let's discuss the assembler in a little more depth. As we mentioned earlier, the assembler is a program that accepts an assembly language program as input. The latter is referred to as the **source module.** The assembler generates two *files,* a **listing** and an **object module.** The former file contains the source module *together* with the machine language code that the assembler generates along with some other generated information that is helpful to the programmer for debugging purposes. The latter file contains the machine language code that eventually will be **executed (run)** as was discussed earlier. Figure 4.44 illustrates these concepts.

The source module is illustrated in Figure 4.45; Figure 4.46 illustrates the object module produced by the assembler; and Figure 4.47 shows the listing generated by the assembler over the source module of Figure 4.45.

4.4.2 Source Module

Let's examine the format of a source module more closely. Each line of the source module contains an **assembly language** statement. These statements can be classified either as

---

[22] Other assemblers do not follow this convention.

[23] *n* is a decimal integer representing the appropriate register address.

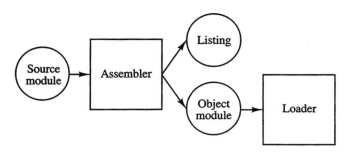

Figure 4.44

```
; This is a line comment
          org     $000000
_main     sub     d1,d1
          movea   d1,a0
          move    24(a0),d0          ; This is
          move    26(a0),d1          ; a comment.
          add     d1,d0             ; All text
          move    d0,28(a0)         ; after a
          move    30(a0),d0         ; semicolon
          trap    #0                ; is ignored
x         dc      11                ; by the
          dc      -1                ; assembler.
          ds      1
          dc      3
          end
```

Figure 4.45   Source module.

```
000000 E 924130413028001832280016D041
00000E E 3140001C3028001E4E40000BFFFF
00001C 2 0003
```

Figure 4.46   Object module generated by assembler over source module shown in Figure 4.45.

LOCATION	OBJECT CODE	STMT	SOURCE CODE
000000		1	; This is a line comment
000000		2	org $000000
000000	9241	3	_main sub d1,d1
000002	3041	4	movea d1,a0
000004	3028 0018	5	move 24(a0),d0 ; This is
000008	3228 001A	6	move 26(a0),d1 ; a comment.
00000C	D041	7	add d1,d0 ; All text
00000E	3140 001C	8	move d0,28(a0) ; after a
000012	3028 001E	9	move 30(a0),d0 ; semicolon
000016	4E40	10	trap #0 ; is ignored
000018	000B	11	x dc 11 ; by the
00001A	FFFF	12	dc -1 ; assembler.
00001C		13	ds 1
00001E	0003	14	dc 3
		15	end

Figure 4.47   Listing generated by assembler over the source module of Figure 4.45.

assembly language **directives** or as assembly language **instructions**. Their difference lies in the fact that directives do not generate machine language instructions; they are simply requests to the assembler to perform certain tasks, whereas assembly language instructions generate machine language instructions. In Figure 4.47 one can see that statements numbered 2 and 11 through 15 represent directives, whereas all other statements represent instructions. The SIM68 assembly language provides us with four directives. Before we discuss directives, notice that the source module can be considered conceptually as consisting of two parts. The first part constitutes the **data area** defined by statements 11 through 14, and the second part constitutes the **instruction area** defined by statements 3 through 10.

Each assembly language statement consists of a single line of input or some part thereof, and its format is given subsequently.

Name_Field	Opcode_Field	Operand_Field	Comment_Field
[symbol]	mnemonic	operands	[; text]

A brief explanation of these fields follows.

Name_field   Recall that in the derivation of the machine language program code we were forced via the pencil-and-paper approach to calculate both addresses of all instructions, as well as the value of the displacement, when we were to access a memory location. From now on, these tasks become a function of the assembler. Specifically, notice the presence of the **symbols** _main and x in the Name_Field of statements number 3 and 11, respectively. The assembler will assign each its corresponding memory address, $000000 and $000018, respectively (in this case). Hence, symbols represent addresses, or equivalently a symbol is a constant whose value is the address that it represents.

```
LOCATION   OBJECT  CODE   STMT    SOURCE           CODE
000000                     1      ; This is a line comment
000000                     2              org   $000000
000000     9241            3      _main    sub   d1,d1
000002     3041            4               movea d1,a0
000004     3028  0018      5               move  x(a0),d0    ; This is
000008     3228  001A      6               move  x+2(a0),d1  ; a comment.
00000C     D041            7               add   d1,d0       ; All text
00000E     3140  001C      8               move  d0,x+4(a0)  ; after a
000012     3028  001E      9               move  x+6(a0),d0  ; semicolon
000016     4E40           10               trap  #0          ; is ignored
000018     000B           11      x        dc    11          ; by the
00001A     FFFF           12               dc    -1          ; assembler.
00001C                    13               ds    1
00001E     0003           14               dc    3
                          15               end
```

Figure 4.48   Listing generated by the assembler over new source module. Notice that object code generated is identical to that of Figure 4.47.

The reader who compares the source listings of Figures 4.47 and 4.48 should notice that the object code generated by the assembler is identical despite the fact that the source modules seem different. Notice that in the former case we had calculated the displacement (statements 5, 6, 8, and 9) via the pencil-and-paper approach. In the latter case, the assembler performs this task for us. Namely, the assembler assigns to the symbol X the value $000018 and then it replaces every occurrence of that symbol in the displacement field with this value. From now on, symbols can be used freely.

The assembler recognizes that it has encountered a symbol by finding either an alphabetical character or an underscore (_) in column 1 of the input line. In particular, a valid symbol is a character string between 1 and 11 characters in length, where the first character must be an alphabetical character or the underscore (_) character, and any subsequent character must be either an alphanumeric character or an underscore (_). Finally, symbols are case sensitive. For example,

HERE, NUMBER1, NUMBER2_, _A_1, here, Number1,

are valid symbols,[24] whereas

```
#HERE,  1A,  SYMBOLTOOLONG,  A+B,
```

are not.

Although symbols may be used freely, the *same* symbol may never be in the Name_Field of two statements. The reason is that each symbol represents a memory address; therefore, the assembler just cannot assign two distinct addresses to the same symbol. In either case incorrect syntax or multiple declarations of the same symbol will cause an **assembly time** error to occur.

Finally the preceding discussion suggests that if anything other than the blank character appears in column 1, the assembler assumes that the string represents a symbol. This is true with one exception; if the character appearing in column 1 is a semicolon, the assembler will assume this line to be a **comment line**. The assembler will simply output the contents of that input line in the listing and proceed with the assembly of the next statement.

Opcode_field.   The opcode field contains the **mnemonic** of a machine language instruction or a directive. Examples of some are add, muls, move, and dc. Although mnemonics will be discussed extensively, we will mention here that valid opcodes are represented by alphabetical character strings of length between 1 and 5. It should be clear then that here1 and 1there, as well as opcode, are not valid opcodes. Moreover, mnemonics are not case-sensitive; for example, the two strings ADD and add denote the same opcode.

Finally, recall that our assembler assumes that strings that represent symbols start in column 1; similarly, our assembler assumes that strings that represent opcodes start in column 13.

Operand_field.   The operand field contains the operands required by the instruction whose mnemonic appears in the opcode field of instruction. The number of operands in this field depends entirely on the type of instruction. In the case of no-operand instructions, this field should be empty; in the case of one-operand instructions, only one operand should appear, whereas in the case of two-operand instructions, the two operands that should appear must be separated by a comma.

The **syntax** employed in specifying an operand conveys to the assembler the *mode specification* of the operand. For example, the syntax

```
dn
```

where n specifies in decimal an unsigned integer conveys to the assembler that the operand specifies a data register and that the mode employed is data register direct. The syntax

```
an
```

where n specifies in decimal an unsigned integer conveys to the assembler that the operand specifies an address register and that the mode employed is address register direct. Consider now the expression

```
exp(an)
```

---

[24] Notice that HERE and here are different symbols.

where n is the decimal integer representation of an unsigned integer and exp denotes a signed integer that represents the displacement. Therefore, this syntax is employed whenever the operand's addressing mode is address register indirect with displacement.

Of course, the programmer should be careful to provide values for n and exp that are within the expected range. In particular, if n is specified as any integer other than 0, 1, 2, or 3, an assembly time error will occur. At the other extreme, if the specified displacement field is outside the required range $-2^{15} \le m \le 2^{15} - 1$, the assembler will *left truncate* the displacement by employing only the four rightmost hex digits of the displacement's hex representation. For example, if the displacement is specified as $65FA10, the assembler will use as displacement the value $FA10. On the other hand, if the specified displacement is specified with fewer than 16 bits, such as $A10, the assembler will left pad the expression with as many binary zeroes as required to bring the displacement to size. In our example, the assembler will use the value $0A10 as the displacement.

Finally, the first operand (if in fact the operand field is not empty) should start at column 21.

Syntax of exp.   As mentioned earlier, exp represents a signed decimal integer that is interpreted by the assembler as representative of a 16-bit signed displacement. Because our assembler is supposed to be a flexible tool, the syntax of exp permits one to indicate the displacement in several different ways that are formally defined in the following paragraph. In its simplest form, an exp could be a signed decimal integer or a symbol. In the former case, the decimal integer's value will be converted to its 2's complement representation and placed in the displacement field of the machine language instruction. In the latter case, the value of the symbol (i.e., the address represented by the symbol) will be converted to its 16-bit 2's complement representation and be employed as the displacement.

We are ready to define the syntax of the exp formally. To do this, we will define a *relative expression* rel_exp to be a symbol. In BNF (Backus-Naur Form) notation,

$$rel\_exp ::= symbol$$

An *arithmetic constant* arithm_cons, is by definition either a decimal, hex, octal, or binary integer. For example, the following are representing valid arithmetic constants:

$$55 \quad \$5f \quad -@55 \quad \%0101011$$

It is clear that arithm_cons can be combined via arithmetic operators to produce an *arithmetic expression* (arithm_exp). The precedence of the arithmetic operators is the standard. The unary minus (−) has the highest precedence, followed by multiplication (∗) and division (/). Finally, the operations of addition (+) and subtraction (−) have the lowest precedence. Note that as one would expect, parentheses override precedence.

Formally, an arithm_exp is defined via the the grammar of Table 4.14 where BNF notation is used. For example, the following constitute a valid arithm_exp:

$$\% \ 10101 + 55 \ -32 + @67$$

It is important to see that all arithmetic operations are **integer** operations, and all such expressions are evaluated from left to right and the operations ∗ and / are performed before the operations of + and −.

TABLE 4.14

```
arithm_exp     ::= arithm_exp + term | arithm_exp - term | term
term           ::= term * primary | term / primary | primary
primary        ::= ( arithm_exp ) | -primary | arithm_cons
arithm_cons    ::= decimal_int | $hex_int | @octal_int | %binary_int
decimal_int    ::= decimal_digit | decimal_int decimal_digit
hex_int        ::= hex_digit | hex_int hex_digit
octal_int      ::= octal_digit | octal_int octal_digit
binary_int     ::= binary_digit | binary_int binary_digit
decimal_digit  ::= 0|1|2|3|4|5|6|7|8|9
hex_digit      ::= 0|1|2|3|4|5|6|7|8|9|A|B|C|D|E|F|a|b|c|d|e|f
octal_digit    ::= 0|1|2|3|4|5|6|7
binary_digit   ::= 0|1
```

We can now define an *absolute expression* (abs_exp) to be an arithmetic expression. In BNF notation

$$abs\_exp ::= arithm\_exp$$

Moreover, one could combine rel_exp and abs_exp to obtain new expressions. *But,* one should be very careful when combining one or more rel_exp. By definition, the rules that govern these combinations are illustrated in Table 4.15.

TABLE 4.15   Combining Relative and Absolute Expressions

Expression	Valid	Result
rel_exp + abs_exp	Yes	rel_exp
abs_exp + rel_exp	Yes	rel_exp
rel_exp - abs_exp	Yes	rel_exp
rel_exp - rel_exp	Yes	abs_exp
rel_exp + rel_exp	No	
abs_exp - rel_exp	No	

Now we formally define an exp to be either a rel_exp or an abs_exp. In symbols

$$exp ::= rel\_exp | abs\_exp$$

Therefore, the preceding discussions suggest that the following expressions are valid exp's where here, there represent two symbols

```
3               3+4    3-4       3*4-5  3/4+6
HERE+4          4+3*2+HERE    HERE-22*(HERE-THERE)
```

whereas the following are invalid exp's

```
(HERE + THERE)      (5 -   THERE)    (2*HERE)
```

Comment_field. The assembler allows the programmer to provide his or her own brief explanations of each assembly language statement via **comments**. When the assembler encounters a semicolon ";" it understands that whatever text follows on the current line is a comment and is ignored by the assembler.[25]

4.4.3 ASM68 Instructions

ASM68 supports all the instructions of SIM68. We will use the following notation. dn represents the data register n, an represents the address register n, rn represents either the data or address register n. Furthermore, either dmem or smem can represent the memory location defined via exp(an); however, we will use smem and dmem whenever this memory location is a source or destination operand, respectively. Their mnemonic and valid operands are given subsequently for each case.

Binary integer addition					
Data register to data register					
Mnemonic	Opcode	Action	Operands	Format	Length
add	$ D_4	Add word from data register to data register.	dn,dn	F1	1

Data register to address register					
Mnemonic	Opcode	Action	Operands	Format	Length
adda	$ D_4	Add lower-order word of the indicated data register to address register. Before addition, source is sign extended to a longword.	dn, an	F1	1

Binary integer subtraction					
Data register to data register					
Mnemonic	Opcode	Action	Operands	Format	Length
sub	$ 9_4	Subtract word in data register from data register.	dn, dn	F1	1

Binary integer multiplication					
Data register to data register					
Mnemonic	Opcode	Action	Operands	Format	Length
muls	$ 67_7	Multiply signed word from register to signed word in data register. Result, a longword, replaces contents of the destination register.	dn, dn	F3	1

---

[25] The comment is printed in the listing.

Binary integer division

Data register to data register

Mnemonic	Opcode	Action	Operands	Format	Length
divs	$ 47_7	Divide signed longword in data register by a signed word from register. Remainder and quotient of the division are inserted in high-order word and the low-order word of data register, respectively.	dn, dn	F3	1

Compare instructions

Data register to data register

Mnemonic	Opcode	Action	Operands	Format	Length
cmp	$ b_4	Compare word of data register to a word in data register.	dn, dn	F2	1

Swap instructions

Data register to data register

Mnemonic	Opcode	Action	Operands	Format	Length
swap	$ 0908_{13}	Swap two words of data register.	dn	F7	1

Moving instructions

Register to data register

Mnemonic	Opcode	Action	Operands	Format	Length
move	$ 0_2	Move lower order word from register to data register.	rn, dn	F4	1

Register to address register

Mnemonic	Opcode	Action	Operands	Format	Length
movea	$ 0_2	Move word from register to address register. Before move source is sign extended to longword.	rn, an	F4	1

Register to memory

Mnemonic	Opcode	Action	Operands	Format	Length
move	$ 0_2	Move word from register to memory.	rn, dmem	F4	2

Memory to register

Mnemonic	Opcode	Action	Operands	Format	Length
move	$ 0_2	Move word from memory to data register.	smem, dn	F4	2

| movea | $ 0_2 | Move word from memory to address register. Before move the source is sign extended to longword. | smem, an | F4 | 2 |

Memory to memory

Mnemonic	Opcode	Action	Operands	Format	Length
move	$ 0_2	Move word from memory to memory.	smem, dmem	F4	3

Branch instructions

The opcode is $ 6_4$.   If e = s,b (e=w) then a byte (word) displacement is forced.

Unconditional branches

Mnemonic	Condition	Action	Operands	Format	Length
bra.e	$ 0	Branch unconditionally.	exp	F5	1,2

Conditional branches

Mnemonic	Condition	Action	Operands	Format	Length
beq.e	$ 7	Branch on equal. Branch is taken if $Z = 1$.	exp	F5	1,2
bgt.e	$ E	Branch on greater than. A branch is taken if $(N \cdot V + \bar{N} \cdot \bar{V}) \cdot \bar{Z} = 1$.	exp	F5	1,2
blt.e	$ D	Branch on less than. Branch is taken if $N \cdot \bar{V} + \bar{N} \cdot V = 1$.	exp	F5	1,2

Stop and dump instructions

Mnemonic	Opcode	Action	Operands	Format	Length
trap	$ 4E4_{12}	If [d0 < 0:15 >= 3] then stop. If [d0 < 0:15 >= 2] then register dump. If [d0 < 0:15 >= 1] then memory dump. If [d0 < 0:15 >= 0] then memory and register dump.	#0	F5	1

4.4.4 ASM68 Directives

ORG and END directives.   In our discussions about SIM68 we have indicated that a user is capable of loading his or her program in specific memory locations.[26] We did actu-

---

[26] Assuming of course that the operating system permits this.

ally see the object code (as well as the object module) for the cases in which the data area is adjacent to the instruction area as in version I and where it was not adjacent as in version II.

The assembler maintains its own program counter, which for distinction we will refer to as the *assembler's location counter* (APC). In particular, the assembler initially sets its (APC) to the value $000000. We show that in version I the loading origin is assumed to be at $000000, and everything will be fine; however, in version II we assume that the program would be loaded at location $000400. Moreover, we wish to load the data at location $000520. Hence, in several instances, there is a need to instruct the assembler to adjust its location counter.

The directive provided for this purpose is the **origin** (ORG), and its format is given subsequently.

Name_Field	Opcode_Field	Operand_Field
[valid symbol]	org	abs_exp

where abs_exp represents a constant as it was defined earlier.[27] For example, if we consider the declaration

$$\text{here} \qquad \text{org} \qquad \$1000$$

the value of the symbol here is equal to $001000, and on encountering this statement, the assembler sets the contents of its location counter to $001000.

In Figure 4.49 the assembly language programs for versions I and II, respectively, are presented. The reader is encouraged to observe the use of the origin directive. The generated object code for each of the two versions of Figure 4.49 are presented in Figure 4.50.

Every module should end with the directive end. In the previous sentence the word every suggests that a program could consist of more than one module! Although our

STM		ASSEMBLER CODE			ASSEMBLER CODE	
1		org	$000000		org	$000400
2	_main	sub	d1,d1	_main	sub	d1,d1
3		movea	d1,a0		movea	d1,a0
4		move	x(a0),d0		move	x(a0),d0
5		move	x+2(a0),d1		move	x+2(a0),d1
6		add	d1,d0		add	d1,d0
7		move	d0,x+4(a0)		move	d0,x+4(a0)
8		move	x+6(a0),d0		move	x+6(a0),d0
9		trap	#0		trap	#0
10	;				org	$000520
11	x	dc	11	x	dc	11
12		dc	-1		dc	-1
13		ds	1		ds	1
14		dc	3		dc	3
15		end			end	

Version I	Version II

Figure 4.49   Source modules for version I and II, respectively.

---

[27] Note that the binary representation of the integer *n* should require less than 24 bits.

STM	LOCATION	OBJECT CODE	LOCATION	OBJECT CODE
1	000000		000000	
2	000000	9241	000000	9241
3	000002	3041	000002	3041
4	000004	3028 0018	000004	3028 0520
5	000008	3228 001A	000008	3228 0522
6	00000C	D041	00000C	D041
7	00000E	3140 001C	00000E	3140 0524
8	000012	3028 001E	000012	3028 0526
9	000016	4E40	000016	4E40
10	000018		000018	
11	000018	000B	000018	000B
12	00001A	FFFF	00001A	FFFF
13	00001C		00001C	
14	00001E	0003	00001E	0003
15	00001E		00001E	

       Version I   Version II

Figure 4.50   Generated object code for versions I and II.

assembler can assemble these modules independently, the discussion of this topic will be delayed for a later chapter. Therefore, for the time being we will assume that each program consists of a **single** module.

Define constant (DC) and define storage (DS) directives

The ASM68 assembler provides the user with two directives that will enable him or her to either store a set of integers (of word length) in contiguous memory locations or to allocate a set of consecutive word locations for future use. The mnemonics for the two directives are dc and ds.

DC directive.   The format of this directive is the following:

Name_Field	Opcode_Field	Operand_Field
[valid symbol]	dc	exp{,exp}

First note the brackets enclosing the expression "valid symbol"; these brackets indicate that this is an optional expression. Second, notice that exp represents the expression discussed earlier, that is, it represents a signed integer, and one such integer is expected to be present.

     The assembler, on encountering this directive, will perform two things. It will examine the contents of *its* location counter[28] to see if the contents represent a word boundary. If it does not, the assembler will increment its location counter so that the new contents represent a word boundary that is nearest to the old location.[29] Second, the signed decimal integer exp is converted by the assembler to its corresponding 2's complement representation and is "stored" in this location. After these two steps have been completed, the assembler increments its program counter by $2 and proceeds with assembling the next assembly statement. As one would expect, an *assembly time error* will occur if the operand "expres-

---

[28] The assembler maintains its own program counter.

[29] Therefore, the assembler performs the required alignments that were the responsibility of the programmer under machine language programming.

sion" represents a decimal integer that is outside the allowable bounds. Recall that the range of integers of word size that can be accommodated is between -2^{15} and $2^{15} - 1$.

Example

Assume that the assembler has generated the following code from statement number 15.

LOCATION	OBJECT	CODE	STMT	SOURCE	CODE	
......	....		14	......	....	....
000002	03		15	......	....	....
			16		dc	-1

At this point the assembler's location counter points to $000003 (because only one byte of code was generated); the next source statement (number 16) contains the directive dc. Therefore, the contents of the location counter are incremented by one so that the word boundary alignment is ensured; and, code consisting of the word %1111111111111111 (the 2's complement representation of the signed decimal integer -1) is generated. Hence, the listing will be as the next figure illustrates (after the code generation yielded by statement number 16).

LOCATION	OBJECT	CODE	STMT	SOURCE	CODE	
......	....		14	......	....	....
000002	03		15	......	....	....
000004	FFFF		16		dc	-1

DS directive.   The format of this directive is the following.

Name_Field	Opcode_Field	Operand_Field
[valid symbol]	ds	abs_exp

The name field is optional, whereas abs_exp represents an unsigned decimal integer. Unlike the dc directive, the purpose of this directive is to allocate storage space and not to generate code.

Hence the assembler, on encountering such a statement, will perform only one function. First, it will examine the contents of *its* location counter to see if the contents represent a word boundary. If it does not, the assembler will increment its location counter so that the new contents represent a word boundary that is nearest to the old location. After this step has been completed, the assembler increments its program counter by $n \cdot \$2$, where n is the decimal value represented by the expression abs_exp and it proceeds with assembling the next statement.

Example

Assume that the assembler has generated the following code from statement number 15.

LOCATION	OBJECT	CODE	STMT	SOURCE	CODE	
......	....		14	......	....	....
000002	0312		15	......	....	....
			16		ds	5

At this point the assembler's location counter points to $000004 (because only one word of code was generated); the next source statement (number 16) contains the directive ds and the operand 5. Therefore, the contents of the location counter are incremented by $5 \cdot \$2 = \$A$ and nothing else occurs. Hence, the listing will be as the next figure shows after assembling statement number 16.

```
LOCATION    OBJECT    CODE    STMT    SOURCE          CODE
--------    --------------    ----    --------------------
......      ....              14      ......    ....    ....
000002      0312              15      ......    ....    ....
000004                        16                ds      5
```

4.4.5 Example

Consider the last example of the previous section. Recall that the algorithm that performs this task is given in Table 4.16.

TABLE 4.16

[1]. Zero out d0 (so sum=0).
[2]. Move d0 into a0 (so the a0=0).
[3]. Move into d2 the number_of_integers.
[4]. Move increment/decrement into d3 (so d3=1).
[5]. Move "next"_integer into d1.
[6]. Add d1 to d0 (so sum is accumulated in d0).
[7]. Increment a0 by the contents of d3 twice.
[8]. Decrement d2 by the contents of d3 (so the number_of_integers is reduced by one).
[9]. If the contents of d2 is not equal to zero (so there are more numbers to add) go to 5.
[10]. Move RESULT from d0 into d1.
[11]. Zero out d0.
[12]. Increment d0 by the contents of d3 twice (so a register dump can be issued).
[13]. Dump registers.
[14]. Increment d0 by the contents of d3 (so a stop instruction may be issued).
[15]. Stop.

The assembly language code together with the generated machine language code is given in Table 4.17.

TABLE 4.17   An ASM68 program

LOCATION	OBJECT CODE	STMT	SOURCE CODE		
		1		org	$000000
000000	9040	2		sub	d0,d0	; d0 ← 0
000002	3040	3		movea	d0,a0	; a0 ← 0
000004	3428 002A	4		move	x(a0),d2	; d2 ← number of integers
000008	3628 002C	5		move	x+2(a0),d3	; d3 ← 1
00000C	3228 002E	6	loop	move	num(a0),d1	; loop : d1 ← next integer
000010	D041	7		add	d1,d0	; add next integer to the sum
000012	D0C3	8		adda	d3,a0	; a0 ← a0+1
000014	D0C3	9		adda	d3,a0	; a0 ← a0+1
000016	9443	10		sub	d3,d2	; d2 ← d2-1
000018	6E00 FFF0	11		bgt	loop	; if d2 ≠ 0 go to LOOP
00001C	3200	12		move	d0,d1	; d1 ← sum
00001E	9040	13		sub	d0,d0	; d0 ← 0
000010	D043	14		add	d3,d0	; d0 ← d0+1
000022	D043	15		add	d3,d0	; d0 ← d0+1
000024	4E40	16		trap	#0	; register dump
000026	D043	17		add	d3,d0	; d0 ← d0+1
000028	4E40	18		trap	#0	; stop (exit)
00002A	000A	19	x	dc	10	; number of integers
00002C	0001	20		dc	1	; increment
00002E	000A	21	num	dc	10	; first integer
000030	0009	22		dc	9	; second integer
000032	0008	23		dc	8	; third integer
000034	0007	24		dc	7	; fourth integer
000036	0006	25		dc	6	; fifth integer
000038	0005	26		dc	5	; sixth integer
00003A	0004	27		dc	4	; seventh integer
00003C	0003	28		dc	3	; eighth integer
00003E	0002	29		dc	2	; ninth integer
000040	0001	30		dc	1	; tenth integer
		31		end		

4.5 EXERCISES

1. Describe the general architecture of the SIM68 hypothetical computer.
2. What are the last 5 bits of the status register called collectively? What is the low-order byte of the status register referred as? What are the names of each bit?
3. What addressing modes are supported by SIM68? How are these modes represented in an instruction?
4. What are the settings of the condition codes after an add to address register?

5. What is the result of multiplying the d0 as source and d1 as destination if d0 = $1234ABCD d1 = $45670012. What are the condition code settings?

6. What is the result of the divide operation of the preceding registers? What are the condition code settings?

7. Describe three ways to determine the sign of a number that was just moved to a data register from memory.

8. Explain what the following SIM68 code does. Also comment on each line.

```
1001000001000000
0011000001000000
0011000000101000
0000000000101100
0011001000101000
0000000000101110
0011011000101000
0000000000110000
1001000001000001
1101000011000001
1101000011000001
0011010000101000
0000000000110000
1100011111000010
1001000001000001
0110111011110010
1001000001000000
1101000001000001
1101000001000001
0100111001000000
1101000001000001
0100111001000000
0000000000001010
0000000000000001
0000000000001000
0000000000000001
0000000000000010
0000000000000010
0000000000000100
0000000000000001
0000000000000010
0000000000000100
0000000000000001
1111111111111111
```

9. Determine what the following code does. Also comment on every line.

```
1001000001000000
0011000001000000
0011001000101000
0000000000001100
0110011100000110
0110110111111000
```

```
1101000001000001
0110000011110110
0100111001000000

0000000000000000
0001011011110000
1111111111111111
1000000000000000
0000000000000001
```

10. What does an assembler do?

11. Describe the fields of an assembly language instruction. Where does each field start for our assembler?

12. What is the purpose of a "loader"? How will you use it?

13. What do the following assembler directives do?
    a. dc   100, $120, 4, 'A'
    b. org $9000
    c. ds   4
    d. end

14. What does the following code segment do?

```
            org     $1000
_main       sub     d1,d1
            move    d1,a0
            move    x(a0),d0
            move    neg_one(a0),d1
            add     d1,d0
            move    d0,y(a0)
            move    exitcode(a0),d0
            trap    #0
x           dc      15
neg_one     dc      -1
y           ds      1
exitcode    dc      3
            end
```

15. What does the following code segment do?

```
            org     $2000
            sub     d0,d0
            move    d0,a0
            move    X(a0),d1
            move    X+2(a0),d2
            muls    d1,d2
            move    X+4(a0),d0
            trap    #0
X           dc      11
            dc      41
            dc      3

            end
```

16. What does the following code segment do? Hand assemble each line.

```
        org     $0000
        sub     d0,d0
        move    d0,a0
        move    X(a0),d1
        move    X+2,d2
        muls    d1,d2
        move    X+4,d0
        trap    #0
X       dc      11
        dc      41
        dc      3

        end
```

17. What does the following code segment do? Hand assemble each line.

```
        org     $0000
        sub     d0,d0
        move    d0,a0
        move    X(a0),d1
        move    X+2(a0),d2
        muls    d1,d2
        move    X+4(a0),d0
        trap    #0
X       dc      11
        dc      41
        dc      3

        end
```

18. What is the content of register d2 after multiplying it by d1? d1 is the source, and d2 is the destination. What are the condition code settings?

```
a. d1 = $398AED49   d2 = $12345678
b. d1 = $75DE89FF   d2 = $ABCDEF01
c. d1 = $00001040   d2 = $89750020
d. d1 = $10010010   d2 = $00000001
e. d1 = $A45A0020   d2 = $00000000
f. d1 = $8EDA8391   d2 = $8EFEEE00
g. d1 = $0A0B0C0D   d2 = $E1F25092
```

19. What is the content of register d2 after dividing it by d1? d1 is the source, and d2 is the destination. What are the condition code settings?

```
a. d1 = $398AED49   d2 = $12345678
b. d1 = $75DE89FF   d2 = $ABCDEF01
c. d1 = $00001040   d2 = $89750020
d. d1 = $10010010   d2 = $00000001
e. d1 = $A45A0020   d2 = $00000000
```

```
f. d1 = $8EDA8391   d2 = $8EFEEE00
g. d1 = $0A0B0C0D   d2 = $E1F25092
```

20. Assume that contents of the assembler's location counter is $5501. Indicate what action the assembler will do when the next statement that it encounters is

```
a. DC 23,$4A34, 990, ';'
b. DC 669,987,%1001000100101111,$1000
c. DS 48
d. DS $34
e. DS '*'
f. ORG $9002
   DC $95
   DS 8
   DC 'a'
g. DS @87
h. ORG %10101+55-32+@74
i. DC $8-%0100+@10
j. DC 12-$@4 + 'a'
```

21. How many times does the *x* labeled statement execute? Assuming that d0 = $0071 and d1 = $0004

```
a. x   sub d0,d1              b. x   sub do,d1
       bra x                         sub d0,d1
                                     beq x
```

22. What is the result after the instructions are executed?

```
divs    d0,d1
divs    d1,d0
```

Given:

```
a.  d0 = $1001871F     d1 = $00000008
b.  d0 = $00010000     d1 = $00000008
c.  d0 = $0000FBCD     d1 = $00000018
d.  d0 = $FADE0000     d1 = $00000023
e.  d0 = $ABCDEF10     d1 = $01234567
f.  d0 = 1024          d1 = 89
g.  d0 = 1990          d1 = 200
```

23. Given d0 = $0000F010, d1 = $00000000, d2 = $00000002, and d3 = $00000000, what is the result of the following segments?

```
a.  x   divs    d2,d0
        add     d2,d2
        cmp     d0,d3
        ble     x

b.  x   divs    d2,d0
        add     d2,d2
        ble     x
```

```
c.  x    divs   d2,d0
         adda   d2,a0
         ble    x

d.  x    divs   d0,d2
         add    d2,d2
         sub    d2,d0
         ble    x
```

24. Hand assemble the following:

```
         org    $1000
         sub    d0,d0
         movea  d0,a0
         movea  d0,a1
next     move   one(a0),d0
         move   stop(a0),d1
         swap   d2
         cmp    d1,d0
         bne    next
         adda   d1,a0
         move   exit(a1),d0
         trap   #0

one      dc     1,4,98,209,4,76,14,87
stop     dc     14
exit     dc     3
```

5

System Component Implementation

Recall that the fundamental unit of a digital computer is the gate. In Chapter 2 we examined how a gate is constructed from transistors, and how gates are combined to make simple combinational and sequential circuits. In this chapter we show how these simple components are combined together into more complex building blocks, which in turn are combined to realize a computer system.

As with the rest of this text, we will use SIM68 as a model where appropriate to demonstrate how a simple computer is designed. We note at the outset, however, that the SIM68 instruction set was designed for instructional purposes rather than efficiency. Similarly, the hardware design has been developed to demonstrate the full complement of building blocks we will discuss. We are not suggesting that the MC68000 is in any way architecturally similar to the SIM68 design outlined later, nor are we suggesting that the design is optimal (in fact several of the homework exercises are "improvements" on SIM68 circuit elements). SIM68 is an interesting architecture, however, which incorporates many of the concepts seen in more complex central processors.

5.1 BUILDING BLOCKS

The building blocks to be described in this section are as follows: **encoders**, **decoders**, **multiplexers**, **demultiplexers**, **main memory**, an **arithmetic and logic unit** (ALU), and a **barrel shifter** (not used in SIM68). Where appropriate, we will provide information regarding "off-the-shelf" SSI components from the TI TTL-7400 series.[1]

5.1.1 Encoders and Decoders

Recall from Chapter 2 that we may represent numbers using *codes*. In particular the coding of integers in binary is known as a binary encoding (i.e., $0, 1, 10, 11, 100, 101, 110, 111$, etc.). One useful combinational circuit provides as output the binary representation of a selected input line, assuming that the input lines are ordered sequentially starting from 0. This device is known as an **encoder**. For example, given that line 5 is high (i.e., line I_5 in

---

[1] Texas Instruments TTL Logic Data Book, Texas Instruments, 1988.

Figure 5.1) into the encoder, the output lines corresponding to the binary representation of 5 (i.e., 101) will be high (i.e., lines O_2 and O_0).

From the previous discussion it should be clear that an encoder is a hardware component with 2^n inputs and n outputs. The block diagram for this is shown in Qigure 5.1(a) (supply and ground lines omitted) with a corresponding truth table given in Table 5.1. Notice that we have the inputs on the left, control and enable lines on the top and bottom, and outputs on the right. To implement this component, consider the circuit in Figure 5.1(b). As you can see each output is simply the **or** of those lines, which will set the appropriate output line true. These values may be obtained directly from the truth table by observing that the input values, when high, contribute to a particular output line being high. For example O_0 is high when any of I_1, I_3, I_5, I_7 are high. Notice that we include an **enable line E**, which, when reset, will force an output zero regardless of the inputs. This permits the encoder to be connected with other outputs using a wire or design.[2]

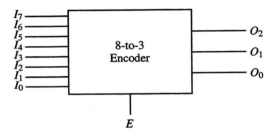

(a) A 2^n-to-n (where $n = 3$) encoder

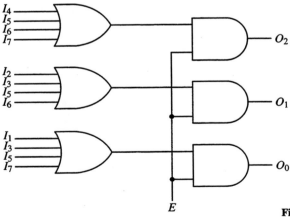

(b) Circuit realization

Figure 5.1   A 2nd-to-n (where $n = 3$) encoder (a) and circuit realization (b).

The converse of an encoder is a **decoder**. A decoder selects a single output line determined by the set of input lines that are assumed to be the binary representation of some number that corresponds to a particular output line. For example, the binary number 001, which corresponds to $\overline{I_2}\,\overline{I_1}\,I_0$, will cause the output line O_1 to be high with all other output

---

[2] Notice that some chips invert the interpretation of the enable bit, that is, it *disables* the output. Others use the term chip select.

TABLE 5.1   Truth table for 8-to-3 encoder

I_0	I_1	I_2	I_3	I_4	I_5	I_6	I_7	E	O_2	O_1	O_0
1	0	0	0	0	0	0	0	1	0	0	0
0	1	0	0	0	0	0	0	1	0	0	1
0	0	1	0	0	0	0	0	1	0	1	0
0	0	0	1	0	0	0	0	1	0	1	1
0	0	0	0	1	0	0	0	1	1	0	0
0	0	0	0	0	1	0	0	1	1	0	1
0	0	0	0	0	0	1	0	1	1	1	0
0	0	0	0	0	0	0	1	1	1	1	1
x	x	x	x	x	x	x	x	0	0	0	0

lines low. From this discussion we establish that there are n input lines to the decoder and 2^n output lines. Figure 5.2(a) shows a diagram of an 8-to-3 decoder (supply and ground lines omitted) with the truth table as given in Table 5.2. In Figure 5.2(b) one possible hardware realization is given. Notice that we require n inverters and 2^n n-input **and** gates. We arrive at this realization by noting that the output from a particular **and** gate is high only when all its inputs are high, which occurs only when the inverted inputs to the gate were originally low, and the noninverted inputs were originally high.

We conclude this section by noting that encoders and decoders come in a variety of different configurations, some of which permit circuit optimization (see exercises). Because encoders and decoders are so useful, they are packaged as individual integrated circuits. Looking at the 7400 series chips, we provide examples in Table 5.3.

TABLE 5.2   Truth table for 8-to-3 decoder

I_2	I_1	I_0	E	O_0	O_1	O_2	O_3	O_4	O_5	O_6	O_7
0	0	0	1	1	0	0	0	0	0	0	0
0	0	1	1	0	1	0	0	0	0	0	0
0	1	0	1	0	0	1	0	0	0	0	0
0	1	1	1	0	0	0	1	0	0	0	0
1	0	0	1	0	0	0	0	1	0	0	0
1	0	1	1	0	0	0	0	0	1	0	0
1	1	0	1	0	0	0	0	0	0	1	0
1	1	1	1	0	0	0	0	0	0	0	1
x	x	x	0	0	0	0	0	0	0	0	0

TABLE 5.3   Sample encoders/decoders from 7400 Series TTL

Code	Function
74137	3-line to 8-line decoder/demultiplexer with address latches
74138	3-line to 8-line decoder/demultiplexer
74139	Dual 1 of 4 decoder
74148	Octal priority encoder 8-line to 3-line

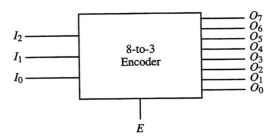

(a) A n-to-2^n (where $n = 3$) encoder

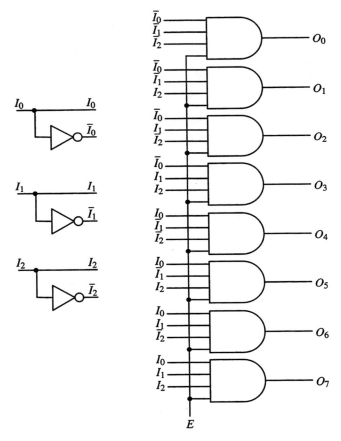

(b) Circuit realization

Figure 5.2   A n-to-2^n (where $n = 3$) decoder.

5.1.2 Multiplexers and Demultiplexers

Another common component in digital circuits is the **multiplexer**. The multiplexer has a number of input lines (usually 2^n), a single output line, and a number of **control lines** (n). The control lines are used to select one of the 2^n input lines and connect it to the output line (i.e., the output line will be the same logical value as the selected input line). Notice that in addition to the 2^n inputs there is a chip enable line. According to the truth table, the output lines will be all zeros regardless of the inputs, unless the chip is enabled (i.e., the enable input is 1). This is a common feature of the more complex building blocks that we will introduce, and is reflected in the diagrams, truth tables, and circuit realizations. We also note for future reference that component enable lines and control lines together constitute the **control points** of the system. Thus, by specifying the values of the control points for each component, we specify the data flow through the system.

Figure 5.3(a) shows a 4-input multiplexer (supply and ground lines omitted) with the truth table given in Table 5.4. Given that the control lines are set to binary 10 and that the device is enabled, the output will be the same as input line 2. The circuit used to achieve this is given in Figure 5.3(b).

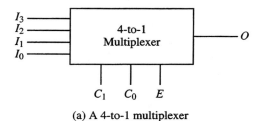

(a) A 4-to-1 multiplexer

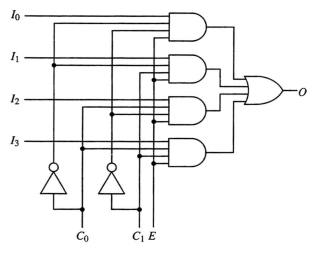

(b) Circuit realization

Figure 5.3   A 4-to-1 multiplexer.

TABLE 5.4   Abbreviated truth table for a 4-to-1 multiplexer; B denotes a boolean value and x a don't-care condition

I_0	I_1	I_2	I_3	c_1	c_0	E	O
B	x	x	x	0	0	1	B
x	B	x	x	0	1	1	B
x	x	B	x	1	0	1	B
x	x	x	B	1	1	1	B
x	x	x	x	x	x	0	0

Notice that the circuit is essentially the **or** of all the input lines; however, only one of the input lines is selected. The line selection is achieved by **and**ing each line with the appropriate logic combination from the control lines such that the output will be high only if the input is high. You should notice the similarity with the decoder, in fact, every multiplexer has a decoder within it. The control lines correspond to a binary number and will set all of the inputs into one **and** gate high, with the exception of a single line. This line is the input line and will therefore determine whether the output is 0 or 1. Thus, the output will be determined by the value of the selected input. Finally, we point out that an n-bit word may be selected from one of several n-bit words by using n multiplexers with common control and enable lines. This extension to word operations also applies to demultiplexers.

As you might expect, the converse of the multiplexer is the **demultiplexer**. The demultiplexer directs a single input to one of many possible outputs. Typically the demultiplexer has 1 input, n control (output selection) lines, an enable line, and 2^n output lines. Figure 5.4(a) shows a 4-output demultiplexer (supply and ground lines omitted) with the corresponding truth table in Table 5.5. The circuit used to realize this component is given in Figure 5.4(b). Again, as you might expect, the circuit realization is rather similar to the decoder, with the addition of a common input (the input line) to each of the **and** gates.

Like encoders and decoders, multiplexers and demultiplexers may be purchased as integrated circuit packages. The examples in Table 5.6 are taken from the 7400 series.

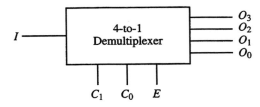

(a) A 4-to-1 demultiplexer

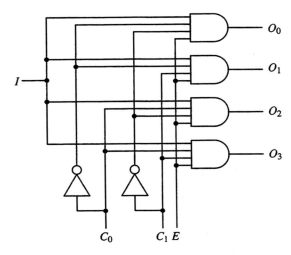

(b) Circuit realization

Figure 5.4 A 1-to-4 demultiplexer.

TABLE 5.5 Abbreviated truth table for a
1-to-4 Demultiplexer; B denotes a boolean
value and x a don't-care condition

I	c_1	c_0	E	O_0	O_1	O_2	O_3
B	0	0	1	B	x	x	x
B	0	1	1	x	B	x	x
B	1	0	1	x	x	B	x
B	1	1	1	x	x	x	B
B	0	0	1	x	x	x	0
x	x	x	0	0	0	0	0

TABLE 5.6 Sample multiplexers/demultiplexers,
7400 series TTL

Code	Function
74155	Dual 1 of 4 decoder/demultiplexer
74151	1 of 8 data selector/multiplexer
74153	Dual 4-line to 1-line data selectors/multiplexers

5.1.3 Tristate Buffers

Another important building block used in computers is the **tristate buffer** (or **tristate line
driver**). The function of a tristate buffer is to permit more than one device to be connected
to the same wire without damaging the components. A bus driver is in one of three states
0,1, or high impedance. The circuit representation for the bus driver is presented in Figure
5.5.

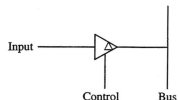

Input

Control   Bus   **Figure 5.5**   Tristate bus driver.

Consider the case in which many I/O devices wish to communicate with one another.
To achieve this, we use a common bus (see Section 1.2) to which all the devices are connected. Consider what happens if we simply connect the outputs of each I/O device to the
same wire. Each output may be either a 0 or 1. In both cases, however, the devices are
attempting to hold that value constant. With one device at 0 and another at 1, we see that a
short circuit will occur. The problem is that both devices are attempting to drive the bus at
the same time. To solve this, we need a driver between the device and the bus that, to the
bus, is in one of three states: read, write, or high impedance. When in read mode, the
driver connects the inputs of the device to the bus; when in write mode, the driver connects
the outputs of the device to the bus, and when in high-impedance mode the driver "discon-
nects" the device from the bus. The disconnection is achieved by placing the driver in its
high-impedance state. We then ensure by control logic that the drivers for only one device
is selected in write mode, one is selected as read mode, and all the others are in the high-
impedance mode. This creates a "path" between the device writing the data and the device
reading the data.

Typically when two devices communicate, what actually happens is that the contents of a register in the source device are latched into the destination device. This implies that a circuit between the source and destination registers exist. To permit many devices to communicate with one another, and still provide a circuit, it is usually the case that registers are connected to a bus. To achieve this, each bit of the register is connected to its corresponding bus line using bus drivers. In Figure 5.6 we show a register that is connected to the bus via a pair of bus drivers, one for reading, the other for writing. A single logic line is used to select the direction, whereas another is used to enable the action. Thus, the register may be in either read or write mode, or may be disabled.

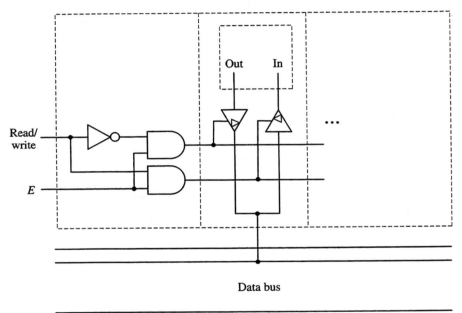

Figure 5.6.   Register connected to bus using tristate buffers.

5.2 MAIN MEMORY

Recall that the function of **main memory** (see Chapter 2) is to store user programs and data during execution. In this section we show how memory is realized. First we show how a **memory chip** is composed of **single storage cells**. A storage cell remembers the state of a single bit while power is applied to the circuit. We then take advantage of the benefits derived from circuit integration using these cells to form memory chips. These chips come in a variety of different configurations. For example, the Intel 2114[3] a 1024 by 4-bit static ram chip is a single integrated circuit that possesses 1024 addressable 4-bit words of storage. Finally, we demonstrate using the SIM68 4 Kb memory how a main memory configuration may be constructed using a number of 2114 memory chips, multiplexers, and some combinational logic.

Starting then with the memory chip, Figure 5.7(a) shows a block diagram corre-

---

[3] Intel TTL Memory Components Handbook, Intel Corporation, 1990.

sponding to a single chip. Notice that there are three inputs to the chip: (1) the $R/\overline{W}$ (read/write) line, which selects whether the operation to the chip is a read (1) or a write (0); (2) the E (enable) line, which makes the chip activate; and (3) the I (input) lines, which are used to specify the value of data to be stored. In addition there is one output, the O (output) lines. For our hypothetical memory chip, the 4×4-bit chip, there would be 4 addressable (4-bit) words, therefore we would require 2 address lines. Because the word size is 4 bits, there will be 4 input lines and 4 output lines.

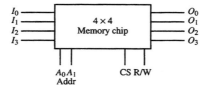

(a) Block diagram of 4×4 bit memory cell

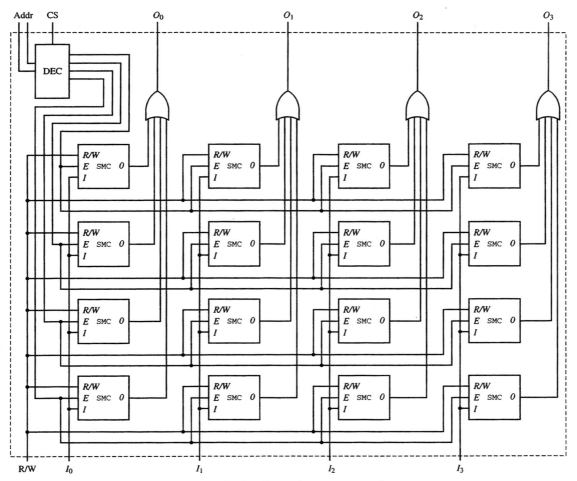

(b) Circuit realization of 4×4 bit memory cell

Figure 5.7 4×4-bit memory chip.

The chip consists of a decoder that is enabled by CS (chip select), 16 storage cells (4*4) and 4 **or** gates (one for each bit in the output word). The decoder is used to select a particular word from those addressable by enabling only those cells in that word. Each input line is connected to all bits of equal significance; however, only those cells enabled (i.e., one word) will be affected, and then only if the $R/\overline{W}$ line is low. The output for each bit is the **or** of the outputs from each word; however, only at most one word will be enabled, yielding the correct value on the output lines. Notice that the memory would require connecting to the data bus using bidirectional tristate buffers.

Memory chips may be purchased in many different configurations. Table 5.7 shows some of the more popular chips from the mid 1970s. Included are some of the newer VLSI memory chips.

TABLE 5.7   Sample RAM memory chips

Code	Function	Type
National 5255	1 K * 4	Static
Texas 74S400	4 K * 1	Static
Intel 2167	16 K * 1	Static
Intel 2107B	4K * 1	Dynamic
Intel 2116-2	16K * 1	Dynamic
Intel 2164	64K * 1	Dynamic
NEC D41256L-12	256K * 1	Dynamic

In fact there are two classes of RAM, **static RAM**, and **dynamic RAM**. The difference between the two is that with static RAM the data in the cell remains at the same value while power is applied (because of the action of a JK flip-flop), whereas in dynamic RAM the value decays after a short period (because of the action of a capacitor). Thus for dynamic RAM to be useful, each bit must be *dynamically* read and rewritten to keep the contents fresh. We now consider the internal construction of both static and dynamic RAM.

5.2.1 Static RAM

The circuit described in Figure 5.8 is also known as a **static RAM** cell (clock and ground lines omitted). Recall that the outputs (Q and $\overline{Q}$) of a JK flip-flop remain unchanged until the inputs (J and K) are altered. First we notice that while the enable line is low, the output will be low and the JK flip-flop will not change. Thus the device is disabled. The output (O) will be the value of Q, provided that the cell is enabled (E is high) and that the cell is in write mode ($R/\overline{W}$ is low) because the value of the output gate will be determined solely by Q. To modify the cell, the user places the value to be stored on the I line, places the cell into write mode (sets $R/\overline{W}$ low) and again enables the cell by setting E high. In the next clock cycle the value of I will be clocked into the cell (with I as the input to J and $\overline{I}$ as the input to K). Notice that during a write operation the output is disabled. The effects of the input lines on the cell are summarized in Table 5.8.

5.2.2 Dynamic RAM

Unlike static RAM that uses a flip flop to hold the current state, **dynamic RAM** uses a capacitor to maintain the current state. A single cell of a dynamic ram chip is shown in Figure 5.9.

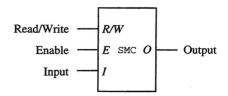

(a) Single memory cell

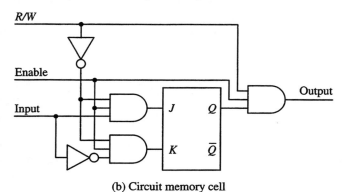

(b) Circuit memory cell   **Figure 5.8**   Static RAM storage cell

TABLE 5.8   Excitation table for storage cell

Inputs			Output	Effect
E	R/W	I		
1	1	1	Q	Output is stored value, I has no effect.
1	1	0	Q	Output is stored value, I has no effect.
1	0	1	0	Output disabled, I=1 saved in cell.
1	0	0	0	Output disabled, I=0 saved in cell.
0	X	X	0	Output disabled, cell disabled.

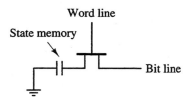

Figure 5.9   Dynamic RAM storage cell.

The principal advantage in using dynamic RAM is that it requires fewer transistors (one as opposed to two). Therefore, by using dynamic RAM, it is possible to manufacture cheaper chips with higher densities than with static RAM (higher densities means that the manufacturer can offer more storage than with a static RAM of the same size). As you might expect there is a tradeoff. Because the storage component is a capacitor (which loses its charge), the cell will forget its value unless refreshed. To refresh the capacitor, the cell value is read and rewritten. The act of rewriting to the cell thus recharges the capacitor.

Clearly the frequency at which the cell is refreshed must be greater than the decay time of the capacitor; typically the refresh rate for a single cell is 2 ms. To perform the refresh, a simple circuit must be included that performs a read/write on each cell in turn. Once it was the case that refresh logic would be external to the memory chip (either as an explicit logic circuit, or as another task for the CPU to perform). With the advent of VLSI, however, it is now possible to incorporate the refresh logic onto the chip. The attraction of this is a reduction in the number of integrated circuit components. Care must be taken that memory refresh does not interfere with normal memory accesses. In addition to requiring refresh, dynamic RAM is somewhat slower than static ram.

5.3 GENERAL-PURPOSE COMPUTATION UNIT

As was discussed in Chapter 3 a general-purpose computer is expected to support a complete set of arithmetic and logic operators. These operators are made available to the user via the different **op codes** in the instruction set. As we have already seen, the typical programmer's model of a CPU is several registers that may be used as operands to the operators provided by the instruction set. In this text we define the **computation unit** to be those hardware components that provide the arithmetic, logic, and shift operations. Typically the computation unit is composed of two units: the **arithmetic and logic unit** (ALU) and the **barrel shifter**. Each of the units is a combinational circuit that provides several microinstructions (a **microinstruction** is defined to be a single function that may be completed in one clock cycle). The units are typically arranged in one of two organizations, as shown in Figures 5.10 and 5.11. Simple arithmetic operations (such as integer **add** and **subtract**), and logic operations (such as **and**, **or**, and **not**) are performed by the ALU. Data-shifting operations (such as **shift** and **rotate**) are performed by the barrel shifter. More complex operators such as integer **multiply** and **divide** are usually performed as a *sequence* of microinstructions using these three units together with additional control logic.

In Figure 5.10, we see two inputs to the computation unit, *A* and *B*. Each of the inputs is a bus (i.e., a set of wires) to which would be connected registers (either directly, through a multiplexer, or through three-state line drivers). The computational unit also possesses a single output bus *F*, which would go to the destination (again a register). A multiplexer is used to select which of the units (arithmetic, logic, or shift) the output data is

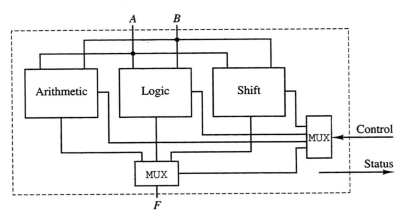

Figure 5.10   Overview of ALU internal organization.

selected from. The control lines to the multiplexer would be selected by some decoding function on the currently executing instruction. Notice in this example that only one of the three units will be selected at a time. Notice also that there will typically be some status output from the computational unit that will depend on the inputs and operation selected.

An alternative organization of the computational unit is provided in Figure 5.11. Notice in this instance that either of the outputs from the arithmetic unit or logic unit may be used as input to the barrel shifter. The advantage of this organization is that instructions such as **add then shift** may be executed as a single microinstruction. Instructions of this form are useful for implementing multiplication and division. The disadvantage is the additional delay incurred in the shift logic for nonshifted data.

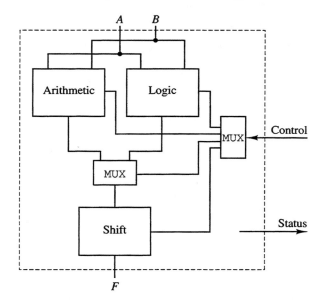

Figure 5.11   Alternative Implementation for ALU.

5.3.1 ALU

Clearly the ALU is an important component in the CPU; thus we will spend some time discussing it in detail. We note, however, that explaining the design of these circuits alone would take a book by itself (particularly the pipelined models used in modern processors). Thus we will take the more conservative approach of presenting a simple ALU based on the **cascade adder**, and discussing its implementation and operation. A n-bit ALU has two n-bit data inputs, a n-bit data output, a number of control lines, and a number of status lines. A block diagram for a general n-bit ALU is given in Figure 5.12. An important characteristic of an ALU is that each operation (specified via the control lines) takes *exactly one t-state* (see Section 2.4.1). Thus an ALU may easily be "plugged" into a CPU design.

Clearly the functions provided by the ALU should be a reflection of the operations performed by the computer system that it will form the basis of. As we just noted, however, it is not the case that the ALU be required to directly support every computer instruction. This is because a single computer instruction may be implemented by a sequence of several ALU operations. Because the goal of the this section is to demonstrate how a simple computer (the SIM68 computer) could be realized, we will briefly review the SIM68 instruction set (see Table 5.9).

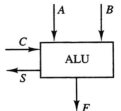

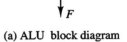

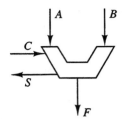

(a) ALU block diagram   (b) Alternative representation   **Figure 5.12**   General-purpose ALU.

TABLE 5.9   SIM68's instruction set

SIM68's instruction set		
Opcode	Operands	Q value
add	sD_n, dD_n	q_0
add	sD_n, dA_n	
sub	sD_n, dD_n	q_1
cmp	sD_n, dD_n	q_2
swap	sD_n, dD_n	q_3
move	sD_n, dD_n	q_4
move	sD_n, dA_n	
move	sA_n, dD_n	
move	sA_n, dA_n	
move	$sA_n, dmem$	
move	$sD_n, dmem$	
move	$smem, dA_n$	
move	$smem, dD_n$	
move	$smem, dmem$	
bra	mem	q_5
beq	mem	
bgt	mem	
blt	mem	
trap	#0	q_6
muls	sD_n, dD_n	q_7
divs	sD_n, dD_n	q_8

Notice that in essence the instruction set is composed of only a few different types of instruction—move (swap), add (subtract, compare), branch, and mult (divide), which vary in complexity. The 16-bit ALU as described by the block diagram in Figure 5.12 provides the system with a restricted set of operations (determined by the control lines C_0 to C_3) that is more than adequate for the task. The arithmetic and logical instructions that we will define are given in Table 5.10.

TABLE 5.10   Overview of SIM68 ALU

Code	c_2	c_1	c_0	Function
XFR	0	0	0	$F \leftarrow A$
NEG	0	0	1	$F \leftarrow \bar{A}$
AND	0	1	0	$F \leftarrow A \wedge B$
OR	0	1	1	$F \leftarrow A \vee B$
PLUS	1	0	0	$F \leftarrow A + B$
MINUS	1	0	1	$F \leftarrow A - B$

Notice that there are two 16-bit input data buses (labeled A and B) and a single 16-bit output bus (labeled F), three control lines (labeled $C_0 - C_2$), and 5 status lines (labeled $S_0 - S_4$). With 3 control lines, it would be possible to specify 8 different ALU instructions; notice from Table 5.10, however, that of these 8, only 6 have been defined. Remember also that each ALU instruction is a microinstruction (executes in a single t-state). The status lines are set according to Table 5.11. Now that we have details on the input, output, control, and status lines, we are in position to discuss the internals of the ALU. We do this in two sections; first we discuss how the output is generated from the inputs, then we describe how the status lines are set.

TABLE 5.11   Status bits

Code	Function
S_0	Carry-out from ALU (C)
S_1	Overflow from ALU (V)
S_2	Zero in ALU (Z)
S_3	Negative value in ALU (N)
S_4	Extended carry from ALU (same as C) (X)

Looking again at Table 5.9, we see two types of instruction: logical and arithmetic. For each bit position (e.g., bit n) the output bit (F_n) of each logical instruction depends *only* on the input bits (A_n and B_n). When we consider the arithmetic instructions, however, the output bit depends not only on the input bits but also on the carry-out from next lowest bit (bit $n - 1$). Even with this complication, the ALU design becomes clear when we consider the design of a single cell.

A single cell for bit n of the SIM68 ALU is provided in Figure 5.13. As you might have guessed, the control lines $C_0 - C_2$ are used to select one of the functions blocks to the 8-to-1 multiplexer. Thus the output for cell n is the output of the selected function block. The A and B input bits are inputs to each of the function blocks. In addition, the arithmetic function blocks make use of the carry from cell $n - 1$ and provide a carry to cell $n + 1$. All that is necessary now is to define the circuitry inside each function block, which we will proceed to do.

XFR function block.   The XFR function transfers the input A to the output F. Thus the output for the bit n function block will be just A_n. The circuit realization for this is simply a pass through line as given in Figure 5.14.

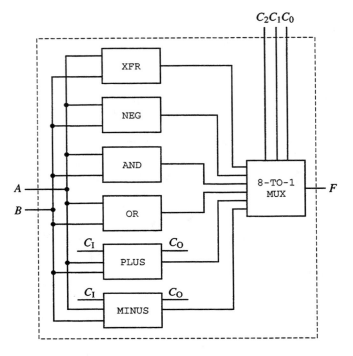

Figure 5.13   Single bit of ALU.

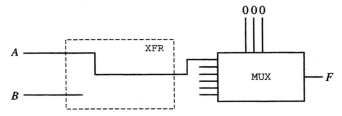

Figure 5.14   XFR cell.

NEG function block.   The NEG function places the complement of the input A on the output F. Thus the output for the bit n function block will be just $\overline{A_n}$. The circuit realization for this is a **not** gate as given in Figure 5.15.

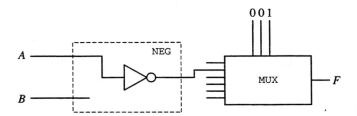

Figure 5.15   NEG cell.

AND function block.   The AND function places the logical AND of the inputs A and B (according to Table 2.16) on the output F. Thus the output circuit realization is simply a two-input AND gate, as shown in Figure 5.16.

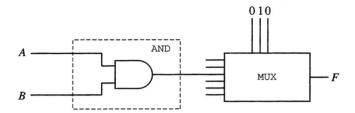

Figure 5.16   AND cell.

OR function block.   The OR function places the logical OR of the inputs A and B (according to Table 2.16) on the output F. Thus the output circuit realization is simply a two-input OR gate, as shown in Figure 5.17.

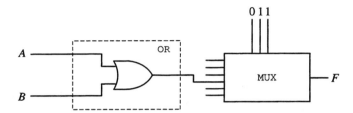

Figure 5.17   OR cell.

PLUS function block.   The PLUS function performs the arithmetic addition of the inputs A and B. Recall from Section 2.1 that the output of a particular bit n depends on the inputs A_n, B_n and the carry from the previous cell C_{n-1}. The circuit realization for this is given in Figure 5.18. Notice that the Y input is the **xor** of B_i and 0, which is simply B_i. The reason for this will become apparent shortly. Note also that the input to the first cell would have a 0 as the carry-in.

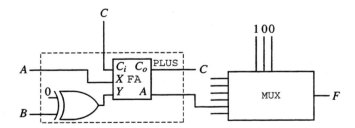

Figure 5.18   PLUS cell.

MINUS function block.   The MINUS function performs the arithmetic subtraction of input B from input A. Recall from Section 2 that subtraction may be realized by performing the **add** function between A and the complement of B, and then adding 1. The circuit realization for this is given in Figure 5.19. Notice that again for cell n the Y input is a **xor**, this time with B_n and a 1. The output from this (recall Table 2.16) is the complement of B_n. Note also that the input to the first cell would have a 1 as the carry-in. This would have the effect of adding one to $A + \bar{B}$ yielding, $A + \bar{B} + 1 = A - B$.

Process of putting it all together.   Now that each function has been specified, we are finally in a position to look at the complete conceptual circuit realization for a

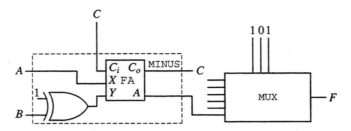

Figure 5.19 MINUS cell.

single cell (or bit) in the ALU, as given in Figure 5.20. Notice that the control lines will select one of the six operations. This philosophy of computing all operations concurrently and selecting the appropriate one is very common in hardware design.

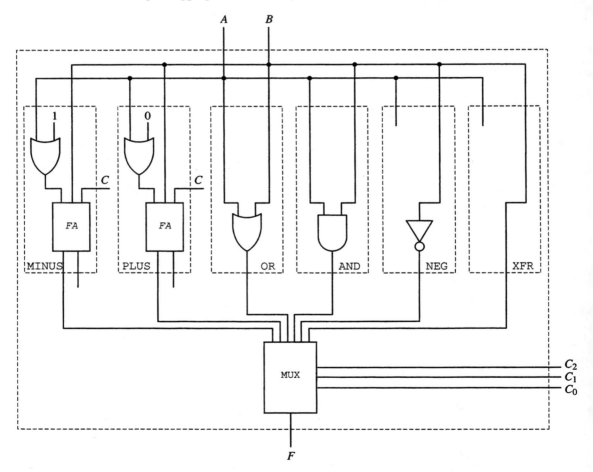

Figure 5.20 Conceptual circuit realization of single cell of ALU.

Notice the similarity between the **PLUS** function block and the **MINUS** function block. By using the **xor** gate and a control line we can implement both the add and subtract circuits with the same full adder. If the instruction is a **minus** we want a 1 as input into the **xor** gate, yielding a complemented input to the full adder; otherwise we want a 0, yielding an uncomplemented input. Looking at the PLUS/MINUS units of the complete ALU we see

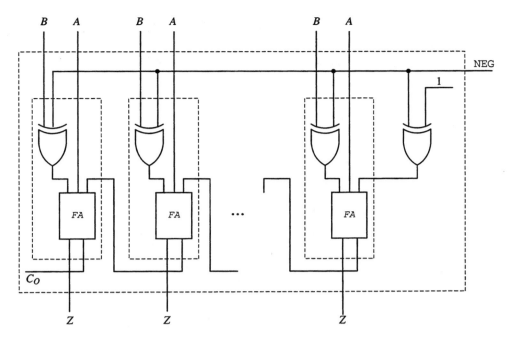

Figure 5.21   Circuit realization for PLUS/MINUS unit.

that a circuit realization like Figure 5.21 would satisfy our needs. The outputs (Z) will be directed into multiplexer ports 4 and 5 simultaneously.

With this improvement we finally show the circuit realization for the computational component of the ALU in Figure 5.22.

5.3.2 ALU Status Lines

In addition to computing the results of a particular operation, in our design the ALU is also responsible for providing status information about the result (S), to the condition code register, shown in Figure 5.23. This is somewhat different from an off-the-shelf ALU in which the status lines would be set by logic circuits external to the ALU. The reason for the integration of the ALU and status logic in this example is purely for convenience and aesthetics. By combining the two, we provide a single functional unit as was shown in Figure 5.12, which will then connect to the condition code register. As before, we will now consider how each of the status bits is set and will present the circuit realization for it.

Note also that the ALU is connected to the condition codes via an additional logic circuit as shown in Figure 5.24. This combinational logic is required to provide additional control over *when* particular bits in the condition code register should be set. This control is exercised by the CPU control logic to ensure that the condition code register is updated only when required.

Z Bit.   The Z bit is set when the result from the ALU for any operation is zero and reset otherwise. In other words, the Z bit is set when $(f_0 = 0) \wedge (f_1 = 0) \wedge \cdots \wedge (f_{15} = 0)$. This may be written as $(\overline{f_0} \wedge \overline{f_1} \wedge \cdots \wedge \overline{f_{15}})$. Using DeMorgan, this simplifies to $(\overline{f_0 \vee f_1 \vee \cdots \vee f_{15}})$. With this observation in mind we arrive at the circuit realization given in Figure 5.25.

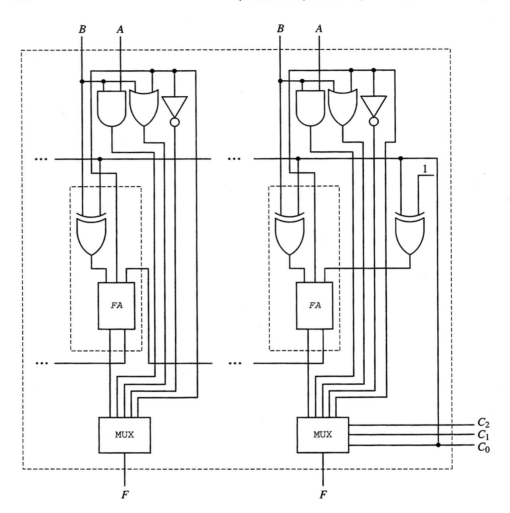

Figure 5.22 Circuit realization for computational component of ALU.

V Bit. The V bit is set when there is an overflow in the arithmetic operation and reset otherwise. Recall from Chapter 2 (see Figure 2.11) that an overflow occurs when the carry into the most significant bit is different from the carry out of the most significant bit. Recall that the arithmetic component of the ALU is based on the cascade adder as shown in Figure 5.26.

Using the logical **xor** of the carry-in and carry-out bits of the most significant bit, we are able to achieve the required function. The circuit realization for the V bit is therefore given as in Figure 5.27.

You may have noticed that as it stands now, the V bit may be set during a logical operation, which is contrary to correct operation of the CPU. This problem will be handled by logic outside the ALU, which we will discuss during the design of the CPU.

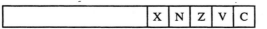

Figure 5.23 Condition codes.

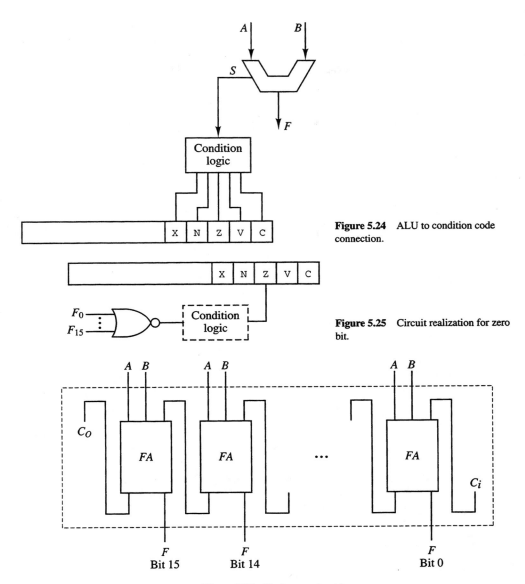

Figure 5.24 ALU to condition code connection.

Figure 5.25 Circuit realization for zero bit.

Figure 5.26 Basic cascade adder.

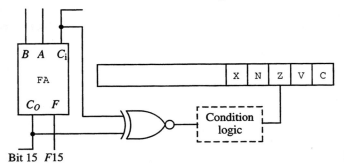

Figure 5.27 Circuit realization for V bit.

N bit. The N bit is set when the result of an arithmetic operation is negative and reset otherwise. In other words, the N bit is set when the most significant bit of the result is set. The circuit realization for this is given in Figure 5.28.

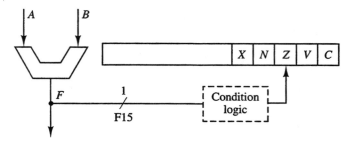

Figure 5.28 Circuit realization for N bit.

C and X bits. For the MC68000 instructions that we are implementing, both the X and C bits behave identically.[4] These bits are set when the carry-out of the most significant bit in the ALU is a 1 and reset otherwise. The circuit realization for this corresponds simply to a line from the carry out of the most significant bit in the ALU as given in Figure 5.29.

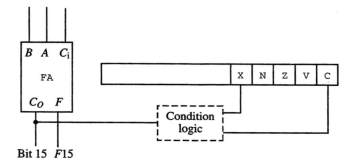

Figure 5.29 Circuit realization for X and C bits.

Process of putting it all together. With all the status bits defined; we are now in a position to see the complete picture for the status lines. Figure 5.30 shows the output status lines as controlled by the ALU.

5.3.3 Shift/Rotate Unit

The other important component in the computational unit is the barrel shifter. The reader should recall from Chapter 2 that we implemented a parallel load register with left and right shift, using a similar design. Figure 5.31 shows how a barrel shifter may be used to shift data in a single cycle. Notice that unlike Figure 2.71 there is no register required, because the barrel shifter is composed of combinational logic only.

5.3.4 CPU Control Design

State table logic design. The term **state table logic design** corresponds to the use of simple components connected together such that the correct output value results

---

[4] In the full MC68000 instruction set there exist instructions that treat these bits differently.

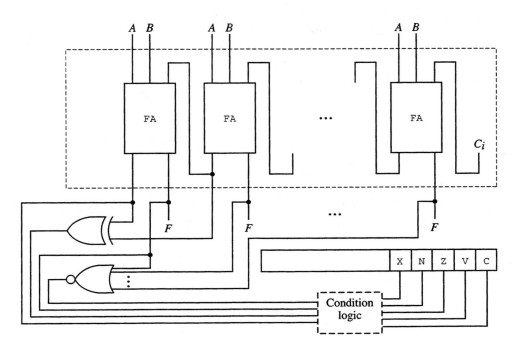

Figure 5.30   Output status lines as controlled by ALU.

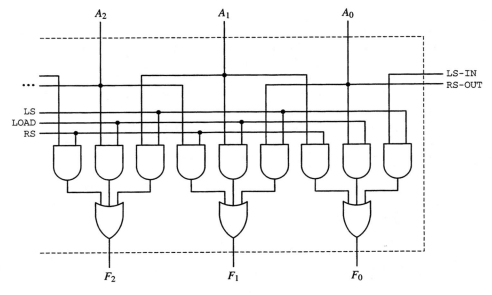

Figure 5.31   Shift/rotate logic.

from the specified inputs. In these terms, basic flip-flops such as the JK flip-flop may be considered constructed by state table logic design. Such a design procedure with a CPU may be considered rather ad hoc or random. Clearly we are not suggesting that the circuits are wired at random! Rather we do not impose artificial structure on the problem; instead we use the minimal combination of gates necessary to give the correct output (e.g., by determining the state tables and minimizing the combinational logic to realize the function). In the case of the computer, the inputs are the current instruction, the current value of the program counter, and the current value of all of the registers. Consider the case of a simple 4-bit computer, with only 4 instruction, 1 register, and 16 memory locations. The number of states in which the central processor may be is $2^4 * 2^4$. The instruction to be executed may be any of 2^4 values leading to as many as $2^4 * 2^4 * 2^4$ possible results, with the output function as the PC, the register, and perhaps a memory location. To compute this without structuring the problem would be impossible. In fact, the state tables would become enormous, even if we make some simplifying assumptions by using some of the building blocks that we have constructed. The task is simply beyond our reach. In addition to the overwhelming complexity of the task, we will discover that our design procedure is such that we are unable to verify whether the central processor operates in accordance with our expectations, or whether we have made some slight error in our design that went unnoticed. Finally we notice that looking toward the future any modification in the instruction set requires that the entire system be redesigned from scratch. Clearly, designing a central processor using this design procedure is a rather unsatisfactory technique. In fact, we discover that in the design of real systems only circuits of modest complexity are designed using state tables.

Clocked sequence implementation. The second design methodology is the so-called **clocked sequence** implementation. In fact, as we have seen, all of the building blocks of the central processor are either clocked registers or are combinational logic units. The design methodology used in the clocked sequence implementation is to use a single-system clock to coordinate the activity of all control points in the system. We define a single CPU instruction as a **macroinstruction** that will be composed of a sequence of **microinstructions** (or **micro-operations**). Each microinstruction is a well-defined action on one or more of the registers in the CPU. A well-defined operation might be, for example, adding two integers using the ALU and storing the result in a register, or loading a register from a bus, or incrementing a register by 1, or in fact anything that can be performed in a single clock cycle (or t-state). We will decompose the macroinstruction cycle into a few **named cycles**. We have already seen an example of this in Chapter 3 in which we introduced the **fetch cycle** and the **execute cycle**. During each of these cycles, a well-defined CPU function occurs, for example fetching data from main memory, or executing a register-to-register instruction. The current named state (i.e., the named cycle that the processor is currently in) is maintained by one or more 1-bit registers. Each named cycle is given a subscripted label, e.g., $c_0, \ldots, c_n$ where the subscript corresponds to the numerical representation of the control bits. Notice that a macroinstruction may consist of several named cycles, and a named cycle may consist of several microinstructions. Within a single named cycle, the execution of individual microinstructions is controlled by a single sequential counter driven by the system clock. The first cycle in the sequence is labeled t_0, the second t_1, etc. Typically, this counter will possess reset control to start the sequence from t_0 on the next cycle. Notice that the number of t-states must be sufficient to complete all the microinstructions required in any single named cycle. The transition between different named cycles is controlled explicitly, by loading the named cycle control bits with the appropriate value during the last microcycle of the previous named cycle.

The concept of using a synchronized clock to coordinate all register transfer events leads naturally to the idea of a register transfer language. A register transfer language is a language used to define CPU operations in a clocked system at the register level.[5] In a clocked system the state of the system is precisely defined by the contents of the registers in the system, at the start of a new cycle.[6] Thus by specifying system control in terms of updating registers based on the current contents of the control registers (i.e., the current named cycle, the current t-state, and any other control information required) and other internal registers (i.e., user programmable registers, PC, MAR, MBR, etc.) we uniquely specify the next state that the machine will enter. This fact may be used in design by modeling the system as a set of registers and specifying when data are transferred between registers. A language that permits us to describe such models is called a register transfer language. Modern register transfer languages (e.g., VHDL, which is a comprehensive hardware description language)[7] have the general appearance and expressive power of a high-level programming language. In keeping with a more modest design philosophy, we introduce a simple register transfer language,[8] which is sufficient for the purposes of this text.

Register Transfer Languages.   The register transfer language to be discussed later is rather generic. The introduction is informal and the language has only those features necessary to support the definitions required later in the text. Extensions to this generic language are easy to imagine (see questions at the end of the text) but are omitted for brevity. The language is composed of two **blocks**: a **definition block** followed by a **statement block**. The definition block is composed of a sequence of **definitions**, and the statement block is composed of a sequence of **statements**. This organization is shown subsequently.

```
;
; Generic Register Transfer Language Program
;
; Definition block
;
DEFINITION₁;
DEFINITION₂;
DEFINITIONₙ;
;
; Statement Block
;
STATEMENT₁;
STATEMENT₂;
STATEMENTₙ;
;
```

---

[5] During the design of a system there are languages available at many different levels, from the system level (e.g., ISPS) all the way to the circuit level (e.g., Magic).

[6] The addition of external interrupts invalidates this model, however, by expanding the model so that external interrupt lines are considered as another register that requires attention at the start of the cycle so that we may accommodate them.

[7] VHDL—Very High Speed Integrated Circuit (VHSIC) Hardware Description Language, IEEE standard 1076.

[8] Based on CDL, a Computer Design Language developed by J. Bara.

Notice that each definition and statement is terminated by a semicolon, with text after the semicolon to the end of the line considered a comment and thus ignored.

Let's start then with the definitions. The definition block is used to specify the components of the design. These include register names and sizes, which may be considered analogous to a register diagram of the system, clocks (i.e., simple binary counters with reset lines), and control lines composed of combinational circuits using output from the registers. Thus the definition block represents those elements that compose the state of the system.

A clock element is a simple sequential counter that may be reset to its first state. The specification for a clock is the keyword CLOCK followed by a list of clocks and their specification. The specification indicates the size and ordering of the bits in the clock, and is given as a numeric range enclosed in parentheses, using the range operator "-" to separate the integers. The range is mapped to the bit cells with the left-hand range specifier corresponding to the left-hand cell, and the right-hand range specifier corresponding to the right hand cell. Thus, the general form of a clock specification is as follows:

```
CLOCK reg₁(x₁-y₁), reg₂(x₂-y₂), ..., regₙ(x₃-y₃);
```

Thus we might define the system clock of a simple computer as follows:

```
CLOCK CLK(1-0);
```

indicating a 2-bit sequential counter. We assume the right hand bit is the least significant (i.e., changes most rapidly). Thus in binary, the counting is 0, 1, 2, 3, 0, 1, 2, 3, . . . etc.

We define a register as a collection of single bits. We are able to specify a complete register using the keyword REGISTER followed by a list of register names and their specification. Register names may be a single capitalized name (e.g., MAR, A0, SR, etc.). Thus, the general form for a register specification is as follows:

```
REGISTER reg₁(x₁-y₁), reg₂(x₂-y₂), ..., regₙ(x₃-y₃);
```

Thus we might define the register components of a simple computer as follows:

```
REGISTER PC(15-0);  16-bit program counter register
REGISTER MAR(15-0); 16-bit memory address register
REGISTER MBR(15-0); 16-bit memory buffer register
REGISTER CTRL(0-3); 4-bit control register (note reverse bit ordering)
REGISTER A(7-0),B(7-0),C(7-0),D(7-0); 8-bit registers
```

Notice that the size of the register is implied by the integer range and the order of the cells in the register is implied by the relative sizes of the range specifiers. Notice also that the contents of these represent the central processing unit's state at any time.

A combinational logic circuit may be defined and assigned to a label by using the boolean operators (+,.,') on selected fields of the registers (indicated by the bit number within the register) and other combinational circuits. The resulting line may then be used in the statement block to control the microinstruction sequence as a function of the contents of the internal registers. The circuit is defined by using the keyword LINE followed by a boolean expression using registers. Thus, the general form for a line specification is as follows:

```
LINE L1 (MBR(0)+MBR(1)+MBR(2)).(CTRL(0).CTRL(1)'.CTRL(2)'.CTRL(3)')
LINE L2 L1+(MBR(3).MBR(4))
```

This specifies that L1 will be true if any of the three low order bits of the MBR are high and we are in named state c_1.[9] Similarly L2 will be true if L1 is true or if both MBR bits 3 and 4 are true.

Let's now consider the statements block. The statement block specifies the actions (i.e., register transfers) to occur at each microcycle. Thus, the statement block may be thought of as the dynamic component of the design. In fact, as we shall see later, the statements actually specify the control logic which governs the runtime characteristics of the system. Each statement is composed of two parts, a **condition** part, and an **action** sequence (corresponding to one or more comma separated microinstructions, which may be executed concurrently). The remainder of the line is considered a comment. Thus:

Condition : Action$_1$, Action$_2$, ... , Action$_n$;

may be read as:

IF Condition THEN perform Action$_1$, Action$_2$ ... , Action$_n$

Thus, at the start of a microcycle, we may imagine that the *Condition* is evaluated and if true the corresponding microinstructions $Action_1, \ldots, Action_n$ are initiated.[10] These actions will cause some change in the state of the system that may change the condition in the next cycle. We consider first with the *action* part of the statement. Individual bits within a register are accessed by their bit position, with the bits assumed to correspond to the register specification given in the definition block. Thus, MBR(2) corresponds to the third bit counting from the right. A range of consecutive bits may be specified using the range operator "-" and multiple bit selections are comma separated. For example PC(6,4-0), specifies the bits 6, 4, 3, 2, 1, 0. During a single microoperation a register may take on a new value based on some logic function of the other registers. This is depicted using the assignment operator ←. The functions available may be any boolean expression (.,+,'), the concatenate operator (|), or may be a symbolic name corresponding to a well-defined microoperation (e.g., add for an ALU add microinstruction or inc for a register increment). Notice the number of bits specified on the left must equal the number of bits specified on the right of the assignment operator. The following are example register assignments (assume all registers are 8-bit parallel load registers).

```
A ← B;                              ;Load register A with the contents
                                    ;of register B.
A(7-0) ← C(2-0)|M  BR(0)|D(6-4);    ;Load bits 0-7 of register A with
                                    ;the concatenated bits specified
                                    ;on the left.
A ← A.B, B ← A;                     ;Multiple actions.
PC ← inc PC;                        ;Increment program counter
A ← B minus C;                      ;ALU minus function.
A ← MBR(15-8).(B(7-0) plus C(7-0)); ;Compound functions.
A(7-0) ← A(6-1)|A(7);               ;Rotate register right.
```

---

[9] Indicated by the value %0001.

[10] In fact of course the "evaluation" is realized by a combinational circuit, which we compute from the inputs to the conditional clause.

Notice that the same register may be selected as a source as well as the destination; this is a result of using clocked circuits. Notice also that we may easily specify arbitrary boolean expressions or serial operations such as rotate left. The complete set of symbolic functions will be up to the user. Typically, however, if an ALU is to be used; then the functions plus and minus usually will be available; if a barrel shifter is available, the operations lshift, rshift, and so on, usually will be available. Many languages define a complete set of operators for the users and provide an additional mechanism for users to define their own operators. In fact any operation that can be completed in a single cycle (i.e., uses only combinational circuits) may be defined.

Now we'll look at the *condition*. We require that the actions occur only when the condition part is true. Recall that each register (and several other building blocks) possess an enable line. Thus the register will accept data on the next clock cycle, provided the enable line is high. In other words, an *assignment* in the action part will occur if the enable line corresponding to the register on the left-hand side of the assignment is high. Thus, considering the *condition* as a logical function, we see that the register should be enabled when this condition is high. To restate this, if the output from the conditional expression *condition* is 1, the assignment will occur; otherwise, it will not. Clearly this may be implemented by using the condition function to enable the registers in that statement. Let us demonstrate this with some examples:

```
c0.t0   : MAR ← PC,   PC ← inc PC;
c0.I.q0 : MBR ← M[MAR];
c2.I.b  : PC ← MBR;
c2.I.b' : PC ← inc PC;
```

Notice that we may use combinational logic (.,+,') to construct boolean functions for the condition field. Notice, also, that the actions are only dependent on the condition field; there is not an implied sequential execution of the statements. Typically condition fields consist of several conjunctive clauses.

It is also extremely important to notice that in a register transfer language, any number of statements (microinstructions) could occur during a particular cycle, assuming their condition parts are satisfied. Also note that the order of the statements is completely unimportant (think about the condition part). This is distinctly different from sequential programming languages (including assembly programming) in which precisely one instruction is executed at a time with the sequence of execution defined by the order of the instructions in the code.

Sequence Control.   With the notion of a register transfer language defined, it is now easy to describe control of the clocked sequence implementation. Each statement has associated with it at least two terms in the condition clause, the named cycle number, and the t-state. Thus, each statement may only occur at a particular time, during a particular cycle. For example, consider a circuit with two named cycles ($c0, c1$) determined by a single bit C, and a four t-states ($t0, \cdots, t3$) determined by counter T. Then the statement set below

```
c0.t0 : MAR ← PC;
c0.t1 : MBR ← M[MAR], PC ← inc PC, T ← 0, C← 1;
```

might form the sequence of events for the **fetch** cycle ($c0$). The microinstructions would occur in sequence because the counter (T) would be incremented automatically each clock cycle. Notice that several microinstructions occur during $c0.t1$ including resetting T and moving to the next named cycle ($c1$).

Applying the division of instruction execution into named cycles and sequences within named cycles provides us with a systematic way of specifying all the events to occur within the CPU and the times at which they are to occur. To actually realize the sequence control logic, we notice that each register is enabled at different times during the instruction cycle. Thus, for *each* register we need only specify the conjunction of all the timing conditions during which that register is enabled. This expression will correspond precisely to those microcycles during which the register is to be loaded with data. We now discuss these concepts using a simple demonstration architecture. A detailed example using the clocked sequence implementation is presented in Section 5.4 using SIM68.

Consider the architecture in Figure 5.32 and the simple instruction format as defined in Table 5.12. The instruction is divided into three fields: opcode, indirect data flag, and address. There are 3-bit positions in the opcode giving rise to 8 possible instructions. In fact, the complement instruction requires no arguments and, therefore, may be used to provide an additional instruction format if required (e.g., immediate data, clear accumulator, etc.). The instruction set is defined in Table 5.13. The indirect data flag is used to indicate if an indirect cycle is required (indicated by an i after the instruction mnemonic) and may be used with all but the not instruction. In memory direct addressing ($I = 0$), the address field is used to select the memory location for the operand. Thus, the instruction lda $1000 will load the accumulator with data from location $1000. Similarly, sta $0000 will cause data in accumulator to be stored at location $0000. In memory indirect addressing ($I = 1$), the address field is used to fetch the *address* of the location in question. Thus the instruction ldai $1000 will load the data located at the *address* indicated by the contents of location $1000.

The ALU is assumed to be similar to that discussed earlier except that the condition codes are reduced to a single Z bit.

The task before us, therefore, is how to define the control logic for instruction execution using clocked sequence control. We will divide our macroinstruction execution into four named cycles: the **fetch cycle** (c_0), the **indirect cycle** (c_1), the **data cycle** (c_2), and the

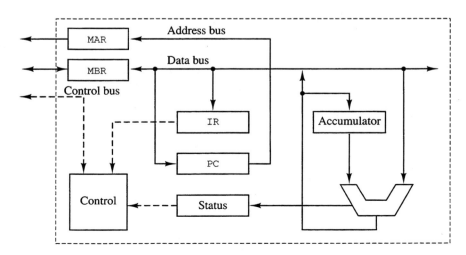

Figure 5.32 Simple single operand CPU architecture.

TABLE 5.12 Instruction format: Opcode field (bits 15–13) specifies the instruction required; the *I* field (bit 12) specifies indirect data; the address field (bits 11–0) specifies the address

Opcode		*I*	Address field
15	13	12	11 0

TABLE 5.13 Instruction set for Simple CPU

Mnemonic	Opcode			Function
LDA x	0	0	0	Load accumulator with data.
STA x	0	0	1	Store data into memory.
ADD x	0	1	0	Add data to accumulator.
SUB x	0	1	1	Subtract data from accumulator.
AND x	1	0	0	AND data with accumulator.
BEQ x	1	0	1	Branch to address if accumulator zero.
BRA x	1	1	0	Branch always.
NOT	1	1	1	Complement accumulator.

execute cycle (c_3). Each named cycle will consist of up to three *t*-states ($t_0, \ldots, t_2$). Below we specify the system description and microinstruction sequence using the generic register transfer language introduced earlier.

```
;
; Definition Block
;
CLOCK T(1-0);                  2-bit clock, counts 0,1,2,3,0,... with reset
REGISTER MAR(15-0);            Memory address register
REGISTER MBR(15-0);            Memory buffer register
REGISTER ACCUM(15-0);          Accumulator
REGISTER PC(15-0);             Program counter
REGISTER IR(2-0);             Instruction register
REGISTER STATUS(0);            Status bit
REGISTER C1(0),C0(0);          Labeled cycle control register
LINE I MBR(12);                Indirect line
LINE b ACCUM(0)'.ACCUM(1)'. ... .ACCUM(15)';   true if ACCUM = 0
LINE q0 (IR(15).'IR(14)'.IR(13)');    LDA instruction
LINE q1 (IR(15)'.IR(14)'.IR(13));     STA "
LINE q2 (IR(15)'.IR(14).IR(13)');     ADD "
LINE q3 (IR(15)'.IR(14).IR(13));      SUB "
LINE q4 (IR(15).IR(14)'.IR(13)');     AND "
LINE q5 (IR(15).IR(14)'.IR(13));      BEQ "
LINE q6 (IR(15).IR(14).IR(13)');      BRA "
LINE q7 (IR(15).IR(14).IR(13));       NOT "


;
; Statement Block
;
;FETCH
c0.t0          : MAR ← PC, PC ← inc PC;      Load MAR, inc PC
c0.t1          : MBR ← M[MAR];               Fetch instruction
```

```
c0.t2              : IR ← MBR(15-13)
c0.t2.I            : C0 ← 1;                      Go to indirect cycle, or
c0.t2.I'           : C1 ← 1;                      Go to data cycle

;INDIRECT
c1.t0.I.q7'        : MAR ← MBR(11-0);             Load MAR with address
c1.t1.I.q7'        : MBR ← M[MAR];                Fetch address
c1.t2              : C1 ← 1, C0 ← 0;              Goto data cycle

;DATA
c2.t0.q7'          : MAR ← MBR(11-0);             Load MAR with address
c2.t1.q7'          : MBR ← M[MAR];
c2.t3              : C1 ← 1, C0 ← 1;              Goto execute cycle

;EXECUTE
;lda
c3.t0.q0           : A ← MBR;                     Load accumulator
c3.t3              : C1 ← 0, C0 ← 0;              Goto fetch cycle (all instns)

;sta
c3.t0.q1           : MAR ← MBR, MBR ← A;          Load MAR and MBR
c3.t1.q1           : M[MAR] ← MBR;

;add
c3.t0.q2           : A ← A plus MBR;              Do the add

;sub
c3.t0.q3           : A ← A minus MBR;             Do the subtract

;and
c3.t0.q4           : A ← A and MBR;               Do the AND

;bra
c3.t0.q5           : PC ← MBR;                    Branch to new location

;beq
c3.t0.q6.b         : PC ← MBR;                    If b = 1 branch

;not
c3.t0.q7           : A ← not A;                   Complement A
```

To see how the macroinstruction execution occurs, we follow the microinstruction execution for a typical instruction, addi. At the start of the macroinstruction, the clock will be at state t_0, and the named cycle registers will be at state c_0. Looking at the statements in the statement block, we see that we are about to start an instruction fetch. The two micro-operations enabled are: load the IR and MAR from the PC, and increment the PC. At the start of the next cycle the clock will be t_1. Because the named cycle register has not been altered the current condition is $c_0.t_1$; thus an instruction fetch will occur, with the resulting instruction (addi) loaded into the MBR. Notice that without the IR, the current instruction would be lost, making further decoding impossible. In the next cycle ($c_0.t_2$) we set the named cycle register to either c_1 or c_2 depending on the value of I (defined as bit 12 in the IR). If I is high, the named state is changed to c_1; otherwise, it is changed to c_2. Because there is no $c_0 . t_3$, the next microcycle results in a no-op.

Because the instruction is `addi`, the next named cycle will be the indirect cycle c_1 with the clock counter back to t_0. Looking at the indirect cycle, we see that if the instruction isn't the `not` instruction (which cannot be indirect), we first load the MAR with the indirect address (bits 11 to 0 of the MBR) and then perform a memory fetch using this address. Finally we change the named cycle to c_2.

During the data cycle, the data is loaded from memory into the MBR. Notice that regardless of the instruction (NOT excepted) the effective address of the data has now been loaded into the MBR. The data cycle, therefore, consists of moving the effective address from the MBR to the MAR and performing a memory load. The final operations in the data cycle are to set the named cycle to c_3.

The final stage in processing a single macroinstruction is instruction execution. Notice that each condition in the execution phase has appended to it a q value, which corresponds to the desired macro-operation (decoded from the IR). Notice also that in general the actual instructions may be executed in a single microcycle. In the case of the `addi` instruction, the condition is $c_3 . t_0 . q_2$, with the microinstruction as the `plus` code to the ALU. The remaining cycles will be no-ops until the final t-state $c_3 . t_3$, which resets the named cycle to be the fetch cycle (c_0). Thus, the next cycle to be executed will be $c_0 . t_0$, which is the start of a new instruction fetch.

Notice the following points:

1. Not all cycle/t-state combinations are specified, indicating that nothing happens during these cycles.

2. The indirect cycle will only be executed if the indirect bit in the IR is set ($I = 1$).

3. During the indirect cycle we check to see that this is not the complement instruction. Notice that because the **not** instruction does not require an effective address, we could use these extra fields to implement additional instructions (e.g., I/O instructions).

4. The **beq** instruction is conditional on the value of the **b** line. This line is high when the accumulator output is zero and low otherwise. Thus, a branch will only occur if the data in the accumulator is zero.

To see how the sequence control logic operates, consider as an example the Simple CPU at the start of fetching a new instruction. Assume the program counter contains $100 and location $100 contains the instruction LDA $200 to load the contents of location $200 into the accumulator. The named cycle is c_0 and the current t-state is t_0. Looking at the conditional clauses in the microinstruction list, we see that only one of the conjunctions is true ($c_0 t_0$); thus, the microinstructions to occur will be MAR $\leftarrow$ PC and PC $\leftarrow$ inc PC which occur simultaneously. Thus, the MAR now contains $100 and the PC contains $102. Of course the t-state is also incremented to t_1. During the next microcycle the new condition is ($c_0 t_1$), which causes the microinstruction MBR $\leftarrow$ M[MAR] to be executed. The MBR now contains the LDA instruction. In the next microcycle ($c_0 t_2$), the instruction is loaded into the IR while the named cycle is changed to c_2 (because bit 12 of the IR is reset). The new t-state will be 0, because T resets after three clock ticks; thus, the next microcycle will be ($c_2 t_0$). Because the IR is loaded with LDA the selected q line will be q_0; all other q values will be 0. Thus, the microinstruction defined at ($c_2 t_0 \overline{I}$) will occur. We proceed in this manner noting that in each microcycle only specific microinstructions will be eligible to occur. Subsequent sets of microinstructions are determined by the new conditions that prevail as a result of the current operations.

We conclude this section by stressing that the sequencing action in the CPU is determined by incrementing the T register, coupled with a named cycle register C that maintains the current state of the system. These two registers are used in conjunction with external conditions (e.g., the i or q lines) to determine which microinstructions may occur. The register transfer specification should not be thought of as a sequential programming language.

Microprogramming implementation.   The final and most flexible approach to CPU implementation is **microprogramming**. It may not be obvious at this point, but it is the case that the clocked sequential approach becomes unwieldy as the processor design becomes more complex. This is particularly the case when we have multiple data registers and include MUX and bus control. In addition to design complexity, we note that the design itself becomes difficult to change, making the process of correcting design errors expensive and limiting the growth of the architecture.

A tidy solution to the sequence control problem is the use of a technique known as microprogramming. The idea behind microprogramming is simple. A small high-speed memory known as **control store** resides within the CPU. Each location in control store is directly addressable and specifies a subset of all possible micro-operations, bus enables, and line enables that are available to the CPU in a single microcycle. In addition, the control store encodes (either directly or indirectly) the next control store address to be examined. Another component known as the **sequencer** is responsible for stepping through the control store in an orderly manner. At the start of each microcycle, output from the control store determines which particular lines and buses will be enabled, which micro-operations are selected, and the address of the control store word to be selected in the next microcycle. Thus, the microprogrammed implementation can follow a sequence of events in exactly the same fashion as the clocked sequence implementation. The difference is that the entire control unit is now *programmable*. By changing the control store (which we may think of as a program), the designer changes the behavior of the CPU. Because the control store effectively defines the instruction set, and control store programs are extremely complex, usually end-users of the system will not make any modifications; thus, control store is often implemented using high-speed ROM. It is possible, however, for control store to be writable (called **writable control store**). In such a case, the control store is loaded from some device when the machine starts up. Under these circumstances, corrections or improvements in control store programs are relatively easy to install. We now consider the control store and sequence in more detail.

The control store typically has far fewer locations than main memory (usually 4K to 64K), but each location has many more bits (usually 20 to 100) and may be either **read only** or may be **writable**. If the former is the case, the control store is essentially high-speed ROM and is programmed by the manufacturers. If the latter, then the control store is essentially high-speed RAM and is loaded when the machine is powered up. Again the information is programmed by the manufacturers. The advantage of the latter is that changes to the control store are easily implemented on existing machines, without hardware modification. A location in the control store is called a **control word**, and is divided into two sets of fields called the **sequence control fields** and the **function fields**. The sequence control field is in turn typically divided into the **address field, condition field**, and **instruction field**. The sequence control fields are used to determine the state of the sequencer in the next microcycle. The **instruction fields** are highly system dependent and are used to control all CPU internals; this might include one or more ALUs, bus enables, line enables, register enables, and anything else in the CPU that requires control. Note that there is no confusion with macroinstruction terminology because of the context in which they are used. A simple control store and control word are shown in Figure 5.33. Notice that in this example, the condition control field and instruction field have been grouped together.

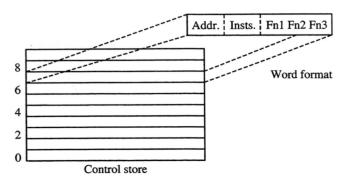

Word format

Control store

Figure 5.33   Microprogramming control store and control word format.

Using a single control word, the microprogrammer has complete control of all register, MUX, and bus enables during a single clock cycle. Thus, we may think of bits in the function fields as being wired directly to the different registers enables and so on.[11] Thus, any combination of microinstructions that may be legitimately executed in a single t-state may be represented by setting the appropriate bits in the function fields of the control word.

To see how the sequencer and control store operate together, consider Figure 5.34 and Table 5.14. At the start of a new cycle, the **microprogram counter** will contain the address of a word in control store memory, whereas the contents of this memory word will be resident in the **microinstruction register**. The function field from this register specifies function lines used to set all control points in the CPU for the current microinstruction. The instruction field specifies the sequencer control lines (c_0, c_1, c_2), which determines the actions of the sequencer during this microcycle. Finally the address field specifies a control store address, which may optionally be used in microprogram branching. The question of when and where to branch is determined by the instruction field and external conditions.

From Figure 5.34, the µPC may be either incremented or loaded with a new value, depending on the MUX control line. This control line is determined by the sequencer controls c_1 and c_2. As can be seen from Table 5.14, an input of 00 ($c_1 = 0, c_2 = 0$) will enable the increment path. An input of 01 ($c_1 = 0, c_2 = 1$) will cause a branch to occur. Thus, the address of control word in the next microcycle will be determined by c_0. The other two possibilities are dependent on condition code inputs. If a cc input (cc_1 or cc_2) is selected **and** the corresponding cc line is high, a branch will occur; otherwise, the next microinstruction will be loaded. This mechanism permits the microprogram execution flow to depend on external circumstances. The other sequence control line (c_0) selects as a branch address either some external source ($c_0 = 0$), or from the address specified in the microinstruction register address field ($c_0 = 1$). One possible use of the external address is to select a particular microcode sequence (starting at some control word address) based on the value of the IR. Thus the sequence of microinstructions executed will be controlled by the IR, which in turn is determined by the user's program.

---

[11] Actually there may be some decoding performed; see horizontal and vertical microprogramming later.

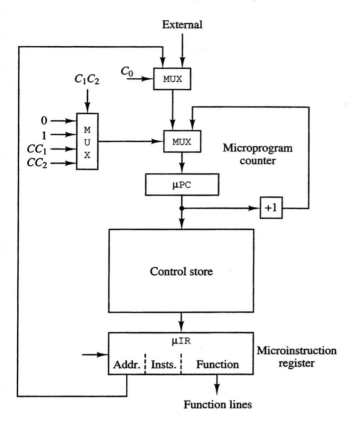

Figure 5.34 Sequencer and control store.

Without any complex decoding, the sequencer instruction field may be used to control the sequencer control points directly $(c_0 \cdots c_2)$. Thus, the instruction field will be 3 bits wide, with 1 bit for each of the control lines. Looking at Table 5.14, we see all the sequencer controls points and their actions listed. Notice, however, that several of the eight possible combinations make little sense. Using Table 5.14 we are able to construct a set of "useful" instructions as listed in Table 5.15. We associate with each of these sequencer instructions a mnemonic to indicate that appropriate action. Thus, the **cont** instruction (000) simply selects the next control word address for execution in the following cycle.

TABLE 5.14 Sequencer instruction fields

Sequence Control			Function
c_0	c_1	c_2	
0			Map from external address.
1			Address field.
	0	0	Continue with next instruction.
	0	1	Branch to address field.
	1	0	Conditional branch on cc_1 to address field.
	1	1	Conditional branch on cc_2 to address field.

TABLE 5.15   Useful sequencer instruction fields (selected from Table 5.14)

Sequence Control c_0	c_1	c_2	Function
0	0	0	CONT—Continue with the next microinstruction in control store.
1	0	1	BRA—Branch to address as given in address field.
0	0	1	MAP—Branch to address given externally.
1	1	0	BRcc_1—(Conditional branch (cc_1) as given in address field.
1	1	1	BRcc_2—(Conditional branch (cc_2) as given in address field.

To see the sequencer in operation, we now consider an example based on the fetch/execute cycle discussed earlier. We assume that the control store is 256 * 16. Because we are now working with a microprogrammable architecture the actions of the CPU are controlled explicitly by the control store. The precise contents of the control word are specified in Table 5.16. We mentioned earlier we have divided the word into its logical constituents.

TABLE 5.16   Control word address field

Sequencer control		Function fields		
Address	Instn.	ALU	Regs.	Misc.
16 bits	3 bits	3 bits	5 bits	2 bits

Although we have not specified the CPU design for this simple system, we assume that the indirect bit is used as an input to cc_1. Thus, $BRcc_1$ will permit a change in the flow of microprogram control based on the indirect bit. Also, we assume two MUXs: one selecting as an input to the PC, either the incremented PC or the contents of the MBR; the other selecting as an input to the MBR, either the accumulator or memory (i.e., M[MAR]). These MUXs are controlled by two 1-bit fields in the control word.

TABLE 5.17   Microprogram worksheet

Location	Sequencer control		Function fields		
	Address	Instn.	ALU	Regs.	Misc.

Using the worksheet, we may write the microprogram control store program. Recall each line of control store corresponds to a single t-state. As an example Table 5.18 shows the fetch cycle for the preceding CPU design.

TABLE 5.18 Microprogram Fetch cycle using worksheet

Location	Sequencer control		ALU	Function fields						
	Address	**Instn**		**Regs**					**Misc**	
				MAR	MBR	ACC	PC	IR	PC Mux	MBR Mux
$0000	$0000	%000	%000	%1	%0	%0	%1	%0	%0	%0
$0001	$0000	%000	%000	%0	%1	%0	%0	%0	%0	%1
$0002	$nnnn	%110	%000	%0	%0	%0	%0	%1	%0	%0

Clearly, writing microcode using the worksheets is cumbersome. In fact, you should recognize the same problems as were encountered when writing machine-level programs. Fortunately, the solution is similar. We define a **microprogram assembly language** in which the microprogrammer writes code, and we use a **microprogram assembler** to translate the code into control store words. These are then loaded into the store effectively loading the CPU's instruction set. Looking at the assembler language we base the syntax closely on the generic register transfer language. Notice that there are four primary fields: **location field**, **address field**, **instruction field**, and **function field(s)**. We now consider each of these fields separately. The location field specifies the address at which this control word will be loaded into control store. Notice in the example below that instruction sequences start at "random" addresses; the reason for this will become clear later. The address field specifies the branch address should a branch be taken. Notice that as before we specify the micro-instructions, these will correspond to function fields. For example, the ALU that we defined previously (and required three control lines) would be one of the function fields. Additional function fields might be bus selection, MUX selection, and register enables.

```
;Loc.  Addr.Field  InstField    FunctionFields

;FETCH CYCLE
   00      00       CONT     MAR ← PC, PC ← inc PC
   01      00       CONT     MBR ← M[MAR]
   02      nn       BRcc1
   03      00       MAP

;INSTRUCTIONS (Reached by MAP from IR)
;
;ADD instruction
   80      00       BRA      PLUS

;SUB instruction
   88      00       BRA      MINUS

;BEQ instruction
   90      92       BRcc₁    MINUS
   91      00       BRA
   92      00       CONT     MAR ← PC, PC ← inc PC
   93      00       CONT     MBR ← M[MAR]
   94      00       BRA      PC ← MBR

;BLT instruction
   ..      ..
;INDIRECT
   nn      ..
```

Each line in the microcode program corresponds to a set of micro instructions (given in the function field). We assume that the μPC starts (is reset) at location $00. During the first three microcycles, the next macro instruction is fetched from main memory. Notice that for the first two cycles the sequence controller is set to CONT; thus, the μPC is incremented each cycle. The next microprogram instruction will depend on the contents of the IR. In the case that the I-bit is set, the next microinstruction taken is at location $nn, otherwise it is at location $03. The sequence control field at location $03 corresponds to a MAP, thus the address of the next microcode instruction will be determined by the external lines, which in our simple example will be address **1opcode000**. Thus, microcode routines for each instruction will start at control store location $80 (opcode 0) and will be located every $8 words. Notice that if a particular instruction requires more than $8 locations we may BRA to some region of control store not used and continue there.

Horizontal and Vertical Microprogramming.   Three terms commonly used in conjunction with control store bit assignments are horizontal, vertical, and functional microprogram architectures. The difference between these lies in the amount of decoding logic required to drive the control points.

A control store is described as **horizontally microprogrammed**, if each control point in the design is directly controlled by a single bit in the control word. This is demonstrated in Figure 5.35.

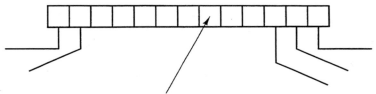

Each bit is used to specify a single control point

Figure 5.35   Horizontal encoding of control points.

Clearly, the width of a control word will be determined by the number of control points in the design and will typically be quite large (from 30 to several hundred bits). Notice that with horizontal microprogramming we permit the maximum possible parallelism in the architecture. The use of a single bit per control point allows the microprogrammer to enable any and all of the control points during a single microcycle. Notice also that typically there will only be a few of the control points actually set during any single microinstruction. For example, we will typically only enable one or two registers at any one time; similarly we will only select one device as writing to each bus. Thus, most of the bits in the control word will be zeros. With the expense of control store, we might consider such a scheme wasteful.

This observation regarding the sparsity of the map between the control word bits and control points permits some simplification. For example, if we know that seven control points are mutually exclusive we could save 4 bits of the control word by adding a decoder. The control word bits are used to drive the decoder, with the output from the decoder used to set the different control points (we would reserve one output for the do-nothing case). This is shown in Figure 5.36.

Another observation that permits a reduction in control word size is the division of the control points into classes (members in the same class are set/reset together). Clearly each class requires only one bit in the control word to set/reset it.

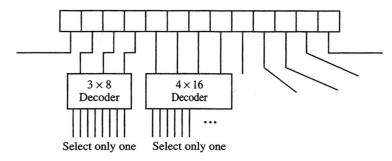

Figure 5.36   Mapping control word bits to control points.

With these comments in mind, a control word is described as **vertically encoded** if a high degree of decode logic is used between the bits in the control word and the control points. The advantage is clear—a much-reduced width in the control word. The disadvantage, however, is that to achieve this reduction we were required to make assumptions regarding when the control points would be set. Specifically, it is necessary to define completely the dependencies between different control points. Thus, a change to the design will be difficult to accommodate, that is, we have lost the flexibility provided by the use of microprogramming. Figure 5.37 shows vertical encoding.

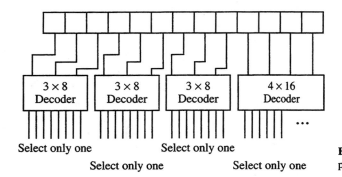

Figure 5.37   Vertical encoding of control points.

Between the high flexibility/width of horizontal encoding and low flexibility/width of vertical encoding lies a happy medium. This is typically called **function** encoding. We make use of the observation that although some control point groups have well defined functions (for example ALU control points), others are treated individually (e.g., register enables). With this in mind, we encode each control point group that has some well-defined function and leave the others. This is demonstrated in Figure 5.38.

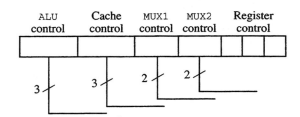

Figure 5.38   Function encoding of control points.

5.4 ADDITIONAL ARCHITECTURE TERMINOLOGY

No chapter on computer architectures would be complete without a brief description of some of the "buzz words" that are often applied when referring to computer architectures. In particular we describe here the following terms: **Von Neumann architecture**, **Harvard architecture, functional unit, pipelining**, and **cache**. The terms complex instruction set computer (CISC) and reduced instruction set computer (RISC) are described in greater detail in the next section.

5.4.1 Von Neumann Architecture

The term Von Neumann architecture (the term was coined in the late 1940s in honor of John Von Neumann, often called the father of computing) refers to a class of computers into which most traditional computers (including the MC68000) fall. The characteristics of Von Neumann architectures are a single memory in which both code and data are stored and a single CPU that performs the work. We consider the machines to possess a single instruction stream and a single data stream. Each instruction is fetched from memory and executed, possibly modifying the data stream. Often the term **Von Neumann** bottleneck is used. This refers to an inherent bottleneck in these architectures whereby the instruction stream and data streams are both competing for the same resource, the CPU-to-memory buses.

5.4.2 Harvard Architecture

The Harvard architecture is an alternative to the Von-Neumann architecture. Developed at Harvard University about the same time as Von Neumann's it has been increasingly popular in the last few years. The Harvard architecture assumes two separate memories, one for code (instructions) and the other for data. The obvious advantage of the Harvard architecture is that it alleviates the Von Neumann bottleneck. It also avoids potentially unpleasant errors caused by mixing data and instructions, that is, it is implicitly a tagged scheme. The disadvantage is that separate buses are required for the instruction and data streams at considerable extra cost. Only recently have manufacturers been forced to consider the additional expenses to achieve the throughputs that are now required.

5.4.3 Functional Unit

A functional unit is a unit of hardware that performs a single function. Typical functions are integer arithmetic $(+, -, *, /)$, the logic unit, floating point arithmetic $(+, -, *, /$, reciprocal, etc.), load/store, and so on. A function may either possess its own hardware unit or may share a unit with other functions. The advantage of specialized functional units is that during a particular cycle, several functional units may be operational simultaneously. Again, this offers improved performance over sequential execution. The disadvantage is the increased cost and complexity of individual functional units.

5.4.4 Pipelining

The term *pipelining* (or staging) refers to subdividing a single task into a number of stages such that each stage performs some well-defined subtask. The output from one stage is used as the input to the next. Thus, the entire sequence of subtasks may be likened to a pipeline, in that the input enters at one end, and the corresponding output appears some time later at the other end. An example of pipelining is an assembly line in manufacturing. In the context of computers, we note that many instructions require several cycles to execute. In a pipelined architecture, each phase of instruction execution is overlapped in time with the other phases. Thus, while we are completing the ith instruction (e.g., writing a result back to memory), we may be executing the $(i-1)^{th}$, decoding the $(i-2)^{th}$, and fetching the $(i-3)^{th}$, providing of course that these stages do not interfere with one another!

Clearly the advantage of pipelining is that in a system with k stages, provided the pipeline is full, we obtain a result every cycle, even though the time for any particular instruction to execute would be k cycles. Thus, we have increased performance of the non-pipelined system by a factor of k.[12]

In addition to pipelining instruction execution, we may apply similar techniques to individual functional units within the CPU. Notice that pipelining places a heavy burden on hardware requirements. For the preceding instruction pipeline, we must now be able to access three words of memory (one for instruction fetch, one to read a memory source, and one to write to a memory destination) *every cycle*!

5.4.5 Cache

In the early days of architecture design it was quickly realized that fetching data from memory is far slower than fetching it from registers. It was also recognized that often data is written out to memory only to be read back in a short time later. If then it were possible for the CPU to delay writing the data, we might be able to use the data value again without performing a memory read. We stress that this mechanism is completely transparent to the programmer. Such a device is a **cache**. Thus, a cache is a set of registers and associated hardware control that acts as an interface between the CPU and memory.

The design of caches is quite complex because they must store not only the data but also the address of the data. Also, they must be able to deliver a result very quickly; otherwise, the CPU will be unable to continue processing. In addition, they require a mechanism to write old data values to memory when full and to recognize when data scheduled to be written to memory should update a current cache entry. These issues are further complicated when multiple CPUs are connected on the same bus concurrently sharing a single memory. Caches vary in size from a few bytes (as in the case of the Intel 8086) to several thousand bytes (as in the case of the MC68030). In addition they are defined as either on-chip or off-chip. Because of the close relationship between cache and memory management units, they are often combined.

5.5 GENERAL CPU DESIGNS

In the following paragraphs we will discuss the general CPU architectures for successively more complex systems. Recall from Chapter 2 that all CPUs possess common elements such as a **program counter, instruction register, ALU,** and **status register.** There are, how-

---

[12] In fact because of instruction dependencies and hardware limitations pipeline speedups are never quite this high.

ever, significant hardware differences between a simple single-register 8-bit microprocessor (such as the Mostech 6502, used in popular early personal computers), a complex 32-bit processor (such as the MC68030), and the new high-speed RISC processors (such as the MC88100)! A detailed examination of any of these processors is outside the scope of this text; instead, we will concentrate on gross architectural issues associated with the different types.

5.5.1 Single-register Designs

Perhaps the simplest CPU organization is the single-register microprocessor as depicted in Figure 5.39. Notice that there is a single register to hold user data, usually called the **accumulator** connected directly to one of the inputs of the ALU. The output from the ALU may be routed to either the system data bus or back into the accumulator. The other input to the ALU would typically come from memory via the data bus. The instructions would typically be one word in length with an optional word specifying a memory address or immediate data. To see this instruction execution, recall from Chapter 2 the *fetch/execute* cycle. First the instruction is fetched into the MBR, and then moved to the IR, while the PC is incremented. In the next cycle, the instruction would then be decoded and any additional operands (e.g., immediate data or a memory address) would be fetched into the MBR (MAR for addresses). An optional cycle would then be executed to fetch the data from the memory location given in the MAR, had the operand been a memory reference (again incrementing the PC). Finally, in the next cycle the instruction would be executed (e.g., add MBR to **accumulator**). The cycle would then repeat with a new instruction fetch. Notice that the PC may be loaded from the MBR in the event that a branch is required. An architecture thus arranged would support instructions of the following form:

lda $10	Load accumulator from memory location $10.
sta $10	Store accumulator to memory location $10.
add $20	Add memory location $20 to the accumulator.
add #18	Add immediate data 18 to the accumulator.
blt $30	Branch to location $30 if *N*-bit set.

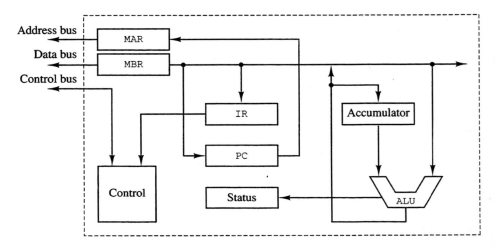

Figure 5.39 Typical structure of single-operand CPU.

Typically the data buses would be 8-bits and the address bus 16-bits; the microprocessor implementation would require about 20,000 gates. We would classify these as 8-bit microprocessors.

The control logic to coordinate these events would be a complex combinational logic circuit based on the current state of the machine. Details of how the control would operate are best explained by an example and are therefore left to the SIM68 component realization in Section 5.6. For now we simply state that the control mechanism for the preceding could be easily handled using the **discrete logic implementation** (defined later).

5.5.2 Muliple-register Designs

A modest extension to Figure 5.39 involving several on-chip registers results in a computer organization, as depicted in Figure 5.40. The advantage of having several registers is clear. The instruction set may now be extended to include instructions with two operands. This permits register-to-register operations, reduces the number of memory references, and permits additional addressing modes (e.g., using one of the registers as an **index** when accessing memory. With this architectural improvement, the instruction set may offer the following types of instruction:[13]

```
add  b          Add register B to the accumulator.
mov  a,b        Move register A to register B.
lda  $10(i)     Load accumulator with memory location defined by
                index register I plus a displacement of $10.
inc  i          Increment index register I.
```

Notice that the additional register file permits considerable flexibility with the instruction set. Additional features which *may* be provided include special registers for particular operations (e.g., index registers, stack registers, and multiply/quotient registers.

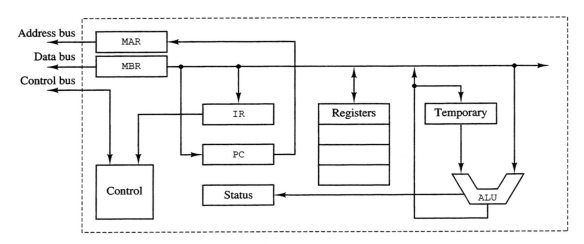

Figure 5.40   Typical structure of one-and-one-half–operand CPU.

---

[13] The RISC philosophy questions some of these observations, as discussed at the end of Chapter 6.

Excellent examples of this microprocessor organization are the Intel 8085, Zilog Z80, and the MC6809 microprocessors. The control logic to drive these would typically be discrete logic. The data bus would typically be 8/16 bits, whereas the address bus would be 16/20 bits, and the implementation would require approximately 40,000 gates. Developments from these architectures include the Intel 8088 (used in the original IBM PC) and the 8086, which we would classify as 16-bit microprocessors.

5.5.3 General-purpose Register Designs

The next major step in microprocessor organization is the removal of special-purpose accumulator(s). Additional internal data buses are included, with the register file connected to each. The advantage of this is that now any of the registers may be specified as sources with the output directed to any other register. We note that an internal bus and logic may be saved, if the destination register is the same as one of the source registers. A typical organization for a two- (or three-) operand organization is shown in Figure 5.41. With the increased flexibility in the organization, there are typically many registers to use (e.g., 16) and a wide selection of addressing modes. Because of the increased number of instruction formats and the hardware complexity **microprogramming** is used. Such processors would possess 32-bit data buses and at least 32-bit address buses. The implementations usually require in excess of 70,000 gates and may properly be called 32-bit microprocessors.

   A good example of the two-operand instruction set architectures are the Intel i286, i386, i486, and the MC680X0 series (the series name was in fact derived from the gate count). Although the MC68000 has fourteen addressing modes and five data types, it does not provide complete two-operand addressing. It offers more than the **load/store instruction set**, however, in that one operand may be in memory while the other must be in register. As the number of addressing modes and data types increases, the architecture is usually

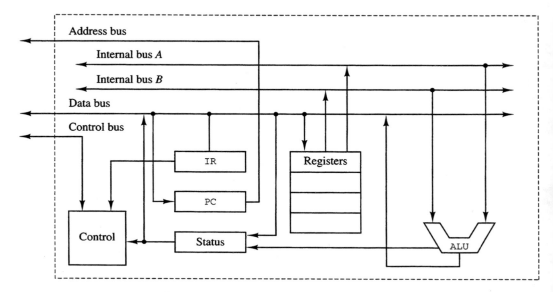

Figure 5.41 Typical structure of three single-operand CPU.

referred to as a CISC. The MC68000 is a simple CISC machine. Typical examples of the MC68000 instruction set are as follows:

```
add r1,r2          Add register 1 to register 2.
mov 20(a1),d0      Move the data in location
                   (a2)+20 to register d0.
```

Instruction sets may contain any number of additional features that the manufacturer considers necessary. An excellent example of a highly complex instruction set is the DEC VAX 11/780 instruction set. The architecture is a complete three-operand processor that would permit instructions of the following form:

```
add3 r1,r2,r3           Add register r1 with register r2
                        placing the result in register r3.
add3 $10, $20, $30      Add the contents of memory
                        location $10 to that of memory
                        location $20 placing the result in
                        memory location $30.
```

CISC design philosophy. Notice that the programmer may specify both the sources and destination as memory locations, thus bypassing the register file completely. In addition to providing the programmer with three-operand instructions the VAX instruction set provides many instructions to aid assembly programming. In fact, compared with the MC68000's 120+ instructions (including different modes) the VAX weighs in with more than 300 instructions! The scope of the VAX instruction format is demonstrated by a sample of the instruction details as listed subsequently.

Data Types. The VAX supports seven different data types including five forms of the integer type (with both quadword—64 bits, and octaword—128 bits!), four forms of the floating-point type, packed decimal, character string, variable length bit fields, numeric strings, and queues (to support bi-directional linked list operations).

Addressing Modes. The VAX supports sixteen different addressing modes including immediate, register, register deferred, autodecrement and autoincrement, autoincrement and autodecrement deferred, absolute, displacement, displacement deferred, and indexed.[14] In general the modes and instructions are orthogonal (i.e., operands specified in instructions may use any of the modes).

Special-purpose Instructions. The VAX supports many specialized instructions to "assist" the assembly language programmer. Examples of specialized instructions are add compare and branch, case (as in the HLL case selection mechanism), convert (different formats from one to another), edit packed to character, find first clear byte, insert/delete from queue, locate character, evaluate polynomial, and scan character, to name but a few.

The success of this instruction set may be gauged from the popularity of the VAX during the 1970s and 1980s. Although CISC machines are currently unfashionable, they have much to offer.

RISC design philosophy. Recently much attention has been given to RISCs; we shall therefore briefly explain the characteristics that make up a RISC computer and

---

[14] See Chapter 6 for an explanation of addressing modes.

discuss their popularity. In one sense, RISCs may be thought of as a step back in terms of instruction set design! Rather than providing a complex set of instructions that offers the assembly-level programmer a rich environment (as with the CISC architectures) at the expense of some loss in performance, the RISC architectures assume the philosophy that today programming is done using high-level programming languages and that only the compilers make use of the machine instruction set. Because compilers are typically unable to make full use of complex instructions and addressing modes, it is argued that a simple load/store architecture with faster execution speeds is more useful. The extra space on the chip (real estate in computer architects terminology) resulting from the simpler architecture is instead used to provide a larger register file and cache. Another point argued in favor of RISC architectures is that they are more easily scaled to meet future demands.

Figure 5.42 shows the typical structure of a RISC central processor. We now provide the general characteristics that define a RISC computer and discuss in some detail the reasons for the drive to RISC architectures.[15]

1. A relatively small number of instructions (typically less than 100).
2. Few addressing modes (perhaps only two, register and indexed).
3. Single cycle execution of all instructions.
4. A load/store architecture, that is, memory is accessed using only the load and store instructions.
5. A hardwired control unit. Recall from Section 5.3 that the control unit may be either hardwired or microprogrammed. With a simple instruction set and computer-aided design methods the control unit may be reasonably designed using sequence control logic.
6. A large register file. The savings in chip real estate from a simplified design may be used to support a register file size of more than one hundred 32-bit registers.
7. Instructions are designed to facilitate compiler-generated code rather than programmer-generated code.

It would be unfair to discuss the virtues of RISC architectures without some discussion of the perceived problems associated with them.

1. Clearly, if the instruction set is less complex it will in general require more instructions to achieve a complex operation. Consider a single MC68000 instruction versus a sequence of MC88100 instructions as shown below:

```
; MC 68000 loads d3 with (100+(a1)+(d2))
move.w  #100(a1,d2),d3          ; MC68000 instruction

; MC88100 loads r3 with (100+(r1)+(r2)) using r4 as temp.
lda     #100,r4                 ; load $100
add     r2,r4                   ; add in r2
lda     [r1,r4],r3              ; using indexed mode to fetch dat
```

---

[15] D. Tabak, *RISC Architecture*. Letchworth, Hertfordshire, England: Research Studies Press, 1987.

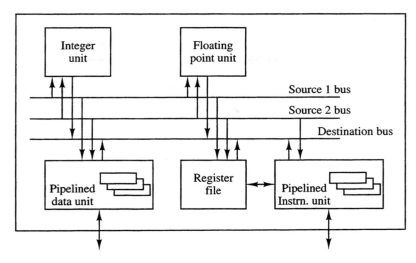

Figure 5.42   Typical structure of RISC CPU.

Notice that although the number of instructions is greater (three versus one) when we consider length, in bytes of code generated, we notice that the difference is less profound. The MC68000 code requires 4 bytes, whereas the MC88100 requires 12.

2. The additional size of the RISC code places additional requirements on all components of the computer system. More main memory is required to hold the programs while they are executing, additional backing store is required to hold them, and assembly language programming will take longer because of the limited instruction set.[16]

3. It has been argued that the performance advantage of RISC machines is due only to the larger register size. It has been suggested that if the CISC instruction sets were to embrace a large register file they too would experience significant performance improvements.

4. Several vendors have suggested that it is possible to obtain the best of both worlds— single cycle execution for simple instructions and support for complex instruction formats. Often these processors are described as possessing a RISC engine at the heart of a CISC processor. The MC68040 has been described (by employees of Motorola!) in this sense.

At present the final word on whether RISCs are an improvement on CISCs has yet to be said. It is often the case that when the pendulum swings from one extreme, it will swing through to the other.

5.6 SIM68 CPU DETAIL DESIGN

During the previous sections, we introduced all of the necessary components to construct a digital computer. In particular, we have examined the functions of multiplexers, demultiplexers, encoders, decoders, registers, memory, and the ALU. We also discussed the organi-

---

[16] This problem may be addressed by writing macros.

zation of different classes of microprocessor including 8-, 16-, and 32-bit processors including CISC and RISC architectures. In this section we will use some of these basic blocks and concepts to construct a simple 16-bit microprocessor based on the SIM68 instruction set. As we have just seen, there are three primary approaches to the design of a digital computer: random logic, clocked sequence implementation, and microprogramming. In Section 5.6, we demonstrate a clocked sequence hardware realization of SIM68 using the ALU developed earlier. Finally in Section 5.6.3, we demonstrate how the circuit may be modified to make use of microprogramming based on the sequencer discussed in Section 5.3.4.

Before describing in detail the central processor implementation, timing, and sequence control, we review the SIM68 instruction set. To refresh your memory we present the instruction set in Table 5.19 with some additional information that will prove useful in the future.

As has already been noted there are nine different instructions, ADD, SUB, COMP, SWAP, MOVE, Bcc, TRAP, MULT, and DIV, which we have labeled q_0 to q_8. We

TABLE 5.19 SIM68 instruction set

Timing and sequence		
Opcode	Operands	Q value
add	sD_n, dD_n	
add	sD_n, dA_n	q_0
sub	sD_n, dD_n	q_1
cmp	sD_n, dD_n	q_2
swap	sD_n, dD_n	q_3
move	sD_n, dD_n	
move	sD_n, dA_n	
move	sA_n, dD_n	
move	sA_n, dA_n	
move	$sA_n, dmem$	q_4
move	$sD_n, dmem$	
move	$smem, dA_n$	
move	$smem, dD_n$	
move	$smem, dmem$	
bra	mem	
beq	mem	
		q_5
bgt	mem	
blt	mem	
trap	#0	q_6
muls	sD_n, dD_n	q_7
divs	sD_n, dD_n	q_8

also recall that some of these instructions have several different modes. In particular, the MOVE instruction uses three different modes: **data register direct, address register direct,** and **address register indirect with a displacement.** These modes may be specified for either the source or destination register. Table 5.20 lists these modes with appropriate acronyms for use later. We also notice that the Bcc instruction has four different forms depending on the condition under which the branch will occur.

TABLE 5.20   Addressing Modes

Addressing Modes	
Notation	Mode
sD_n	Data register direct (source)
dD_n	Data register direct (destination)
sA_n	Address register direct (source)
dA_n	Address register direct (destination)
smem	Address register indirect with displacement (source)
dmem	Address register indirect with displacement (destination)
mem	Program counter relative (branch address)

5.6.1 Timing and Sequencing

Cycles.   Looking at the instruction set, we identify a maximum of four different *cycles* for any particular instruction. The four cycles are given in Table 5.21 below.

TABLE 5.21   Instruction Cycles

Cycle specification				
Cycle name	C1	C0	Fn.	Comment
Fetch	0	0	c_0	Fetch the instruction from memory, load into the IR.
Indirect source	0	1	c_1	Compute the effective address of the source (optional).
Indirect destination	1	0	c_2	Compute the effective address of the destination (optional).
Execute	1	1	c_3	Execute the instruction

Notice that we have associated with each cycle (c_0 to c_3) a state represented by the bits of C0 and C1. Thus, we are in the fetch cycle (c_0) when bits C0 and C1 are both 0. We will use these bits to control which activities occur by ensuring that every microinstruction is associated with a single cycle. This is accomplished by **and**ing the cycle with any additional fields in the timing side of the microinstruction.

The cycles, as the table indicates, are fetch, indirect source, indirect destination, and execute. These cycles have the following interpretation. The **fetch** cycle is used to fetch the instruction from memory. To do this the program counter will be loaded into the MAR and a read from memory will be issued. The result is loaded into the MBR which will be moved into a temporary instruction register (IR). The next cycle is the **indirect source** cycle. During this cycle, if the instruction requires it, the effective address for source address register indirect data required by an instruction is computed, and the operand is fetched into a temporary register. Notice that in the SIM68 only the MOVE instruction possesses this address mode. The third cycle is the **indirect destination** cycle. During this cycle, again if the instruction requires it, the effective address of the destination address register indirect data required by an instruction is computed, and the operand is fetched into a temporary register. Notice again that in SIM68 only the MOVE instruction possesses this mode. The final cycle is the **execute** cycle. With the operands now directly available to the processor in either a user register or an internal temporary register the instruction may be executed. Should the instruction write data back to memory (e.g., in the MOVE instruction) the destination effective addresses will have been computed in cycle c_2. Once the current instruction has completed the cycle repeats starting again with the fetch cycle c_0. Notice that transition from one cycle to the next is under sequence control, at the end of each cycle the control logic will set C0 and C1 to the values appropriate for the next cycle. For example, at end of the fetch cycle the cycle register would be modified to either c_1 (indirect source cycle) by setting C0 or c_3 (execute cycle) by setting C1 and C0.

Recall also that at some point during the instruction the program counter will have been modified (otherwise we will keep executing the same instruction!). The program counter will be incremented at least during the fetch cycle, and it may be incremented again during the indirect source and indirect destination cycles.

t-States.

In addition to dividing the instruction processing into four cycles, we note that a single clock tick (or microcycle or *t*-state) is insufficient to perform all the operations that we require during the cycle. For example, consider the fetch instruction. We know that to perform a fetch we are required to load the MAR with the memory address to be fetched. This will take one microcycle. *Then* we must load the MBR with the data from memory which requires another microcycle. Thus the fetch cycle requires *at least* two microcycles. In fact as we shall see some cycles consist of up to five microcycles. Within a single cycle the microcycles occur in order starting from 0, labeled t_0. During each microinstruction the system clock increments the *t*-state counter so that a new *t*-state will be entered at the start of the next clock pulse. Notice that any number of microinstructions occur during a single *t*-state provided they do not interfere with one another. The *t*-states associated with SIM68 are given in Table 5.22.

TABLE 5.22   *t*-states

t-states			
T2	T1	T0	
0	0	0	t_0
0	0	1	t_1
0	1	0	t_2
0	1	1	t_3
1	0	0	t_4

In the same way that the current cycle is maintained by a 2-bit register, so the current t-state within the cycle is maintained by a parallel load cyclic 5-bit shift register (see later discussion). The shift register is clocked by the master clock so that successive t-states are selected. In the same way that each microinstruction has a cycle code c_0 to c_3 associated with it, so each instruction has a t-state that corresponds to when the microinstruction is valid. Thus a single microinstruction in the clocked sequence implementation has the form as given in Table 5.23.

TABLE 5.23   Microinstruction in clocked sequence implementation

Condition control	Actions
$c_x t_y \cdot$ other conditions	Set of microinstructions to perform during this micro-cycle

5.6.2 CPU Design

As a first attempt at our design we might consider the block diagram representation of the circuit as in Figure 5.43. Notice that the computer design makes use of the basic architectural features discussed earlier. There are two internal buses (the SBUS and the DBUS), which connect together the major components of the system. The SBUS is used for the source operands, and the DBUS is used for destination operands. Because of the complexity of address calculation the effective addresses are computed using a separate adder and temporary register area.

Although Figure 5.43 is ideal for a high-level representation of SIM68, we are interested in a more thorough view. To this end, we have decided to implement SIM68 using no common buses, only multiplexers. Although this decision makes the design more complex, it also shows each data path and permits several functions to occur simultaneously.

Using only the basic blocks discussed earlier then, the design of the CPU is given in Figure 5.44. Notice that in the overall design there are five basic regions: arithmetic, register control, memory control, address computation, and timing and control. The design makes use of seventeen registers, of which the programmer "sees" ten, thirteen 16-bit-wide two-to-one multiplexers, a decoder, an adder, the ALU designed in Section 4.1, and some control logic. In fact, the CPU design outlined here is sufficient to support more complex instruction formats than that of SIM68. We now discuss each of the basic regions in some detail.

Memory access region.   The memory access region consists of main memory (actually connected externally to the processing unit) as shown in Figure 5.45, component A. Notice that memory is composed of $2K \times 8$ bit memory cells attached directly to the address bus. The data lines from each memory cell are attached to the data bus via tristate buffers as explained in Section 2.4. A read/write operation is determined by the value of the $R/\overline{W}$ line, which in turn is controlled by the sequencing logic of the processor.

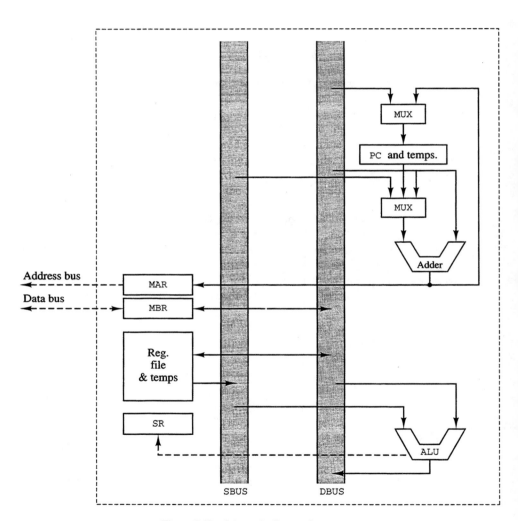

Figure 5.43   Schematic diagram for SIM68.

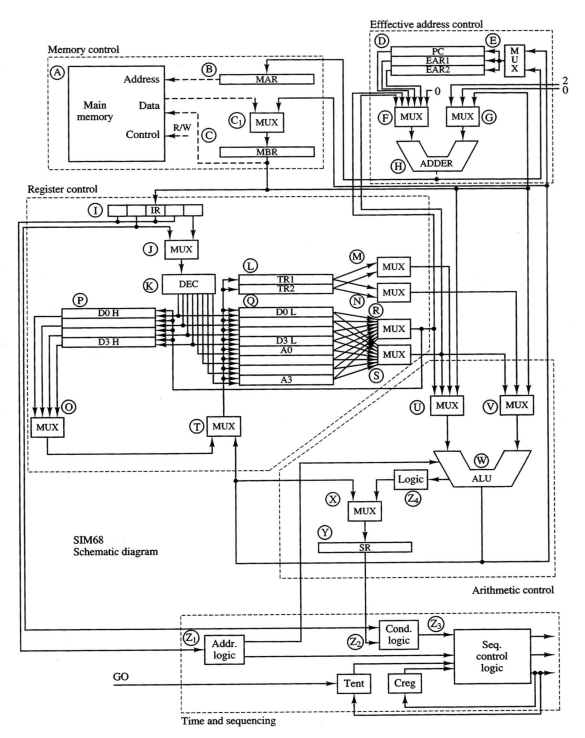

Figure 5.44   SIM68 circuit design.

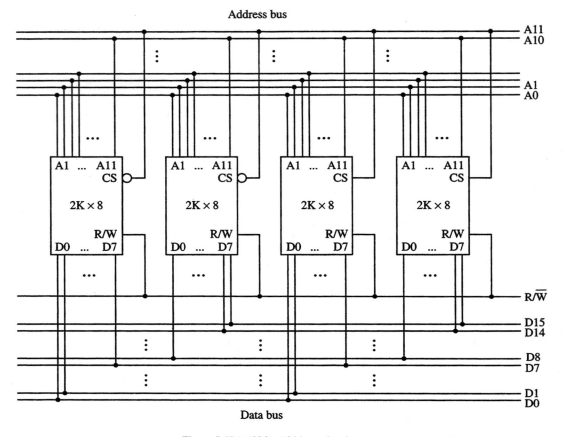

Figure 5.45 A 4096 × 16-bit word main memory, component A.

The other components of the memory access region are two 16-bit registers, the MAR (Figure 5.46, component B) and the MBR (Figure 5.47, component C), and a multiplexer (Figure 5.48, component C_1).

For the purposes of SIM68, we may think of the MAR as being directly connected to the address bus (thus B_MAR_OUT could actually be the address bus), and the MBR as

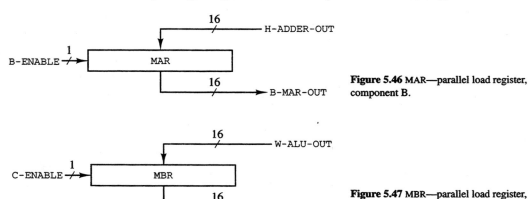

Figure 5.46 MAR—parallel load register, component B.

Figure 5.47 MBR—parallel load register, component C.

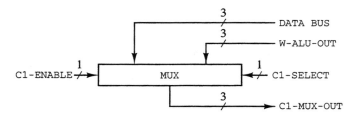

Figure 5.48   Two-input MUX, component C_1.

indirectly connected to the data bus. Input to the MAR comes from the adder and is loaded only when enabled via B-ENABLE. Input to the MBR is from either the ALU or from the data bus. With the processor design using no internal bidirectional buses we must select this input using a two-input multiplexer (Figure 5.49, component C_1). The selection is based on the sequencing logic. The MBR is connected to the data bus through a set of three-state line drivers. The read/write line associated with the data bus is enabled based on the sequencing logic.

Effective address region.   The effective address computation region (Figure 5.49) consists of three registers (D) three multiplexers (see E, F, G) and an Adder (H).

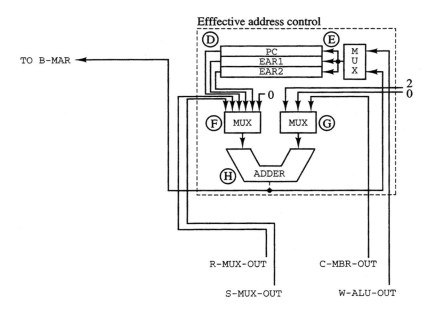

Figure 5.49   Effective address computation.

The function of the effective address computation is to permit the calculation of the source and destination effective addresses. Recall that the only effective address mode available in SIM68 is address register indirect with a displacement. Thus, the computation unit is only required to add two values, the contents of an address register and a displacement. Notice that the displacement will be obtained from main memory via the MBR. The result from this addition may be either saved in EAR1, EAR2, or may be written directly to the MAR.

Figure 5.50 shows the three 16-bit parallel load registers used in effective address computation. Notice that each register has a register enable line that is under the control of the sequence logic.

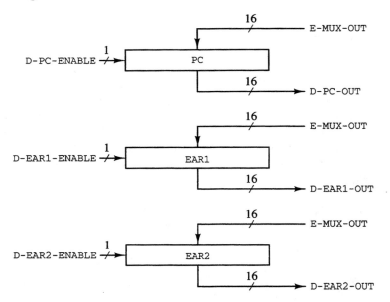

Figure 5.50 PC and temps—parallel load registers, component D.

Figure 5.51 shows the two-input multiplexer. The inputs may be either the output from the adder, or the output from the ALU. The multiplexer is controlled by an enable line and a single select line. Input selection details are given in Table 5.24. Notice from the diagram that the multiplexer output goes to all three registers, permitting any of the registers to receive the selected data.

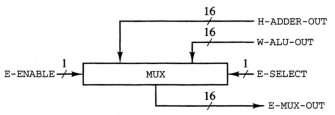

Figure 5.51 Two-input MUX, component E.

TABLE 5.24 Truth table, component E

E-SELECT	Input
0	W_ALU_OUT
1	H_ADDER_OUT

Figure 5.52 shows multiplexer F controlling input to the A side of the adder. There are six possible inputs: the three registers, the constant 0, output from multiplexer R, and output from multiplexer S. The latter two indicate that that inputs could either be a source

or destination register, determined by the appropriate fields in the IR. As with all multi-plexers there is an enable line and a set of select lines. Table 5.25 shows the input selection based on the value of the select lines.

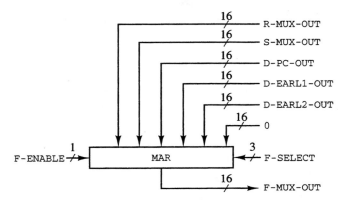

Figure 5.52 Five-input MUX, component F.

TABLE 5.25 Truth Table, component F

F-SELECT			Inputs
0	0	0	R_MUX_OUT
0	0	1	S_MUX_OUT
0	1	0	D_PC_OUT
0	1	1	D_EAR1_OUT
1	0	0	D_EAR2_OUT
1	0	1	0

Figure 5.53 shows the three inputs to the multiplexer attached to the B side of the adder. The inputs correspond to the constants 0, 2, and the output from the MBR. Input selection line control details are given in Table 5.26.

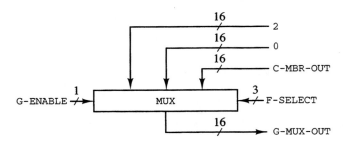

Figure 5.53 Three-input MUX, component G.

TABLE 5.26 Truth Table, component G

C-SELECT		Inputs
0	0	2
0	1	0
1	0	C_MBR_OUT

In fact, we see that any of the three effective address control registers may be loaded from either the adder or from the ALU output. The left side of the adder may select inputs either from the internal registers (*D*), a source register as dictated by the IR, a destination register as dictated by the IR, or the constant 0. The right side of the adder may select as inputs either the MBR or the constants 0 or 2. With this in mind, you should verify that following effective addresses are easily obtainable.

```
PC,MAR ← PC              ; PC
       ← PC + 2          ; PC increment
       ← PC + MBR        ; PC relative addressing (PC + disp)

EAR1,EAR2 ← An + MBR     ; Address Register Indirect (An + disp)

MAR ← EAR1,EAR2          ; load a precomputed effective address
```

In fact, many other addressing modes could also be obtained; however, this is unnecessary for the SIM68 instruction set.

Figure 5.54 shows the adder unit. The two inputs are the multiplexers previously discussed. This unit could be realized using the cascade adder discussed in Chapter 2. As with the ALU, the circuit is composed of combinational logic only.

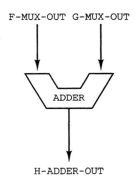

F-MUX-OUT G-MUX-OUT

ADDER

H-ADDER-OUT

Figure 5.54 A 16-bit adder, component H.

Register access region.   The register access region consists of fifteen 16-bit registers (see Figures 5.55, 5.58, 5.62, and 5.63) composed of the instruction register (IR), two temporary registers, four address registers, and four data registers (low word and high word); seven multiplexers (see Figures 5.56, 5.59, 5.60, 5.61, 5.64, 6.65, and 5.66) and a decoder (see Figure 5.57).

The IR (Figure 5.55) is loaded from the MBR during the fetch cycle with the first word of the instruction. From this word, we are able to determine the following information: the opcode, source address mode, the source address register (if any), the destination address mode, and the destination address register (if any). This information is available by considering particular output lines from the IR, as shown in Figure 5.55. Because of the complexity of the MC68000 instruction set, tasks such as instruction decoding will require some combinational logic as discussed in timing and sequencing.

Figure 5.56 shows a two-input 16-bit multiplexer. The multiplexer selects either the source or destination address register specification from the IR. Thus, looking at Figure

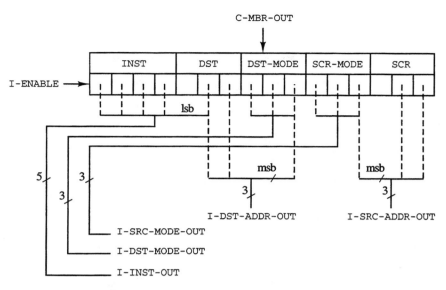

Figure 5.55   Instruction register—parallel load register, component I.

5.56 with an instruction in the IR and the J multiplexer enabled, exactly one of the address/data registers will be selected. The register is, therefore, selected directly by the contents of the IR, not by the control logic. Table 5.27 indicates the select line details.

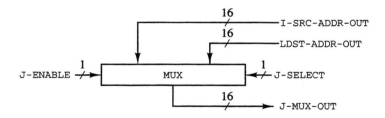

Figure 5.56   Two-input MUX, component J.

TABLE 5.27   Truth Table,
component J

J-SELECT	Inputs
0	I_SRC_ADDR_OUT
1	I_DST_ADDR_OUT

Figure 5.57 shows the decoder used to select one of the user-programmable registers. As was mentioned earlier, this selection is based entirely on the contents of the IR and is not directly coordinated by the control logic. Notice that the decoder includes an enable line to allow the case in which no register selection is required. Table 5.28 provides details on the decoder outputs given the input lines.

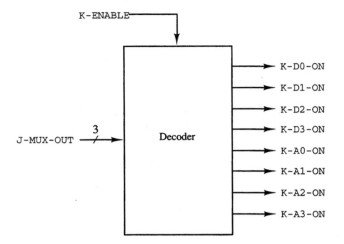

Figure 5.57   Three-to-eight decoder.

TABLE 5.28   Truth Table,
component K

F-SELECT			Inputs
0	0	0	K_D0_ON
0	0	1	K_D1_ON
0	1	0	K_D2_ON
0	1	1	K_D3_ON
1	0	0	K_A0_ON
1	0	1	K_A1_ON
1	1	0	K_A2_ON
1	1	1	K_A3_ON

Figure 5.58 shows the two temporary registers used to hold the source operand values. Notice each register is individually controlled by enable lines.

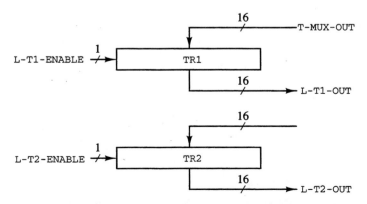

Figure 5.58   Temporary registers—parallel load register, component L.

Figure 5.59 shows the two-input mux that selects either of the temporary registers TR1 and TR2 as an input to the A side of the ALU. Table 5.29 provides details for the select control logic.

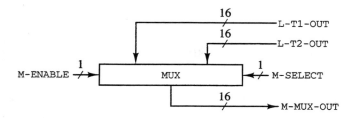

Figure 5.59 Two-input MUX, component M.

TABLE 5.29 Truth Table, component M

M-SELECT	Inputs
0	L_T1_OUT
1	L_T2_OUT

Figure 5.60 shows the two input mux which selects either of the temporary registers TR1 and TR2 as an input to the B side of the ALU. Table 5.30 provides details for the select control logic.

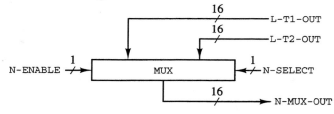

Figure 5.60 Two-input MUX, component N.

TABLE 5.30 Truth Table, component N

M-SELECT	Inputs
0	L_T1_OUT
1	L_T2_OUT

Figure 5.61 shows the four-input mux used in the swap instruction. The inputs may be any of the data register high words. The select lines (O_SELECT) are attached directly to the the two least significant bits of the source register specifier (I_SRC_ADDR_OUT). Thus, the register will be selected directly by the current instruction in the IR. Table 5.31 specifies these select line assignments.

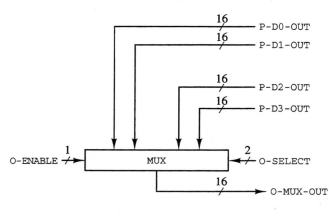

Figure 5.61 Four-input MUX, component O.

TABLE 5.31   Truth Table, component O

O-SELECT		Inputs
0	0	P_D0_OUT
0	1	P_D1_OUT
1	0	P_D2_OUT
1	1	P_D3_OUT

Figure 5.62 shows the four parallel load registers used to maintain the high words of the data registers. Notice that the registers are enabled only when both the appropriate register has been selected via the decoder and the P-REG-ENABLE line is high. This prevents the registers from changing when the low words of the data registers are enabled during the move instruction.

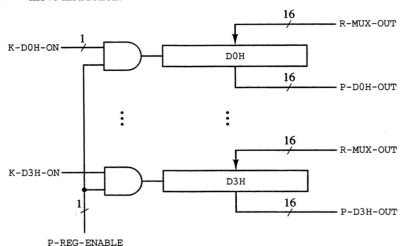

Figure 5.62   Data regs (high)—parallel load registers, component P.

Figure 5.63 shows the main register file. Notice that the registers are selected directly by the decoder (see Figure 5.57), which in turn is controlled by the either the source or destination fields of the instruction register.

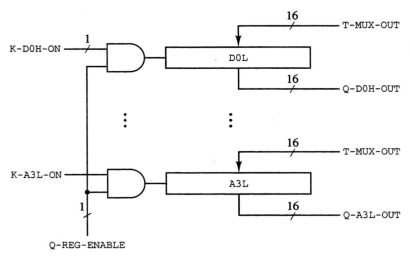

Figure 5.63   Data regs (low)—parallel load registers, component Q.

Figure 5.64 shows the eight-input multiplexer which selects which of the registers to place on the *A* side of the ALU (or adder). Note that, as with the decoder, the select lines are driven directly from the IR source register field. Table 5.32 specifies these select line assignments.

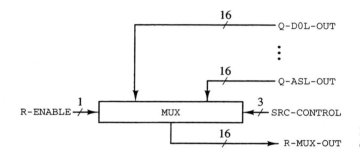

Figure 5.64 Eight-input MUX, component R.

TABLE 5.32 Truth Table, component R

SRC-CONTROL			Inputs
0	0	0	Q_D0L_OUT
0	0	1	Q_D1L_OUT
0	1	0	Q_D2L_OUT
0	1	1	Q_D3L_OUT
1	0	0	Q_A0L_OUT
1	0	1	Q_A1L_OUT
1	1	0	Q_A2L_OUT
1	1	1	Q_A3L_OUT

Like Figure 5.64, Figure 5.65 shows the eight-input multiplexer, which selects which of the registers to place on the *B* side of the ALU (or adder). Again, the select lines are driven directly from the IR destination register field. Table 5.33 specifies these select line assignments.

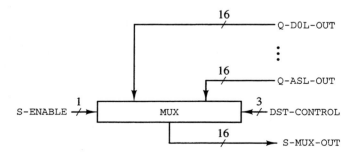

Figure 5.65 Eight-input MUX, component S.

Figure 5.66 shows the two-input MUX used to select either output from the ALU or data register high words as input to the data register low words. Notice that since the IR selects the same data register low and high words, the swap instruction is easily accomplished. Table 5.34 specifies the select line assignments.

TABLE 5.33 Truth Table, component S

DST-CONTROL			Inputs
0	0	0	Q_D0L_OUT
0	0	1	Q_D1L_OUT
0	1	0	Q_D2L_OUT
0	1	1	Q_D3L_OUT
1	0	0	Q_A0L_OUT
1	0	1	Q_A1L_OUT
1	1	0	Q_A2L_OUT
1	1	1	Q_A3L_OUT

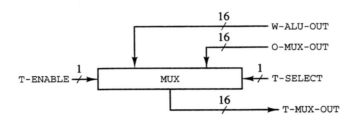

Figure 5.66 Two-input MUX, component T.

TABLE 5.34 Truth Table, component T

T-SELECT	Inputs
0	O_MUX_OUT
1	W_ALU_OUT

Notice the following points. The two multiplexers R and S select a register based on the value in the IR source and destination fields only. Looking at the control lines to the multiplexers we see that, for example, a value of XXXX X01X X0XX 1X11 in the IR will select register A3 as the source (i.e., an input to MUX-U) and register D1 as the destination (i.e., an input to MUX-V). Whether or not these registers are actually used, depends of course on whether the control lines to MUX-U and MUX-V select these inputs to the ALU. Thus data/address registers are made available to the ALU A and B inputs based on the value selected directly by the IR. Notice also that MUX-J may be selected to transfer either the source or destination fields to the decoder. Finally notice that the multiplexer MUX-T may select as input either the ALU or one of the data registers (high word). Again the choice of register will depend on the value in the IR destination field. Thus a data/address register may be loaded from either the ALU or from a data register high word.

Arithmetic region. The arithmetic region is primarily composed of an ALU, as we described in section 5.3 (see Figure 5.69), three multiplexers (see Figures 5.67, 5.68, and 5.70), and the status register (see Figure 5.71).

Figure 5.67 shows a four-input MUX (U), which controls access to the A side of the ALU. Notice that ALU input may come from either a source register field, a destination register field, the MBR, or one of the two registers TR1 or TR2. Table 5.35 specifies the select line assignments.

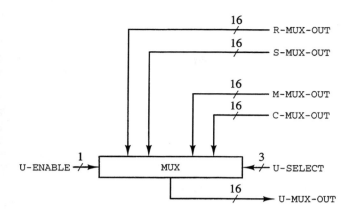

Figure 5.67   4-input multiplexer, component U.

TABLE 5.35   Truth Table, component U

U-SELECT		Inputs
0	0	R_MUX_OUT
0	1	S_MUX_OUT
1	0	M_MUX_OUT
1	1	C_MUX_OUT

Figure 5.68 shows a three-input MUX (V) controlling access to the B side of the ALU. Notice that the inputs may come from either a destination register field, the MBR, or one of the two temporary registers TR1 or TR2. Table 5.36 indicates the select-line specification.

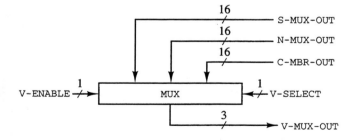

Figure 5.68   Three-input multiplexer, component V.

TABLE 5.36   Truth Table, component V

V-SELECT		Inputs
0	0	S_MUX_OUT
0	1	N_MUX_OUT
1	1	C_MBR_OUT

Figure 5.69 shows the 16-bit ALU specified in Section 4.1. Notice that the input control lines will be used to specify which ALU function is to be performed. Similarly the five status lines will be used to control branch instructions.

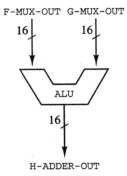

F-MUX-OUT G-MUX-OUT

H-ADDER-OUT

Figure 5.69   A 16-bit ALU, component W.

Figure 5.70 shows a two-input MUX used to control how the SR is loaded. In the case of SIM68, the input will always be from the ALU; however, the MUX gives the opportunity to load the SR directly. Table 5.37 indicates the select line specification.

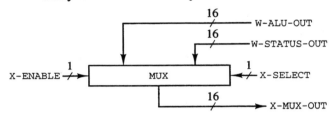

Figure 5.70   Two-input multiplexer, component X.

TABLE 5.37   Truth Table, component X

X-SELECT	Inputs
0	W_ALU_OUT
1	W_STATUS_OUT

Figure 5.71 shows the SR as a set of five individual 1-bit parallel-load registers. These registers are enabled during the arithmetic/logic instructions. Notice that a single enable line could be used for the purposes of SIM68.

From the above discussion we see that the inputs to the ALU are selected through two multiplexers V_MUX and W_MUX. The inputs to V_MUX may be either a source register (R_MUX), a destination register (S_MUX), an effective address (M_MUX), or the MBR (C_MBR). The inputs to V_MUX may be either a destination register (S_MUX), an effective address (N_MUX), or the MBR (C_MBR). The control inputs into the ALU are determined by an address mapping from the instruction register (I_REG) through the function map to select the appropriate ALU instruction based on the contents of the IR. Thus, the CPU design provides for a rich set of arithmetic functions. The status register may be loaded from either the ALU output or may be loaded directly from the ALU (from W_ALU), depending on X_MUX control inputs.

Timing and control region.   The timing and control region consists of three combinational logic circuits (grouped by functionality): the address and control map (see Figure 5.72), the condition code logic (see Figure 5.75), and the timing and control logic (see Figure 5.77). We now consider each of these in turn.

The address logic (Figure 5.72) will be used to control which instruction is executed, and which registers are selected by the R and S MUXs. The inputs will be selected lines from the IR. Notably I_INST_OUT, I_DST_OUT, and I_SRC_OUT. The outputs will be a

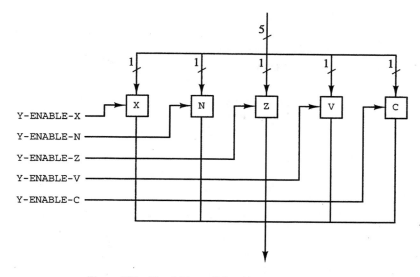

Figure 5.71   Five 1-bit parallel registers, component Y.

single line for each instruction (enabled when that instruction is in the IR) and a single line for each addressing mode (enabled when that mode has been selected). A function diagram of this is shown in Figure 5.72.

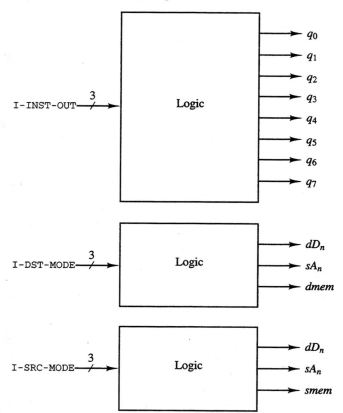

Figure 5.72 Instruction and register control logic, component Z1.

Recall from Table 5.9 that each instruction has associated with it a q number. The mapping between the instruction format and the q number may be seen by considering Table 5.38. Although the mapping is somewhat complex, it may be easily realized using the combinational logic circuit given in Figure 5.73.

TABLE 5.38 Map for instruction control lines

Code	Instruction	Opcode bits
q_0	add	1101X
q_1	sub	1001X
q_2	comp	1011X
q_3	swap	01000
q_4	move	0011X
q_5	bcc	0110X
q_6	trap	01001
q_7	mult	1100X
q_8	div	1000X

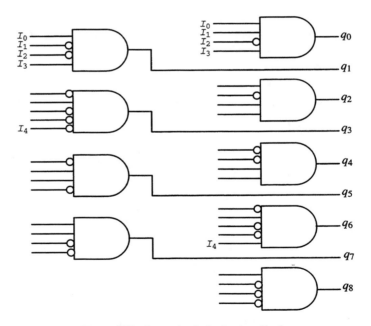

Figure 5.73   Instruction logic circuit realization.

In a similar way, the register control logic may be specified using Table 5.39. Notice that the logic is the same for both the source and destination register selection. The circuit realization for this is provided in Figure 5.74.

The second logic function shown in Figure 5.75. The logic coordinates the activity of the conditional branch instructions. To see how this operates, we first need to consider precisely what is meant by a **condition**.

In the SIM68 instruction set there are four conditions under which a branch may be taken: bra, bgt, blt, and beq. These correspond to branch always, branch on less than,

TABLE 5.39   Map for register mode control lines

Code	Mode	Register mode bits
sD_n	Source data register direct	000
sA_n	Source address register direct	001
smem	Source address register indirect with displacement	101
dD_n	Destination data register direct	000
dA_n	Destination address register direct	001
dmem	Destination address register indirect with displacement	101

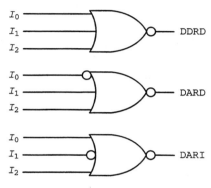

Figure 5.74   Register control circuit realization.

branch on greater than, and branch on equal to. These conditions are satisfied by particular boolean expressions using the five status register bits (N, Z, V, C, X). The expressions have already been discussed in Chapter 3; however, to refresh your memory we provide Table 5.40.

TABLE 5.40   Boolean expressions to realize SIM68 branch conditions using status register bits

Cond.	I-DST-MODE	Status Reg. Logic
bra	000	-
beq	011	Z
bgt	111	$\bar{Z} \wedge (N \otimes V)$
blt	110	$(N \oplus V)$

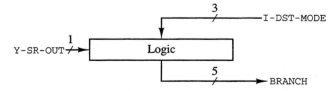

Figure 5.75   Branch control logic, component Z2.

Notice that included in Table 5.40 are the instruction register bits used to select which condition is to be satisfied. The bit positions correspond to I-DST-MODE field in the IR

The Z2 logic circuit in Figure 5.75 will, therefore, realize a single function called the **branch line**. The inputs will be the condition code select bits (I-DST-MODE), and the status register bits (Z,V,N,C,X), whereas the output will be a single line indicating whether or not a branch should occur. A branch will occur if, and only if, one of the conditions in Table 5.40 is realized **and** the corresponding condition code bits in the IR have been set. For example, the **branch line** should be set, if the Z bit is set **and** the bits corresponding to the beq condition occurs. The full circuit realization for the **branch line** therefore corresponds to the **or** of each of the conditions provided. This realization is shown in Figure 5.76.

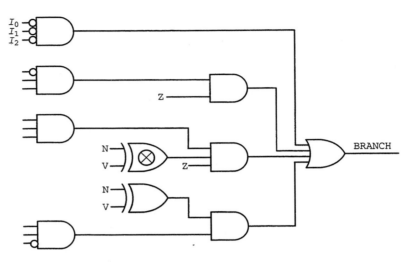

Figure 5.76   Branch control circuit realization, component Z3.

The final logic control unit is the sequence control logic (Figure 5.77). The function of this unit is conceptually simple; however, the combinational logics are complex. The inputs to the unit are the nine instruction control lines (q_0 to q_8), the three destination mode lines (dD_n, dA_n, dmem), the three source mode lines (sD_n, sA_n, smem), and the branch line. The outputs are lines controlling all register enables and MUX selects. The functional realization of this unit is shown in Figure 5.77. The details of how the logic circuit is realized will be discussed after a discussion of microinstruction sequencing.

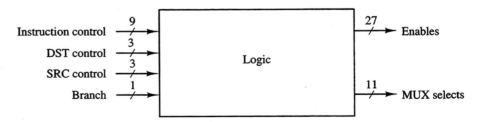

Figure 5.77   Register enable and multiplexer control logic, component Z3.

Microinstruction sequencing.   Even though we have discussed each of the CPU components in some detail, you are probably still wondering how the processor will operate! In fact, with the processor as designed, it is now simply a matter of selecting the appropriate micro-operations to occur at each t-state, which in turn transforms to enabling the appropriate registers, and selecting the appropriate inputs to the multiplexers, in other words specifying unit Z3. To determine the timing and control we will use the format shown in Table 5.41.

TABLE 5.41   Table format for control and timing

		CPU Cycle (c_n)		
Condition	Action	MUX	ALU	Comments
$c_0 t_1$	MAR←PC	(F-MUX,D-PC-OUT)		
		(G-MUX,0)		

The **Condition** field identifies the logical condition under which this sequence of micro instructions will operate. Every microinstruction occurs during one of the four cycles and occurs at a particular t-state in the cycle; therefore, each CONDITION field starts with the conjunction $c_x t_y$ indicating a particular cycle and t-state within the cycle (in the example $c_0 t_0$)—exactly like the condition field in our register transfer language.

The **Action** field specifies the micro-operations to be performed. The register on the left-hand side of the micro-operation will be loaded with the result from the right-hand side. Thus the left-hand side register must be **enabled** during this micro-operation, one of the tasks performed by the timing logic Z3. Again, note the similarity with the register transfer language.

The **MUX** field identifies the multiplexers to be enabled and the input lines to be selected; the format is (MUXNAME,SELECT) where MUXNAME is the name of the multiplexer and SELECT specifies the line to be selected. Control of these select lines is the other task of Z3. Notice that some of the Multiplexers have their input lines selected automatically via the contents of the source/destination fields in the IR. These multiplexers still require enabling by the sequence logic in Z3.

The **ALU** field is used to indicate the ALU function to be selected during this micro operation. The function is set by the sequence logic Z3, enabling the appropriate control lines to the ALU.

The **Comment** field is used to annotate each micro-operation.

We now discuss the micro-instruction sequencing within each of the four cycles in some detail.

Instruction Fetch Cycle.   The first cycle consists of the instruction fetch (Table 5.42). First the MAR is loaded from the PC; next the instruction loaded from main memory into the MBR; at the same time the PC is incremented by two in anticipation of the next fetch. The newly obtained contents of the MBR are moved into the IR in preparation of execution. Finally the next cycle is started. Note that if the next cycle does not possess a source memory address, the memory source cycle is skipped.

Instruction Indirect Source Cycle.   The function of the memory source cycle is to load the source data into a temporary register TR1 (Table 5.43). If the source is a register (i.e., mode 0 = SDRD or mode 1 = SADR) then the register as designated by the source field is copied into the temporary register. If the source is a memory reference (i.e., mode 5 = SARI); then the next word of memory (i.e., the displacement) is fetched, added to the appropriate address register, and the result loaded into both a temporary register (EAR1) and the memory address register. The data at this memory location are then loaded into the temporary register. In either event, the result at the end of the cycle is that the temporary register EAR1 contains the address of the source memory location (if mode 5) and the temporary register TR1 contains the source data.

TABLE 5.42

	Instruction Fetch (c_0)		
Condition	Action	MUX	ALU
$c_0 t_0$	MAR←PC	(F-MUX,D-PC-OUT)	
		(G-MUX,0)	
$c_0 t_1$	MBR←M[MAR]		
	PC←PC+2	(F-MUX,D-PC-OUT)	
		(G-MUX,2)	
		(E-MUX,H-ADDER-OUT)	
$c_0 t_2$	IR←MBR		
$c_0 t_3$	CLK←0		
$c_0 t_3 (q_3 + q_6)$	C1←1		
	C0←1		
$c_0 t_3 (q_0 + q_1 + q_2 + q_4 + q_5)$	C1←0		
	C0←1		

TABLE 5.43

	Source cycle (c_1)		
Condition	Action	MUX	ALU
$c_1 t_0 (SDRD + SARD)$	TR1←SrcReg	(R-MUX,I-SRC-ADDR-OUT)	XFR
		(U-MUX,R-MUX-OUT)	
		(T-MUX,W-ALU-OUT)	
	CLK←0		
	C1←1		
	C0←0		
$c_1 t_0 SARI$	MAR ← PC	(F-MUX,D-PC-OUT)	
		(G-MUX,0)	
$c_1 t_1 SARI$	MBR←M[MAR]		
	PC←PC+2	(F-MUX,D-PC-OUT)	
		(G-MUX,2)	
		(E-MUX,H-ADDER-OUT)	
$c_1 t_2 SARI$	EAR1,MAR←Disp+SrcReg		
		(F-MUX,R-MUX-OUT)	
		(R-MUX,I-SRC-ADDR-OUT)	
		(G-MUX,C-MBR-OUT)	
$c_1 t_3 SARI$	MBR←M[MAR]		
$c_1 t_4 SARI$	TR1←MBR	(U-MUX,C-MBR-OUT)	
		(T-MUX,W-ALU-OUT)	
	CLK←0		
	C1←1		
	C0←0		

Instruction Indirect Destination Cycle.   The function of the memory destination cycle is to load the destination data into a temporary register TR2. If the destination is a register (i.e., mode 0 = DDRD or mode 1 = DADR), then the register as designated by the destination field is copied into the temporary register TR2 (Table 5.44). If the destination is a memory reference (i.e., mode 5 = DARI), then the next word of memory (i.e., the displacement) is fetched, added to the appropriate address register, and the result loaded into

TABLE 5.44

	Destination cycle (c_2)		
Condition	Action	MUX	ALU
$c_2 t_0 (\text{DDRD} + \text{DARD}) \bar{q}_5$	TR2←DstReg	(S-MUX,I-DST-ADDR-OUT)	XFR
		(U-MUX,S-MUX-OUT)	
		(T-MUX,W-ALU-OUT)	
	CLK←0		
	C1←1		
	C0←1		
$c_2 t_0 \text{DARI} \bar{q}_5$	MAR←PC	(F-MUX,D-PC-OUT)	
		(G-MUX,0)	
$c_2 t_1 \text{DARI} \bar{q}_5$	MBR←M[MAR]		
	PC←PC+2	(F-MUX,D-PC-OUT)	
		(G-MUX,2)	
		(E-MUX,H-ADDER-OUT)	
	EA2,MAR<-Disp+DstReg	(F-MUX,S-MUX-OUT)	
		(S-MUX,I-DST-ADDR-OUT)	
		(G-MUX,C-MBR-OUT)	
$c_2 t_3 \text{DARI} \bar{q}_5$	MBR←M[MAR]		
$c_2 t_4 \text{DARI} \bar{q}_5$	TR2←MBR	(U-MUX,C-MBR-OUT)	XFR
		(T-MUX,W-ALU-OUT)	
	CLK←0		
	C1←1		
	C0←1		
$c_2 t_0 q_5$	MAR←PC	(F-MUX,D-PC-OUT)	
		(G-MUX,0)	
$c_2 t_1 q_5$	MBR←M[MAR]		
	PC←PC+2	(F-MUX,D-PC-OUT)	
		(G-MUX,2)	
		(E-MUX,H-ADDER-OUT)	
$c_2 t_2 q_5$	EAR2←Disp+PC	(F-MUX,D-PC-OUT)	
		(G-MUX,C-MBR-OUT)	
	CLK←0		
	C1←1		
	C0←1		

the both a temporary register (EAR2) and the memory address register. The data at this memory location are then loaded into the temporary register TR2. In either event, the result at the end of the cycle is that the temporary register EAR2 contains the address of the destination memory location (if mode 5), and the temporary register TR2 contains the destination data.

Another case that requires consideration during this cycle is the branch instruction. The branch instruction uses PC relative addressing to obtain the effective address of the branch memory address. To accommodate this we check to see if the instruction is a branch, and if so, we compute the effective address and save it in the temporary register EAR2. Thus, if the branch condition turns out to be true, the "branch" will simply involve loading EAR2 into the PC.

Instruction Execution Cycle. During the final cycle, instruction execution occurs. The particular sequence of microinstruction to execute is determined by **and**ing the appropriate q value with the other conditions. In this implementation, we will only consider the first seven instructions, that is, we will omit the mul and div instructions.

The add instruction simply involves adding together the two temporary registers TR1 and TR2 and placing the result in destination specified by the destination register field (Table 5.45). The add is performed by the ALU **plus** operation, and the status registers are set by the ALU status outputs through X-MUX. The next cycle is clearly the start of a new instruction.

TABLE 5.45

	Instruction cycle (c_3)		
	Add instruction		
Condition	Action	MUX	Comments
$c_3 t_0 q_0$ SDRD(DDRD + DARD)	DstReg←TR1+TR2	(M-MUX,L-TR1-OUT)	PLUS
		(U-MUX,M-MUX-OUT)	
		(N-MUX,L-TR2-OUT)	
		(V-MUX,N-MUX-OUT)	
		(T-MUX,W-ALU-OUT)	
		(J-MUX,I-DST-ADDR-OUT)	
		(X-MUX,W-STATUS-OUT)	
	CLK←0		
	C1←0		
	C0←0		

In a similar vein to the add instruction, sub simply involves subtracting TR1 from TR2 and placing the result in destination specified by the destination register field (Table 5.46). The subtraction is performed by the ALU **minus** operation, and the status registers are set by the ALU status outputs through X-MUX.

The CMP is the same as the sub instruction, with the exception that the result of the subtraction is not saved into the destination register (Table 5.47).

TABLE 5.46

Subtract instruction			
Condition	Action	MUX	ALU
$c_3 t_0 q_1$ SDRD(DDRD + DARD)	DstReg←TR2-TR1	(M-MUX,L-TR2-OUT)	MINUS
		(U-MUX,M-MUX-OUT)	
		(N-MUX,L-TR1-OUT)	
		(V-MUX,N-MUX-OUT)	
		(T-MUX,W-ALU-OUT)	
		(J-MUX,I-DST-ADDR-OUT)	
		(X-MUX,W-STATUS-OUT)	
	CLK←0		
	C1←0		
	C0←0		

TABLE 5.47

Compare instruction			
Condition	Action	MUX	ALU
$c_3 t_0 q_2$ SDRD(DDRD + DARD)	DstReg←TR2-TR1	(M-MUX,L-TR2-OUT)	MINUS
		(U-MUX,M-MUX-OUT)	
		(N-MUX,L-TR1-OUT)	
		(V-MUX,N-MUX-OUT)	
		(X-MUX,W-STATUS-OUT)	
	CLK←0		
	C1←0		
	C0←0		

The swap instruction exchanges the high and low words of the source data register (Table 5.48). This is a achieved in a single cycle by simply selecting the appropriate paths through the R, O, and T multiplexers.

TABLE 5.48

Swap instruction			
Condition	Action	MUX	ALU
$c_3 t_0 q_3$ DDRD	SrcReg(H)←SrcReg(L)		XFR
	SrcReg(L)←SrcReg(H)	(R-MUX,I-SRC-ADDR-OUT)	
		(O-MUX,I-SRC-ADDR-OUT)	
		(T-MUX,O-MUX-OUT)	
		(J-MUX,I-SRC-ADDR-OUT)	
	CLK←0		
	C1←0		
	C0←0		

The source data for the `move` instruction is already in the temporary register TR1 (Table 5.49). There are, therefore, only two cases to consider. If the destination is a register (modes 0 or 1), the register is selected according to the destination register field. If the destination is a memory location, then the effective address was computed during the destination indirect cycle and is available from register EAR2. Thus, we have simply to load the MBR with TR1 and the MAR with EAR2 and issue a **write** to complete the operation.

TABLE 5.49

	Move instruction		
Condition	Action	MUX	ALU
$c_3t_0q_4$DDRD	DstReg←TR1	(M-MUX,I-SRC-ADDR-OUT)	XFR
		(U-MUX,M-MUX-OUT)	
		(T-MUX,W-ALU-OUT)	
		(X-MUX,W-STATUS-OUT)	
	CLK←0		
	C1←0		
	C0←0		
$c_3t_1q_4$DARI	MAR←EAR2	(F-MUX,D-EAR2-OUT)	XFR
		(G-MUX,0)	
	MBR←TR1	(M-MUX,L-TR1-OUT)	
		(U-MUX,M-MUX-OUT)	
		(X-MUX,W-STATUS-OUT)	
$c_3t_2q_4$DARI	M[MAR]←MBR		
	CLK←0		
	C1←0		
	C0←0		

With the **Bcc** instruction, there is only one case to consider, whether or not to branch (Table 5.50). If the decision is yes (which is determined by the **branch** (or **b**) bit from the combinational logic unit Z2), the PC is loaded with the contents of EAR2. Otherwise, we simply move to the start of the next instruction.

TABLE 5.50

	Branch instruction		
Condition	Action	MUX	ALU
$c_3t_0q_5$b	PC←EAR2	(F-MUX,D-EAR2-OUT)	
		(G-MUX,0)	
		(E-MUX,H-ADDER-OUT)	
$c_3t_1q_5\bar{b}$	CLK←0		
	C1←0		
	C0←0		

The `trap` instruction simply disables the go flag. This flag is **and**ed with the clock pulse, thus, when set low the CPU stops instruction fetch. Notice that we also reset the CLK and cycle registers in preparation for a restart.

TABLE 5.51

	Trap instruction		
Condition	Action	MUX	ALU
$c_3 t_0 q_6$	GO← 0		
	CLK←0		
	C1←0		
	C0←0		

Realization of Sequence Unit Z3.   With the instruction sequencing identified, we are now in a position to determine the control logic in unit Z3. To establish the sequencing logic, we notice that each microinstruction involves moving the data *from* a particular location t_0 another location during each t-state. Thus the data will be clocked into the correct destination register, if the register is enabled and the appropriate multiplexers have been selected during this t-state. Thus, for each register, we must establish those microcycles when its enable line is to be high. This will be a boolean expression based on current micro-cycle and the inputs to Z3. We now show by example how the sequencing logic is implemented for register enables, and multiplexer selections using this approach.

Example: MBR

Consider the case of the MBR. To see when the MBR is enabled, we inspect all the micro-operations in all of the sequence tables and list those in which it occurs on the left-hand side (because the register will require enabling *only* when it is a destination. For the MBR this is

$c_0 t_1$	MBR ← M[MAR]
$c_1 t_1 \text{SARI}$	MBR ← M[MAR]
$c_1 t_3 \text{SARI}$	MBR ← M[MAR]
$c_2 t_1 \text{DARI} \overline{q_5}$	MBR ← M[MAR]
$c_2 t_3 \text{DARI} \overline{q_5}$	MBR ← M[MAR]
$c_2 t_1 q_5$	MBR ← M[MAR]
$c_3 t_1 \text{DARI}$	MBR ← TR1

Thus, we enable MBR whenever any of these conditions applies. That is (because the MBR enable is line **C-ENABLE**) we have

C-enable (MBR) = $c_0 t_1 + c_1 t_1 \text{SARI} + c_1 t_3 \text{SARI} + c_2 t_1 \text{DARI} \overline{q_5} + c_2 t_3 \text{DARI} \overline{q_5} +$
$\qquad c_2 t_1 q_5 + c_3 t_1 q_4 \text{DARI}$

This logic expression would be simplified to reduce the number of gates and the appropriate logic would be included in the processor design to drive the enable line to the MBR.

With this in mind we now provide the line enable functions for each register in the design.

B-enable (MAR) $= c_0t_0 + c_1t_0\text{SARI} + c_1t_2\text{SARI} + c_2t\text{DARI}\overline{q_5} + c_2t_1\text{DARI}\overline{q_5} +$
                 $c_2t_0q_5 + c_3t_1q4\text{DARI}$

C-enable (MBR) $= c_0t_1 + c_1t_1\text{SARI} + c_1t_3\text{SARI} + c_2t_1\text{DARI}\overline{q_5} + c_2t_3\text{DARI}\overline{q_5} +$
                 $c_2t_1q_5 + c_3t_1q_4\text{DARI}$

R/W $= c_3t_2q_4\text{DARI}$

D-PC-enable (PC) $= c_0t_1 + c_1t_1\text{SARI} + c_2t_1\text{DARI}\overline{q_5}c_2t_1q_5 + c_3t_0q_5b$

D-EA1-enable (EAR1) $= c_1t_2\text{SARI}$

D-EA2-enable (EAR2) $= c_2t_1\text{DARI}\overline{q_5} + c_2t_2q_5$

I-enable (IR) $= c_0t_2$

L-T1-enable (TR1) $= c_1t_0(\text{SDRD}+\text{SARD}) + c_1t_4\text{SARI}$

L-T2-enable (TR2) $= c_2t_0(\text{DDRD}+\text{DARD})\overline{q_5} + c_2t4\text{DARI}\overline{q_5}$

Y-enable (SR) $= c_3t_0(q_0+q_1+q_2+q_3+q_4)$

Z3-C0-enable (C) $= \text{Z3-C0-high} + c_1t_0(\text{SDRD}+\text{SARD}) +$
                 $c_1t_4\text{SARI} + c3t_0(q_0+q_1+q_2)\text{SDRD}(\text{DDRD}+\text{DARD}) + c_3t_0q_3\text{DDRD} + c_3t_0q_4\text{DDRD} +$
                 $c_3t_2q_4\text{DARI} + c_3t_1q_5\overline{b} + c_3t_0q_6$

Z3-C0-high (C0) $= c_0t_3(q_3+q_6) + c_0t_3(q_0+q_1+q_2+q_4+q_5) +$
                 $c_2t_0(\text{DDRD}+\text{DARD})\overline{q_5} + c_2t_4\text{DARI}\overline{q_5} +$
                 $c_2t_2q_5$

Z3-C1-enable (C) $= \text{Z3-C1-high} + c_0t_3(q_0+q_1+q_2+q_4+q_5) +$
                 $c_3t_0(q_0+q_1+q_2)\text{SDRD}(\text{DDRD}+\text{DARD}) + c_3t_0(q_3+q_4)\text{DDRD} +$
                 $c_3t_2q_4\text{DARI} + c_3t_1q_5\overline{b} + c_3t_0q_6$

Z3-C1-high (C1) $= c_0t_3(q_3+q_6) + c_1t_0(\text{SDRD}+\text{SARD}) +$
                 $c_1t_4\text{SARI} + c_2t_0(\text{DDRD}+\text{DARD})\overline{q_5} +$
                 $c_2t_4\text{DARI}\overline{q_5} + c_2t_2q_5$

Z3-rst (CLK-RST) $= c_0t_3 + c_1t_0(\text{SDRD}+\text{SARD}) + c_2t_0(\text{DDRD}+\text{DARD})\overline{q_5} +$
                 $c_2t_4\text{DARI}\overline{q_5} + c_2t_2q_5 + c_3t_0(q_0+q_1+q_2)\text{SDRD}(\text{DDRD}+\text{DARD}) +$
                 $c_3t_0q_3\text{DDRD} + c_3t_0(q_3+q_4)\text{DDRD} + c_3t_2q_4\text{DARI} +$
                 $c_3t_1q_5\overline{b} + c_3t_0q_6$

GO (GO) $= c_3t_0q_6$

In a similar vein to the MBR, each input line to a multiplexer is selected based on the situations in which it is used. Thus, like the register enables, the multiplexer control lines must be enabled at the appropriate time.

Example: F-MUX

Looking in the MUX column we see for example that the F-MUX is used to select the following:

(F-MUX,R-MUX-OUT) $= c_1t_2\text{SARI}$
(F-MUX,S-MUX-OUT) $= c_2t_2\text{DARI}\overline{q_5}$
(F-MUX,D-PC-OUT) $= c0t_1 + c0t_1 + c_1t_1\text{SARI} + c_2t_1\text{DARI}\overline{q_5} + c_2t_1q_5 + c_2t_1q_5 + c_2t_2q_5$
(F-MUX,D-EAR1-OUT) $= 0$
(F-MUX,D-EAR2-OUT) $= c_3t_1q_4\text{DARI} + c_3t_1q_5b$

Thus, the boolean logic for each of the MUX select lines would be included in the sequencing logic (using Tables 5.42 to 5.51) as follows:

F-select$_0$ $= c_2t_2\text{DARI}\overline{q_5}$
F-select$_1$ $= c_0t_0 + c_0t_1 + c_1t_0\text{SARI} + c_2t_0\text{DARI}\overline{q_5} + c_2t_1\text{DARI}\overline{q_5} + c_2t_0q_5 + c_2t_2q_5$
F-select$_2$ $= c_3t_1q_4\text{DARI} + c_3t_1q_5b$

Notice that there is a high degree of repetition involved in these expressions; thus, we would expect the expressions could be simplified using expression minimization techniques.

As with the register enables below we now provide the complete set of register select control functions.

$$\text{C1-select}_0 = c3t_1\text{DARI}$$

$$\text{E-select}_0 = c_0t_1+c_1t_1\text{SARI}+c_2t_1\text{DARI}\overline{q_5}+c_2t_1q_5+c_3t_0q_5b$$

$$\text{F-select}_0 = c_2t_2\text{DARI}\overline{q_5}$$

$$\text{F-select}_1 = c_0t_0+c_0t_1+c_1t_0\text{SARI}+c_2t_0\text{DARI}\overline{q_5}+c_2t_1\text{DARI}\overline{q_5}+c_2t_0q_5+c_2t_2q_5$$

$$\text{F-select}_2 = c_3t_1q_4\text{DARI}+c_3t_1q_5b$$

$$\text{G-select}_0 = c_0t_0+c_1t_0\text{SARI}+c_2t_0\text{DARI}\overline{q_5}+c_2t_0q_5+c_3t_1q_4\text{DARI}+c_3t_0q_5b$$

$$\text{G-select}_1 = c_1t_1\text{SARI}+c_2t_1\text{DARI}\overline{q_5}+c_2t_2q_5$$

$$\text{J-select}_0 = c_3t_0(q_0+q_1)\text{SDRD}(\text{DDRD}+\text{DARD})$$

$$\text{N-select}_0 = c_3t_0(q_0)\text{SDRD}(\text{DDRD}+\text{DARD})$$

$$\text{M-select}_0 = c_3t_0(q_1+q_2)\text{SDRD}(\text{DDRD}+\text{DARD})$$

$$\text{T-select}_0 = c_1t_0(\text{SDRD}+\text{SARD})+c_1t_4\text{SARI}+c_2(\text{DDRD}+\text{DARD})\overline{q_5}+$$
$$c_2t_4\text{DARI}\overline{q_5}+c_3t_0(q_0+q_1)\text{SDRD}(\text{DDRD}+\text{DARD})+c_3t_0q_4\text{DDRD}$$

$$\text{U-select}_0 = c_1t_4\text{SARI}+c_2t_0(\text{DDRD}+\text{DARD})\overline{q_5}$$

$$\text{U-select}_1 = c_1t_4\text{SARI}+c_2t_4\text{DARI}\overline{q_5}+c_3t_0(q_0+q_1+q_2)\text{SDRD}(\text{DDRD}+\text{DARD})+$$
$$c_3t_0q_4\text{DDRD}+c_3t_1q_4\text{DARI}$$

$$\text{V-select}_0 = c_3t_0(q_0+q_1+q_2)\text{SDRD}(\text{DDRD}+\text{DARD})$$

$$\text{X-select}_0 = c_3t_0(q_0+q_1+q_2)\text{SDRD}(\text{DDRD}+\text{DARD})+c_3t_1q_4(\text{DDRD}+\text{DARI})$$

We have seen that implementation of SIM68 could be accomplished by hard coding the logic of all multiplexers and register control lines according to the microinstructions to be executed. As you have probably realized, there is much opportunity for error during this process. In addition to ensuring that the design is correct, we also notice that an error in the design is extremely difficult to correct: This is particularly the case when the expressions have been simplified. There is hope, however, as we shall see from the next section!

5.6.3 Microprogrammed Implementation

We have mentioned that an alternate to clocked sequence logic is microprogramming. Recall that in microprogramming, sequencing is performed by a microprogram sequencer under the direction of a control store. Each macroinstruction is composed of several microinstructions that are executed in sequence. The microinstructions specify which control lines to set and where from to obtain the next microprogram instruction. A hardware realization of SIM68 using a microprogram sequencer is given in Figure 5.78.

To understand the microprogram sequencer, we require a specification of the microinstruction word. Again, recall that the control word is composed of sequencing fields and function control fields. The sequence fields are the sequence instruction field and the address field. The function control fields include control lines to the functional units (ALU etc.), to the multiplexers, and to the register enables. Looking at the fields of the microcode instruction word in the context of SIM68, we see the specification as shown in Table 5.52.

To perform the required instructions of SIM68, the microprogram sequencer must be slightly more complex than that of Figure 5.34. The modifications are shown in Figure 5.79. Notice that we have enlarged the external condition selection lines from 4 to 8; this enables us to jump to different microstore locations based on the addressing modes obtained from the IR. Notice also that there are two registers in the sequencer. The **return register** and the **count register**. The return register may be used to save a microprogram return address. Thus, the microcode may make use of microprogram subroutines (!) by saving the return address while issuing a branch. We may then return by loading the micro-

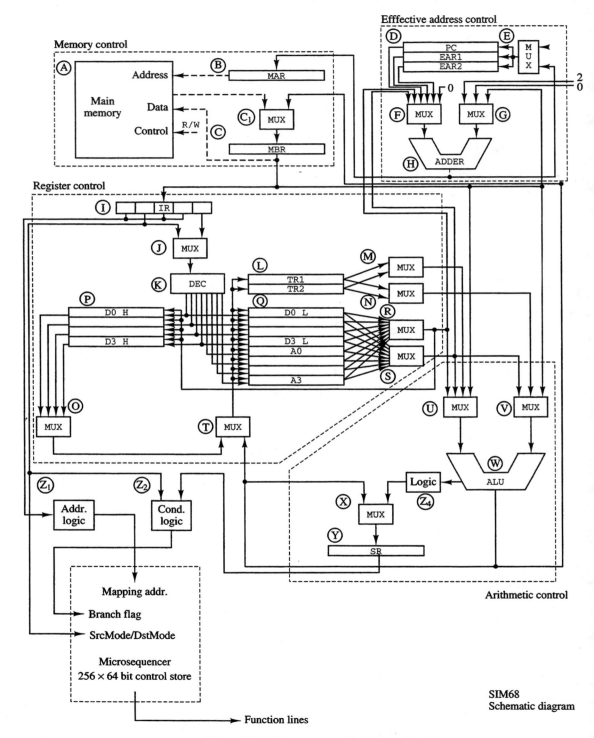

Figure 5.78 Microprogrammed implementation of SIM68.

TABLE 5.52 Control word format for SIM68

Sequencer			Control	
Instr.	Addr.	ALU	MUXs	Registers
8 bits	8 bits	3 bits	32 bits	13 bits
			E, F, G, J, M, N, O, T, U, V, X	MAR, MBR, R/W, EAR1, EAR2, T1, T2, Y-ENABLEs

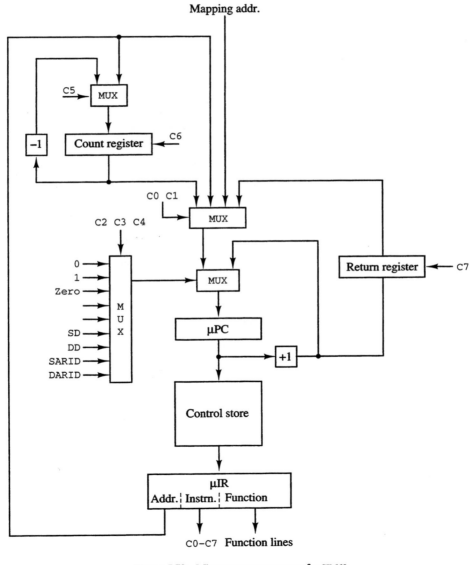

Figure 5.79 Microprogram sequencer for SIM68.

program counter from this register. The count register may be used as a counter; thus, we may specify that a particular microprogram sequence be repeated a selected number of times. The initial value is loaded into the register using the same field as used for jump addresses. When the register contains the value 0 the unused MUX input line (selected by %011 on $C_4C_3C_2$) is set to one. We may use this register to perform multiply and divide operations. On SIM68 these cannot be implemented in a single cycle but require several cycles.

There are clearly many more instructions that may be offered using the improved sequencer. A few of the possible ones are identified in Table 5.53; you are encouraged to study them closely in the context of Figure 5.79.

TABLE 5.53 Instructions for microsequencer used in SIM68

Sequence Control					Function
$c_{0,1}$	$c_{2,3,4}$	c_5	c_6	c_7	
XX	001	X	0	0	CONT - Continue with the next microinstruction in control store.
01	000	X	0	0	BRA - Branch to address as given in address field.
10	000	X	0	0	MAP - Branch to address given externally.
01	010	X	0	0	BR_flag - Conditional branch as given by branch logic.
01	100	X	0	0	BR_SrcData - Conditional branch if source mode 1.
01	101	X	0	0	BR_DstData - Conditional branch if destination mode 1.
01	000	X	0	1	JSR - Microprogram subroutine jump to address as given in address field.
01	110	X	0	1	JSR_SrcARID - Conditional subroutine jump if source mode 5.
01	111	X	0	1	JSR_DstARID - Conditional subroutine jump if destination mode 5.
11	000	X	0	0	RET - Subroutine return.

Notice the following points regarding the SIM68 control word format:

1. The **instruction** (8 bits) is used to control the sequencer and performs the functions given in Table 5.53. Notice that $C_2C_3C_4$ are derived from the branch control logic.

Thus, where appropriate, we can jump to a new address in control store if a branch has occurred, we may even use microprogram subroutines!

2. The **address** field (8 bits) contains the branch address to be taken in the event of a BRA, BRflag, BRA_SrcData or a BR_DstData. The value is unimportant for the other instructions because we will not be using the count register.

3. The ALU field (3 bits) is used to select one of the functions of the ALU defined in Table 5.10. Notice that additional functions could be provided, if required.

4. The MUX field contains control bits for each MUX in the system. Thus, we may program any data path through the processor by selecting the appropriate MUXs.

5. The **registers** field contains the control bits for each register. Using this we are able to latch selected data into any of the registers under program control.

We admit that in terms of the functionality of SIM68, the sequencing control is overkill in the sense that we may now implement far more than needed. We wish to demonstrate that the control logic may be replaced by a microsequencer unit with few other changes, however. In fact the only other change that we must consider is the logic for Z1. Recall that we must permit a change in the microinstruction flow based on the contents of the IR. After the fetch cycle has completed the IR will contain a macroinstruction opcode. This opcode is used to run the appropriate microprogram for that instruction. Unfortunately looking at Table 5.38 again we see that the opcode bits of SIM68 are rather messy. This is because SIM68 is a proper subset of the MC68000, and we are only partially decoding a full MC68000 instruction. In fact, the opcode format for the MC68000 is rather messy even in the complete implementation! We notice that the X bit in the opcode could be either a zero or a one. This could cause problems when the MAP instruction is used because it would result in a jump to one of two locations depending on the value of X. This may be resolved by noting that the X bit is the least significant bit; thus, for those instructions in which there is an X, we will use the same control information in both locations with a jump to the remaining code. With this determined, we notice that the logic Z1 is unnecessary! The start locations for microprogram code segments for each macroinstruction are given in Table 5.53.

Notice that by using some combinational logic in Z1 we could map the opcodes to other starting locations. In this this instance we have chosen to leave them unmodified.

TABLE 5.38 Microprogram start locations

Instruction	Op code bits	Start location(s)
(Fetch)		00
add	1101X	26, 27
sub	1001X	18, 19
comp	1011X	22, 23
swap	01000	8
move	0011X	6, 7
bcc	0110X	12, 13
trap	01001	9
mult	1100X	24, 25
div	1000X	16, 17

Thus, the external input to the microprogram sequence will be **000opcode$_5$**. With these modifications we are now in a position to write microprograms. We use a coding sheet similar to that discussed in Section 5.3.

```
;Loc.   Sequence Fields Control Fields   ; Comment
;       Address  Instn.

;FETCH CYCLE
                                  ; MAR ← PC.
  00       00    CONT     MAR,F=%010,G=%01
                                  ; MBR ← M[MAR],PC ← PC+2.
  01       00    CONT     MBR,PC,F=%010,G=%00,E=%1
                                  ; IR ← MBR.
  02       00    MAP      IR

;INSTRUCTIONS (Reached by MAP from IR)
;
;MOVE instruction
  06             CONT              ; Fall thru to next microinstructi
  07       41    BRA               ; Branch to move code-segment

;SWAP instruction
  08       00    BRA      ...      ; SrcReg(H) ← SrcReg(L) and visa-v

;TRAP instruction
                                  ; Branch to 00 and stop
  09       00    BRA      Stop_processor
  10
  11

;Bcc instruction
  12             CONT              ; Fall thru to next microinstructi
  13             BR_flag  ...      ; IF BR_flag then PC ← EAR2
  14       00    BRA

;DIV instruction
  16             CONT              ; Fall thru to next microinstructi
  17       x     BRA      ...      ; Branch to division routine

;SUB instruction
  18             CONT              ; Fall thru to next microinstructi
  19       32    BR_SrcData
  20       200   BRA               ; Error, illegal src mode

;CMP instruction
  22             CONT              ; Fall thru to next microinstructi
  23       35    BRA               ; Branch to Comp routine

;MUL instruction
  24             CONT              ; Fall thru to next microinstructi
  25       y     BRA               ; Branch to multiplication routine
```

```
;ADD instruction
  26              CONT                  ; Fall thru to next microinstruction
  27      29      BR_SrcData            ;
  28     200      BRA                   ; Error, illegal src mode

; ADDITIONAL MICROPROGRAM STORAGE
; Memory may be used to either complete
; instructions or store subroutines
; used by one or more programs.
;
;Remainder of the microprogram for the Bcc instruction
  29              ...       ...
  30              ...       ...
  31              ...       ...

;Remainder of the microprogram for the SUB instruction
  32              ...       ...
  33              ...       ...
  34              ...       ...

;Remainder of the microprogram for the CMP instruction
  35              ...       ...
  36              ...       ...
  37              ...       ...

; Remainder of the microprogram for the ADD instrn.
  38      40      BR_DARID              ; Check for Dst=ARD or DRD.
                                        ; OK, so Dst ← Src+Dst and set SR.
  39      00      BRA        PLUS,U=%00,V=%00,T=%1,X=%1,J=%1,K,Y_X,Y_N,Y_Z,
                                    Y_V,Y_C
  40     200      BRA                   ; Error, illegal dst mode.

;Remainder of the microprogram for the MOVE instrn
  41     100      JSR_SrcARID           ; Subroutine for src address
                                        ;  register indirect?
  42     110      JSR_DstARID           ; Subroutine for dest address
                                        ;  register indirect?
  43      46      BR_DstData
                                        ; MAR ← EAR2, MBR ← TR1
  44              CONT      ...
                                        ; M[MAR] ← MBR
  45      00      BRA       ...
  46      00      BRA       ...         ; DestReg ← TR1

;SUBROUTINES - Called by one or more microprograms.
;Source ARID Cycle
 100     106      Br_SrcData
                                        ; TR1 ← SrcReg
 100              CONT      XFR,U=%00,T=%1,L_TR1
                                        ; MAR ← PC
 101              CONT      F=%010,G=%01,B
                                        ; MBR ← M[MAR], PC ← PC + 2
```

```
102          CONT      C1=0,C,F=%010,G=%00,E=%1,D_PC
                                ; EAR1,MAR ← Disp+SrcReg
103          CONT      E=%1,F=%000,G=%10,C1=%1,C,D_EAR1
                                ; MBR ← M[MAR]
104          CONT      C1=0,C1
                                ; TR1 ← MBR
105          RET       XFR,M=%0,U=%10,T=%0,L_TR1
                                ; TR1 ← SrcReg
106          RET       XFR,m=%0,U=%00,T=%0,L_TR1

;Dest ARID Cycle

110          ...       ...
111          ...       ...
112          ...       ...
113          ...       ...
114          ...       ...
115          ...       ...

;
;ERROR Routine - where we come if an illegal Intn/Mode occurs.
200    00    BRA                   ; Return to instruction fetch.
```

As can be seen from the preceding code, when microprogramming we are required to write short code segments. Each control word specifies the functional unit operation, the registers to receive data, and multiplexer inputs. Thus, we are able to implement the macroinstructions as a sequence of control words. Notice that because of the opcode decoding, several instructions have two entry points. For simplicity we permit the lower numbered entry point to "fall through" to the next instruction. You may wish to consider a more elegant solution. Notice also that we use microprogram subroutines to handle the source and destination address register indirect with displacement mode. This concept could be readily expanded to accommodate a variety of different addressing modes if we were interested in supporting them. Finally, notice that there are several control words where we make use of conditional branches using some external condition (e.g., checking for address register indirect, checking for data register direct etc.) These condition tests were defined during the design of the microsequencer and are given in Table 5.52. We have left portions of the microprogram incomplete (indicated with ellipses) for exercises at the end of this chapter. The reader is encouraged to study the microprogram most carefully as it draws together many concepts discussed earlier in the text.

Although writing the microprogram at this low level is a time-consuming and complex task there are several steps that we may take to reduce the work. The first step is to write a symbolic assembler for writing microcode! This would allow us to specify labels for branch targets and would remove the need for our computing the addresses. This may sound odd but it's worth the effort if the microprogram is large. Second, we can make use of assembler macros (see Chapter 8) to provide us with a set of "higher-level" functions. For example, we could define a macro to perform MAR ← PC as follows:

```
MARfromPC    macro
             MAR,F=%010,G=%01
             endm
```

This macro could then be used as required within in microprogram. In fact, the microcode programmer may start his or her task by writing out a set of useful macros for the program ahead. Finally there are several checks and optimizations that may be made both manually and automatically to the microprogram. The reader is invited to "optimize" the preceding microprogram; there are many instances where microcycles could be saved by reordering microinstructions. We now examine some of the points raised by our simple example. First we must consider the advantages:

1. You may be wondering where the savings are in microprogramming. Looking back at the hard-wired circuit realization for control unit Z3 you will see many complex boolean expressions. These have now been completely replaced by the microprogram sequencing.

2. We now see that to modify (or correct!) the macroinstruction set we need only change the microprogram. This procedure is easy when compared with the task of recomputing the boolean expressions for Z3 and developing a new control circuit.

3. Unlike the hard-wired implementation, the microprogrammed implementation may be easily extended to facilitate new instructions or addressing modes. Notably, with only a few additional hardware modifications the MUL and DIV instructions may now be included by using the shift and add algorithm introduced in Chapter 2. This would be coded using the temporary registers to store the partial product. To do this one would need a counter which could be initialized to the number of loops in the multiplication, could be decremented, and would signal an external condition to the sequencer when it reached zero. Similarly, a slight change to the way that the IR lines control the sequencer would permit additional modes to be easily added.

Against these, we must consider the disadvantages.

1. We now have a control store of 256×60 bits! This is 15,360 bits, or 30,000 gates! Clearly this represents a tremendous overhead when compared with the rest of the architecture. Of course by writing the microprogram carefully we may be able to manage with only 128 (possible), or 64 (unlikely), control words, but this is still large.

2. The other obvious disadvantage of microprogramming is the delay. Notice in particular that microprograms tend to require several steps (e.g., establishing the mode) that are encoded as a combinational circuit in the hard-wired implementation. Again, of course, we could increase the expressive power of the sequencer to alleviate this.

We conclude this section by noting that the movement toward RISC architectures is precisely to reduce the control logic. In doing this, it is possible to move the design back from a microprogrammed design to a hard-wired one. This permits some improvement in performance.

5.7 ILLUSTRATIVE ARCHITECTURES

We now show architectures from the CISC and RISC, courtesy of Motorola Incorporated.

5.7.1 MC68000 — 16/32-bit Architecture

The MC68000, as you should by now be aware, is a CISC processor. It was the first of a highly successful family of 16/32-bit single chip microprocessors. The MC68000 has a 16-bit data bus and a 24-bit address bus. The full architecture provides for 32-bit address and data buses. As with many families, the MC68000 is upward code compatible to the MC68010, MC68020, and MC68030. That is, any user-mode program written using the MC68000 instruction set will execute on the other processors. The MC68000 itself is composed of seventeen 32-bit registers (eight data registers and nine address registers). The instruction set supports fifty-six different instruction types, five data types, and fourteen different addressing modes. Only integer arithmetic is directly supported. Floating point operations are available via the MC68881 floating point coprocessor to the more sophisticated models (MC68020 and MC68030). Instructions supported include the usual arithmetic and logic instructions; load/store instructions; branch, jump, and link support for subroutines and procedures; and limited BCD support.

A minor upgrade to the MC68000 is the MC68010. The MC68010 is pin compatible to the MC68000; however, unlike the MC68000, it permits virtual address translation. The MC68000 is unable to respond gracefully to an address bus error, as would be generated during virtual address references. The result of this is that the MC68000 will not support virtual memory. The MC68010, however, internally maintains the state of instruction execution and permits instruction restarts.[17]

This is sufficient to permit virtual memory systems. In addition, the MC68010 possesses an internal "loop mode," which permits (via use of an instruction and data cache) execution of tight loops without the need for instruction fetches.

Another version of the MC68000 is the MC68008, an 8-bit data bus version of the MC68000. The MC68008 is available in either 48-pin DIL package or 52-pin quad plastic package. The user model of the system is identical to the MC68000. In fact, the MC68008 is completely code compatible with the MC68000, that is, object code that executes on one will also execute on the other.

5.7.2 MC68020 and MC68030 Modern CISC Architectures

We mention the MC68020 and MC68030 to demonstrate the design component that goes into an architecture family. The typical lifetime for a computer architecture is about 10 years, although some last far longer (IBM's 370 architecture is a good case in point). During this period the product is expected to evolve. Thus growth must be planned from the start of the product. Often architectures have been suffocated by design limitations that were not noticed when the product was originally delivered.

The MC68020, is the first full 32-bit implementation of the MC68000 architecture; it uses both 32-bit address and data paths, using a 114-pin grid array package. Perhaps the most important difference from the MC68000 is a significant increase in the number of

---

[17] This is discussed further at the conclusion of Chapter 9.

addressing modes available to the programmer, this is discussed in greater detail in Section 6.6. In addition to the addressing modes, the MC68020 has five new control registers; these permit relocation of the exception vector table in memory, improved support for virtual memory, and programmer manipulation of the on-chip instruction cache. The MC68020 also has much improved support for virtual memory and floating-point operations via coprocessors (the MC68881 and MC68851 units). The MC68020 also has two new data types: the bit field type to support graphics and quad word integers (64 bits). Finally there are several new instructions including support for high level modules and instructions to assist in multiprocessor environments.

Motorola claims that the MC68030, shown in Figure 5.80, is a second-generation enhanced microprocessor. Although the MC68030 represents a major advance over the MC68020, there is little difference from the programmer's perspective. The MC68030 has another five control registers that are used to control the new on-chip memory management system. The differences are primarily internal and result in significant performance improvements. The MC68030 contains on-chip 256-byte instruction, data caches, and a paged memory management unit. The architecture is highly pipelined and makes use of multiple gate types to achieve high performance in a single package.

5.7.3 MC68040—CISC Architecture, RISC engine

The MC68040 probably represents the end of the product life for the MC68000 architecture. Again, from the programmer's perspective it is similar to the MC68020. The MC68040 is manufactured with 0.8-micron high-speed CMOS technology and is composed of 1.2 million transistors! Like the MC68030 the MC68040 is contained in a 179-pin grid array but is not pin compatable. The design makes extensive use of pipelining; in fact with the pipeline full, the MC68040 will execute an instruction every 1.4 clock cycles! The MC68040 contains an integral floating point unit that is compatible with IEEE 754 standard and is object code compatable with the MC68881/2 used on the earlier processors. The MC68040 also contains large instruction and data caches that are kept consistent with main memory by control logic using a technique called "bus snooping."

Notice that throughout the product lifetime (which is drawing to a close), there is a clear evolutionary path from the MC68000 all the way to the MC68040. The success that this product has enjoyed is a reflection of the planning that has gone into its growth.

5.7.4 MC88100—Modern RISC Architecture

The MC88100, shown in Figure 5.81, is a modern RISC-based microprocessor. The processor is available in a 180-pin grid array package containing approximately 1 million transistors. The MC88100 contains fifty-one instructions, the majority of which execute in one machine cycle. The Harvard architecture is used. This is ideally suited in situations that call for high performance because the separate code and data memories permit concurrent access. Thus the MC88100 has separate code and data-area address and data buses, permitting parallel fetchs from the two memories. There are thirty-two general purpose registers with the MC88100 designed as a register-to-register architecture. Three register-to-register addressing modes are supported (triadic, register with 10-bit immediate displacement, and register with 16-bit immediate displacement), three data memory addressing modes (register indirect with dispacement, register indirect with index, and register indirect with scaled

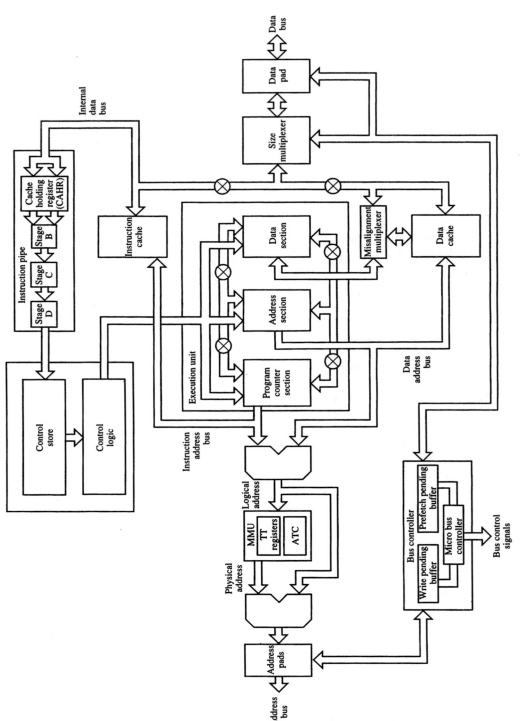

Figure 5.80 Internal structure of the MC68030.

index), and four code memory addressing modes (triadic, register with vector table index, register with 16-bit immediate displacement, and 26-bit branch displacement). As may be seen from Figure 5.81 the MC88100 supports IEEE 754 floating-point arithmetic and has four fully independent execution units. As with all RISC architectures the MC88100 makes extensive use of internal pipelines to improve performance and permits programmer controlled delayed branching. In addition the MC88100 may make use of memory management functions provided on a sister chip, the MC88200.

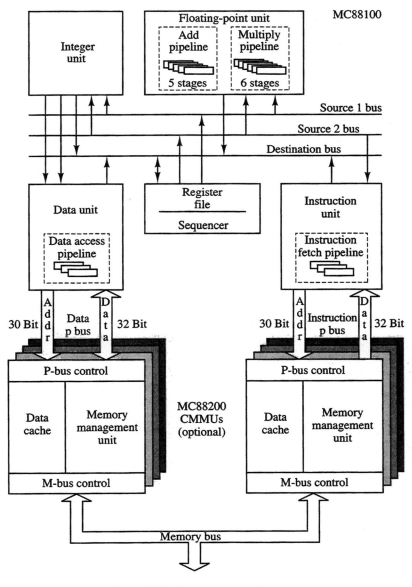

Figure 5.81   Internal structure of MC88100.

5.8 EXERCISES

1. Design an 8-to-3 encoder using only two-input **and** gates.

2. Approximately how many gates would be required to build a 16-bit 4-to-1 multiplexer?

3. Show how a multiplexer and demultiplexer pair might be used to reduce the number of wires between two circuits.

4. Design a 32-bit ALU using 4-bit ALUs similar to those defined in Figure 5.20. Specifically, show the circuits connecting the 4-bit slices together.

5. Extend the functionality of the ALU defined in Figure 5.20 to include the operations **xor** and **co-in**.

6. Explain how clocked sequence logic operates. What is the distinction between the named cycle and the t-state?

7. Explain the term microprogramming. What are the advantages of microprogramming over hard-wired operation?

8. Explain the function of a register transfer language.

9. Explain the difference between horizontal and vertical microprogramming. What are the trade-offs?

10. What class of microprogram control word is the one given in Table 5.52? Why?

11. Explain the term Harvard architecture. What is the principal disadvantage with the Harvard architecture?

12. Explain the term functional unit. In the context of central processors name four different functional units (the ALU counts as only one!).

13. Explain the term pipelining. What difficulties might we expect to encounter if we use an instruction pipeline in a processor?

14. Define a cache. What advantages do using a cache offer over noncached systems. What would we have to change during instruction fetch if a cache were used.

15. Explain the hardwired condition $c_3 t_0 q_2$ SDRD(DDRD + DARD). Which instruction is being executed at this instance? What cycle are we in?

16. Explain the hardwired condition $c_3 t_0 q_5 b$. Which instruction is being executed at this instance? What cycle are we in? What ALU related condition is currently true?

17. A `bra` instruction always branches, therefore the `bra` conditions make no use of the branch line—true or false? (Explain your reasons.)

18. The effective address computation unit of SIM68 (see Figure 5.44) is far more complex than is required by SIM68. Show how it could be used to permit register indirect with an index and displacement. Use Table 5.43 as a model and assume a control mode ARIID with the index register contents already loaded into EAR1. Use the hard-wired model.

19. Show how SIM68 could implement a CLR instruction that clears the specified register. Assume the q-line exits. Use the hard-wired model.

20. Approximately how many gates are required to implement the control logic for the circuits Z1, Z2, and Z3?

21. Explain the sequence of operations for the instruction `move (4[a0],5[a1])` assuming the SIM68 hard-wired implementation.

22. Complete line 44 on page 319.

23. Complete the microprogram subroutine for the DestARID cycle (pg 319).

24. Using SIM68, complete the microprograms for each instruction defined.

25. Answer problem 15 using the appropriate portion of the microprogrammed model instead of hard-wired control.

26. Answer problem 16 using the appropriate portion of the microprogrammed model instead of hard-wired control.

27. Consider an integer multiplier that takes two 8-bit inputs and produces a 16-bit result. Write an algorithm for this operation. Assume that you had available the microprogram sequencer defined in Figure 5.79, the registers, and the adder, design such a multiplier show the micro-program required to control it.

28. Assuming the necessary additional hardware components for SIM68, write the microprogram code to implement MUL instruction in it's entirety. Show clearly the additional components used and any changes made to the sequencer.

29. Discuss what changes would be necessary to modify the microprogrammed version of SIM68 so that absolute addressing would also be supported.

30. Discuss what changes would be necessary to modify the microprogrammed version of SIM68 so that addres register indirect with an index and displacement would also be supported. (*Hint*: you need to be able to decode the extension word and extract the index and displacements.)

31. Explain the advantages of CISC processors over RISC processors. Which is currently in fashion?

32. Could a processor that uses microprogramming classify as a RISC processor? How?

33. What is the MC88100? To what class of architecture does it belong?

ADDITIONAL READING

ABD-ALLA, A. M. *Principles of Digital Computer Design.* Englewood Cliffs, N.J.: Prentice Hall, 1976.

ARMSTRONG, J. R. *Chip-Level Modeling with VHDL.* Englewood Cliffs, N.J.: Prentice Hall, 1989.

BARA, J. *A Computer Design Language.* Masters Thesis, Michigan Technological University, 1975.

DASGUPTA, S. *Computer Architecture: A Modern Synthesis*, vol. 1. New York: John Wiley, 1989.

GEAR, C. W. *Computer Organization and Programming*, 2nd ed. New York: McGraw-Hill, 1974.

HAYES, J. P. *Computer Architecture and Organization*, 2nd ed. New York: McGraw-Hill, 1988.

KORN, G. A. *Minicomputers for Engineers and Scientists.* New York: McGraw-Hill, 1973.

MANO, M. M. *Computer System Architecture.* Englewood Cliffs, N.J.: Prentice Hall, 1982.

MOTOROLA, *M68000 Family Reference*, 2nd ed. Englewood Cliffs, N.J.: Prentice Hall, 1989.

MOTOROLA, *MC68000 8-/16-/32-Bit Microprocessor User's Manual*, 6th ed. Englewood Cliffs, N.J.: Prentice Hall, 1989.

MOTOROLA, *MC68020 32-Bit Microprocessor User's Manual*, 3rd ed. Englewood Cliffs, N.J.: Prentice Hall, 1989.

MOTOROLA, *MC68030 32-Bit Microprocessor User's Manual*, 3rd ed. Englewood Cliffs, N.J.: Prentice Hall, 1989.

MOTOROLA, *MC88100 User's Manual.* Englewood Cliffs, N.J.: Prentice Hall, 1989.

MOTOROLA, *MC88200 User's Manual.* Englewood Cliffs, N.J.: Prentice Hall, 1989.

TANENBAUM, A. S. *Structured Computer Organization*, 3rd ed. Englewood Cliffs, N.J.: Prentice Hall, 1990.

TEXAS INSTRUMENTS, *TTL Logic Data Book*, 2nd ed. Dallas: Texas Instruments, 1988.

WAKERLY, J. F. *Microcomputer Architecture and Programming: The 68000 Family.* New York: John Wiley, 1989.

6

Addressing Schemes
and the MC68000

In this chapter we examine, with examples, all the major addressing modes used on the popular computers today. A subset of these addressing schemes is found in DEC's PDP/11 and VAX architectures, Motorola Inc.'s MC68000, MC68010, MC68020, MC68030, MC68040, and MC88100 architectures, Intel Inc.'s 8086, 80186, i286, i386, i486, and i860 architectures, Sun's Sparc architecture, and many others. We then introduce the MC68000 processor. We present an overview of the architecture including the main memory organization and the CPU before introducing the principles of the MC68000 machine language. It is our belief that the previous study of SIM68 computer together with a broad knowledge of addressing modes will aid in the transition to the MC68000. We conclude the chapter with a brief discussion of the addressing modes provided in the MC68020, MC68030, MC68040, and RISC processors.

6.1 ADDRESSING MODES

The reader should already be somewhat familiar with the concept of addressing modes from the SIM68 simulator. Recall the SIM68 simulator had **data register direct addressing**, **address register direct addressing**, and **address register indirect with displacement addressing**. The term *addressing mode* refers to the manner in which data are accessed. During the execution of a program the data may be either part of a machine instruction, in one of the CPU's registers, in primary memory, or in secondary storage. When in secondary storage the data are not directly available for access, so we will ignore this case. When the data are part of the instruction, there is no problem in referencing it because it is already immediately available. In the other two situations, however, we need mechanisms for selecting (or modifying) the desired data element. We thus define three classes of data access: **immediate data**, **register addressing schemes**, and **memory addressing schemes**. To explain the sequence of operations by which data are chosen, we introduce in Table 6.1 some terms used in register description language (RDL) definitions. The notion of an RDL is introduced in Chapter 5, however, for those unfamiliar with the concept an RDL is simply a language to represent the flow of data between storage elements (registers and memory) within a computer.

In the preceding notation we use the symbol Mem[] to indicate "the memory contents of." Thus, the RDL statement Mem[$1000] would indicate that the data to be accessed are at memory location $1000. The statement $1000, on the other hand, would indicate that the data to be accessed *are the literal value* $1000. Again, the statement EA

TABLE 6.1 Register description language to represent data access within the CPU

Register description language	
Symbol	Definition
EA	Effective address (an expression that yields a memory address)
const	Integer constant; subscript indicates the number of bits
disp	Integer constant; subscript indicates the number of bits
s	Integer constant; subscript indicates the number of bits
R[n]	Contents of general-purpose register Rn
A[n]	Contents of address register n (for MC68000 only)
D[n]	Contents of data register n (for MC68000 only)
X[n]	Contents of index register n (for MC68000 only)
PC	Program counter
Mem[]	"The memory contents of"
←	"Is replaced by"
=	"Is equal to"
+	Integer addition
−	Integer subtraction

= R[1] + const would indicate that the effective address of the data was equal to the contents of register R1 added with the constant const. The RDL descriptions below indicate the sequence of steps that the computer must go through to access the data according to the addressing mode. Notice that the question of whether we want the actual data (as a source operand) or the address of the data (as a destination) will be determined by whether the addressing mode is used as a source or as a destination within an instruction. The RDL will be the same in either case. Notice also that constants and displacements are simply signed integers that are stored in the machine instruction.

We now consider each of the addressing schemes. Because most of the modes are best explained by using an example, we will use the generic two operand move instruction, move source, destination, as was explained in the ASM68 section. One feature in common with all the major architectures is the ability of the user to select the data size of the operand (i.e., the operation will be applied to either a byte, a word, or a long word). In this general section, we assume that the operands are words (for simplicity and consistency with SIM68). Notice, however, that in the section discussing the MC68000, the operand size depends on the instruction.

6.1.1 Immediate Addressing Schemes

There is only one immediate mode addressing scheme and it is described in Table 6.2.

TABLE 6.2 RDL description of immediate addressing

Name	Symbol	RDL definition	Comment
Immediate	#const	dest ← const	Data are defined in machine code

Recall that a machine instruction is composed from several different fields. It is often the case that the data value is a constant; thus, we may store this value as *part* of the instruction (i.e., one of the fields in the instruction). By doing this, the data are made immediately available to the processor without additional memory accesses. Clearly, immediate mode addressing acts only as a source operand. An example using immediate data is shown in Table 6.3.

TABLE 6.3 Example showing use of immediate data. Notice that actual data are specified in the instruction

Mnemonic	Action	State before	State after
move #1234,R1	Move the immediate value #1234 into register R1.	R1: ????????	R1: ????1234

6.1.2 Register Addressing Schemes

Typically a computer possesses only a few registers. Why? Because the registers operate at high speeds, must be physically close to the arithmetic and logic units of the central processor, and are expensive to manufacture. A limitation on the size of the register set is not as serious as one might expect. By making careful use of the limited registers available we are able to maintain a **working set** of data associated with our current computations. This will change as results are stored to memory, thus freeing up registers, and new data are loaded into registers. The number of registers varies from machine to machine with typical numbers being 1, 4, 8, 16, 32, 128, and 256, depending on the size and complexity of the machine. Notice that all of these numbers are quite small (machines with the larger register sets are also usually large machines). Recall from Chapter 2 that to represent n states we need only $\log_2 n$ bits. Thus only $\log_2$ bits are required to index (or select) a particular location. If we label the registers starting from zero we can uniquely identify an individual register using only a few bits, for the register sets above we need 0, 2, 3, 4, 5, 7, and 8 bits, respectively. Clearly, with these small numbers the addressing schemes must be kept simple. Another point to consider is that because registers keep only a working set of data for current computations it is unusual to maintain tables or complex structures in the central processor register sets; thus, the more sophisticated addressing schemes available to main memory are unnecessary. With this in mind, the only useful addressing mode is direct addressing as shown in Table 6.4.

The address of the register is specified in the instruction. As we mentioned earlier, only a few bits are required, so that there is no problem in specifying the entire address of the register. Therefore, the machine instruction contains several bits sufficient to permit the

TABLE 6.4 RDL description of register direct addressing

Name	Symbol	RDL definition	Comment
Register direct	Rn	R[n]	The specification is register n, thus the "data" is the contents of register R[n].

user to identify uniquely the register he or she wishes to access. Suppose, for example, that the processor had eight registers. Then only three bits are required to identify which of the registers is to be used. In addition, we notice that because structures are not kept in registers, **register direct addressing** is sufficient for all our needs.[1]

Table 6.5 shows our move example.

TABLE 6.5 Example showing use of register direct data; Notice that we are assuming that move is of word width only, therefore high-order word of the destination is unaffected

Mnemonic	Action	State before	State after
move R1,R2	Move the contents of R1 into R2.	R1: `0000F000` R2: `????????`	R1: `0000F000` R2: `????`**F000**

6.1.3 Memory Addressing Schemes

In contrast to registers, memory is typically very large. Although the exact size dependents on a particular system, it varies from 64 Kb (for small machines) to 64 Mb (medium-size machines) up to hundreds or thousands of Mb for large machines. If all operands had to be identified using a memory index only the instructions would become very large.[2]

Clearly, these address spaces require additional modes of access if the instructions are to remain compact and efficient. Another point to consider with main memory is the use to which it is put. Unlike registers, main memory will often hold tables of data that are accessed sequentially, perhaps structures that contain data fields of different sizes, perhaps even tables of pointers to such structures. Whatever complex data structures the user requires, the memory addressing facilities should make the task of retrieving this data reasonably efficient. With this in mind, computer designers have developed several different memory addressing schemes that permit many different structures to be quickly traversed. Because of the different schemes, we use the notion of an **effective address** (EA). An effective address is a value that results from the calculation of an expression and indicates (or "points to") a memory address. As mentioned earlier, this address is derived by the processor from a sequence of simple arithmetic operations on data. The exact nature of the operations and data values used to determine the effective address are features that distinguish different memory addressing schemes. We now introduce many of the popular memory addressing schemes using RDL descriptions.

Absolute (or memory direct) addressing. The simplest form of addressing is to refer directly to the memory location in question. As with immediate addressing, the absolute address is stored as a part of the machine instruction. In general, absolute addresses are either one or two words in length. The RDL description is given in Table 6.6 and an example of its use is given in Table 6.7.

---

[1] The reader might wish to speculate whether there would perhaps be some value in permitting other addressing modes on registers.

[2] Consider, two operands in a 32-bit address space would require 64 bits in the instruction *just to identify the data.*

TABLE 6.6 RDL description of absolute addressing

Name	Symbol	RDL definition	Comment
Absolute	`const`	`EA = const`	Effective address, EA, is defined by a constant that is encoded as part of the machine instruction, data are therefore the contents of location `const`.

TABLE 6.7 Example showing use of absolute data; Notice that address of data is specified in instruction

Mnemonic	Action	State before	State after
`move $1236,R1`	Move the contents of memory location `$1236` into R1.	R1: `????????` Memory 1230: `????????` 1234: `0000FA01` 1238: `????????`	R1: `????FA01` Memory 1230: `????????` 1234: `0000FA01` 1238: `????????`

Register indirect addressing. In register indirect addressing, one of the registers is assumed to contain the address of the memory location to be accessed. Thus, the effective address of the data is derived by using the contents of the appropriate register. The data is therefore accessed *indirectly* through the user-specified register. The RDL description demonstrating register indirect addressing is provided in Table 6.8 and an example using the move is given in Table 6.9.

Notice that had the instruction specified memory indirect addressing for the destination operand (e.g., move R1, (R2)), the source data (register direct addressing) would have been in register R1, and the destination would have been a memory location (register indirect addressing) whose effective address is given in R2.

TABLE 6.8 RDL description of register indirect addressing

Name	Symbol	RDL definition	Comment
Register indirect	(Rn)	`EA = R[n]`	Effective address, EA, is defined as memory location given in register R[n].

TABLE 6.9 Example showing use of register indirect addressing; Notice that source *data* is stored in memory and is obtained by using contents of register to specify memory address

Mnemonic	Action	State before	State after
`move (R1),R2`	Use the contents of register R1 as a memory address; move the data stored at this memory address into register R2	R1: `00001230` R2: `????????` Memory 1230: `0000ABCD` 1234: `0000DCBA` 1238: `????????`	R1: `00001230` R2: `????0000` Memory 1230: `0000ABCD` 1234: `0000DCBA` 1238: `????????`

Indirect addressing with displacement.   Indirect addressing with a displacement is similar to indirect addressing. In fact it may be thought of as an extension of register indirect addressing in which a constant displacement is added to the effective address computed in register indirect addressing. Thus, the final address is the sum of the contents of the specified register and the displacement. As with immediate mode and absolute addressing, the displacement is stored as part of the machine instruction and may not be changed during program execution.[3]

This addressing scheme is particularly useful for accessing elements of record structures as we shall see later. The RDL description is given in Table 6.10, and an example demonstrating register indirect with a displacement is provided in Table 6.11.

TABLE 6.10   RDL description of register indirect addressing with displacement

Name	Symbol	RDL definition	Comment
Base displacement	`disp(Rn)`	`EA = disp+R[n]`	Effective address, EA, is computed by the addition of the contents of `R[n]` and a displacement

TABLE 6.11   Example showing use of register indirect addressing with displacement

Mnemonic	Action	State before	State after
`move 1(R1),R2`	Add 1 to contents of register R1 to form effective address; move data at location specified by effective address to R2	R1: `00001233` R2: `????????` Memory 1230: `0000ABCD` 1234: `0000DCBA` 1238: `????????`	R1: `00001233` R2: `????0000` Memory 1230: `0000ABCD` 1234: `0000DCBA` 1238: `????????`

Indirect addressing with index.   As indirect addressing with a displacement extends indirect addressing by allowing a displacement, so indexed addressing extends the former by allowing the contents of another register to be added when forming the effective address of the data. Thus, the effective address is the sum of three components: the contents of two different registers, and a displacement. This mode is particularly useful for accessing tables, in which one register is loaded with the start address of the table, and the other is used to step through the table item at a time. This will be discussed in greater detail later. Table 6.12 provides a RDL description, and Table 6.13 demonstrates using indirect addressing with an index register and a displacement.

Scaled indirect addressing with index.   Scaled indirect addressing with an index is an extension to indexed addressing with an index in which the indirect address is scaled (multiplied) by a small integer constant 2^n. Thus, the effective address is computed as the sum of three components: the contents of a register, the contents of a register

---

[3] Code segments that change during runtime are called self-modifying code. This is considered poor programming practice because of the difficulty in identifying programmer errors.

TABLE 6.12 RDL description of register indirect addressing with index

Name	Symbol	RDL definition	Comment
Indexed	`disp(Rn,Rm)`	`EA = disp+R[n]+R[m]`	Effective address, EA, is formed by adding the contents of register R[n] with the contents of register R[m] and a displacement

TABLE 6.13 Example showing use of register indirect addressing with index

Mnemonic	Action	State before	State after
`move $6(R1,R2),` `R1`	Move the data in memory location given by adding the contents of registers R1, R2 and the displacement $6 to register R1	R1: `00001100` R2: `00000130` Memory 1230: `0000ABCD` 1234: `0000DCBA` 1238: `????????`	R1: `0000`**DCBA** R2: `00000130` Memory 1230: `0000ABCD` 1234: `0000DCBA` 1238: `????????`

scaled by a small constant, and a displacement. The utility of this lies in the fact that tables that are of different word sizes (e.g., byte, word, long word, etc.) may be conveniently accessed. Table 6.14 provides an RDL description and Table 6.15 demonstrates the use of scaled indirect addressing with an index.

Register indirect addressing with postincrement. In register indirect with postincrement addressing, two steps are taken. First the effective address is computed as with indirect addressing on a register n. Register n is *then* incremented by a constant value (which depends on the size of the data item fetched by the instruction, usually this is either 1, 2, or 4). The utility of such an instruction becomes apparent when one considers the operation of a stack. Table 6.16 provides an RDL description and Table 6.17 demonstrates register indirect addressing with postincrement.

Register indirect addressing with predecrement. This mode complements the previous mode. Again the mode is performed in two stages. First register n is decremented by a constant (again this typically depends on the size of the data item accessed). The effective address is then computed as per an ordinary indirect address on register n. Note the symmetry with the previous mode. Again the value of this becomes

TABLE 6.14 RDL description of scaled register indirect addressing with index

Name	Symbol	RDL definition	Comment
Indexed	`disp(Rn*s,Rm)`	`EA = disp+R[n]*s+R[m]`	Effective address, EA, is formed by multiplying the contents of register Rn by scale factor s and adding contents of register Rm and displacement `disp`.

TABLE 6.15 Example showing the use of scaled register indirect addressing with index

Mnemonic	Action	State before	State after
`move $4(R1*4,R2),` `R1`	Move the data in memory location given by summing the contents of registers R1 (multiplied by 4) with R2 and $4, to register R1.	R1: `00000440` R2: `00000130` Memory 1230: `0000ABCD` 1234: `00000000` 1238: `????????`	R1: `00000000` R2: `00000130` Memory 1230: `0000ABCD` 1234: `0000DCBA` 1238: `????????`

TABLE 6.16 RDL description of register indirect addressing with postincrement

Name	Symbol	RDL definition.	Comment
Postincrement	`(Rn)+`	`EA = R[n];` `R[n] ← R[n]+disp;`	`disp` is a constant defined by the data word length

TABLE 6.17 Example showing use of register indirect addressing with postincrement

Mnemonic	Action	State before	State after
`move (R1)+,R2`	Move the contents of the memory location given by the contents of register R1 into R2, then increment the contents of register R1 by 2 (assuming a word instruction)	R1: `00001234` R2: `????????` Memory 1230: `0000ABCD` 1234: `00000000` 1238: `????????`	R1: `00001236` R2: `????**DCBA**` Memory 1230: `0000ABCD` 1234: `0000DCBA` 1238: `????????`

apparent when one considers the operation of a stack. Table 6.18 provides an RDL description, and Table 6.19 demonstrates the use of register indirect addressing with predecrement.

Program counter relative addressing.   There are often occasions when we would like to access data *relative to the position of the program counter*. This may be achieved by the PC relative addressing modes. In these modes, the programmer (or assembler) computes a displacement, which when added to the program counter will yield the desired memory location. On execution of the instruction, the processor adds this displace-

TABLE 6.18 RDL description of register indirect addressing with predecrement

Name	Symbol	RDL definition	Comment
Predecrement	`-(Rn)`	`R[n] ← R[n]-disp;` `EA = R[n];`	`disp` is a constant defined by the data word length

TABLE 6.19 Example showing use of register indirect addressing with predecrement

Mnemonic	Action	State before	State after
move -(R1),R2	Decrement the contents of register R1 by 2 and move contents of the memory location given by contents of register R1 into R2	R1: `00001236` R2: `000ABCD` Memory 1230: `0000ABCD` 1234: `0000DCBA` 1238: `????????`	R1: `00001234` R2: `00000000` Memory 1230: `0000ABCD` 1234: `0000DCBA` 1238: `????????`

ment to the program counter and uses this as the effective address. The advantage in using PC-relative addressing becomes apparent when one considers data areas that are referred to by symbolic labels only. Table 6.20 provides an RDL description and Table 6.21 demonstrates the use of PC relative addressing. Notice that in some architectures (including the MC68000) the PC is automatically incremented by 2 in PC-relative addressing. This is shown in the example.

The notion of PC-relative addressing may be further extended by allowing **PC-relative addressing with an index.**

Deferred (or double-indexed) addressing. One useful feature possessed by several machines is to permit double indirect addressing. By double indirect addressing, we mean that one of the previous modes is used to compute the address of a memory loca-

TABLE 6.20 RDL description of PC relative addressing

Name	Symbol	RDL definition	Comment
PC relative	disp(PC)	EA = disp + PC;	Effective address, EA, is computed as sum of a displacement and contents of program counter
PC relative indexed	disp(PC,Rn)	EA = disp + (PC) + (R[n]);	Effective address, EA, is computed as sum of a displacement, the contents of the program counter, and the contents of register Rn

TABLE 6.21 Example showing use of PC-relative addressing

Mnemonic	Action	State before	State after
move $34(PC),R2	Move the data $34+2=$36 bytes further on from the PC into register R2	PC: `00001200` R1: `0000ABCD` R2: `0000ABCD` Memory 1230: `0000ABCD` 1234: `0000DCBA` 1238: `????????`	PC: `00001200` R1: `0000ABCD` R2: `0000`**DCBA** Memory 1230: `0000ABCD` 1234: `0000DCBA` 1238: `????????`

tion, which *is then used to compute* the effective address. If this sounds confusing, think of it in the following terms. In deferred addressing we use whatever data value was obtained by a previous mode specification, as an effective address. Table 6.22 provides an RDL description and Table 6.23 demonstrates the use of deferred addressing.

TABLE 6.22 RDL description of deferred addressing

Name	Symbol	RDL definition	Comment
Deferred	`@(other mode)`	EA = (EA');	Where EA' is effective address of another mode; we therefore have indirection on some previous effective addressing mode

TABLE 6.23 Example showing the use of deferred addressing

Mnemonic	Action	State before	State after
`move @(R1),R2`	Move the contents of the memory location pointed by the contents of the memory location pointed to by the contents of register R1 into R2 (assuming word sized data).	R1: 00001236 R2: 0000DCBA Memory 1230: 0000ABCD 1234: 00001232 1238: ????????	R1: 00001234 R2: 0000**ABCD** Memory 1230: 0000ABCD 1234: 00001230 1238: ????????

We would point out that deferred addressing may be used to "extend" any addressing mode. Examples would be `@(R1)` (i.e., deferred register indirect addressing), `@(R1)+` (i.e., deferred register indirect addressing with postincrement), and `@disp(PC)` (i.e., deferred PC relative addressing). The reader might wonder whether perhaps some architectures support additional levels of indirection. The answer is yes! For example, the Burroughs B5000 computer designed in 1960 permits unlimited levels of indirection by tagging each memory location with an "indirect bit" which is interpreted by the CPU when the location is accessed. We conclude this section by noting that although the MC68000 does not provide deferred addressing, the MC68020 does provide variations on this format. These modes are called **memory indirect addressing** by Motorola and are briefly discussed at the end of this chapter.

6.1.4 Use of Addressing Modes

Having outlined the different ways of accessing data, that is, the different addressing modes, we are now in position to consider the way in which they may be used. As we said previously, there are essentially only two places to put data: memory and registers.[4] A machine instruction is composed of two elements: an operation code (opcode) and zero or more operands. If the instruction uses data, the data are specified by these operands. In most machines the number of operands is limited to either zero, one, two, or three. We now consider each of these cases separately.

Zero-operand instructions. Some instructions require no data; these are the zero operand instructions. Clearly instructions that do not require data have limited applications. Examples are the `stop` instruction, or the `rts` (return from subroutine) instruction available on the MC68000.

One-operand instructions. Single-operand instructions are those instructions that require only one operand. Examples are the `jsr` (jump to subroutine) and `clr` (clear data) in which only a single effective address is required (i.e., the address of the subroutine for the first example, or the memory location to be cleared for the second example).

Two-operand instructions. Most instructions in a microprocessor are two-operand instructions. Typically the instruction format is `opcode EA1,EA2`. The instruction either operates on the data from the first effective address (EA1) and places the result in the second effective address (EA2) or the instruction uses the data from both the first *and* second effective addresses, and places the result back in the second effective address. Examples of the these two instances are

```
move 3(R1,R2),R3
```

Here, the data is copied from the location given by the effective address of the leftmost operand (indirect addressing with an index) to the location given by the effective address of the rightmost operand (register direct addressing).

```
add (R3),(R1)+
```

Here, the data given by the effective address of the leftmost operand (register indirect addressing) is added to the data in the location given by the effective address of the rightmost operand (indirect addressing with post increment).

Three-operand instructions. The final addressing form permits the specification of three effective addresses: EA1, EA2, and EA3. The opcode is assumed to be diadic (i.e., requires two operands), which are EA1 and EA2, with the result placed in EA3. For example,

```
add (R1),R2,15(R1,R2)
```

Here, the data in the locations given by the effective addresses of the two leftmost operands are added together, and the result is placed in the location given by the effective address of the rightmost operator.

6.1.5 Why So Many Modes?

In Chapters 3 and 4 we introduced the concept of a linear address space. Using the simple SIM68 model, we observed that a large proportion of the instructions executed by the CPU consist of moving data within primary memory and performing simple numeric operations on these data. Recall the SIM68 model has four registers and a limited memory. To move data around the addressing modes available were:

---

[4] Notice that peripheral devices are either memory mapped, in which case they are accessed as memory, or they are special ports (or channels) in which case they are a combination of registers and dedicated machine instructions.

1. **Data register direct.** The user may specify one of the four data registers to be either the source or destination of an operation.

2. **Address register direct.** The user may specify one of the four address registers to be either the source or destination of an operation.

3. **Address register indirect with displacement.** The user may specify a register to contain a base address, and access the data using a specified displacement from this base.

As we have seen, these addressing modes are only a fraction of the more popular addressing schemes that are available. The observant reader will probably be wondering why there are so many modes, when SIM68 manages quite well with only three. To answer this fully, the reader is invited to examine the code segments provided in Appendix F. The answer is simply convenience, however. The fact remains that all of the addressing modes may be simulated provided the user has direct and indirect addressing. Consider the indirect indexed addressing mode.

```
move 123(a1,a2),(a3,a4)
```

If we only had the an and (an), modes we could still achieve this instruction using the following sequence:

```
move #123,a5
add  a1,a5
add  a2,a5    ; The effective address of 123(a1,a2) is now in a5
move (a5),a6  ; Move the data into a temporary register
move a3,a5
add  a4,a5    ; The effective address of (a3,a4) is now in a5
move a6,(a5)  ; Move the data to the required address.
```

The resulting code is much more cumbersome and requires additional registers to store intermediate results. In fact, it is always the case that addressing modes are implemented for code efficiency and convenience, as opposed to necessity.[5]

6.2 MC68000 COMPUTER

It is our belief that a good assembly language programmer for some target machine must at least first *understand* the machine language for that machine and second be able to *read* the code generated by the assembler. Debugging of assembly language programs more often than not can be done more easily and efficiently when one inspects the machine language code generated from the assembler as well as interprets the memory and register dumps. To this end, this section presents an overview of the architecture of the MC68000. Later, we will briefly discuss the principles of the machine language of the MC68000 such as the different addressing modes supported; the different machine language formats of the instructions; and, several examples of these instructions. Despite the high number of addressing modes, we think that the previous section along with SIM68 computer will aid in transition to this machine. Finally, in the following sections we will discuss the similarities of the two machines and the additional features of the MC68000.

---

[5] This is not to suggest that providing few addressing modes is unpopular. In fact, quite the opposite it true. RISC architectures provide few addressing modes to reduce control logic and increase CPU performance.

6.3 MAIN MEMORY ORGANIZATION

The main memory organization of the MC68000 resembles that of SIM68's in that the smallest addressable unit is the byte and its address bus is 24 bits wide. Unlike the SIM68, user programs cannot be loaded at location $000000, because as we will see, the first 1K of memory is used by the processor as well as by the operating system and users for other useful purposes.

6.3.1 Data Information

MC68000's data bus is (like SIM68's) 16 bits wide. Unlike SIM68, on the other hand, MC68000 provides instructions that permit operations on both signed as well as unsigned integer data; in addition, their representations are not limited as in SIM68 to only *word* size. MC68000 supports also byte as well as longword representations.[6] Furthermore, MC68000 provides a set of instructions that permits one to operate on integer data that are represented on yet another internal representation referred to as **binary coded decimal** (BCD).[7] In addition, as we will see with the use of the provided instructions that operate on data of byte size, one can easily manipulate character or character strings. Finally, floating-point instructions are not supported by the chip.[8]

6.4 CPU

The MC68000 processor resembles that of SIM68's because it provides the programmer with an assortment of data, and address registers as well as a program counter and a status register. In this section, issues and the basic concepts associated with these registers are discussed.

6.4.1 Data Registers

MC68000's CPU makes available to the user a total of eight data registers numbered consecutively from %000 to %111; each has a width of 32 bits. As we mentioned earlier MC68000 permits manipulation of bytes (8 bits), words (16 bits), and longwords (32 bits). If a longword is to be addressed or operated on, the contents of the entire register in question are accessed; if the manipulation involves a word, then the word accessed is always the least significant word of the register (bits 15 through 0); if a byte is to be operated on then the byte accessed is always the low-order byte (bits 7 through 0). Figure 6.1 illustrates these concepts.

6.4.2 Address Registers

There are a total of eight address registers; each is 32 bits wide and numbered consecutively from %000 to %111 so that they can be accessed at any instant. In reality, the eighth

---

[6] Longword data *should* be aligned at word boundaries.

[7] BCD representations are discussed in Chapter 7.

[8] Operations can be simulated, however, as explained in Chapter 7.

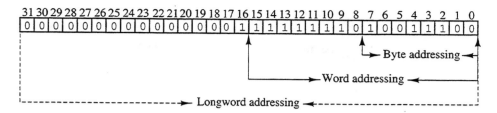

Figure 6.1   Addressing a data register.

register is really two registers. One is referred to as the **user stack pointer** (USP), the other as the **system stack pointer** (SSP); which one is addressed at any instant depends on the setting of the **mode** bit in the status register, which is discussed in the next section.

Unlike data registers, only word and longword operations are permitted in the case of address registers. In particular, when a word is to be addressed, the word is always the least significant word of the register (bits 15 through 0) as Figure 6.2 illustrates.

At this point, we should repeat that whenever a memory location must be accessed (pointed to by that address register), only the low order 24 bits will be utilized for the formation of that address (Figure 6.3).

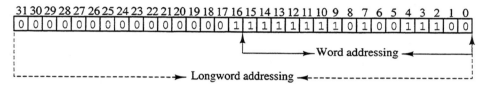

Figure 6.2   Addressing an address register.

6.4.3 Program Counter Register

There is only one program counter register that is 32 bits wide; however, there are two points to be made here. First, although this register is 32 bits wide, only the 24, low-order bits are used in the formation of a memory address as illustrated in Figure 6.3. In addition *only* longword operations are permitted in this register.

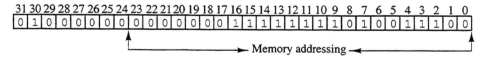

Figure 6.3.   Memory addressing mechanism via the program counter or address register. Recall that the program counter points to the next instruction.

6.4.4 Status Register

There is only one status register, and it is 16 bits wide. Its 5 lower order bits have the same meaning as in SIM68. That is, bit 4 is the **extend** (X) bit; bit 3 is the **negative** (N) bit; bit 2 is the **zero** (Z) bit; bit 1 is the **overflow** (V) bit; and bit 0 is the **carry** (C) bit. There are five more bits in the status register that are of special interest to the programmer.

The most significant bit of the status register, bit 15, is referred to as the **trace** bit. Whenever that bit is set, then we say that the processor is in **trace mode**. Whenever a program is executed in this mode, the processor will inform the monitor[9] each and every time an instruction has been executed. The monitor will execute its own piece of code that performs a register and possibly a memory dump, so the programmer will be able to monitor the result of the execution of each instruction and then control will be passed back to the users program, which will proceed with the execution of the next instruction.[10] Despite the fact that the trace mode provides one with a very important and helpful facility, running an entire program in the trace mode will cause tremendously long delays in its execution. We will see later that there is a way to trace only a *specified set* of instructions by introducing the notion of *breakpoints*.

The MC68000 has two operating modes: the **supervisor mode** and the **user** or **problem mode**. The mode under which the machine is operating at any instant is specified by the **mode** bit, bit 13, of the status register. Specifically, whenever this bit is set, it indicates the supervisor mode; otherwise, the user mode. When the machine runs under the latter mode, it is assumed that a user's program is executing, whereas under the supervisor mode it is assumed that system routines are executing. In addition to this conceptual difference, it is important to notice that *all* the instructions supported by MC68000 can be executed *only* in supervisor mode. In other words, a set of instructions, referred to as **privileged** instructions, cannot be executed in user mode. Furthermore, when the processor operates in user mode, only the user stack pointer register is accessible by the running program, whereas both the user and system stack pointer registers are accessible whenever the processor is running under supervisor mode.

Finally, bits 10, 9, and 8 of the status register are collectively referred to as the **interrupt mask**. The MC68000 provides seven levels of interrupts, 1 through 7. The interrupts are prioritized in such a way that interrupts bearing higher numbers are considered of higher priority than those bearing lower numbers. Setting the interrupt mask to an integer value n causes the processor to service all higher-order (than n) interrupts and *ignore*[11] all other interrupts. For example, if the value of the mask was as in Figure 6.4, then only the seventh-level interrupt will be acknowledged, and all other interrupts, levels 1 through 6, will be ignored. At the other extreme, a setting of the interrupt to %000 will cause all interrupt levels to be acknowledged. Figure 6.5 illustrates the basic components of a MC68000 architecture consisting of the CPU and main memory.

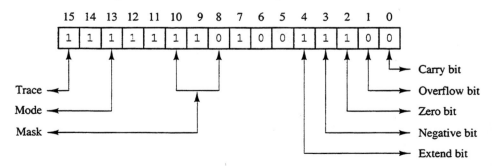

Figure 6.4 Status register bit assignment.

[9] Recall that a monitor is an operating system.

[10] The exact mechanism is explained in Chapter 9.

[11] The only exception to this rule is that all level seven interrupts are serviced irrelevant of the current interrupt mask value.

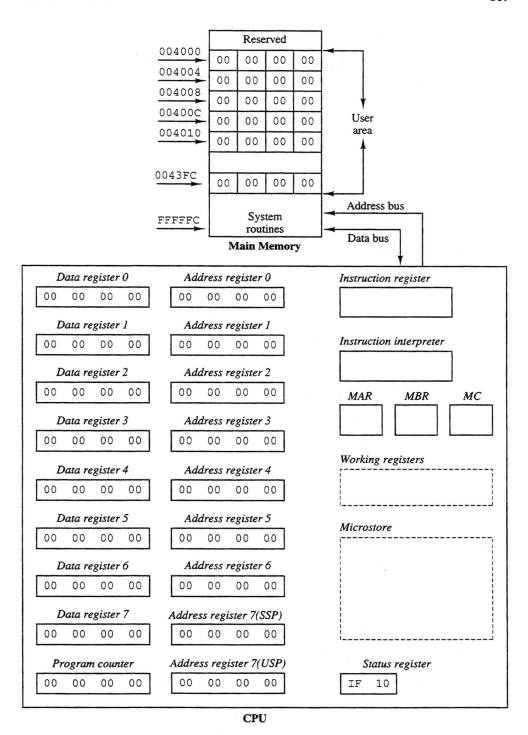

Figure 6.5 Principal components of the MC68000. Note that the memory contents vary from system to system; hence, contents are labeled for illustration purposes only.

6.5 MC68000 MACHINE LANGUAGE

At this time we briefly discuss the machine language of the MC68000. Specifically, we will
first present an overview of the instructions provided as well as their associated formats; the
various addressing modes supported will follow. Finally, we will explain how a machine
language instruction is coded by giving an example for each possible addressing mode.

6.5.1 Instructions

There are more than 1000(!) machine language instructions. Two instructions are zero-
operand instructions, and the remaining are one-operand and two-operand instructions.
The instructions have varying length (from 1 to 5 words) and can be classified according to
the format of their first word, which will be referred to as the format of the instruction. We
may distinguish a total of over 25 formats (F1 through F25). These are illustrated in Table
6.24. Even though these formats (in Table 6.24) will be discussed in detail in the following
paragraphs, we will present a synopsis of the fields as well as their significance.

- OP_n denotes an n-bit opcode.
- dMS_6 and sMS_6 denote the 6-bit mode specification of the destination and the source,
  respectively.
- ddn_3 and sdn_3 denote the 3-bit address of the destination and the source data register, respectively.
- srn_3 and dRn_3 denotes the 3-bit address of the source and destination register (data
  or address register), respectively.
- V_4 denotes a 4-bit (vector) address.
- $displacement_8$ denotes an 8-bit signed integer.
- dir_1, denotes a 1-bit field.
- om_n denotes a n-bit field known as the **operation mode** field.
- $Cond_4$ denotes a 4-bit code known as the **condition**.

6.5.2 MC68000 Addressing Modes

We demonstrated during our discussions of SIM68 that the effective address of an operand
is specified via the mode specification; we have studied the three possible addressing
schemes: mode 0, 1, and 5. MC68000 supports a total of twelve addressing modes. The
mode specification fields are summarized in Table 6.25.

You may have noticed that the mode field is labeled from 0 to 7. Therefore, several
addressing schemes share the same mode number 7. The factor distinguishing any two
such modes, however, is the register field. For example, if a register field contains %001,
we speak of *absolute long* addressing, whereas if it contains %100, we speak of *immediate*
addressing.

The curious reader should be wondering why the designers grouped several addressing schemes under the same number. The answer is that the dedication of a unique mode
number to each addressing mode would require a larger number of bits for its specification

TABLE 6.24 Machine language formats (according to first word), bit assignments, and length (in words) of instructions supported by MC68000

F1	OP_4	drn_3	om_3	sMS_6		
F2	OP_4	sdn_3	om_3	dMS_6		
F3	OP_4	drn_3	OP_3	sMS_6		
F4	OP_2 om_2	ddn_3	dM_3	sMS_6		
F5	OP_4	$Cond_4$	$displacement_8$			
F6	OP_{12}	V_4				
F7	OP_{13}	ddn_3				
F8	OP_8	om_2	dMS_6			
F9	OP_4	$QData_3$ OP_1	om_2	dMS_6		
F10	OP_4	rn_3 OP_1	om_2	OP_2 dir_1	rn_3	
F11	OP_4	dan_3 OP_1	om_2	OP_3	san_3	
F12	OP_4	rn_3 OP_1	om_5	rn_3		
F13	OP_7	om_3	OP_3	Dn_3		
F14	OP_{16}					
F15	OP_4	ddn_3 OP_1	$IData_8$			
F16	OP_{10}	MS_6				
F17	OP_4	$Cond_4$	OP_5	ddn_3		
F18	OP_4	dn_3 OP_1	ds_2 cs_1	OP_2	ddn_3	
F19	OP_4	$Cond_4$	OP_2	dMS_6		
F20	OP_4	dn_3	OP_3	dMS_6		
F21	OP_8	$displacement_8$				
F22	OP_{13}	an_3				
F23	OP_4	drn_3	OP_5	om_1 srn_3		
F24	OP_{12}	dir_1 an_3				
F25	OP_5	dir_1	OP_3	sz_1	MS_6	

TABLE 6.25 Summary of addressing modes supported by MC68000;
Dn and An represent address of data and address register, respectively

Addressing modes	Mode specification	
	Mode	Register
Data register direct addressing	0	dn
Address register direct addressing	1	an
Address register indirect addressing	2	an
Address register indirect addressing with postincrement	3	an
Address register indirect addressing with predecrement	4	an
Address register indirect addressing with displacement	5	an
Address register indirect addressing with index and displacement	6	an
Absolute short addressing	7	0
Absolute long addressing	7	1
Program counter relative addressing with displacement	7	2
Program counter relative addressing with index and displacement	7	3
Immediate addressing	7	4

than the three that are required with the scheme adopted. In addition, notice that the values 5, 6 and 7 have not been assigned to the register field of the address mode 7. Hence, there is a potential for 15 (7 + 8) different modes, of which only 12 are used by the MC68000.[12]

6.5.3 Coding Machine Language Instructions

The purpose of this section is to indicate how one codes a machine language instruction of MC68000. Consequently, when we talk about the assembler, it will be much easier for one to understand how the instructions are coded by the assembler. To this end, we will explain the required bit assignment for the different addressing modes. We will use three specific instructions to provide the reader with a complete set of examples for each case that arises. First, we will consider the move instruction whose format is F4 and the bit assignment of its first word which are shown in Figure 6.6.

F4 | OP_2 | om_2 | dDn_3 | dM_3 | sMS_6 | **Figure 6.6** The F4 format.

Specification of data size.

As mentioned earlier, MC68000 instructions act on either bytes, words, or longwords. The data size is identified to the interpreter via the **operation mode** field. Notice that this field is denoted in Table 6.24 by om_n. In the case of the move instruction, this field is 2 bits wide; if its setting is %11 (as in the corresponding SIM68 instruction), this indicates a word operation; if %01, a byte operation; and if %10, a longword operation.

---

[12] Note that the MC68020 and upwards use additional modes.

In the following sequence, we will assume that the move instruction is a word operation and that the destination is always data register 1. With this assumption, the first word of the instruction will have the format illustrated in Figure 6.7; the length of the instruction will depend entirely on the addressing mode employed for the addressing of the source operand. We will examine these cases subsequently.

move   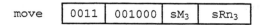   **Figure 6.7**   First word of move to data register 1 instruction.

The boxes show: | 0011 | 001000 | sM₃ | sRn₃ |

First five modes.   The length of the instruction will be equal to one word, independent of which of the five modes is employed for the specification of the source operand. The interpreter will be able to identify the mode; consequently, it will be able to determine the action to access the source operand. In particular, there are five distinct possibilities (one for each addressing mode); each of these possibilities is illustrated in Figure 6.8.

Mode 0	0011	001000	000	101
Mode 1	0011	001000	001	101
Mode 2	0011	001000	010	101
Mode 3	0011	001000	011	101
Mode 4	0011	001000	100	101

Figure 6.8   Moving a word into data register 1. Source operand is specified via any of first five modes.

As a result of each of the preceding instructions, the following moves and actions will occur.

Mode 0.   The lower-order word of data register 5 will be moved to the lower order word of data register 1.

Mode 1.   The lower-order word of address register 5 will be moved to the lower order word of data register 1.

Mode 2.   The word from the memory location whose address is indicated by the 24 low-order bits of address register 5 will be moved to the lower order word of data register 1.

Mode 3.   The word from the memory location pointed to by the 24 low-order bits of the address register 5 will be moved to the lower order word of data register 1; furthermore, the contents of address register 5 will be incremented by two.

Mode 4.   First the contents of the address register 5 will be decremented by two and the word from the memory location pointed to by the 24 low-order bits of address register 5 will be moved to the lower order word of data register 1.

Mode 5. Despite the fact that we have extensively discussed this particular mode in Chapter 5, we must state for the sake of completeness that the size of the instruction in this case will be equal to two words. The reason for this is that the displacement that occupies a word should be known. For example, in the case of mode 5, the machine language instruction is as illustrated in Figure 6.9.

Mode 5	0011	001000	101	101
	displacement$_{16}$			

Figure 6.9 Source memory location is specified via mode 5.

In this case, the word from the memory location indicated by the 24 low-order bits, and found by the sum of the contents of address register 5 and the indicated displacement,[13] will be moved to the lower-order word of data register 1.

Mode 6. In this case the length of the instruction will again be equal to two words. The second word (usually referred to as the **extension word**), however, contains the required information relative to both the index register and the displacement. Its format is shown in Figure 6.10.

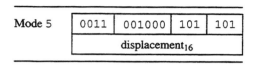

EW	rt_1	Xn_3	s_1	und_3	displacement$_8$

Figure 6.10 Format of extension word associated with mode 6.

The first field, the one-bit field rt_1 indicates the type of register employed as an index register; if this bit is set, then the index register is an address register. Otherwise, it is a data register. The 3-bit field Xn_3 indicates the address of the index register. The 1-bit field is_1 indicates whether the longword ($is_1 = 1$) or the lower-order word ($is_1 = 0$) contents of the index register should be considered in the formation of the effective address. The 3-bit field und_3 is an unused field; and, the 8-bit displacement is indicated by the last field displacement$_8$. For example, consider the instruction in Figure 6.11.

Mode 6	0011	001000	110	101
	1	010	1	000	00001110

Figure 6.11 Example of instruction where source memory location is specified via mode 6.

Execution of this instruction will cause a word of data to be moved from memory location (EA) to be moved into data register 1. The effective address EA will be equal to the 24 low order bits of the longword (AD) which will be calculated as follows:

AD = (longword contents of address register 5) +
        (longword contents of the index register (address register 2))+
        (longword signed extension of the 8-bit displacement field)

Mode 7 (absolute short and long). In certain instances, one may wish to specify the effective address in **absolute** mode. In other words, the effective address could be indicated directly (without any intermediate calculations). Given that an effective address can be specified by at most 24 bits, the MC68000 permits one to use either a *short* or *long* format to indicate this address. One should use the short format if the address can be specified

---

[13] Recall that the 16-bit displacement is sign extended to a longword before addition occurs.

(with the appropriate 24-bit extension) with 16 or less bits; otherwise, he or she should use the long format. In the former case, the effective address is placed in an extension word that follows the first word; in the latter case, the effective address is placed into two consecutive extension words that follow the first word as Figure 6.12 illustrates. Notice, that the advantage of the short over the long format is the saving in storage. Notice that in the short format case (mode 70), the effective address is formed by sign extending the 16-bit displacement to a 24-bit address; in the long format case (mode 71), only the 24 low-order bits of the extension longword are used in forming the address.

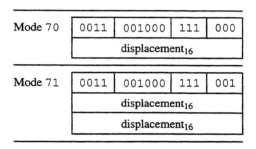

Figure 6.12   Absolute short vis à vis absolute long addressing. Notice that former mode leads to a savings of one word vis à vis the latter.

PC-relative instructions.   Both PC-relative machine language instructions provided have the same formats as modes 5 and 6 that were discussed earlier. Therefore, further discussion of these modes is omitted.

Immediate addressing.   The immediate addressing mode permits one to indicate the data (and not its address) in the machine language instruction. MC68000 supports two distinct ways to accomplish this task via *immediate data* and *quick data* instructions. The former method allows one to use immediate data of byte, word, or longword size. On the other hand, the quick data operation permits a data size equal to only three bits[14] that restricts the range of the decimal integers that can be represented from 1 to 7. Each one is examined in turn.

Immediate data instructions.   The addressing mode employed here is *immediate addressing*. Recall from earlier discussions that this mode permits the data to be specified in any of three allowable sizes. Because the data are stored in extension word(s), it is clear that only one such word is required for byte and word data; however, two such words are needed for longword data.

We will begin by considering the add immediate instruction whose 8-bit opcode is $06, and whose format F8 is presented in Figure 6.13.

F8

Figure 6.13   The F8 format.

The 2-bit field, om_2, indicates the size of the immediate data. If this field is set to %00, this indicates byte data; %01, word data; and %10, longword data. The machine language instructions for these three possible cases (where the destination is data register 4) are illustrated in Figure 6.14. When byte data are indicated, the data are assumed to be in the lower-order byte of the extension word.

---

[14] With one exception relative to the move instruction.

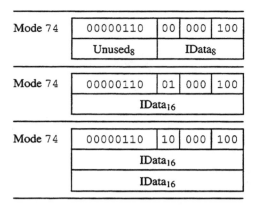

Figure 6.14 Adding immediate data to data register 4. All three versions (add byte, word, or longword) are shown.

Quick data instructions. It is important to notice that despite the fact that quick data instructions can be and are considered a part of the immediate instructions, *no* particular mode is associated with their addressing. In other words, the interpreter realizes that an instruction operates in quick data by examining the opcode of the instruction alone. For example, for add quick instructions, the 5-bit opcode is $0A_5$ and its format can be seen in Figure 6.15.

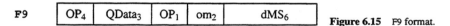

Figure 6.15 F9 format.

The setting of the om_2 field is used to extend the quick data $QData_3$ to a byte (setting %00), to a word (setting %01), or to a longword (setting %10) before the operation occurs. For example, the instruction in Figure 6.16 will add the data %101 (extended to a longword before the addition) to the contents of data register 1.

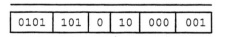

Figure 6.16 Adding decimal integer 5 to the longword contents of data register 1 by using quick instruction.

It is important to notice that representation of the immediate data is in two's complement, whereas that of the quick data is in unsigned integer representation. Moreover, the quick data field's setting to %001, 010, through %111 will have its usual meaning (i.e., representing the unsigned integers 1 through 7.) On the other hand, the designers realized that no one would ever operate with quick data whose value is equal to zero. Therefore, the bit setting of the $QData_3$ field to %000 is interpreted as though it represented the unsigned decimal integer 8.

6.6 MC68020/030/040 ADDRESSING MODES

In concluding this chapter we discuss those addressing modes supported by the newer (and more complex) central processors in the MC68000 family, i.e., the MC68020, MC68030, and MC68040 processors. We stress at the outset that these are provided for interest only. The MC68000 and MC68010 do not support these addressing modes, and the text will not discuss in detail how they are used. The MC68020 and newer processors support 18 different

TABLE 6.26 Assembly language notation used to specify operand
of MC68020/030/040 instruction

Addressing modes	Assembly
Data register direct addressing	dn
Address register direct addressing	an
Address register indirect addressing	(an)
Address register indirect addressing with postincrement	(an)+
Address register indirect addressing with predecrement	-(an)
Address register indirect addressing with displacement	$disp_{16}(an)$
Address register indirect addressing with index (8-bit displacement)	$(disp_8,an,xn.e)$
Address register indirect addressing with index (base displacement)	$(disp_{6\ or\ 32},an,xn.e)$
Memory indirect addressing postindexed	$([disp_{6\ or\ 32},an],xn.e,disp_{16\ or\ 32})$
Memory indirect addressing preindexed	$([disp_{16\ or\ 32},an,xn.e],disp_{16\ or\ 32})$
Absolute short addressing	(addr).w
Absolute long addressing	(addr).l
Program counter relative addressing with displacement	$(disp_{16}pc)$
Program counter relative addressing with index (8-bit displacement)	$(disp_8,pc,xn.e)$
Program counter relative addressing with index (base displacement)	$(disp_{16\ or\ 32},pc,xn.e)$
PC Memory indirect postindexed	$([disp_{16\ or\ 32},pc],xn.e,disp_{16\ or\ 32})$
PC Memory indirect preindexed	$([disp_{16\ or\ 32},pc,xn.e],disp_{16\ or\ 32})$
Immediate addressing	#data

addressing modes as shown in Table 6.26. Notice that the most important addition is the new addressing mode **memory indirect**. Using this addressing mode we are able to use data retrieved from an effective address as the basis for *another* effective address!

The additional addressing modes are **address register indirect with index (base displacement), PC relative addressing with index (base displacement), memory indirect addressing postindexed, memory indirect addressing preindexed, PC memory indirect postindexed,** and **PC memory indirect preindexed**. With the reader's understanding of computing effective addresses from the previous sections, it should be clear that the first two modes are similar to their MC68000 counterparts and differ only in the size of their displacements (16 or 32 bits as opposed to only 8 bits). The remaining four modes are related to the deferred addressing discussed earlier. We now discuss these modes in additional detail.

Memory indirect addressing postindexed.   As may be observed from Table 6.26, the effective address for memory indirect addressing postindexed is computed as follows: first, an *inner effective address* is formed by adding an *inner displacement* (16 or 32 bits) to the contents of address register an; second, the long word located by this inner displacement is then obtained from memory; finally, this long word is then used to compute the *final effective address* by adding to it an *outer displacement* (16 or 32 bits) and the contents of index register Xn.E (the "index register"). This effective address may be used in instructions as either a source or destination address for data.

Memory indirect addressing preindexed.   As may be observed from Table 6.26, the effective address for memory indirect addressing preindexed is computed as follows: first, an *inner effective address* is formed by adding an *inner displacement* (16 or 32 bits) to the contents of address register an and the contents of index register Xn.E (the "index register"); second, the long word located by this inner displacement is then obtained from memory; finally, this long word is then used to compute the *final effective address* by adding to it an *outer displacement* (16 or 32 bits). This effective address may be used in instructions as either a source or destination address for data.

PC memory indirect postindexed.   As may be observed from Table 6.26, the effective address for PC memory indirect addressing postindexed is computed as follows: first, an *inner effective address* is formed by adding an *inner displacement* (16 or 32 bits) to the contents of the program counter; second, the long word located by this inner displacement is then obtained from memory; finally, this long word is then used to compute the *final effective address* by adding to it an *outer displacement* (16 or 32 bits) and the contents of index register Xn.E (the "index register"). This effective address may be used in instructions as either a source or destination address for data.

PC memory indirect preindexed.   As may be observed from Table 6.26, the effective address for PC memory indirect addressing preindexed is computed as follows: first, an *inner effective address* is formed by adding an *inner displacement* (16 or 32 bits) to the contents of the program counter PC and the contents of index register Xn.E (the "index register"); second, the long word located by this inner displacement is then obtained from memory; finally, this long word is then used to compute the *final effective address* by adding to it an *outer displacement* (16 or 32 bits). This effective address may be used in instructions as either a source or destination address for data.

6.7 RISC ADDRESSING MODES

One of the characteristics associated with RISC architectures is that they possess a simple load/store[15] instruction set. By keeping the instruction set simple and only offering a few addressing modes the CPU designers are able to reduce the clock cycle time of the processor and provide a high degree of pipelining. The results of these efforts is a processor that is able to execute instructions very quickly indeed. In fact, the improvement derived from the reduced instruction set philosophy more than compensates for the extra instructions required to access data.

Typically a RISC processor will provide **register indirect with displacement** and possibly **register indirect with an index** in byte, word, and longword sizes. These modes are *only* available on the load and store instructions. Absolute addressing is supported by providing one "register" which when read, returns the constant zero. The register file is usually 32

---

[15] The term load/store indicates that all operands for an ALU operation must be in the register file. The RISC processors provide load and store instructions to move data from, and to, memory.

registers or more to allow space for temporary computations. The ALU instructions offer immediate data (i.e., constants in the instruction) and take three operands. To see the relationship between the MC68000 and RISC processors we conclude with an short example comparing the MC68000 with a hypothetical RISC processor.

```
; Code segments to move data from one memory location to
; another.  We assume the appropriate registers are loaded
; with the byte count (register 2) and source and target
; memory addresses (registers 0 and 1).
;
; Example code for MC68000:


Loop    move.l    (a0)+,(a1)+; memory to memory transfer
        subi.l    #1,d0      ; decrement count
        bgt       Loop       ; loop until count = zero


; Example code for hypothetical RISC machine:


Loop    load.l    0(r0),r3   ; load element from source
        store.l   r3,0(r1)   ; store to target
        add       #4,r0,r0   ; increment source index
        add       #4,r1,r1   ; increment target index
        sub       #1,r2,r2   ; decrement count
        bgt       Loop       ; loop until count = zero
```

6.8 EXERCISES

1. Where is data stored for an instruction using immediate addressing? In which operand of the instruction?
2. Why do computers have relatively few address registers?
3. How many bits are required to specify an address register identity in SIM68 (four registers) and MC68000 (eight registers)?
4. Why is register indirect addressing sufficient for all our needs?
5. What is meant by an "effective address"?
6. Explain the absolute addressing mode.
7. Explain the register indirect addressing mode.
8. Explain the indirect addressing with a displacement mode.
9. Explain the indirect addressing with an index mode.
10. Explain the scaled indirect addressing with an index mode.
11. Explain the register indirect addressing with postincrement mode.
12. Explain the register indirect addressing with predecrement mode.
13. Explain the PC relative addressing mode.
14. Explain the deferred (or double-indexed) addressing mode.
15. Give examples of zero-operand, one-operand, two-operand, and three-operand instructions.

16. Identify the correct addressing mode for each of the operands in each of the following instructions:
    - **a.** `move  89(pc),d2`
    - **b.** `move  d4,d1`
    - **c.** `move  (a2)+,-(a6)`
    - **d.** `move  #52,d7`
    - **e.** `move  (d2,a5),(a3)`
    - **f.** `move  8(a0),d3`
    - **g.** `move  875(a2,a5.w),345`
    - **h.** `move  $2000,a3`
    - **i.** `move  @2354(pc,d3),d3`
    - **j.** `move  #$30,d5`
    - **k.** `move  -(a3),986(a2,a4)`

17. Replace each instruction with an equivalent sequence of instructions using only the three addressing modes from SIM68.
    - **a.** `move  2(a3),(a2)`
    - **b.** `move  34(a3,a2),d3`
    - **c.** `move  (a1),d2`
    - **d.** `move  #135,(a1)+`
    - **e.** `move  $200,(a3)`

18. Compare and contrast the hypothetical SIM68 and the MC68000.

19. Define the user stack pointer and the system stack pointer. At what times are they accessible?

20. What is bit 15 of the status register called? What happens when this bit is set? Reset?

21. What is bit 13 of the status register called? What happens when this bit is set? Reset?

22. Describe the function of the interrupt mask.

23. What are the possible addressing modes of the MC68000? Describe a possible usage for each mode.

24. What is the difference between quick data and immediate data?

25. What is the decimal value of the Quick data field %000? %111? %010?

ADDITIONAL READING

LEVY, H. M., and ECKHOUSE, R. H. *Computer Programming and Architecture: The VAX-11.* Bedford, Mass.: Digital Press, 1980.

MOTOROLA, *MC68000 8-/16-/32-Bit Microprocessor User's Manual,* 6th ed. Englewood Cliffs, N.J.: Prentice Hall, 1989.

OVERBEEK, R. A., and SINGLETARY, W. E. *Assembler Language with Assist and Assist/1.* Chicago: Computer Research Associates, 1983.

SCHNIDER, G. M., DAVIS, R., and MERTZ T. *Computer Organization and Assembly Language Programming for the VAX.* New York: John Wiley, 1987.

7

Assembly Language
for the MC68000

This chapter focuses on the study of the basic features of the assembly language for the MC68000 and its assembler. First, directives provided are presented later followed by examples of the different addressing modes supported by the MC68000. Next, examples of how assembly language instructions are assembled are illustrated. The instructions of the MC68000 are then discussed; and the chapter closes with a brief discussion of floating-point representation and manipulation of real numbers in a general manner.

Discussions of certain directives and instructions of MC68000 that are designed to support particular tasks are deferred to later, more relative chapters. Specifically, instructions that are designed to be used with subroutines, as well as directives that have been designed to be employed with macros, external subroutines, and conditional assembly are presented in Chapter 8. A discussion of instructions that will generate or can be used to handle exceptions occurs in Chapter 9, whereas instructions that are intrinsic to I/O operations are featured in Chapter 10.

7.1 BASIC CONCEPTS

As one might expect, the assembly language and the assembler, ASM68K,[1] for the MC68000 resemble the corresponding assembly language and assembler for the SIM68 that was one of the central topics of Chapter 4. They resemble each other to the extent that the syntax employed for the two assembly languages is the same. For example, each assembly language statement (as in ASM68) consists of a single line of input or some part thereof; its format is given subsequently. Each field is separated by one or more spaces (blanks) or tab characters.

Name-Field	Opcode-Field	Operand-Field	Comment-Field
[symbol[:]]	mnemonic	operands	[[;]text]

---

[1] The assembly language for the MC68000 is not a standard one. Consequently, assemblers differ considerably. The discussions concerning the assembly language in the remainder of the textbook are relative to our own assembler (see Appendix B).

7.1.1 Symbols

If **symbols (labels)** are present, they should start at column 1 of the input line;[2] unlike ASM68, however, ASM68K supports two types of symbols : **nonlocal** and **local**.

Nonlocal symbols are similar to those symbols supported in ASM68. In particular, a valid nonlocal symbol is a character string whose first character must be an alphabetical character, an underscore (_) character, or a period (.). Any subsequent characters must be alphanumeric, an underscore, or a period. The symbol may optionally be followed by a colon (:). If a colon is present, it is ignored by the assembler. As in the case of ASM68, symbols are case-sensitive; incorrect syntax or multiple declarations of the same symbol will lead to an **assembly time** error; however, unlike ASM68, the symbol length is limited only by the line length, which is set to 128 characters. Any characters beyond this limit are ignored.

Local symbols, on the other hand, are character strings between two and four characters in length. The last character must always be a dollar, "$", sign; and, every other character must be a numeric character. For example, each of the following strings denote a valid local label 32$, 1$, 678$.

Nonlocal and local symbols are similar because they represent symbolic addresses; however, they are different in that nonlocal labels are valid in the entire module (therefore they cannot be reused in the same module). Local symbols are valid between any two nonlocal symbols (therefore they can be reused). Consider the following code:

```
 1 →        proc    move.w   LoopCount,d1
 2 →                bra      2$
 3 →                clr.w    d0
 4 →        1$      addq.w   #2,d0
 5 →        2$      dbra     d1,1$
 6 →
 7 →        exit    cmp.w    #$20,d0
 8 →                beq      1$
 9 →                clr.w    d0
10 →        1$      rts
```

In the preceding segment of code there are only two nonlocal symbols, proc and exit, whereas there are three local symbols 1$, 2$, and 1$. But the former two local symbols 1$ and 2$ are valid only in the code between the two, nonlocal labels proc and exit. In other words, these two local labels cease to exist outside the set of statements 1 through 7. Therefore, the operand 1$ in instruction 8 refers to the location of instruction 10.

7.1.2 Opcodes

The **opcode** field contains the **mnemonic** of a machine language instruction or an assembler **directive**. Although mnemonics will be discussed extensively, we should mention here that the number of mnemonics (for instructions as well as for directives) available in the

---

[2] If the character appearing in column 1 is a semicolon ";" or an asterisk "*", the assembler assumes that this is a **comment line**.

ASM68K assembly language is considerably larger than that in ASM68. There is one more fundamental difference: MC68000 instructions (unlike SIM68 instructions that default to word size instructions) act on either bytes, words, or longwords. The size is identified to the assembler by the extension field `.b`, `.w`, and `.l` that is placed immediately after the opcode's mnemonic. Thus, if the instruction is an add (`add`) instruction,[3] the opcode could be `add.b` meaning to add a byte, `add.w` meaning to add a word, or `add.l` meaning to add a longword. When an extension is expected and is not provided, the assembler assumes that the extension is a `w`. In other words, if the opcode provided in the source is `add`, the assembler will assemble the instruction as though its mnemonic were defined via `add.w`.

Nonetheless, all MC68000 assembly language instructions as well as directives will be discussed extensively, in this chapter we will first present the mnemonic for directives and instructions in Tables 7.1 and 7.2, respectively. In the latter case, the mnemonics of the instructions have been classified according to their corresponding machine language format.

TABLE 7.1   ASM68K directives

Assembly language directives
`dc, ds, org, equ, end, include, list, nolist, cnop`
`set, endm, endc, macro, xref, xdef, section, ifeq`
`ifne, ifgt, ifge, iflt, ifle, ifc, ifnc, ifd, ifnd`

Mnemonics are case insensitive; the assembler makes no distinction between uppercase, lowercase, or mixed-case mnemonics.

7.1.3 Operands

The **operand** field contains the operands required by the instruction/directive whose mnemonic appears in the opcode field. The number of operands in this field depends entirely on the type of instruction/directive.

In the case of no-operand instructions, this field should be empty. In the case of one-operand instructions, only one operand should appear that represents the **destination**, whereas in the case of two-operand instructions, the two operands should be separated by a comma; by convention the first operand represents the **source** and the second one represents the **destination**. Do not use (unquoted) spaces within an operand or use spaces to separate operands; the assembler interprets a space as terminating the operand field. Finally, as in ASM68, the syntax employed to define the operands conveys their address specification to the assembler. Given that the addressing modes supported by the ASM68K are larger than those of ASM68, the reader should be familiar with these extra modes; they are presented in a subsequent section.

Before we discuss operands in any more detail, we will define absolute and relative expressions.

---

[3] A different mnemonic is used for certain categories of instructions. For example, `addq` and `addi` are employed when the instruction is a quick or an immediate instruction, respectively.

TABLE 7.2 Classification of ASM68K instructions according to their machine language format

Format	MC68000 Assembly language instructions Mnemonic
F1	add, adda, sub, suba, cmp, cmpa
F2	$add_{dn,mem}$, $sub_{dn,mem}$, $and_{dn,mem}$, $or_{dn,mem}$, eor
F3	muls, mulu, divs, divu, lea
F4	move
F5	bcc
F6	trap
F7	swap
F8	tst, addi, subi, neg, negx, clr, andi, ori, eori, not
F9	addq, subq
F10	addx, subx
F11	cmpm
F12	exc
F14	$andi_{sr}$, ori_{sr}, $eori_{sr}$ trapv, illegal, rte, rts, rtr
F15	moveq
F16	asr_m, asl_m, lsl_m, lsr_m, $move_{sr}$, $move_{ccr}$ ror_m, rol_m, $roxl_m$, $roxr_m$, nbcd, pea, stop jmp, tas, $bchg_{dn}$, $bclr_{dn}$, $bset_{dn}$, $btst_{dn}$, jsr
F17	dbcc
F18	asl, asr, lsl, lsr, rol, ror, roxl, roxr
F19	scc
F20	$bchg_{dmem}$, $bclr_{dmem}$, $bset_{dmem}$, $btst_{dmem}$, chk
F21	bsr
F22	link, unlk
F23	abcd, sbcd
F24	$move_{usp}$
F25	movem

Absolute and relative expressions. An *arithmetic constant* (arithm_cons) in ASM68K is defined in nearly the same way as an arithmetic constant in ASM68. That is, it is an arithmetic constant that can be expressed as a decimal, hexadecimal, octal, or binary integer. An arithmetic constant may also be expressed as a string of (up to four) characters enclosed in single quotes. Example arithmetic constants are shown in Table 7.3.

TABLE 7.3 Examples of arithmetic constants

Constant	Example
Decimal integer	18
Hex integer	$18
Octal integer	@1327
Binary string	%0101111
Character string	'ABC3'

It is important to note that if a character string contains the single quote (') character, then this character should appear twice. For example, to specify the string "it's", one should use the syntax

'it''s'

Arithmetic constants are always right justified and padded with binary zeros if necessary. Overflows on hexadecimal, binary, and character constants are detected by the assembler, and a warning is issued. Overflows are left truncated on the "hexadecimal level." For example, the hexadecimal constant $123 that is "used" as a byte will be truncated to $23. Similarly, the decimal constant 300 that is "used" as a byte is truncated to $2C.

In ASM68K, as in the case of ASM68, one can use arithmetic constants and a set of operators to form *arithmetic expressions* that will be denoted in the sequence as arithm_expr. Unlike ASM68, however, this assembler permits the use of additional operators in the formation of an arithmetic expression. In particular, ASM68K also permits the use of modulo, shifts, and logical operations. Formally, we define an arithm_expr via the following productions where BNF notation is used.

```
arithm_exp     ::= arithm_exp + term | arithm_exp - term | term
term           ::= term * factor | term / factor | term %% factor |
                   factor
factor         ::= factor & shift_op | factor ! shift_op |
                   factor ^ shift_op | factor
shift_op       ::= shift_op << primary | shift_op >> primary | primary
primary        ::= ( arithm_exp ) | -primary | ~primary | arithm_const
arithm_const   ::= decimal_int | $hex_int | @octal_int | %binary_int |
                   'char_string'
decimal_int    ::= decimal_digit | decimal_int decimal_digit
hex_int        ::= hex_digit | hex_int hex_digit
octal_int      ::= octal_digit | octal_int octal_digit
binary_int     ::= binary_digit | binary_int binary_digit
char_string    ::= character | char_string character
decimal_digit  ::= 0|1|2|3|4|5|6|7|8|9
hex_digit      ::= 0|1|2|3|4|5|6|7|8|9|A|B|C|D|E|F|a|b|c|d|e|f
octal_digit    ::= 0|1|2|3|4|5|6|7
binary_digit   ::= 0|1
character      ::= any printable character
```

The precedence[4] of the operators as well as the notation of each operator is illustrated in Table 7.4.

TABLE 7.4   Precedence and notation of the operators that are supported by ASM68K in the formation of arithm_expr

Precedence level	Operators
1	Unary minus (−), logical NOT (~)
2	Left shift (<<), right shift (>>)
3	Logical AND (&), logical OR (!), logical XOR (^)
4	Multiply (*), divide (/), modulo (%%)
5	Add (+), subtract (−)

---

[4] Parentheses override precedence.

We now define an *absolute expression* (abs_expr) to be an arithm_expr; in symbols,

$$abs\_exp ::= arithm\_exp$$

By definition (as in ASM68), a *relative expression* rel_exp is a symbol.[5] Moreover, one could combine relative and absolute expressions, and obtain valid absolute or relative expressions according to the rules that appear in Table 7.5.

TABLE 7.5 Combining relative and absolute expressions

Expression	Result
rel_exp + abs_exp	rel_exp
abs_exp + rel_exp	rel_exp
rel_exp - abs_exp	rel_exp
rel_exp - rel_exp	abs_exp

Any other rule that does not appear in Table 7.5 yields an invalid expression. For example, the rule rel_exp + rel_exp yields an invalid expression. An exp is now defined to be either a rel_exp or an abs_exp. In symbols

$$exp ::= rel\_exp \mid abs\_exp$$

Therefore, the above discussions suggest that the following expressions are valid exp's where here, there represent two symbols.

```
    3    3+4   3-4   3*4-5    3/4+6
HERE+4    4+3*2+HERE    HERE-22*(HERE-THERE)
```

However, the following are invalid exp's.

```
(HERE + THERE)    (5 - THERE)    (2*HERE)
```

Operands of instructions. An operand of an instruction could be either a register address or a memory address. Before the format of the operands according to their addressing mode is described, we note that the assembler recognizes the following *special* (insensitive case) *symbols*, pc, sp, dn, an, ccr, sr, usp, *, whenever they appear in the operand field of an instruction to have a preassigned and fixed meaning.[6] In particular, the first seven symbols represent register addresses, whereas the last symbol represents a constant. All these symbols are discussed subsequently.

7.1.4 Register Notation

As in ASM68, we denote by dn and an the data and address register n, respectively. In addition, our assembler recognizes the notation pc to refer to the program counter, sr to

---

[5] There is only one exception to this rule. A symbol that is equated to an arithm_expr is considered to be an arithm_cons.

[6] There is another special symbol narg whose discussion is delayed until Chapter 8.

refer to the status register, and ccr to refer to the condition code register. Furthermore, the notation sp can be used interchangeably with a7. The notation usp is used only with the "move user stack pointer" instruction. The discussion of this paragraph is summarized in Table 7.6.

TABLE 7.6   Assembly language notation of operands that address registers

Assembly	dn	an	pc	sr	ccr	usp	sp
Data register	√						
Address register		√				a7	a7
Program counter			√				
Status register				√			
Condition code register					√		

Second, the notation rn will be used throughout this textbook to represent either data register dn or address register an. Similarly, by xn, we will represent either the data register dn or address register an. The notation xn, however, will be used whenever the register in question is employed as an index register.[7]

7.1.5 Mode Specification and Operand Notation

The syntax employed to define an operand of an instruction conveys its address specification to the assembler. Table 7.7 summarizes the applicable syntax for each of the available 12 addressing modes.

TABLE 7.7   Assembly language notation used to specify operand of instruction; Syntax conveys to assembler address specification (Note that $disp_n$, addr, and data are specified via exps)"

Addressing modes	Assembly
Data register direct addressing	dn
Address register direct addressing	an
Address register indirect addressing	(an)
Address register indirect addressing with postincrement	(an)+
Address register indirect addressing with predecrement	-(an)
Address register indirect addressing with displacement	$disp_{16}$(an)
Address register indirect addressing with index and displacement	$disp_8$(an,xn.e)
Absolute short addressing	(addr).w
Absolute long addressing	(addr).1
Program counter relative addressing with displacement	$disp_{16}$(pc)
Program counter relative addressing with index and displacement	$disp_8$(pc,xn.e)
Immediate addressing	#data

---

[7] The assembler does not recognize either symbol xn or rn.

The reader will be provided shortly with an example of each addressing scheme. He or she should pay special attention to the two *program counter relative* addressing schemes because the assembler assembles each such instruction differently depending on whether or not the associated displacement $disp_n$ is specified via an abs_exp or a rel_exp.

Data register direct addressing. Under this mode, the effective address is data register dn; thus, the "data" is the contents of data register dn. Data register direct addressing is the same as register direct addressing but is restricted to MC68000 data registers only. Because a data register has been specified, the data size may be either a byte, a word, or a longword. The syntax employed in specifying the operands of the assembly language instruction

move.b d2,d1

indicates that the mode of the source and destination operand is data register direct. The code generated by the assembler, as well as the action that will be taken during run time, is illustrated in Figure 7.1.

Instruction move.b d2,d1	Object code 1202	
Action	State before	State after
Move low-order byte of data register d2 to low-order byte of data register 1.	d1: AB12F10A d2: CFDCB3ED	d1: AB12F1**ED** d2: CFDCB3ED

Figure 7.1 Sample addressing illustration.

Address register direct addressing. The effective address is address register an; thus, the "data" is the contents of address register an. Address register direct addressing is the same as register direct addressing but is restricted to address registers only. Unlike data register direct addressing, because we are dealing with an address register, the only valid sizes are the word and longword. As an example, the syntax employed in specifying the operands of the assembly language instruction

movea.w d2,a1

indicates that the mode of the source operand is data register direct, whereas that of the destination operand is address register direct. The code generated by the assembler, as well as the action that will be taken during run time, is illustrated in Figure 7.2.

Instruction movea.w d2,a1	Object code 3242	
Action	State before	State after
Move low-order word of data register d2 to address register a1. Notice that in such a move the word is sign extended to a longword before the move is performed.	d2: AB12F10A a1: CFDCB3ED	d2: AB12F10A a1: **FFFFF10A**

Figure 7.2 Address register direct addressing.

Address register indirect addressing. The effective address EA is defined by the memory location given in address register an. Address register indirect addressing is the same as register indirect addressing with the restriction to address registers only. As we shall see from now on, only address registers may be used in computing effective addresses for memory. The syntax employed in specifying the operands of the assembly language instruction

move.w (a1),d2

indicates that the mode of the source operand is address register indirect and that of the destination operand is data register direct. The code generated by the assembler, as well as the action that will be taken during run time, is illustrated in Figure 7.3.

Instruction move.w (a1),d2	Object code 3411	
Action	State before	State after
Move word from the memory location whose address is specified by 24 low-order bits of address register a1 to low-order word of data register d2.	a1: 00001230 d2: C1F0DC00	a1: 00001230 d2: C1F0**F180**
	Memory	Memory
	1230: F180ABCD 1234: 0000DCBA	1230: F180ABCD 1234: 0000DCBA

Figure 7.3 Address register indirection addressing.

Address register indirect addressing with postincrement. Address register indirect addressing with postincrement is the same as register indirect addressing with postincrement, with the restriction that only an address register may be used. Note that the increment will be a function of the data size selected by the opcode (byte, word, or longword). If the instruction is a byte instruction, the increment will be 1 unless the register is a7 where the increment will be[8] 2. If the data size specified in the instruction is a word, the increment will be 2; if it is a longword, the increment will be 4. This means that an array of simple data items (either byte, word, or longword) may be sequentially accessed without explicitly changing an index. As an example, the syntax employed in specifying the operands of the assembly language instruction

move.w (a1)+,d2

indicates that the mode of the source operand is address register indirect with postincrement and that of the destination operand is data register direct. The code generated by the assembler, as well as the action that will be taken during run time, is illustrated in Figure 7.4.

---

[8] Recall that both postincrement and predecrement modes are used to emulate the push and pop operations. If the register used is a7 the processor maintains word boundaries for this stack pointer. Therefore, if the size of the data is a byte the processor increases if the mode specified is postincrement (decreases in the case of predecrement mode) the contents of the stack pointer by 2 in order to maintain this alignment.

Instruction move.w (a1)+,d2	Object code 3419	
Action	State before	State after
Move contents of memory location pointed to by 24 low-order bits of register a1 into d2, and then increment contents of register a1 by 2 (the operation mode size).	a1: `00001230` d2: `87C3187A` Memory 1230: `320D0005` 1234: `0000DCBA`	a1: `00001232` d2: `87C3320D` Memory 1230: `320D0005` 1234: `0000DCBA`

Figure 7.4   Address register indirect addressing with postincrement.

Address register indirect addressing with predecrement.   Address register indirect addressing with predecrement is the same as register indirect with predecrement. As with postincrement (explained above), the decrement will depend on the data size used (unless if the register is a7 and the data size is 1, in which case it decrements by 2). The syntax employed in specifying the operands of the assembly language instruction

```
move.w -(a1),d2
```

indicates that the mode of the source operand is address register indirect with predecrement and that of the destination operand is data register direct. The code generated by the assembler, as well as the action that will be taken during run time, is illustrated in Figure 7.5.

Instruction move.w -(a1),d2	Object code 3421	
Action	State before	State after
Decrement contents of register a1 by 2 (the operation mode size), and then move contents of memory location pointed to by 24 low-order bits of register a1 into the low-order word of register d2.	a1: `00001234` d2: `87C3187A` Memory 1230: `320D0005` 1234: `0000DCBA`	a1: `00001232` d2: `87C30005` Memory 1230: `320D0005` 1234: `0000DCBA`

Figure 7.5   Addressing register indirect with predecrement.

Address indirect addressing with displacement.   The effective address, EA is computed by the addition of the contents of an and a displacement. Address indirect addressing with a displacement is the same as indirect addressing with a displacement; however, only the address registers may be used. Conceptually, the displacement may be either a byte or a word. Within a machine instruction, however, the size is always a word. As an example, the syntax employed in specifying the operands of the assembly language instruction move.w $14(a1),20(a2)

indicates that the mode of both the source and destination operands is address register indirect with displacement. The code generated by the assembler, as well as the action that will be taken during run time, is illustrated in Figure 7.6.

Instruction move.w $14(a1),20(a2)	Object code 3569 0014 0014			
Action	State before		State after	
Move word from memory location whose effective address is formed by 24 low-order bits of the sum of sign extended displacement ($14) and the longword contents of register a1 to memory location whose effective address is formed by 24 low-order bits of sum of sign extended displacement (20) and the longword contents of register a2.	a1:	0000121E	a1:	0000121E
	a2:	00001224	a2:	00001224
	Memory		Memory	
	1230:	F1267DEA	1230:	F1267DEA
	1238:	64ACB320	1238:	**7DEA**B320

Figure 7.6   Address register indirect with displacement.

Address indirect addressing with index and displacement.   The effective address, EA is formed by adding the contents of address register an, the contents of register xn, and the indicated displacement.

Address indirect addressing with an index is the same as indirect addressing with an index, with the restriction that the indirect register must be an address register. The syntax employed in specifying the operands of the assembly language instruction

move.w $12(a1,a2.1),20(a3,a4.w)

indicates that the mode of both the source and destination operands is address register indirect with displacement and index. The code generated by the assembler, as well as the action that will be taken during run time, is illustrated in Figure 7.7.

Instruction move.w $12(a1,a2.1),20(a3,a4.w)	Object code 37B1 A812 C014			
Action	State before		State after	
Move word from memory location whose effective address is formed by 24 low-order bits of the sum of sign extended displacement ($12), longword contents of register a1 and longword contents of register a2 to the memory location whose effective address is formed by 24 low-order bits of the sum of sign extended displacement (20), longword contents of register a3 and sign-extended, low-order word of register a4.	a1:	00001100	a1:	00001100
	a2:	00000134	a2:	00000134
	a3:	00008120	a3:	00008120
	a4:	00000034	a4:	00000034
	Memory		Memory	
	1246:	F18D190F	1246:	F18D190F
	8168:	0000DCBA	8168:	**F18D**DCBA

Figure 7.7   Address indirect addressing with index and displacement.

Absolute short (long) addressing. The effective address, EA is defined by a single word constant is encoded as part of the machine instruction. This instruction is synonymous with the absolute addressing mode previously described. The term "short addressing" refers to the fact that, when using this mode, the absolute address is restricted to only 16 bits. This 16-bit address is sign extended (at run time) to 32 bits. Thus, the only addresses that are accessible with this addressing mode are those in the first 32K of memory and the last 32K of memory. For larger addresses, the long form must be used. The syntax employed in specifying the operands of the assembly language instruction

```
move.b ($61234).w,d1
```

indicates that the mode of the source operand is absolute short and that of the destination operand is data register direct. The code generated by the assembler, as well as the action that will be taken during run time, is illustrated in Figure 7.8.

Instruction move.b ($61234).w,d1	Object code 1238 1234	
Action	State before	State after
Move contents of memory location with effective address $001234 into data register d1.	d1: FF12DCA8	d1: FF12DC88
	Memory	Memory
	001234: 88825F44	001234: 88825F44
	061234: 6A01FAB2	061234: 6A01FAB2

Figure 7.8. Absolute short addressing.

On the other hand, the syntax employed in specifying the operands of the assembly language instruction

```
move.b ($61234).l,d1
```

indicates that the mode of the source operand is absolute long and that of the destination operand is data register direct. The code generated by the assembler as well as the action that will be taken during run time is illustrated in Figure 7.9.

Instruction move.b ($61234).l,d1	Object code 1239 0006 1234	
Action	State before	State after
Move the contents of memory location with effective address $061234 into data register d1.	d1: FF12DCA8	d1: FF12DC6A
	Memory	Memory
	001234: 88825F44	001234: 88825F44
	061234: 6A01FAB2	061234: 6A01FAB2

Figure 7.9 Absolute long addressing.

PC-relative addressing with displacement. The effective address, EA is computed as the sum of a displacement and the contents of the PC at the start of the instruction and an offset of 2.

In essence, this instruction is similar to PC-relative addressing. The major difference is that the effective address is computed by the sum of the PC at the start of the instruction, the constant 2, and the displacement. If the object code is generated by an assembler and labels are used, the user will not be affected by this. If, however, one is programming in machine code, it is important to be aware of the offset of 2. Note also that the displacement is a single word, giving rise to a displacement of -32768 to +32767 bytes. The syntax employed in specifying the operands of the assembly language instruction

```
move.w $30(pc),d1
```

indicates that the mode of the source operand is PC indirect with displacement and that of the destination operand is data register direct. The code generated by the assembler, as well as the action that will be taken during run time, is illustrated in Figure 7.10.

Instruction move.w $30(pc),d1	Object code 323A 0030	
Action	State before	State after
Move the word located $30 bytes further on from pc into the low-order word of register d1.	pc: 00000034 d1: FF87ABCD Memory 0066: F2863409	pc: 00000038 d1: FF87**F286** Memory 0066: F2863409

Figure 7.10 PC-relative addressing with displacement using numeric constants.

On the other hand, one should be very careful when a relative expression is used to specify the displacement. For example, if we replace the previous assembly language instruction by

```
move.w   num(pc),d1
```

the effect is that we are asking the assembler to generate code in such a way so that the word at *location* num is moved to d1; however, the calculation of the effective address is to be made via the PC-relative mode. Figure 7.11 illustrates this concept under the assumption that the instruction is assembled and subsequently loaded at location $000034 whereas the value of the symbol num is $000030.

Instruction move.w num(pc),d1	Object code 323A FFFA	
Action	State before	State after
Instruction requests that the word at location num (value $30) be moved into low-order word of data register d1.	pc: 00000034 d1: FF87ABCD Memory 0030: F2863409	pc: 00000038 d1: FF87**F286** Memory 0030: F2863409

Figure 7.11 PC-relative addressing with displacement using labels.

PC-relative addressing with index and displacement. The effective address, EA is computed as the sum of a displacement, the contents of the pc, and the contents of register rn. This instruction is an extension of PC-relative indexed addressing. As with the previous instruction, the effective address is composed of the pc at the beginning of the instruction, plus 2, plus the contents of the index register, plus the displacement. With this instruction the displacement is restricted to one a byte giving rise to a displacement in the range of −128 to +127 bytes. As an example, the syntax employed in specifying the operands of the assembly language instruction

```
move.w $12(pc,a2.w),20(a3)
```

indicates that the mode of the source operand is pc indirect with index and displacement and that of the destination operand is address register indirect with displacement. The code generated by the assembler, as well as the action that will be taken during run time, is illustrated in Figure 7.12.

Instruction move.w $12(pc,a2.w),20(a3)		Object code 377B A012 0014	
Action	State before		State after
Move the word from memory location whose effective address is formed by 24 low-order bits of sum of sign extended displacement ($12), program counter contents and sign-extended low-order word of register a2 to the memory location whose effective address is formed by 24 low-order bits of the sum of the sign-extended displacement (20) and the longword contents of register a3.	pc: 00000026 a2: 0000001A a3: 00000100 Memory 0054: F268FDA1 0114: 9467AAB2		pc: 0000002B a2: 0000001A a3: 00000100 Memory 0054: F268FFDA1 0114: **F268**AAB2

Figure 7.12 PC-relative addressing with index and displacement using numeric constants.

On the other hand, if the instruction were

```
move.w  num(pc,a2.w),20(a3)
```

the assembler would generate the code in Figure 7.13 under the assumptions that the instruction is assembled at location $000026 and the value of the symbol num was $000012.

Immediate addressing. The data is defined in the machine language instruction. The MC68000 immediate addressing mode is synonymous with the general immediate mode. As an example, the syntax employed in specifying the operands of the assembly language instruction

```
move.w #1234,d1
```

indicates that the mode of the source operand is immediate addressing and that of the destination operand is data register direct. The code generated by the assembler as well as the action that will be taken during run time is illustrated in Figure 7.14.

Instruction `move.w num(pc,a2.w),20(a3)`	Object code 377B A0EA 0014	
Action	State before	State after
Assuming that the symbol num represents the symbolic address $12. The instruction requests that a word from the memory location whose effective address is formed by 24 low-order bits of the sum of the sign- extended displacement (the displacement here is equal to the distance between the symbol num and the current contents of location counter pc + 2). $12-$(000026+2) = EA, the program counter contents, and the sign-extended, low-order word of register a2 be moved to the memory location whose effective address is formed by 24 low-order bits of the sum of the sign extended displacement (20) and the longword contents of register a3.	pc: `00000026` a2: `0000001A` a3: `00000100` Memory 002C: `F268FDA1` 0114: `9467AAB2`	pc: `0000002B` a2: `0000001A` a3: `00000100` Memory 002C: `F268FDA1` 0114: `F268AAB2`

Figure 7.13   PC-relative addressing with index and displacement using labels.

Instruction `move.w #1234,d1`	Object code 323C 04D2	
Action	State before	State after
Move immediate data `1234` into low-order word of data register d1.	d1: `087A5467`	d1: `087A04D2`

Figure 7.14   Immediate addressing.

7.2 CATEGORIES OF ADDRESSING MODES

Before we proceed, we will classify the addressing modes into four major overlapping categories that are presented in Table 7.8 and briefly discussed subsequently.

1. *Data references.* Every addressing mode except address register direct may be used (when permitted by the instruction at hand) to reference data. Address register direct is not allowed, because the contents of an address register contain *addresses* and not data.

2. *Memory references.* All addressing modes with the exception of data register direct, address register direct, or immediate addressing, address memory. Hence, there is a total of nine modes that one may use to access memory. Furthermore, memory references can be divided into two overlapping categories: *control* vis à vis *alterable* memory references.

3. *Control references.* Into this category fall all memory addressing modes that are allowed to be employed to specify branch addresses, that is, addresses to which the program should branch to.

TABLE 7.8 Categories of effective addresses

Addressing modes	Data	Memory	Control	Alterable
Data register direct addressing	√			√
Address register direct addressing				√
Address register indirect addressing	√	√	√	√
Address register indirect addressing with postincrement	√	√		√
Address register indirect addressing with predecrement	√	√		√
Address register indirect addressing with displacement	√	√	√	√
Address register indirect addressing with index and displacement	√	√	√	√
Absolute short addressing	√	√	√	√
Absolute long addressing	√	√	√	√
PC-relative addressing with displacement	√	√	√	
PC-relative addressing with index and displacement	√	√	√	
Immediate addressing	√			

4. *Alterable references.* Into this category fall all modes that are allowed for modification of the contents of the location indicated by the operand. As Table 7.8 indicates, both direct register modes are allowed together with all memory references with the only exception being the PC-relative modes. In other words, PC-relative modes are not permitted to address a memory location if the contents of that location are to be modified.

In this textbook, five different symbols will be used to classify the memory references of the four overlapping categories and they are presented in Table 7.9. It should be noted that smem (an acronym for "source memory") specifies the set of memory references. On the other hand, dmem (an acronym for "destination memory") specifies the set of alterable memory references, whereas smem* and dmem* specify two non-disjoint sets of control references. Finally, absmem specifies an absolute address that could be specified by either a relative or an absolute expression.

TABLE 7.9 Grouping of operands that address memory locations in sets smem, smem*, dmem, dmem*, and absmem

Assembly	smem	dmem	smem*	dmem*	absmem
(an)	√	√	√	√	
(an)+	√	√			
-(an)	√	√			
disp$_{16}$(an)	√	√	√	√	
disp$_8$(an,xn.e)	√	√	√	√	
addr.w	√	√	√	√	√
addr.l	√	√	√	√	√
disp$_{16}$(pc)	√		√		
disp$_8$(pc,xn.e)	√		√		

7.3 DIRECTIVES AND CONSTANTS

In ASM68K, there are several constants that can be defined and used. There are two disjoint classes of constants, the **run-time** and **assembly-time** constants. Their principal difference is that the former constants *occupy* storage area in the user's program, whereas in the latter constants *no storage is allocated;* instead the values of the constants are used by the assembler.

7.3.1 Run-time Constants

Defined constants

The ASM68K assembler provides the user with two directives that enable him or her to either store data or allocate storage for future use. The mnemonics for the two directives are dc (define constant) and ds (define storage).

DC directive.   The format of this directive is the following:

Name-Field	Opcode-Field	Operand-Field
[valid symbol]	dc.e	exp[,exp]

The brackets enclosing the expression "valid symbol" indicate that this expression is optional. The operand field expects at least one operand that may be either an abs_exp or a rel_exp. Finally, there are several variations of this directive depending principally on the size of the data that should be stored.

The value of the extension e (b, w or l) provides the assembler with two pieces of information; first, the size of the representation that must be generated, and second, the alignment that is desired.

If the extension of the directive is w or l, the data is aligned on word boundaries. If the extension of the directive is b, no added data alignment occurs.

The assembler handles character constants in a special way when the extension is b. Each character in the character string is converted byte-by-byte to its corresponding ASCII code; no truncation occurs. To use a single quote in a string, use two quotes.

Example

The code generated by the assembler as a result of the source directives.

LOCATION	OBJECT	CODE	STMT	SOURCE		CODE
......	....		14	......	....	....
000002	03		15	......	....	....
000003	16		16		dc.b	22
000004	0016		17		dc.w	22
000006	0000 0016		18		dc.l	22
00000A	22		19		dc.b	$22
00000C	0022		10		dc.w	$22
00000E	0000 0022		11		dc.l	$22
000012	414243		12		dc.b	'ABC'
000016	4243		13		dc.w	'ABC'
000018	00004142		14		dc.l	'AB'
00001C	48656C6C6F00		15		dc.b	'Hello',0
......	....		..	......	....	....

DS directive.   The format of this directive is the following:

Name-Field	Opcode-Field	Operand-Field
[valid symbol]	ds.e	abs_exp

The name field is optional, whereas "abs_exp" represents a positive integer arithmetic expression. Unlike the dc directive, the purpose of this directive is to allocate storage space and not to generate code; therefore, the extension field e is required. As before, the extension indicates the boundary alignment and the size of storage that must be allocated for each copy of the data. The positive integer represented by "abs_exp" indicates the number of copies of the data or, equivalently, the number of locations that are to be allocated.

This directive can be used also to force the assembler to align his program counter. In particular, if the operand of this directive is the decimal integer zero the assembler performs the alignment without allocating any storage.

Example

The assembly of several defined storage directives is given subsequently.

LOCATION	OBJECT CODE	STMT	SOURCE CODE
000002		15	....
000004		16	ds.b 3
000007		17	ds.w 0
000008		17	ds.b 1
00000A		18	ds.w 2
00000E		14	....

7.3.2 Assembly-time Constants

EQU, *

A user may define the *value* of a symbol via the **equivalence** (equ) directive. The format of this directive follows.

Name-Field	Opcode-Field	Operand-Field
valid symbol	equ	exp

A symbol should be present in the Name-Field of the statement; the effect caused by this directive is that the assembler will assign the value associated with the "exp" to the symbol. Consider the declaration

setit   equ $1000

The assembler will make the following assignment setit=$1000 and will *replace* every occurrence of the symbol setit with its value $1000. Notice that no storage is allocated to that symbol. Two important observations should be made here. First, the value of a symbol defined via the `equ` directive cannot be changed by any other statement;[9] second, the declaration of this symbol should *precede* any reference to it.

Recall that the assembler maintains its own location counter. The assembler permits one to extract the *current* contents of its location counter via the special symbol asterisk "*". Consider the following statement:

```
        setit      equ     *
```

If we assume that the assembler's location counter contains $001000, then the assembler will perform the assignment `setit`=$001000. A reference to the assembler's location counter provides one with a flexible and powerful tool. Consider the declaration

```
        string    dc.b      'I LOVE MC68000'
        length    equ       14
```

and, assume that we will assign to the symbol `length` the length of the string `string`. One way is to calculate that length (as we did earlier); the other, and more preferable way, is to let the assembler calculate it for us! It is not difficult to see that the piece of code outlined below performs this task.

```
        string    dc.b      'I LOVE MC68000'
        length    equ       *-string
```

As a second example, consider the statement

```
        here     bra       *
```

Execution of this statement will cause an infinite loop. The reason is that the value of "*" is equal to the value indicated by the assembler's location counter. The value of the latter is equal to the value of the symbol `here`; therefore, the program will branch to this location.

7.3.3 ORG and END Directives

Recall that programs should not be loaded in low addresses because these addresses are reserved by the processor. Hence, there is a need to instruct the assembler to generate code according to the address where the machine language program will be loaded. For example, if we knew that the program could be loaded starting at location $010000 and thereafter, the assembler should be instructed to generate code as though this were the **loading origin**.

The directive that is provided for this purpose is the **origin** (ORG); its format is given subsequently. Consider the declaration

Name-Field	Opcode-Field	Operand-Field
[valid symbol]	org	abs_exp

```
        here      org    $1000
```

---

[9] Nor even via another `equ` directive.

Then, the value of the symbol here will be equal to $1000; on encountering this statement, the assembler will set the contents of its location counter to $001000.

As with ASM68, every module should end with the directive end. The word "every" in the previous sentence suggests that a program could consist of more than one module! Although our assembler can assemble these modules independently, we will delay the discussion of this topic to the next chapter. Therefore, for the time being, assume that each program consists of a **single** module.

7.3.4 INCLUDE Directive

Name-Field	Opcode-Field	Operand-Field
	include	'filename'

The include directive instructs the assembler to obtain its input from the file specified in the operand field. The assembler opens this file and continues to read from it until either another include directive is found or the end of the file is reached. When the end of a file is reached, the assembler closes the file and starts reading from the most recent file it opened. include directives may be nested up to a total of three times. An error message is issued if this nesting depth is exceeded. Observe that the name field of this directive should be empty.

7.3.5 LIST and NOLIST Directives

The nolist and list directives (whose format is presented subsequently) allow the user to suspend and resume sending output to the listing file.

Name-Field	Opcode-Field	Operand-Field
	[no]list	

These directives are useful for bracketing an include directive that will prevent the included file from appearing in the listing file. The name field of these directives should be empty.

7.3.6 CNOP Directive

Even though the ds directive can be used to align data in desired boundaries, another directive is also provided, the cnop directive, which will allow the alignment of either code or data on any boundary. The format of the directive is the following:

Name-Field	Opcode-Field	Operand-Field
[valid symbol]	cnop	abs_exp1,abs_exp2

The alignment is performed in two steps. In the first step, the nearest (greater than or equal to) address to the location counter that is evenly divisible by the second operand expression, abs_exp2, is calculated. In the second step, the first expression, abs_exp1, is assumed to represent an offset that is added to the boundary address calculated in the previous step. Consider the following piece of code:

```
LOCATION    OBJECT    CODE    STMT    SOURCE          CODE
--------    --------------    ----    --------------------
......                                ....    ....    ....
  000002                        2     here      sub.w    d0,d1
  00000A                        3               cnop     2,8
  00000A                        4               add.w    d0,d1
  00000C                        5     ......    ....    ....
```

After the instruction at the address here is assembled the assembler's location counter contains $000002; now, the nearest boundary to that address that is divisible evenly by 8 is $000008. Finally, the offset defined in the cnop directive of 2 is added to $000008 yielding $00000A. We close this section by noting that use of this directive in the form

```
          cnop      0,2
```

will cause alignment of code/data on a word boundary.

Comments.   The assembler provide for his or her own benefit brief explanations of each assembly language statement via **comments**. When the assembler encounters (an unquoted) semicolon ";", it understands that whatever text follows is a comment and is ignored by the assembler.

Moreover, an asterisk (*) in the first column of an input line specifies that the entire line is a comment. Blank lines are also considered to be comments. Finally, comment text can follow any complete instruction or directive as long as at least one space (blank) separates the instruction/directive and the comment.

7.4 POSITION-DEPENDENT VERSUS POSITION-INDEPENDENT CODE

By definition, a machine language program that can be loaded anywhere in main memory and still run correctly is said to be **position independent**; the assembly language code employed in this case is said to be **position independent code**. One example of a position dependent program is given in Figure 7.15 whose listing is provided by ASM68. Before we begin this discussion, notice that from the assembly language code, it appears that the program will always run as it is expected and produce the result of the multiplication of 11 and 41. In reality, the program is guaranteed to be executed, if and only if, its loading origin is really $000000, assuming that this area of memory is not protected by the operating system.

To understand that the code is position dependent, consider what would occur during execution of this program, if the assumption is made that it is loaded at location $1000.

The instruction specified by statement 4 will be executed as was expected. When statement number 5 is executed, however, what will be moved into register d1 will not be the binary equivalent of the decimal integer 11; instead, whatever is at location $0016 at that time will be moved; this is due to the *machine language instruction* specifications. The same problem appears whenever the instruction at statement 6 must be executed. The

```
LOCATION  OBJECT   CODE    STMT   SOURCE          CODE

                            1
000000                      2           org     $0000
                            3
000000    90C8              4           sub     a0,a0
000002    3228 0016         5           move    X(a0),d1
000006    3439 00000018     6           move    X+2,d2
00000C    C5C1              7           muls    d1,d2
00000E    3039 0000001A     8           move    X+4,d2
000014    4E40              9           trap    #0
000016    000B             10  X        dc      11
000018    0029             11           dc      41
00001A    0003             12           dc      3
                           13
00001C                     14           end
```

Figure 7.15 Position-dependent code.

reason that this occurs is because in the assembly language instruction the *absolute mode* is used to access the data. Therefore, one solution would have been to employ PC-relative modes to access those memory locations that are specified by *relative expressions*.[10] The assembly language code presented in Figure 7.16 is one example that would solve this particular problem.

Notice that this technique will not solve all problems relative to producing position-independent code. One reason for this is outlined via the assembly language program that is presented in Figure 7.17. Even though we may replace all first operands of the instructions with PC-relative modes, the destination of the move instruction in statement number 9

```
LOCATION  OBJECT   CODE    STMT   SOURCE          CODE

                            1
000000                      2           org     $0000
                            3
000000    90C8              4           sub     a0,a0
000002    323B 880E         5           move    X(pc,a0.1),d1
000006    343A 000C         6           move    X+2(pc),d2
00000A    C5C1              7           muls    d1,d2
00000C    303A 0008         8           move    X+4(pc),d0
000010    4E40              9           trap    #0
000012    000B             10  X        dc      11
000014    0029             11           dc      41
000016    0003             12           dc      3
                           13
000018                     14           end
```

Figure 7.16 Position-independent code using PC-relative addressing modes.

---

[10] Certain assemblers aid in achieving this, with the use of the PC-relative mode as the default whenever an absolute address mode, specified via a relative expression, is encountered. For example add here,d0 will be assembled as though it were written as add here(PC),d0; however, add $1000,d0 will be assembled in absolute mode.

```
LOCATION  OBJECT      CODE    STMT   SOURCE         CODE

                               1
000000                         2            org     $0000
                               3
000000    90C8                 4            sub     a0,a0
000002    3228 001C            5            move    X(a0),d1
000006    3430 0000001E        6            move    X+2,d2
00000C    C5C1                 7            muls    d1,d2
00000E    3039 00000020        8            move    X+4,d0
000014    33C1 00000022        9            move    d1,X+6
00001A    4E40                10            trap    #0
00001C    000B                11      X     dc      11
00001E    0029                12            dc      41
000020    0003                13            dc      3
000022                        14            ds      1
000024                        15            end
```

Figure 7.17 Position-dependent code that cannot be replaced with PC-relative addressing.

cannot be replaced with a PC-relative mode; that is because this mode is not supported. MC68000, however, permits the second operand of this instruction to be specified via address register indirect addressing. Therefore, the lea instruction in statement 9, instead of the move instruction, can be employed to load the effective address of X + 6 (using a PC-relative mode again) into an address register, a1 in this case. Now we may move the word by issuing the move instruction in statement 10. The assembly code is presented in Figure 7.18. Moreover, the techniques outlined earlier require a considerable amount of work; furthermore, it will never work if the *distance* of the data from the program changes.

All of these problems can be solved by employing a *relocatable assembler* and writing *relocatable code*. A relocatable assembler generates code so that every address that could be affected by the relocation of the program is flagged. This information is passed to

```
LOCATION  OBJECT     CODE  STMT   SOURCE         CODE

                            1
000000                      2            org     $0000
                            3
000000    90C8              4            sub     a0,a0
000002    323B 8814         5            move    X(pc,a0),d1
000006    343A 0012         6            move    X+2(pc),d2
00000A    C5C1              7            muls    d1,d2
00000C    303A 000E         8            move    X+4(pc),d0
000010    43FA 000C         9            lea     X+6(pc),a1
000014    3281             10            move    d1,(a1)
000016    4E40             11            trap    #0
000018    000B             12      X     dc      11
00001A    0029             13            dc      41
00001C    0003             14            dc      3
00001E                     15            ds      1
000020                     16            end
```

Figure 7.18 Position-independent code using lea and PC-relative addressing.

a **relocatable loader**, which is able to replace the flagged addresses with the appropriate ones. This can be accomplished by adding the *relocatable factor* to the flagged address.

At this point the reader should realize why assembly expressions have been classified as either relative or absolute. Relative expressions (constants) are *affected* by the relocation of a program, whereas absolute expressions are not. The programmer should be aware of this important difference.

Even so, these issues will be clarified later. The following definitions are set forth, however. A loader that resolves external references, relocates object modules, and then loads them is called a **linking loader**. In some systems, a separate program referred to as the **link editor (linker)** resolves external references and concatenates object modules into one contiguous[11] relocatable object module without loading it. The relocatable loader can now be loaded anywhere in memory.

7.5 INSTRUCTIONS

The remainder of this chapter is dedicated to the discussion of most instructions that are supported by MC68000. These instructions have been divided into five different subsets according to the logical function that they perform and are discussed subsequently.

Section 7.5.1 *Binary Integer Arithmetic.* In this set, all instructions have been placed that will perform integer arithmetic such as addition, multiplication, and so on. In addition, special instructions that are used to test the sign of integers or compare them also belong in this category. It should be emphasized that instructions in this group assume that the binary strings that they operate on represent integers in two's complement.

Section 7.5.2 *Moving Instructions.* The type of instructions that belong in this group are those that perform the copying of data from one place to another. This "place" could be a data register, an address register, the status register, the condition code register, or a memory location.

Section 7.5.3 *Branching and Looping.* All instructions that will permit one to "jump around" in the code belong in this group.

Section 7.5.4 *Bit Manipulation Instructions.* Here we have placed the logical instructions such as the or instructions and the instructions that perform shifts, as well as those that are used for rotation. In general, the instructions in this group are usually employed to manipulate bit patterns.

Section 7.5.5 *Decimal Arithmetic.* The set of instructions that are employed to perform arithmetic on decimal integers have been placed in this group.

Section 7.5.6 *Real Number Arithmetic.* Here we present the methods that are employed in representing real numbers internally. In particular, conversion algorithms are presented and examples are given which would indicate how one could emulate binary or floating-point instructions by using instructions that have been designed to be used with binary or decimal integers.

---

[11] A linker is discussed in Chapter 8.

Before proceeding, it should be emphasized that all examples that will be provided have been assembled with our own assembler and run on the educational computer board (ECB).[12]

7.5.1 Binary Integer Arithmetic

MC68000 provides us with a rich assortment of instructions that allows us to perform the basic arithmetic operations of *addition, subtraction, multiplication, division,* and *negation.* In addition, instructions are provided that permit one to *compare* and *clear* data as well as to manipulate the contents of the registers (such as *swapping, exchanging,* and *extending*). These instructions are presented and discussed in the following paragraphs.

Which form of an instruction to be used depends entirely on the task at hand. It is the responsibility of the programmer, however, to use that particular instruction that leads to the most efficient code. In other words, the programmer should select that particular instruction (or set of instructions) that requires the least amount of storage and execution time. For example, if the programmer needs to add the decimal integer 4 to data register d0, then he or she should employ a quick instruction.

Before we proceed with discussion of the available instructions, the reader should be very careful whenever she or he codes an instruction (i.e., in particular when specifying the operands of an instruction). For example, a coded instruction such as add smem, dmem will lead to an assembly time error. Although such an instruction as this is desirable, the MC68000 does not support it. Therefore, whenever in doubt, consult your manual for the allowable addressing modes of the instruction that needs to be coded.

Addition

Earlier, was mentioned that the set of provided *addition* instructions has been classified into groups. In the case at hand, four groups are under consideration. The *regular* operations are instructions that require at least one of the operands to reside in a register, whereas the other may reside either in a register or in memory. The *immediate* as well as the *quick* operations allow the destination to be either a register or a memory location. The last group, the *extended* operations group, requires that both operands be either in data registers or in memory.

The mnemonic employed depends primarily on whether or not the destination is an address register. In the latter case, the mnemonic is simply add; in the former, the character "a" is appended to the mnemonic (i.e., adda) to indicate this fact. Second, an extra character is appended to the mnemonic indicating to which group the instruction belongs. The appended character is either "i," "q," or "x" when the group is *immediate, quick,* or *extended*, respectively.

Condition code.   All the instructions presented here, as well as all the instructions in the *immediate* and *quick* groups except the adda instructions, set the condition code in the same fashion as the add instruction in SIM68. In particular,

---

[12] See Chapter 10 and the relative appendices.

- If a carry was generated as a result of the operation, then both the **carry** and **extend** bits are *set*. Otherwise, both are *reset*.
- If the result of the operation is a negative number, then the **negative** bit is *set;* otherwise, it is *reset*.
- If the result of the addition is equal to the number zero, then the **zero**[13] bit is *set* to reflect this fact; otherwise, it is *reset*.
- Finally, the **overflow** bit is *set* when an overflow has occurred; otherwise, this bit is *reset*.

It is important to notice that the result of the operation as well as the condition code setting also depends on the operation mode size (i.e., the size of the data). Consider the operation in its general form add d1,d2. The different results as well as the different settings of the condition code are illustrated by the following three distinct cases and presented in Figure 7.19.

Action with Byte Specified. According to the initial data presented in Figure 7.19 and the specified size in the instruction, the low-order byte of data register 1 will be added to the low-order byte of data register 2; in symbols we should add $FF + $00; and, the result ($FF) will replace the low-order byte of the destination. Given that the result is a negative integer and that no overflow occurred, the negative bit will be set, whereas all other bits of the condition code will be reset.

Action with Word Specified. In this case, the low-order words of the two registers must be added. Again referring to Figure 7.19, we see that the addition $F0FF + $F000 will not yield an overflow. In this case, the 16-bit result $E0FF replaces the low-order word of the destination; because an overflow did not occur, the overflow bit is reset, whereas both the carry and the extend bits are set because a carry was generated. Notice that it is the responsibility of the application program to detect that an overflow was generated; otherwise, the program could be completed successfully and provide us with erroneous output.

Action with Longword Specified. In this last case, the two binary integers $0000F0FF and $008FF000 are to be added. The result of the addition will yield the positive integer $0090E0FF; thus, all bits of the condition code will be reset.

State before		State after execution of instruction					
		add.b d1,d2		add.w d1,d2		add.l d1,d2	
d1	0000 F0FF	d1	0000 F0FF	d1	0000 F0FF	d1	0000 F0FF
d2	008F F000	d2	008F F0**FF**	d2	008F **E0FF**	d2	**0090 E0FF**
cc	00000	cc	**01000**	cc	**11001**	cc	00000

Figure 7.19   Effect of executing each of three indicated instructions. Notice that contents of registers are in hex, whereas those of condition code are in binary.

---

[13] The setting of this bit is different in the extended instructions.

Regular operations.   A complete listing of all allowable operations is presented in Table 7.10 as well as a discussion of the notation that we will employ throughout the manuscript. The significance of each of the entries in this table follows.

TABLE 7.10   Adding two binary integers

Binary integer addition					
Group 1 : Regular operations					
Action					
Add data from the source to the destination. The size of the data is indicated by the extension except when the destination is an address register in which case the data are sign-extended to longwords before the instruction is executed.					
Mnemonic	Opcode	User byte (X,N,Z,V,C bits)	Operands	Format	Length
Register to data register					
add.b	SD_4	E M M M E	dn,dn	F1	1
add.w	SD_4	E M M M E	rn,dn	F1	1
add.l	SD_4	E M M M E	rn,dn	F1	1
Register to address register					
adda.w	SD_4	P P P P P	rn,an	F1	1
adda.l	SD_4	P P P P P	rn,an	F1	1
Memory to data register					
add.b	SD_4	E M M M E	smem,dn	F1	1, 2, 3
add.w	SD_4	E M M M E	smem,dn	F1	1, 2, 3
add.l	SD_4	E M M M E	smem,dn	F1	1, 2, 3
Memory to address register					
adda.w	SD_4	P P P P P	smem,an	F1	1, 2, 3
adda.l	SD_4	P P P P P	smem,an	F1	1, 2, 3
Data register to memory					
add.b	SD_4	E M M M E	dn,dmem	F2	1, 2, 3
add.w	SD_4	E M M M E	dn,dmem	F2	1, 2, 3
add.l	SD_4	E M M M E	dn,dmem	F2	1, 2, 3

The first column labeled with the header MNEMONIC provides us with the appropriate syntax for the allowable mnemonic. The FORMAT of the instruction as well as its length (that depends on the mode specification of the operands) is presented in the columns labeled by the headers FORMAT and LENGTH, respectively. The opcode of the corresponding machine language instruction is presented in the column labeled by the header OPCODE. The numeric subscript n indicates the number of bits in the opcode. The convention that we employ is that the opcode should be formed by the n *rightmost* bits of the given hexadecimal representation. All affected bits of the condition code resulting from execution of the instruction are labeled as follows. Whenever the value of a bit can possibly be changed, we employ one of the following symbols: M, R, S, or E. In particular, if the value of the bit is set, we use the symbol S; if it is reset, we use the symbol R. Both symbols M and E signify the fact that the value of this bit is possibly modified; however, the symbol E is reserved to indicate that the corresponding bits have been set to the same value. U is a symbol that is used whenever the value of a bit becomes undefined. Whenever the value of a bit is not affected, the symbol P is used to indicate that this bit preserves its previous value. Finally, the operation that will occur at run time as a result of the corresponding instruction is presented under the header ACTION.

At this point, the reader should be warned that whenever the destination register is an address register, the operations are performed in *longword* mode irrespective of the size of the data. As an example, we repeat in Figure 7.20 the examples of Figure 7.19 by replacing the opcode by `adda` and the destination register by `a2`.

State before		State after execution of instruction			
		adda.w d1,a2		adda.l d1,a2	
d1	0000 F0FF	d1	0000 F0FF	d1	0000 F0FF
a2	008F F000	a2	**008F E0FF**	a2	**0090 E0FF**
cc	00000	cc	00000	cc	00000

Figure 7.20   Effect of executing each of two indicated instructions. Notice that contents of the registers are in hex, whereas those of condition code are in binary.

In the first instruction (`adda.w  d1,a2`), the low-order word of the source register $FOFF is extracted; it is sign extended to a longword (i.e., $FFFFF0FF). This longword is added to the longword ($008FF000) in the destination register producing the result $008FE0FF. On the other hand, the second instruction adds the two longwords as expected, producing $0090E0FF.

Immediate and quick operations.   These two groups are similar in that the data is a part of the instruction; they are faster in general (in terms of execution times) than their regular group operations counterpart; the setting of the condition code parallels that of the regular operations. The available instructions in each group are given in Tables 7.11 and 7.12, respectively.

It is the responsibility of the programmer to issue the appropriate instruction so that the assembler can generate the correct code and so that the size of the machine language instruction is minimal. For example, if the range of the immediate data is between -2^7 and $2^7 - 1$, a byte immediate instruction should be issued; otherwise, if it is in the range between -2^{15} and $2^{15} - 1$, a word immediate instruction should be issued; otherwise, (i.e., if it is between -2^{31} and $2^{31} - 1$), a longword immediate instruction should be issued. At the other extreme, a quick instruction can be issued, if and only if, the range of the immediate data is between 1 and 8.

The difference between these two groups lies in the fact that quick instructions require one word of storage, whereas storage of immediate instructions requires between two and three words, depending on the data size. Moreover, quick instructions may be used only for data in the range between 1 and 8.

Consider the following two instructions:

```
addq.l  #8,D3
addi.l  #8,D3
```

TABLE 7.11 Addition of two binary integers

Binary integer addition
Group 2 : Immediate operations

Action

Add immediate data to destination. Size of data is indicated by extension except when destination is address register in which case data are sign extended to longwords before instruction is executed.

Mnemonic	Opcode	User byte (X,N,Z,V,C bits)	Operands	Format	Length
		Add to data register			
addi.b	06_8	E M M M E	$IData_8, dn$	F8	2
addi.w	06_8	E M M M E	$IData_{16}, dn$	F8	2
addi.l	06_8	E M M M E	$IData_{32}, dn$	F8	3
		Add to address register			
addi.w	D_4	P P P P P	$IData_{16}, an$	F1	2
addi.l	D_4	P P P P P	$IData_{32}, an$	F1	3
		Add to memory			
addi.b	06_8	E M M M E	$IData_8, dmem$	F8	2, 3, 4
addi.w	06_8	E M M M E	$IData_{16}, dmem$	F8	2, 3, 4
addi.l	06_8	E M M M E	$IData_{32}, dmem$	F8	3, 4, 5

TABLE 7.12 Adding two binary integers

Binary integer addition
Group 3 : Quick operations

Action

Add quick data ($1 \le data \le 8$) to the destination. Data is extended to size indicated by extension except when destination is address register in which case indicated data are sign extended to longwords.

Mnemonic	Opcode	User byte (X,N,Z,V,C bits)	Operands	Format	Length
		Add to data register			
addq.b	$0A_5$	E M M M E	$QData_3, dn$	F9	1
addq.w	$0A_5$	E M M M E	$QData_3, dn$	F9	1
addq.l	$0A_5$	E M M M E	$QData_3, dn$	F9	1
		Add to address register			
addq.w	$0A_5$	P P P P P	$QData_3, an$	F9	1
addq.l	$0A_5$	P P P P P	$QData_3, an$	F9	1
		Add to memory			
addq.b	$0A_5$	E M M M E	$QData_3, dmem$	F9	1, 2, 3
addq.w	$0A_5$	E M M M E	$QData_3, dmem$	F9	1, 2, 3
addq.l	$0A_5$	E M M M E	$QData_3, dmem$	F9	1, 2, 3

Despite the fact that the execution of each will generate the same result in register d3, the assembler will generate (in hex) the code

5083

for the first instruction, while it will generate (in hex) the code

0683 0000 0008

for the second instruction. Hence, one can see the considerable time[14] and storage savings of the addq vis à vis the addi instruction. As another example, consider the initial situation as illustrated in Figure 7.21. As a response to the first instruction (addi.b), the immediate data $5 (of byte size) will be added to the low-order byte of the destination register d1 (i.e., $FF). The result will replace the low-order byte of the destination. On the other hand, execution of either of the other two instructions will cause a *longword* to be added to the destination register. In the first case (addi.w), the word size immediate data $1000 will be sign extended to the longword $00001000, which will be added to the destination address register. The reader is encouraged to verify the results of these examples as well as the condition code setting.

State before		State after execution of instruction					
		addi.b #$5,d1		addi.w #$1000,a2		addi.l #$11000,a2	
d1	F0F0 FFFF	d1	F0F0 FF**04**	d1	F0F0 FFFF	d1	F0F0 FFFF
a2	000E F000	a2	000E F000	a2	**000F 0000**	a2	**0010 0000**
cc	00000	cc	**10001**	cc	00000	cc	00000

Figure 7.21 Effect of executing each of three indicated instructions. Notice that the contents of the registers are in hex, whereas those of condition code are in binary.

Extended operations.   The MC68000 provides one with another type of instruction, the *add with extend* addx instruction, which permits one to perform binary addition. This instruction differs from the add instruction we discussed in the previous section in that three binary numbers are now added: the source, the destination, and the extended extend bit of the condition code. As an example, consider the initial situation as illustrated in Figure 7.22.

As a response to the first instruction in Figure 7.22(a), the low-order byte of the source $FA will be extracted; the extend bit %1 will be extended to a byte $01; finally these two integers will be added to the low-order byte of d2, producing the result $FD that will replace the low-order byte of the destination. In Figure 7.22(b), the operation will produce the same result as the add.b instruction because extending the extend bit %0 produces the byte $00, which does not affect the addition.

As mentioned earlier, that particular setting of the condition code of this group of instructions differs from the one in the previously discussed groups in one respect.

---

[14] Refer to the timing table.

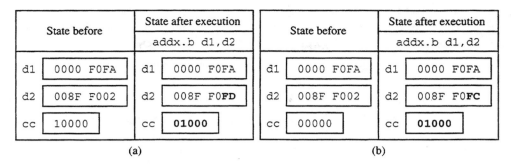

Figure 7.22   Effect of executing each of two indicated instructions. Notice that
contents of the registers are in hex. whereas those of condition code are in binary.

Namely, if the result is different than zero, the zero bit is reset; however, if the result is
zero, the zero bit is *unchanged*. Therefore, if the programmer must test the bit to determine if it is set, he or she should set it before the instruction is issued.

At this point the reader should wonder why this extra instruction has been provided.
The answer lies in the fact that with the use of the extended operations, one can perform
multiprecision arithmetic. Before this topic is discussed, we will present the group of
extended addition operations in Table 7.13.

Multiprecision arithmetic.   Let's consider the following task. Assume that we
would like to add two signed integers that are so large that their two's complement representation requires more than 32 bits of storage. Moreover, with no loss of generality
(to our proposed solution), assume that their representations require less than 64 bits of
storage. Because the dc directives cannot be used for such large integers, assume that
through the pencil-and-paper approach we have found that their representations are

TABLE 7.13   Adding two binary integers

Binary integer addition					
Group 4 : Extended operations					
Action					
Add data from source and (extended to size of data) extend bit to destination. Size of data is indicated by extension.					
Mnemonic	Opcode	User byte (X,N,Z,V,C bits)	Operands	Format	Length
Data register to data register					
addx.b	$6C_7	E M M M E	dn,dn	F10	1
addx.w	$6C_7	E M M M E	dn,dn	F10	1
addx.l	$6C_7	E M M M E	dn,dn	F10	1
Memory to memory					
addx.b	$6C_7	E M M M E	-(an),-(an)	F10	1
addx.w	$6C_7	E M M M E	-(an),-(an)	F10	1
addx.l	$6C_7	E M M M E	-(an),-(an)	F10	1

$00010201AB12345B and $FF0D033B12D8F230, respectively. We may now use two directives to store each integer as two consecutive longwords in memory. Specifically, let's code

```
        org     $4000
num1    dc.l    $00010201
        dc.l    $AB12345B
num2    dc.l    $FF0D033B
        dc.l    $12D8F230
```

Now let's move num1 into the two consecutive registers d0 and d1 and num2 into the two consecutive registers d2 and d3.[15] Now if we add the contents of the two data registers via an add.l d1,d3, data register d3 would contain the *exact*, low-order longword of the desired result. One may think that if we also issue an instruction of the form add.l d0,d2, then register d2 would contain the high-order longword of the result. This would have been the case if the carry out of the sign bit position of register d3 on completion of the addition add.l d1,d3 was equal to zero. If it were equal to one, then that one should have been added on to the least significant bit of register d2 so that it would contain the exact result. In other words, the exact result of the high-order longword of the result is found by adding the contents of the data registers containing the high-order words of the 64-bit integers *and* the carry-out of the sign-bit position of the data register that holds the low-order longword of the result. The carry out of the sign-bit position has been placed into the extend bit of the status register, however. Therefore, we need to add the two data registers as well as the extend bit. This is exactly the function of the extended operations. Therefore, the complete code that will perform this task is given as follows:

```
        org     $4000

num1    dc.l    $00010201
        dc.l    $AB12345B
num2    dc.l    $FF0D033B
        dc.l    $12D8F230

start   move.l  num1,d0
        move.l  num1+4,d1
        move.l  num2,d2
        move.l  num2+4,d3
        add.l   d1,d3
        addx.l  d0,d2
        ....    ....
```

We note here that one could have used the predecrement mode to add these two long integers in memory.

Subtraction

As in the case of SIM68, MC68000 provides one with a subtraction counterpart to each of the addition instructions. Therefore, here again we may distinguish the same four groups

---

[15] Not necessary.

of operations as in the previous section. Given the similarity of these subtract instructions with the SIM68 subtract instructions on the one hand and the groups of addition instructions presented earlier, any further discussion of the subtraction instructions is omitted except that of the condition code setting.

Condition code.   All the subtraction instructions presented **except** the suba instructions set the condition code in the same fashion as the sub instruction in SIM68. In particular,

- If a borrow was generated as a result of the operation, then both the **carry** and **extend** bits are *set*. Otherwise, both are *reset*.
- If the result of the operation is a negative number, then the **negative** bit is *set;* otherwise, it is *reset*.
- If the result of the subtraction is equal to the number zero, then the **zero**[16] bit is *set* to reflect this fact; otherwise, it is *reset*.
- Finally, the **overflow** bit is *set* when an overflow has occurred; otherwise, this bit is *reset*.

Regular operations.   These instructions are summarized in Table 7.14. As in the case of the addition instructions, the result as well as the setting of the condition code depends on the size of the data. Figure 7.23 illustrates via three examples this dependency.

TABLE 7.14

Binary integer subtraction
Group 1 : Regular operations

Action
Subtract data in source from destination. Size of data is indicated by extension except when destination is address register in which case data are sign extended to longwords before instruction is executed.

Mnemonic	Opcode	User byte (X,N,Z,V,C bits)	Operands	Format	Length
		Register from data register			
sub.b	9_4$	E M M M E	dn,dn	F1	1
sub.w	9_4$	E M M M E	rn,dn	F1	1
sub.l	9_4$	E M M M E	rn,dn	F1	1
		Register from address register			
suba.w	9_4$	P P P P P	rn,an	F1	1
suba.l	9_4$	P P P P P	rn,an	F1	1
		Memory from data register			
sub.b	9_4$	E M M M E	smem,dn	F1	1, 2, 3
sub.w	9_4$	E M M M E	smem,dn	F1	1, 2, 3
sub.l	9_4$	E M M M E	smem,dn	F1	1, 2, 3

---

[16] The setting of this bit is different in the extended instructions.

TABLE 7.14 (*Continued*)

Mnemonic	Opcode	User byte (X,N,Z,V,C bits)	Operands	Format	Length
Memory from address register				
suba.w	9_4$	P P P P P	smem, an	F1	1, 2, 3
suba.l	9_4$	P P P P P	smem, an	F1	1, 2, 3
Data register from memory				
sub.b	9_4$	E M M M E	dn, dmem	F2	1, 2, 3
sub.w	9_4$	E M M M E	dn, dmem	F2	1, 2, 3
sub.l	9_4$	E M M M E	dn, dmem	F2	1, 2, 3

In particular, as a response to the first instruction sub.b d1,d2, the low-order byte of d1 will be subtracted from the low-order byte of d2; in symbols $00 −$FF; the result ($01) will replace the low-order byte of the destination. Moreover because a borrow was generated, both the carry and extend bits are set. Execution of the second instruction sub.w d1,d2 will cause the low-order word $F0FF of the source data register to be subtracted from the low-order word $F000 of the destination data register; and, the result ($FF01) will replace the low-order word of the destination. Because an overflow has occurred, the overflow bit as well as the carry and extend bits are set. Finally, execution of the third instruction sub.l d1,d2 will replace the entire contents of d2 with the result of the subtraction $008FF000 −$0000F0FF.

State before		State after execution of instruction					
		sub. b d1, d2		sub. w d1, d2		sub. l d1, d2	
d1	0000 F0FF	d1	0000 F0FF	d1	0000 F0FF	d1	0000 F0FF
d2	008F F000	d2	008F **F001**	d2	008F **F001**	d2	008E **F001**
cc	00000	cc	**10001**	cc	**11001**	cc	**00000**

Figure 7.23 Effect of executing each of three indicated instructions. Notice that contents of registers are in hex, whereas those of condition code are in binary.

Immediate and quick operations.   These two groups are similar because they permit the subtraction of a literal from a register or a memory location. The available instructions in each group are given in Tables 7.15 and 7.16, respectively.

The same issues that were discussed before concerning immediate and quick instructions apply here. In particular, which instruction in these groups must be used depends on the range of the literal that must be subtracted. Because of the similarity of these instructions with those of their addition counterparts, any further discussion is omitted; this section closes with the presentation of three examples illustrated in Figure 7.24. The reader is encouraged to verify the results.

TABLE 7.15

<table>
<tr><td colspan="7" align="center">Binary integer subtraction
Group 2 : Immediate operations</td></tr>
<tr><td colspan="7" align="center">Action</td></tr>
<tr><td colspan="7">Subtract immediate data from destination. Size of data is indicated by extension, except when destination is address register, in which case data are sign-extended to longwords before instruction is executed.</td></tr>
<tr><td>Mnemonic</td><td>Opcode</td><td>User byte (X,N,Z,V,C bits)</td><td></td><td>Operands</td><td>Format</td><td>Length</td></tr>
<tr><td colspan="7" align="center">Subtract from data register</td></tr>
<tr><td>subi.b</td><td>04_8</td><td>E M M M E</td><td></td><td>$IData_8$, dn</td><td>F8</td><td>2</td></tr>
<tr><td>subi.w</td><td>04_8</td><td>E M M M E</td><td></td><td>$IData_{16}$, dn</td><td>F8</td><td>2</td></tr>
<tr><td>subi.l</td><td>04_8</td><td>E M M M E</td><td></td><td>$IData_{32}$, dn</td><td>F8</td><td>3</td></tr>
<tr><td colspan="7" align="center">Subtract from address register</td></tr>
<tr><td>subi.w</td><td>9_4</td><td>P P P P P</td><td></td><td>$IData_{16}$, an</td><td>F1</td><td>2</td></tr>
<tr><td>subi.l</td><td>9_4</td><td>P P P P P</td><td></td><td>$IData_{32}$, an</td><td>F1</td><td>3</td></tr>
<tr><td colspan="7" align="center">Subtract from memory</td></tr>
<tr><td>subi.b</td><td>04_8</td><td>E M M M E</td><td></td><td>$IData_8$, dmem</td><td>F8</td><td>2, 3, 4</td></tr>
<tr><td>subi.w</td><td>04_8</td><td>E M M M E</td><td></td><td>$IData_{16}$, dmem</td><td>F8</td><td>2, 3, 4</td></tr>
<tr><td>subi.l</td><td>04_8</td><td>E M M M E</td><td></td><td>$IData_{32}$, dmem</td><td>F8</td><td>3, 4, 5</td></tr>
</table>

TABLE 7.16

<table>
<tr><td colspan="7" align="center">Binary integer subtraction
Group 3 : Quick operations</td></tr>
<tr><td colspan="7" align="center">Action</td></tr>
<tr><td colspan="7">Subtract quick data ($1 \le$ data ≤ 8) from destination. Data are extended to size indicated by extension except when destination is address register in which case indicated data are sign extended to longwords before instruction is executed.</td></tr>
<tr><td>Mnemonic</td><td>Opcode</td><td>User byte (X,N,Z,V,C bits)</td><td></td><td>Operands</td><td>Format</td><td>Length</td></tr>
<tr><td colspan="7" align="center">Subtract from data register</td></tr>
<tr><td>subq.b</td><td>$0B_5$</td><td>E M M M E</td><td></td><td>$QData_3$, dn</td><td>F9</td><td>1</td></tr>
<tr><td>subq.w</td><td>$0B_5$</td><td>E M M M E</td><td></td><td>$QData_3$, dn</td><td>F9</td><td>1</td></tr>
<tr><td>subq.l</td><td>$0B_5$</td><td>E M M M E</td><td></td><td>$QData_3$, dn</td><td>F9</td><td>1</td></tr>
<tr><td colspan="7" align="center">Subtract from address register</td></tr>
<tr><td>subq.w</td><td>$0B_5$</td><td>P P P P P</td><td></td><td>$QData_3$, an</td><td>F9</td><td>1</td></tr>
<tr><td>subq.l</td><td>$0B_5$</td><td>P P P P P</td><td></td><td>$QData_3$, an</td><td>F9</td><td>1</td></tr>
<tr><td colspan="7" align="center">Subtract from memory</td></tr>
<tr><td>subq.b</td><td>$0B_5$</td><td>E M M M E</td><td></td><td>$QData_3$, dmem</td><td>F9</td><td>1, 2, 3</td></tr>
<tr><td>subq.w</td><td>$0B_5$</td><td>E M M M E</td><td></td><td>$QData_3$, dmem</td><td>F9</td><td>1, 2, 3</td></tr>
<tr><td>subq.l</td><td>$0B_5$</td><td>E M M M E</td><td></td><td>$QData_3$, dmem</td><td>F9</td><td>1, 2, 3</td></tr>
</table>

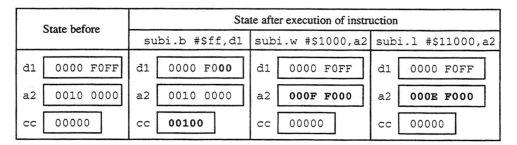

Figure 7.24 Effect of executing each of three indicated instructions. Notice that contents of registers are in hex, whereas those of condition code are in binary.

Extended operations. The MC68000 provides one with another type of instruction, the *subtract with extend* subx instruction, which permits one to perform binary subtraction. This instruction differs from the sub instruction that we discussed in the previous section in that three binary numbers are involved in this operation. Specifically, the source as well as the unsigned-extended extend bit of the condition code is subtracted from the destination. As an example, consider the initial situation as illustrated in Figure 7.25. As a response to the first instruction (in Figure 7.25[a]), the low-order byte of the source $FF will be extracted, the extend bit %1 will be extended to a byte $01; and finally these two integers will be added producing the result $00. This result is subtracted from the low-order word $00 of the destination yielding $00. In the second example, extension of the extend bit produces the byte $00; its addition to the low-order byte of the source will produce the result $FF; this result is subtracted from the low-order word $00 of the destination yielding $01.

As mentioned earlier, that setting of the condition code of this group of instructions differs from those of the previously discussed groups in one respect. Namely, if the result is different than zero, the zero bit is reset; however, if the result is zero, the zero bit is *unchanged.* Therefore, if the programmer must test the bit to determine if it is set, he or she should set it before the instruction is issued. This group of instructions is presented in Table 7.17.

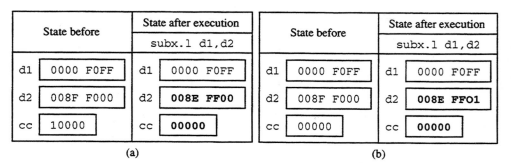

Figure 7.25 Effect of executing each of two indicated instructions. Notice that contents of registers are in hex, whereas those of condition code are in binary.

TABLE 7.17

Binary integer subtraction
Group 4 : Extended operations

Action
Subtract data from source and (extended to size of data) carry bit from destination. Size of data is indicated by extension.

Mnemonic	Opcode	User byte (X,N,Z,V,C bits)	Operands	Format	Length
		Data register from data register			
subx.b	$4C₇	E M M M E	dn,dn	F10	1
subx.w	$4C₇	E M M M E	dn,dn	F10	1
subx.l	$4C₇	E M M M E	dn,dn	F10	1
		Memory from memory			
subx.b	$4C₇	E M M M E	-(an),-(an)	F10	1
subx.w	$4C₇	E M M M E	-(an),-(an)	F10	1
subx.l	$4C₇	E M M M E	-(an),-(an)	F10	1

Multiplication

MC68000 provides us with two instructions, `muls` and `mulu`, which permit one to multiply two word-length binary integers and produce a longword result. The first instruction *multiply signed* `muls` is identical to that supported by SIM68.[17] The second instruction *multiply unsigned* `mulu` performs multiplication of the binary integers as though they were unsigned integers. Figure 7.26 illustrates the effect of the execution of either of the two instructions. The source data A (of word size) is multiplied with the low-order word B of the destination data register. The longword result $A \times B$ replaces the entire contents of the destination register.

All versions of the multiply instructions that are summarized in Table 7.18 affect certain bits of the condition code. Specifically, the **carry** as well as the **overflow** bits are reset regardless of the value of the result. The **extend** bit retains its old value. If the result of the

State before		State after execution of instruction			
		muls d1,d2		mulu d1,d2	
d1	1111 FFFF	d1	1111 FFFF	d1	1111 FFFF
d2	1111 0005	d2	**FFFF FFFB**	d2	**0004 FFFB**
cc	00000	cc	**01000**	cc	**00000**

Figure 7.26 Effect of executing either of two multiplication instructions `muls d1,d2` or `mulu d1,d2`.

---

[17] Except the fact that MC68000 also permits the source operand to be in main memory.

TABLE 7.18

Binary integer multiplication
Action
Multiply data word from source with low-order word of destination data register. The result, a longword, replaces contents of destination. muls and mulu assume that both operands represent signed and unsigned binary integers, respectively. muls produces signed result, whereas mulu produces unsigned result.

Mnemonic	Opcode	User byte (X,N,Z,V,C bits)	Operands	Format	Length
Data register by data register					
muls	67_7$	P M M M R	dn,dn	F3	1
mulu	63_7$	P M M M R	dn,dn	F3	1
Memory by data register					
muls	67_7$	P M M M R	smem,dn	F3	1, 2, 3
mulu	63_7$	P M M M R	smem,dn	F3	1, 2, 3
Immediate data by data register					
muls	67_7$	P M M M R	IData$_{16}$,dn	F3	2
mulu	63_7$	P M M M R	IData$_{16}$,dn	F3	2

operation is a negative number, then the **negative** bit is *set;* otherwise, it is *reset.* If the result of the multiplication is equal to the number zero, then the **zero** bit is *set* to reflect this fact; otherwise, it is *reset.*

We close this section by providing the reader with two examples. According to the initial data of Figure 7.27, execution of the muls d1,d2 instruction will cause the signed integer represented by the low-order word of data register 1, $FFFF, to be multiplied with the signed integer represented by the low-order word of data register 2, $0005. The result is a longword signed integer, $FFFFFFFB, which replaces the contents of data register 2. Given that the result is a negative integer and that no overflow occurred, the negative bit will be set, whereas all other bits of the condition code will be reset.

Execution of the mulu d1,d2 instruction, on the other hand, will cause the unsigned integer represented by the low-order word of data register 1, $FFFF, to be multiplied with the unsigned-integer represented by the low-order word of data register 2, $0005. The result is a longword unsigned integer, $0004FFFB, which replaces the con-

	State before		State after execution of instruction		
			muls d1,d2		mulu d1,d2
d1	1111 FFFF	d1	1111 FFFF	d1	1111 FFFF
d2	1111 0005	d2	**FFFF FFFB**	d2	**0004 FFFB**
cc	00000	cc	**01000**	cc	**00000**

Figure 7.27 Effect of executing each of two indicated instructions. Notice that contents of registers are in hex, whereas those of condition code are in binary.

tents of data register 2. The result, though it is assumed to be an unsigned integer, is treated as a signed integer in setting the condition code.

Division

MC68000 provides us with two instructions, divs and divu, which permit one to divide a longword binary integer by a word-length binary integer and produce a word-length quotient and a word-length remainder. The first instruction *divide signed* divs is identical to that supported by SIM68.[18] The second instruction *divide unsigned* divu performs the division of the binary integers as though they were unsigned integers. These instructions are summarized in Table 7.19.

TABLE 7.19

Binary integer division

Action

Divide data longword in data register by data word in source. Remainder and quotient of division are inserted in high-order word and low-order word of data register, respectively. divs and divu assume that both operands are representing signed and unsigned binary integers, respectively; divs produces a signed result, whereas divu produces unsigned result.

Mnemonic	Opcode	User byte (X,N,Z,V,C bits)	Operands	Format	Length
Data register by data register					
divs	47_7	P M M M R	dn, dn	F3	1
divu	63_7	P M M M R	dn, dn	F3	1
Data register by memory					
divs	47_7	P M M M R	smem, dn	F3	1, 2, 3
divu	63_7	P M M M R	smem, dn	F3	1, 2, 3
Data register by immediate data					
divs	47_7	P M M M R	$IData_{16}$, dn	F3	2
divu	63_7	P M M M R	$IData_{16}$, dn	F3	2

Recall from the relevant discussions in Chapter 4 that the binary integer division operation assumes a longword dividend A, a word divisor B, and it produces an *integer* **quotient** Q of word size and an integer **remainder** R. Those four variables are related via the equation

$$A = Q \cdot B + R$$

where quotient Q is determined via

$$Q = \begin{cases} \lfloor A/B \rfloor & \text{if } (A \cdot B) \geq 0 \\ \lceil A/B \rceil & \text{if } (A \cdot B) < 0 \end{cases}$$

---

[18] Except the fact that MC68000 also permits the source operand to be in main memory.

It is important to notice that unless the division is perfect,[19] the sign of the remainder is the *same* as that of the dividend.

Figure 7.28 illustrates the effect of execution of either of the two instructions. The dividend data A (of longword size) is divided by the low-order word B of the source data register. The calculated remainder R and quotient Q will be stored in the *high-order* and the *low-order* word of the destination data register, respectively. It is important to notice that if the divisor is equal to zero, then the operating system will suspend execution of the instruction. On the other hand, the hardware can detect an overflow[20] *during* execution of the instruction. In the latter case the overflow bit will be set, the operands will not be affected, and execution will resume with the next instruction. In all other cases, the hardware, at completion of the execution of the instruction, sets or resets the value on the *carry, overflow, zero,* and *negative* flag bits of the *status register* according to the rules specified subsequently.

State before			State after		
	High-order word	Low-order word		High-order word	Low-order word
d1	????	B	d1	????	B
d2	A		d2	R	Q

Figure 7.28   Effect of executing either of two division instructions `divs d1,d2` or `divu d1,d2`.

The **carry** bit is reset. If the quotient generated is a negative number, the **negative** bit is *set;* otherwise, it is *reset.* If the quotient generated is equal to the number zero, the **zero** bit is *set* to reflect this fact; otherwise, it is *reset.* Finally, the **overflow** bit is *set* when an overflow has occurred; otherwise, this bit is *reset.*

We conclude this section by providing the reader with two examples. According to the initial data of Figure 7.29, execution of the `divs d1,d2` instruction will cause the signed integer represented by the longword contents of data register 2, $00020001, to be divided by the signed integer represented by the low-order word of data register 1, $8000. The word size remainder of the division, $0001, is placed in the high-order word, whereas the word size quotient of the division, $FFFC, is placed in the low-order word in data register 2. Given that the result is a negative integer and that no overflow has occurred, the negative bit will be set, whereas all other bits of the condition code will be reset.

Execution of the `divu d1,d2` instruction, on the other hand, will cause the unsigned integer represented by the longword contents of data register 2, $00020001, to be divided by the unsigned integer represented by the low-order word of data register 1, $8000. The word size remainder of the division, $0001, is placed in the high-order word, whereas the word size quotient of the division, $0004, is placed in the low-order word in data register 2.

---

[19] In this case the remainder is equal to zero.

[20] An overflow occurs when a quotient is either greater than $2^{15} - 1$ or less than -2^{15} in which case it would require more than 16 bits to be specified.

State before	State after execution of instruction	
	divs d1,d2	divu d1,d2
d1	1111 8000	d1	1111 8000	d1	1111 8000
d2	0002 0001	d2	0001 FFFC	d2	0001 0004
cc	00000	cc	01000	cc	00000

Figure 7.29   Effect of executing each of two indicated instructions. Notice that contents of the registers are in hex, whereas those of condition code are in binary.

Negation of binary integers.   Despite the fact that the negation of a binary integer can be accomplished with the aid of instructions previously discussed (either via its multiplication by −1 or via its subtraction from zero), MC68000 provides one with an instruction designed specifically for this purpose—the *negate* (neg) and its execution is considerably faster than other methods previously discussed.

The instructions available can be divided into two groups: the *regular* and the *extended* operations that are presented in Tables 7.20 and 7.21, respectively.

Regular operations.   All the negate instructions in this group set the condition code according to the following rules. If the result is zero, both the **carry** and **extend** bits are *reset*. Otherwise, both are *set*. If the result of the operation is a negative number, the **negative** bit is *set;* otherwise, it is *reset*. If the result is zero, the **zero** bit is *set* to reflect this fact; otherwise, it is *reset*. Finally, the **overflow** bit is *set* when an overflow has occurred; otherwise, this bit is *reset*.

TABLE 7.20

Negating a binary integer					
Group 1 : Regular operations					
Action					
Negate the data in destination. Size of data is indicated by extension.					
Mnemonic	Opcode	User byte (X,N,Z,V,C bits)	Operands	Format	Length
In data register					
neg.b	44_8	E | M | M | M | E	dn	F8	1
neg.w	44_8	E | M | M | M | E	dn	F8	1
neg.l	44_8	E | M | M | M | E	dn	F8	1
In memory					
neg.b	44_8	E | M | M | M | E	dmem	F8	1, 2, 3
neg.w	44_8	E | M | M | M | E	dmem	F8	1, 2, 3
neg.l	44_8	E | M | M | M | E	dmem	F8	1, 2, 3

As in the case of all instructions discussed so far, the result as well as the setting of the condition code depends on the size of the data. Figure 7.30 illustrates this dependency via three examples. As a response to the first instruction (neg.b), the low-order byte of the source $01 will be extracted; and, its two's complement representation $FF will replace it. In the second example, execution of the instruction neg.w will cause the low-order word of the destination register ($F001) to be replaced by $0FFF, whereas the third instruction (neg.l) will produce the longword $FFFF0FFF, is the negative of the binary integer that has the representation $0000F001.

State before	State after execution of instruction		
	neg.b d1	neg.w d1	neg.l d1
d1 `0000 F001`	d1 `0000 F0FF`	d1 `0000 0FFF`	d1 **`FFFF 0FFF`**
cc `00000`	cc `11001`	cc `10001`	cc `11001`

Figure 7.30   Effect of executing each of three indicated instructions. Notice that contents of the registers are in hex, whereas those of condition code are in binary.

Extended operations.   The *negate with extend* negx instruction differs from the neg instruction that we discussed in the previous section in two respects which are discussed later. First, two binary numbers are involved in this operation: Specifically, the source as well as the unsigned-extended extend bit of the condition code. These two numbers are added; the result is negated (by subtracting it from zero).

Second, all the negate extended instructions set the condition code slightly different from those of their regular operation counterparts. Specifically, the **negative** as well as the **overflow** bits are set or reset in the same fashion. If a borrow is generated (during the subtraction of the operand from zero), then both the **carry** and **extend** bits are *set*. Otherwise, both are *reset*. If the result is zero, then the **zero** bit is *set;* otherwise, it is *reset*.

TABLE 7.21

Negating a binary integer					
Group 2 : Extended operations					
Action					
Negate sum of data in destination and of extended bit. Size of data is indicated by extension.					
Mnemonic	Opcode	User byte (X,N,Z,V,C bits)	Operands	Format	Length
In data register					
negx.b	40_8$	E M M M E	dn	F8	1
negx.w	40_8$	E M M M E	dn	F8	1
negx.l	40_8$	E M M M E	dn	F8	1
In memory					
negx.b	40_8$	E M M M E	dmem	F8	1, 2, 3
negx.w	40_8$	E M M M E	dmem	F8	1, 2, 3
negx.l	40_8$	E M M M E	dmem	F8	1, 2, 3

As an example, consider the initial situation as illustrated in Figure 7.31. As a response to the first instruction (in Figure 7.32[a]), the low-order byte of the source $FF will be extracted, the extend bit %1 will be extended to a byte $01. Finally these two integers will be added producing $00; the result so obtained will be negated, yielding $00, which will replace the low-order byte of the data register d1. In the second example, the operation will produce the same result as the neg.b instruction because extending the extend bit %0 produces the byte $00 whose addition to the low-order byte of d1 does not affect its value. At any rate, the result $FF is negated producing $01, which replaces the low-order word of the d1.

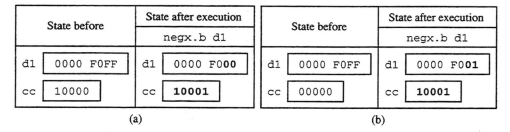

State before	State after execution negx.b d1	State before	State after execution negx.b d1
d1 0000 F0FF	d1 0000 F000	d1 0000 F0FF	d1 0000 F001
cc 10000	cc **10001**	cc 00000	cc **10001**
(a)		(b)	

Figure 7.31   Effect of executing each of the two indicated instructions. Notice that contents of the registers are in hex, whereas those of condition code are in binary.

Comparison of data

Consider the simple task of determining the largest of two byte-long binary integers residing in the low-order words of data registers d1 and d2 respectively. According to our previous discussions, this task can be accomplished by subtracting the two integers via the instruction sub.b d2,d1 and then examining the setting of the condition code. But after execution of the instruction, the low-order byte of register d2 has been replaced by the result; therefore, the integer has been lost. To avoid the destruction of any of the compared data, the designers of MC68000 have provided us with the *compare* cmp instruction that functions identically to the subtract instruction; however, the result *does not* replace the destination.

The result of this comparison is reflected via the setting of the condition code. In particular:

- If a borrow is generated as a result of the (subtraction) operation, the **carry** bit is *set.* Otherwise, it is *reset.*
- If the source data is greater than the destination data, the **negative** bit is *set;* otherwise, it is *reset.*
- If the source data is equal to the destination data, the **zero** bit is *set* to reflect this fact; otherwise, it is *reset.*
- The **overflow** bit is *set* when an overflow has occurred during the subtraction operation; otherwise, this bit is *reset.*
- Finally, the **extend** bit is *not affected* and retains its previous value.

As an example consider the initial situation as illustrated in Figure 7.32. As a response to the first instruction, the low-order bytes $00 and $00 of data registers d1 and d2, respectively, will be compared. Because they are equal, the zero bit is set to reflect this fact.

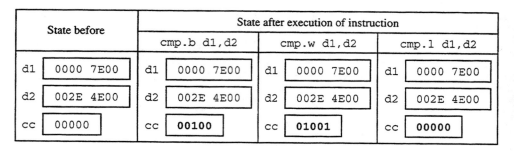

Figure 7.32 Effect of executing each of the three indicated instructions. Notice that contents of the registers are in hex, whereas those of condition code are in binary.

Execution of the second instruction will cause the low-order words $7E00 and $4E00 of data registers d1 and d2, respectively, to be compared. The result of the comparison is reflected by the condition code setting. Finally, the result of the longword contents of the two registers is again conveyed to the application program by the setting of the condition code. The reader is encouraged to study the last example.

TABLE 7.22

Comparing data
Group 1 : Regular operations

Action
Compare data from source with that of destination. Size of data is indicated by extension except when destination is address register in which case indicated data are sign extended to longwords.

Mnemonic	Opcode	User byte (X,N,Z,V,C bits)	Operands	Format	Length
		Register to data register			
cmp.b	B_4	P M M M M	dn,dn	F1	1
cmp.w	B_4	P M M M M	rn,dn	F1	1
cmp.l	B_4	P M M M M	rn,dn	F1	1
		Register to address register			
cmpa.w	B_4	P M M M M	rn,an	F1	1
cmpa.l	B_4	P M M M M	rn,an	F1	1
		Memory to data register			
cmp.b	B_4	P M M M M	smem,dn	F1	1, 2, 3
cmp.w	B_4	P M M M M	smem,dn	F1	1, 2, 3
cmp.l	B_4	P M M M M	smem,dn	F1	1, 2, 3
		Memory to address register			
cmpa.w	B_4	P M M M M	smem,an	F1	1, 2, 3
cmpa.l	B_4	P M M M M	smem,an	F1	1, 2, 3
		Memory to memory			
cmpm.b	$B9_8$	P M M M M	(an)+,(an)+	F11	1
cmpm.w	$B9_8$	P M M M M	(an)+,(an)+	F11	1
cmpm.l	$B9_8$	P M M M M	(an)+,(an)+	F11	1

TABLE 7.23

Comparing data
Group 2 : Immediate operations

Action

Compare immediate data from source with that of destination. Size of data is indicated by extension except when destination is address register in which case indicated data are sign-extended to longwords.

Mnemonic	Opcode	User byte (X,N,Z,V,C bits)	Operands	Format	Length
		Compare to data register			
cmpi.b	$0C_8	P M M M M	$IData_8$,dn	F8	2
cmpi.w	$0C_8	P M M M M	$IData_{16}$,dn	F8	2
cmpi.l	$0C_8	P M M M M	$IData_{32}$,dn	F8	3
		Compare to address register			
cmpa.w	$0C_8	P M M M M	$IData_{16}$,an	F8	2
cmpa.l	$0C_8	P M M M M	$IData_{32}$,an	F8	3
		Compare to memory			
cmpi.b	$0C_8	P M M M M	$IData_8$,dmem	F8	2, 3, 4
cmpi.w	$0C_8	P M M M M	$IData_{16}$,dmem	F8	2, 3, 4
cmpi.l	$0C_8	P M M M M	$IData_{32}$,dmem	F8	3, 4, 5

Immediate operations

Instructions in this group allow one to compare data to a literal. As an example, consider the initial situation as illustrated in Figure 7.33. In response to the first instruction, the low-order byte $00 of data register d1 will be compared to byte $00. On the other hand, as a response to the second instruction, the low-order word $7F00 of the data register d1 will be compared with the word $4E00. Finally, execution of the third instruction will cause the longword contents $00007F00 of the data register d1 to be compared with the long-word $002E4E00. The result of each comparison is conveyed by the setting of the condition code whose setting parallels that of the subtraction operation, except that the extend bit is not affected.

State before	State after execution of instruction		
	cmpi.b #$0,d1	cmpi.w #$4e00,d1	cmpi.l #$2e4e00,d1
d1 0000 7F00	d1 0000 7F00	d1 0000 7F00	d1 FFFF 7F00
cc 00000	cc 00100	cc 00000	cc 01001

Figure 7.33 Effect of executing each of three indicated instructions. Notice that contents of the registers are in hex, whereas those of condition code are in binary.

Testing of Sign of binary integer

Sometimes we may be interested in examining the sign of a binary integer at run time. The reader should have noticed that we can compare a binary integer with the integer zero and then examine the condition code. MC68000 provides us with an instruction, the *test* tst instruction, which tests the sign of an integer and sets the condition code to indicate its sign. In particular:

TABLE 7.24

		Testing the sign of a binary integer			
		Action			
		Test data in source. Size of data is indicated by extension.			
Mnemonic	Opcode	User byte (X,N,Z,V,C bits)	Operands	Format	Length
		In data register			
tst.b	$48₈	P M M R R	dn	F8	1
tst.w	$48₈	P M M R R	dn	F8	1
tst.l	$48₈	P M M R R	dn	F8	1
		In memory			
tst.b	$48₈	P M M R R	dmem	F8	1, 2, 3
tst.w	$48₈	P M M R R	dmem	F8	1, 2, 3
tst.l	$48₈	P M M R R	dmem	F8	1, 2, 3

if the tested data represent a negative number, the **negative** bit is *set;* otherwise, it is *reset.* If the tested data represent the integer zero, the **zero** bit is *set* to reflect this fact; otherwise, it is *reset.* Finally, the **overflow** and the **carry** bits are *reset,* whereas the **extended** bit is *not affected* and retains its previous value.

As an example, consider the initial situation as illustrated in Figure 7.34. In response to the first instruction, the low-order byte $00 represents the integer zero; in the second instruction, the word to be tested $0400 represents a positive integer, whereas in the third instruction the longword to be tested $FFFF0400 represents a negative integer. The result of the comparisons in each case is reflected by the condition code setting. In the first case, the zero bit is set (and the negative bit reset); in the second case both the zero and negative bits are reset; and in the third case the negative bit is set (and the zero bit reset). Finally, both the overflow and the carry bits are reset, and the extend bit is unaffected.

State before	State after execution of instruction		
	tst.b d1	tst.w d1	tst.l d1
d1 [FFFF 0400]	d1 [FFFF 0400]	d1 [FFFF 0400]	d1 [FFFF 0400]
cc [00000]	cc [00100]	cc [00000]	cc [01000]

Figure 7.34 Effect of executing each of three indicated instructions. Notice that contents of the registers are in hex, whereas those of condition code are in binary.

Clearing of data

In certain instances, we are interested in zeroing data. One way this can be accomplished is by subtracting the data from itself. As one might expect, the designers of MC68000 provided an instruction designed especially for that purpose, the *clear* clr instruction. All available clear instructions are presented in Table 7.25.

TABLE 7.25

<table>
<tr><th colspan="6">Clearing data</th></tr>
<tr><th colspan="6">Action</th></tr>
<tr><td colspan="6">Clear data in destination. Size of data is indicated by extension.</td></tr>
<tr><th>Mnemonic</th><th>Opcode</th><th>User byte (X,N,Z,V,C bits)</th><th>Operands</th><th>Format</th><th>Length</th></tr>
<tr><th colspan="6">In data register</th></tr>
<tr><td>clr.b</td><td>$42₈</td><td>P R S R R</td><td>dn</td><td>F8</td><td>1</td></tr>
<tr><td>clr.w</td><td>$42₈</td><td>P R S R R</td><td>dn</td><td>F8</td><td>1</td></tr>
<tr><td>clr.l</td><td>$42₈</td><td>P R S R R</td><td>dn</td><td>F8</td><td>1</td></tr>
<tr><th colspan="6">In memory</th></tr>
<tr><td>clr.b</td><td>$42₈</td><td>P R S R R</td><td>dmem</td><td>F8</td><td>1, 2, 3</td></tr>
<tr><td>clr.w</td><td>$42₈</td><td>P R S R R</td><td>dmem</td><td>F8</td><td>1, 2, 3</td></tr>
<tr><td>clr.l</td><td>$42₈</td><td>P R S R R</td><td>dmem</td><td>F8</td><td>1, 2, 3</td></tr>
</table>

The clear instructions affect the condition code in the following way. The extend bit retains its previous value; the zero bit is always set; and the other three bits—overflow, carry, and negative—are always reset. The results of execution of these types of instructions are illustrated in Figure 7.35.

State before	State after execution of instruction		
	clr.b d1	clr.w d1	clr.l d1
d1 E28D FABC	d1 E28D FA00	d1 E28D 0000	d1 0000 0000
cc 11011	cc 10100	cc 10100	cc 10100

Figure 7.35   Effect of executing each of three indicated instructions. Notice that contents of the registers are in hex, whereas those of condition code are in binary.

The first instruction causes the low-order byte of the register to be cleared; the second instruction causes the low-order word of the register to be cleared; and the last instruction causes the entire register to be cleared.

Exchanging of Contents of Two Registers

MC68000 provides us with the *exchange* exg instruction, which permits exchange of the contents of two registers. The types of instructions which are allowable are summarized in Table 7.26.

TABLE 7.26

Exchanging of contents of two registers					
Mnemonic	Opcode	User byte (X,N,Z,V,C bits)	Operands	Format	Length
exg	19_5	P P P P P	dn, dm	F12	1
exg	19_5	P P P P P	dn, an	F12	1
exg	19_5	P P P P P	an, am	F12	1

Figure 7.36 provides us with an example where the contents of the data registers d1 and d2 are exchanged. Execution of this instruction *does not* affect the condition code setting.

State before	State after execution
	exg d1, d2
d1 98AB F0FF	d1 **0000 D012**
d2 0000 D012	d2 **98AB F0FF**
cc 01011	cc 01011

Figure 7.36 Effect of executing the exg d1, d2 instruction. Notice that contents of the registers are in hex, whereas those of condition code are in binary.

Swapping of words of data register

MC68000 supports the swap instruction that was discussed in Chapter 4; it permits swapping of the low-order and high-order words of a data register. This instruction is presented in Table 7.27.

TABLE 7.27

Swapping high-low words of a data register					
Mnemonic	Opcode	User byte (X,N,Z,V,C bits)	Operands	Format	Length
swap	0908_{13}	P M M R R	dn	F7	1

Execution of this instruction affects the condition code as follows. The extend bit is unaffected; the overflow and carry bits are always reset. If the longword resulted from the swap is a negative number, the negative bit is set; otherwise, it is reset. The zero bit is set, if and only if, the longword represents the number zero; otherwise, it is reset. These concepts are illustrated in Figure 7.37.

State before	State after execution
	swap d1
d1 98AB F0FF	d1 **F0FF 98AB**
cc 10011	cc **11000**

Figure 7.37 Effect of executing the swap d1 instruction. Notice that contents of the registers are in hex, whereas those of condition code are in binary.

Extending of data in a data register

One can sign-extend bytes to words and words to longwords of a data register via the *extend* ext instruction presented in Table 7.28.

TABLE 7.28

Sign extending bytes and words in a data register					
Action					
Extend low-order byte ext.w (word ext.1) of the destination data register to word (longword).					
Mnemonic	Opcode	User byte (X,N,Z,V,C bits)	Operands	Format	Length
ext.w	220_{10}	P M M R R	dn	F13	1
ext.1	220_{10}	P M M R R	dn	F13	1

As Figure 7.38 illustrates, execution of the instruction ext.w d1 causes the low-order byte of the indicated data register $8A to be sign-extended to the word $FF8A, which replaces the low-order word of the data register.

State before	State after execution of instruction	
	ext.w d1	ext.1 d1
d1 A288 708A	d1 A288 **FF8A**	d1 **0000 708A**
cc 00011	cc **01000**	cc **00000**

Figure 7.38 Effect of executing each of two indicated instructions. Notice that contents of the registers are in hex, whereas that of the condition code are in binary.

On the other hand, execution of the instruction ext.1 d1 causes the low-order word of the indicated data register $708A to be sign-extended to the longword $0000708A, which replaces the entire contents of the data register.

Finally as Figure 7.38 illustrates, execution of this instruction causes the condition code to be affected in the same way as the swap instruction. Specifically, the extend bit is unaffected; the overflow and carry bits are always reset. If the data resulting from the extension (word or longword depending on the instruction issued) represent a negative number, then the negative bit is set; otherwise, it is reset. The zero bit is set, if and only if, the data represents the number zero; otherwise, it is reset.

7.5.2 Moving Data

During our discussions in SIM68, three versions of the move instruction were presented. MC68000 provides one with a very rich collection of such instructions that permits one to copy data from a source to a destination. In this section we will attempt to classify this set of instructions into different classes.[21] These are briefly discussed.

1. *Regular operations.* This class of instructions permits the transfer of data between two registers, a register and a memory location, and two memory locations (Table 7.29).

2. *Immediate operations.* This class of instructions permits the transfer of immediate data to a register or to a memory location (Table 7.30).

3. *Quick operations.* This class contains a single instruction that permits the transfer of quick (byte) data to a data register (Table 7.31).

4. *USP operations.* This class of instructions permits the transfer of data between an address register and the usp register (Table 7.32).

5. *SR/CCR operations.* This class of instructions permits the transfer of byte data to ccr or word data to sr. The data in both cases could be immediate or could reside in a data register or a memory location. Moreover, the contents of the sr could be moved to a data register or a memory location (Table 7.33).

6. *Saving/restoring the contents of a set of registers.* This class of instructions permits the transfer of the contents of a user selected set of registers to memory area and conversely (Table 7.34).

7. *Pushing/loading an effective address.* These two instructions permit one to push onto the stack or to load into an address register the effective address of a memory location; as we will see, by employing these instructions we will be able to write position-independent code.

Before these groups are discussed in a more detailed fashion, the following general observations should be made:

1. Whenever the source or destination is an address register, only word or longwords operations are permitted.

2. Whenever the destination is an address register and the size of the operation is a word operation, the word data is sign extended to a longword before the move occurs, irrelevant of the addressing mode of the source. It is important to note that the contents of the source do not change as a result of the sign extension because this extension takes place in a working register.

3. Execution of *all* move instructions in which the destination is an address register, as well as *all* the instructions in groups 6 and 7, do not affect the condition code. All remaining instructions, except the ones that perform moves to ccr and sr, set the condition code the same way.[22] In particular, the **extend** bit retains its value and both the **carry** and **overflow** bits are *reset.* If the moved data represent a negative integer, the **negative** bit is *set;* otherwise, it is *reset.* If the moved data represent the integer zero, the **zero** bit is *set;* otherwise, it is *reset.*

---

[21] The discussion of the movep instruction is deferred to Chapter 8.

[22] The setting of the condition code for these exceptions is discussed later.

Regular operations

With the aid of the instructions in the group that are summarized in Table 7.29, one may move data between any two registers, any register and a memory location, as well as between two memory locations.

TABLE 7.29   Regular move instructions

<table>
<tr><td colspan="7" align="center">Moving instructions
Group 1 : Regular operations</td></tr>
<tr><td colspan="7" align="center">Action</td></tr>
<tr><td colspan="7">Move data from source to destination. Size of data is indicated by extension except when destination is address register in which case data are sign extended to longword before instruction is executed.</td></tr>
<tr><td>Mnemonic</td><td>Opcode</td><td>User byte (X,N,Z,V,C bits)</td><td>Operands</td><td>Format</td><td>Length</td></tr>
<tr><td colspan="6" align="center">Register to data register</td></tr>
<tr><td>move.b</td><td>0_2</td><td>P M M R R</td><td>dn,dn</td><td>F4</td><td>1</td></tr>
<tr><td>move.w</td><td>0_2</td><td>P M M R R</td><td>rn,dn</td><td>F4</td><td>1</td></tr>
<tr><td>move.l</td><td>0_2</td><td>P M M R R</td><td>rn,dn</td><td>F4</td><td>1</td></tr>
<tr><td colspan="6" align="center">Register to address register</td></tr>
<tr><td>movea.w</td><td>0_2</td><td>P P P P P</td><td>rn,an</td><td>F4</td><td>1</td></tr>
<tr><td>movea.l</td><td>0_2</td><td>P P P P P</td><td>rn,an</td><td>F4</td><td>1</td></tr>
<tr><td colspan="6" align="center">Memory to data register</td></tr>
<tr><td>move.b</td><td>0_2</td><td>P M M R R</td><td>smem,dn</td><td>F4</td><td>1, 2, 3</td></tr>
<tr><td>move.w</td><td>0_2</td><td>P M M R R</td><td>smem,dn</td><td>F4</td><td>1, 2, 3</td></tr>
<tr><td>move.l</td><td>0_2</td><td>P M M R R</td><td>smem,dn</td><td>F4</td><td>1, 2, 3</td></tr>
<tr><td colspan="6" align="center">Memory to address register</td></tr>
<tr><td>movea.w</td><td>0_2</td><td>P P P P P</td><td>smem,an</td><td>F4</td><td>1, 2, 3</td></tr>
<tr><td>movea.l</td><td>0_2</td><td>P P P P P</td><td>smem,an</td><td>F4</td><td>1, 2, 3</td></tr>
<tr><td colspan="6" align="center">Data register to memory</td></tr>
<tr><td>move.b</td><td>0_2</td><td>P M M R R</td><td>dn,dmem</td><td>F4</td><td>1, 2, 3</td></tr>
<tr><td>move.w</td><td>0_2</td><td>P M M R R</td><td>dn,dmem</td><td>F4</td><td>1, 2, 3</td></tr>
<tr><td>move.l</td><td>0_2</td><td>P M M R R</td><td>dn,dmem</td><td>F4</td><td>1, 2, 3</td></tr>
<tr><td colspan="6" align="center">Address register to memory</td></tr>
<tr><td>move.w</td><td>0_2</td><td>P M M R R</td><td>an,dmem</td><td>F4</td><td>1, 2, 3</td></tr>
<tr><td>move.l</td><td>0_2</td><td>P M M R R</td><td>an,dmem</td><td>F4</td><td>1, 2, 3</td></tr>
<tr><td colspan="6" align="center">Memory to memory</td></tr>
<tr><td>move.b</td><td>0_2</td><td>P M M R R</td><td>smem,dmem</td><td>F4</td><td>1, 2, 3</td></tr>
<tr><td>move.w</td><td>0_2</td><td>P M M R R</td><td>smem,dmem</td><td>F4</td><td>1, 2, 3</td></tr>
<tr><td>move.l</td><td>0_2</td><td>P M M R R</td><td>smem,dmem</td><td>F4</td><td>1, 2, 3</td></tr>
</table>

Consider the situation given in Figure 7.39. The first instruction, move.b, will cause the low order byte $00 of data register d1 to be moved into the low-order byte of data register d2. The overflow and carry bits of the condition code are reset; the extend bit retains its previous value; and because the moved data represents the integer zero, the zero bit is set, whereas the negative bit is reset.

The second instruction, move.w, will cause the low order word $F200 of data register d1 to be moved into the low-order word of data register d2. The overflow and carry bits of the condition code are reset; the extend bit retains its previous value, because the moved data represents a negative integer, the zero bit is reset, whereas the negative bit is set.

Finally, the third instruction, move.l, will cause the entire contents of data register d1 $6BCDF200 to be moved into data register d2. The overflow and carry bits of the condition code are reset; the extend bit retains its previous value; because the moved data represents a positive integer, both the zero and negative bits are reset.

State before		State after execution of instruction		
		move.b d1,d2	move.w d1,d2	move.l d1,d2
d1	6BCD F200	d1 6BCD F200	d1 6BCD F200	d1 6BCD F200
d2	008F 7189	d2 008F 7100	d2 008F **F200**	d2 **6BCD F200**
cc	11011	cc **10100**	cc **11000**	cc **10000**

Figure 7.39 Effect of executing each of three indicated instructions. Note that contents of the registers are in hex, whereas those of the condition code are in binary.

The situation is different when the destination register is an address register; Figure 7.40 illustrates such an example. First, notice that only word and longword instructions are permitted when the destination register is an address register. Moreover, execution of the first instruction, movea.w, will cause the low-order word $F200 of data register d1 to be accessed; the word is transferred to a working register where it is sign extended to the longword $FFFFF200 that eventually is moved and which will replace the contents of address register a2. On the other hand, execution of second instruction, movea.l, will cause the longword $6BCDF200 of data register d1 to be moved into address register a2. Finally, observe that these latter moves did not affect the condition code.

State before		State after execution of instruction	
		movea.w d1,a2	movea.l d1,a2
d1	6BCD F200	d1 6BCD F200	d1 6BCD F200
a2	008F 7189	a2 **FFFF F200**	a2 **6BCD F200**
cc	10011	cc 10011	cc 10011

Figure 7.40 Effect of executing each of two indicated instructions. Note that contents of the registers are in hex, whereas those of condition code are in binary.

Immediate operations

With this set of instructions presented in Table 7.30, one may move data into a data register, address register, or a memory location where the data are defined in the first operand of the instruction. To repeat, notice that only word or longword instructions may be issued when the destination is an address register; moreover, when a word is moved, the word is sign extended to a longword.

TABLE 7.30   Immediate move instructions

<table>
<tr><td colspan="6" align="center">**Moving instructions**
Group 2 : Immediate operations</td></tr>
<tr><td colspan="6" align="center">**Action**</td></tr>
<tr><td colspan="6">Move immediate data from source to destination. Size of data is indicated by extension except when the destination is an address register; if it is, then data are sign extended to longwords before instruction is executed.</td></tr>
<tr><td>Mnemonic</td><td>Opcode</td><td>User byte (X,N,Z,V,C bits)</td><td>Operands</td><td>Format</td><td>Length</td></tr>
<tr><td colspan="6" align="center">**To data register**</td></tr>
<tr><td>move.b</td><td>0_7</td><td>P M M R R</td><td>$IData_8$, dn</td><td>F4</td><td>1</td></tr>
<tr><td>move.w</td><td>0_7</td><td>P M M R R</td><td>$IData_{16}$, dn</td><td>F4</td><td>1</td></tr>
<tr><td>move.l</td><td>0_7</td><td>P M M R R</td><td>$IData_{32}$, dn</td><td>F4</td><td>1</td></tr>
<tr><td colspan="6" align="center">**To address register**</td></tr>
<tr><td>movea.w</td><td>0_7</td><td>P P P P P</td><td>$IData_{16}$, an</td><td>F4</td><td>1</td></tr>
<tr><td>movea.l</td><td>0_7</td><td>P P P P P</td><td>$IData_{32}$, an</td><td>F4</td><td>1</td></tr>
<tr><td colspan="6" align="center">**To memory**</td></tr>
<tr><td>move.b</td><td>0_7</td><td>P M M R R</td><td>$IData_8$, dmem</td><td>F4</td><td>1</td></tr>
<tr><td>move.w</td><td>0_7</td><td>P M M R R</td><td>$IData_{16}$, dmem</td><td>F4</td><td>1</td></tr>
<tr><td>move.l</td><td>0_7</td><td>P M M R R</td><td>$IData_{32}$, dmem</td><td>F4</td><td>1</td></tr>
</table>

The first example in Figure 7.41 illustrates that one should be very careful when he or she specifies the size of the data in an instruction. In particular, the operand field of all three instructions in Figure 7.41 is the *same*; however, what is moved depends entirely on the operation mode. Therefore, execution of the first instruction, move.b, will cause the low-order *byte* of the immediate data $00 to be moved to the low-order byte of data

State before	State after execution of instruction		
	move.b #$8f6400,d2	move.w #$8f6400,d2	move.l #$8f6400,d2
d2 1234 5678	d2 1234 5600	d2 1234 **6400**	d2 **008F 6400**
cc 11111	cc 10100	cc 10000	cc 10000

Figure 7.41   Effect of executing each of three indicated instructions. Note that contents of the registers are in hex, whereas those of condition code are in binary.

register d2. Execution of the second instruction, `move.w`, will cause the movement of the low-order *word* of the immediate data $6400 to be moved into the low-order word of data register d2. Finally, execution of the third instruction, `move.l`, will cause the immediate data $8F6400 to be extended to a longword $008F6400; the longword will be moved to data register d2. The reader should try to verify the setting of the condition code in each of the preceding cases.

We close this section by noting that seemingly simple typing errors can lead to errors that are more difficult to catch at run time. Consider the result of the execution of each of the following two instructions:

`move.w $6400,d1   move.w #$6400,d1`

As Figure 7.42 indicates, execution of the first instruction will cause the word at location X = $006400 to be moved to the low-order word of data register d2 whereas execution of the second instruction will cause the low-order *word* of the immediate data $6400 to be moved into the low-order word of data register D2. One can argue that the probability of making two typing errors in the same instruction is quite low. Most assemblers, however, do not support a different syntax for the mnemonic of the opcode for the regular and immediate `move` operations. In other words, they do not support the `movei` mnemonic, which compounds the problem.

State before	State after execution of instruction	
	move.w $6400,d1	move.w #$6400,d1
x `1023 4567`	x `1023 4567`	x `1023 4567`
d1 `238F 8976`	d1 `238F 1023`	d1 `238F 6400`
cc `00111`	cc `00000`	cc `00000`

Figure 7.42 Effect of executing each of two indicated instructions. Value of the symbol x is $006400. Note that contents of register d1 and of memory location x are in hex, whereas those of the condition code are in binary.

Figure 7.43 provides one more example that may further emphasize the point made earlier. One should attempt to verify the results.

State before	State after execution of instruction	
	move.w x,d1	move.w #x,d1
x `0000 F0FF`	x `0000 F0FF`	x `0000 F0FF`
d1 `238F 8123`	d1 `238F 0000`	d1 `238F 6400`
cc `00111`	cc `00100`	cc `00000`

Figure 7.43 Effect of executing each of the two indicated instructions. Value of symbol x is $006400. Note that contents of register d1 and of memory location x are in hex, whereas those of the condition code are in binary.

Quick operations

There is only one instruction in this group that permits the movement of quick data into a data register and is presented in Table 7.31.

TABLE 7.31   Quick move instruction

Moving instructions				
Group 3 : Quick operations				
Action				
Move quick byte data to data register. Data are sign extended to longword before the instruction is executed.				
Mnemonic	Opcode	User byte (X,N,Z,V,C bits)	Operands	Format	Length
moveq	$0E$_5$	[P][M][M][R][R]	QData$_8$,dn	F15	1

Unlike any other quick instruction the `moveq` instruction permits the data to represent a signed integer of byte length. Moreover, the data is sign extended to a longword before the move occurs. Figure 7.44 provides two examples.

State before	State after execution of instruction	
	moveq #$6a,d2	moveq #$8a,d2
d2 1234 5678	d2 0000 006A	d2 FFFF FF8A
cc 11111	cc 10000	cc 11000

Figure 7.44   Effect of executing each of the two indicated instructions. Note that contents of the registers are in hex, whereas those of condition code are in binary.

Finally, notice that the condition code setting is the same as when the `move` instructions were used.

USP Operations

When register `a7` must be accessed the register that is accessed depends on the mode. If the processor is running in supervisor mode, the `sp` register is accessed; otherwise the `usp`. The supervisor, however, should be able to access *any* register particularly since it is responsible for maintaining the system. Hence, the MC68000 designers have made available a *privileged* instruction that is presented in Table 7.32 and allows access of the supervisor to the user stack pointer.

CCR/SR operations

There are several instructions as shown in Table 7.33 that are designed so that one can move data to and from the `ccr/sr`; moves involving the `ccr` can be done freely in any mode, user or supervisor mode, because the user (or the system for that matter) should be able to set the condition code anyway that he or she chooses. Instructions that involve moves into the status register, however, can be executed only in the supervisor mode; otherwise, any user would be able to "break" in the system just by setting the supervisor bit.

TABLE 7.32 usp move instructions

Moving instructions
Group 4 : USP moves

Action

Move longword contents of user stack pointer register to or from indicated address register an. Following instructions are privileged.

Mnemonic	Opcode	User byte (X,N,Z,V,C bits)	Operands	Format	Length
To and from USP					
move	$09C6_{12}$	P|P|P|P|P	an,usp	F24	1
move	$09C6_{12}$	P|P|P|P|P	usp,an	F24	1

TABLE 7.33 ccr/sr move instructions

Moving instructions
Group 5 : CCR/SR moves

To CCR

Action

Move byte to ccr. If source is a data register, its low-order byte is moved.

Mnemonic	Opcode	User byte (X,N,Z,V,C bits)	Operands	Format	Length
move	$10B_{10}$	4|3|2|1|0	IData$_8$,ccr	F16	2
move	$10B_{10}$	4|3|2|1|0	dn,ccr	F16	1
move	$10B_{10}$	4|3|2|1|0	smem,ccr	F16	1, 2, 3

To and from SR

Action

Move word to/from sr. If source or destination is data register, its low-order word is accessed. Instructions that perform moves to sr are privileged.

Mnemonic	Opcode	User byte (X,N,Z,V,C bits)	Operands	Format	Length
To SR					
move	103_{10}	4|3|2|1|0	IData$_{16}$,sr	F16	2
move	103_{10}	4|3|2|1|0	dn,sr	F16	1
move	103_{10}	4|3|2|1|0	smem,sr	F16	1, 2, 3
From SR					
move	103_{10}	P|P|P|P|P	sr,dn	F16	1
move	103_{10}	P|P|P|P|P	sr,dmem	F16	1, 2, 3

Saving/Restoring the Contents of a Set of Registers

It is apparent that the number of data registers, as well as the number of address registers, is not adequate when one must code a large program. It is easy to derive several different scenarios where during the running of a program *all* data registers contain data that are the result of some calculations. For the program to proceed, a new calculation involving four data values is needed. Because we have assumed that all registers at this instant contain some useful information and that there is a need to allocate four data registers, the only thing that we could do would be to store the contents of the four registers in main memory, thereby freeing four data registers so that they could be used to load the four new values. When this new operation is completed, the previous contents of the four involved data registers must be reloaded. Of course as some would say "nothing to it"; only four move (store) instructions are needed to *save* the contents of these four registers plus four more move (load) instructions to *restore* their contents.

Another scenario is the case of multiprogramming. Recall that the dispatcher is that component of the operating system that ensures that the computer resources are allocated between users in an equitable fashion. In other words, each job that runs for a fixed (by the operating system) period is referred to as the *quantum*; if it is not completed in that interval, the job is suspended, and another one is started. The suspended job must wait until its turn comes around again. Assume a job is suspended once and now its time has come to run again. Of course, the job should start running from the point at which it was suspended; however, the contents of the data, as well as of the address registers, have been corrupted since the jobs that have been run in between have used the *same* registers! Therefore, one of the very first tasks the dispatcher must do is to *save* the contents of *all* registers by storing them in main memory when a program is suspended and to *restore* them in exactly the same way when the program is restarted by reloading them from memory.[23] Easy again, we need only sixteen move instructions to store and sixteen more move instructions to restore the contents of the registers. Assuming that a program was interrupted ten times before it is completed, we will need $10 \cdot 16 + 11 \cdot 16 = 336$ move instructions to store and restore the registers just for this job!

The designers of MC68000 realized that to save storage and execution time, a single instruction should be provided that would perform the storing and also the restoring of any number of registers. This instruction is the *move multiple registers*, movem, instruction, and its allowable versions are presented in Table 7.34.

Notice that one of the operands of each of these instructions is denoted by reglist, an acronym for *register list*. The syntax employed in the specification of this list indicates *which* registers are to be stored or restored, but *not* the order in which they are stored or restored. The order, as we will see shortly, is indicated *implicitly* from the addressing mode of the other operand. First, we will discuss the syntax of the reglist.

The reglist syntax consists of a finite list of ordered disjoint sets s_i where any two sets are separated by a slash. For example, the expression

$$s_1 / s_2 / s_3$$

represents a reglist of three sets.

---

[23] The code for a dispatcher is presented in Chapter 10.

TABLE 7.34   Storing and Restoring contents of registers

<table>
<tr><td colspan="6" align="center">Moving instructions
Group 6 : Storing and restoring the contents of registers</td></tr>
<tr><td colspan="6" align="center">Action</td></tr>
<tr><td colspan="6">Contents of specified registers are stored (in stack fashion) in memory starting at specified memory location one at a time. Conversely, contents of specified registers are restored by moving data from main memory.</td></tr>
<tr><td>Mnemonic</td><td>Opcode</td><td>User byte (X,N,Z,V,C bits)</td><td>Operands</td><td>Format</td><td>Length</td></tr>
<tr><td colspan="6" align="center">Save registers in memory</td></tr>
<tr><td>movem.w</td><td>49_8</td><td>P P P P P</td><td>reglist,-(an)</td><td>F25</td><td>2</td></tr>
<tr><td>movem.w</td><td>49_8</td><td>P P P P P</td><td>reglist,dmem*</td><td>F25</td><td>2, 3, 4</td></tr>
<tr><td>movem.l</td><td>49_8</td><td>P P P P P</td><td>reglist,-(an)</td><td>F25</td><td>2</td></tr>
<tr><td>movem.l</td><td>49_8</td><td>P P P P P</td><td>reglist,dmem*</td><td>F25</td><td>2, 3, 4</td></tr>
<tr><td colspan="6" align="center">Restore registers from memory</td></tr>
<tr><td>movem.w</td><td>49_8</td><td>P P P P P</td><td>(an)+,reglist</td><td>F25</td><td>2</td></tr>
<tr><td>movem.w</td><td>49_8</td><td>P P P P P</td><td>smem*,reglist</td><td>F25</td><td>2, 3, 4</td></tr>
<tr><td>movem.l</td><td>49_8</td><td>P P P P P</td><td>(an)+,reglist</td><td>F25</td><td>2</td></tr>
<tr><td>movem.l</td><td>49_8</td><td>P P P P P</td><td>smem*,reglist</td><td>F25</td><td>2, 3, 4</td></tr>
</table>

Each set s_i is a collection of registers of the same type. Moreover, the collection of registers belonging to a set must be numbered consecutively. For example, the following are valid sets:

$$s_1 = \{d0\}, s_2 = \{d3,d4,d5,d6\}, s_3 = \{a2,a3,a4,a5,a6\}, s_4 = \{a0\}$$

Furthermore, we must use the following notation. A set of one element is represented by its element register, whereas a set of more than one element is denoted by its first register element followed by a hyphen and finally followed by its last register element. With this convention, the preceding sets can be rewritten as

$$s_1 = d0, s_2 = d3-d6, s_3 = a2-a6, s_4 = a0$$

Hence, the reglist takes the form

$$d0/d3-d6/a2-a6/a0$$

and the assembler will use only these registers to store or restore their contents. In other words, registers that do not appear in the reglist do not participate in data transfers. We are now ready to examine the *order* in which the registers in the register list are stored or restored.

First, notice from Table 7.34 that if the destination is a memory address and the mode is *address register indirect with predecrement*, then only a register to memory operation is allowed. Moreover, the order in which the registers are stored is address register 7 to address register 0, then data register 7 to data register 0. Hence, the storage of the registers in the register list d0/d3-d6/a2-a6/a0 will be stored in the following order:

$$a6, \; a5, \; a4, \; a3, \; a2, \; a0, \; d6, \; d5, \; d4, \; d3, \; d0$$

Second, when one must restore a set of registers by using the *address register indirect with postincrement* mode, he or she should be aware that the order in which the registers are restored is the *reverse* of that defined for the store operation where predecrement mode is used. In other words, the order of register restoration would be data register 0 to data register 7, then address register 0 to address register 7. Hence the restoration of registers appearing in the register list a0/d0/d3-d6/a2-a6 would follow the order:

```
d0, d3, d4, d5, d6, a0, a2, a3, a4, a5, a6
```

Finally, we would like to mention that irrelevant of the addressing mode employed, whenever a word size *save* instruction is issued, the low-order words of the indicated in reglist registers are moved. On the other hand, whenever a word size *restore* instruction is issued, a word is accessed from main memory; however, it is sign extended to a longword before it is moved into the indicated register in reglist.

As an example consider the fragment of code

```
movem.w    d6/a2-a3,-(a4)
movem.w    (a4)+,a2-a3/d6
```

and consider the initial situation as indicated in Figure 7.45(a). According to our earlier discussions the low-order words of the registers in the order a3, a2, d6 will be stored in locations $01010A (Fig 7.45[b]), $010108 (Fig 7.45[c]), and $010106 (Fig 7.45[d]), respectively.

On the other hand, during the restore operation the registers will be restored in the order d6, a2, a3; however, each accessed word is sign-extended to a longword before it is transferred into the corresponding register (Figure 7.46). In other words, by storing the low-order words of the registers, it is highly unlikely that after the restoration process is completed that the registers will contain the same high-order word as before their initial storage.

Finally, for all other instructions of this group, the order in which the registers will be saved or restored is data register 0 to data register 7 followed by address register 0 to address register 7. Hence, the storage of the registers in the register list d0/d3-d6/a2-a6/a0 will be stored in the following order:

```
d0, d3, d4, d5, d6, a0, a2, a3, a4, a5, a6
```

As an example consider the situation in Figure 7.47.

Pushing/loading of an EA

Recall from earlier discussions that instructions such as

```
move.l    d1,x
```

are the critical problem in writing and generating relocatable code. The reason for this is that the MC68000 instruction set does not allow an alterable memory refence to be specified via PC-relative modes. The observant reader should have noticed that if one replaces the preceding instruction with the set of the following two instructions

```
movea.l    #x,a1
move.l     d1,(a1)
```

then the second instruction is position independent but now the first instruction is not!

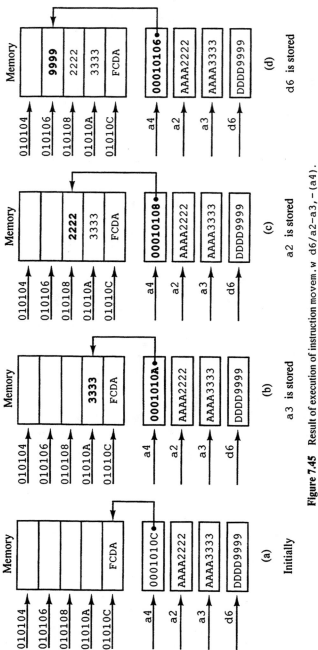

Figure 7.45 Result of execution of instruction movem.w d6/a2–a3, –(a4).

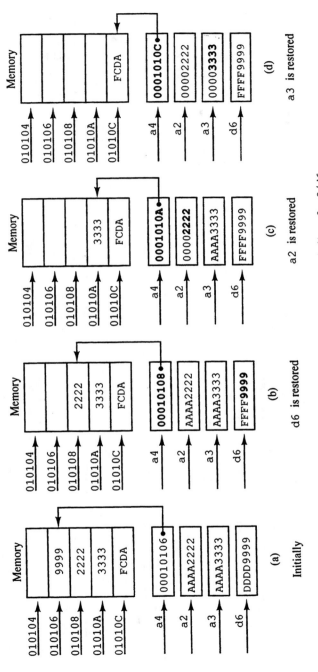

Figure 7.46 Result of execution of instruction movem. w (a4) +, a2–a3/d6.

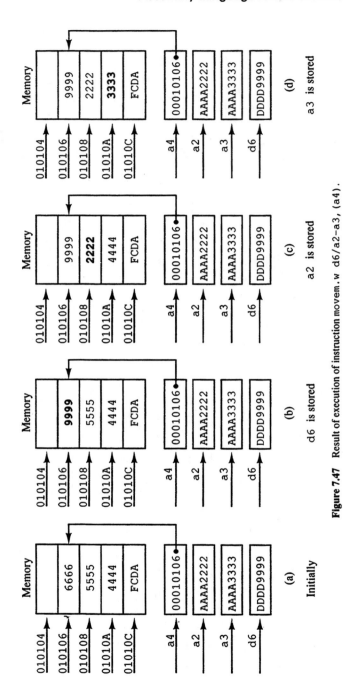

Figure 7.47 Result of execution of instruction movem.w d6/a2–a3,(a4).

Therefore, a new instruction the `Load Effective Address` (`lea`), instruction is provided. This instruction, which at run time accomplishes the same result such as the `movea.l   #x,a1`, loads the value of the symbol x into the indicated address register. In addition, however, one may use *PC-relative mode,* as illustrated in Table 7.35, that makes the code relocatable. In other words, the code that will accomplish this task is

```
lea       x(pc),a1
move.l    d1,(a1)
```

TABLE 7.35   `lea` instruction

Load effective address
Action
Calculate and load the EA (32-bits) of indicated memory location into indicated address register.

Mnemonic	Opcode	User byte (X,N,Z,V,C bits)	Operands	Format	Length
lea	$27₇	P|P|P|P|P	smem*,an	F3	1

As an example, assuming the initial situation as in Figure 7.48 and also assuming that the value of the symbol x is equal to $3000, we will obtain the following.

State before	State after execution lea x,a2	State before	State after execution lea x(a1),a2
a1 0000 6002	a1 0000 6002	a1 0000 6002	a1 0000 6002
a2 0000 8260	a2 **0000 3000**	a2 0000 8260	a2 **0000 9002**
cc 00000	cc 00000	cc 00000	cc 00000
(a)		(b)	

Figure 7.48   Effect of executing each of the two indicated instructions assuming that x=$3000. Notice that contents of registers are in hex, whereas the condition code is in binary.

Before we close this section we should note that the two instructions that follow

```
lea       x,a3
movea.l   x,a3
```

are *not* equivalent. To see this consider the following two pieces of code:

```
          org     $2000                    org     $2000
here      dc.l    64            here       dc.l    64
          movea.l here,a0                  lea     here,a0
there     ....... .......       there      ...     .......
```

Notice that when the instruction at location `there` is reached in the first example, register a0 will contain $00000040 because the contents of location `here` were moved via the `movea` instruction. On the other hand, register `a0` will contain `$00002000` when the instruction at location `there` is reached since the value of the symbol `here` was moved via the `lea` instruction.

There is one more instruction that may be used when one wishes to push the effective address of a relocatable expression onto the stack pointed to by the stack pointer (register `a7`). The instruction is the `Push Effective Address` (`pea`) (Table 7.36); and, because of its similarity with the `lea`, any further discussion is omitted.

TABLE 7.36　`pea` instruction

Push effective address				
Action				
Calculate and push (onto stack pointed to by `a7`) effective address (32 bits) of indicated memory location.				

Mnemonic	Opcode	User byte (X,N,Z,V,C bits)	Operands	Format	Length
pea	27_7$	P|P|P|P|P	smem*	F3	1

7.5.3 Branching and Looping

Earlier we stated that in a number of instances one would like to "jump" around in the code; in SIM68 we show that one could employ several available *branch* instructions. When employing these instructions, a branch will be taken, if and only if, a single specified condition is true. MC68000 supports a richer superset of all these instructions plus another set of instructions, the *loop* instructions that permit one to branch, if and only if, *two* conditions are met. Finally, an instruction, known as the *jump* instruction, is supplied that performs unconditional branches. Each of these sets will be discussed in the following paragraphs. Note that the condition code will not be affected when any of these instructions is executed.

Jump instruction. Whenever this instruction is executed, an unconditional branch is taken to the specified memory address x. The `jump` instruction is distinguished by the instructions provided by the other groups in two respects. First, the branch address is specified *explicitly* by the instruction, and not via the displacement, relative to the program counter value mechanism.[24] In other words, the jump address is not affected by relocation of the program.[25] Therefore, the user must be very careful when he or she uses this instruction. Second, although instructions in the other groups limit the length of the jump to either 8 bits for byte displacement or 16 bits for word displacement from the current value of the program counter, the `jump` instruction permits one to jump anywhere via its absolute long addressing mode. At any rate, characteristics of this instruction are illustrated in Table 7.37.

---

[24] Unless the branch address has been explicitly defined via a PC-relative mode.

[25] Unless if a relocatable assembler and a linker are used (see Chapter 9).

TABLE 7.37 `jmp` instruction

Jump Instruction					
Mnemonic	Opcode	Action	Operands	Format	Length
`jmp`	$13B_{10}$	Jump Unconditionally.	smem[*]	F16	1, 2, 3

Branch instructions. The set of *branch* instructions, conveniently denoted by `bcc`, permits one to branch if the condition that is conveyed via the `cc` acronym of the opcode is met; otherwise, the "next" instruction is executed. The `cc` acronym can take fifteen different values as summarized in Table 7.38.

As one can see, one of these instructions, the `bra` instruction, is referred to as an unconditional branch; the reason is that whenever this instruction is executed, the indicated branch is always taken. The other fourteen branch instructions do force a branch, if and only if, the condition is met.

TABLE 7.38

Branch instructions Opcode for all instructions is 6_4					
Action					
If condition indicated by `cc` code is false, then the next instruction is executed. Otherwise, branch is taken. Notice that the extension e takes the values s (b) or w. In the first instance, the assembler will generate a byte size relative displacement; otherwise, it will generate a word size relative displacement.					
Mnemonic					
Unconditional branches					
`bra`	$0	Branch Unconditionally.	absmem	F5	1, 2
Conditional branches					
`bcc.e`	$4	Branch on carry clear; branch if $C = 0$	absmem	F5	1, 2
`bcs.e`	$5	Branch on carry set; branch if $C = 1$	absmem	F5	1, 2
`beq.e`	$7	Branch on equal; branch if $Z = 1$	absmem	F5	1, 2
`bge.e`	$C	Branch on greater or equal; branch if $N \cdot V + \bar{N} \cdot \bar{V} = 1$	absmem	F5	1, 2
`bgt.e`	$E	Branch on greater than; branch if $(N \cdot V + \bar{N} \cdot \bar{V}) \cdot \bar{Z} = 1$	absmem	F5	1, 2
`bhi.e`	$2	Branch on high; branch if $\bar{C} \cdot \bar{Z} = 1$	absmem	F5	1, 2
`ble.e`	$F	Branch on less or equal; branch if $Z + N \cdot \bar{V} + \bar{N} \cdot V = 1$	absmem	F5	1, 2
`bls.e`	$3	Branch on low or same; branch if $C + Z = 1$	absmem	F5	1, 2
`blt.e`	$D	Branch on less than; branch if $N \cdot \bar{V} + \bar{N} \cdot V = 1$	absmem	F5	1, 2
`bmi.e`	$B	Branch on minus; branch if $N = 1$	absmem	F5	1, 2
`bne.e`	$6	Branch on not equal; branch if $\bar{Z} = 1$	absmem	F5	1, 2
`bpl.e`	$A	Branch on plus; branch if $\bar{N} = 1$	absmem	F5	1, 2
`bvc.e`	$8	Branch on overflow clear; branch if $\bar{V} = 1$	absmem	F5	1, 2
`bvs.e`	$9	Branch on overflow set; branch if $V = 1$	absmem	F5	1, 2

Consider the piece of code presented in Table 7.39. Whenever the `bvs there` instruction is executed, the overflow bit of the condition code is examined. If the current value of this bit is `%1`, then the condition is true and a branch is taken to location `there`; otherwise, the condition is false, and the instruction to be executed next is the one at location `here`.

TABLE 7.39

there	add.w	d1,d2
	.....	.....
	.....	.....
	.....	.....
	bvs	there
here	add.b	d3,d7
	.....	.....

Loop instructions.   The set of *Loop* instructions, conveniently denoted by `dbcc` has been designed so that it operates similarly to the "repeat until condition(`cc`)" provided by the Pascal programming language. These instructions permit one to branch to the indicated address, if and only if, two conditions are met. The first condition is conveyed via the `cc` acronym of the opcode as in the case of the `bcc` instructions discussed in the previous section; the second condition is conveyed via the contents of the indicated in the instruction data register `dn`.

Specifically, when the instruction `dbcc dn,X` is executed, the events that occur are illustrated in the flowchart of Figure 7.49 and are explained briefly.

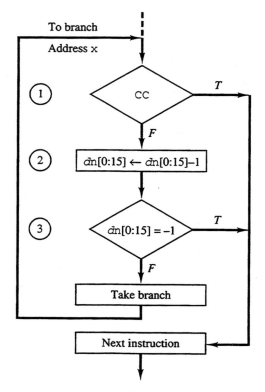

Figure 7.49   Steps required for execution of the `dbcc dn,X` instruction.

In step 1 the cc is examined. If the condition is met, the "next" instruction is executed; otherwise, in step 2 the low-order word of data register dn is decremented by one. A test, in step 3, is performed to verify whether the low-order word of the data register represents the decimal integer −1. If the test is successful, the "next" instruction is executed; otherwise, the branch is taken to the instruction at address x.

The cc acronym can take fifteen different values as summarized in Table 7.40.

TABLE 7.40   dbcc instructions

Loop instructions
The opcode for all instructions is $0B9_9$
Action
If condition indicated by cc code is true, the next instruction is executed. Otherwise, if condition indicated by cc code is not true, low-order word of indicated data register is decremented by one. If the updated, low-order word of the data register is different from -1, then indicated branch is taken; otherwise, next instruction is executed. Notice that extension e takes the values s (b) or w. In the first instance the assembler will generate byte size, relative displacement; otherwise, will generate word size, relative displacement.

Mnemonic	Condition	Branch taken	Operands	Format	Length
Unconditional loops					
dbra.e	$1	Unconditionally	dn,absmem	F17	2
dbf.e	$1	On false	dn,absmem	F17	2
Conditional loops					
dbcc.e	$4	if $C = 1$ and Dn $[0:15] - 1 \neq -1$	dn,absmem	F17	2
dbcs.e	$5	if $C = 0$ and Dn $[0:15] - 1 \neq -1$	dn,absmem	F17	2
dbeq.e	$7	if $Z = 0$ and Dn $[0:15] - 1 \neq -1$	dn,absmem	F17	2
dbge.e	$C	if $N \cdot V + \bar{N} \cdot \bar{V} = 0$ and Dn $[0:15] - 1 \neq -1$	dn,absmem	F17	2
dbgt.e	$E	if $(N \cdot V + \bar{N} \cdot \bar{V}) \cdot \bar{Z} = 0$ and Dn $[0:15] - 1 \neq -1$	dn,absmem	F17	2
dbhi.e	$2	if $\bar{C} \cdot \bar{Z} = 0$ and Dn $[0:15] - 1 \neq -1$	dn,absmem	F17	2
dble.e	$F	if $Z + N \cdot \bar{V} + \bar{N} \cdot V = 0$ and Dn $[0:15] - 1 \neq -1$	dn,absmem	F17	2
dbls.e	$3	if $C + Z = 0$ and Dn $[0:15] - 1 \neq -1$	dn,absmem	F17	2
dblt.e	$D	if $N \cdot \bar{V} + \bar{N} \cdot V = 0$ and Dn $[0:15] - 1 \neq -1$	dn,absmem	F17	2
dbmi.e	$B	if $N = 0$ and Dn $[0:15] - 1 \neq -1$	dn,absmem	F17	2
dbne.e	$6	if $\bar{Z} = 0$ and Dn $[0:15] - 1 \neq -1$	dn,absmem	F17	2
dbpl.e	$A	if $\bar{N} = 0$ and Dn $[0:15] - 1 \neq -1$	dn,absmem	F17	2
dbvc.e	$8	if $\bar{V} = 0$ and Dn $[0:15] - 1 \neq -1$	dn,absmem	F17	2
dbvs.e	$9	if $V = 0$ and Dn $[0:15] - 1 \neq -1$	dn,absmem	F17	2
dbt.e	$0	if Dn $[0:15] - 1 \neq -1$	dn,absmem	F17	2

Consider the piece of code presented in Table 7.41. Whenever the instruction dbeq d3,there is executed, the 0 bit of the condition code is examined. If the current value of this bit is %1, the condition is true and the instruction that is executed next is the one at location here; otherwise, the low order word of register d3 is decremented by 1. If the low-order word of this register contains the decimal integer −1, the next instruction to be executed is the one at location here; otherwise, the one at location there is executed.

TABLE 7.41

```
there      add.w   d1,d2
...        .....
...        .....
...        .....
dbeq       d3,there
here       sub.w   d1,d2
...        .....
```

It must be apparent that whenever a loop should be executed n times, the number $n-1$ is loaded into the low order word of a data register, say d0; the instruction dbra d0,loop is issued. It is also clear that the largest number that can be stored in the low-order word of a data register is $2^{15} - 1$. So it will seem that the maximum number of times that a loop can execute is equal to 2^{15}. This is only partially true because if one loads the number −1 into d0, then the loop will execute approximately 2^{16} times!.

The question now is how can one execute a loop for a number n that is larger than 2^{15} and less than 2^{31} (i.e, it cannot fit in a word, but it can fit in a longword)? The answer is via programming; such an example is provided in Table 7.42. Specifically, the execution of that piece of code causes a specified number of bytes (starting at the location pointed to by a1) to be cleared. This number (which has been loaded in d0) could represent an integer that could require more than 16 bits to be specified. The reader is encouraged to trace the execution of this code.

TABLE 7.42 Clearing a number of bytes

```
....       ......    .........
....       ......    .........
           move.l    number,d0    ; number of bytes to be cleared

           bra.s     loop2
loop0      swap      d0           ; swap again
loop1      clr.b     (a1)+
loop2      dbra      d0,loop1     ; clear for as long as ( d0[0:15] ≠ -1)
           swap      d0           ; make upper word low word
           dbra      d0,loop0     ; decrement (previous upper) word by 1

....       ......    .........
```

Example

We close this section by giving a complete example of a program that incorporates several instructions introduced so far. The code presented in Table 7.43 is employed to compare two strings, string_1 and string_2, where both strings are assumed to be terminated by a null byte. The result of this comparison is reflected via the value found in d0. In particular, d0 will contain 1 if string1 > string2; 0 if string1 = string2; and, −1 if string1 < string2. This program has been run on the TUTOR environment.[26]

TABLE 7.43   String comparison code

```
data        org     $0F00
tutor       equ     228
string_1    dc.b    'This is the first string',0
string_2    dc.b    'It could have been read in at runtime',0

program     org     $1000           ; loading origin

            move.l  #string_1,a0    ; a0 contains the address of
                                    ; the first string
            move.l  #string_2,a1    ; a1 contains the address of
                                    ; the second string

1$          tst.b   (a0)            ; check for null byte in first string
            beq     2$              ;
            cmpm.b  (a0)+,(a1)+
            bgt     3$              ; if (a1) > (a0)
            blt     4$              ; if (a0) > (a1)
            bra     1$              ; keep looping 'til null
                                    ; or (a1) ≠
2$          cmpm.b  (a0)+,(a1)+     ;
            beq     5$              ; (a0) = (a1)
3$          moveq   #-1,d0          ; string1 < string2, -1→ d0
            bra     done
4$          moveq   #1,d0           ; string1 > string2, 1→ d0
            bra     done
5$          moveq   #0,d0           ; string1 = string2, 0→ d0

done        move.w  #tutor,d7       ; get ready to exit
            trap    #14             ; normal TUTOR's exit

            end
```

7.5.4 Logical and Bit Operations

MC68000 provides numerous instructions that permit us to manipulate any subset of bits in a bit string. A *bit string* is a string of binary digits such as %01101100. The *length*, *l*, of a

---

[26] TUTOR is discussed in Appendix D.

given bit string is defined as the positive integer which is equal to the number of bits in the bit string. For example, the length of the bit string %0011 is equal to 4, whereas the length of the bit string %00100101 is equal to 8.

The bits in a bit string are labeled with an integer whose value reflects their position in the bit string. By convention the bits are labeled consecutively with the leftmost bit bearing the label $l - 1$, whereas the rightmost bit bears the label 0.

The instructions that permit us to perform the manipulation of bit strings can be classified into four major categories. These categories are briefly discussed and broadly compared.

1. *Logical operations.* These are instructions that implement the binary boolean functions and, or, and eor as well as the unary boolean operation not that was discussed in Chapter 2. Characteristic of these instructions is their ability to directly manipulate any subset of bits in a string given that their length is 8, 16, or 32.

2. *Shift operations.* These are instructions that permit one to shift (to the left or right) the bits of a bit string by a certain amount. In addition, not only are certain bits repositioned during the shift, but also a number of bits (equal to the amount of the shift) are lost. The vacated positions are replaced by bits whose values are conveyed to the processor via the opcode of the instruction. The bit string is again permitted to have the same size as it does when logical instructions are used.

3. *Rotate operations.* These are instructions that permit one to shift (to the left or right) the bits of a bit string by a certain amount. Unlike in shift instructions, however, the "lost" bits are fed back to the string at its other end. The bit string is again permitted to have the same size as it does in the case of the two previous categories.

4. *Test and set/clear operations.* These are instructions[27] that permit one to directly test the value of a specific bit in a given string; according to the value of that bit, the string is set or reset.

Logical operations. The instructions that belong in this category are the binary boolean functions and, or, and eor as well as the unary boolean operation not which are all discussed subsequently.

AND, OR, and EOR Instructions. With the use of the instructions provided from this group, one is capable of manipulating any subset of bits in a given string. A bit string of length l that is to be manipulated is referred to as the *target* string and is denoted by T_l. The desired manipulation requires the use of one or more of the provided instructions. These instructions are binary, however, meaning that another operand is required. The other operand, as one could expect, is a bit string of length l, and is referred to as the *mask* string and is denoted by M_l.

Let @ denote any of the operations belonging to this group. By definition, the result of the operation between the two strings denoted by M_l @ T_l yields a string of the same length R_l. This operation is performed bitwise between bits that occupy the same relative positions within each of the strings M_l and T_l. In other words, if we denote the *ith*

---

[27] The discussion of the tas instruction is deferred to Chapter 10.

$(i = l - 1, l - 2, \ldots, 1, 0)$ bit of the strings M_l, T_l, and R_l, by $(M_l)_i$, $(T_l)_i$, and $(R_l)_i$, respectively, the following l equations hold:

$$(R_l)_i = (M_l)_i \ @ \ (T_l)_i$$

for each $i = l - 1, l - 2, \ldots, 1, 0$.

Therefore, one can think of the logical operations between strings as logical operations performed in parallel between corresponding bits of the two strings. Therefore, calculation of the result can be found via the definitions presented in Chapter 2 or via the truth tables for these operations as Table 7.44 demonstrates.

TABLE 7.44 Truth tables for three operators and, or and eor

M	T	M and T		M	T	M or T		M	T	M eor T
0	0	0		0	0	0		0	0	0
0	1	0		0	1	1		0	1	1
1	0	0		1	0	1		1	0	1
1	1	1		1	1	1		1	1	0

These concepts will be illustrated via three specific examples. Assume that the target T_8 and mask M_8 strings are defined via:

```
M = M8  = %0001 1001 and T = T8 = %1101 0011
```

We have that

```
R = M and T
  = %0001 1001 and %1101 0011 =
  = %(0 and 1)(0 and 1)(0 and 0)(1 and 1)(1 and 0)(0 and 0)(0 and 1)(1 and 1)
  = %    0        0        0        1        0        0        0        1
  = %0001 0001
```

On the other hand,

```
R = M or T
  = %0001 1001 or %1101 0011 =
  = %(0 or 1)(0 or 1)(0 or 0)(1 or 1)(1 or 0)(0 or 0)(0 or 1)(1 or 1)
  = %   1       1       0       1       1       0       1       1
  = %1101 1011
```

Finally,

```
R = M eor T
  = %0001 1001 eor %1101 0011 =
  = %(0 eor 1)(0 eor 1)(0 eor 0)(1 eor 1)(1 eor 0)(0 eor 0)(0 eor 1)(1 eor 1)
  = %    1         1         0         0         1         0         1         0
  = %1100 1010
```

As is apparent, whenever a user must manipulate a certain bit or bits of a given target string, he or she must decide which operation or set of operations should be selected, and what mask he or she should define to accomplish the desired result. Despite the fact that initially this task seems to be complicated, some simple rules will be derived below detailing how one can accomplish this task with a minimum amount of effort.

Because these operations are performed in a bitwise fashion, it is enough to restrict our attention to the effect of each operation on two strings of length 1. Each scenario will be discussed later. First let's give one more definition. Consider the two strings *target (T)* and *mask (M)*. The *selected* bits of *T* will be defined to be the set of all bits in the *target* string whose positions correspond to the positions of the bits in the *mask* that are set. The *unselected* bits will be defined to be the set of all bits in the *target* string whose positions correspond to the positions of the bits in the *mask* string that are reset. For example, consider the two bit strings *target (T)* and *mask (M)* of length 8 defined by M = %0001 1001 and T= %1101 0011. The selected bits are the ones whose positions are 4, 3, and 0 whereas the unselected bits are the ones at positions 7, 6, 5, 2, 1.

Notice the truth table of the and operation presented in Table 7.44. When a bit is *unselected* (value of M=0), irrelevant of the value of the corresponding bit of the *target* string, the result will be that this bit is *reset*. On the other hand, when a bit is *selected* (value of M=1), the result will have the *same* value as the corresponding bit of the *target* string. These observations can be formulated as the following rule:

> *The effect of the* and *operation on a target string is that the selected bits remain unchanged, whereas the unselected bits will be reset.*

These concepts are illustrated in Figure 7.50 where the *mask* = %01011101 is anded with the *Target* = %11010100 to produce the result %01010100.

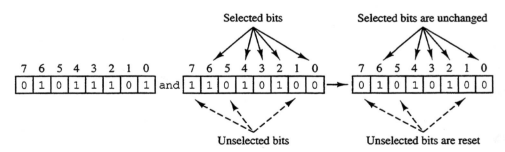

Figure 7.50 Effect of and operator.

Similarly, close examination of the truth table of the or operation (Table 7.44) reveals that when a bit is *selected* (value of $M = 1$), irrelevant of the value of the corresponding bit of the *target* string, the result will be that this bit will be *set*. On the other hand, when a bit is *unselected* (value of $M = 0$), then the result will have the *same* value as the corresponding bit of the *target* string. The following rule is formulated from the observations previously made.

> *The effect of the* or *operation on the target string is that selected bits will be set, whereas unselected bits remain unchanged.*

These concepts are illustrated in Figure 7.51, where the *mask* = %01011101 is ored with the *target* = %11010100 to produce the result %11011101.

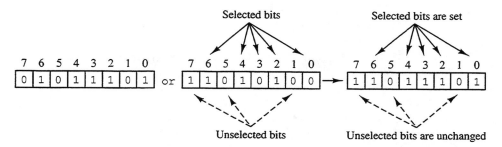

Figure 7.51   Effect of or operator.

Finally, we can see from the truth table of the (Table 7.44) eor operator that when a bit is *unselected* (value of $M = 0$), irrelevant of the value of the corresponding bit of the *target* string, the result will be that this bit will remain *unchanged*.   On the other hand, when a bit is *selected* (value of $M = 1$), the result has the *complement* value of the corresponding bit of the *target* string.   Therefore, the observations made above lead to the following rule:

> *The effect of the* eor *operation on the target string will be that the selected bits are complemented, whereas unselected bits remain unchanged.*

These concepts are illustrated in Figure 7.52 where the *mask* = %01011101 is eored with the *target* = %11010100 to produce the result %10001001.

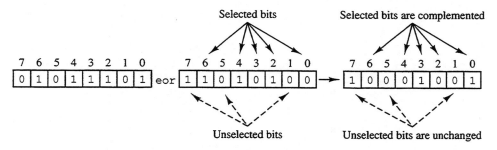

Figure 7.52   Effect of eor operator.

The rules derived above are summarized in Table 7.45 and indicate that whenever a bit or a collection of bits must be set, one employs the or operator. The mask is formed via selecting the bits that must be set and not selecting the ones that remain. Similar observations can be made for the other two operations.

TABLE 7.45   Effect of each of three logical operations on selected and unselected bits of target string

Operator	Selected bits	Unselected bits
and	Unchanged	Reset
or	Set	Unchanged
eor	Complemented	Unchanged

The AND operation. MC68000 provides us with the and operation. According to our convention, the source operand always represents the mask, whereas the destination operand always represents the target string. The instructions can be divided into two groups: regular operations and immediate operations. No instruction in either of these two groups permits any of the operands to be an address register. Moreover, one can manipulate the bits of either the condition code register or the status register via certain provided instructions.

Condition code. Before each group is discussed, we must state that the condition code is set in exactly the same fashion for all versions of and operations *except* the two immediate instructions in which the destination is either the status register or the condition code register.[28] Specifically, the **carry**, as well as the **overflow**, bits are reset. The **extend** bit will retain its value. If the result is equal to the number zero, the **zero** bit is *set* to reflect this fact; otherwise, it is *reset*. Finally, the **negative** bit is *set* when the result represents a negative integer; otherwise, this bit is *reset*.

Regular operations. This set of instructions is presented in Table 7.46 requires that at least one of the operands be a data register, whereas the other operand could either be a data register or a memory location. An example is provided in Figure 7.53.

Immediate operations. When this type of operations is used, the source (mask) is defined via immediate data, whereas the destination (target) could be a data register, a

TABLE 7.46   and regular instructions

AND operator					
Group 1 : Regular operations					
Action					
and data from source to destination. Size of data is indicated by extension.					
Mnemonic	Opcode	User byte (X,N,Z,V,C bits)	Operands	Format	Length
Data register with data register					
and.b	$C_4	P|M|M|R|R	dn,dn	F1	1
and.w	$C_4	P|M|M|R|R	dn,dn	F1	1
and.l	$C_4	P|M|M|R|R	dn,dn	F1	1
Data register with memory					
and.b	$C_4	P|M|M|R|R	dn,dmem	F2	1, 2, 3
and.w	$C_4	P|M|M|R|R	dn,dmem	F2	1, 2, 3
and.l	$C_4	P|M|M|R|R	dn,dmem	F2	1, 2, 3
Memory with data register					
and.b	$C_4	P|M|M|R|R	smem,dn	F1	1, 2, 3
and.w	$C_4	P|M|M|R|R	smem,dn	F1	1, 2, 3
and.l	$C_4	P|M|M|R|R	smem,dn	F1	1, 2, 3

---

[28] The setting of the condition code for these two special cases will be discussed later.

State before	State after execution of instruction		
	and.b d1,d2	and.w d1,d2	and.l d1,d2
d1 B23F A562	d1 B23F A562	d1 B23F A562	d1 B23F A562
d2 A4D1 68BC	d2 A4D1 68**20**	d2 A4D1 **2020**	d2 **A011 2020**
cc 10011	cc **10000**	cc **10000**	cc **11000**

Figure 7.53 Effect of executing each of the three indicated instructions. Notice that contents of the registers are in hex, whereas contents of condition code are in binary.

memory location, the status register,[29] or the condition code register. The set of all these instructions is presented in Table 7.47.

TABLE 7.47 and immediate instructions

<table>
<tr><th colspan="7">AND operator
Group 2 : Immediate operations</th></tr>
<tr><th colspan="7">Action</th></tr>
<tr><td colspan="7">and immediate data from source to destination. Size of data is indicated by extension. Instruction where destination is status register is a privileged instruction.</td></tr>
<tr><th>Mnemonic</th><th>Opcode</th><th>User byte (X,N,Z,V,C bits)</th><th>Operands</th><th>Format</th><th>Length</th></tr>
<tr><th colspan="7">With data register</th></tr>
<tr><td>andi.b</td><td>02_8</td><td>P M M R R</td><td>$IData_8$,dn</td><td>F8</td><td>2</td></tr>
<tr><td>andi.w</td><td>02_8</td><td>P M M R R</td><td>$IData_{16}$,dn</td><td>F8</td><td>2</td></tr>
<tr><td>andi.l</td><td>02_8</td><td>P M M R R</td><td>$IData_{32}$,dn</td><td>F8</td><td>3</td></tr>
<tr><th colspan="7">With condition code register</th></tr>
<tr><td>andi.b</td><td>$023C_{16}$</td><td>4 3 2 1 0</td><td>$IData_8$,ccr</td><td>F14</td><td>2</td></tr>
<tr><th colspan="7">With status register</th></tr>
<tr><td>andi.w</td><td>$023C_{16}$</td><td>4 3 2 1 0</td><td>$IData_{16}$,sr</td><td>F14</td><td>2</td></tr>
<tr><th colspan="7">With memory</th></tr>
<tr><td>andi.b</td><td>02_8</td><td>P M M R R</td><td>$IData_8$,dmem</td><td>F8</td><td>2, 3, 4</td></tr>
<tr><td>andi.w</td><td>02_8</td><td>P M M R R</td><td>$IData_{16}$,dmem</td><td>F8</td><td>2, 3, 4</td></tr>
<tr><td>andi.l</td><td>02_8</td><td>P M M R R</td><td>$IData_{32}$,dmem</td><td>F8</td><td>3, 4, 5</td></tr>
</table>

Condition code.   We stated earlier that the condition code setting is the same for all and instructions except those that operate in either the status register or in the condition code register. Specifically, the setting of the condition code is dictated by the result of the operation; however, it can also be stated as follows. The bits X, N, Z, V, and C, of the

---

[29] This is a privileged instruction.

condition code register are placed in a one-to-one correspondence with bits 4, 3, 2, 1, and 0 of the immediate data. Whenever one of these latter bits has the value %0 (i.e., it is an unselected bit) the corresponding bit in the condition code is reset; otherwise, it retains its previous value. The following example in Figure 7.54 illustrates these concepts.

State before	State after execution of instruction	
	andi.b #$6d,ccr	andi.w #$26d,sr
sr FF FF	sr FF 6D	sr 02 6D

Figure 7.54   Effect of executing each of two indicated instructions. Notice that contents of status register are in hex.

One more illustration of the usefulness of these instructions can be seen by considering the following task. The processor operates in trace and supervisor modes. The application program requires disabling the trace mode and a return to the user mode. This task is equivalent to the following. Reset the trace and supervisor bits, or equivalently reset bits 15 and 13 of the status register, whereas all other bits retain their values. According to the rules that were derived in an earlier section (Table 7.45), an and instruction should be issued where the only unselected bits are bits 15 and 13. In other words, our mask should be as follows:

$$\%0101\ 1111\ 1111\ 1111 = \$5FFF$$

Because we are operating (according to our assumption) in supervisor mode, we may issue the

```
andi.w     $5FFF,sr
```

to accomplish the desired result.

We must point out at this time that bit manipulation instructions are not only used to set, complement, or reset bits. In addition, they may be used to perform several other tasks. As a simple example would be to consider the situation where it would be desired to truncate a word size positive integer to a multiple of four. Note that this task is equivalent to the resetting of the two low-order bits of the two's complement representation of the integer. Hence, assuming that the integer has been loaded onto d2, the only instruction needed to accomplish this task is

```
andi.w     $FFFC,d2
```

OR operator.   MC68000 provides the same exact set of or instructions as and instructions. Moreover, the condition code setting for these instructions is exactly the same as for their and counterpart, except for those of the immediate instructions whose destination is either the status register or the condition code register. This setting is presented in the next section.

Regular operations.   This set of instructions is presented in Table 7.48. As an example, consider the situation as given in Figure 7.55. The first instruction, or, will cause the low-order byte $00 of data register d1 to be ored with the low-order byte of data register d2. The overflow and carry bits of the condition code are reset, the extend bit retains its previous value, and because the result $89 represents a negative integer zero, the zero bit is reset, whereas the negative bit is set. The reader is encouraged to verify the result of the other two instructions.

TABLE 7.48 or regular instructions

OR operator
Group 1 : Regular operations

Action
or data from source to destination. Size of data is indicated by extension.

Mnemonic	Opcode	User byte (X,N,Z,V,C bits)	Operands	Format	Length
Data register with data register					
or.b	$8₄	P|M|M|R|R	dn,dn	F1	1
or.w	$8₄	P|M|M|R|R	dn,dn	F1	1
or.l	$8₄	P|M|M|R|R	dn,dn	F1	1
Data register with memory					
or.b	$8₄	P|M|M|R|R	dn,dmem	F2	1, 2, 3
or.w	$8₄	P|M|M|R|R	dn,dmem	F2	1, 2, 3
or.l	$8₄	P|M|M|R|R	dn,dmem	F2	1, 2, 3
Memory with data register					
or.b	$8₄	P|M|M|R|R	smem,dn	F1	1, 2, 3
or.w	$8₄	P|M|M|R|R	smem,dn	F1	1, 2, 3
or.l	$8₄	P|M|M|R|R	smem,dn	F1	1, 2, 3

State before	State after execution of instruction		
	or.b d1,d2	or.w d1,d2	or.l d1,d2
d1 6BCD F200	d1 6BCD F200	d1 6BCD F200	d1 6BCD F200
d2 008F 7189	d2 008F 7189	d2 008F **F389**	d2 **6BCF F389**
cc 11011	cc **11000**	cc **11000**	cc **10000**

Figure 7.55 Effect of executing each of three indicated instructions. Contents of the registers are in hex, whereas that of cc is in binary.

Immediate operations.   or operations, that have a destination of either the status or the condition code register sets the condition code differently than it would with other or instructions. Specifically, because the setting of the condition code is dictated by the result of the operation, and given our earlier discussions, the rule can also be stated as follows. The bits X, N, Z, V, and C of the condition code register are placed in a one-to-one correspondence with bits 4, 3, 2, 1, and 0 of the immediate data. Whenever one of these latter

TABLE 7.49   or immediate instructions

OR operator					
Group 2 : Immediate operations					
Action					
or immediate data from source to destination. Size of data is indicated by extension. ori with status register is a privileged instruction.					
Mnemonic	Opcode	User byte (X,N,Z,V,C bits)	Operands	Format	Length
With data register					
ori.b	00_8$	P M M R R	$IData_8$, dn	F8	2
ori.w	00_8$	P M M R R	$IData_{16}$, dn	F8	2
ori.l	00_8$	P M M R R	$IData_{32}$, dn	F8	3
With condition code register					
ori.b	$003C_{16}$	4 3 2 1 0	$IData_8$, ccr	F14	2
With status register					
ori.w	$007C_{16}$	4 3 2 1 0	$IData_{16}$, sr	F14	2
With memory					
ori.b	00_8$	P M M R R	$IData_8$, dmem	F8	2, 3, 4
ori.w	00_8$	P M M R R	$IData_{16}$, dmem	F8	2, 3, 4
ori.l	00_8$	P M M R R	$IData_{32}$, dmem	F8	3, 4, 5

bits has the value %1 (i.e., it is selected), the corresponding bit in the condition code is set; otherwise, it retains its previous value.

As one illustration of the usefulness of these instructions, consider the following task. We would like to set all bits in the low and high order nibbles of data register 0; however, all other bits would retain their current value. Recalling the rules that were derived in an earlier section (Table 7.45), an or instruction must be issued where the selected bits are the ones that occupy the positions in both the high- and low-order bytes of a 32-bit mask. In other words, our mask should be as follows.

%1111 0000 0000 0000 0000 0000 0000 1111 = $F000000F

Therefore, the task at hand may be accomplished by issuing the following instruction.

```
ori.l      $F000000F,d0
```

EOR operation.   The only difference between the provided eor instructions vis à vis the set of and and or instructions is that with the regular eor operations set, the source is restricted to being a data register or immediate data. In other words, eor cannot be used when the source is a memory location. Besides this difference, MC68000 provides the exact same set of eor instructions with and and or instructions, which are shown in Tables 7.50 and 7.51. Moreover, the condition code setting for these instructions is exactly the same as their and counterpart except that of immediate instructions whose destination is either the status or the condition code register.

TABLE 7.50 eor regular instructions

		EOR operator Group 1 : Regular operations			
		Action			
		Exclusive or data from source to destination. Size of data is indicated by extension.			
Mnemonic	Opcode	User byte (X,N,Z,V,C bits)	Operands	Format	Length
		Data register with data register			
eor.b	$B_4	[P|M|M|R|R]	dn,dn	F2	1
eor.w	$B_4	[P|M|M|R|R]	dn,dn	F2	1
eor.l	$B_4	[P|M|M|R|R]	dn,dn	F2	1
		Data register with memory			
eor.b	$B_4	[P|M|M|R|R]	dn,dmem	F2	1, 2, 3
eor.w	$B_4	[P|M|M|R|R]	dn,dmem	F2	1, 2, 3
eor.l	$B_4	[P|M|M|R|R]	dn,dmem	F2	1, 2, 3

Specifically, and to make a direct analogy with the andi and ori counterparts, the bits X, N, Z, V, and C of the condition code register are placed in a one-to-one correspondence with bits 4, 3, 2, 1, and 0 of the immediate data. Whenever one of those latter bits has the value %1, the corresponding bit in the condition code is complemented; otherwise, it retains its previous value. The following example in Figure 7.56 illustrates these concepts.

TABLE 7.51 eor immediate instructions

		EOR operator Group 2 : Immediate operations			
		Action			
		Exclusive or data from source to destination. Size of data is indicated by extension.			
Mnemonic	Opcode	User byte (X,N,Z,V,C bits)	Operands	Format	Length
		With data register			
eori.b	$0A_8	[P|M|M|R|R]	$IData_8$,dn	F8	2
eori.w	$0A_8	[P|M|M|R|R]	$IData_{16}$,dn	F8	2
eori.l	$0A_8	[P|M|M|R|R]	$IData_{32}$,dn	F8	3
		With condition code register			
eori.b	$0A3C6	[4|3|2|1|0]	IData,ccr	F14	2
		With status register			
eori.w	$0A7C6	[4|3|2|1|0]	$IData_{16}$,sr	F14	2
		With memory			
eori.b	$0A_8	[P|M|M|R|R]	$IData_8$,dmem	F8	2, 3, 4
eori.w	$0A_8	[P|M|M|R|R]	$IData_{16}$,dmem	F8	2, 3, 4
eori.l	$0A_8	[P|M|M|R|R]	$IData_{32}$,dmem	F8	3, 4, 5

State before	State after execution of instruction	
	eori.b #$35,ccr	eori.w #$5635,sr
sr	A1 61	sr	A1 54	sr	**F7** **54**

Figure 7.56   Effect of executing each of two indicated instructions. Notice that contents of status register are in hex.

NOT operator.   This operation is a unary operation; therefore, only one operand is required. As Table 7.52 illustrates, MC68000 permits the operand to be either a data register or a memory location. Execution of this instruction causes each bit of the target destination to be complemented.

TABLE 7.52   not instructions

NOT operator					
Action					
Not indicated data. Size of data is indicated by extension.					
Mnemonic	Opcode	User byte (X,N,Z,V,C bits)	Operands	Format	Length
Data register					
not.b	$46₈	P M M R R	dn	F8	1
not.w	$46₈	P M M R R	dn	F8	1
not.l	$46₈	P M M R R	dn	F8	1
Memory					
not.b	$46₈	P M M R R	dmem	F8	1, 2, 3
not.w	$46₈	P M M R R	dmem	F8	1, 2, 3
not.l	$46₈	P M M R R	dmem	F8	1, 2, 3

The condition code is set in exactly the same fashion as it is for the regular operations of the and, or and eor instructions. Specifically, the Carry, as well as the Overflow, bits are reset. The Extend bit retains its value. If the result is equal to the number zero, then the Zero bit is *set* to reflect this fact; otherwise, it is *reset*. Finally, the Negative bit is *set* when the result represents a negative integer; otherwise, this bit is *reset*.   The following example in Figure 7.57 illustrates these concepts.

State before	State after execution of instruction		
	not.b d1	not.w d1	not.l d1
d1	2B86 A7FF	d1	2B86 A7**00**	d1	2B86 **5800**	d1	**D479 5800**
cc	10011	cc	10**100**	cc	1**0000**	cc	**11000**

Figure 7.57   Effect of executing each of three indicated instructions. Notice that contents of registers are in hex, whereas contents of condition code are in binary.

Shifts.   We saw earlier how one can manipulate and alter a collection of bits via logical operations. Now we will study two classes of instructions, the *shift* and *rotate* instructions, which were designed so that one may "move" bit patterns about. Also, there are some other welcomed side effects of these instructions, which if one employs, will lead to more elegant code and programs that run faster.

Even though the discussion of rotate instructions is deferred to a later section, we should state some general rules that govern the execution of both of these classes of instructions.

1. All shifts/rotations take place in either a data register or in a memory location.
2. The *count* of a shift/rotation is a nonnegative integer that indicates the number of bits that a pattern must be shifted/rotated left or right. The following rules govern the permissible values for the count:
   a. If the pattern that must be shifted/rotated resides in a memory location, then it is assumed that
      i.   The size of the data is a word (therefore the location is a word boundary).
      ii. The count of the shift/rotation is *one*.
   b. If the pattern that must be shifted/rotated is in a data register then
      i.   The size of the data may be a byte, word, or a longword.
      ii. The count of the shift/rotation is between 0 and 63. Moreover, the count can be specified either *explicitly* or *implicitly*. In the former case, the count is specified as immediate data in the operand of the instruction, whereas in the latter case, the value of the count can be placed into a data register.

The class of shift instructions that we are ready to discuss is divided into two categories, the *arithmetic* and *logical* shifts. Moreover, each of these categories is further divided into two group of instructions, the *left* and *right* shifts. Hence, we can distinguish between *arithmetic left shifts* (**ALS**) instructions, *arithmetic right shifts* (**ARS**) instructions, *logical left shifts* (**LLS**) instructions, and *logical right shifts* (**LRS**) instructions.

We begin our discussion with arithmetic shifts.

Arithmetic Shifts.   The MC68000 instructions that perform arithmetic left and right shifts are presented in Tables 7.53 and 7.54, respectively. Moreover, note that each category consists of two groups: the instructions that perform register shifts and one instruction that performs memory shifts.

To visualize the effect of the left arithmetic shifts, consider the instruction

```
asl.b    #3,d2
```

and assume that immediately before this instruction is executed both the extend and carry bit of the condition code are reset and that the contents of the low-order byte of data register d2 are $AA. Figure 7.58 illustrates the step-by-step execution of this instruction. During the first shift, the most significant bit, %1, is shifted out and is fed into both the carry and extend bits; the remaining bits are shifted one position to the left. This leaves a vacated position, bit number 0, where a bit of value %0 is inserted. During the second shift this process is repeated. The most significant bit, %0, is shifted out and is fed into both the carry and extend bits; the remaining bits are shifted one position to the left. This leaves a vacated position, bit number 0, where a bit of value %0 is inserted. Finally, the process is repeated once more.

TABLE 7.53   `asl` immediate instructions

Arithmetic left shifts

Group 1: Data register shifts

Explicit count

Action

Arithmetically left shift contents of indicated data register by count ranging between 1 and 8, as indicated by the $IData_3$ field.

Mnemonic	Opcode	User byte (X,N,Z,V,C bits)	Operands	Format	Length
asl.b	74_7	M M M M M	$IData_3$,dn	F18	1
asl.w	$ 74_7$	M M M M M	$IData_3$,dn	F18	1
asl.l	$ 74_7$	M M M M M	$Data_3$,dn	F18	1

Implicit count

Action

Arithmetically left shift contents of the indicated data register by count ranging between 0 and 63, as indicated by the contents (modulo 64) of data register Dm field.

Mnemonic	Opcode	User byte (X,N,Z,V,C bits)	Operands	Format	Length
asl.b	74_7	M M M M M	dm, dn	F18	1
asl.w	74_7	M M M M M	dm, dn	F18	1
asl.l	74_7	M M M M M	dm, dn	F18	1

Group 2 : Memory (word) shifts

Action

Arithmetically left shift word indicated by memory address *dmem* by 1 bit.

Mnemonic	Opcode	User byte (X,N,Z,V,C bits)	Operands	Format	Length
asl	387_{10}	M M M M M	dmem	F16	1, 2, 3

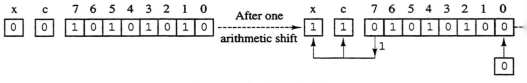

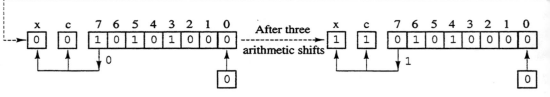

Figure 7.58   Effect of arithmetic left shift with a count of three.

TABLE 7.54 `asr` instructions

Arithmetic right shifts					

Group 1: Data register shifts					

Explicit count					

Action					

Arithmetically right shift contents of indicated data register by count ranging between 1 and 8, as indicated by $IData_3$ field.

Mnemonic	Opcode	User byte (X,N,Z,V,C bits)	Operands	Format	Length
asr.b	$70_7	M M M M M	$IData_3$,dn	F18	1
asr.w	$70_7	M M M M M	$IData_3$,dn	F18	1
asr.l	$70_7	M M M M M	$IData_3$,dn	F18	1

Implicit count					

Action					

Arithmetically right shift contents of indicated data register by count ranging between 0 and 63, as indicated by contents (modulo 64) of data register Dm field.

Mnemonic	Opcode	User byte (X,N,Z,V,C bits)	Operands	Format	Length
asr.b	$70_7	M M M M M	dm, dn	F18	1
asr.w	$70_7	M M M M M	dm, dn	F18	1
asr.l	$70_7	M M M M M	dm, dn	F18	1

Group 2 : Memory (word) shifts					

Action					

Arithmetically right shift word indicated by memory address dmem by 1 bit.

Mnemonic	Opcode	User byte (X,N,Z,V,C bits)	Operands	Format	Length
asr	$383_{10}	M M M M	dmem	F16	1, 2, 3

The preceding discussion can be summarized more formally by indicating what effect execution of **left arithmetic shift** instructions has on the other bits of the condition code. In the following discussion, we will assume that the shift count is denoted by n.[30]

1. The leftmost n bits are lost.
2. The value of the last bit shifted out of the sign bit position is inserted into the carry and extend bit of the condition code. If the count is equal to zero, the carry bit is reset and the extend bit retains its previous value.
3. If *during* the shift, the value of the bit in the sign bit position is different than the sign-bit of the number that was initially shifted, the overflow bit is set to reflect this fact. Otherwise, the overflow bit is reset.

---

[30] Recall that in the case of a memory shift, the value of n is either 0 or 1.

4. The rightmost n bit vacated positions are replaced by zeros.

5. The zero and negative bits are set to indicate whether the result is negative, positive, or zero.

The effect of right arithmetic shifts, can be seen by tracing the execution of the instruction

```
asr.b    #3,d2
```

and by assuming the same initial conditions as in the example given earlier. Thus, assume that immediately before this instruction is executed, both the extend and carry bit of the condition code are reset and that the contents of the low-order byte of data register d2 are $AA. Figure 7.59 illustrates the step-by-step execution of this instruction. During the first shift, the least significant bit, %0, is shifted out and is fed into both the carry and extend bits; the remaining bits are shifted one position to the right. This leaves the most significant bit position vacated where a copy of the sign-bit, %1, can be inserted.

The process just previously discussed is repeated two more times to obtain the result given in Figure 7.59.

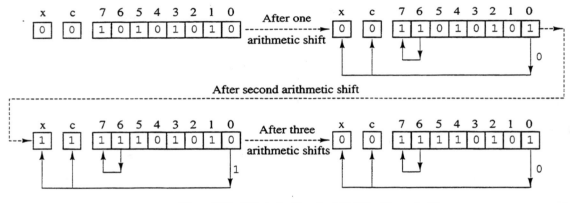

Figure 7.59   Effect of arithmetic right shift with count of three.

The effect of execution of **right arithmetic shift** instructions is more formally summarized below. Again, assume that the shift count is denoted by n.[31]

1. The rightmost n bits are lost.

2. The value of the last bit shifted out from the least significant bit position is inserted into the carry and extend bit of the condition code. If the count is equal to zero, the carry bit is reset, whereas the extend bit retains its previous value.

3. The overflow bit is reset.

4. The leftmost n bit vacated positions are replaced by a copy of the most significant bit.

5. The zero and negative bits are set to indicate whether the result was negative, positive, or zero.

---

[31] When a memory shift occurs, the value of n is either 0 or 1.

Logical shifts.   Each instruction that performs an arithmetic shift, either left or right, has a corresponding instruction that performs a logical shift. Despite this fact, for the sake of completeness, the MC68000 instructions that perform left and right logical shifts are presented in Tables 7.55 and 7.56, respectively. Execution of left logical shifts is performed in exactly the same fashion as arithmetic left shifts, except that the overflow bit is always cleared. The rationale behind this difference is that when one deals with arithmetic shifts, the patterns are assumed to represent two's complement representations; therefore, the sign bit is important. On the other hand, logical shifts treat the patterns as though they were representing characters; therefore, the sign bit has no special significance. In other words, the sign bit is treated like any other bit in the pattern. Figure 7.60 illustrates the effect of executing the instruction

```
lsl.b    #3,d1
```

to the low-order byte of data register d2. During each shift the most significant bit is shifted out and is fed into both the carry and the extend bits; the remaining bits are shifted

TABLE 7.55 lsl instructions

Logical left shifts					
Group 1: Data register shifts					
Explicit count					
Action					
Logically left shift contents of indicated data register by count ranging between 1 and 8, as indicated by $IData_3$ field.					
Mnemonic	Opcode	User byte (X,N,Z,V,C bits)	Operands	Format	Length
lsl.b	$75_7	M M M R M	$IData_3$,dn	F18	1
lsl.w	$75_7	M M M R M	$IData_3$,dn	F18	1
lsl.l	$75_7	M M M R M	$IData_3$,dn	F18	1
Implicit count					
Action					
Logically left shift contents of indicated data register by count ranging between 0 and 63, as indicated by contents (modulo 64) of data register Dm field.					
Mnemonic	Opcode	User byte (X,N,Z,V,C bits)	Operands	Format	Length
lsl.b	$75_7	M M M R M	dm,dn	F18	1
lsl.w	$75_7	M M M R M	dm,dn	F18	1
lsl.l	$75_7	M M M R M	dm,dn	F18	1
Group 2 : Memory (word) shifts					
Action					
Logically left shift word indicated by memory address *dmem* by 1 bit.					
Mnemonic	Opcode	User byte (X,N,Z,V,C bits)	Operands	Format	Length
lsl	$38F_{10}	M M M R M	dmem	F16	1, 2, 3

TABLE 7.56 `lsr` instructions

Logical right shifts					

Group 1: Data register shifts					

Explicit count					

Action

Logically right shift contents of indicated data register by count ranging between 1 and 8, as indicated by $IData_3$ field.

Mnemonic	Opcode	User byte (X,N,Z,V,C bits)	Operands	Format	Length
lsr.b	$71_7	M M M R M	$IData_3$,dn	F18	1
lsr.w	$71_7	M M M R M	$IData_3$,dn	F18	1
lsr.l	$71_7	M M M R M	$IData_3$,dn	F18	1

Implicit count					

Action

Logically right shift contents of indicated data register by count ranging between 0 and 63, as indicated by contents (modulo 64) of data register Dm field.

Mnemonic	Opcode	User byte (X,N,Z,V,C bits)	Operands	Format	Length
lsr.b	$71_7	M M M R M	dm,dn	F18	1
lsr.w	$71_7	M M M R M	dm,dn	F18	1
lsr.l	$71_7	M M M R M	dm,dn	F18	1

Group 2 : Memory (word) shifts					

Action

Logically right shift word indicated by memory address dmem by 1 bit.

Mnemonic	Opcode	User byte (X,N,Z,V,C bits)	Operands	Format	Length
lsr	$38B_{10}	M M M R M	dmem	F16	1, 2, 3

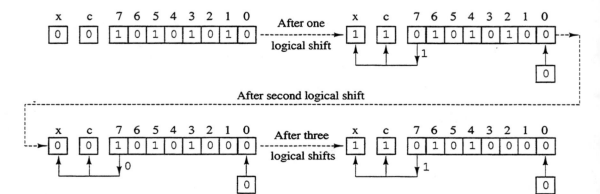

Figure 7.60　Effect of logical left shift with count of three.

one position to the left. This leaves a vacated position at the least significant bit where a bit of value %0 is inserted. If one should compare the result of execution of the instruction lsl.b #3,d1 that appears in Figure 7.60 vis à vis that of instruction asl.b #3,d1 that appears in Figure 7.58, he or she will arrive at the conclusion that the effect of both instructions in the pattern is the same. The only difference (that is not shown) is that the overflow bit for the former instruction has been reset, whereas for the latter instruction it has been set. As a matter of fact, if the pattern represented a non-negative integer, then the results relative to the pattern, as well as the condition code setting would have been *exactly* the same.

Right logical shifts differ from their arithmetic counterparts in one respect. Namely, during arithmetic shifts the leftmost vacated positions are filled with copies of the sign bit value; in logical shifts, the vacated positions are filled with zeroes.

Figure 7.61 illustrates the step-by-step execution of the instruction

$$\text{lsr.b} \quad \text{#3,d1}$$

During each shift the least significant bit is shifted out and is fed into both the carry and the extend bits; the remaining bits are shifted one position to the right. This leaves the most significant bit vacated, where a bit value of %0 is inserted. Notice that the results are identical when the bit pattern represents a nonnegative integer.

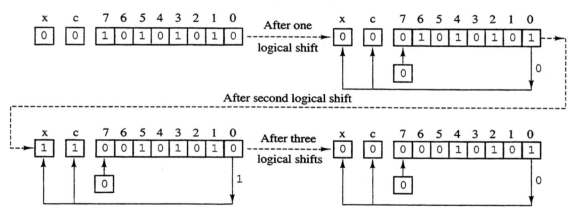

Figure 7.61   Effect of logical right shift with count of three.

Examples

Consider the following declarations:

```
data            org         $1000
Bit1            ds.b        1
Bit2            ds.b        1
```

Bit1 and Bit2 contents represent two nonnegative integers in the range 0 to 15 that are computed at run time. We will demonstrate the piece of code required to set (at the *same time*) the two bits, Bit1 and Bit2, of the low-order word of data register 0.

The first task is to build a mask of word size where the bit positions corresponding to the contents of Bit1 and Bit2 are set, whereas all other bits are reset. To do this, we begin with a pattern of the form $8000. Two distinct logical shifts to this pattern are performed so that the first shift produces a mask in which the only bit set will be the one corresponding to the contents of Bit1, whereas the second shift produces a mask where the only bit set will be the one corresponding to the contents of Bit2. Finally, these two masks are ored to produce the desired mask. The following code performs this task.

```
. . . . . .        . . . . . . . .
move.w       #$8000,d1       ; d1.w has $8000
move.w       d1,d2           ; d2.w has $8000
clr.l        d3              ; d3.l has 0
clr.l        d4              ; d4.l has 0
move.l       #15,d3          ; d3 has 15
sub.b        Bit1,d3         ; d3 has the count for the first shift
move.b       #15,d4          ; d4 has 15
sub.b        Bit2,d4         ; d4 has the count for the second shift
lsr.w        d3,d1           ; Bit1 bit position is set
lsr.w        d4,d2           ; Bit2 bit position is set
or.w         d1,d2           ; bits at Bit1 and Bit2 positions are set
. . . . .        . . . . . .
```

$\rightarrow$

To set the bits at the Bit1 and Bit2 positions of d0, the instruction

```
or.w         d2,d0
```

should be inserted in the position marked by the arrow ($\rightarrow$) in the preceding code. If the problem were to invert (complement) these 2 bits of d0, one would have to use an appropriate mask string and then exclusive or it with the target string. In other words, the only difference in the code would be that the last instruction or.w   d2,d0 would be replaced with

```
eor.w        d2,d0
```

Finally, the code required for resetting these two bits is quite similar. A mask must first be built that contains 0's in bit positions Bit1 and Bit2 and 1's everywhere else; then, this mask must be anded with the target string. Hence, this task could be accomplished this task by inserting the following piece of code in the position marked by the arrow ($\rightarrow$).

```
not.w     d2      ; all bits are reset except those at positions Bit1
                      and Bit2
and.w     d2,d0   ; bits at Bit1 and Bit2 positions of d0.w are reset
```

Rotations. The instruction set for MC68000 provides us with a rotate instruction which is the counterpart of each shift instruction; moreover, rotate instructions take the same form of operands as their shift instruction counterparts.

The primarily conceptual difference between shifts and rotations is that during the former, bits that were shifted out were lost, whereas, during rotations, bits are shifted out, *but* they are not lost. Instead, they are fed back to the other end into the vacated positions. For that reason, rotations may be thought of as circular shifts.

The class of rotation instructions is divided into two categories: *simple* and *extended* rotations. Moreover, each of these categories is further divided into two group of instructions: *left* and *right* rotations. Hence, we can distinguish between *left (simple) rotation* (rol) instructions, *right (simple) rotation* (ror) instructions, *extended left rotation* (roxl) instructions, and *extended right rotation* (roxr) instructions.

Rotations.   The instructions that perform left and right rotations are presented in Tables 7.57 and 7.58, respectively. Moreover, note that each category consists of two groups: instructions that perform register rotations and one instruction that performs memory rotations.

TABLE 7.57 rol instructions

Left rotations					
Group 1: Data register rotations					
Explicit count					
Action					
Rotate contents of indicated data register by count ranging between 1 and 8, as indicated by $IData_3$ field.					
Mnemonic	Opcode	User byte (X,N,Z,V,C bits)	Operands	Format	Length
rol.b	73_7$	P M M R M	$IData_3$,dn	F18	1
rol.w	73_7$	P M M R M	$IData_3$,dn	F18	1
rol.l	73_7$	P M M R M	$IData_3$,dn	F18	1
Implicit count					
Action					
Rotate contents of indicated data register by count ranging between 0 and 63, as indicated by contents (modulo 64) of data register dm field.					
rol.b	73_7$	P M M R M	dm,dn	F18	1
rol.w	73_7$	P M M R M	dm,dn	F18	1
rol.l	73_7$	P M M R M	dm,dn	F18	1
Group 2 : Memory (word) rotations					
Action					
Rotate left word indicated by memory address dmem by 1 bit.					
Mnemonic	Opcode	User byte (X,N,Z,V,C bits)	Operands	Format	Length
rol	$39F$_{10}$	P M M R M	dmem	F16	1, 2, 3

Rotations may be visualized as circular shifts. Consider the instruction

```
rol.b    #3,d2
```

and assume that immediately before this instruction is executed the carry bit of the condition code is reset and that the contents of the low order byte of data register d2 are $AA. Figure 7.62 illustrates the step-by-step execution of this instruction. During the first rotation, all bits are shifted one position to the left. The most significant bit, %1, that was shifted out initially is fed into both the carry bit and the vacated position (bit position 0). During the second rotation, this process is repeated. All bits are shifted one position to the left. The most significant bit, %0, which was shifted out, is fed into both the carry bit and the vacated position (bit position 0).

TABLE 7.58   `ror` instructions

Right rotations					
Group 1: Data register rotations					
Explicit count					
Action					

Rotate right contents of indicated data register by count ranging between 1 and 8, as indicated by $IData_3$ field.

Mnemonic	Opcode	User byte (X,N,Z,V,C bits)	Operands	Format	Length
ror.b	73_7	P | M | M | R | M	$IData_3$, dn	F18	1
ror.w	73_7	P | M | M | R | M	$IData_3$, dn	F18	1
ror.l	73_7	P | M | M | R | M	$IData_3$, dn	F18	1

Implicit count					
Action					

Rotate right contents of indicated data register by count ranging between 0 and 63, as indicated by contents (modulo 64) of data register dm field.

ror.b	73_7	P | M | M | R | M	dm, dn	F18	1
ror.w	73_7	P | M | M | R | M	dm, dn	F18	1
ror.l	73_7	P | M | M | R | M	dm, dn	F18	1

Group 2 : Memory (word) rotations					
Action					

Rotate right word indicated by memory address dmem by 1 bit.

Mnemonic	Opcode	User byte (X,N,Z,V,C bits)	Operands	Format	Length
ror	$39B_{10}$	P | M | M | R | M	dmem	F16	1, 2, 3

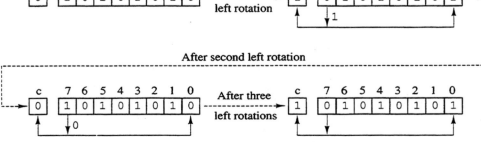

Figure 7.62   Effect of left rotation with count of three.

We can summarize the preceding discussion more formally by indicating the effect of the execution of **left rotation** by a count of n as follows:

1. The leftmost n bits are replacing the n rightmost vacated positions.
2. The value of the last bit shifted out of the sign bit position is inserted into the carry bit, whereas the overflow bit is reset. If the count is equal to zero, the carry bit is reset. The extend bit retains its previous value.
3. The negative and zero bits are set or reset in the usual fashion so that they reflect the value of the result.

The effect right rotations have on a bit pattern, as well as on the condition code, is identical to that of left rotations, except that a right rotation causes the least significant bit to be shifted out and to be fed into both the carry bit and the most significant bit position.

Figure 7.63 provides us with a step-by-step example of the right rotation of an 8-bit string with a count of 3; the reader is encouraged to verify the result.

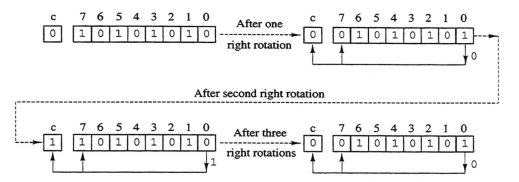

Figure 7.63   Effect of right rotation with count of three.

Before concluding this section, one example will be used to demonstrate the usefulness of several bit manipulation instructions. Our task wll be to convert the eight-hex digit representation of the integer that has been loaded into register d1 to its equivalent ASCII string representation and to store it into memory starting at the location pointed to by register a0. If the contents of register d1 were $000F2A00, we should store at the location pointed to by a0 the ASCII representation of the string '000F2A00', which is $3030304632413030. The algorithm is basically a loop that executes eight times. Each time, one hex digit (the most significant hex digit first) is isolated by first moving it into the low order nibble of d1. Then a byte is moved to the low-order byte of d2 where the hex digit in question can now be isolated by clearing the high order nibble of the low-order byte of d2. The value of the hex digit is now converted to its ASCII representation by using the following technique. A 16-byte table is used whose base address is digits and contains the ASCII representation of the digits 0 through F. Then the ASCII representation of a hex digit say n will be located n bytes from the beginning of the table. Therefore, the hex value of the digit can be used as an offset from the beginning of the table to access its character representation. With this in mind, we present the code in Table 7.59.

TABLE 7.59   Converting hex string to ASCII string

```
      . . . . . .        . . . . . .
; a0 points to a storage area where the ASCII string will be stored
; d1 contains the hex representation

        clr.w    d2              ; prepare to get nibble
        moveq    #7,d0           ; prepare to loop 8 times

loop    rol.l    #4,d1           ; next digit to be converted to low
                                 ; order nibble
        move.b   d1,d2           ; move a byte
        andi.l   #$F,d2          ; isolate the digit to be converted
        movea.w  d2,a1           ; get ready to use the digit as an
                                 ; offset
        move.b   digits(a1),(a0)+ ; get the character representation
                                 ; of the digit
        dbra     d0,loop         ; get next digit
        . . . . . .        . . . . . .

digits dc.b     '0123456789ABCDEF'     ; the ASCII table
```

Extended rotations.   The extended left and right rotation instructions presented in Tables 7.60 and 7.61 differ from simple rotations in only two respects, namely, that during a rotation the bit that is shifted out will be fed into the extend bit and that the vacated position will receive a copy of the *previous* value of the extend bit.

TABLE 7.60   `roxl` instructions

Extended left rotations					
Group 1: Data register rotations					
Explicit count					
Action					
Rotate extended left contents of indicated data register by count ranging between 1 and 8 as indicated by $IData_3$ field.					
Mnemonic	Opcode	Meaning	Operands	Format	Length
roxl.b	76_7	M M M R M	$IData_3$,dn	FI8	1
roxl.w	76_7	M M M R M	$IData_3$,dn	FI8	1
roxl.l	76_7	M M M R M	$IData_3$,dn	FI8	1
Implicit count					
Action					
Rotate extended left contents of indicated data register by count ranging between 0 and 63 as indicated by contents (modulo 64) of data register dm field.					
Mnemonic	Opcode	User byte (X,N,Z,V,C bits)	Operands	Format	Length
roxl.b	76_7	M M M R M	dm,dn	FI8	1
roxl.w	76_7	M M M R M	dm,dn	FI8	1
roxl.l	76_7	M M M R M	dm,dn	FI8	1

TABLE 7.60   (*Continued*) roxl instructions

Group 2 : Memory (word) rotations				
Action				
Rotate extended left word indicated by memory address dmem by 1 bit.				
Mnemonic	Opcode	Meaning	Operands	Format	Length
roxl	397_{10}$	M M M R M	dmem	F16	1, 2, 3

Consider the instruction:

$$\text{roxl.b} \quad \#3, d2$$

and assume that immediately before this instruction is executed, both the carry and extend bits of the condition code are reset and that the contents of the low-order byte of data register d2 are $AA. Figure 7.64 illustrates the step by step execution of this instruction. During the first rotation, all bits are shifted one position to the left. The most significant bit, %1, which was shifted out is now fed into the carry bit, and the old value of the extend bit is fed into the vacated position (bit position 0). Finally, the value of the new carry bit is fed into the extend bit.

TABLE 7.61   roxr instructions

Extended right rotations					
Group 1: Data register rotations					
Action					
Rotate extended right contents of indicated data register by count ranging between 1 and 8, as indicated by IData$_3$ field.					
Mnemonic	Opcode	User byte (X,N,Z,V,C bits)	Operands	Format	Length
Explicit count					
roxr.b	72_7	M M M R M	IData$_3$, dn	F18	1
roxr.w	72_7	M M M R M	IData$_3$, dn	F18	1
roxr.l	72_7	M M M R M	IData$_3$, dn	F18	1
Action					
Rotate extended right contents of indicated data register by count ranging between 0 and 63, as indicated by contents (modulo 64) of data register dm field.					
Implicit count					
roxr.b	72_7	M M M R M	dm, dn	F18	1
roxr.w	72_7	M M M R M	dm, dn	F18	1
roxr.l	72_7	M M M R M	dm, dn	F18	1
Group 2 : Memory (word) rotations					
Action					
Rotate extended right word indicated by memory address dmem by 1 bit.					
Mnemonic	Opcode	User byte (X,N,Z,V,C bits)	Operands	Format	Length
roxr	393_{10}	M M M R M	dmem	F16	1, 2, 3

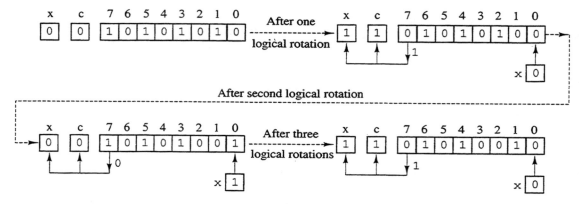

Figure 7.64 Effect of extended logical left rotation with count of three. Note that bit marked by x contains *previous* value of extend bit.

An example of the use of such instructions can be seen by considering the following task. We would like to perform a left logical shift by a count of 1 on the 64-bit string whose high-order 32 bits have been loaded onto d1 whereas its low-order 32 bits have been loaded into d2. Equivalently stated, our problem is to perform a left logical shift of a 64-bit quantity by a count of 1. If a left logical shift of d2 by count of 1 is performed the bit shifted out has been copied into the extend bit. Henceforth, if we follow with an extended left rotate of d1 by a count of 1, the most significant bit of this register would be lost; all other bits would be shifted one position to the left; and, the vacated least significant bit would be replaced by a copy of the extend bit as initially desired. Summarizing, the following two instructions are sufficient to accomplish this task:

```
; Left logical shift by a count of 1 of the 64-bit string loaded in
; d1 and d2

        lsl.l   #1,d2
        roxl.l  #1,d1
```

Figure 7.65 provides one with an example of an extended right rotation. The reader is encouraged to verify the result.

Test and set/clear operations.   Instructions in this group allow the manipulation of a single bit of a pattern or the manipulation of an entire byte. The two classes of instructions that belong to this group are discussed subsequently.

Testing and Setting of Bits.   MC68000 provides a set of four instructions that permit one to examine the status of a single specific bit of a bit pattern by appropriately setting the zero bit of the condition code;[32] it also allows the manipulation of the value of the "tested" bit. Specifically, four instructions available just for that purpose are listed subsequently.

---

[32] Making it possible for this bit to be tested.

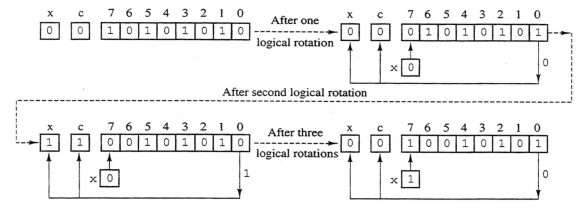

Figure 7.65 Effect of extended logical right rotation with count of three. Note that bit marked by x contains *previous* value of extend bit.

1. Execution of the bchg instruction causes the value of the bit to be complemented.
2. Execution of the bclr instruction causes the value of the bit to be reset.
3. Execution of the bset instruction causes the value of the bit to be set.
4. Execution of the btst instruction does not affect the value of that bit.

These instructions permit the bit position being accessed to be specified either via immediate data or by placing it into a data register. Moreover, they permit the bit pattern to be in a data register or in main memory as illustrated in Tables 7.62 and 7.63, respectively.

In the former case, the bit position could be any of the 32-bit positions; therefore, the position is calculated via a modulo 32 operation. In the latter case the bit pattern is restricted to a byte size; hence, the position of the bit is determined via a modulo 8 operation.

We close this section with the note that only the zero bit of the condition bit may be affected in this case.

TABLE 7.62   Set, reset, complement, and test bit instructions

<table>
<tr><td colspan="6" align="center">Testing and setting bits
Group 1: Data register testing</td></tr>
<tr><td colspan="6" align="center">Explicit bit position</td></tr>
<tr><td colspan="6" align="center">Action</td></tr>
<tr><td colspan="6">Reflect status of bit number (IData mod 32) of data register dn by appropriately setting the Z bit of status register; then, set, reset or complement that bit according to the specific instruction.</td></tr>
<tr><td>Mnemonic</td><td>Opcode</td><td>In addition</td><td>Operands</td><td>Format</td><td>Length</td></tr>
<tr><td>bchg</td><td>021_{10}</td><td>Complement that bit</td><td>$IData_8$, dn</td><td>F16</td><td>2</td></tr>
<tr><td>bclr</td><td>022_{10}</td><td>Reset that bit</td><td>$IData_8$, dn</td><td>F16</td><td>2</td></tr>
<tr><td>bset</td><td>023_{10}</td><td>Set that bit</td><td>$IData_8$, dn</td><td>F16</td><td>2</td></tr>
<tr><td>btst</td><td>020_{10}</td><td>No change</td><td>$IData_8$, dn</td><td>F16</td><td>2</td></tr>
</table>

TABLE 7.62 *(Continued)* Set, reset, complement, and test bit instructions

		Implicit bit position			

Action

Reflect status of bit number ([Dm[31:0]] mod 32) of data register dn by setting appropriately the Z bit of the sr; then, change status of indicated bit according to the opcode.

Mnemonic	Opcode	In addition	Operands	Format	Length
bchg	021_{10}	Then complement that bit	dm, dn	F20	2
bclr	022_{10}	Then clear (reset) that bit	dm, dn	F20	2
bset	023_{10}	Then set that bit	dm, dn	F20	2
btst	020_{10}	No change	dm, dn	F20	2

TABLE 7.63 Set, reset, complement, and test bit instructions

		Testing and setting bits			
		Group 2: Memory byte testing			

Explicit bit position

Action

Reflect status of bit number (IData mod 8) of byte in memory location dmem by appropriately setting the Z bit of the sr; then, change status of indicated bit according to the opcode.

Mnemonic	Opcode	User byte (X,N,Z,V,C bits)	Operands	Format	Length
bchg	05_7	Then complement that bit	$IData_8$, dmem	F16	2
bclr	06_7	Then clear (reset) that bit	$IData_8$, dmem	F16	2
bset	07_7	Then set that bit	$IData_8$, dmem	F16	2
btst	04_7	No change	$IData_8$, dmem	F16	2

Implicit bit position

Action

Reflect status of bit number ([Dm[31:0]]$_8$) of byte in memory location dmem by appropriately setting the Z bit of the sr; then, change status of indicated bit according to the opcode.

Mnemonic	Opcode	User byte (X,N,Z,V,C bits)	Operands	Format	Length

Mnemonic	Opcode	Meaning	Operands	Format	Length
bchg	05_7	Then complement that bit	dm, dmem	F20	2
bclr	06_7	Then clear (reset) that bit	dm, dmem	F20	2
bset	07_7	Then set that bit	dm, dmem	F20	2
btst	04_7	No change	dm, dmem	F20	2

Set or Clear Byte Instructions.   Finally, an assortment of instructions, the `Scc` instructions permit one to either set or clear a byte according to whether or not the condition being specified is true or false. Execution of these instructions that are presented in Table 7.64 does not affect the condition code; moreover, it expects the byte being tested to either be in a data register or in memory.

7.5.5 Decimal Arithmetic

So far we have indicated that integers can be represented internally in their two's complement representation. `MC68000`, as well as other processors, facilitates another representation of integers by using **binary coded decimal** (BCD) representation of each of its digits. A BCD representation of a decimal digit is equivalent to its 4-bit, unsigned integer representation. For example, the `bcd` representation of the digit 7 is `%0111`, whereas that of the decimal digit 3 is `%0011`. An unsigned decimal integer is a sequence of decimal digits; therefore, its internal representation, referred to as the **packed decimal**, is the sequence of its corresponding BCD digits. For example, the internal representation of the integer 190567 will be `$190567`. Note that each decimal digit requires a nibble of storage; therefore, if the decimal number consists of a sequence of n decimal digits, with n being even, then exactly $n/2$ bytes will be required for its internal representation. On the other hand, if the number n is odd, the internal representation is padded to the left with the BCD decimal digit 0; therefore, $(n + 1)/2$ bytes will be be reserved for its internal representation. As an example, the internal packed decimal representation of the decimal integer 19056 is `$019056`.

Finally, **unpacked decimal** representation requires that each decimal digit of a given decimal integer be represented by a *byte*. The high-order nibble of the byte is the BCD representation of the decimal digit 0 and is referred to as the **zone** of the byte, whereas the low-order nibble of the byte is occupied by the BCD representation of the digit. This scheme necessitates that n bytes of storage are required for the unpacked decimal representation of an n digit, unsigned decimal integer. Table 7.65 provides one with a few examples of the two different representations.

`MC68000` provides one with three instructions that permit the *addition* and *subtraction* of two packed decimal integers and also the *negation* of a packed decimal integer. The packed decimal integers that can be manipulated via a single such instruction, however, are restricted to packed decimal integers whose storage requires *exactly* one byte. Before a discussion of each of these instructions is initiated, we should first note that one can take advantage of the predecrement mode and perform multiple precision packed decimal arithmetic of long integers in a similar way as was performed with the extended instructions.[33] Second, packed decimal representation can be used to represent real numbers;[34] with the aid of packed decimal integer instructions, one can perform real number operations and produce high-precision results.

---

[33] See the relevant discussion in Section 7.5.1.

[34] See the relevant discussion in Section 7.5.6.

TABLE 7.64 Conditional setting or clearing byte instructions

Set or clear byte instructions

Action

If condition specified is true, then byte indicated by operand is set; otherwise, it is cleared. If operand specifies data register, then its low-order byte is affected. Opcode of all instructions is $\$17_6$

Mnemonic	Condition	Action	Operands	Format	Length
\multicolumn{6}{c}{**Data register**}					
sf	$1	Set byte on false	dn	F19	1
scc	$4	Set byte on carry clear (if $C = 0$).	dn	F19	1
scs	$5	Set byte on carry set (if $C = 1$)	dn	F19	1
seq	$7	Set byte on equal (if $Z = 1$)	dn	F19	1
sge	$C	Set byte on greater or equal (if $N \cdot V + \bar{N} \cdot \bar{V} = 1$)	dn	F19	1
sgt	$E	Set byte on greater than (if $(N \cdot V \cdot + \bar{N} \cdot \bar{V}) \cdot \bar{Z} = 1$)	dn	F19	1
shi	$2	Set byte on high (if $\bar{C} \cdot \bar{Z} = 1$)	dn	F19	1
sle	$F	Set byte on less or equal (if $Z + N \cdot \bar{V} + \bar{N} \cdot V = 1$)	dn	F19	1
sls	$3	Set byte on low or same (if $C + Z = 1$)	dn	F19	1
slt	$D	Set byte on less than (if $N \cdot \bar{V} + \bar{N} \cdot V = 1$)	dn	F19	1
smi	$B	Set byte on minus (if $N = 1$)	dn	F19	1
sne	$6	Set byte on not equal (if $\bar{Z} = 1$)	dn	F19	1
spl	$A	Set byte on plus (if $\bar{N} = 1$)	dn	F19	1
svc	$8	Set byte on overflow clear (if $\bar{V} = 1$)	dn	F19	1
svs	$9	Set byte on overflow set (if $V = 1$)	dn	F19	1
st	$0	Set byte on true (if always set byte).	dn	F19	1
\multicolumn{6}{c}{**Memory**}					
sf	$1	Set byte on false	dmem	F19	1, 2, 3
scc	$4	Set byte on carry clear (if $C = 0$).	dmem	F19	1, 2, 3
scs	$5	Set byte on carry set (if $C = 1$)	dmem	F19	1, 2, 3
seq	$7	Set byte on equal (if $Z = 1$)	dmem	F19	1, 2, 3
sge	$C	Set byte on greater or equal (if $N \cdot V + \bar{N} \cdot \bar{V} = 1$)	dmem	F19	1, 2, 3
sgt	$E	Set byte on greater than (if $(N \cdot V \cdot + \bar{N} \cdot \bar{V}) \cdot \bar{Z} = 1$)	dmem	F19	1, 2, 3
shi	$2	Set byte on high (if $\bar{C} \cdot \bar{Z} = 1$)	dmem	F19	1, 2, 3
sle	$F	Set byte on less or equal (if $Z + N \cdot \bar{V} + \bar{N} \cdot V = 1$)	dmem	F19	1, 2, 3
sls	$3	Set byte on low or same (if $C + Z = 1$)	dmem	F19	1, 2, 3
slt	$D	Set byte on less than (if $N \cdot \bar{V} + \bar{N} \cdot V = 1$)	dmem	F19	1, 2, 3
smi	$B	Set byte on minus (if $N = 1$)	dmem	F19	1, 2, 3
sne	$6	Set byte on not equal (if $\bar{Z} = 1$)	dmem	F19	1, 2, 3
spl	$A	Set byte on plus (if $\bar{N} = 1$)	dmem	F19	1, 2, 3
svc	$8	Set byte on overflow clear (if $\bar{V} = 1$)	dmem	F19	1, 2, 3
svs	$9	Set byte on overflow set (if $V = 1$)	dmem	F19	1, 2, 3
st	$0	Set byte on true (if always set byte)	dmem	F19	1, 2, 3

TABLE 7.65   Packed and unpacked decimal integer representations

Decimal	Packed	Unpacked
12	12	01 02
8913	89 13	08 09 01 03
18913	01 89 13	01 08 09 01 03

Addition.   The *add binary coded decimal* abcd instruction permits the addition of two packed decimal numbers of 1 byte in length, provided that either both operands are in data registers or both are in main memory. These two versions of the instruction are presented in Table 7.66.

TABLE 7.66   Adding two packed decimal integers

Decimal integer addition					
Action					
Add packed decimal byte from source and byte extended extend-bit to destination.					
Mnemonic	Opcode	User byte (X,N,Z,V,C bits)	Operands	Format	Length
Data register to data register					
abcd	190_9$	E U M U E	dn,dn	F23	1
Memory to memory					
abcd	190_9$	E U M U E	-(an),-(an)	F23	1

Execution of this instruction causes the addition of the byte indicated by the source operand to the (byte-extended) value of the extend bit; the result will be added to the byte indicated by the destination operand. The resultant (byte) replaces the contents of the destination. In addition, execution of this instruction causes the condition code to be affected. Specifically, the Negative, as well as the Overflow, bits become undefined. The Extend bit is set equal to the value of the Carry bit. If a carry is generated during execution of the instruction, then the Carry bit is *set*; otherwise, it is *reset*. If the result is equal to the number zero, then the Zero bit is *set* to reflect this fact; otherwise, it is *reset*.

Figure 7.66 illustrates the result of execution of the addition of the packed decimal number $13 to the packed decimal $85. In Figure 7.66(a), the extend bit is equal to %0; the result is the packed decimal number $98. In Figure 7.66(b), the extend bit is equal to %1; the result of this addition is the packed decimal number $99.

We close this section by presenting in Table 7.67 the code that performs addition of the two unsigned packed decimal integers at locations x and y, respectively (whose length [in decimal digits] does not exceed 80); the result is stored in location result.

Let lengthx be the length of x and lengthy be the length of y. The algorithm, that the reader is encouraged to study, consists of three basic steps. First, the *shorter* number (in terms of digits) is copied right justified in the storage area reserved for the result. Second, the remaining uninitialized bytes of this 80 byte area are cleared. Third, the two numbers are added via the abcd instruction. The algorithm assumes no overflow.

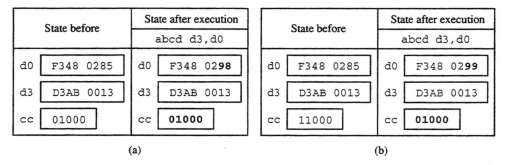

Figure 7.66 Memory and register contents immediately before and after execution of the abcd d3,d0 instruction. All contents are in hex except that of the status register, which is in binary.

Subtraction. The *subtract binary coded decimal* sbcd instruction permits one to subtract two packed decimal numbers of 1 byte in length, provided that either both operands are in data registers or both are in main memory. These two versions of the instruction are presented in Table 7.68.

Execution of this instruction causes the byte indicated by the source operand to be added to the (byte extended) value of the extend bit; the result will be subtracted from the byte indicated by the destination operand. The resultant byte replaces the contents of the destination. In addition, when this instruction is executed the condition code will be affected in the same way as it was by the abcd instruction. Specifically, the negative bit, as well as the overflow bit, is undefined; the extend and carry bits are set if a borrow is generated; otherwise, they are reset. The zero bit is set if the result is equal to zero; otherwise, it is reset.

Figure 7.67 shows the result of subtraction of the packed decimal number $13 from the packed decimal number $85. In Figure 7.67(a), the extend bit is equal to %0; the result of the subtraction is the packed decimal number $72. In Figure 7.67(b) the extend bit is equal to %1; the result of the subtraction is the packed decimal number $71.

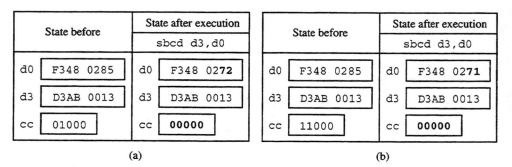

Figure 7.67 Memory and register contents immediately before and after execution of sbcd d3,d0 instruction. All contents are in hex except that of status register, which is in binary.

TABLE 7.67   Adding two long integers via decimal arithmetic

```
; Assumptions : No overflow occurs, and the arguments of the addition
; are no longer than 20 longwords.  The answer is stored beginning at memory
; location 'result'.  All decimal integers are padded to the left by zeroes.
          org    $1000
          move   #lengthx,d2      ; lengthx is equal to the number of digits of x
          move   #lengthy,d3      ; lengthy is equal to the number of digits of y
          cmp    d2,d3            ; lengthy - lengthx = (- if x is larger)
;  d2 will contain the length of the longer number,  a2 will point to end of the
;  longer number,  whereas a0 will point to the rightmost byte of the 'result'
;  where the shorter number has been moved (right justified).
;
          blt.s  xislarger
          bra.s  yislarger

xislarger move   #y,a3
          move   #x,a2
          bra.s  setup

yislarger exg.l  d2,d3
          move   #x,a3
          move   #y,a2

setup     adda   d3,a3
          sub    #1,d3
          move   #there,a0

          move   #79,d4           ; number of bytes to store the result
store     move.b -(a3),-(a0)      ; stores the shorter number in 'result'
          subi   #1,d4            ; one less byte to clear
          dbra   d3,store         ; copy the smallest number into result

pad       move.b #0,-(a0)         ; pad to the left with zeros
          dbra   d4,pad
          adda   d2,a2            ; advance a2 to point to end of longer number
          move   #there,a0

; this loop does binary coded decimal arithmetic adding in memory.

begin     subq   #1,d2
          move   #0,CCR           ; clear extend bit
go        abcd   -(a2),-(a0)
          dbra   d2,go

          move   #228,d7
          trap   #14              ; exit

x         dc.l   $78321567        ; The first number x (up to 160 digits long)
lengthx . equ    *-x              ; Length of x is 8 digits (in this example)

y         dc.l   $13468912        ; The second number y
          dc.b   $78
          dc.l   $78838588        ; Notice the packed decimal representation
lengthy   equ    *-y              ; Length of y is 16 digits
result    ds.l   20               ; Here is the result
there     equ    *

          end
```

TABLE 7.68   Subtracting two packed decimal integers

Decimal integer subtraction					
Action					
Subtract packed decimal byte from source and byte extended Extend bit from destination.					
Mnemonic	Opcode	User byte (X,N,Z,V,C bits)	Operands	Format	Length
Data register to data register					
sbcd	110_9$	E U M U E	dn,dn	F23	1
Memory to memory					
sbcd	110_9$	E U M U E	-(an),-(an)	F23	1

Negation of decimal integer.   The *negate binary coded decimal* nbcd instruction permits computation of either the 9's or 10's complement of a (byte) packed decimal number. This instruction is presented in Table 7.69.

TABLE 7.69   Negating a packed decimal integer

Negating a decimal integer					
Action					
If the extend bit is set, indicated byte is replaced by its 10's complement; otherwise, it is replaced by it's 9's complement.					
Mnemonic	Opcode	User byte (X,N,Z,V,C bits)	Operands	Format	Length
Data register					
nbcd	120_{10}$	E U M U E	dn	F16	1
Memory					
nbcd	120_{10}$	E U M U E	dmem	F16	1, 2, 3

Execution of this instruction causes the byte indicated by the single operand to be replaced by its 9's complement if the extended bit is set; otherwise, it will be replaced by its 10's complement. The result is a packed decimal integer formed by subtraction of the target byte from the packed decimal number 99, in the former case, and from the packed decimal number 100, in the latter case. Execution of this instruction also causes the condition code to be affected in the same fashion as during execution of the sbcd instruction.

Figure 7.68 shows the result of negation of the packed decimal number $13.

7.5.6 Real Number Arithmetic

In this section we will deal with the problem of handling real numbers. A real number consists of an *integral* part and a *fractional* part. For example, the real number 136.7275 has as its integral part the number 136; its fractional part is the number 0.7275. In Chapter 2 we indicated how one could convert an integral part from one base to another; the different methods of the internal representation of the signed integers have also been discussed. In

| State before | State after execution |
| | nbcd d3 |

d3	D3AB 0013	d3	D3AB 0087
cc	01000	cc	11001

Figure 7.68 Effect of executing nbcd d3 instruction. Notice that contents of register are in hex, whereas condition code is in binary.

this section we will first present the methods that permit one to convert a fractional part from one base to another; then, a discussion of the array of possible internal representations of real numbers and their operations will be undertaken.

Converting from one base to another.   All the numbers that we have dealt with so far are implicitly assumed to represent either signed or unsigned integers. The method for handling real numbers involves manipulation of their fractional portion. In particular, the value of the fractional portion of the decimal real number

$$0. \alpha_1 \alpha_2 \cdots \alpha_n$$

is computed as

$$(0. \alpha_1 \alpha_2 \cdots \alpha_n)_{10} = \alpha_1 \times 10^{-1} + \alpha_2 \times 10^{-2} + \alpha_3 \times 10^{-3} + \ldots + \alpha_n \times 10^{-n} \qquad [1]$$

For example, the value of the fractional part of the real number 0.93 is

$$9 \times 10^{-1} + 3 \times 10^{-2} = \frac{9}{10} + \frac{3}{100} = \frac{93}{100} = 0.93$$

Equation [1] is a special case of the general equation

$$(0. \alpha_1 \alpha_2 \cdots \alpha_n)_r = \alpha_1 \times r^{-1} + \alpha_2 \times r^{-2} + \alpha_3 \times r^{-3} + \ldots + \alpha_n \times r^{-n} \qquad [2]$$

that is used to find the *value* of a functional part of a number in radix r $(0. \alpha_1 \alpha_2 \cdots \alpha_n)_r$. As another example, the value of the binary number 0.10011 in view of equation 2 is given by

$$(0.10011)_2 = 1 \times 2^{-1} + 0 \times 2^{-2} + 0 \times 2^{-3} + 1 \times 2^{-4} + 1 \times 2^{-5} =$$

$$= \frac{1}{2^1} + \frac{0}{2^2} + \frac{0}{2^3} + \frac{1}{2^4} + \frac{1}{2^5} = \frac{1}{2} + \frac{1}{16} + \frac{1}{32} =$$

$$= \frac{19}{32} = 0.59375$$

The calculations required for the conversion from any radix r to decimal can be simplified as the following sequence indicates.

Consider equation 2 again. Multiplication of both sides of the equation by r^n yields

$$(0.\alpha_1\alpha_2\cdots\alpha_n)_r \times r^n = \left(\alpha_1 \times r^{-1} + \alpha_2 \times r^{-2} + \alpha_3 \times r^{-3} + \ldots + \alpha_n \times r^{-n}\right) \times r^n$$

or

$$(0.\alpha_1\alpha_2\cdots\alpha_n)_r \times r^n = \left(\alpha_1 \times r^{n-1} + \alpha_2 \times r^{n-2} + \alpha_3 \times r^{n-3} + \ldots + \alpha_n \times r^0\right)$$

Hence,

$$(0.\alpha_1\alpha_2\cdots\alpha_n)_r = \frac{(\alpha_1\alpha_2\cdots\alpha_n)_r}{r^n} \tag{3}$$

As an example consider the hexadecimal real number $\$0.2AB$. Then, in view of equation 3, its value is given by

$$\$0.2AB = \frac{\$2AB}{(16^3)_{10}} = \left(\frac{2 \times 16^2 + 10 \times 16^1 + 11 \times 16^0}{16^3}\right)_{10} = \left(\frac{683}{4096}\right) \approx 0.166748$$

The method analyzed earlier can be summarized in the form of the algorithm presented in Table 7.70 and can be used when conversion of a fraction from base r to its decimal equivalent is desired.

TABLE 7.70 Algorithm that converts base r fraction to its decimal equivalent

```
Convert x=(0.a₁a₂...aₙ)ᵣ to y=(0.b₁b₂...bₘ)₁₀

[1].  Multiply (0.a₁a₂...aₙ)ᵣ by rⁿ
[2].  Convert the integer result (a₁a₂...aₙ)ᵣ of step 1 to decimal
[3].  Divide the result of step [2] by rⁿ
```

On the other hand, conversion of a decimal fraction $x = 0.\alpha_1\alpha_2\cdots\alpha_n$ to a fraction in some other base r can be accomplished via the algorithm presented in Table 7.71.

TABLE 7.71 Algorithm that converts decimal fraction to its base r equivalent

```
Convert x=(0.a₁a₂...aₙ)₁₀ to y=(0.b₁b₂...bₘ)ᵣ

[1].     i = 0
[2].     while [(x<>0) and (error=<tolerance)] do
             begin
                 i = i + 1;
                 z = x × r;
                 bᵢ = integer_part_of(z);
                 x = fractional_part_of(z);
                 error = calculate_error;
             end;
[3].     m = i;
[4].     y = (0.b₁b₂...bₘ)ᵣ
```

The preceding algorithm is quite straightforward. The index i (step 1) that counts the number of r digits is initialized to zero. The loop in step 2 is executed until the number x becomes equal to zero or less than a (user defined) threshold. At each step, the number x is multiplied by the radix r to which the given number must be converted. The integer portion of the result z is recorded; and, its fractional portion is assigned to x. The error that will be generated, if the conversion is terminated at this step, is returned by the function `calculate_error` (whose code is an exercise for the reader); and, the process is repeated. When step 3 is reached, the number formed by the sequence of recorded integer portions (in the order in which they were derived) is the required number.

Example

Consider the task of converting the real number 0.59375 to its equivalent binary representation. In this case $x = 0.59375$ and $r = 2$. The successive iterations are displayed below.

```
number x        base        number z      integer_part_of(z)
--------        ----        --------      ------------------
0.59375    ×    2           1.1875        b₁  = 1
0.1875     ×    2           0.375         b₂  = 0
0.375      ×    2           0.75          b₃  = 0
0.75       ×    2           1.5           b₄  = 1
0.5        ×    2           1.0           b₅  = 1
```

Hence, $0.59375 = (b_1 b_2 b_3 b_4 b_5)_2 = (0.10011)_2$.

The algorithm previously outlined could be illustrated for the sake of convenience in tabular form, as Figure 7.69 indicates.

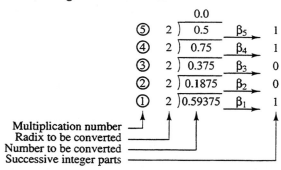

Multiplication number
Radix to be converted
Number to be converted
Successive integer parts

Figure 7.69. Tabular illustration of successive multiplication algorithm. Converting decimal fraction 0.59375 to its equivalent binary representation %0.10011.

Figure 7.70 provides us with another example where a decimal fraction is converted to its hex equivalent fraction. It is important to notice that the result $0.2AAFF is only an approximation. Stopping after the fifth iteration produces an error equal to $0.166748 - 0.166747 = 0.000001$. If greater accuracy is desired, then simply a greater number of iterations must be performed. This loss of accuracy is a common phenomenon when one deals with fractions.

The following general remarks are in order before concluding:

1. The algorithm presented earlier works well even if the fraction under consideration for conversion is not a decimal fraction, that is, this algorithm can be applied whenever the number that must be converted is in any base s given that all operations will be performed in base s.

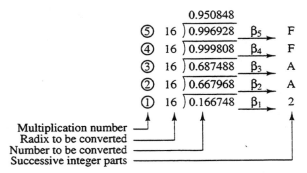

Figure 7.70 Converting decimal fraction 0.166748 to its equivalent hex representation 0.2AAFF.

2. The result is formed by the integer parts of the results obtained after each multiplication (in the order they were derived).

3. The algorithm terminates if either the fractional part of a multiplication is equal to zero or the desirable accuracy has been obtained. In certain instances the algorithm (as in the example of Figure 7.70) does not necessarily produce a fractional part of zero irrelevant of the number of iterations.

Internal representation of real numbers.   The problem that arises with real numbers is how to internally represent their decimal point because its position is of crucial importance when arithmetic operations must be performed involving real numbers. For example, to add the real numbers 1.234 and 254.2 the decimal points must first be aligned before this type of the operation is performed. In the sequence below we discuss three principal ways to represent real numbers; these points are outlined and briefly compared subsequently.

1. *Binary arithmetic.* This method requires that the programmer be responsible for representing numbers in a suitable form, the *binary form*. The programmer also is responsible for providing routines, that will emulate real instructions by using ordinary *integer* arithmetic instructions.

2. *Decimal arithmetic.* Certain processors, as well as the MC68000, provide an assortment of instructions that permit the operation on integers that have been represented internally as decimal integers. A programmer could internally represent the reals as decimal integers and employ these instructions to manipulate these numbers; however, he or she is responsible for keeping track of the position of the decimal point.

3. *Floating-point arithmetic.* Under this method the reals are represented internally in a specific format referred to as *floating point*. In addition, certain processors provide specialized instructions that will perform real number operations.

The commonality of all these methods lies in the fact that in none of these representations is the position of the decimal point represented internally; instead its position is *implied*. In the first two methods, the *programmer* is responsible for keeping track of the position of the decimal point, whereas the hardware keeps track of its position in the third method. Each of these three methods is briefly discussed in the following sections.

Binary Arithmetic.   This method allows the programmer to use only binary integer arithmetic operations. Therefore, when this method is employed, the format of the internal representation of a real number must be suitable for these operations to be performed correctly. Consequently, a programmer must allocate three fields to represent such a number.

1. The sign-bit field, a 1-bit field, stores the sign of the number.
2. The integral part field, an i-bit field, stores the *magnitude* of the integral part of the number.
3. The fractional part field, an f-bit field, stores the *magnitude* of the fractional part of the number.

With this representation, the decimal point is *implicitly* defined. Hence, if a real number must be stored in a longword, then its binary representation must be as shown in Figure 7.71.

sb	Integral part	Fractional part
1	i bits	f bits

Figure 7.71   Binary representation of a real number. Notice that 1 bit is allocated for the sign, followed by i bits for integral part, followed by f bits for fractional part.

As an example, the internal representation of the decimal integer 63.59375 with $i = 13$ and $f = 18$ would be as illustrated in Figure 7.72.

31 30 29 28 27 26 25 24 23 22 21 20 19 18 17 16 15 14 13 12 11 10 9 8 7 6 5 4 3 2 1 0
0 0 0 0 0 0 0 0 1 1 1 1 1 1 1 1 0 0 1 1 0 0 0 0 0 0 0 0 0 0 0 0

| sb | Integral part = 63 = %111111 | Fractional part = 0.59375 = %10011 |

Figure 7.72   Binary representation of decimal number +63.59375 with 32 bits. Notice that 13 bits are allocated for integral part; therefore, (32-13-1)=18 bits are allocated for fractional part.

Earlier we stated that the programmer must implicitly handle the binary point. The following example illustrates how this can be accomplished. Assume a 16-bit representation of real numbers with i equal to 8 bits. Then the representation of 63.59375 would be %0001111111001100, or equivalently $1FDC. Also assume that this number is stored in the low-order word of d0 and that the low-order word of d1 contains $0040. According to the conventions that we have established, these latter contents represent the decimal real number 0.5. Let's also assume that we would like to multiply these two numbers together, that is, to multiply 63.59375 × 0.5 and obtain 31.796875. We issue a muls d1,d0 instruction; $0007F700 will be returned in data register d0, which (longword contents) is equivalent to the decimal integer 521,984. This is what would be expected if the integers $1FDC = 8156 and $0040 = 64 were multiplied together. To get the desired representation of the result, the decimal point must be **aligned**; this can be accomplished by *shifting* the result so obtained to the right by (f) 7 bits. Then, the low-order word of register d0 will contain $0FEE = %0000111111101110. Notice that the sign bit is zero, the integral part %00011111 = 31, and the fractional part %0.1101110 = 0.796875. Hence, the result is equivalent to 31.796875 as expected.

Decimal Representation.   This method parallels that of binary arithmetic in that the position of the decimal point is implied; it is the programmer's responsibility to "align" it properly according to what operation is performed at the time. It differs from the previous method because this type of representation does not require any conversions (i.e., the real number 1234. 565 is represented internally as the decimal integer 1234565); in addition, a greater degree of precision can be attained with no additional effort because, as we demonstrated in Section 7.5.4, decimal integers can be arbitrarily long.

Floating-point Representation. This method is similar to scientific notation where a decimal number such as -1.75 is written as the product of three terms:

$$-0.175 \times 10^1$$

The first term is the *sign* of the number; the second term is the *mantissa* of the number (i.e., 0.175); the third term is the *scale factor* (i.e., 10^1). The scale factor is always of the form r^n where r is the *base* of the scale factor and n is the *true exponent*.

In practice, the base of the scale factor is either $r = 2$ or $r = 16$. The conversion of a number with a scale factor of base 10 to either base 2 or 16 is simple. Consider the real number

$$-0.0175 \times 10^1$$

and assume that we want to convert this number to base 2. First, note that $10 = 1.25 \times 8 = 1.25 \times 2^3$. Hence the given number can be rewritten as

$$-0.0175 \times 10^2 = -0.0175 \times (1.25 \times 2^3)^2 = -0.0175 \times (1.25^2) \times 2^6$$

$$= -0.0175 \times (1.5625) \times 2^6 = -0.02734375 \times 2^6$$

Now, 0.02734375 must be converted to its equivalent binary representation. Following the method outlined in a previous section, we obtain $0.0273475 = \%0.00000111$. Hence, the number can be written with a scale factor base of 2 as

$$-\%0.00000111 \times 2^6$$

The floating-point representation of this number in 32 bits again requires three fields as illustrated in Figure 7.73.

sb	Biased exponent	Mantissa
1	e bits	f bits

Figure 7.73 Three fields of floating point representation.

Assuming that $e = 7$ and $f = 24$, consider the number $-\%0.00000111 \times 2^6$. The sign bit must now be set because the number is negative. Second, the mantissa is equal to 0000011100000000 and can be stored as is. Clearly, however, if five of the leading zeros could be eliminated then future accuracy would increase. In other words, it is more desirable to make the first bit of the mantissa equal to one;[35] this is known as *normalizing* the number. Normalization can very easily be attained by shifting the mantissa to the left by n bit positions where n is the number of leading zeros of the mantissa. Each such shift, however, is equivalent to multiplying the number by the base. This action can be countered by decrementing the true exponent by one. Hence, when a left shift is made by a count of n

---

[35] Unless the mantissa is equal to zero.

the true exponent must also be *decreased* by n. As an example, the preceding number can be normalized by left shift of its mantissa by five positions. In other words,

$$- \%0.00000111 \times 2^6 = - \%0.111 \times 2^1$$

and the mantissa will be %1110 0000 0000 0000.

The remainder of our discussion will concentrate on the representation of the true exponent. In Figure 7.73 the corresponding field has being labeled *biased exponent* because the true exponent is not explicitly represented; instead is represented *implicitly*. One may wonder what would be the motivation for this type of representation. A true exponent can be either negative or positive. Hence, if it were to be represented explicitly, its representation would require the representation of its sign. For example, if the chosen representation was a 2's complement with 7 bits, the size of the true exponent would have been in the range of [−64, 63]; however, the sign would be presented explicitly, which would require special attention during arithmetic, as well as during normalizing transformations. For these reasons the true exponent n is not stored. What *is* stored is the *biased exponent* (or *characteristic*) of the number, which is defined to be the *unsigned* integer $q + n$ where q is a preassigned, unsigned integer equal to 2^{e-1} and where e is the number of bits allocated to the biased exponent field. In our case $e = 7$; hence, $q = 2^6 = 64$. Because the range of unsigned integers that can be stored in this 7-bit field is [0, 127] and because *biased exponent = true exponent + 64*, one can see that the range of true exponents that can be accommodated is in the range of [−64, 63]. This notation is referred to as *excess q-notation*.

Assuming this representation, the biased exponent of our *normalized* number

$$- \%0.111 \times 2^1$$

is equal to $64 + 1 = 65 = \%1000001$. Hence, its floating point representation is as shown in Figure 7.74.

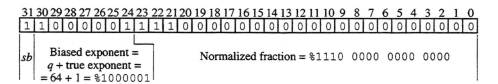

Figure 7.74   Floating-point representation of normalized decimal number +63.59375 with 32 bits and a base 2 for scale factor. Notice that excess-64 notation is used, with 7 bits allocated to biased exponent and 24 bits to mantissa.

This section concludes by noting that a number of computer systems use a base 16 scale factor. The conversion of a decimal number to base 16 parallels what has been discussed earlier. For example,

$$- 0.0175 \times 10^2 = - 0.0175 \times (0.625 \times 2^4)^2 = - 0.0175 \times (0.625^2) \times 16^2$$

$$= - 0.0175 \times (0.390625) \times 16^2 = - 0.0068359375 \times 16^2$$

$$= - \$0.01C \times 16^2$$

Hence, normalizing $- \$0.1C \times 16^1$ is obtained; the floating point representation will be as illustrated in Figure 7.75.

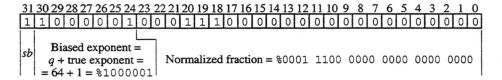

Figure 7.75   Floating-point representation of normalized decimal number +63.59375
with 32 bits and a base 16 for scale factor. Notice that excess-64 notation is used,
with 7 bits allocated to biased exponent and 24 bits to mantissa.

Finally, observe that when the base of the scale factor is 16, the number is normalized if the
first *hex* digit of the mantissa is other than zero.

   With this type of representation, the *hardware* can easily perform the arithmetic operations because alignment of the decimal point can be done by simply "manipulating" the
biased exponents. In Table 7.72 the algorithm that performs the addition of two real numbers r_1 and r_2 with the same sign and with the biased exponents chr_1 and chr_2 and
mantissas m_1 and m_2, respectively, is presented. Recall that when two real numbers are to
be *added* and before this operation is performed, the decimal point must be aligned. This
occurs, if and only if, $chr_1 = chr_2$ (steps 1 and 2). If not, then alignment is accomplished
by shifting the mantissa of the number with the smaller biased exponent to the right by an
amount equal to the absolute value of the difference between the two biased exponents and
by adding this quantity to the smaller biased exponent (step 3). The biased exponent of the
result chr_r is set to the value of chr_1; the mantissa of the result, m_r, is set to the sum of
the mantissas of the two operands (steps 4, 5). If during that addition a carry is generated
out of the most significant digit, the mantissa is shifted to the right by one; the biased
exponent of the result is incremented by one (step 6). The algorithm for subtraction is
almost identical to the one for addition and is left as an exercise for the reader.

   The assembly language code for the emulation addition of two floating point numbers
that was just presented in Table 7.72 is given in Table 7.73. The reader is encouraged to
trace it. As far as multiplication is concerned, the algorithm itself is also straightforward.
First, the mantissa of the result is equal to the product of the mantissas of the operands,
whereas its biased exponent is equal to the sum of the biased exponents of the operands
minus the excess q quantity. Now all these instructions can be emulated by using integer
operations in the same fashion as illustrated in Table 7.73.

   IEEE standard.   Even though all these operations can be emulated, the time required
for their execution is prohibitively high. Therefore, manufacturers provide coprocessors,
that is, another processor that performs floating point operations within the hardware.

Implicit in our previous discussions is the fact that the internal representation of real numbers is not always accurate. Furthermore, even if the representation of two real numbers is
accurate, the result of an operation may not be accurate. In other words, representations of
real numbers almost invariably approximate the real number. The amount they differ from
the exact representation is referred to as a *round-off* error.

   The magnitude of the round-off error is of crucial significance in scientific applications; therefore, numerical analysis techniques allow one to account for this difference.
Those techniques are based on an estimation of the round-off error; moreover, these techniques are portable across different machines, if and only if, they all generate the same
amount of round-off error.

TABLE 7.72 Adding two floating point numbers with same sign

$r_1 + r_2 = r_r$

[1].   diff_chr = chr_1 - chr_2;

[2].   if diff_char = 0 then go to step [4];

{ if biased exponents are not equal, then shift right by an appropriate
  amount the representation of the real number with the smaller biased
  exponent }

[3].   if diff_chr < 0 then
                              begin
                                  chr_1 = chr_1 + |diff_chr|;
                                  m_1 = shift_right(m_1,count=|diff_chr|);
                              end
                       else
                              begin
                                  chr_2 = chr_2 + diff_chr;
                                  m_2 = shift_right(m_2,count=diff_chr);
                              end;

[4]. chr_r = chr_1;
[5]. m_r = m_1 + m_2;

{ if a carry was generated out of the high order digit of the mantissa,
compensate }

[6].   if carry generated
                              then
                                  begin
                                      m_r = shift_right(m_r,count=1)
                                      chr_r = chr_r + 1;
                                  end;

It must be clear by now that for this to occur one must use the *same* internal representation for real numbers and produce the *same* results. Therefore, IEEE has proposed a standard referred to as the *IEEE Standard for Binary Floating-Point Arithmetic* that all machines that conform to this standard[36]

1. Accept the same format.
2. Employ the same rounding mode.
3. Provide the same precision.

---

[36] In addition, the *IEEE Specification for Binary Floating-Point Arithmetic* specifies that such a (co)processor must support the four standard arithmetic operations *add*, *subtract*, *multiply*, and *divide* as well as *square root*, *compare*, *remainder*, and *integer part*.

TABLE 7.73   Adding two floating point numbers with same sign

```
;   The following code is written to emulate the addition of two
;   floating-point numbers (num1 and num2) of the same sign.  The
;   result is stored in memory location 'result'.
;
                org     $1000
                move.l  num1,d2         ; get num1 from mem
                move.l  num2,d3         ; get num2 from mem
                rol.l   #8,d2           ; d2 = chr1 in low byte
                rol.l   #8,d3           ; d3 = chr2 in low byte
                move.l  d2,d4           ; prepare to get mantissa of num1
                                        ; into d4
                move.l  d3,d5           ; prepare to get mantissa of num2
                                        ; into d5
                clr.b   d4              ; clear chr1
                clr.b   d5              ; clear chr2
                ror.l   #8,d4           ; d4 = m1
                ror.l   #8,d5           ; d5 = m2

;   find diff_chr, and store in d2, then branch to appropriate code
                sub.b   d3,d2           ; d2 = diff_chr = chr1 - chr2
                move.l  num1,d3
                rol.l   #8,d3           ; d3 = chr1
                cmp.b   #0,d2           ; cmp diff_chr to zero
                blt     less
                beq     do_m

;   diff_chr > 0, chr1 > chr2
greater         asr.l   d2,d5           ; d5 = m2 = shift_right(m1, count =
                                        ; diff_chr )
                bra     do_m

;   diff_chr < 0, chr1 < chr2, the following code finds the absolute
;   value of diff_chr and uses that to perform operations on m1
less            move.l  num2,d2
                rol.l   #8,d2           ; d2 = chr2
                sub.b   d3,d2           ; chr2 - chr1 = d2 = |diff_chr|
                add.b   d2,d3           ; d3 = chr1 = |diff_chr| + chr1
                asr.l   d2,d4           ; m1 = shift_right( m1, count =
                                        ; |diff_chr| )

;   diff_chr = 0, chr1 = chr2, assuming all proper changes to any
;   numbers have been made this code will add the two mantissas,
;   checking for a carry, and then proceed store the result.
do_m            add.l   d4,d5           ; mr = m1+m2
                btst    #24,d5
                beq     doresult
                asr.l   #1,d5           ; mr = shift_right(mr,count=1)
                add.b   #1,d3
```

```
doresult       rol.l      #8,d5
               move.b     d3,d5        ; put chr in with mr
               ror.l      #8,d5        ; d5 holds end result
               move.l     d5,result    ; store result


exit           move.l     #228,d7      ; exit
               trap       #14


               org        $3000
num1           dc.l       $41E00000    ; floating-point representation
                                              of 1.75

num2           dc.l       $42A00000    ; floating-point representation
                                              of 2.08

result         ds.l       1


               end
```

Two formats have been proposed: *single*-precision and *double*-precision. Both formats use base 2 as the scale factor. The former format, however, employs excess 127 notation, an 8-bit, biased exponent and a 23-bit normalized mantissa. The latter format employs excess 1023 notation, an 11-bit, biased exponent, and a 52-bit mantissa. Both are shown in Figure 7.76.

sb	exp + 127	Normalized mantissa
1	8 bits	23 bits

(a) Single-precision format

sb	exp + 1023	Normalized mantissa
1	11 bits	52 bits

(b) Double-precision format

Figure 7.76 Two formats, single-precision (a) and double-precision (b), as defined by the IEEE standard. Notice that exp denotes the true exponent.

Observe that the range of the biased exponent in the single-precision format is between 0 and 255. The values of the biased exponent of zero and 255, however, *do not* represent the true exponents −127 and 128, respectively, as one would expect. Instead, a biased exponent of 0 represents either +0 or −0 (depending on the sign), whereas a biased exponent of 255 represents infinity or the *not a number* (NAN) as it is otherwise known.

Furthermore, the magnitude of the numbers that can be represented in this format is from 2^{-126} to 2^{+127}; however, the equation $10^m = 2^n$ yields $\log_{10}(10^m) = \log_{10}(2^n)$. Then $m = n \times \log_{10}(2) = n \times 0.3010305$. Therefore, the range of magnitude represented in this single precision format is from $2^{-126} \approx 10^{-37}$ to $2^{127} \approx 10^{+38}$. Finally, one can demonstrate that the precision of a real number represented in this format is up to 7 decimal digits.

This precision can be extended to 11 decimal digits when the double-precision format is employed. In this case the magnitude of the number that can be represented also increases considerably. As before, the values $000 and $FFF of the biased true exponent are reserved to represent the numbers ± 0 and NAN, respectively. Therefore the effective range becomes from 2^{-1022} to 2^{+1023}, or equivalently from 10^{-307} to 10^{+307}.

7.6 EXERCISES

1. Compare and contrast run-time and assembly-time constants.
2. What do the following assembler directives do?
   a. dc.b   'A', 7, $3
   b. dc.w   'Why are lions not aardvarks'
   c. dc.l $25347
   d. ds.b   3
   e. ds.w   4
   f. ds.l   2
3. What do the following assembler directives do?
   a. start   equ $2000
   b. string   dc   'Why are aardvarks not lions? '
             length   equ   *-string
   c. org $1000
             setit   equ   *
4. What is relocatable code?
5. What do the following instructions do?
   a. moveq   #$a2,d5
   b. moveq   #$3E,d4
   c. move   #$1F,ccr
6. What will happen when the following two instructions are executed?
   ```
   movem.w   a7/d3-d7,-(a7)
   movem.w   (a7),d3-d7/a7
   ```
7. What will be the contents of register d0 when the nop instruction is reached?

   ```
                 move.l   #0,d0
                 move.w   #-1,d4
   loop          addq.l   #1,d0
                 dbra     d4,loop
                 nop
   ```

8. Convert the following PASCAL program into MC68000 code.

   ```
   Program BubbleSort(output);

   var a : array [0..4] of integer;
           i : integer;
           n : integer;
   sortflag : boolean;
       temp : integer;
   ```

```
begin

    a[0] := 5;
    a[1] := 4;
    a[2] := 3;
    a[3] := 2;
    a[4] := 1;

    n := 4 - 1;
    sortflag := false;

    while ((n >= 0) and (sortflag = false)) do
       begin
          sortflag := true;
          for i := 0 to n do
             begin
                if (a[i+1]) < (a[i]) then
                   begin
                      temp := a[i];
                      a[i] := a[i+1];
                      a[i+1] := temp;
                      sortflag := false;
                   end;
             end;
           n := n - 1;
       end;

    for i := 0 to 4 do
        writeln(a[i]);

end.
```

9. Hand assemble the code segments

```
count       equ       10
tutor       equ       228
program     equ       $1000
            org       program
            move.w    #0,d0
            move.w    #count,d1
loop        subq      #1,d1
            addq      #1,d0
            tst       d1
            bne.s     loop
            move.w    d0,result
            move.w    #tutor,d7
            trap      #14
result      ds.w      1
            end
```

10. Hand assemble the code segment

```
tutor       equ     228
program     equ     $1000
            org     program
            moveq   #0,d1
            moveq   #31,d2
loop        roxl.l  #1,d0
            roxr.l  #1,d1
clear       dbra    d2,loop
            move.l  d1,d0
            move    #tutor,d7
            trap    #14
            end
```

11. Hand assemble the code segment

```
            org     $4000
string      dc.b    'make me backwards'
strlen      equ     *-string
new         ds.b    strlen
            org     $1000
            lea     new,a1
            lea     string,a0
            move    #strlen,d0
            add.w   d0,a0
            subq    #1,d0
loop        move.b  -(a0),(a1)+
            dbra    d0,loop
            move    #228,d7
            trap    #14
            end
```

12. Convert the following code segment into relocatable code.

```
            org     $2000
            clr.w   d0
            move.w  d0,(a0)
            move.w  $500(a0),d3
            org     $3000
            ds.l    2
            move.l  $504(a0),$3000(a0)
            end
```

13. Convert the following code segment into relocatable code.

```
            org     $4000
num         dc.w    $30
            clr.w   d1
            move.w  d1,a1
            move.w  num(pc),d1
            move.w  100(a1),d2
```

```
                    move.w   d1,50(pc)
                    move.w   8(a1,d1),num(a1)
                    end
```

14. Convert the following code segment into relocatable code.

```
                    org      $3000
    first           dc.w     100
    second          dc.w     200
                    clr.w    d3
                    move.w   d3,a4
                    move.w   first,a1
                    move.w   second,a2
                    move.l   12(a1,a2),1000(pc)
                    move.l   8(pc),first(a4)
                    move.l   8(pc),second(a4)
                    ds.l     2
                    end
```

15. Given the following data, what is the result of the operations on it? If an instruction is illegal, clearly state the reason in one sentence. All instructions are independent of each other.

```
    d0 = $98765432    d1 = $A68B3237   (a0) = $00009802   (a7) = 288
    d2 = $000300FF    d7 = $FF00F2D0
```

```
    a.  and.w    d2,d0
    b.  eor.l    d7,d0
    c.  or.b     (a7),d1
    d.  and.l    (a0),d2
    e.  or.l     d2,(a0)
    f.  or.w     (a7)+,(a0)+
    g.  eor.b    (a0),d7
    h.  and.b    d1,d2
    i.  andi.l   #0378,d7
    j.  eori.b   #49,(a7)+
    k.  ori.w    #%010011101,d0
```

16. What is the effect of the following instructions given the same data as previously?

```
    a.  nop
    b.  ext.w    d2
        cmp.l    #0,d2
    c.  lsl      (a7)
    d.  lsl.b    #9,d2
    e.  lsr.w    d1,d2
    f.  asl      (a7)+
    g.  asr.l    #893,d7
    h.  rol.l    #18,d7
    i.  rol.b    #8,d1
    j.  roxr.l   (a0)+
    k.  roxl     #38,d7
    l.  roxr.w   (a7)
```

17. What do the following code segments do? Note all changes to registers and memory.

```
a.    org      1024
      move.l   #FF00FF00,d0
      move.l   #2,d1
      move.w   #1000,d7
loop  divs     d1,d0
      dbvs     d7,loop
      move.w   #228,d7
      trap     #14


b.    org      $1000
      move.w   #100,d7
      moveq.l  #$83,d6
      cmpi.l   #0,d6
      bge.s    exit
      move.l   #4,d0
exit  move.w   #228,d7
      trap #14
```

18. Given a list of integers of word length terminated by a zero, write the algorithm to find which integers are prime. Turn this algorithm into a working MC68000 program. Use as few instructions as possible.

19. You are to write a small piece of code to take commands from the keyboard and execute the appropriate instructions. You are given the subroutines ReadCH which places the ASCII representation of the character just pressed into register d0. If an invalid instruction is entered, do nothing. Instructions are terminated by carriage returns. Furthermore, you should support only the following commands:

    add - adds d6 to d5.
    load1 xx - loads xx integer into d5.
    load2 xx - loads xx integer into d6.

20. Write a MC68000 program that will determine if any of a set of 10 integers is relatively prime to the others in the set. You need only find if one number is relatively prime. When you find a number that is prime, output it with an appropriate message. You are provided with the subroutine WriteString, which will output a string terminated with a null byte; if you pass the address of the ASCII, string in a0.

21. A number is placed in register d0. If the number has even parity, set the overflow bit; if the parity is odd, reset the overflow bit. Furthermore, if the integer is a negative number, check the parity of its absolute value to set the overflow bit.

22. Using logical operations for manipulations of the data, devise a program that can detect negative numbers and convert them to their positive representation.

23. Write a MC68000 program that will take the contents of a register, all 32 bits, and interleave the bits 2:1. In other words, reshuffle the bits so that the order of the bits is 0,16,1,17,2,18,3,19,4.... Use as few registers as possible.

24. Write an MC68000 program that will scan a file and decrypt it according to a key that is provided to you in memory location KEY. Your program should use the formula $x + x*x - 12x + 83$. If you scan the decrypted file and find the character $11, you should redecrypt the remainder of the file using the next word length integer as the key. When the file is decrypted, output it using the subroutine WriteString described in problem 21.

8

Subroutines and Macros

As is often the case in writing an assembly language program, it happens that a particular segment of code is used in more than one place. Consider the following scenario. We wish to provide a utility that enables us to square the word contents at location x. Clearly this code segment can be very useful in many different situations. Let's assume that we have written the code segment as outlined in Table 8.1.

TABLE 8.1 Squaring
the word at location x

```
move.w    x,d0
muls      d0,d0
move.w    d0,x
```

Let's now define a **subroutine** to be a set of statements that performs a certain task. According to this definition the set of statements in Figure 8.1 is a subroutine. Now whenever in an assembly language program we need to square a word-size integer we can either

1. Use only one "copy" of this code and use it whenever it is needed. Such a subroutine is referred to as a **closed subroutine** or simply a **subroutine**.
2. Include a "copy" of this code at each place it is needed. Such a subroutine is referred to as an **open subroutine** or a **macro**.

After a little reflection, the reader may think that subroutines are preferable to macros because it is quite possible that the code segment that has been written will occupy many bytes of storage. Consequently, every time it is duplicated, the size of the assembly program is increased by the size of that segment. Clearly, this leads to a considerable waste of storage because the code remains the same. As we will see in the following sequence of discussions, however, in several instances macros can be preferable to subroutines. We will begin our discussion with subroutines.

8.1 SUBROUTINES

Earlier the remark was made that only one *common* "copy" of the code is used with subroutines; whenever we wish to use the segment, a *jump* is made to it. Jumping to a common code segment is a simple matter. If the assumption is made that the main program *knows* the address of the first instruction of the subroutine, referred to as the **entry point**, a simple jmp instruction will suffice.

Returning from a subroutine to its caller, however, presents some problems. One should realize that if a jump to the common code segment is made, there is no way to know from *where* the jump occurred, so we are unable to return to the code that was executing before the jump. The solution to this problem is to save the address of the **re-entry point** (i.e., the instruction that follows the instruction that caused the jump and whose address is referred to as the **return address**) before the jump to the common code segment in a known location; this way the common code segment may use this information to jump back to the correct instruction.

The use of a subroutine is summarized and depicted in Figure 8.1. Notice that the main program *calls* the subroutine suba three times. Notice, also, that the entry point to suba is unique; but, the re-entry point (and consequently the return address which is always the address of the instruction that follows the call) *depends* on the call.

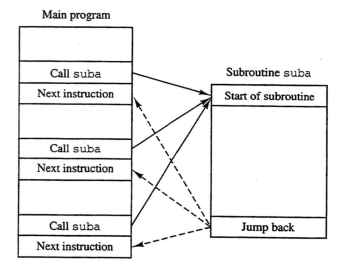

Figure 8.1 Using a subroutine. Notice that entry point is always the same, whereas re-entry point depends on the call.

In Table 8.2 a piece of code is presented that implements the sequence of subroutine calls and returns as illustrated in Figure 8.1.

In the code segment in Table 8.2 the subroutine is labeled suba. It is assumed that this code segment will be executed at three different locations in the main program where each of the jmp instructions is located. Recall that for the program to return to the proper location at the end of execution of the subroutine it is necessary to save the **return address**. This can be accomplished by the instruction of the form move.l #nextXXX, save_return (XXX=1, 2, or 3, depending on the location of the call), which stores the return address in the longword labeled by save_return. We are now free to jump to the subroutine using the jmp suba instruction. On termination of the subroutine, a return is affected by loading the location of the return address into an address register (using the lea save_return, a0) and executing the jump using address register indirect mode (jmp (a0)).

TABLE 8.2   Subroutine calls and returns for Figure 8.1

```
main        equ      *
;
; first call
;
            move.l      #next1,save_return    ; save return address
            jmp         suba                  ; jump to subroutine
next1       ...         ......                ; this is where we will continue
            ...         ......
;
; second call
;
            move.l      #next2,save_return    ; save new return address
            jmp         suba                  ; jump to subroutine
next2       ...         ......                ; this is where we will continue
            ...         ......
;
; third call
;
            move.l      #next3,save_return    ; save new return address
            jmp         suba                  ; jump to subroutine
next3       ...         ......                ; this is where we will continue
;
; Code of subroutine suba, notice that suba "knows" the symbols x &
; save_return
;
suba        equ      *                        ; entry point
            move.w      x,d0
            muls        d0,d0
            move.w      d0,x
            lea         save_return,a0         ; put the correct return address
                                               ; into a0
            jmp         (a0)                   ; return
; end of subroutine
            ...         ......
save_return    ds.l                           ; storage for the return address
```

There are three major points to observe about this code.

1. It is not elegant because a considerable amount of bookkeeping is involved in the establishment of the correct return address.

2. The code is not very efficient because every subroutine call requires four extra instructions.

3. It is not possible for a subroutine to call itself either directly or through a chain of calls. (Why not?)

To remedy this situation most central processors provide a set of several special instructions that make the task of calling and returning from subroutines easier for the programmer and more efficient to run. In the next section, we will examine the mechanisms provided by the MC68000 for working with subroutines.

To appreciate better the mechanisms used to support subroutines in the MC68000, it is necessary that one be familiar with the concept of a stack.

8.1.1 What Is a Stack?

A stack is a list of similar items arranged in a structure so that the last item added to the structure is the first item to be removed. One can make an analogy with spring-loaded plate holders in a cafeteria. As a plate is added to the holder, the plate previously on top becomes inaccessible. We use the terminology of **pushing** an element onto the stack when one is added; conversely, when a plate is removed from the stack, the next plate underneath now becomes available. We use the terminology of **popping** an element from the stack when one is removed.

In terms of assembler structures, a stack is a contiguous block of memory and an associated **stack pointer**, which is a register in the central processor. For simplicity, the elements are assumed to be either words or longwords. The stack pointer originally points to (i.e., contains the location of) the beginning of the block of memory. To push an element on a stack, we first decrement (or increment) the stack pointer. We then move the element to be pushed into the memory location pointed to by the stack pointer. Conversely, to pop an element from the stack, we first move the data pointed to by the stack pointer to our destination. We then increment (or decrement) the stack pointer. Observe that address register indirect with predecrement or postincrement is precisely the sequence of operations performed by the two addressing modes mentioned earlier. Thus, if we assume that a7 is loaded with the high address of the region of memory that we will use as a stack, then the instruction sequence move.l d0,-(a7) will push the contents of data register d0 onto this stack, whereas the instruction move.l (a7)+,d0 will pop it back into d0. Notice also, in this convention, the stack pointer is normally pointing to the *last element pushed onto the stack*; another convention that could have been adopted for the push operation would be to move the element, *then* increment (or decrement) the stack pointer. In this case, the stack pointer would normally point to the *next free location in the stack*. Whichever method is adopted, we must be careful that when pushing or popping an element from a stack, we are consistent. Thus, if the convention is adopted that to push an element, we decrement the stack pointer and move the data, then to pop an element from the same stack, the element must be moved and the stack pointer must be incremented. As we shall see, the stack is such a useful mechanism that *within* the MC68000 certain instructions automatically make use of a stack; thus, a standard convention has already been defined. This convention states that *the predecrement instruction is used to push elements onto the stack*, whereas *the postincrement mode is used to pop elements from the stack*. When using this convention, the stack starts at some high address and **grows** toward low memory. In addition, the MC68000 assumes that one register in particular is used as a stack pointer, namely register a7. Register a7 is referred to as *the* stack pointer, and is given the special symbol sp by the assembler. Thus move d0,-(a7) and move d0,-(sp) are synonymous. Figure 8.2 illustrates the state of the stack pointer and memory through a sequence of pushes and pops.

Referring to Figure 8.2 notice that the stack is initialized to address $1010C and that the stack grows toward low memory. The first instruction (ii) pushes the immediate data #$1234 onto the stack and the stack pointer (sp) points to the address containing this

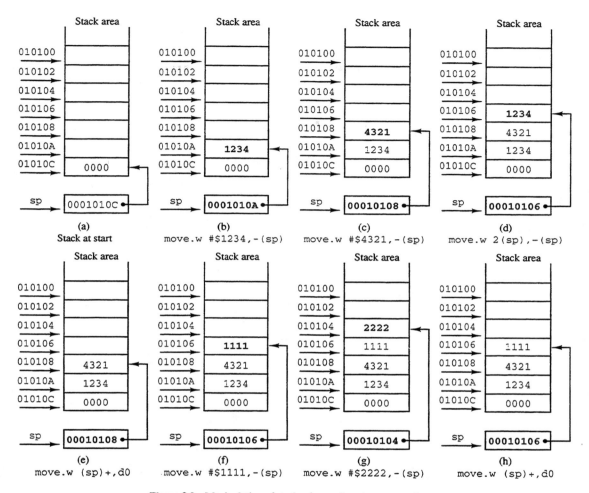

Figure 8.2   Manipulation of stack using push-and-pop operations.

value after execution of this instruction. The second instruction (iii) pushes another value #$4321 onto the stack. The third instruction (iv) exemplifies how elements within the stack may be accessed; in this case pushing an element already on the stack. The next instruction shows how the top of the stack may be popped off; in this case into d0. The final three examples show two more push operations followed by a pop operation.

Notice that during the push operations, the stack "grows larger." Clearly, we must be careful to ensure that there is sufficient stack space for our needs; otherwise, the stack will overwrite some portion of memory that contains other code or data. Notice also that the top of the stack may be accessed directly using (sp).

8.1.2 Calling Subroutines

Recall from previous discussions and with the instructions presented thus far, that the programmer must *explicitly* save the return address *before* we jump to a subroutine. Recalling Table 8.2 again the following two instructions were used for this purpose:

```
; call
;
          move.l      #next1,save_return      ; save return address
          jmp         suba                    ; jump to subroutine
next1     ...         ......                  ; this is where we will continue
          ...         ......
;
          ...         ....
save_return     ds.l                          ; storage for the return address
```

One of the major problems that also arose was that this particular way of calling a subroutine did not permit a subroutine to call itself either directly or through a chain of calls. The MC68000 solves these problems by providing two instructions for calling subroutines; the first is the jump subroutine instruction jsr, and the second is the branch subroutine instruction bsr. Each one is illustrated in Table 8.3. Both perform similar functions because they first save the return address onto the *stack*; then they load the program counter with the start address of the subroutine.

TABLE 8.3

Jump and branch to subroutine

JSR

Action

Jump to subroutine. Address (longword) of next instruction is pushed onto stack; address of subroutine specified in jsr instruction is loaded into pc. Then the instruction pointed to by pc is executed.

Mnemonic	Opcode	User byte (X,N,Z,V,C bits)	Operands	Format	Length
jsr	$13A_{10}$	P|P|P|P|P	smem*	F16	3

BSR

Action

Branch to subroutine. Address (longword) of next instruction is pushed onto stack; byte or word displacement, depending on extension (B, W) is added to the pc. Then the instruction pointed to by pc is executed.

Mnemonic	Opcode	User byte (X,N,Z,V,C bits)	Operands	Format	Length
bsr.b	61_8	P|P|P|P|P	absmem	F21	1
bsr.w	61_8	P|P|P|P|P	absmem	F21	2

The two instructions differ in the way in which the address of the subroutine is computed; and, as you would expect, they correspond to the jmp and bcc instructions.

The jsr instruction takes a single operand which is an effective address. Execution of this instruction causes the longword address of the next instruction to be pushed onto the stack. The effective address specified in the operand of the instruction is then used to jump to the subroutine. Unlike the original discussion (Table 8.2), the return address is not saved in a particular area; instead, it is pushed onto the stack, (i.e., pointed to by register a7). Thus the MC68000 *implicitly uses the stack when calling subroutines*. To complement subroutine calling, we shall see shortly that the MC68000 provides special return instructions which expect to find the return address on the stack. Note also that since the jsr instruction uses an effective address, the address of the subroutines can be specified either as an absolute address, placed in a register, or even placed on the stack!

The second way of calling a subroutine is by using the `bsr` instruction. The `bsr` instruction takes a single operand which can be a label. The effect of this instruction is the same as that of the `jsr`; the difference arises in its implementation. With the `bsr` instruction, a signed displacement is added to the program counter to determine the address of the subroutine. This is either an 8- or 16-bit displacement and is computed by the assembler at assembly time. Because the displacement is at most 16 bits, the start address of the subroutine must be within the range $-32,768$ to $32,767$ bytes from the current position. The advantage in using the branch subroutine instruction over the jump subroutine is that the code is position independent. That is, the branch is relative to the current value of the `pc`; thus, the subroutine may be placed anywhere in memory within the displacement range.

The difference between the `jsr` instruction and the `bsr` instructions is clearly demonstrated in Figures 8.3 and 8.4, which show the stack during execution of each instruction.

8.1.3 Returning from Subroutines

The converse to calling a subroutine is returning from it. Just as the MC68000 provides instructions for calling subroutines, so too it provides two instructions to assist in returning.

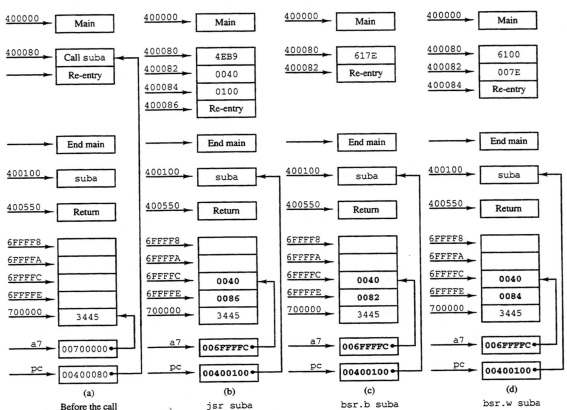

Figure 8.3 Effect of three calls (`jsr`, `bsr.b`, `bsr.w`).

These instructions are the "return from subroutine" `rts` and the "return and restore" `rtr` instructions (Table 8.4). Both instructions pop a longword, the return address (originally pushed by a `jsr` or `bsr`), from the stack and load it into the program counter. This affects a jump back to the calling program. The difference between the returns is that the `rtr` instruction *first* pops a word from the stack placing its low byte into the condition code register. To make effective use of the `rtr` instruction it is therefore necessary to save the condition code registers, as a word, on the stack immediately upon entry to the subroutine. Thus the combination of a `move.w sr,-(sp)` at the start of the subroutine and an `rtr` at the end will ensure that the condition code register is unchanged by the subroutine call. In other words, whatever condition code bits were set prior to the call will be set after completion of the subroutine. This sequence, coupled with the `movem` instruction, permits programmers to perfectly preserve the state of the computer during a subroutine call. Notice that in the event that an `rtr` is used when the programmer has not originally stacked the condition code registers, the low order word of the return address will be popped and loaded into the `ccr`. The PC will then be loaded with the next two words, clearly an erroneous situation! This is demonstrated in Figure 8.4 (c).

TABLE 8.4

RTS and RTR Instructions					
Mnemonic	Opcode	Action	Operands	Format	Length
rts	$4E75$_{16}$	Return from subroutine. Top (longword) of the stack is popped off and loaded into the pc. Then the instruction pointed to by the pc is executed.		F14	1
rtr	$ 4E77$_{16}$	Return and restore. Top (word) of stack is popped off and loaded into sr; stack is popped off (longword) one more time and loaded into the pc. Then instruction pointed to by pc is executed.		F14	1

The effects of these returns are illustrated in Figure 8.4. Note that `rtr` instruction is used erroneously! To better understand how these instructions are used in conjunction with the `jsr` (`bsr`) instructions to call and return from subroutines, in Table 8.5 we present the equivalent of the code given in Table 8.2. Table 8.5 corresponds to a main program and subroutine using the subroutine call and return instructions provided by the MC68000.

TABLE 8.5   Calling and returning from `suba`

```
main       equ      *
;
; code to make call
;
           jsr      suba            ; first call
next1      ...      ......          ; this is where we will continue
           ...      ......
           jsr      suba            ; second call
```

TABLE 8.5 (*Continued*) Calling and returning from `suba`

```
next2      ...        ......        ; this is where we will continue
           ...        ......
           jsr        suba          ; third call
next3      ...        ......        ; this is where we will continue
;
; Code of subroutine suba, notice that suba "knows" the symbol x
;
suba       equ        *             ; entry point
           move.w     x,d0
           muls       d0,d0
           move.w     d0,x
           rts                      ; return
; end of subroutine
           ...        ....
```

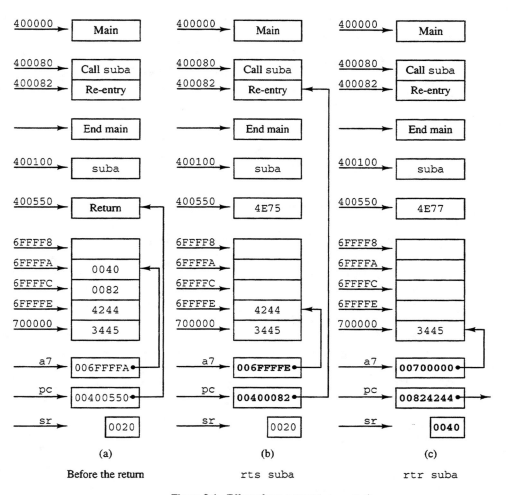

Figure 8.4 Effect of two returns (`rts`, `rtr`).

Notice that we no longer need to be concerned with return addresses; in fact, the labels `next1`, `next2`, and `next3` are unnecessary and are provided only for visual reference. Use of the `jsr` instruction to call the subroutine causes the appropriate return address to be pushed onto the stack. This is complemented by terminating the subroutine with an `rts`, which pops the stack and places the popped value into the program counter. There will still remain some overhead when using subroutines; two instruction delays; however, this is considered insignificant compared to the advantages of a reduction in code size and the development of modular programs. The reader is encouraged to compare these two programs to better appreciate the simplicity provided by these new instructions.

8.1.4 Passing Parameters

Although there are situations where a subroutine requires no data from the calling program, it typically is the case that the subroutine will use data. Consider the example discussed earlier in which the word-size integer at location x was to be squared. Clearly, the subroutine should have access to that location. But, if this subroutine were used, we would not be able to square the word that resides in location y despite the fact that the code required for this task is almost the same. This problem can be eliminated by passing data to the subroutine.

Data that are passed to a subroutine are called **parameters**. In general, a subroutine may require any number of parameters. It is important that the number and type of parameters expected by the subroutine match the number and type passed by the calling program. Clearly the assembler program has no way of checking that the correct parameters have been passed. Thus it is the programmer's responsibility to ensure that the parameters that are passed correspond exactly with those that are expected!

To present the concept of parameters in an orderly manner, we must first define two classes of parameters; **in** and **in-out** parameters. An **in** parameter is one which, to the calling program, is unchanged by the subroutine. Thus a subroutine may **use** or modify a **copy** of the original data; however, it should not change the original data. An **in-out** parameter is one which can be modified by the called subroutine; thus, the calling program may see changes to the data after a call to the subroutine. So, changes to the original data in the subroutine are reflected in the calling program after the subroutine has returned. One final class of parameters which the reader may see elsewhere in other texts is called an **out** parameter. Here the calling program is not expected to provide data as input; but, instead, **out** parameters are used by a subroutine to convey information to the calling program. This is clearly equivalent to an uninitialized **in-out** parameter and will be treated as such in this text.

One effective way of managing **in** and **in-out** parameters is to pass a copy of the data to the subroutine if the parameter is **in**, and to pass *the location* of the data if the parameter is **in-out**. The former technique is called passing an **in** parameter by **value**, whereas the later technique is called passing an **in-out** parameter by **reference**. The advantage of this should be clear. In passing the data by value for **in** parameters, the subroutine only has a *copy* of the data. It is not *possible* to modify the version that is seen by the calling program. Thus the parameter is truly an **in** parameter. Conversely, with **in-out** parameters the address of the data is passed. Thus any changes to this location will be reflected in the calling program.[1] It is also possible to pass **in-out** parameters to a subroutine by value, provided it

---

[1] As we shall see later, for complex parameters such as arrays and strings the address of the structure is passed even if no modification is intended. This results in a considerable savings of space and time.

is understood that the calling program must "update" its version of the parameter after the subroutine has returned. This technique is called passing an **in-out** parameter by **copy-back** and will not be discussed any further.

We now are ready to describe the different ways that are employed to pass parameters. In all the examples that will be presented we will assume that a subroutine `convert` is used whose function is to convert an eight character ASCII string that represents an integer whose base address is `string` to its equivalent 2's complement binary representation. Two parameters are passed: an **in** parameter (the numeric string which is used but is not modified) and an **out** (or **in-out**) parameter (the unsigned integer which is computed by the subroutine).

Using Registers.   The simplest method to pass parameters is to use registers. The calling program places whatever parameters that need to be passed in particular registers and calls the subroutine. Because the programmer presumably knows what he or she is doing, the subroutine will expect the appropriate parameters to be in particular registers. Thus it becomes a simple matter for the subroutine to access the parameters. The code required to perform this task is given in Table 8.6. Registers `a1` and `d1` to pass the parameters.

TABLE 8.6 Parameter passing by registers

```
;
; Main program
;
main       equ       *                 ; start of code
           ...       ...
           ...       ...
           lea       string,a1         ; move the start address of the string
                                       ; to a1
           jsr       convert           ; call subroutine
           ...       ...               ; now result is in d1
           ...       ...
           ...       ...               ; end of code
;
; Subroutine convert
;
; This subroutine converts a string to a signed integer.  Upon return
; register a1 is still pointing to the string and d1 contains the result.
; Parameters:
;    - IN      a1    numeric string
;    - IN-OUT d1    resulting integer
;
convert    equ       *                 ; start of subroutine
           movea.1   a1,a2             ; copy string pointer to a2
           ...       ...
           ...       ...               ; assume result in d1
           rts                         ; return
;
; Data area
;
string     ds.b      20                ; storage for string
           end
```

Using parameter blocks. Another method of passing parameters is by way of a parameter block. Again since a subroutine is aware of the order and type of all passed parameters, the size of the block will be known to both the calling program and the subroutine. From a programming point of view then, the calling program reserves a block of memory in which it stores these parameters. Thus the only piece of information required by the subroutine is the start address of the parameter block which may be passed through a single address register. After the subroutine has been invoked, all parameters may be referenced relative to the start of the parameter block. If the example just discussed is used, we can now show the code using parameter block passing in Table 8.7.

As may be seen from the example, there is some overhead in using parameter blocks as opposed to registers. The advantages in using parameter blocks becomes more apparent when the number of parameters to be passed becomes large. In this case passing by registers is either impossible or becomes inefficient. This becomes clear if we consider that

TABLE 8.7   Parameter passing by parameter block

```
;
; Main program
;
main      equ     *               ; start of code
          ...     ...             ;
          ...     ...             ;
          lea     block,a0        ; move address of parameter block to a
          move.l  #string,(a0)    ; move the string address to the block
          jsr     convert         ; call subroutine
          ...     ...             ; the result is in the block (four
                                  ; bytes offset)
          ...     ...             ;
          ...     ...             ;
          ...     ...             ; end of code
;
; Subroutine convert
;
; Converts a string to a signed integer.  The parameters are passed
; through a parameter block pointed to by a0.
; Parameters:
;     - IN      longword   -    address of string
;     - IN-OUT  word       -    return status code
; The first parameter is left unchanged upon subroutine exit
;
convert   equ     *               ; start of subroutine
          movea.l block,a2        ; copy string pointer to a2
          ...     ...
          ...     ...             ; assume result in d0
          move.w  d0,4(a0)        ; save the result in the block
          rts                     ; return
;
; Data area
;
string    ds.b    20              ; storage for string
block     ds.l    1               ; first param: base address of the stri
          ds.w    1               ; second param: resulted signed integer
          end
```

when all the registers are used for parameter passing, the subroutine will have no registers left to work with! A conceptual view of parameter blocks is given in Figure 8.5.

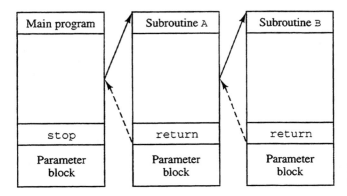

Figure 8.5 Conceptual view of parameter blocks.

Using stacks.   Finally parameters can be passed to a subroutine by making use of the stack. Recall that two of the addressing modes are indirect addressing with predecrement that corresponds to the **push** operation, and indirect addressing with postincrement which corresponds to the **pop** operation. These instructions are ideally suited for supporting the passing of parameters using the **stack** structure.

When a stack is used for parameter passing, the calling program pushes each parameter onto the stack one element at a time. Once all the parameters have been pushed, the subroutine is called. Remember that a subroutine call will also push a longword, the return address, onto the stack. Therefore, any access to parameters by the subroutine will require that an additional offset of four be added to the relative position of the parameters on the stack. Thus if three longword parameters, p1, p2, and p3 are pushed on the stack they will be accessed from the subroutine using indirect addressing as 12(sp), 8(sp), and 4(sp), respectively. Thus the subroutine may then access parameters relative to the stack pointer *as if it were at the beginning of the subroutine* by adding an additional displacement of four. Note that changes to the stack pointer will interfere with accessing the parameters; this problem will be addressed later. When the subroutine has finished, the rts instruction will pop the return address from the stack, leaving the original parameters as they were pushed. Because the parameters are not automatically unstacked by the subroutine, the stack pointer must be adjusted by the calling program after the subroutine has been called. This is achieved by incrementing a7 by the number of bytes that the parameters occupied. Notice also that any **in-out** parameters must first be saved. Using the example previously discussed, we now show the code using parameter passing in Table 8.8. It should be apparent by now, given our earlier discussion, that this method should be the method of choice and should be deviated from only in special circumstances and for a good reason. Clearly when passing parameters on the stack, it is important to make absolutely sure that all displacements are correct. This chore can be accomplished by making generous use of symbolic constants using the equ directive.

8.1.5 Recursive Routines

One of the principal advantages in using the stack for parameter passing is that subroutines may now be called **recursively**. A recursive subroutine is one which may call itself directly

TABLE 8.8 Parameter passing using the stack

```
;
; Main program
;
main      equ       *                   ; start of code
          ...       ...                 ;
          ...       ...                 ;
          lea       string,-(sp)        ; move the start address of the string
                                        ; stack
          clr.w     -(sp)               ; reserve space for the result
          jsr       convert             ; call subroutine
          move      (sp)+,d0            ; since result in (sp) save it
          addi      #4,sp               ; clean up the stack
          ...       ...                 ;
          ...       ...                 ;
          ...       ...                 ; end of code
;
; Subroutine convert
;
; Converts a string to a signed integer.  Parameters are passed using
; the stack.  The address of the string is pushed first, then space
; is allocated for the result.
;
; Parameters may be accessed on the stack as follows:
;     - IN         longword  - string pointer   6(sp)
;     - IN-OUT     word      - signed integer    4(sp)
;
;
convert   equ       *                   ; start of subroutine
          movea.l   6(sp),a2            ; first param (pointer to the string)
                                        ; is at 6(sp)
          ...       ...                 ; second param (signed integer)
                                        ; is at 4(sp)
          ...       ...                 ;
          move.w    d1,4(sp)            ; assume result was in d1
          rts                           ; return
;
; Data area
;
string    ds.b      20                  ; storage for string
          end
```

or is called indirectly via another subroutine. Recall that when using the stack the parameters are *appended* to the stack just beforfe calling the subroutine. Because the data is appended dynamically, (i.e., was not allocated by the assembler), we say that the parameters are **dynamically allocated**. This contrasts with the parameter block which is a fixed area in memory and is therefore **statically allocated**. The advantages of dynamically allocating parameter space is that the subroutine may now call itself, passing to it a new set of parameters each and every time it is called. With the parameters being pushed onto the stack each time, the set corresponding to the previous invocation will not be corrupted, as would be the case with a parameter block.

Each time a subroutine calls itself, additional parameters are pushed. This continues until the recursion terminates at which point successive subroutine returns occur; each such return is followed by a clearing of the parameters from the stack. To understand how recursion might be affected in practice, consider the recursive computation of $n!$. $n!$ is defined as follows:

$$n! = \begin{cases} n*(n-1)! & \text{for } n > 0 \\ 1 & \text{if } n = 0 \end{cases}$$

Consider a subroutine to compute $n!$ We will assume that it takes one in parameter which will be n on entering; we will assume that it returns $(n-1)!$ in d0. Therefore, the subroutine will first subtract 1 from the input; if the result is zero, it will unstack the parameter, which will be a 1, place it in d0, and return. Otherwise, it will unstack the parameter, which will be n, multiply it by the contents of d0, which contains $(n-1)!$, and return. The code for the algorithm to calculate the factorial of 3 is given in Table 8.9.

The action of using the stack to pass parameters is shown clearly by the code trace as given in Figure 8.6. Notice that the stack increases by six bytes for every recursive call, four for the return address, and two for the integer parameter. The recursion is terminated after the parameter is pushed, decremented, and determined to be zero; thus, in the last call the stack was incremented by only 2 bytes.

TABLE 8.9 Assembled code for recursive subroutine `factor`

			1			
006000			2	data	equ	$6000
004000			3	program	equ	$4000
007000			4	stack	equ	$7000
0000E4			5	tutor	equ	228
			6			
006000			7		org	data
006000	0003		8	number	dc.w	3
006002			9	result	ds.w	1
			10			
004000			11		org	program
004000	3E7C	7000	12	main	movea.w	#stack,a7
004004	3038	6000	13		move.w	number,d0
004008	6100	000C	14		bsr	factor
00400C	31C0	6002	15		move.w	d0,result
004010	3E3C	00E4	16		move.w	#tutor,d7
004014	4E4E		17		trap	#14
			18			
004016	3F00		19	factor	move.w	d0,-(a7)
004018	5340		20		subq.w	#1,d0
00401A	6600	0008	21		bne	push
			22			
00401E	301F		23		move.w	(a7)+,d0
004020	6000	0006	24		bra	return
			25			
004024	61F0		26	push	bsr	factor
004026	C0DF		27		mulu	(a7)+,d0
004028	4E75		28	return	rts	
			29			
00402A			30		end	

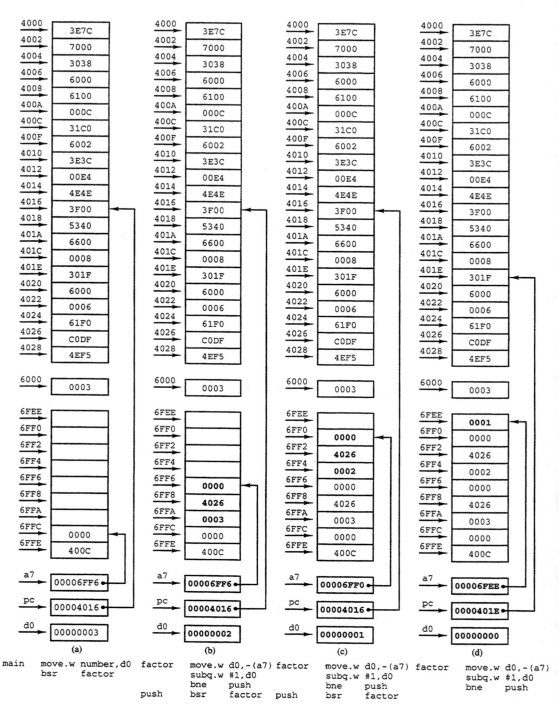

Figure 8.6   Tracing recursive routine `factor`.

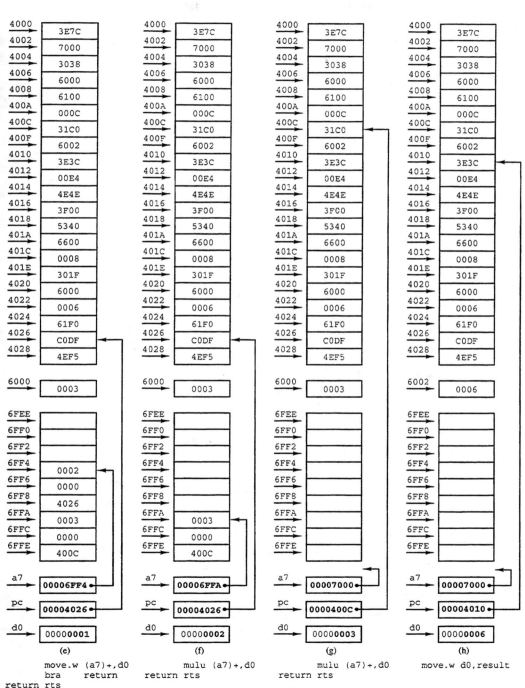

Figure 8.6 (*Continued*) Tracing recursive routine `factor`

8.1.6 Subroutines in a High-level Language Environment

Concept of a frame.   The reader may begin to get the feeling that passing parameters on the stack is somewhat complex; however, there are excellent reasons for using this convention over others. To make the task of passing parameters easier by using the stack, the designers of the MC68000 have provided us with the instructions `link` and `unlk` which help considerably. Before discussing these instructions, it is necessary to develop a standard model for subroutines. The intention with the use of these instructions is that all parameters and data local to a subroutine can be located on the stack. Thus there are no data areas (i.e., `ds` or `dc` directives) declared in the subroutine. We will now introduce the concept of a **frame** or **activation record** which is associated with a particular instance of a subroutine (or program module). A frame contains all the data necessary for the subroutine to execute. This may include pointers to different data objects, local variables, and pointers to previous frames so that the data in calling subroutines may be accessed. As we mentioned earlier, each frame resides on the stack. A conceptual frame is illustrated in Figure 8.7.

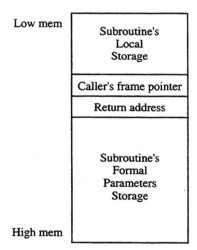

Low mem

| Subroutine's Local Storage |
| Caller's frame pointer |
| Return address |
| Subroutine's Formal Parameters Storage |

High mem

Figure 8.7   Conceptual frame

As Figure 8.7 illustrates, a frame consists of four *ordered* fields; the first field, referred to as **formal parameter storage** area, contains the formal parameters; the second field, longword wide, contains the return address; the third field of the frame is a pointer referred to as the **frame pointer**, which points to the caller's frame pointer and whose function will be explained shortly. Finally, all local variables are pushed into the **local storage** area. Figure 8.8 illustrates the frame when a subroutine accepts six parameters and employs three local variables each of longword size. It is important to remember, as was stated in previous discussions, that address register `a7` serves as the stack pointer and points to the top of the stack. In addition, another address register (usually `a6`), referred to as the **frame pointer register** (`fp`), is employed by the application programmer to point to the *caller routine's* frame pointer field of the active frame. In Figure 8.8 our example assumes that the local variables are each a longword; therefore, the contents of this register should be equal to the contents of the stack pointer (`sp`) plus $C (Why?). At this time the dual purpose of the frame pointer must be explained.

In the previous section on parameter passing it was noted that the stack pointer may only be used to access parameters *immediately* after the subroutine has been called. The

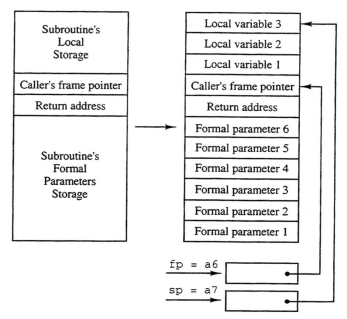

Figure 8.8   Conceptual frame and its storage.

reason for this is that while the subroutine is executing, the size of the stack will probably change, as it does when one must save temporary values during computation. The problem that emerges is how does a programmer access the local variables and parameters on the stack? The stack pointer may no longer be used since it will change as the stack grows and shrinks. Instead another pointer is needed; this pointer, known to as the frame pointer, will point to the location where the stack pointer was pointing *immediately after the invocation to the subroutine*. Because this pointer remains fixed during the life of the subroutine, it is used as a basis that will permit all local variables and formal parameters for this frame (subroutine) to be accessed relative to it. In the preceding example, the sixth formal parameter is at location $(fp)+ $8; the fifth formal parameter's address is $(fp)+$0C, whereas the second local variable is at $(fp)-$8. Thus, all the local variables and formal parameters of a subroutine are easy to reach via the frame pointer.

To better understand the second function of the frame pointer, consider the contents of the stack during execution of a typical program. Assuming that subroutine A calls B and in turn subroutine B calls C, then three frames will coexist in the stack at the same time (Figure 8.9). But only subroutine C is **active** at this time; hence, the second function served by the frame pointer is that it points to the active frame.

Our previous discussions focused on the fact that the pointer stored in an activation record's formal pointer field points to the caller's frame pointer field. Thus by following this pointer, we reach the "start" of the activation record of the subroutine that called us. This is particularly useful because we are now able to access the local storage and parameters of the calling subroutine. In fact, looking more carefully, we can see that we are actually pointing to *its* frame pointer, which in turn allows us to access the activation record of its calling routine. One can immediately see that this may be continued "indefinitely." Thus the frame pointer allows us to "chain back" through preceding subroutines all the way to the original program module. This permits us to access all the local variables associated with these subroutines.

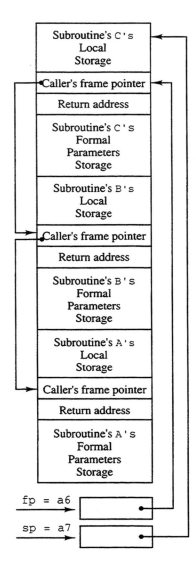

Figure 8.9. The stack and the three frames corresponding to routines A, B, and C.

Using LINK/UNLK instructions. Now we are in a position to examine the action of the `link` and `unlk` instructions which can be very useful to an assembly language programmer whenever he or she needs to maintain activation records. These instructions are presented in Table 8.10. The `link` instruction requires two operands. The first operand is an address register an (assumed to be the frame pointer register, usually a6); the second, is an immediate data constant. When executed, the `link` instruction first causes the contents of the address register an to be pushed onto the stack; the stack pointer is then copied into the address register an; finally the stack pointer's contents are incremented by the immediate data constant.

In terms of using the `link` instruction, it is intended to be the first one executed by the subroutine. Before calling a subroutine, one must recall that the formal parameters must have been pushed onto the stack. When the subroutine is called, the return address is

TABLE 8.10

LINK and UNLK Instructions					
Mnemonic	Opcode	Action	Operands	Format	Length
link	$09CA$_{13}$	Link. Longword contents of address register an are pushed onto stack. Contents of stack pointer are loaded into address register an. Contents of stack pointer are then incremented by amount equal to 16-bit sign-extended displacement indicated by immediate data field in instruction.	an, IData$_{16}$	F22	2
unlk	$ 09CD$_{13}$	Unlink. Longword contents of address register an replace current contents of stack pointer. Top (longword) is popped off stack and is loaded into an.	an	F22	1

pushed onto the stack. Thus by executing the link instruction on entry to the subroutine, the old frame pointer is pushed onto the stack. The frame pointer register is then set to be equal to the value of the current stack pointer; storage is reserved on the stack for the local variables by decrementing the stack pointer by an appropriate amount.

The converse of the link instruction is the unlk instruction. The unlk instruction has only one operand that must be an address register (assumed to be the frame pointer) an. When it is executed, the unlk instruction causes the contents of the address register an to be copied into the stack pointer; the address register's an contents are replaced by a number equal to contents of a7 minus 4.

Again, in terms of using the unlk instruction, it is intended that unlk be the last instruction to be executed before return from the subroutine via the rts instruction. The effect of the unlk is to restore the frame pointer (because it points to the subroutine's caller's frame pointer field) and leave the stack ready for the rts (i.e., with the return address on top of the stack). Thus when the rts is executed, the stack will contain only the formal parameters which were pushed by the calling program. One should remember that removing these formal parameters is the responsibility of the caller.

The code of the recursive procedure that calculates the factorial of 3 is given in Table 8.11 where the link and unlk instructions are employed. The student is encouraged to trace the code in a similar fashion as the one in Figure 8.6.

Although it may not be obvious, there is a close correspondence between the data area and the *dynamic scope* (i.e., what variables are available to a subroutine) of a high level, programming language subroutine and a MC68000 frame. To see this relationship, consider a typical high level programming language. Using the C programming language as an example, consider a typical subroutine (or **function** in C terms) as defined in Table 8.12.

Do not be concerned if the C programming language is not a familiar one. The language C was chosen only to demonstrate the relationship between the data structures and frames. Looking at the C code earlier, there are three parameters to the subroutine, x, y and z. The first two are **in** parameters; the third is an **in-out** parameter (indicated by the "*"). Within the function there are three local variables, u, v, and w. These variables are *local* to this function in the sense that they are available only to this function, and exist only

TABLE 8.11 Calculating factorial of 3 recursively

```
data      equ       $6000
program   equ       $4000
stack     equ       $7000
tutor     equ       228

          org       data
number    dc.w      3
result    ds.w      1
          org       program

main      movea.w   #stack,a7
          move.w    number,d0
          bsr       factor
          move.w    d0,result
          move.w    #tutor,d7
          trap      #14

factor    link      a6,#-2
          move.w    d0,-2(a6)
          subq.w    #1,d0
          bne       push

          moveq     #1,d0
          bra       return

push      bsr       factor
          mulu      -2(a6),d0

return    unlk      a6
          rts

          end
```

TABLE 8.12 Simple C language function

```
/* SumSquared: Computes z=(x+y)² using the formula x²+2xy+y². */

void SumSquared (int x,y, *z)

{
   int u, v, w;

   u = x*x; v = y*y; w = 2*x*y;
   *z = u+v+w;
}
```

when the function is called. Thus local variables are dynamically allocated when the function is called, and are deallocated when the function returns.

In Table 8.13 the MC68000 code is presented which will perform the same task as the C program in Table 8.12; it will implement the function SumSquared; and, it will dynamically allocate and deallocate the local variables u, v, and w.

TABLE 8.13 The equivalent routine in MC68000 code

```
;------------------------------------------------------------------
; SumSquared: Computes the square of the sum of two numbers using the
; formula (x+y)² = x²+2xy+y².  The parameters are passed using the
; stack.  Local variables are stored on the stack using the frame
; concept; three local variables are used u, v, w (words) allocated
; on the stack in that order.  Parameters are (in order pushed):
;       IN:     - word.  Value of x, accessed by $10(a6)
;       IN:     - word.  Value of y, accessed by $0E(a6)
;       IN-OUT: - longword.  Address of z, accessed by $0A(a6)
; Locals are:
;               - word.  Storage for u, accessed by -2(a6)
;               - word.  Storage for v, accessed by -4(a6)
;               - word.  Storage for w, accessed by -6(a6)
; Notice that once the link instruction is used, parameters and locals
; are referenced via the frame pointer.
;------------------------------------------------------------------
;

XOff    equ         $10
YOff    equ         $0E
ZOff    equ         $0A
UOff    equ         -2
VOff    equ         -4
WOff    equ         -6


SumSquared
        move        sr,-(sp)            ; push the condition codes
        link        a6,#-6              ; save the A6, prepare locals
        movem.l     d0-d7/a0-a5,-(sp)   ; save all registers
;
; start code
;
        move.w      XOff(a6),d0         ; get x
        muls        d0,d0
        move.w      d0,UOff(a6)         ; u=x²
        move.w      YOff(a6),d0         ; get y
        muls        d0,d0
        move.w      d0,VOff(a6)         ; v=y²
        move.w      XOff(a6),d0         ; get x
        move.w      YOff(a6),d1         ; get y
        muls        d1,d0               ; xy
        asl.w       #1,d0               ; 2xy
```

TABLE 8.13 (*Continued*) The equivalent routine in MC68000 code

```
        move.w      d0,WOff(a6)          ; w=2xy
        movea.l     ZOff(a6),a0          ; get address of z
        move.w      UOff(a6),d0          ; get u
        add.w       VOff(a6),d0          ; add v
        add.w       WOff(a6),d0          ; add w
        move.w      d0,(a0)              ; save in z
;
; finished, return
;
        movem.l     (sp)+,d0-d7/a0-a5    ; restore all registers
        unlk        a6
        rtr

        end
```

The following points should be noted concerning the MC68000 code segment shown in Table 8.13.

1. The subroutine saves all registers and condition codes prior to the main body. These registers are restored upon termination; thus, the subroutine is nonintrusive. This is accomplished by the `movem.l` and `move sr,-(sp)` instructions at the beginning of the routine and the `movem.l` and `rtr` instructions at end of the routine.

2. All references to parameters and local variables have been made by using the frame pointer (`a6`) rather than the stack pointer. Thus during execution of this subroutine, the frame pointer will remain unchanged.

3. The stack may now be used for temporary storage allocation during the life of this subroutine. When the subroutine is completed, the `unlk` instruction will "clear" the stack and restore the frame pointer for the calling subroutine. These actions, when followed by the `rtr` instruction, will affect the desired return.

4. In the event that this subroutine required access to local variables from the *calling* routine (which it does not), it would be easy to locate them. We would first load the effective address of the previous frame into an address register `an`. This is obtained via (`a6`) with zero offset. The parameters and local variables of the calling subroutine may then be accessed using register indirect addressing on register `an`. This mechanism may be applied repeatedly to reference successively earlier subroutines on the stack.

This discussion should make it clear that nested subroutines are well supported by the MC68000; however, there is some cost involved. Originally, register `a7` was reserved to play the role of a stack pointer. Now it can be seen that when using frames, we must reserve another register, `a6`, as a frame pointer. In addition, most high level programming languages provide global variables, which normally would also be accessed through *another* address register (e.g., `a5`). Given now that the number of address registers actually available for general use is substantially less than eight, one can see that by the time support is provided for high level programming languages, there may be only four or five address registers that remain for general use.

8.2 MODULES, AND INTERNAL AND EXTERNAL SUBROUTINES

So far during the discussion of assembly programming, we have assumed that the entire program is coded as a single module. That is, the entire program is presented to the assembler which is then responsible for generating the code. If this were always the case it would be a simple matter for the assembler to determine the addresses of all symbols and consequently compute all required addresses and offsets. There are frequently occasions when it is desirable to have more than one assembly module, however. The primary instances in which this would occur are (1) when the assembler program is very large (perhaps the kernel of an operating system) with different sections written by a number of programmers, and (2) when we wish to provide a library of subroutines which may be used by other programs. With these situations in mind, most assemblers will assemble an assembly language module which is *incomplete* and that may later be **linked** with others to form a complete program.

In providing this flexibility, there is additional information that must be conveyed to the assembler so that it will perform this type of function correctly. First, we must differentiate between **internal** and **external** subroutines as defined later. Second, we must introduce the notion of a **standard parameter passing convention** and use it to demonstrate external subroutines. Finally, in the next section we will introduce the notion of a **subroutine library**; the concepts of **statically** and **dynamically linked libraries** will be addressed.

8.2.1 Internal Subroutines

An internal subroutine is one that is local to a module. That is, the subroutine will be called only by routines within the module it resides and will not be directly called by code from another module. Because the subroutine is internal, programmers may make whatever decisions they wish regarding parameter passing conventions. In addition because the subroutine is internal, the assembler may resolve all references to this routine during assembly of the module. In this text all the subroutines described so far have been internal.

8.2.2 External Subroutines

An external subroutine is one that may be called from another module; clearly because another module may call the subroutine, there is the need for much tighter control on how the parameters are passed and how results are returned. In particular, a standard convention must be developed so that when parameters are being passed between external subroutines, there is some consistency. Consider the converse of this situation. If modules can be written so that subroutines are available externally, should we not also be able to access external subroutines? The answer is yes! This presents a problem for the assembler, however, because the address of the external subroutine clearly will not be known. We will explain how all these problems are addressed by discussing a simple example in detail.

Assume that in a file, `File2`, we have already coded two subroutines, `sqr` and `mlt`, where the function of the first subroutine is to square the word size integer at location x, whereas the function of the second subroutine is to replace the word size integer at location y with the result of its multiplication of the word size integer at location x (Figure 8.10). Given that this code has been written, we can square the number 3 and multiply 3*9 by coding the driver that appears in Figure 8.10.

File1 (source)   File2 (source)

```
        section  simple, code              section  dimple, code
        xdef     x, y                      xdef     sqr, mlt
        xref     sqr, mlt                  xref     x,y

        jsr      sqr               sqr     move     x,d0
        jsr      mlt                       muls     d0,d0
        rts                                move     d0,x
                                           rts
    x   dc.w     3
    y   dc.w     9                 mlt     move     x,d0
                                           move     y,d1
                                           muls     d0,d1
        end                                move     d1,y
                                           rts

                                           end
```

Figure 8.10   Section in `File1` defines and invokes the two external subroutines in `File2`.

Closer examination of Figure 8.10 reveals the definition of two modules. Formally, a module is a segment of assembly language code whose beginning is identified by a new directive, the `section` directive, and its end by encountering either another `section` directive or the `end` directive.[2] The format of this new directive is

Name-Field	Opcode-Field	Operand-Field
	section	name,type

The `name` appearing in the operand field must be a valid symbol and is used to identify the particular section. In Figure 8.10 we see that names of the two sections are `simple` and `dimple`, respectively.[3] The `type` appearing in the operand field specifies the "type" of section; it can be one of the following three symbols: `code`, `data`, or `bss`. If the assembly language statements in the section consist of only directives that define data, then the type of the section must be `data`. If it consists of only directives that define storage, then the type of the section must be `bss`. If assembly instructions (and or data and or storage) are included, then the type of the section must be `code` as the two modules in Figure 8.10 demonstrate.

Now, notice the two symbols x and y as they appear in the source file `File1`. In addition observe that these two symbols are *defined* in the section `simple`; but, they are also *used (referred)* in the section `dimple`; and, the assembler must be informed

---

[2] Notice that the `end` directive is used to indicate to the assembler the "end" of the assembly language code in a file.

[3] As we will see, section names may not be unique.

of this fact.[4] This is the function of the directive xdef; it indicates to the assembler that the symbol(s) that appear in its operand field are *defined* in this section; and, that they may be referred to in other sections. The format of this directive is presented subsequently.

Name-Field	Opcode-Field	Operand-Field
	xdef	symbol[,symbol]

Furthermore, when the contents of File1 are assembled, the assembler *does* encounter the symbols sqr and mlt; however, these symbols are not defined in this section! Ordinarily the assembler will generate an error to indicate this fact *unless* it has been instructed that these symbols are defined elsewhere. This is the function of the xref directive whose syntax is presented subsequently.

Name-Field	Opcode-Field	Operand-Field
	xref	symbol[,symbol]

The xref directive informs the assembler that the symbols that appear in its operand field are referenced in this section; however, they have been defined elsewhere.

Let's now indicate the method that the assembler employs to assemble each of the files whose listings are given in Figure 8.11. First, the assembler assumes that the loading origin of the section is $000000; and, it processes the source normally. But, during assembly of a section when symbols are encountered that have been referenced, such as the symbols sqr and mlt that it encountered during the assembly of File1, the assembler does not know their values. It does "know," however, that those are externally defined symbols (because of the xref directive). Therefore, because it cannot resolve the address at that time, it simply generates a longword (marked by 00000000 [*]) in the listing,[5] and makes a note that it was unable to resolve this address; a note, which as we will see shortly, is passed to the linker. Figure 8.11 provides us with a number of examples. In particular, notice, that the assembler, during assembly of the section simple, supplied zeros in the second and third word of the machine language code of both jsr instructions because at that time the value of the symbols sqr and mult was unknown to it.[6] Similarly, during assembly of the section dimple, the assembler supplied zeros in each machine language instruction that it generated that needed the value of the symbols x and y that were defined externally.

Referring to Chapter 7 one should recall that the object code files of all modules (and libraries) are passed through a program called the **linker** to resolve any external references. The machine code has already been generated; thus, the only tasks the linker must perform will be filling in the addresses of all symbols that were externally defined to each module and loading the modules for execution. Another function that the assembler performs is the "passage" of notes to the linker relative to the references that must be resolved. These "notes" are part of the object modules that the assembler generated. In Figure 8.12 the object modules generated for the files File1 and File2 by our assembler are displayed. Closer examination of each object module reveals that it consists of up to four components. The first component identifies its type, its size (in bytes), and its name. The second compo-

---

[4] So it can pass this information to the linker.

[5] The assembler generates 00000000. We supplied the asterisk in Figure 8.11 for the purpose of clarity.

[6] Shortly, one can see that the linker will supply the required longword.

File1 (assembly listing)

```
                                 1          section    simple code
                                 2
                                 3          xdef       x,y
                                 4          xref       sqr,mlt
                                 5
000000   4EB9   00000000*        6          jsr        sqr
000006   4EB9   00000000*        7          jsr        mlt
00000C   4EB5                    8          rts
                                 9
00000E   0003                   10   x      dc.w       3
000010   0009                   11   y      dc.w       9
                                12
000012                          13          end
```

File2 (assembly listing)

```
                                 1          section    dimple code
                                 2
                                 3          xdef       sqr,mlt
                                 4          xref       x,y
                                 5
000000   3039   00000000*.       6   sqr    move       x,d0
000006   C1C0                    7          muls       d0,d0
000008   33C0   00000000*        8          move       d0,x
00000E   4E75                    9          rts
                                10
000010   3039   00000000*       11   mlt    move       x,d0
000016   3239   00000000*       12          move       y,d1
00001C   C3C0                   13          muls       d0,d1
00001E   33C1   00000000*       14          move       d1,y
000024   4E75                   15          rts
                                16
000026                          16          end
```

Figure 8.11 Assembler listing of File1 and File2. Contents of fields marked by asterisk will be "replaced" by the linker at link time with the proper values.

nent contains the code generated by the assembler (in S-record format). The third and fourth components form the "notes" that the assembler passes to the linker so that the unresolved addresses can be resolved. Notably, the third component contains the symbols that are defined in this section along with their addresses *relative* to the loading origin of this section. In other words, this address, is only the *offset* of the symbol from the beginning of the section. Finally, the fourth component contains each symbol that is referenced in this section together with the list of offsets from the beginning of the section where the linker is supposed to supply their addresses. From Figure 8.12 one can see that the information contained in the object module and corresponding to section dimple indicates that the value (address) of the symbol x must replace the longword contents of the object code in three different locations. The first is $00000002 bytes off the beginning of the section; the second, $0000000A bytes; and, the third $00000012 bytes. The linker, will now use the information contained in the object module corresponding to the section to resolve the address.

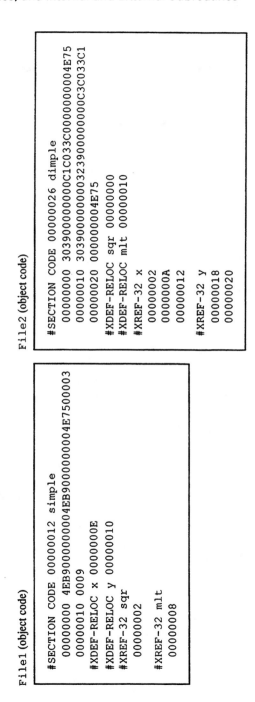

Figure 8.12 Object code generated by assembler for two files File1 and File2, respectively.

Our linker[7] is invoked via a command of the form

```
link <loading_origin> [-s <filename> ] [-m] filelist
```

where `filename.s` is the name of a file that the linker will build by *linking n* object modules

```
object_1.o object2.o object_3.o .. object_n.o
```

denoted by `filelist`.

The previous command was a request to the linker to take these object modules,[8] `object_1.o`, `object_2.o`, `object_3.o,.....,` `object_n.o`, in this order and produce an executable file[9] with all external references resolved. The linker will link the modules so that the object codes are sequential in memory: in the order in which they appeared in `filelist` with the loading origin `loading_origin` being the one specified in the `link` command. This is illustrated in Figure 8.13.

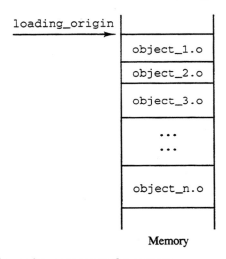

Figure 8.13 Conceptual placement of object modules by the linker in response to `link loading_origin -s example object_1.o object_2.o .. object_n.o`.

The linker as its response to the request

```
link 1000 -s example File_1.o File_2.o
```

will produce the executable S-record format file `example.s` presented in Table 8.14. Notice that the same S-record file would have been produced by the assembler over the source that appears in the listing in Table 8.15.

Despite the fact that the linker is also discussed in Appendix D we should note here that if a filename is not specified, the linker will produce an S-record format file under the name `firstfile.s` where `firstfile` is the filename of the first object file in

---

[7] See Appendix D.

[8] Each object module is obtained by assembling each source file `object_i.asm` via our assembler by entering the command asm68k object_i -r.

[9] An *S-record* format file in which all external references have been resolved.

TABLE 8.14   Executable file `example.s`

```
S0030000FC
S2140010004EB9000010124EB9000010224E750003B3
S21400101000930390000100EC1C033C00000100EA9
S2140010204E7530390000100E323900001010C3C063
S20C00103033C1000010104E75DC
S804000000FB
```

TABLE 8.15

00001000	4EB9 00001012	1	jsr	sqr
00001006	4EB9 00001022	2	jsr	mlt
0000100C	4E75	3	rts	
		4		
0000100E	0003	5 x	dc.w	3
00001010	0009	· 6 y	dc.w	9
		7		
		8		
00001012	3039 0000100E	9 sqr	move	x,d0
00001018	C1C0	10	muls	d0,d0
0000101A	33C0 0000100E	11	move	d0,x
00001020	4E75	12	rts	
		13		
00001022	3039 0000100E	14 mlt	move	x,d0
00001028	3239 00001010	15	move	y,d1
0000102E	C3C0	16	muls	d0,d1
00001030	33C1 00001010	17	move	d1,y
00001036	4E75	18	rts	

`filelist`. For example, the command `link 1000 File_1.o File_2.o` will produce the file `File_1.s`. Finally, the switch -m, when present, requests the linker to produce a memory map as indicated in Appendix D.

We close this section with the following remarks. Whenever our assembler is to be invoked with the the relocatable switch (-r) the programmer should be aware of the following restrictions.

- The assembler and linker only support 32-bit relocatable references.
- PC-relative addressing modes can only be used to access memory locations within the same section.
- Branches via the `bcc`, `dbcc` and `bsr` instructions can only be made to addresses within the same section. To span sections, one should use either a `jmp` or a `jsr`.
- The displacement in both modes, the address indirect with displacement and address indirect with displacement and index must be defined only via absolute expressions.
- Only absolute long addressing may be used.

8.2.3 Standard Parameter Convention

To present a consistent mechanism for sample programs, we will introduce the notion of a **standard parameter convention**.

1. For *all subroutines*, registers $d0$, $d1$, $a0$, and $a1$ are considered temporary registers. Thus, a routine should not expect these registers to contain the same contents after a call and return from a subroutine. Register $d0$ will be designed as a status register for subroutine returns. A successful completion will be indicated by a zero; different kinds of errors will be reported as other values.

2. For *external subroutines*, the method of passing all parameters will be through the stack. For *internal subroutines*, registers may be used if the number of parameters is small.

3. For *external subroutines*, the calling convention is that all **in** parameters are pushed first, followed by all **in-out** parameters. This permits an easy access to the results by the calling program after the subroutine has been called.

4. If a subroutine employs local variables, the space for these local variables must be allocated by using the `link` and `unlk` instructions (mechanisms). No routine may allocate static data space.

5. The only parameters which may be passed by value are "simple" parameters (i.e., integers, reals, and logical values); strings and complex structures (such as arrays, etc.) are all passed by reference regardless whether the parameters are **in** or **in-out**. Clearly subroutines should not modify parameters unless they have been declared as **in-out**.

8.3 SUBROUTINE LIBRARIES

A **subroutine library** is a single file that contains one or more object modules. As the name suggests, the library is a repository for storing frequently used subroutines and any associated constants or variables. The principal difference between a linkable object module and a library is that subroutines may either be added or deleted from the library, whereas an object module is unmodifiable. Thus one may consider a library to be a collection of object modules with some additional information used for indexing. The advantages of using libraries become apparent only when complex systems are involved. A typical operating system will have a set of libraries, each of which provides the programmer with useful functions in a particular domain. Example libraries are discussed subsequently.

Language support.   Each programming language has a set of standard functions that the user may call to either perform a complex calculation or interface with the outside world. For example the programming language FORTRAN has the routines OPEN, CLOSE, WRITE, and READ to allow formatted input-output. These subroutines would reside in a FORTRAN LIBRARY. The programming language Pascal has similar routines, although the parameters passed to each routine differ somewhat from those passed to FORTRAN subroutines. These routines would reside in a PASCAL LIBRARY. Thus different libraries exist for each programming language.

Operating system support.   Chapter 1 discusses the fact that the operating system provides a support environment for the programmer by offering functions to access a file system, create new processes, share information between different processes, and perform other miscellaneous activities. These functions are provided to the user as a set of **operating system calls** that would reside in the **operating system library**. This library is so important that frequently it is automatically linked with the users' program without their explicit request. A special case of this is input-output to the file system which will be discussed next.

Input-output.   Although different programming languages provide different interfaces to the user, at some point they all access the operating system input-output routines. These routines allow files to be opened/closed and data to be read/written. Typically these routines are "low-level" because they are complex to access and they use raw data. For example, these routines may fetch only individual blocks of a file. The programming language routines are therefore intermediaries because they present an easier interface to the file system. In fact, one will notice that many of the functions offered in a language support library will actually translate the users language specific request into a sequence of calls to the input-output library. For example, the FORTRAN library function `WRITE` causing data to be written to a file would typically format the data appropriately for the underlying system and call the operating system `write(...)` function to actually write the data. Although we have discussed only files, the same is true for access to terminals and other devices.

Special applications.   Another use of libraries is to provide support functions for application programs. Examples are *mathematical* libraries that perform matrix manipulations, solve calculus problems, and so on; *graphics* libraries provide the necessary routines that permit one to draw lines, points, circles, and so on; and, *windowing* libraries provide window manipulation primitives for workstations with graphical user interfaces.

Note that because of the instructional nature of the tools in this text, the assembler has no facility for defining libraries; however, the format would be similar to a sequence of external subroutine object code modules with a library index at the beginning of the file that would specify the locations and lengths of subroutines within the library.

8.3.1 Static versus Dynamically Linked Libraries

There are two principal classes of libraries **static** (or **statically linked**) and **dynamic** (or **dynamically linked**). These are characterized as follows. In the case of a statically linked library, each library file is opened by the linker, the subroutines required for the program are located and appended to the object module, then linked (as discussed earlier in this chapter) to the original code by resolving the external references. The object module that is produced may either be a new object module or it may be a complete **executable image**. The latter will be the case if all external references have been resolved and the object module has an entry point (i.e., a starting point from which to run). Each executable image will contain all subroutines for those library calls that it required. Because these subroutines could be quite complex (and may have called subroutines in other libraries, which must also be included) it is understandable that the statically linked executable image could be many times larger than the object module prior to linking. Notice also that none of the resulting code is sharable; that is, the program is completely self-contained. The reader may feel uncomfortable with this arrangement because each executable image in memory will have a copy of all subroutine libraries that it requires (e.g., open, close, read, write, etc.); and, these will be the same code sequences as those used by other executables in memory. This is an extremely wasteful arrangement for main memory, however. In addition, the size of the executables will be increased by the size of the statically linked routines.

This problem was identified many years ago and was resolved by using dynamically linked libraries. Dynamic libraries avoid the resolution of external references until the program is actually executed. This is accomplished by having a special **library monitor routine** statically linked to the object module and executed prior to the initial entry point of the executable image. This routine links and resolves those undefined external references *at runtime*. Clearly, to accomplish this task, the routine must be able to search through portions of the file system for those specified libraries; and, it must be able to include and link (i.e., resolve) the appropriate code segments. Thus the library monitor routine performs the same activities as the linker (in fact, in many systems it is a special version of the linker!). The advantage of this technique is that the library monitor routine can keep track of those dynamically linked subroutines that are already in main memory. Now, if a copy of the same subroutine is requested by another program it is simply linked to the code segment already in use. This implies that instead of having multiple copies of frequently used subroutines in memory we have only one. The savings are twofold; not only is main memory storage saved by sharing subroutines; however, the size of the executable modules in secondary storage is significantly reduced. Of course there is always a tradeoff; the disadvantage is that there is some overhead processing performed by the library monitor routine *each time* the program is executed.

One must be very careful when providing dynamically linked libraries. Consider a library that not only defines a number of subroutines but also defines storage (initialized and uninitialized variables, etc.) for the programmer to use. Clearly *each* user that links this library will require a separate copy of the storage space; however, they may still share the pure code segments. It is for this reason that the `type` (`code`, `data`, `bss`) of each code segment must be identified within the object module. Thus, for a library already in use, the runtime library monitor needs to only allocate and initialize storage for `data` sections and allocate storage for `bss` sections; the `code` sections already exist. Dynamically linked libraries are quite easy to support when the computer has a virtual memory system and segmented addressing. In this case, the operating system can allocate a separate segment for the pure `code` section of each library required; it can allocate another segment for each process that requires storage for the library. The library monitor routine then keeps track of those pure code segments that correspond to different libraries; and, it only loads those that are not already in memory. One potential problem that may occur with dynamic libraries is discerning *which* library routine is being linked at runtime. Consider that a program could be written to call a function `fn()` which resides in library `lib1`. If the program is moved to a different system, when the library monitor routine, is searching its list of libraries, could possibly find another library `lib2` (not on the original machine) with the same function and thereby link the incorrect function. The confusion that results can only be imagined! Fortunately, this problem can be overcome by a using a standard convention when searching for libraries so that the order is known in advance.

8.4 MACROS

Assume that in several positions within an assembly language program a word size integer stored at location `x` must be squared. Assuming that it is not desirable to use a subroutine to perform this task, invariably in each and every one of these positions the set of three instructions illustrated in Table 8.16 must be typed. Alternatively, it would have been considerably more preferable if there were an opcode such as `sqr` that could be used in each of these positions; and, the function of the opcode would be equivalent to the set of three statements as in Table 8.16. This idea could be expanded further by having the additional capability to define operands of that opcode so that `sqr  x` could be used to square the word at location x or `sqr  y` could be used to square the word at location y, and so on. Fortunately, such a facility, the *macro* facility, a *text substitution* facility, is available that will allow a programmer to define his or her own opcodes and potentially his or her own operands.

TABLE 8.16   Squaring
word at location x

move.w	x,d0
muls	d0,d0
move.w	d0,x

This macro facility provides a powerful aid to assembly language programmers since it permits them to create *in-line subroutines*. These in-line subroutines avoid the overhead of a subroutine call (which requires a minimum of a `jsr` and a `rts` instruction) because the code associated with the macro is actually inserted into the program. In actuality, code that is associated with the macro definition does not generate code. Code is only generated when the macro statement is actually used (we will use the term "called," although at run time there is no such call). Thus, unlike subroutines, there is no runtime penalty associated with macro calls. Notice however, that unlike subroutines, every time a macro is called, additional code is generated. Thus there is a tradeoff between speed and code size when comparing macros with subroutines.

Formally, a macro is an opcode (user defined) that represents a set of one or more assembly language statements, directives, or other macros.

Defining and invoking a macro.   Macros (as with subroutines) must be defined and invoked (called). The definition of a macro, which is presented in Table 8.17, consists of three basic components.

The first component, the **header**, establishes the *name (opcode)* of the macro which is conveyed by the `symbol` in the name field of the very first statement followed by the directive `macro`. The syntax of the symbol, which serves as the name of the macro, must be the same as that of a valid symbol; but, it must not be identical to any MC68000 assembly language opcodes, directives, or macros. For example, `add,  asl,` or `adda` are unfortunate choices whereas `sqr,  there,` or `sqrt` are perfectly legal.

The second component of the macro definition is the **body of the macro**, which consists of a set of any valid assembly language statements but not a macro definition.

The last component of the macro definition consists of a statement, the **trailer**, which contains the no-operand directive `endm`; it signals the end of the macro definition to the assembler.

TABLE 8.17   Format of macro definition

symbol	macro
	<body of macro>
	endm

For example, the definition of the macro that calculates the square of the word size integer at location x is presented in Figure 8.14.

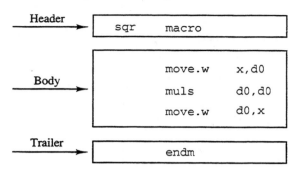

Figure 8.14   Definition of sqr macro.

A macro is invoked via a statement of the form

```
macroname     [parameter_list]
```

The macroname is the name of the macro as has been defined in the macro definition; whereas, the parameter_list appearing in the operand field may or may not be present and will be discussed shortly.

As an example, when the application programmer needs to calculate the square of the word at location x, he or she may invoke the macro defined in Figure 8.14 via the call

```
sqr
```

When this macro call is encountered by the assembler, the macro is **expanded** in the sense that the assembler "replaces" the call statement with the body of the macro. To state this action differently, the assembler "inserts" the body of the macro at the point where the macro is called. This is similar to the *block copy* operation found in many text editors and word processors. In addition, when a statement has been generated by a macro invocation, the assembler appends the plus "+" sign to the number of that statement in the listing to indicate this fact. For illustration purposes, consider the following portion of an assembly language source where the number inside the brackets represents input source file number lines. Then the listing provided by the assembler can be viewed as in Table 8.18.[10] Note that the two

```
[ 1].    sqr      macro
[ 2].             move.w    x,d0
[ 3].             muls      d0,d0
[ 4].             move.w    d0,x
[ 5].             endm
[ 6].    ...      ......    ......
         ...      ......    ......
[20].             sqr
[21].             sub       d4,d5
[22].             sqr
         ...      ......    ......
```

------

[10] Assuming that no other macro invocations or conditional assembly language statements appear in between lines 6 and 20.

calls to the macro appear in the listing (statements [20+], and [25+]); however, they are not assembled by the assembler.

TABLE 8.18   Listing including macro expansion

```
        STMT
         1      sqr     macro
         2              move.w    x,d0
         3              muls      d0,d0
         4              move.w    d0,x
         5              endm
         6      ...     ......    ......
                ...     ......    ......
        20+             sqr
        21+             move.w    x,d0
        22+             muls      d0,d0
        23+             move.w    d0,x
        24              sub       d4,d5
        25+             sqr
        26+             move.w    x,d0
        27+             muls      d0,d0
        28+             move.w    d0,x
                ...     ......    ......
```

In closing, a macro definition can appear anywhere in the source; however, it must be defined before it is invoked.

Parameters.   An application programmer can define (as with subroutines) parameters. The maximum number of parameters permitted is equal to 9; these parameters must appear in the operand field of the invocation statement and be separated by a comma. For example, if we assume that add3 is a defined macro, then the call

$$\text{add3} \quad \text{d2,d5,d6,d0}$$

establishes that there are four parameters: d2, d5, d6, and d0. First, one should be aware that parameters to the assembler are only ordinary character strings; second, the order of the listing of the parameters is particularly *important*. The reason is elaborated later. The assembler assigns the symbol \1 to the first parameter, the symbol \2 to the second parameter, and so on. The programmer (now knowing this simple type of correspondence) can refer to the parameters *in the body* of the macro's definition with these latter special symbols. The assembler, at the time of expansion of the macro, will make the necessary *substitutions* of the parameters into this block based on the correspondence previously described. As an example, assume that a macro, add3, is defined via

```
add3        macro
            move.l    \1,\4
            add.l     \2,\4
            add.l     \3,\4
            endm
```

If the macro is invoked via the call

$$\text{add3} \quad \text{d2,d5,d6,d0}$$

the assembler will assign the string variable d2 to \1, the string variable d5 to \2, the string variable d6 to \3, and the string variable d0 to \4. Finally, during the expansion of the macro, each occurrence of each of the special symbols of the form \n will be substituted by its assigned character string. In other words, the expansion due to the call above will be as shown in Table 8.19.

TABLE 8.19

00000000	2002		9+	move.1	d2,d0
00000002	D085		10+	add.1	d5,d0
00000004	D086		11+	add.1	d6,d0

We close this section by giving one more example. The code fragment shown in Table 8.20 was assembled; and, the corresponding listing file is shown in Table 8.21. The assembler denotes each line of a macro expansion with a plus (+) sign.

Finally it is necessary to note that if the number of parameters that appear in the operand field of a macro call is less than the number indicated by the operands of the statements

TABLE 8.20   Assembly source code including definition of add3 macro and two calls

[1]	add3	macro	
[2]		move.1	\1,\4
[3]		add.1	\2,\4
[4]		add.1	\3,\4
[5]		endm	
[6]			
[7]		org	$000000
[8]		add3	d2,d5,d6,d0
[9]			
[10]		add3	#2,d2,d3,d7

TABLE 8.21   Assembler list file

			1	add3	macro
			2		move.1	\1,\4
			3		add.1	\2,\4
			4		add.1	\3,\4
			5		endm
			6		
			7		org	$000000
			8+		add3	d2,d5,d6,d0
00000000	2002		9+		move.1	d2,d0
00000002	D085		10+		add.1	d5,d0
00000004	D086		11+		add.1	d6,d0
			12		
			13+		add3	#2,d2,d3,d7
00000006	2E3C 00000002		14+		move.1	#2,d7
0000000C	Ce82		15+		add.1	d2,d7
0000000E	Ce83		16+		add.1	d3,d7

included in the body of the macro, the assembler will assign the null string to the excess operands of the form \n.

Local macro labels.   Consider the macro BusyWait whose definition is given in Table 8.22. It should be clear that the function of this macro is to force the CPU to wait for some period; this period is determined by the parameter supplied in the macro call. Even though this macro definition is absolutely correct, its use could lead to assembly time errors. Specifically, if this macro is invoked more than once, each of its expansions will yield the symbols outer and inner. This will lead to multiple declarations of the same symbol.

This problem can be corrected by using two local symbols and two extra parameters. In other words, the macro could be defined as in Table 8.23.

TABLE 8.22

```
BusyWait     macro

             movem.l  d0-d1,-(a7)
outer        move.w   \1,d1
             move.w   #$FFFF,d0
inner        dbra     d0,inner
             dbra     d1,outer
             movem.l  (a7)+,d0-d1

             endm
```

TABLE 8.23

```
BusyWait     macro

             movem.l  d0-d1,-(a7)
\3           move.w   \1,d1
             move.w   #$FFFF,d0
\2           dbra     d0,\2
             dbra     d1,\3
             movem.l  (a7)+,d0-d1

             endm
```

We must ensure that each time the macro is invoked, a new set of parameters is provided and that they are *generated* so that no multiple declarations occur. For example, the first three calls to the macro could be

```
BusyWait    x,outer1,inner1
BusyWait    x,outer2,inner2
BusyWait    x,outer3,inner3
```

Instead of having to keep track of the labels so generated, this task can be handled by the assembler which is capable of automatically generating unique labels each time a specific macro is expanded.

The mechanism is conceptually very simple. When the assembler encounters the symbol \@ in the source, it replaces it with .nnn where .nnn is the number of macro expansions that have already occurred. The first invocation to the macro yields the string .001 as the replacement for \@. Thus, if a label of the form label\@ is encountered during the macro expansion, it will be replaced in the generated code by label.001. Continuing in the same fashion, the same label, label\@, will be replaced in the generated code by the label label.002 at the time of the macro expansion because of the second call. This process can be repeated up to 999 times!

With the preceding discussion in mind, Table 8.24 presents the modified code for the macro BusyWait as well as an assembly language code fragment and its corresponding listing file generated due to the two calls

```
            BusyWait    $4000
            BusyWait    $2000
```

We remarked earlier that macro definitions cannot be nested; however, one *may* nest macro calls. An example of nested macro calls will be given in the next section.

TABLE 8.24 Demonstration of macro definition and expansion using local labels

		4	BusyWait	macro	; count
		5			
		6		movem.l	d0-d1,-(a7)
		7	outer\@	move.w	\1,d1
		8		move.w	#$FFFF,d0
		9	inner\@	dbra	d0,inner\@
		10		dbra	d1,outer\@
		11		movem.l	(a7)+,d0-d1
		12			
		13		endm	
		14			
		15			
		16+		BusyWait	$4000
		17+			
00001000	48E7C000	18+		movem.l	d0-d1,-(a7)
00001004	3238 4000	19+outer.001		move.w	$4000,d1
00001008	303C FFFF	20+		move.w	#$FFFF,d0
0000100C	51C8 FFFE	21+inner.001		dbra	d0,inner.001
00001010	51C9 FFF2	22+		dbra	d1,outer.001
00001014	4CDF0003	23+		movem.l	(a7)+,d0-d1
		24+			
		25+		BusyWait	$2000
		26+			
00001018	48E7C000	27+		movem.l	d0-d1,-(a7)
0000101C	3238 2000	28+outer.002		move.w	$2000,d1
00001020	303C FFFF	29+		move.w	#$FFFF,d0
00001024	51C8 FFFE	30+inner.002		dbra	d0,inner.002
00001028	51C9 FFF2	31+		dbra	d1,outer.002
0000102C	4CDF0003	32+		movem.l	(a7)+,d0-d1
		33+			
		34			

8.5 CONDITIONAL ASSEMBLY

So far the assembler has processed statements in an assembly language program in the order in which they have been encountered. This natural processing sequence can be modified by using a new set of directives referred to as *control directives*. More precisely, the use of these directives affects the outcome of the assembly process since the code that is generated depends on these control directives and the values of the certain variables. The use of conditional directives provides an assembly language programmer with another powerful tool: *conditional assembly*. Furthermore, the combination of macros and conditional assembly provides an even more powerful and versatile tool.

We begin our discussion by presenting a directive, the `set` directive, and a variable `narg`.

Set and narg.   A programmer may define the *value* of a symbol via the `set` directive. The format of the directive follows.

Name-Field	Opcode-Field	Operand-Field
valid symbol	set	exp

Note that a symbol should be present in the Name-Field of the statement; the effect will be that the value associated with the exp will be assigned to the symbol. For example, consider the declaration:

```
here     set     100
```

The assembler will make the following assignment `here = 100`. This directive is similar to the `equ` directive that was encountered earlier. It is similar because it permits one to assign a value to a symbol; no storage is allocated to the symbol; and, declaration of this symbol should *precede* any reference to it. It is different because the value of the symbol defined by the `set` directive can be *changed* at a later time.

An *assembly variable* is defined to be a symbol whose value can be used *only* by the assembler. In other words, neither the symbol or its value are assembled into the object module. An example of an assembly variable is the one represented by the special symbol `narg`. Furthermore, this variable is recognized as such when it is encountered in the body of the definition of a macro; its value is set by the assembler to be equal to the number of parameters in the *call* to the macro. For example, consider the definition of the following macro.

```
example  macro
         .....
number   set     narg
         .....
```

Then, *during* expansion of the macro because of the call

```
example  here,there
```

the value of the symbol `number` will be 2 (because the invocation has two parameters); on the other hand, its value will be 0 *during* the macro expansion because of the call

```
example
```

because the invocation has no parameters. The examples above also illustrate the point that the scope of the variable `narg` is local.

ifxx Directives.   The assembler can test the value of an expression at assembly time and process statements according to the result of the test. The general format for using conditional assembly directives is shown in Table 8.25.

TABLE 8.25 Format of conditional assembly definition; entire set of possible values for *xx* are given in Table 8.26

```
ifxx        <expressions>
<body>
endc
```

The *xx* can assume a number of values and will be discussed later; it indicates the condition that must be tested. The `<expressions>` (see Table 8.26) denotes the expression that must be evaluated. The `<body>` represents one or more assembly language statements, including possibly another conditional directive. Finally, `endc` is yet another directive that is employed to indicate to the assembler the end of the body[11] of the conditional directive.

The decisions that the assembler faces in response to a conditional directive are quite simple. If the condition is true, the assembler processes the body of the conditional directive; otherwise, processing resumes with the statement following the associated `endc` directive.

As an example, consider the `ifeq` conditional directive. This directive expects only one argument that must be an arithmetic expression. The condition is true, if and only if, the value of the expression is equal to zero. Consider also the following macro

```
SmallWait    macro

             ifeq    narg-1
             move.l  d0,-(a7)
             move.w  \1,d0
small\@      dbra    d0,small\@
             move.l  (a7)+,d0
             endc
             endm
```

Notice that as a response to the macro call

```
                    SmallWait    x
```

the value of `narg-1` is zero; therefore, the body of the `ifeq` will be processed so that it will yield the following piece of code:

```
             move.l  d0,-(a7)
             move.w  x,d0
small.001    dbra    d0,small.001
             move.l  (a7)+,d0
```

---

[11] The `endc` directive is always matched with the most recent *ifxx* directive.

On the other hand, as a response to the call

```
SmallWait
```

no code will be generated.

Finally, in Table 8.26 the set of all conditional directives is presented. It must be noted here that by `<string>` we denote any character string. For example `ifc here,there` will evaluate to false whereas `ifc     \1,beq` will evaluate to true if the parameter passed is `beq` (i.e., `\1 = beq`).

TABLE 8.26 Conditional assemblies

Conditional Directives		
Mnemonic	Arguments	Condition
ifeq	`<exp>`	Assemble if (exp $\equiv 0$)
ifne	`<exp>`	Assemble if (exp $\neq 0$)
ifgt	`<exp>`	Assemble if (exp > 0)
ifge	`<exp>`	Assemble if (exp ≥ 0)
iflt	`<exp>`	Assemble if (exp < 0)
ifle	`<exp>`	Assemble if (exp ≤ 0)
ifc	`<string>,<string>`	Assemble if character strings are identical
ifnc	`<string>,<string>`	Assemble if character strings are not identical
ifd	`<symbol>`	Assemble if symbol has been defined
ifnd	`<symbol>`	Assemble if symbol has not been defined

Fail and mexit directives.   Here two new directives provided by the assembler are introduced: `fail` and `mexit`. The `fail` directive can be employed to print messages in the listing that will notify the application programmer of the nature of a directive that is failing; its format is given subsequently.

Name-Field	Opcode-Field	Operand-Field
[valid symbol]	fail	[string]

The `mexit` macro can be employed whenever one would like to suspend expansion of the macro after a certain point. In other words, the function of this directive is that of an unconditional branch to the trailer of the macro. The format of this directive is given below.

Name-Field	Opcode-Field	Operand-Field
[valid symbol]	mexit	

Example

   With both macro definitions in Table 8.27, the macro is expected to be called with one argument. Line 4 "decides" if an incorrect number of arguments have been supplied. If so, the assembler encounters the `fail` directive, which prints an error message. The next directive, `mexit`, aborts expansion of the macro. The final directive `endc` closes the `ifne` on line 4. Table 8.27 shows the listing for the corresponding fragment of code. Observe that the assembler handles unique labels (`\@`) correctly even when nested macro calls are made. Notice also that all this activity takes place during assembly; the result of these deliberations is either that the code within the macro is assembled at this point or that an error message is printed.

TABLE 8.27   Assembly list file

```
                       1
                       2 SmallWait    macro    ; count
                       3
                       4              ifne     narg-1
                       5              fail     not enough arguments :
                                               SmallWait
                       6              mexit
                       7              endc
                       8
                       9              move.l   d0,-(a7)
                      10              move.w   \1,d0
                      11 small\@      dbra     d0,small\@
                      12              move.l   (a7)+,d0
                      13
                      14              endm
                      15
                      16
                      17 LargeWait    macro    ; count
                      18
                      19              ifne     narg-1
                      20              fail     not enough arguments :
                                               LargeWait
                      21              mexit
                      22              endc
                      23
                      24              movem.l  d1,-(a7)
                      25 large\@      move.w   \1,d1
                      26              SmallWait  #$FFFF
                      27              dbra     d1,large@
                      28              move.l   (a7)+,d1
                      29
                      30              endm
                      31
                      32
00001000              33              org      $1000
                      34
                      35+             LargeWait   $4000
                      36+
                      37+             ifne     narg-1
                      38+             fail     not enough arguments :
                                               LargeWait
                      39+             mexit
                      40+             endc
                      41+
00001000  48E74000    42+             movem.l  d1,-(a7)
00001004  3238 4000   43+large.001   move.w   $4000,d1
                      44+             SmallWait  #$FFFF
                      45+
                      46+             ifne     narg-1
```

TABLE 8.27   (*Continued*) Assembly list file

			47+	fail	not enough arguments : SmallWait
			48+	mexit	
			49+	endc	
			50+		
00001008	2F00		51+	move.l	d0,-(a7)
0000100A	303C	FFFF	52+	move.w	#$FFFF,d0
0000100E	51C8	FFFE	53+small.002	dbra	d0,small.002
00001012	201F		54+	move.l	(a7)+,d0
			55+		
00001014	51C9	FFEE	56+	dbra	d1,large.001
00001018	221F		57+	move.l	(a7)+,d1

8.6 EXERCISES

1. In your own words, define a subroutine.
2. Explain why the subroutine `suba` in Table 8.2 cannot call itself (recursively) given that the code in Table 8.2 is not changed.
3. Define a "stack" as it applies to computer science.
4. What are the conventions (dealing with **push** and **pop**) assumed with stack operations? Under these conventions, which stack instruction causes the stack to grow? to shrink? Which way does the stack shrink in regard to memory locations under standard conventions?
5. Show the difference between the `jsr` and `bsr` instructions by listing the steps which occur in the execution of each of these instructions.
6. Of what must one be careful when using the `rtr` instruction to return from a called subroutine? What is the main purpose of the `rtr` instruction?
7. Explain "pass by reference" and "pass by value" as they pertain to subroutine parameter passing.
8. What are the three ways given in the book to pass parameters into subroutines? Which method is simplest and most efficient for a small number of parameters? a large number of parameters?
9. Draw the structure of a frame (activation record).
10. Explain the action, usage, and need for the `link` and `unlk` instructions.
11. Define and compare the advantages and disadvantages (for both the programmer and the assembler) between internal and external subroutines.
12. State the standard parameter conventions in your own words (paraphrase if you must).
13. Trace the execution of the following program. Show in detail each stack frame as it is built. When the program execution reaches the instruction at location "exit," what are the contents of registers `a6`, `a7`, and `d0`? What does the location "result" contain?

```
            org      $2000
number      dc.l     4
result      ds.l     1

            org      $1000
            move.l   #$6000,a6
```

```
              move.l     #$7000,a7
              move.l     number,-(a7)
              jsr        funcn
              addq       #4,a7
              move.l     d0,result
exit          move       #228,d7
              trap       #14

funcn         link       a6,#-4
              move.l     8(a6),d0
              cmp.l      #1,d0
              beq        return
              move.l     d0,-4(a6)
              sub.l      #1,d0
              move.l     d0,-(a7)
              jsr        funcn
              addq       #4,a7
              move.l     -4(a6),d1
              add.l      d1,d0
return        unlk       a6
              rts

              end
```

14. Write a recursive subroutine FIB that computes the next 25 numbers of the Fibonacci sequence of order 3. The seed values will be found in registers d0, d1, and d2, respectively.

```
** Fibonacci sequence ->   1,     3,     4,
                                 seed1 seed2 seed3

next number of sequence = 1+3+4 = 8
next number of sequence - 3+4+8 = 15   etc.
```

15. Explain the relative advantages and disadvantages of dynamic *versus* static libraries. To which class would operating system libraries be expected to belong? What about small, user-defined libraries?

16. Define the term macro. Under what conditions would a macro be superior to writing a subroutine?

17. Write macros that would simulate the following instructions add3, sub3, mul3, div3; each of which may take two source registers and places the result in a destination register. Use the stack to make space for temporary calculations.

18. Explain the need for local macro labels and conditional macros. Write a conditional macro called copyn Ai Aj n that copies n bytes from the memory address pointed to by Ai to the memory address pointed to by Aj. Try to generate efficient code for small values of n.

19. Discuss the fail and mexit directives. Modify the previous question so that the macro will generate an error message if n > 100.

ADDITIONAL READING

BECK, Leland L. *System Software: An Introduction to Systems Programming*, 2nd ed. Reading, Mass.: Addison Wesley, 1990.

DONOVAN, John J. *Systems Programming* (International Student Edition). New York: McGraw-Hill, 1972.

FREEMAN, P. *Software Systems Principles—A Survey*. New York: Science Research Associates, 1975.

SUN MICROSYSTEMS INC. *Programming Utilities and Libraries*. Sun Microsystems Inc., 1990.

9

Exceptions

We have seen that the next instruction to be executed is determined by the instruction that is currently being executed. We have also seen that this instruction is usually the "next" instruction unless the instruction is a jump, branch, or return instruction. We are about to see that *exceptions,* which are the subject of study in this chapter also alter the order of execution of the instructions.

There are two kinds of exception, **internal** and **external**. Internal exceptions occur when the processor recognizes that an anomalous situation occurred (for example an attempt to divide by zero), whereas external exceptions occur when some external hardware component requires the attention of the processor (for example when a key is depressed on the keyboard). A classification of the exceptions as internal or external is indicated in Table 9.1.

TABLE 9.1 Classification of exceptions

Internal		External
Illegal instruction	Address error	Interrupt
Unimplemented instruction	Divide by zero	Bus error
Privileged instruction	Tracing	External reset
Traps (`trap`, `trapv`)	`chk`	

If we return to the example of attempting to divide by zero, the question becomes what should the processor do? Ignore the operation and proceed with execution of the next instruction or abort execution of the program altogether? No matter what we decide to do, the processor should execute a piece of code that indicates the appropriate action desired. This suggests that the "normal" execution of a program must be suspended and a routine (that contains the appropriate code) must be executed. If we decide that the program should be aborted, a message indicating the reason for the abortion should be given and execution of the program will be terminated. Otherwise, after the routine is executed, we must return to the appropriate instruction of the program. This routine is referred to as the *exception handling routine.*

The next question that arises is how does the processor call the appropriate exception handling routine? The answer here is that the processor (after identifying the exception), will perform a number of actions as illustrated by the flowchart shown in Figure 9.1. First, notice that an exception can occur either during execution of an instruction or immediately after its completion. In either case, the processor should (and does!) determine the nature of the exception. Then an exception handling routine or *exception handler* is invoked. The handler is a piece of code that reflects the appropriate action that must be taken as a response to the "anomaly" that initiated the exception. If the handler detects an error or a condition from which it cannot recover, it suspends execution of the program; otherwise, the handler "handles" the problem and control passes back to the program.

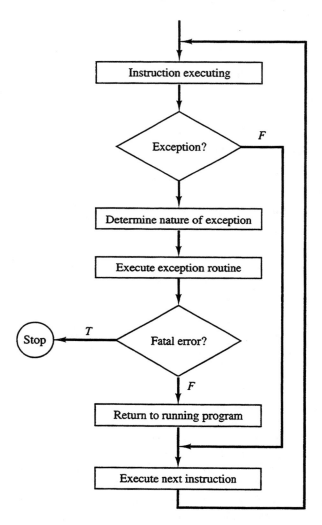

Figure 9.1   High-level view of exception.

The next question to be asked is how does the processor convey the nature of the exception? The answer is that each exception type is mapped to a *unique* number. For example, if the exception is a divide by zero instruction, the exception number is 5; if the exception was caused by an address error, the exception number is 3. The number associated with the exception is an integer ranging from 0 to 255 and is referred to as the *exception vector number*.

Each exception vector number serves as an index to an array of 256 longwords. This array is referred to as the *exception vector table* and is loaded in the first 1K of main memory. When the processor identifies the exception via its vector number v, the processor assumes that the address of the associated exception handler is given by the longword contents of the memory address $v * 4$. The monitor, operating system, or user should store the addresses of the handlers in the appropriate locations in the vector table (see Table 9.4).

Using the exception vector number, the processor invokes the appropriate exception handler. Before the handler is invoked, however, some housekeeping is necessary to be able to branch and execute, and then to return from the exception[1] handler. The number, as well as the sequence of steps that should be performed by the processor, varies according to the type of exception to be handled. Nevertheless, one can separate the exceptions into two disjoint groups as illustrated in Table 9.2.

TABLE 9.2 Two exception groups

	Sequence steps
Group	Exception type
1	Illegal instruction, unimplemented instruction, privilege violation, trace, `trap`, `trapv`, `chk`, zero divide
2	Bus error, address error, (external) reset, interrupt

One can see from Table 9.2, that the first group consists of the set of all internal exceptions except that of the address error, whereas the second group consists of the address error and all external exceptions. All exceptions in the first group require the same sequence of steps, whereas those in the second group require additional steps that are explained later. Outlined subsequently are the sequence of steps that occur for the exceptions that belong in the first group.

We assume that the exception has been identified (Figure 9.2). Recall from our discussion of subroutines that when returning from a subroutine, one should make sure that the status register's `sr` contents are the same upon return from the subroutine as they were before the call. Furthermore, the return address must be saved so that we return to the proper address after servicing the exception. When an exception occurs, the processor does exactly this; it first pushes the return address and then the status register's contents onto the supervisor stack. Also, when an exception takes place, it is implicitly assumed (by the processor) that the exception must be handled by the monitor (operating system). Therefore, from that point on (until return from the exception), the supervisor bit is set[2] so that the processor operates in supervisor mode. Moreover, the processor clears the trace bit so that when the handler is invoked, it is not executing in trace mode.

There is one more point to be made here. Namely, as Table 9.3 indicates, the return address that is pushed onto the stack is the address of either the instruction initiating the exception or the "next" instruction, depending on the type of the exception. Before each exception is discussed in more detail, we would like to emphasize that when an exception occurs, the processor (on its own) performs the necessary steps to invoke the handler. Return from the handler is accomplished, however, *only* by issuing an appropriate return instruction. Some

---

[1] Assuming that no fatal error has been detected.

[2] The exception handler may reset this bit during it's execution.

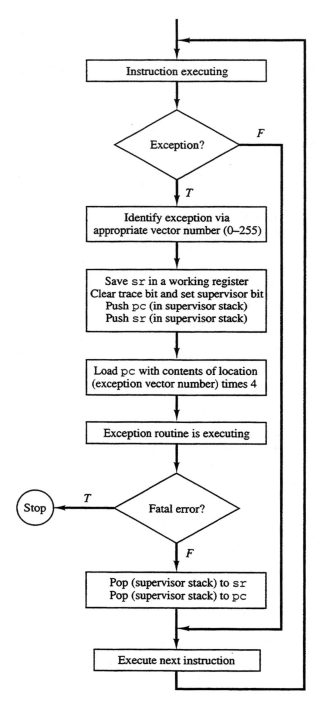

Figure 9.2 Sequence of events that occur in response to exception of internal exception (except that of address error).

TABLE 9.3 Two exception groups

Group	Exception type	Action
	Where to return?	
1	Illegal instruction, unimplemented instruction, privilege violation, address error, bus error	Save the PC of the current instruction
2	Trace, trap, trapv, chk, zero divide, interrupt	Save the PC of the "next" instruction

TABLE 9.4 Exception vector table

Vector number	Address	Assignment
0	$000000	Reset: Initial SSP
1	$000004	Reset: Initial PC
2	$000008	Bus error
3	$00000C	Address error
4	$000010	Illegal instruction
5	$000014	Division by zero
6	$000018	CHK instruction
7	$00001C	TRAPV instruction
8	$000020	Privilege violation
9	$000024	Trace
10	$000028	Line $A emulator
11	$00002C	Line $F emulator
12 13 14	$000030 $000034 $000038	Reserved by Motorola
15	$00003C	Uninitialized interrupt vector
16 23	$000040 .... $00005F	.. Reserved by Motorola
24	$000060	Spurious interrupt
25	$000064	Level 1 Interrupt autovector
26	$000068	Level 2 Interrupt autovector
27	$00006C	Level 3 Interrupt autovector
28	$000070	Level 4 Interrupt autovector
29	$000074	Level 5 Interrupt autovector
30	$000078	Level 6 Interrupt autovector
31	$00007C	Level 7 Interrupt autovector
32 47	$000080 .... $0000BF	.. TRAP Instruction vectors
48 63	$0000C0 .... $0000FF	.. Reserved by Motorola
64 255	$000100 .... $0003FF	.. User interrupt vectors

readers would be quick to point out that the Return and Restore (RTR) instruction will suffice. This instruction pops values off the user stack but *not* from the system stack. Therefore, the counterpart of the rtr instruction provided is the privileged Return from Exception (rte) instruction presented in Table 9.5.

TABLE 9.5   rte instruction

RTE instruction

Action

Execution of this instruction causes top (word size) of system stack to be popped off loaded into sr; then the system stack is popped (longword size) one more time and loaded in pc. This instruction is privileged.

Mnemonic	Opcode	User byte (X,N,Z,V,C bits)	Operands	Format	Length
rte	$4EF3$_{16}$	M M M M M		F14	1

For example, consider the initial situation in Figure 9.3(a). When the rte instruction pointed to by the pc (the instruction in location $480200) is executed, the top word of the system stack, $9623 is popped off and loaded into the sr; then, the top (longword) of the system stack, $00400554 is popped off and loaded into the program counter (Figure 9.3[b]). Execution resumes with the instruction at the latter location.

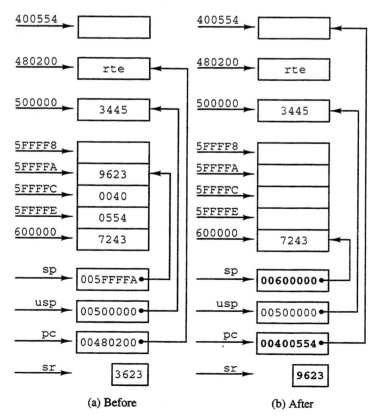

(a) Before   (b) After

Figure 9.3   Effect of execution of rte instruction.

9.1 INTERNAL EXCEPTIONS

This section deals with each of the internal exceptions and provides some examples.

9.1.1 Trace Exception

Recall that when the trace bit of the status register is set, the processor generates a trace exception immediately after execution of each and every instruction of the running program. The trace facility is primarily used as a debugging aid to assist the user in examining the result of execution of each instruction as well as the control flow of the program. Hence, the trace handlers are designed to provide the user with the maximum amount of information. In a number of instances, the handler runs in an interactive mode so the user can request from the handler a display of selected memory contents, a display of register contents and any other pertinent information.

To illustrate the sequence of events, let's assume that our trace handler `trace_handler` dumps the contents of the registers. Moreover, assume that a subroutine `dump_reg`, that performs the register dump, has already been coded and loaded at memory location $6000. Because the vector number associated with the trace exception is vector number 9, the address of our handler should be stored in location 9 * 4 = $24 of the vector table. Here is how the code will look.

```
dump_reg        equ     $6000
trace_vector    equ     $24
   . . .           . . .      . . . . . .


   . . .           . . .      . . . . . .
program         move.l  #trace_handler,trace_vector
   . . .           . . .      . . . . . .
   . . .           . . .      . . . . . .

trace_handler   jsr     dump_reg
                rte

                end
```

Assuming that the trace bit is set after each instruction of our program is executed, the processor will initiate a trace exception sequence that will cause the program to branch to the address indicated by the contents of location $24 where our handler's address have been loaded via the `move.l` instruction. On entering the handler, a branch to subroutine `dump_reg` will occur, a register dump will be performed, followed by a return from the subroutine to the handler, the `rte` instruction will be executed and cause the "next" instruction of our program to be executed, and this sequence will be repeated.

9.1.2 Divide by Zero Exception

When the divisor is zero during execution of a division instruction (i.e., `divs` or `divu`), the processor initiates an exception. As an example, consider the situation in Figure 9.4. During execution of the instruction at location $400550, the processor realizes that an attempt has been made to divide by zero. At this point, the processor initiates the "divide by zero" exception.

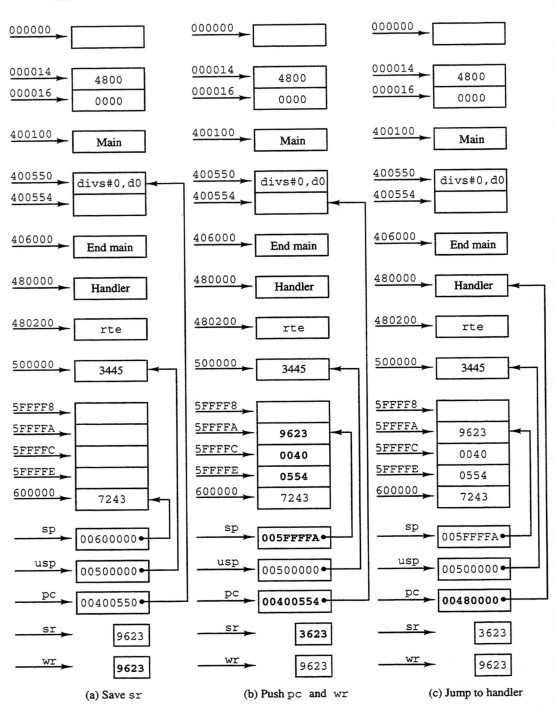

Figure 9.4   Effect of division by zero exception.

First, the processor saves the contents of the `sr` in a working register (`wr`) (Figure 9.4[a]). Second, it resets the trace bit and sets the supervisor bit; then it pushes the address of the "next" instruction, and the contents of the `wr` (in this order) onto the system stack (Figure 9.4[b]). Third, the longword contents of the "division by zero" vector that is located at $000014 are copied into the program counter. The processor then executes the handler for this exception that is at location $48000 (Figure 9.4[c]). For this kind of exception the handler normally provides the user with a message that indicates the type of error and thereafter terminates the user's program.

9.1.3 Privileged Instruction Exception

This exception occurs whenever one attempts to execute a privileged instruction while the processor is running in the user mode. Recall that several MC68000 instructions are privileged, such as `stop` and `rte`. When an application program attempts to execute one of these, a **privileged instruction exception** will occur. The exception vector number for this is exception vector number 8.

9.1.4 Unimplemented and Illegal Instruction Exceptions

There is an assortment of binary strings that do not correspond to any of the valid instructions (privileged or nonprivileged). Distinguishing these invalid "instructions" from valid ones in their machine language representation might seem to be quite a time consuming task. The architecture of the MC68000, however, is such that it permits one to distinguish a number of such instructions in a very straightforward manner. Specifically,

1. No instruction exists whose first nibble is $A. If such an instruction is encountered, a *line $A emulation* exception occurs with associated exception vector 10 (location $28).
2. No instruction exists whose first nibble is $F. If such an instruction is encountered, a *line $F emulation* exception occurs with associated exception vector 11 (location $2C).
3. No instruction exists whose first word is either $4AFA, $4AFB, or $4AFC. If such an instruction or any other instruction (other than those in points 1 and 2) is encountered, an *illegal instruction* exception occurs with associated exception vector 4 (location $10).

For the purposes of distinction, instructions in the first two groups are referred to as *unimplemented instructions*, whereas those in the last group are referred to as *illegal instructions*.

It is worth noting that application programs utilize illegal instructions to their advantage. As the examples that follow will indicate, exceptions of this kind are used to implement additional instructions of our choosing in software or to provide software emulation for instruction formats used by compatible chips.

Unimplemented instructions.   Assume that we have already coded four routines, `real_add`, `real_sub`, `real_mult`, and `real_div` whose functions are to add, subtract, multiply, and divide two real numbers, respectively. Furthermore, assume that the real numbers are represented in binary[3] as longwords with 12 bits dedicated to their fractional part and that the addresses of the real numbers that are to be operated upon are passed to the subroutines via the stack. In other words, before the appropriate subroutine is invoked, we execute the following two instructions:

```
move.l     b,-(a7)              ; push b into the stack
move.l     a,-(a7)              ; push a into the stack
```

In addition, any time that we wish to perform a real operation, instead of using the usual mechanism of calling a subroutine (with either a jsr or bsr instruction), we will generate an exception. In particular, whenever we need to perform a real operation in our program, an unimplemented instruction exception will be generated by using the line A emulator. Moreover, after the exception is generated, our handler must know what real operation it is being requested to perform. This information can be conveyed by a special encoding of the last nibble of the unimplemented instruction. Specifically, we code

```
                              dc.w $A00z
```

where z= 0, 1, 2, or 3 depending on whether an add, subtract, multiply, or divide operation is requested. Figure 9.5 illustrates a portion of the code required.

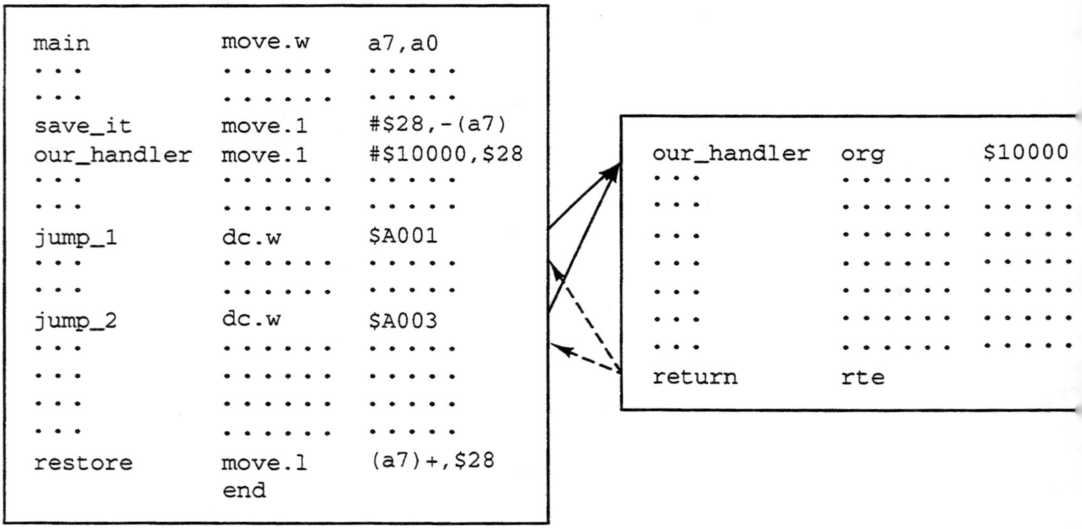

Figure 9.5   Using line A emulator.

Looking at the code of the main, one can we see that initially the system's handler address provided for the line A emulator is saved; then, the handler's address ($10000) is moved into the location of exception vector 11. Note the directive at location jump1. Its execution will cause an exception to occur; our_handler is invoked; the real number subtract operation occurs; we *must* return to the next instruction. The code for the handler is shown in Table 9.6. The reader is encouraged to study it.

---

[3] As described in Chapter 6.

TABLE 9.6

```
our_handler  movem.l  d0/a0,-(sp)      ; save registers

             move.l   usp,a0           ; a0 has usp
             move.l   (a0)+,parm1      ; get a
             move.l   (a0)+,parm2      ; get b
             move.l   a0,usp           ; reset usp
             move.l   10(sp),a0        ; a0 gets address of
                                       ; illegal instruction
             addq     #2,10(sp)        ; fix return address
             clr.w    d0
             move.b   1(a0),d0         ; low order word of
                                       ; d0 has $000z
             asl.w    #2,d0            ; multiply by 4

             move.l   #operation,a0    ; a0 has address of the
                                       ; table
             move.l   0(a0,d0.w),a0    ; a0 has address of
                                       ; proper routine

             jsr      (a0)             ; execute proper real
                                       ; operation
             movem.l  (sp)+,d0/a0      ; restore registers
             rte                       ; return to "next"
                                       ; instruction

parm1        ds.l     1
parm2        ds.l     1
operation    dc.l     real_add,real_sub,real_mult,real_div
```

Illegal instructions.   As discussed earlier, execution of instructions whose the first word is $4AFA, $4AFB or $4AFC, will cause an illegal instruction exception. A user can employ such an instruction with the simple directive

dc.w $4AFC

Certain assemblers provide the assembly language programmer with a no-operand instruction, the illegal instruction presented in Table 9.7, which will achieve the same result.

TABLE 9.7   illegal instruction

Illegal instruction				
Mnemonic	Opcode	Action	Operands	Format	Length
illegal	$ $4AFC_{16}$	Initiate exception at vector number 4		F14	1

A piece of code will now be developed that utilizes the 4AFC instruction to establish breakpoints into an assembly language program. Consider the program discussed in Chapter 8 that calculates the factorial of a number. Also, assume that the user during the debugging process would like the program to pause only at certain points of it (referred to as *breakpoints*) instead of using the trace facility that would cause the program to pause after execution of each and every instruction. The program that we will code gets a machine language program such as the one in Figure 9.6(b) as input.

Location	First word
004004	3038
004016	5540
004020	6000

(a) Breakpoint table

Location object code

006000	
006000	0003
006002	FDFD
004000	
004000	3E7C 7000
004004	3038 6002
004008	6100 000C
00400C	31C0 6002
004010	3E3C 00E4
004014	4E4E
004016	3F00
004018	5540
00401A	6600 0008
00401E	301F
004020	6000 0006
004024	61F0
004026	C0DF
004028	4E75

(b) Input program

Location object code

006000	
006000	0003
006002	FDFD
004000	
004000	3E7C 7000
004004	**4AFC** 6002
004008	6100 000C
00400C	31C0 6002
004010	3E3C 00E4
004014	4E4E
004016	3F00
004018	**4AFC**
00401A	6600 0008
00401E	301F
004020	**4AFC** 0006
004024	61F0
004026	C0DF
004028	4E75

(c) Corrupted program   **Figure 9.6**

The program initially queries the user about which points he or she would like to break; these points are recorded by the program in its *breakpoint table* that is illustrated in Figure 9.6(a). We can see from the first column of this table that the selected breakpoints are at locations $004004, $004016, and $004020. The program then removes the word from each of these memory locations and places it alongside its address in the breakpoint table (second column of the table in Figure 9.6[a]); the word removed is then replaced (in the user's code) by $4AFC (Figure 9.6[c]). In other words, the program *corrupts* the user's program by replacing valid instructions with invalid ones. When such an instruction is executed, an exception occurs; the responsibility of the handler, breakh, is to replace the invalid word with the original word, execute the instruction, corrupt it again, and return to the user's program. The code of this handler is presented in Table 9.8.

TABLE 9.8 Breakpoint handler

```
breakh    movem.l   d0/a0-a1,reg_area        ; save registers
          move.l    2(sp),a0                 ; a0 gets address of illegal
                                             ; instruction

          move.w    (a0),d0                  ; d0.w gets first word of
                                             ; illegal instruction
          cmp.w     #$4afc,d0                ;
          bne       message1                 ; if not $4afc give a message
                                             ; and quit

          jsr       search_breakpoint_tab    ; if address of breakpoint
                                             ; is found in breakpoint
                                             ; table return the address
                                             ; of where it was found in a1
          move.l    a1,d0                    ; set cc
          beq       message2                 ; if zero has been returned
                                             ; give a message and quit

          move.w    4(a1),(a0)               ; restore first word of
                                             ; illegal instruction

          move.l    36,temp                  ; save monitor's trace
                                             ; handler's address
          move.l    #traceh,36               ; store trap handler's address
          or.b      #$80,(sp)                ; set trace bit of "old" SR
          move.l    a0,save                  ; save address of illegal
                                             ; instruction
          movem.l   reg_area,d0/a0-a1        ; restore registers
          rte                                ; return and execute
                                             ; "corrected" instruction

traceh    jsr       trace_handler            ; dumps, etc.
          and.b     #$78,(sp)                ; reset trace bit
          move.w    #$4afc,save              ; make the instruction
                                             ; illegal again!
          move.l    temp,36                  ; restore trap vector
          rte

reg_area  ds.l      3
save      ds.l      1
temp      ds.l      1
```

9.1.5 Trap Exceptions

Traps are instructions that enable a user to generate exceptions via software. They are discussed subsequently.

Trap on overflow.   The `trapv` instruction may be used to "catch" overflows in arithmetic operations. This instruction is illustrated in Table 9.9 and is used in the following manner. A trapv instruction is included in the assembly code immediately after each arithmetic operation that may result in an overflow. The user (or operating system) then provides a trapv exception handler to process this type of exception should it occur. Notice that the start address of this handler must be loaded into exception vector number 7, (i.e, at address $00001C). Whenever the overflow bit is set by an operation, the following trapv will respond by initiating a software exception as discussed earlier.

TABLE 9.9   trapv instruction

Trap on overflow					
Mnemonic	Opcode	Action	Operands	Format	Length
trapv	$4E76$_{16}$	If (V=1) then initiate exception (vector number 7)		F14	1

Traps.   Another use for exceptions is to allow an applications program to communicate with the operating system or monitor. The applications programmer may initiate software exceptions via 16 different available trap instructions outlined in Table 9.10.

TABLE 9.10   trap instructions

Trap instructions					
Mnemonic	Opcode	Action	Operands	Format	Length
trap	$4E4$_{12}$	Initiate exception at vector number $Vector_4 + 32$. $0 \leq Vector_4 \leq 15$.	#Vector$_4$	F6	1

9.1.6 Check Instruction

An instruction that initiates an exception whenever an integer is not within a specified range is known as the chk instruction and is presented in Table 9.11.

This instruction is used primarily to detect the index of an array which is out of bounds. In particular, the index is assumed to have been loaded into data register dn and the upper bound for the index to be specified by the source operand before this instruction is issued.

TABLE 9.11   chk instruction

CHK Instruction					
Action					
If low-order word of data register dn is less than zero or greater than word indicated by word-size source operand (mem), an exception is initiated at vector number 6; mem can be specified via any mode except address register direct.					
Mnemonic	Opcode	User byte (X,N,Z,V,C bits)	Operands	Format	Length
chk	16_{7}$	P M U U U U	mem, dn	F20	1, 2, 3

If we assume that the contents of data register d0 is $000000F2, then execution of the instruction chk #5,d0 will initiate an exception whereas execution of chk #405,d0 will not initiate an exception.

9.1.7 Address Error

This type of exception occurs whenever one attempts to access a longword or a word at a byte boundary. As we mentioned earlier, this exception causes the processor to save three additional pieces of information on the stack than other exceptions that have ben studied so far. In particular, the processor after it pushes the current `pc` and the "old" contents of the `sr` onto the stack, it pushes also (in this order):

1. The first word of the instruction that was in progress and caused the error.
2. The (longword) address that caused the bus error.
3. A word, the *access type word*, that contains information about the type of cycle that was in progress at the time the error occurred. The four most significant bits of this word must be `0000`.

It is highly unusual that a program would ever recover from such an error; all this information is provided to the user to *locate* the error. For this reason we refer the reader to the MC68000 programmer's manual for an explanation of each of the fields concerning the access type word.

9.2 EXTERNAL EXCEPTIONS

External exceptions occur as a result of activity outside the processor and may be classified as either intentional or unintentional. Intentional external exceptions occur either at power on, with the **reset** exception, or when another device wishes to communicate with the central processor by issuing an **interrupt**. As mentioned earlier, the term interrupt is used to indicate that the "normal" flow of execution has been temporarily suspended, or interrupted, while another piece of code is being executed. This code segment is used to service requests by the interrupting device. Unintentional exceptions occur either as **spurious interrupts** to the processor or **address bus errors**. Spurious interrupts are caused by spikes (or glitches) in the interrupt lines that cause the processor to start the interrupt cycle erroneously. We will now consider each of these exception cases in greater detail.

9.2.1 Reset

A reset interrupt is signalled by asserting one of the pins on the MC68000 chip (the $\overline{reset}$ line). This pin is connected to the power on logic of the computer so that the processor is prevented from operating until the circuits surrounding the processor are quiescent. At this stage the reset line is released permitting the MC68000 to begin execution. Consider the state of the MC68000 immediately after a reset. All registers have undetermined values including the system stack pointer and program counter. Thus, without some **reset procedure**, the next operation of the processor would be unpredictable. The reset procedure for the MC68000 therefore operates as follows:

1. Immediately terminate current instruction processing (if any).
2. Set the supervisor status bit, reset the trace bit, set the interrupt priority mask to level seven.

3. Load the system stack pointer with the longword starting at location $000000 in memory.

4. Load the program counter with the longword starting at location $000004 in memory.

5. Begin program execution using the system state as given above (i.e., start the instruction fetch/execute cycle).

Clearly for the processor to perform useful work, there must exist system initialization routines that would be the first ones to be executed after a reset. Notice also that for the system to get started, *at least* two longwords of ROM starting at location $000000 plus enough ROM, at the appropriate location, to contain the initialization routines is required. Starting or **booting** a computer system is a task that requires some explanation.

From a previous discussion, one can see that code can be executed in ROM after a reset. In a typical computer system the code contained in ROM includes a **bootstrap loader**. On simple systems a **basic input/output subsystem** may also be included. For embedded or single board systems such as the TUTOR board the ROM may even include the entire operating system software. In the former case, the bootstrap loader is a short code segment that reads one or more **boot records** from an external device (usually the first track of a default disk drive) into memory. This **bootfile** is presumed to contain enough of the operating system to load in the remainder, initialize external devices, and initialize the complete system. In the case that the ROM contains the I/O subsystem (for example the BIOS of many personal computers) the boot procedure is then required to load only the remaining operating system code into memory. We note here that in many "networked systems" the computer is diskless and may be booted across a network. Whereas the details of this are more complex, the principle is the same; the bootfile is loaded from the device (in this case across the network) into memory and the computer begins its normal operation.

9.2.2 Interrupts

Another intentional form of exception are interrupts. In computer systems interrupts are generated by external devices (i.e., disk-drive controllers, graphics interfaces, or serial communication cards). These devices interrupt the processor to inform it that either data has arrived or that some external state has changed. If data has arrived the system must decide what to do with it; while in the case of a status report, the processor must take the appropriate action. We will first look at precisely what the processor does when an interrupt is signalled. We then indicate how this mechanism is used to greatly improve the performance of a system.

Processor response to interrupt.   Interrupts on most computers, and on the MC68000 in particular, use an interrupt mask register (discussed in Chapter 6) and an external interface to allow interrupt processing. The MC68000 has three interrupt pins on the processor chip. These pins are connected via external logic to the control bus interrupt lines and permit external devices to interrupt the processor. An interrupt is signalled by asserting some combination of these lines; this yields seven **levels** of interrupt numbered one (%001) to seven (%111). Once a device signals an interrupt, it waits for the processor to acknowledge the signal before continuing. If the interrupt mask register is numerically less than the level of the interrupt level, an interrupt occurs as explained below; otherwise, the processor ignores the interrupt until such time the mask register is set below the external level. Notice that during normal operation the processor runs at "level 0", that is, no interrupt. Thus all interrupts should eventually be serviced. Assuming that the processor is about to **service an interrupt** the following actions occur.

1. The processor completes the instruction currently executing.

2. The processor acknowledges the external interrupt by entering an **interrupt acknowledge cycle**. During this cycle the external device either places an **interrupt vector number** on the lower order byte of the data bus (followed by assertion of the **data transfer acknowledge** [DTACK] signal), which is then read by the processor or it indicates to the processor that **autovectoring** must be used by asserting the **valid peripheral address** (VPA) line. If the external device provides an interrupt number, the processor reads this value from the data bus into an internal register. If autovectoring is used, the interrupt number specified on the three interrupt lines is added to 24 to give a number in the range of 25 to 31. This number is used as the interrupt vector. In any event, the processor now has an interrupt vector.

3. The interrupt number defined in action two is now multiplied by four (i.e., we perform an arithmetic shift left two places) and zero extended[4] to 24 bits. This gives a result in the range 0 to 1020 which is used as an address to access a longword from the exception vector table stored in the first 1024 bytes of memory.

4. Exception processing then continues similarly to the processing of internal exceptions discussed earlier with one modification. Thus the status register (a single word) is stored in a working register; and, the status register is modified as follows. The supervisor status bit is set, the trace bit is reset; and, *the interrupt mask is set to the current interrupt level*. The program counter (a longword) is then pushed onto the supervisor stack; the working register is pushed onto the supervisor stack; and, the program counter is loaded with the longword from the exception vector table as discussed in action 3. Recall that an interrupt is only processed if it is at a higher level than the current level. Therefore, new interrupts at the level being processed will now be inhibited.

5. The processor is finally ready to begin processing again; therefore, the instruction fetch/execute cycle is resumed. The new program counter will of course point to the appropriate **interrupt handler** assumed to be a supervisor subroutine that will process the request/status indicated by the external device. This routine will complete using the `rte` instruction, causing a return to the interrupted program.

Notice that saving the status register and program counter permit the interrupt handler to execute an `rte` instruction once it has completed its code. Thus interrupt handlers may be considered as `traps` that are invoked by external circumstance and return using the special `rte` instruction. Also note that when the previous status register is pushed onto the stack, so too is the *then current* interrupt level and privilege status. Thus, when the routine returns with an `rte`, the interrupted program will continue to execute at the same privilege status and interrupt level as it was prior to the interrupt. The reader should realize from this that *interrupts may be nested* in the sense that an interrupt from an external device may occur while we are in the process of handling another, lower level, interrupt. Because

---

[4] Padded to the left with binary zeros.

the previous program context is saved on the supervisor stack this will not cause problems. Later will consider nested exceptions more closely.

Spurious and uninitialized interrupts.   Spurious interrupts are caused by spikes (or glitches) in the interrupt lines that cause the processor to start the interrupt cycle erroneously. The processor realizes this phenomenon from the fact that neither of the signals VPA nor DTACK was asserted during the interrupt acknowledge cycle; and, a spurious interrupt exception will be initiated with exception vector number 24.

Finally, the processor will initiate an uninitialized exception with associated exception vector number 15 if the DACK signal has been asserted but the device that generated the interrupt has not initialized its exception vector register. The 68000-series peripherals have been designed in such a way so a reset operation causes the vector $0F to be loaded into the device's interrupt vector register.

Why we have external interrupts.   The reader may be wondering why it is necessary to have interrupts in the first place. The reason lies in the observation that a processor must communicate with its external environment. Notice that the external environment runs **asynchronously** to the processor. That is, events occur over which the processor has no control and is unable to predict. For example, each character read by a terminal must be loaded into the processor at some point; however, the processor is unable to predict *when* the terminal key will be pressed. Let's assume for this discussion that whenever a character is pressed on the terminal keyboard its equivalent ASCII character "appears" in location $0A00 and remains there until another key is pressed (details on external device interfacing is given in Chapter 10). Without the benefits of interrupts, the processor must periodically check to see if location $0A00 has changed. The process whereby the CPU checks to see if a character has arrived is called **polling**; and, in this context, it is a very inefficient process. To better understand this notice that the processor is required to enter a tight loop which continuously monitors this location until a new character arrives. This code segment is shown clearly in Table 9.12.

TABLE 9.12 Character processing by polling

```
; we assume that the processor alternates between reading a character
; and processing that character.
;
Initialize                              ; prepare to start work
            clr.w   $0A00               ; initialize character register
;
Loop                                    ; begin loop to get a character
            tst.w   $0A00               ; test for a character
            beq     Loop                ; repeat if null character
            move.w  $0A00,d0            ; Yes - we have a character
            clr.w   $0A00               ; ready for next time
;
useful_work                             ; start useful work with character
            ...     ......
            ...     ......
            ...     ......              ; ready for next character
            bra     Loop                ; wait for another character
```

As one can see, there are several problems with the code in Table 9.12. First, the processor spends too much time waiting for a character when it's not there! To see just how wasteful this activity is, consider a typical typist who types 100 words per minute, with an average word length of 6 characters. This produces a stream of characters at the rate of one character every 1/600th of a second. Assuming that the average time to execute a MC68000 instruction is 12 cycles, a 12 MHz MC68000 will execute about one million instructions per second. Thus the MC68000 is able to execute about $1,666$ instructions between each incoming character. Now the question arises, if the time to process the incoming character is of the order of a few instructions, what can the processor do while it is waiting for the next character? The answer, unfortunately, is *nothing*! Recall that the input is asynchronous; thus, we do not know when the next character will appear. Therefore, the processor's computing power is wasted while it awaits for a new input.

Second, notice that if we consider the case of interfacing with several external devices, we see that polling becomes even more complex. Each new device will require that it be checked periodically. This would make the code to respond to external inputs more difficult to write. Additionally, the time required to poll all these devices would be linearly dependent on the number of devices being polled, not on the number of new inputs which is where our interest lies! To summarize, we see that without some extra mechanism, interfacing to external devices by polling is a time consuming and complex activity.

As the reader might suspect, the answer to our problem lies with **interrupt processing**. The user should already be able to see that the external interrupt lines offer a mechanism whereby an external device may interrupt the processor from its normal activities to have it execute a special code segment. This is precisely the action that is required when a new character arrives. Consider our simple terminal as described earlier with the following modifications. Whenever a key is pressed, the character is placed in location $0A00 as before and then an autovectored level one interrupt is signalled to the processor by the terminal controller. Once the interrupt is signalled, the process of acknowledging it and clearing the interrupt lines is performed directly by the processor's hardware. The code segment for this example is presented in Table 9.13. There are two points that require comment regarding Table 9.13. First, the initialization code sets the level one autovector exception vector to be the address of the interrupt routine. Recall from Table 9.3 that level 1 through level 7 autovectors are exception vectors 25 through 31 inclusive. Thus to respond to a level one interrupt, the starting address of CharIntHdlr (a longword) should be loaded at location $4 * 25 = 100$; that is, $0064. The second point to be aware of is that the interrupt routine is called *only* when a character is available; therefore, **no** time is wasted by checking for a valid character. This implies that the processor is now spending 100% of its time performing useful work, as we would wish.

Interrupt processing has therefore resolved both criticisms regarding polling. That is, the processor is now free to perform useful work until such time as a new input value occurs; and, the processing time spent on handling external devices is now linearly dependent on the number of inputs, not the number of devices.

9.2.3 Bus Error

Typical situations when such an exception would occur is whenever one attempts to access a nonexistent or faulty memory address. The steps that the processor follows whenever

TABLE 9.13   Character processing with interrupts

```
; This is the initialization code for the character interrupt handler.
; initialize
          lea       CharIntHdlr,$0064      ; set the location of
                                           ; the handler.
          clr.w     $0A00                  ; ready for a character.
;
; Useful work that its performance does not require characters to be
; input.
;
UsefulWork

          ...       ......
          ...       ......
          ...       ......
          bra       UsefulWork
;
; This is the code for the interrupt handler.  This point is reached
; only if a character is now ready to be read from $0A00 and an
; interrupt has been flagged.  Notice that all previous activity
; has been suspended until this is finished with an rte.
;
CharIntHdlr
;
; To process exception: read character, process it, return.
;
          movem.l   d0-d7/a0-a6,-(sp)      ; save registers.
          move.b    $0A00,d0               ; get character.
          ...       ......
          ...       ......                 ; process character
;
; Exit interrupt handler
;
          movem.l   (sp)+,a0-a6/d0-d7      ; restore registers
          rte
```

such an exception occurs are identical to those that occur whenever an address error exception occurs; a repeated discussion is unnecessary. Table 9.14 demonstrates a simple bus error handler that may be used to print a message to the terminal of the tutor board and return control to TUTOR. Notice that the tutor monitor already contains a similar handler. It is worth pointing out that the information stacked by the bus error exception makes it difficult to locate exactly the instruction causing the error. The reason for this is that the program counter stacked is not necessarily the program counter corresponding to the start of the erroneous instruction, instead it the program counter *some way through* the instruction (in fact, at the point the MC68000 detects the bus error). Thus the handler must use this address, along with the first word of the instruction (also stacked), to search for the correct address. Notice also that this program will not operate

TABLE 9.14 Bus error handler

```
;
; This code segment demonstrates installing a bus error handler to
; print a simple error message and terminate a program.
;
Stop            equ     228
Output          equ     243
                org     $2000
BusHndlr        equ     *                              ; bus error handler
                move.w  (sp)+,FnCode                   ; save function
                                                       ; code info
                move.l  (sp)+,BadAddr                  ; save the offending
                                                       ; address
                move.w  (sp)+,Instruction ; save the
                                                       ; offending instruction
                add     #6,sp                          ; delete stacked sr
                                                       ; and pc
                lea     ErrorStr,a5                    ; prepare to print
                                                       ; message
                movea   #StrEnd,a6
                move.l  #Output,d7                     ; print message
                trap    #14
                move.l  #Stop,d7                       ; go to tutor exit
                trap    #14


FnCode                  dc.w    0
BadAddr                 dc.l    0
Instruction     dc.w    0
ErrorStr        dc.b    'Bus Error detected'
StrEnd                  dc.b    0
;
; User program starts here
;
                org     $3000
Init            equ     *                              ; set up bus
                                                       ; error handler
                move.l  #BusHndlr,$0008
                move.w  $8FFFFF,D0                     ; instrn will
                                                       ; cause bus error
                end
```

correctly on the simulator, this is because the trap vector table and routines are not mod-
ifiable in SIM68K.

   Summarizing the steps.   The previous discussions relative to the steps that the processor takes when an exception occurs can be classified into four groups that are outlined in
Table 9.14.

TABLE 9.14   Four exception groups according to sequence of steps required for handling an exception

Exception sequence steps		
Group	Exception type	Action
1	Illegal instruction, unimplemented instruction, privilege violation, `trap`, `trapv`, `chk`, trace, zero divide	1. Save SR in a WR. 2. Set supervisor bit and clear trace bit. 3. Save "PC" in system stack. 4. Push WR in system stack. 5. Jump to location indicated by exception vector.
2	Bus error, address error	1. Save SR in WR. 2. Set Supervisor bit, clear trace bit. 3. Push "PC" into the system stack. 4. Push WR in system stack. 5. "Invalid" address is pushed into the system stack. 6. Access type word is pushed onto the stack. 7. Jump to location indicated by exception vector.
3	(External) reset	1. Set supervisor bit, clear trace bit, set mask's interrupt level to 7. 2. Move longword contents of location exception vector zero to register a7. 3. Jump to location indicated by the longword contents of exception vector one.
4	Interrupt.	1. Save SR in WR. 2. Set supervisor bit, clear trace bit, set interrupt level to that of the servicing interrupt. 3. Processor informs device that issued interrupt that latter is serviced. 4. Device responds by presenting processor with exception vector number u. 5. Push "PC" into system stack. 6. Push WR in system stack. 7. Jump to location indicated by exception vector u.

9.3   NESTED EXCEPTIONS

In the case of multiple exceptions, the exceptions can be nested. Table 9.15 lists their relative priorities. Observe that level 0 corresponds to the highest priority, whereas level 2 corresponds to the lowest priority.

TABLE 9.15   Exception priorities

Exception priorities		
Level	Exception type	Action
0	Address error, bus error, external reset	Abort current instruction and then cess exception
1	Illegal instruction, unimplemented instruction, trace, interrupt, privilege violation	Complete current instruction and process exception
2	`trap`, `trapv`, `chk`, divide by zero	Instruction execution initiates exetion processing

9.4 EXCEPTION PROCESSING IN THE MC68010/20/30

In concluding this chapter we note that exception processing is significantly different in more powerful models of this architecture. We summarize these differences subsequently.

9.4.1 MC68010

First, the MC68010 includes a **vector base register**. The vector base register contains the address of the exception vector table in memory. Thus, the exception vector table no longer need start at location $000000 in memory. Second, the MC68010 makes some provision for virtual memory support[5]. Recall that in the MC68000 an access type word is pushed onto the stack during a bus or address error. In the case of the MC68010 this is modified to reflect the new processor type. In particular the most significant bits of the access type word must now be `1000` otherwise a trap to a **format error** exception vector takes place. For memory or bus errors, the MC68010 now stacks an additional 22(!) words of information. This additional information describes the internal state of the processor at the time of the bus error. As before the approximate location of the erroneous instruction is stacked. This information permits the MC68010 to control virtual memory using external hardware, a feat which is impossible when using the MC68000. Thus, the bus and memory error handlers are able to detect virtual address errors and load the physical pages into memory before reexecuting the instruction. As the user might expect the `rte`, by recognizing the access type and reading the additional words, correctly restores the machine state once the memory or bus error handler has concluded it's work.

9.4.2 MC68020

Unlike the MC68010, the MC68020 and higher models provide complete support for virtual memory. Thus, while the user programming model looks the same (i.e., 8 data registers, 8 address registers, a program counter, and a condition code register) the supervisor programming model is completely different. In particular, the model now includes the following registers: **interrupt stack pointer, master stack pointer, status register, vector base register,** two **alternate function code registers, cache control register,** and a **cache address register.** Some of these deserve comment. We have now separated out the regular supervisor stack (master stack pointer) from that used for interrupt processing (interrupt stack pointer). The alternate function code registers contain 3-bit function codes, which may be considered extensions of the 32-bit linear address space. This provides up to eight 4-Gb address spaces. The function codes correspond to external pins on the chip and are set according to which memory cycle is being used (e.g., user instruction, user data, supervisor instruction, supervisor data, etc.) and, unlike the MC68010, are used by certain instructions to explicitly specify the function codes for operations. The user may also connect the MC68020 to the MC68851 **paged memory management unit** (PMMU).

In addition, the MC68020 extends the exception vector table assignments to include floating point exceptions and paged memory management unit exceptions. Also, the exception stack frame format is greatly extended from that of the MC68010. In particular, the access type word now specifies one of six different stack frames for exception processing.

---

[5] See Chapter 10 for a discussion on virtual memory.

These include the normal four word stack frame, a throwaway four word stack frame, a six word stack frame, a coprocessor midinstruction stack frame, a 16-word short bus cycle fault stack frame, and a 46-word(!) long bus cycle fault stack frame. Again, these are correctly handled by the `rte` instruction.

Finally, we note that the MC68020 and higher processors have on-chip cache memories.[6] The cache within the MC68020 may be manipulated via the cache control register and cache address register. In particular, the programmer can enable, disable, clear, clear an entry, and freeze, the cache. Detailed operation of the cache is, unfortunately, beyond the scope of this text.

9.4.3 MC68030

The MC68030 is upward compatible to the MC68020 and again provides the user with a familiar programming model. The MC68030 supervisor programming model, however, is significantly different from that of the MC68020. In particular the MC68030 contains the following additional registers, **cpu root pointer register, supervisor root pointer register, translation register, transparent translation register 0, transparent translation register 1,** and **mmu status register.** These registers, along with 256-byte instruction and data caches, enable the MC68030 to manipulate the on-chip memory management unit very efficiently. The root pointer register's point to the roots of the translation trees for the currently executing user and supervisor tasks. The translation control register enables and disables the use of address translation. The transparent translation registers each specify separate blocks of memory that are to be accessed without address translation (for I/O transfers, etc.) The result of these enhancements is a processor that supports virtual memory much more quickly that does the MC68020 but is otherwise similar.

9.5 EXERCISES

1. Explain the difference between *external* and *internal* exceptions and give an example of each.
2. What is the `chk` exception used for? Show a sample code segment that makes use the `chk` exception that checks for the valid array bounds $0 \cdots 100$.
3. What is the `trapv` exception used for? Show a sample code segment that makes use of the `trapv` exception.
4. Why does the MC68000 possess an `rte` instruction in addition to the `rts` instruction. Does the `rte` instruction behave in the same way for all exceptions?
5. Explain exactly what occurs when an autovectored interrupt occurs. Assume for your discussion that the device interrupts at level 2. Write a simple handler to clear the registers `d0 ... d7` whenever this autovectored interrupt occurs. Show how it would be installed.
6. Explain exactly what occurs when an vectored interrupt occurs. Assume that the external device places the value $20 onto the low byte of the data bus after signaling the interrupt. Write a simple handler to clear the registers `d0 ... d7` whenever this autovectored interrupt occurs. Show how it would be installed.
7. Explain the sequence of events that occur after a power-on reset. Is the order of register loads important, if so why?

---

[6] Caches are described in Chapter 5.

8. Show the supervisor stack before and after a bus error exception. Explain each item on the stack and give it's size. Why does the information on the stack differ from that of the `trapv` exception?

9. Write a code segment that will respond to a memory address error by replacing the erroneous instruction with a `jmp (a0)` instruction, where a0 is loaded with $1000 (assumed to be the user's own memory address error handler). Why do we use `jmp (a0)` instruction rather than, say, a `jmp $nnnnnnn`?

10. List the exceptions handled by the MC68000 and explain what each is used for.

11. You are developing an embedded system using the MC68000 which makes frequent use of base conversion on the contents of a register. To save time during execution you decide to implement this as an illegal instruction (a). The instruction will have an assembler syntax `conv #imm,an,am` where imm is an immediate constant (8,10,or 16) indicating the required base; dn is a register containing a non-negative binary integer; and am indicates the address of the result. After the instruction executes a $00 terminated ASCII string, starting at address (am), should indicate the integer's value. Design the instruction and write the exception handler to implement `conv`.

12. What is the problem with trying to trace a program when you generate exceptions?

13. What are the differences between `rts` and `rte`?

14. Trace throughout the exceptions execution cycle for vector number 9.

15. If the pc = $2000 and the sr = $F023, what is the effect of the `rte` instructions? If the pc = $2200 and the sr = $0034, what is the effect of an `rte`?

16. If you were given access to the address of the handler for the privileged violation exception, describe one way that you could get supervisor status for your program.

17. Write the piece of code to set up the line $A emulator exception handler, also write the exception handler to do the following: If the instructions is $A000 you should do nothing, but if the instruction is $A0A0 the sum of registers d3 and d4. On completion of the exception, no registers but d4 should be affected.

18. To prevent an infinite loop what step should be at the end of every exception handler you write for this class.

19. For what reasons are internal and external exceptions handled differently?

20. Demonstrate your understanding of exceptions by writing the code necessary to perform the stopping at break points the tutor provides.

ADDITIONAL READING

BECK, LELAND L. *System Software: An Introduction to Systems Programming*, 2nd ed. Reading, Mass.: Addison-Wesley, 1990.

DONOVAN, JOHN J. *Systems Programming* (International Student Edition). New York: McGraw-Hill, 1972.

FREEMAN, P. *Software Systems Principles—A Survey*. Science Research Associates, 1975.

SUN MICROSYSTEMS INC. *Programming Utilities and Libraries*. Sun Microsystems Inc., 1990.

CLEMENTS, A. *Microprocessor Systems Design*. Boston: Prindle, Weber and Schmidt, 1987.

LIPPIATT, A. G. *The Architecture of Small Computer Systems*. Englewood Cliffs, N.J.: Prentice Hall, 1979.

SCANLON, L. J. *The 68000: Principles and Programming*. Indianapolis: Howard W. Sams, 1981.

10

Communicating with the Outside World

In this chapter the discussion will focus on how the CPU communicates with other devices. We discuss the different methods used for device communications including the two types of I/O module used on the Educational Computer Board (ECB), the asynchronous serial port (the MC6850) used for controlling terminals and printers, and the combined parallel interface and timer unit (the MC68230). An Ethernet controller (the NS32490C, used to attach a workstation to a local area network) is used as an example of a more complex controller. We then consider each of the peripherals from the register transfer level and discuss the programmer's view of these devices. Figure 10.1 shows the typical devices that could be used on a simple, single-board development system. In this instance, the user interface is through a non-graphics, terminal/keyboard combination that is connected to a serial communications port. There is no secondary storage; however, an additional serial I/O interface is available which is connected to a printer. An example of this system is the Motorola ECB.

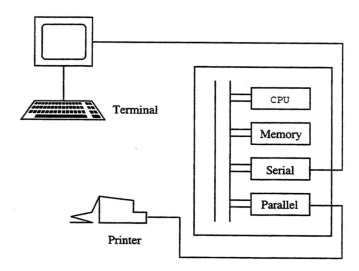

Figure 10.1 Common attachments to single-board computer.

10.1 I/O MODULES

In Chapter 3 several secondary devices such as tape drives and disk drives were presented and their characteristics discussed. Programs and examples presented so far, however, have not involved any I/O operations. The reason for this is that we assumed that our computer system consisted of only a CPU and main memory, both attached to the system bus. We are now ready to discuss how external devices could be added to our system and how programs can be written that will permit data transfer between the CPU and these external devices. To this end consider Figure 10.2, which represents a schematic of two I/O devices, a terminal, and a printer that have been attached to our system.

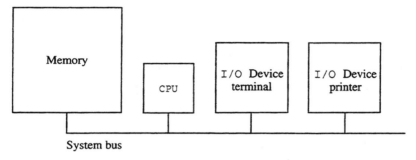

Figure 10.2   Schematic diagram of computer system.

Recall from our discussions in Chapter 3 that

1. The time required to perform a data transfer from/to an external device and the CPU is considerably longer than the time required for a similar data transfer between CPU and main memory. Hence, if the CPU were to wait for I/O operations to complete much time would be wasted.

2. The transfer of data requires many related tasks such as assembling the incoming bits into bytes, performing parity checks, and acknowledging data. If these tasks were to be performed by the CPU via software, significant overhead would be introduced. Hence, to speed up this process we delegate these tasks to specialized hardware units.

3. Each external device type has different characteristics and operates differently as regards data formats and transmission rates. Thus different control logic must be introduced for each device.

In order to perform I/O operations, therefore, external devices are rarely *attached* directly to the bus. Instead, a new hardware component, referred to as an *I/O module*, is employed that serves as an interface between the CPU and the device. In other words, the attachment of each device to the system bus is *not* as direct as could be (mis)interpreted from Figure 10.2. Rather, the connections are as illustrated Figure 10.3 in which each device is linked via a multiwire cable (dashed line) to an I/O module through a *port*, the module is in turn directly connected (solid line) to the system bus.[1]

---

[1] More will be said later.

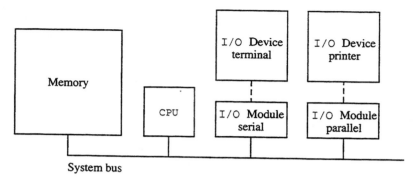

Figure 10.3   Schematic diagram of computer system.

Three new issues emerge that must be addressed relative to the I/O module:

1. **The internal interface.** How is the I/O module connected to the system bus, and how does the assembly language programmer control it?
2. **The external interface.** How is the device connected to the I/O module?
3. **It's minimal components.** What are the minimal components necessary to control an external device?

10.1.1 Internal Interface

The system bus of a typical system is a collection of wires as explained in Chapter 1. In *embedded* systems (i.e., systems that have a specific purpose such as a traffic light controller) and small systems (such as the ECB) the bus may simply be wires etched on a printed circuit board (PCB), which may terminate on the edge of the board in connector. In these instances I/O modules are often integrated onto the PCB to save space. In larger systems the bus is organized as a *backplane*, which contains a number of slots. The bus runs "through" each slot, thus an I/O module may be attached to the bus by plugging it into the backplane. A typical I/O module is therefore a self contained functional unit. The necessary components (a collection of SSI, MSI, and LSI chips) are usually arranged on the I/O board, or *card*.

From the assembly programmer's perspective a memory mapped device may be thought of as a set of user programmable registers as shown in Figure 10.4. The user controls the device (i.e., issues I/O requests) through the **control register** and monitors the status of an I/O request through the **status register**. For character devices, there may also be a **transmit register** and a **receive register**, which are used to write and read the data values. In more complex devices, an entire buffer is defined as shared memory; thus, both the device *and* the bus are able to access this shared memory region simultaneously.

10.1.2 External Interface

Recall that the external interface is provided via a multiwire cable. The wires of this cable can be divided into three distinct sets; the *control* lines, the *status* lines, and the *data* lines. The number of the lines depends on the type of transmission. In particular if the transmis-

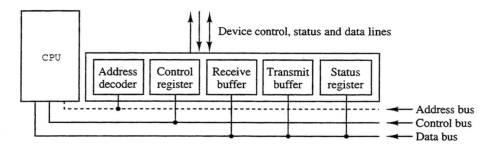

Figure 10.4   Minimal components of I/O module, and its internal and external interfaces.

sion is **serial**, then there is only one data line[2] because (as the name suggests) the data are transmitted serially one bit at a time. If the transmission is **parallel**, then there will be a number of data lines so each byte can be transmitted in parallel, that is, 1 byte at a time, 1 bit on each line. Other external interfaces include coaxial cable (as used in cable television) and fiber optics. In principle, serial transmissions are considerably slower than parallel transmissions; therefore, serial modules are attached to slow devices such as modems and terminals whereas parallel modules are employed with high speed devices such as magnetic tapes and disks. In either case, the receiver and transmitter must be synchronized in such a way that the receiver knows when to sample the data lines to receive data. This synchronization can be done in two modes: either *asynchronously* or *synchronously*. Thus communications over a direct (i.e., point-to-point) link may be either **asynchronous** or **synchronous**. The term *asynchronous* implies that the sender and receiver need not be synchronized; this will be discussed shortly whereas *synchronous* data transfer requires that the sender and receiver synchronize their data transfer clocks. This requires costly controllers; however, once this is done high data rates are attained. We will focus initially on the more modest asynchronous modules used on the ECB. Recall from Chapter 3 that a popular mechanism for low/medium speed data transfer (e.g., 300 bps to 1 Mbps) is asynchronous serial communication.

Serial asynchronous communications.   Recall that the term *serial* implies that a single wire is used to send data with the data sent one bit at a time along the wire. For simultaneous, bidirectional communications, we therefore require two wires, a transmit wire (or line) and a receive wire. Asynchronous communication is achieved by the sender first transmitting a start bit (%1), then the eight data bits (zeros and ones), then one or more stop bits (%0). The receiver uses the start bit as a reference point to determine when to sample the line for incoming data bits.

In other words, the transmission of a byte requires the transmission of a larger quantity of information that will be referred to as a *data packet*. The number of bits in the data packet depends on the format used by the external device. Later on, one can see that the I/O module can be programmed to support one out of a number of different formats; therefore, it can be connected to a number of devices having different characteristics. The next issue that must be addressed is "when and how" the transmitter "puts" the bits to the transmit line and "when and how" the receiver "gets" the data from this line. This is determined by the *baud rate*. The transfer mechanism is very simple. Both the receiver and the transmit-

---

[2] Actually, two lines; one to transmit and one to receive.

ter employ a *baud rate generator*, which is a hardware clock that generates pulses. The generators at both ends generate the same number of clock pulses per second which is referred to as the *baud rate*. This way the transmitter puts a bit in a transmit line in rhythm with the clock pulse. Assuming binary encoding a baud rate of 2400 will yield 2400 bps.

As an example, consider a data packet format consisting of one start bit, seven bits per ASCII character, even parity, and two stop bits. Assuming a baud rate of 2400, each clock pulse occurs every 1/2400 of a second; assume that we would like to send the string "Hello" out. Figure 10.5 illustrates the sequence of events that would occur.

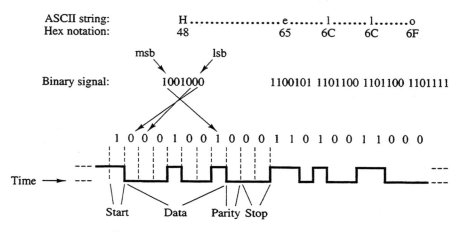

Figure 10.5 Representation of "Hello" on serial line.

For each character of this string we must send a data packet. After, the communication has been established, we send a start bit, a 1. Then at each subsequent clock pulse, the transmitter puts one bit of the ASCII representation of the character "H" (with the least significant bit first to the most significant bit last) followed by the parity bit 0, and the two stop bits. This process is repeated for each character in the string.

To demonstrate more clearly the relationship between internal and external interfaces Figure 10.6 shows the general layout of a serial asynchronous board. The wires on the left side of the board connect to the external device, while the address, data and control buses on the right side connect to the internal interface. The reader is encouraged to refer back to this figure when the ACIA is later discussed.

10.1.3 Programmer's Interface

Before looking at devices in detail, we must first explain the two principal methods by which the CPU controls I/O: **memory-mapped I/O** and **isolated I/O**. Some of this material has already been introduced in Sections 1.2 and 3.3; however, we will repeat it for the sake of completeness.

Memory-mapped I/O. In the case of memory-mapped I/O, we require the CPU to share a common bus with memory and the I/O devices, as shown in Figure 10.7. In essence, with memory mapped I/O, each device takes the place of some portion of memory by providing a number of registers that may be addressed as though they were memory. Thus, writing to the correct memory location amounts to writing to a command register in

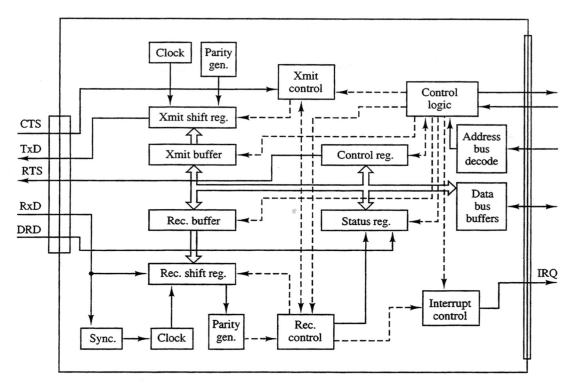

Figure 10.6 Serial communications board.

the device, whereas reading from a memory location amounts to reading from a status register in the device.

    To see how this is accomplished, recall from the section on memory control (Sections 3.3 and 5.2) that physical memory is attached to the CPU through a common system bus comprised of a data bus, an address bus, and control lines (or a control bus). Memory address recognition is performed by partial decoding (i.e., the high-order bits) of the address placed on the address bus. The final address decoding (i.e., the low-order bits) is usually performed by the memory chip itself. With this in mind, we can see that those locations that represent memory vis a vis those that are used to control devices is entirely up to

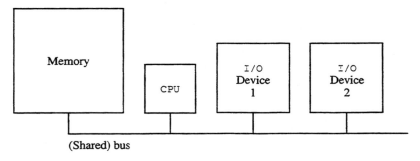

Figure 10.7 Memory-Mapped I/O.

the system designer. Recall also that memory is accessed by placing an address on the address bus, and then issuing a read or write request. In the case of memory mapped I/O, we leave a "hole" in the memory space for devices. That is, we leave a sequence of addresses without any memory assigned to that region. This may be accomplished by having the memory address decoders (see Section 5.2) omit some selected address region. We then attach to the bus the memory mapped I/O module. Each module contains several registers that are "mapped" into a set of sequential address locations.[3] Thus, each controller monitors the address bus; when it recognizes an address which corresponds to one of its own, it either writes the appropriate register into the data bus (in the case of a CPU read), or latches it into the appropriate register (in the case of a CPU write). Since there is no physical memory at these locations, there will be no bus conflict. In other words there is no differentiation between memory reads and inputs on the one hand and memory writes and outputs on the other.

Looking at the MC68000 we see that the first 512 bytes of memory is reserved for exception vectors; any other addresses in the MC68000's 16M bytes of addressable memory are fair game. In fact it is typical to use either low or high memory address locations for attached devices. Thus the address map might be locations $000000-$000FFF reserved for ROM, $001000-$EXXXXX reserved for memory, and $F00000-$FFFFFF reserved for devices. This leaves 1 Mb for the devices. Assuming that no device requires more than 64 bytes for control and status, this permits the attachment of 16000 devices! With this in mind, we have a **memory map** as shown in Table 10.1.

TABLE 10.1 Memory map for typical static memory allocation

Address Region	Device	Size (bytes)
$000000 - $0003FF	ROM	8K
$000400 - $EFFFFF	RAM	8M-8K
$F00000 - $F0003F	Peripheral 1	64
$F00040 - $F0007F	Peripheral 2	64
$F00080 - $F000BF	Peripheral 3	64
$F000C0 - $F000FF	Peripheral 4	64

Isolated I/O

Under this method and unlike memory mapped I/O, the devices use a different address space than the ordinary CPU space as Figure 10.8 indicates. In this case there are two additional control lines: the input and output lines that indicate that the address refers to the I/O space. When isolated I/O is used, one needs specialized *I/O instructions*, to distinguish input/output instructions from ordinary memory reads/writes. The instruction set contains some typical instructions such as `start_io`, `test_io`, `in`, and `out`.

The first instruction, the `start_io`, has an operand that indicates the device's (I/O bus) address; its execution causes an initialization of that device. The second instruction, the `test_io`, is employed to check the completion of a data transfer by a device whose

---

[3] This mapping may be done by selecting the device address using jumpers on the module, or it may be accomplished through some other mechanism.

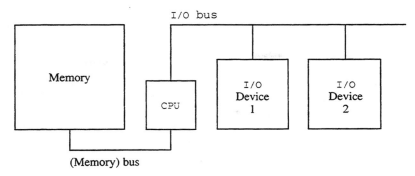

Figure 10.8   Isolated I/O.

address is indicated by the operand of the instruction. Finally, when the last two instructions, in and out, are executed they are requesting the reception or transmission of a block of data respectively from the device whose address is indicated by one of the operands of these instructions.

10.2 METHODS OF I/O

Communications with the I/O device may be either **programmed**, **interrupt driven**, or **direct memory access**. We now consider each of these I/O methods.

10.2.1 Programmed I/O

The simplest I/O method is *programmed I/O*. Under this method, when an application program requires an I/O operation, the CPU issues this request to the device. Then, the CPU (under the program's control) continually checks the device until the operation is completed.[4] The above discussion, as well as the structure of the application program, are summarized in Figure 10.9(a). Notice that initially at the time t_0, an explicit request is made to a specified module to send a character. The program subsequently loops until the transfer is complete; this occurs at time t_1. The net result is that the CPU "wasted" $t_1 - t_0$ units of time by just waiting for the completion of the transfer. The length of that time depends on a number of factors; however, it must be clear that this amount can be prohibitively large.

10.2.2 Interrupt Driven I/O

Interrupt-driven I/O is a method that is employed to minimize the time that is "wasted" by the CPU in waiting for the completion of an I/O request. Under this method when the application program needs an I/O operation to be performed, the CPU issues that request to the appropriate device. At this point (time t_0), the CPU performs a *context switch* as is illustrated in Figure 10.9(b). The latter term indicates that the CPU *saves* all pertinent information[5] (called the *context*) relative to the program that was just executing and

---

[4] As we will see, the CPU examines the value of a specific bit of the I/O module's status register.

[5] Such as data, address, status registers as well as program counter.

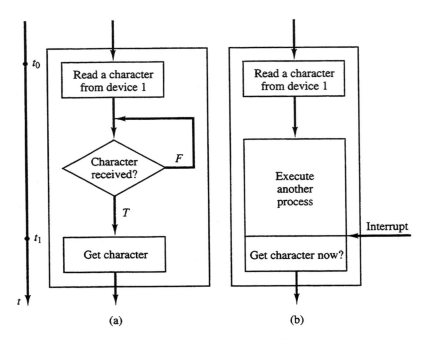

Figure 10.9   Program versus interrupt-driven I/O.

resumes with the execution of another program (process). At time t_1, when the I/O operation is completed, the device *interrupts* the CPU as illustrated in Figure 10.9(b). The CPU eventually serves the interrupt as was discussed in Chapter 10. The net result is that the CPU *did not* wait that $t_1 - t_0$ time that was required under programmed I/O; instead, it did something useful during that time.

We can summarize the above discussion by stating that under interrupt driven I/O, the CPU is relieved of its responsibility of checking for the completion of a pending I/O operation; and, therefore it can continue to execute other programs while the transfer is pending.

Identification and priorities. The reader should have already noticed a dilemma. Namely, under the programmed I/O method, only one I/O request is pending at each instant. On the other hand, it is highly likely that a number of such I/O requests pend at the same time. So the question that naturally arises is whenever an I/O operation is completed and the device interrupts the CPU, then how does the CPU know which of the devices caused the interrupt? We have indirectly provided some answers to this question in Chapter 10; however, we will briefly discuss this topic in general here.

First, notice that certain processors provide one with several different *interrupt levels*. For example, MC68000 provides us with eight such levels. So one could dedicate a different level to each device. This way the identification would be simple. But unfortunately, the number of devices is usually larger than the number of available levels. Increasing the number of levels would require *more* interrupt lines that will add complexity (and cost) to the bus. Therefore, one must leave with the preassigned number of interrupt lines; if the number of devices exceeds that of the levels, then more than one device is tied up in the same set of interrupt lines by sharing the same level. The question now is how one identifies the device that generated an interrupt of level n if there are m $(m > 1)$ devices that could generate that level of interrupt. There are a number of schemes that are designed to solve the identification problem just stated and are outlined below.

Polling.   Under this scheme, whenever an interrupt level n is generated, the exception handling routine polls each of the m devices that share that level to find out which one caused the interrupt.

Daisy Chain.   This method is similar to the one just discussed above in that each device of level n is polled. The poll, however, is not done in software; instead, it is done via a hardware poll. Under this scheme, *all* devices that generate level n interrupts are daisy chained via an interrupt acknowledge line as illustrated in Figure 10.10. When the CPU receives a level n interrupt, it activates the interrupt acknowledge line. The signal, propagates through the attached devices as in Figure 10.11. When the device that caused the interrupt receives that signal it identifies itself to the CPU via the *vectored interrupt* method that is similar to the one discussed in Chapter 10. In particular, the device puts a vector into the lower bits of the data bus that uniquely identifies that device.

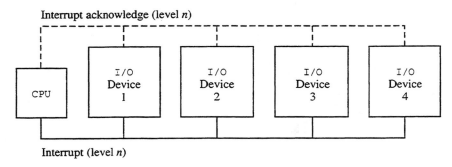

Figure 10.10   Daisy-chain: Physical bus connections.

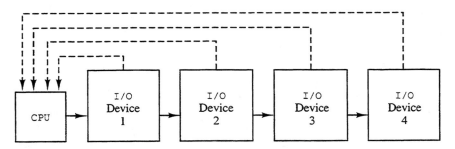

Figure 10.11   Daisy-chain: Logical flow.

Bus Arbitration.   Under this method when a device is ready to notify the CPU of the completion of its pending I/O operation (before it generates an interrupt) it requests **control** of the bus from the *bus arbitrator*. The bus arbitrator is a special piece of hardware logic whose primary function is to give control of the bus to only one device at a time. When the device is given control, it generates the interrupt. When the CPU is ready to service the interrupt, it acknowledges the interrupt; when the device receives this acknowledgment it places its unique address on the data bus from where the CPU retrieves it.

10.2.3 Direct Memory Access (DMA)

Even though interrupt driven I/O is a considerable improvement over programmed I/O, it still does not provide us with optimal CPU utilization. The reason for this is that the CPU is still responsible for transferring the data from/to the device to/from main memory. In other words, the CPU will be best utilized if it is interrupted after the data have been transferred to main memory via a **DMA device**. As its name suggests, this device has a *direct path* from the device to the main memory; therefore, the CPU is relieved of this task. An example of DMA transfer between a disk drive and memory is illustrated in Figure 10.12. Notice that the CPU will initiate all data transfers by informing the DMA device of the details of the data transfer. Once initiated the DMA device will service the request independently of the CPU.

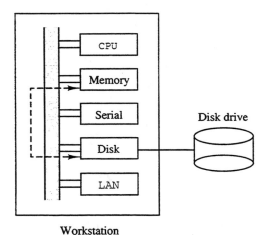

Workstation

Figure 10.12 Disk transfer using DMA.

The DMA device issues an external interrupt (see Section 9.2) when the I/O operation has been completed and the data has been transferred to main memory.

To the observant reader a question must arise. In particular, we stated that the DMA transfers the data to main memory while the CPU executes other programs. Now, programs are residing in main memory so the CPU has to use the bus; on the other hand the DMA device, has to transfer the data to main memory so it needs to use the *same* bus. In addition, only one device can have control of the bus at a time. So what happens? The answer is that whenever the DMA device is ready to transfer data into the main memory, it *steals* control of the bus from the CPU. But, it is important to notice that the DMA device does *not* interrupt[6] the CPU; instead, it performs *cycle stealing* by suspending the CPU at mid-instruction execution if necessary.

As is always the case, the benefits that one gains from the introduction of a more expensive component (as is the case here with the introduction of the DMA I/O over the interrupt driven I/O) should outweigh the additional cost required. As must be apparent by now, the only way that any gains can be felt is when the data transfer involves large volumes of data.

---

[6] In computer science language, interrupt means that the CPU will have to go through the process of handling the exception. Roughly, that is, saving pc, sr, executing the interrupt handler, followed by an rte. This does not occur here.

Hence, the DMA device will need its own local storage where the data can be buffered before their transfer, given the disparity of the fast speed of the system bus transfers vis a vis the external data transfers. Hence, such a module will require additional internal components such as control registers, status registers, and transmit and receive buffers as is illustrated in Figure 10.13.

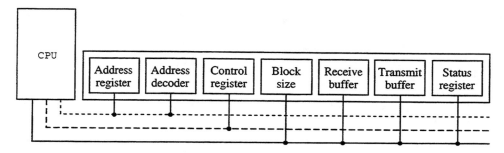

Figure 10.13   Minimal components of DMA I/O module and its internal interface.

Whenever an application program requires the transfer of a block of data, the CPU issues a request to the DMA module in the form of special instructions such as those discussed before. As an example, consider the following DMA request:[7]

```
001000:    Start I/O on device x using control block at address 002000
...

002000:    DMA request type
002004:    Sub-unit number
002008:    Cylinder
00200C:    Track
002010:    Start Memory Address
002014:    Number of bytes
```

Notice that the control block has a well-defined format that would depend on the particular controller used. Once the request has been issued, the CPU is freed to perform other tasks while the DMA device is transferring data. When the data transfer has completed the DMA device interrupts the CPU as was discussed earlier.

Channels.

To further improve performance, the DMA module can be enhanced in such a way so that it can *execute* an I/O program that consists of a set of specialized I/O instructions and is referred to as a *channel program*. In other words, the DMA device has become a processor in its own right. Such DMA devices are classified as *I/O channels* or *I/O processors*. The difference lies in whether or not the DMA device is a "full-blown" processor. In the former case, the channel program will reside in the CPU's memory, whereas in the latter, it will reside in the DMA device's memory.

---

[7] In fact, of course, the request would be encoded as a sequence of binary words which would be interpreted by the DMA controller. We use English for readability.

In channel I/O, the computer is directly connected to I/O device controllers through a dedicated channel[8] (or port). In addition, the instruction set contains special I/O instructions to initiate I/O to the channel. For example, the IBM 370 instruction set includes **start-io, test-io, halt-io,** and **test-channel.** Although I/O is initiated by a CPU instruction, it is still necessary to pass information to the device (i.e., the parameters of the request). These parameters are stored in memory before the I/O request and constitute the control block for a particular I/O request.[9] This is called the **device control block** (DCB) for the I/O operation. The **start-io** request specifies the address of the DCB, which is then read by the device. The I/O sequence is initiated. In addition, the device will read or write data into main memory. Thus we see that the device requires direct access to memory, as well as to the processor.

Illustrative DMA device: NS32490C ethernet controller. Controlling a DMA device may become quite complex as is demonstrated by the National Semiconductor NS32490C Network Interface Controller. This device was selected as representative of a large class of high-speed controllers. A typical workstation or personal computer is networked with other computers using one of a variety of **local area networks** (LANs).[10] These LANs permit data to be transferred from the memory of one computer to another using a high-speed cable. A LAN controller, therefore, is the interface to communicating data from one CPU to another in the same way that the disk controller is the interface to communicate data from a CPU to its secondary storage. The principle difference between disk controllers and network interface controllers is that in the former case the local CPU *always* initiates data transfers, whereas in the latter case either the local CPU or some remote CPU may initiate the transfer. The controller discussed here is designed for the Ethernet, a 10 Mbit/s LAN which allows for blocks of data varying in length from 46 to 1500 bytes to be transferred using coaxial cable (similar to television cable) as the physical medium. The relationship between the workstation and the Ethernet is shown in Figure 10.14. Notice that the Ethernet controller forms part of a network card which plugs into the system bus and that the network card is connected to the Ethernet coaxial cable via another short cable and a medium access unit.[11]

The NS32490C Network Interface Controller is designed to interface with the 8-, 16-, and 32-bit microprocessor systems. It includes two 16-bit DMA channels, one for transfers issued by the local processor, the other for transfers issues by some remote processor; has a 16-byte internal first-in-first-out (FIFO) data queue; and automatically maintains statistics on network access. Included in the controller is address resolution logic to discard data not destined for this computer, and packet generation logic.[12] From the programmers perspec-

---

[8] Channel I/O is highly utilized in IBM mainframe computers; however, we include any system that has dedicated communication paths between the CPU and devices.

[9] In the case of IBM systems, the parameters may actually be an "I/O program" which is executed by the channel attached processor.

[10] An introduction to computer networks is provided in Chapter 11. Although this information is not essential to this section the reader will derive benefit from reading Section 11.6 to see how an Ethernet controller is used.

[11] This assumes traditional (or thick wire) Ethernet, newer specifications (e.g., thin wire) place the medium access unit on the network card.

[12] Blocks of data are sent across the network as **packets**. These packets include source and destination network addresses and additional control fields, see Section 11.6 for more information.

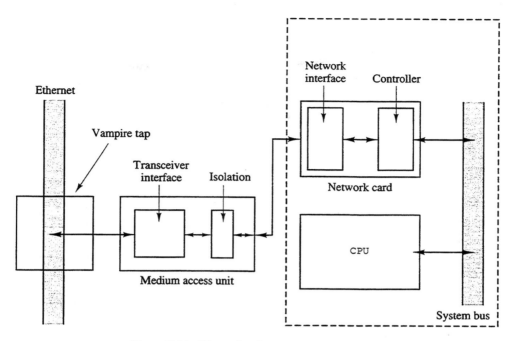

Figure 10.14   Ethernet interface to LAN and workstation.

tive the NS32490C is controlled by a command register; 45 internal read registers organized in three pages of 15 registers each; and 45 internal write registers also organized in three pages of 15 registers each. This is shown in Figure 10.15. The **command register** is used to select one read/write page set, thus the user "sees" 16 contiguous memory mapped read/write registers only. The command register is used to initiate transmissions, enable and disable remote DMA requests, and to select the register pages. The internal read registers include specifying the two DMA addresses, transmit status and receive status registers, next packet pointer registers, and address counters. The write registers include specifying the two DMA addresses, source address registers, transmit and receiver configuration registers, data configuration registers, and interrupt mask registers.

The mechanism used to maintain data for transmission and reception is particularly interesting. The local DMA receive channel makes use of a ring buffer structure composed of a series of contiguous fixed-length 256-byte buffers for storing received packets. The location of the receive buffer ring register is specified by two of the write registers (the **page start register** and the **page stop register**). Recall that Ethernet packets may contain anywhere from 46 bytes to 1500 bytes, thus an incoming data packet may occupy anywhere from one to six buffers. The assignment of buffers for storing incoming packets is controlled by buffer management logic in the controller. Similarly, packets are removed from the ring buffer either by remote DMA or by the local processor. When using remote DMA a send-packet command may be used to forward the received packet to yet another destination. Figure 10.16 illustrates how the buffer memory is organized into the receive buffer ring. Position information as to which buffer should be next accessed is maintained by registers in the controller.

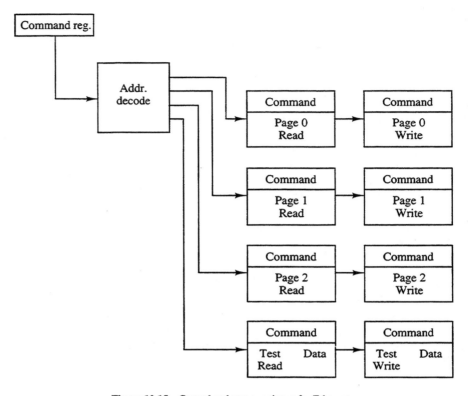

Figure 10.15   Control and status registers for Ethernet.

Packet transmission is accomplished by constructing the entire packet in memory according to Ethernet specifications, initializing a **transmit page start register** and a **transmit byte count register**, and setting the appropriate start transmission bits in the command register. The controller will then transmit the packet across the Ethernet to the specified destination.

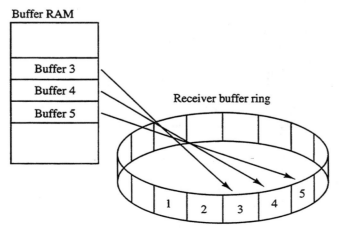

Figure 10.16   Ring buffer used by Ethernet controller.

10.3 MEMORY HIERARCHY

Although one might not consider the memory subsystem as an external device, some aspects of it deserve consideration and this seems an appropriate point. In the text so far, we have made it clear that code and data reside in main memory, which is a sequence of addressable storage locations. We said each instruction is fetched from memory, decoded, all required operands are fetched, the instruction is executed, and finally results may be written back. In fact, we can improve on this model by employing several mechanisms, in particular we can use **caches** to improve performance and **virtual memory** to free the programmer from system constraints and improve memory management. At the heart of these improvements is an observation regarding how memory is referenced which has been emperically verified. The observation is known as the **principle of locality of reference** (also known as the 90/10 rule) and may be stated as follows: "A program spends about 90% of its time in 10% of its code"; in other words, at any instant in time, programs tend to repeatedly access certain regions of code and data. This may be clearly seen if one considers a program loop. In fact, when one considers program execution, we see locality in two dimensions: (1) **temporal locality**, which says, if an item is referenced, it will tend to be referenced again shortly; and (2) **spatial locality**, which says, if an item is referenced, items close to it will tend to be referenced shortly.

10.3.1 Caches

The first mechanism mentioned is a **cache**. The term cache was first introduced in Section 5.4.5. To refresh the reader's memory, a cache is a set of registers and associated hardware control which acts as an interface between the CPU and memory. It is the case that memory references may take 10 times longer than references to the CPU's register file. Thus, during execution of an instruction, the CPU may have to wait (or **stall**), while operands are read from and written to memory. This dramatically reduces the CPU's performance. Making use of the principle of locality of reference defined above, we see that when fetching a word from memory the following are quite likely: (1) we will need it again in the near future, and (2) we will need adjacent items in the near future. A cache, therefore, is located between the CPU and memory. It accepts requests by the CPU for memory (both instruction fetches and operands), and, if it has a copy of the requested word (determined by matching the address with one of those in the cache, and called a *cache hit*) it returns it to the CPU at a rate similar to the register file. If the word is not in the cache (called a *cache miss*), it reads an entire block (also called a **line**, typically in the range of 4 to 32 words) surrounding the requested word.[13]

This all occurs automatically and transparently to the user. Conversely, when the CPU writes a data item, the cache updates it's own entry and *then* writes the item to memory. A cache is demonstrated in Figure 10.17. Cache sizes typically range from 16 to 128K words. Notice that the cache is necessarily much smaller than memory and therefore blocks in the cache will be overwritten with other blocks as the program executes. Notice also that the cache will always initially miss.

---

[13] This is easily accomplished by ignoring the least significant x bits of the requested address (x is typically in the range 2 to 5 bits). For example. a request for location $0000F3, with $x = 2$ would return the block of words $0000F0 to $0000F3 inclusive.

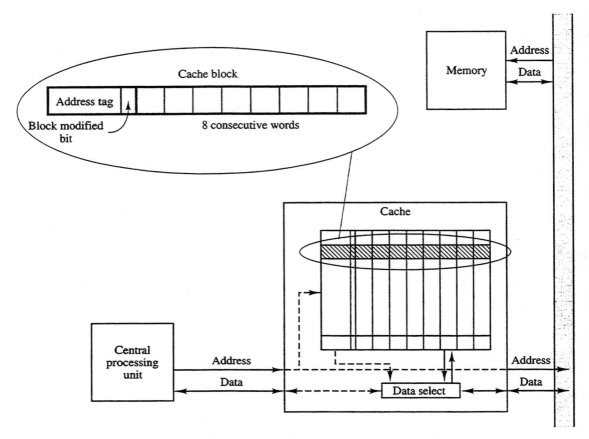

Figure 10.17 Cache located between CPU and memory.

There are several isses to be decided when a cache is used:

1. How large should be cache block be? A large block takes longer to transfer from memory (we can still only transfer one word at a time!) but locality suggests that once loaded we will save time in the future.

2. How large should the cache be? A large cache takes more space on the CPU but improves performance. The relationship between cache size, hit rate, and cost for a particular CPU design, is used to determine the "ideal" cache size.

3. How should blocks be located in the cache? There are several approaches including **direct mapped**, in which bits in the address are used to select where the block is to reside in the cache; **associative**, in which blocks are located randomly and must be obtained by a parallel search of the cache; and a combination of these two approaches called **n-way set associative**.

4. When should blocks be written back to memory? The cache may either **write-through** a modified block to memory immediately that the CPU writes a word; or it may **write-back** the word only when that cache block *must* be replaced. The former technique ensures that the cache and memory are always consistent. The latter technique saves on memory accesses.

We conclude by noting that a large cache will reduce the *average* memory accesses time close to that of the register file. In fact, caches are *essential* in modern computer systems.

10.3.2 Virtual Memory

Virtual memory is a mechanism that provides each process in the system with its own *virtual* address space. That is, each process believes that it has access to all addressable memory (location $000000 onward). There are several advantages to this. First, we have decoupled virtual memory from physical memory limitations. Thus we may execute programs that are larger than physical memory. This is accomplished by having only portions of the program in physical memory at any instant of time. Second, the task of loading a program for execution is much simplified, since each program may now be considered in isolation. Thus the linking loader (see Chapter 9) need not be concerned with making the code relocatable. Third, we may use the same mechanism that supports virtual memory to protect each process's address space from unauthorized access by other processes and to share data if required. To implement virtual memory we require a mapping function that translates virtual addresses into physical ones at run time. This is shown in Figure 10.18.

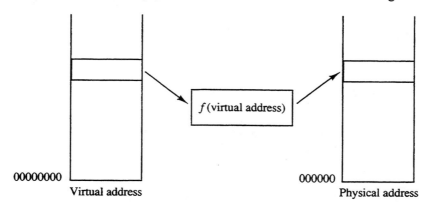

Figure 10.18   Translation from virtual address to physical address.

Although it would be possible to map each virtual address to a physical address this is considered unnecessarily fine grained. Instead, we divide the virtual address space into a block number and an index within the block, and map each virtual block to a physical block. This is shown in Figure 10.19. There are two mapping approaches: **segmentation**, where blocks may vary in size; and **paging**, where blocks are all the same size. These may be applied either separately or together and are discussed subsequently.

b	d

b = block number
d = displacement (or index) in block

Figure 10.19   Viewing virtual address as two components: block and index.

Segmentation.   Segmentation is a mechanism of convenience for assembly programmers and compilers. The virtual address space is treated as a number of individual segments which correspond to self-contained pieces of an application. For example, the code for each function or procedure might each be a separate segment, the user's data might be another segment. Thus, the user writes code using a two dimensional address space [segment number, index within segment] rather than a linear address space. This is shown in Figure 10.20.

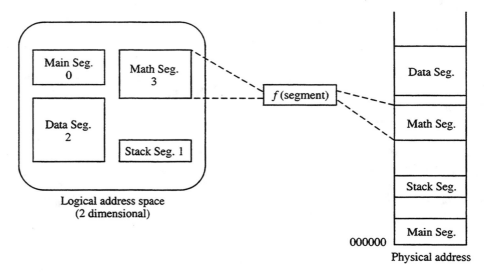

Figure 10.20 Mapping segments to physical addresses.

To accommodate segmentation additional hardware is required. Specifically, for each process the operating system maintains a **segment table** (in memory or as a set of registers) indicating all the segments used by the process and their base addresses in physical memory. The address of the start of the segment table is indicated by a **segment table base register** in the CPU as shown in Figure 10.21.

For each virtual address, hardware within the CPU uses the segment number as an index into the processes segment table to extract the mapping and additional information. First the CPU checks (using a valid bit) that the segment has been loaded into memory. If not it generates an internal exception to the operating system indicating an segment address error. The operating system is then responsible to copying the segment[14] from secondary storage into memory and then reissuing the read or write. Notice that this occurs transparently to the user; and that in a multitasking system the operating system can allow another process to execute while the first process waits for its segment to be loaded using DMA. Second, because segments are different sizes the CPU must check that the index does not exceed the segment's bounds (defined by the programmer or compiler). This is done automatically. Third, if the index is legal, it is added to the segment's base address to generate the actual address in memory. Notice that virtual address translation occurs at run time, thus the above sequence occurs for *every* address computed (instructions and data)! Clearly this is a great deal of work. Fortunately, the principle of locality of reference makes it worth-

---

[14] Or some portion of it. See paging later.

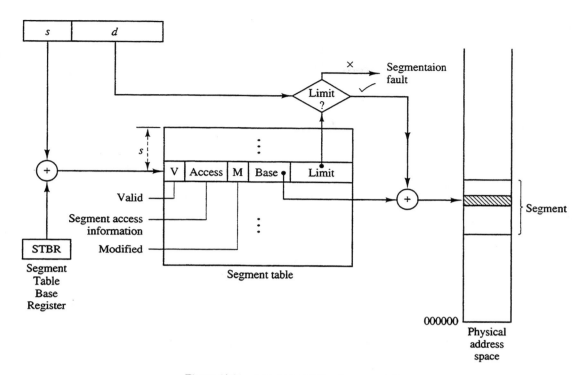

Figure 10.21   Address translation for segmentation.

while. Recall that the segment table is accessed only to obtain the segment base address, thus we can cache virtual-to-physical segment maps in much the same way that we cache data (using **translation lookaside buffers**). Without this advantage virtual address translation would be prohibitively slow.

Apart from the obvious convenience of segmentation, it is now extremely easy to permit several processes to share segments. All the operating system need do is map the appropriate segments (from the different processes) to the same physical base. Notice that in the absence of any additional addressing scheme, *segmentation causes excessive external fragmentation* (i.e., wasted memory outside the processes segments). The reason for this is that we have "holes" inbetween the segments that may be too small to be useful, yet add up to a significant amount of storage. Although we could in principle relocate segments at runtime this is rarely done.

Paging.   In many ways paging is similar to segmentation. The difference lies in the goals and characteristics of paging. In a paged system we divide the virtual address space into small, equally sized blocks called **pages**. Again, this is accomplished by using some bits in the virtual address to indicate the page number and the remainder to indicate the offset within the page. The pages are then mapped into the physical address space where they are called **frames**. This is indicated in Figure 10.22. Pages sizes typically range from 512 bytes to 4 Kb depending on the system. As with segmentation, when a page is referenced that is not currently mapped to a frame, the CPU generates a **page fault** exception

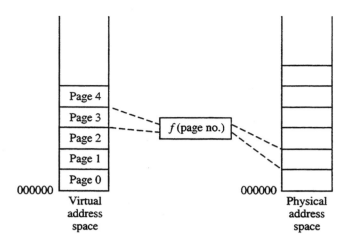

Page 4

Page 3
                          f (page no.)
Page 2

Page 1

Page 0

000000   000000

Virtual   Physical
address   address
space   space

Figure 10.22   Mapping virtual address pages to physical frames.

and the operating system must load the appropriate page into memory before reissuing the request. Again, this is transparent to the user.

Unlike segmentation, the goals in paging are to provide the operating system with a mechanism to manage memory efficiently. Thus, the user is completely unaware that paging is taking place. As far as they are concerned the virtual address space is linear. By having all the "holes" between useful frames multiples of the same size, and page size, the operating system is *always* able to load another page into memory should a process require it (assuming that there is any memory unused). Notice, however, that because the smallest unit of storage that the operating system may allocate is a page, there will be **internal fragmentation** (i.e., a small amount of space wasted at the end of the code and data segments etc.); however, there will be no external fragmentation. This contrasts sharply with segmentation which exhibits the opposite characteristics. Notice also that only a subset of the process' pages need be maintained in physical memory. Again, the principle of locality of reference suggests that a **working set** of pages is all that is necessary for the process to execute for prolonged periods without a page fault.

To accommodate paging the hardware is similar to that used in segmentation with the following exceptions: (1) the operating system maintains a page table for each process, and (2) the page size is known in advance so a limit field is unnecessary. The procedure for mapping the virtual address to a physical one is also similar, as shown in Figure 10.23.

A quick calculation on the size of the page table indicates one problem with paging. Assume a 32-bit virtual address, 16M (2^{24}) bytes of physical memory, and 2K (2^{11}) byte page size. Then the number of entries in the page table for each process is 2^{21}. Each entry requires $24 - 11$ bits for the frame number plus additional bits to indicate protection and access rights, yielding at least 2 bytes per entry. Thus, the page table is 4M bytes long! Notice however, that most of the entries will be empty (programs are not typically 2^{32} bytes long!). In fact, again, according to the principle of locality of reference, there will be small clusters within the table corresponding to active code, stack, and data areas, while the rest

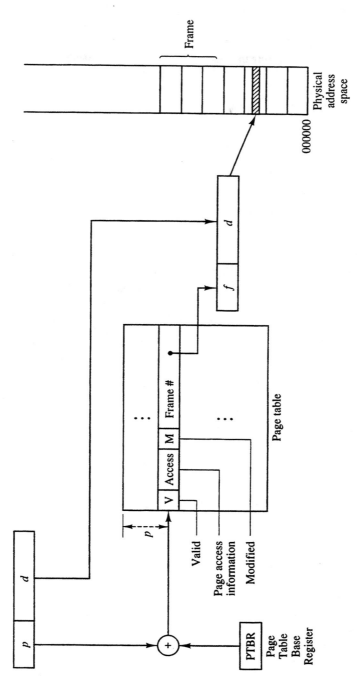

Figure 10.23   Address translation for paging.

need not be in memory. This suggests that the page tables should be segmented, as shown in Figure 10.24, which we know how to accomplish!

Thus, while paging alone, and segmentation alone, each have weaknesses, a combination of them both yields the flexibility and efficiency we seek.

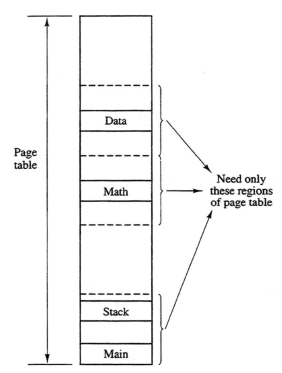

Figure 10.24   Active portions of page table.

Segmentated paging.   Without additional discussion, we show in Figure 10.25 how **segmented-paging** is accomplished. Notice that we must go through two levels of address translation to compute the physical address. Notice also that the programmer "sees" only the logically segmented address space, and the operating system is able to optimize physical memory allocation using paging.

We note in concluding this section that there are many improvements and modifications to the general concepts that we have introduced here. We invite the interested reader to examine the data sheets of one of the popular microprocessors (e.g., Motorola's MC68040 or Intel's i486) to appreciate the gory details! Notice also that whenever the operating system switches processes it must change a number of registers (e.g., the segment table base register) and flush the translation lookaside buffers (because the same virtual addresses may be used). We would finally remind that reader that all of the techniques would be unworkable without translation lookaside buffers and caches to essentially eliminate address translation and memory access overheads.

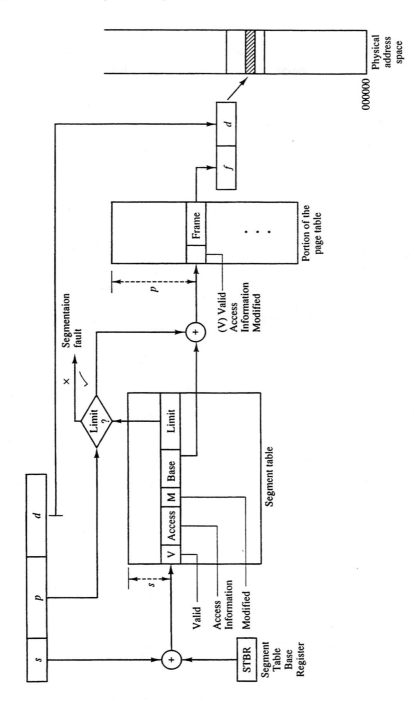

Figure 10.25   Address translation using segmented-paging.

10.4 MULTIPROCESSOR SYSTEMS

It would be impossible to discuss external device interaction without making some mention of communication within multiprocessor systems. Recall from Section 3.5 that there are two principle classes of multiprocessor system, shared memory and message passing. In the following two sections we outline some design considerations for these two classes and introduce the `tas` instruction, used in the MC68000 series to support shared memory multiprocessing.

10.4.1 Design Considerations

The essential issue in multiprocessing is communication between the different processors. We can easily imagine how, once given the code segment and data, an individual processor is able to complete its task. The problem, therefore, is to coordinate communication between different processors. In the case of shared memory multiprocessing there is no requirement for any special devices since we use main memory to pass data between the processors. Thus, a value written by processor A may be read by processor B, etc. So, for example, one could easily see how we could provide a single task queue for a multiprocessor system and allow processors to "take" tasks from it as they become ready. We notice a danger in this, however. Consider the following simplified code segment to check for a task in the queue:

```
CheckQ:   move.b    $1000,d0     ; check queue
          blt       Exit         ; empty queue indicated by 0 or less
          subq.b    #1,$1000     ; decrement task count
          jsr       DeQueue      ; remove from task queue
          jsr       RunTask      ; run it
Exit:     rts                    ; return
```

Suppose in a multiprocessing system we have the following initial sequence:

```
Processor 1:   CheckQ:   move.b    $1000,d0
Processor 2:   CheckQ:   move.b    $1000,d0
Processor 1:             blt       Exit       ; Assume there is a task
                         subq.b    #1,$1000
Processor 2:             blt       Exit       ; ERROR: We examined
                                              ; "old" value!
                         subq.b    #1,$1000
```

We have an error! Processor two read the "old" value at location $1000 before processor one could change it. Clearly the two processors need to synchronize at the instruction level. Notice that this problem is very similar the operating system critical region issue (see Section 1.2), which was resolved using semaphores around the "critical region." In this case we need to be able to set the condition code bits of a processor *and* modify memory, without any other device accessing memory inbetween these actions. This requirement is so important that buses often provide a special **read-modify-write** cycle that allows a bus master to examine a memory location, act on it, and write back to that location, without interference. This is often called an **atomic** or **indivisible** action. Given such an instruction it is an easy matter to ensure that critical code (queue management in this case) be performed properly.

In the case in which processors communicate using message passing, the message channel will be controlled much like any other device. That is, the processor reads/writes bytes or blocks of data from/to it using I/O requests. The reader should feel quite familiar with this concept.

10.4.2 TAS Instruction

The *test and set* (tas) instruction that is presented in Table 10.2, permits one to test a byte and set the negative and zero bits of the condition code so that their value reflects that of the tested byte. Both the carry and overflow bits of the condition code are reset. Furthermore, the sign-bit (i.e., most significant bit) of the byte *being examined* is then set. This modification is made using a **read-modify-write** cycle. The utility of the tas instruction becomes clear in the context of the shared memory multiprocessor systems discussed earlier.

TABLE 10.2   Testing a byte and setting its most significant bit instructions

Testing and setting of a byte				
Action				
Test indicated byte and then set its most significant bit.				
Mnemonic	Opcode	User byte (X,N,Z,V,C bits)	Operands	Format	Length
In data register				
tas	$ 12B$_{10}$	P M M R R	dn	F16	1
In memory				
tas	s 12B$_{10}$	P M M R R	dmem	F16	1, 2, 3

Processors use the tas instruction as a simple semaphore mechanism. By reading the value of a byte, setting the condition codes according to its *old* value, and writing back a modified value, a processor can "lock" access to a word (or group of words) for other processors.[15] The reader is invited to see what modifications would be necessary to the task queue code to prevent multiprocessor errors from occurring.

10.5 THE EDUCATIONAL COMPUTER BOARD (ECB)

In this section we will discuss as well as give examples of I/O operations on the Educational Computer Board (ECB) whose principal components are illustrated in Figure 10.26. The components appearing are the CPU, memory, clock, as well as three I/O modules: two **asynchronous communication interface adapters** (ACIA) (part number MC6850) and a **parallel interface/timer** (PI/T) (part number MC68230). As Figure 10.26 illustrates, the I/O modules are *memory mapped*. In particular, the PI/T is mapped over the range of locations from $010000 to $01003F whereas the two ACIAs are mapped over the range from $010040

---

[15] Provided, of course, that they check!

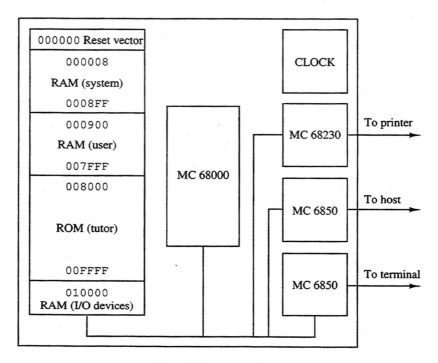

Figure 10.26   ECB architecture.

to $010043. Because the ACIAs addresses are only partially decoded (i.e., the complete address is not checked), their memory mapping is duplicated over the range $010044 to $01FFFF. A detailed memory map for the MC-ECB system is provided in Table 10.3.

10.5.1 Principal Components of ACIA

From a software point of view the principal components of each ACIA are its status register, control register, receive register, and transmit register, as illustrated in Figure 10.27. Even though the significance of each of these one-byte wide registers will be discussed in detail, we will first present a high-level view of their functionality.

TABLE 10.3   Memory map for the MC ECB

Address region	Device	Use
$000000 - $000007	ROM/EPROM	Reset vector
$000008 - $0003FF	RAM	Exception Vector table
$000400 - $0008FF	RAM	Tutor Scratch pad
$000900 - $007FFF	RAM	User memory
$008000 - $00BFFF	ROM/EPROM	Tutor firmware
$00C000 - $00FFFF		Unused
$010000 - $01003F	PI/T	Parallel I/O Module and timer
$010040 - $010043	ACIA 1&2	Serial I/O modules
$010044 - $01FFFF	ACIA 1&2	Duplicate mapping
$020000 - $FFFFFF		Unused

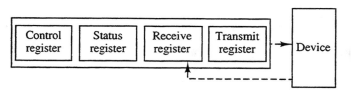

Figure 10.27   Top view of data movement and address mechanism involving ACIA.

First note that, as the name of this module suggests, its communication with the peripheral is of asynchronous nature. Given also that this module must be flexible, in that it can be interfaced with an assortment of peripheral devices, it must be made aware of the different parameters that the peripheral operates, such as format of the data packet, baud rate, etcera. This is the function of the ACIA's *control register*: to indicate (to the ACIA) the parameters of the communication with the device at hand.

Assuming now that the communication has been established, the transmission of data between the processor and device is done in a character by character basis. The arriving character that is transmitted by the device is placed in the ACIA's *receive* register from where the application program retrieves it. Whenever an application program wishes to send a character, then the program should place this byte in the ACIA's *transmit register* (Figure 10.27).

Finally, after a transmission has been initiated, there must be a mechanism by which the application program knows when a transfer has been successfully completed; if not, the nature of the error. This information is conveyed via an appropriate setting of the ACIA's *status register*.

ACIA to Device Communication

Let's assume that an application program is to send a character to a device. Furthermore, assume that the character has been loaded into the appropriate ACIA's transmit register. Notice, that there is a possibility that the device is busy with other tasks and is unable to receive it at this time. If the ACIA sends it anyway, then the character will be lost and *no one* will know about it. In other words the ACIA and the device must follow a common *communication protocol* for the transmission to take place. As an example, the communication protocol that is followed when the ACIA is ready to transmit a character is given subsequently.

```
[1].    ACIA issues a request to send
[2].    repeat
            ACIA is in wait state
        until device is ready.
[3].    device gives its permission to ACIA to transmit the data.
[4].    ACIA transmits the data line.
```

In step 1 the ACIA requests permission to send a character via a *request to send* signal. In step 2 the ACIA is in a wait state until the device is ready to receive the character which it does in step 3 via its explicit *clear to send* signal. At this point, step 4, the ACIA transmits the data packet.

As is clear, these signals are transmitted via dedicated lines that are fed into the control logic of the appropriate devices and trigger what action is to be performed next. In the case at hand, each ACIA can be connected to an external device via a standard RS232 port. Given the ACIA's simplicity, very few of the RS232's pins are used. These pin assignments are illustrated in Figure 10.28, whereas the significance of each of these pins is discussed briefly.

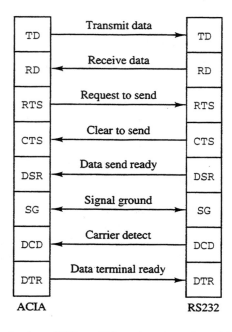

Figure 10.28 ACIA-RS232 pin assignment.

Transmit data (TD). When the ACIA is receives an acknowledgment to transmit data to the external device, it puts the data and transmits them (serially) via this line. When the line is not used, it is set to 1.

Receive data (DD). When the external device is ready to transmit data to the ACIA, it transmits them (serially) via this line. When the line is not used, it is set to 0.

Request to send (RTS). When the ACIA is ready to transmit data, it must request permission from the external device before putting the data in the (TD) line.

Clear to send (CTS). After the external device receives an RTS signal from the ACIA and when it is ready, it issues the permission via a signal that is sent via this line.

Data set ready (DSR). The external device informs the ACIA that it is ready to communicate (with the ACIA).

Data carrier detect (DCD). This pin is used to indicate that the RS232 has an active line of communication with the external device and is ready to transmit data.

Data terminal ready (DTR). The ACIA informs the external device that it is ready to communicate (with the external device).

ACIA's registers. Recall that each ACIA is memory mapped. In particular the first ACIA occupies locations $010040 and $010042 whereas the second ACIA occupies locations $010041 and $010043. The reader should be wondering how it is possible (with *two* addresses dedicated to an ACIA) to access all *four* of its registers. The answer lies in the fact that the control and transmit registers are *write only*, whereas the status and receive registers are *read only*. More specifically, the control and status registers of each ACIA "share" its lower address whereas the receive and transmit register "share" the higher address. But which of the two registers in each pair is accessed depends entirely on the operation; if the operation is a read, then the read-only register is accessed; otherwise, the write-only register.[16] Figure 10.29 illustrates these concepts for the first ACIA.

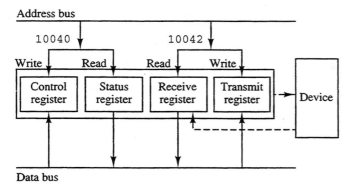

Figure 10.29 Top view of data transfer between ACIA and device that it is connected to.

All I/O operations, given the nature of the I/O, are indicated via ordinary MC68000 instructions. For example, execution of the instruction

```
move.b #$F1,10040
```

will cause the contents of the first ACIA's control register to be replaced by $F1, whereas execution of the instruction

```
move.b #$10040,d0
```

will cause the contents of the first ACIA's status register to be moved to the low-order byte of data register d0.

ACIA's control register.   As was mentioned earlier, this register must be set by the application program in such way so that it ensures proper communication with the device to which it is attached to. In particular, this eight bit register is divided into four fields as Figure 10.30 illustrates.

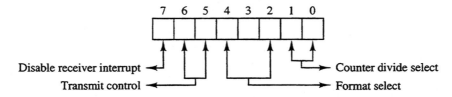

Figure 10.30   ACIA's control register bit assignments.

Each of these fields is discussed briefly.

Disable receiver interrupt.   If this bit is set, whenever ACIA receives a character (receive data register is full), the ACIA will interrupt the CPU to inform it of this fact. Hence, setting of this bit implicitly assumes that the application program will employ interrupt driven I/O; otherwise, programmed I/O.

---

[16] The R/W line acts as chip select.

Transmit control.   This 2-bit field controls the RTS line and whether or not a CPU interrupt should be generated in the case in which the transmit register is empty. The four possible settings together with their meanings are illustrated in Table 10.4.

TABLE 10.4 Transmit control field settings
and their meanings; Notice that in last case
break level is transmitted on transmit data output

Bit Number		Function	
6	5	RTS	Transmitting interrupt
0	0	Low (=1)	Disabled
0	1	Low (=1)	Enabled
1	0	High (=0)	Disabled
1	1	Low (=1)	Disabled*

Counter divide select.   The four possible settings of this field and their meanings are presented in Table 10.5. Notice that one setting, %11, causes the ACIA to reset itself,[17] whereas the other three settings control the timer that in turn controls the baud number generator. Both serial ports can be jumpered for various transmission rates in the range of 110 to 9600 baud.[18]

TABLE 10.5   Counter Divide Select field settings
and their meanings

Bit number		Function
1	0	
0	0	Baud rate = (Timers frequency)
0	1	Baud rate = [(Timer's frequency) ÷ 16]
1	0	Baud rate = [(Timer's frequency) ÷ 64]
1	1	Master reset

Format select.   This 3-bit field allows one to program the ACIA in such a way so that it can select one of eight possible formats of the data packet. The settings and the corresponding formats are illustrated in Table 10.6.

ACIA's status register.

As we mentioned earlier the purpose of the status register is to provide a way so that the application program can be informed of the status of a transfer or why such a transfer failed when the application program is in the process of I/O. In particular, each bit of this 8-bit register corresponds to a field as illustrated in Figure 10.31 and discussed subsequently.

---

[17] The ACIA should be reset before transmission take place via this software reset.

[18] The on-board baud rate generator (part MC 14411) provides eight sets of pairs of pins. One could select only one set of the that would force the baud rate generator to generate one of the following rates: 110, 150, 300, 600, 1200, 2400, 4800, 9600.

TABLE 10.6 Format Select field settings and their meanings

Bit number			Function		
4	3	2	Bits	Parity	Stop bits
0	0	0	7	Even	2
0	0	1	7	Odd	2
0	1	0	7	Even	1
0	1	1	7	Odd	1
1	0	0	8	None	2
1	0	1	8	None	1
1	1	0	8	Even	1
1	1	1	8	Odd	1

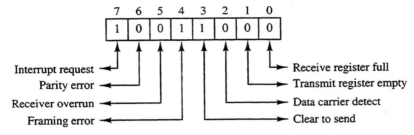

Figure 10.31   ACIA's status register bit assignments.

Interrupt request.   If this bit is set, the ACIA will interrupt the CPU when a character is received (receive data register full). The ACIA attached to the terminal generates an interrupt of level (autovector) 5; whereas the ACIA attached to the host generates a level (autovector) 6.

Parity error.   If such an error occurs when a character is transmitted, the ACIA sets this bit.

Receiver overrun.   When a character arrives in the receive register of the ACIA, the application program must read it before the next one arrives. If such a case arises (different transmission rates), then the corresponding bit is set by the ACIA.

Framing error.   If the detected number of stop bits is different than the number indicated by the format select field, then we say that a framing error has occurred. The ACIA reports this error by setting bit number 4.

Clear to send.   As you recall, the ACIA does not transmit a character unless it receives the clear to send signal. Such a signal is indicated by a value of zero.

Data carrier detect.   If the connection to the device has been lost the ACIA set this bit.

Transmit register empty.   Whenever the transmit register becomes empty (i.e., the transmission of a character to the external device is completed), this bit is set (by the ACIA) to 1. In other words, when the value of this bit is zero, this is an indication that the character (in the transmit register) is about to be transmitted or is in the process of transmitting.

Receive register full. If the receive register is full (i.e., as soon as the transmission of a character from the external device is completed), this bit is set (by the ACIA) to 1. Whenever the value of this bit is zero, then this is an indication that a character is about to be received or is in the process of being received.

10.5.2 I/O Programming the ACIA

The previous discussion suggests that I/O through the ACIA can be done in two ways, programmed or interrupt driven. In the following sections we will give examples of both. But before we begin, we will make some general assumptions in order to avoid further repetitions. First, we used for I/O the ACIA that is memory mapped at location $010040; furthermore, we will assume that the timer is operating at 4800Hz, the input/output device that we communicate with is transmitting/receiving at 300 baud; therefore, the counter divide select field must be set to %01. The data packet consists of eight bits per character, no parity, and one stop bit; hence, the format select field must be set to %101. In addition, the transmit control field will be set to %10. Finally, if programmed I/O is to be employed the disable interrupt bit must be reset; otherwise, it must be set. Summarizing, the control register must be set to $55 in the case in which we intend to employ programmed I/O; whereas, it must be set to $C5 if interrupt driven I/O is to be employed.

Therefore in each of the I/O programs that we ready to develop, we will utilize the following standard naming conventions.

```
acia            equ        $10040
acia_status     equ        $0
acia_control    equ        $0
acia_receive    equ        $2
acia_transmit   equ        $2
acia_reset      equ        $3
acia_mode       equ        $55
```

It is worth mentioning that, first, if interrupt driven I/O, is required the `acia_mode` constant's value must be changed. Second, the symbols `acia_status`, `acia_control`, `acia_receive`, and `acia_transmit` represent the corresponding registers of the ACIA. Actually, only two declarations are needed to access all four registers; however, we "duplicate" them for the reader to see which register is accessed. Finally, the `acia_reset` is needed in order to perform its required master reset.

Programmed I/O. In this section two examples will be presented. In the first example, a program program will be coded that receives a set of up to 200 characters terminated by a carriage return from the external device; it will store them in an array with base address at location $6000. In the second example, the presented program will transmit the string to the external device.

Reading a string. The code required to read the string is given in Table 10.7. Initially, the ACIA's address is placed in a0, the ACIA is reset, the proper data are placed into the ACIA's control register, and a1 gets the `string`'s address. Then the we branch to the subroutine, `get_char`, where the receive 1-bit field of the status register is examined. If the value of this bit is 0, the character has not arrived; this bit is examined one more time. At some point in time the character arrives so the bit is set; in this case, we get the character

TABLE 10.7 Receiving a string via programmed I/O

```
acia            equ       $10040
acia_status     equ       $0
acia_control    equ       $0
acia_receive    equ       $2
acia_reset      equ       $3
acia_mode       equ       $55
                org       $6000

string          ds.b      200

                org       $1000

read_string     movea.l   #acia,a0                      ; a0 gets ACIA's
                                                        ; address
                move.b    #acia_reset,acia_control(a0)  ; reset the ACIA
                move.b    #acia_mode,acia_control(a0)   ; establish proper
                                                        ; communication
                movea.w   #string,a1                    ; a1 gets string's
                                                        ; base
                                                        ; address
loop            jsr       get_char                      ; call subroutine
                cmpi.b    #$0d,(a1)+                     ; if CR we are
                                                        ; done
                bne.s     loop                          ; get next
                                                        ; character

                rts                                     ; all done

get_char        btst      #0,acia_status(a0)            ; is character
                                                        ; here?
                beq.s     get_char                      ; if not wait
                move.b    acia_receive(a0),(a1)         ; get char in
                                                        ; the array
                rts                                     ; return

                end
```

from the receive register[19] and return to the program from the subroutine. In the next step, a comparison is made to determine if the character just received was a carriage return. If not, then we branch to subroutine `get_char` one more time in preparation of receiving the next character; otherwise, we return to our caller.

Transmitting a string.   The code required to transmit the string is almost identical to the one that we presented earlier and is given in Table 10.8. In particular, after the standard housekeeping is performed, the routine `put_char` checks the bit number 1 to see if it is set; if it is, then the transmit register is full which means that the transmission of the "previ-

---

[19] Whenever, a character is read, the ACIA resets the receive bit.

TABLE 10.8 Transmitting a string via programmed I/O

```
acia           equ     $10040
acia_status    equ     $0
acia_control   equ     $0
acia_transmit  equ     $2
acia_reset     equ     $3
acia_mode      equ     $55
               org     $6000
string         dc.b    200

               org     $1000

send_string    movea.l #acia,a0                      ; a0 gets ACIA's
                                                     ; address
               move.b  #acia_reset,acia_control(a0)  ; reset the ACIA
               move.b  #acia_mode,acia_control(a0)   ; establish proper
                                                     ; communication
               movea.w #string,a1                    ; a1 gets string's
                                                     ; base address
loop           jsr     put_char                      ; call subroutine
               cmpi.b  #$0d,(a1)+                     ; if CR we are
                                                     ; done
               bne.s   loop                          ; get next char

               rts                                   ; all done

put_char       btst    #1,acia_status(a0)            ; send character?
               beq.s   put_char                      ; if not wait
               move.b  (a1),acia_transmit(a0)        ; send "next"
                                                     ; char
               rts                                   ; return

               end
```

ous" character has not been completed yet; therefore, we should and do wait. Eventually, when the bit is reset, we send the "next" character and while this is taking place we return to pick-up the next character from the string. Of course, if the cmpi succeeds, we have reached the carriage return and we exit.

Interrupt-driven I/O. In this section we will present the code of two routines that employ the interrupt driven method to perform I/O. In particular, the function of the first routine (Table 10.9) is to read just one character, whereas the function of the second routine (see Table 10.12) is to read a string of up to 200 characters that is terminated by a carriage return.

Before the code is presented some general comments that apply equally well to both examples should be given. First, as we remarked earlier, the control register's setting must be $C5. Second, the base address of the string will be $6000. Third, in both examples, we will store our handler in location $3000. Fourth, both programs use a byte-long integer variable flag that is used to indicate if the transfer has been completed; if its value is zero, the transfer is incomplete; if it is one then it is completed. Fifth, because the ACIA generates an interrupt of level five and asserts the VPA line,[20] we should store at location $74 corresponding to autovector 5 the address of our handler. Finally, notice that if at run time the processor's interrupt mask indicates an interrupt level of greater than or equal to five, our ACIA's interrupt request will not be acknowledged. To make sure that this does not occur we instruct our routines to enable all interrupts by moving the appropriate data in the status register. Notice that this suggests that when control was passed to our program, the processor was operating in *supervisor* mode.[21]

We are now ready to present the programs.

Reading a single character.   The code for this routine is given in Table 10.9. After certain "housekeeping" tasks are performed, such as resetting the ACIA, moving the appropriate data into the ACIA's control register, and resetting the interrupt mask to zero, then our program keeps looping by executing the piece of code

```
wait            tst.b     flag
                beq.s     wait
```

When the interrupt arrives the processor jumps and executes the handler routine. Notice, that as soon as we enter the handler, we set the flag variable because *we know* that the character has been received unlike in the programmed I/O method in which we kept polling the ACIA to see if the transfer was complete. Returning to our code, we can see that the completion of the transfer, and therefore the associated interrupt, can be generated during or at the end of the execution of each of the two instructions in the loop. If the interrupt arrives during (at the end) the execution of the tst instruction, the beq will fail and we will exit; otherwise, the loop will execute one more time before we exit.

There is a way that one can replace the set of three instructions

```
                move.w    #int_mask,sr
wait            tst.b     flag
                beq.s     wait
```

that appear in the code of Table 10.9 with a single instruction, the stop instruction, in the form

```
        stop      #int_mask
```

Execution of this privileged[22] one-operand instruction, that is presented in Table 10.10, causes two events to occur. First, the word-size, immediate data specified in its operand field is moved into the status register; second, the processor suspends execution of any instructions. Execution resumes with the "next" instruction if one of the following three exceptions occurs: either a trace, an interrupt of priority level higher than the one set by this instruction, or an external reset.

Finally, we would like to emphasize here that the program presented earlier does not take advantage of the features supplied by interrupt-driven I/O. The processor does not per-

---

[20] As was explained in Chapter 10.

[21] Actually, as is self evident, as a good practice I/O must be done in *supervisor* mode.

[22] I/O is usually performed in supervisor mode.

TABLE 10.9   Receiving character via interrupt-driven I/O

```
acia            equ       $10040
acia_status     equ       $0
acia_control    equ       $0
acia_receive    equ       $2
acia_reset      equ       $3
acia_mode       equ       $C5
int_mask        equ       $2000

handle          equ       $3000
vector_adres    org       $74
                dc.l      handle

                org       $6000

string          ds.b      1
flag            dc.b      0

                org       $1000

                movea.l   #acia,a0                         ; a0 gets
                                                           ; ACIA's
                                                           ; address
                move.b    #acia_reset,acia_control(a0)     ; reset ACIA
                move.b    #acia_mode,acia_control(a0)      ; establish
                                                           ; proper
                                                           ; communicatio
                movea.w   #string,a1                       ; a1 gets
                                                           ; char's
                                                           ; address

                move.w    #int_mask,sr                     ; enable all
                                                           ; interrupts

wait            tst.b     flag                             ; if flag=1
                                                           ; we are done
                beq.s     wait                             ; otherwise,
                                                           ; wait
                rts                                        ; done,
                                                           ; return
                                                           ; to caller

                org       handle

handler         move.b    #1,flag                          ; set flag=1
                move.b    acia_receive(a0),(a1)            ; get the
                                                           ; character
                rte                                        ; return

                end
```

TABLE 10.10   `stop` instruction

STOP instruction
Action
Word-size immediate data are moved into status register, program counter is incremented by two (so it points to the "next" instruction), and processor stops executing instructions. Instruction execution resumes, if and only if, one of following events occur. Either trace bit was one, an interrupt of priority level higher than one set by this instruction occurs, or an external reset occurs. This instruction is privileged.

Mnemonic	Opcode	User byte (X,N,Z,V,C bits)	Operands	Format	Length
stop	$ 4E72	M|M|M|M|M	$IData_{16}$	F14	4

form any useful work because it keeps checking to see when the flag will be set. It is left as an exercise for the reader to indicate what modifications should be made in the code in question so the use of the processor can be maximized.

Before we conclude this section, we note that the designers of MC68000 have provided one with the `reset` instruction which causes all external devices to be reset[23] when it is executed. This instruction is presented in Table 10.11.

TABLE 10.11   `reset` instruction

RESET instruction
Action
Execution of this privileged instruction causes all external devices to be reset (by asserting ASSERT line for 124 clock cycles). Then execution resumes with the "next" instruction.

Mnemonic	Opcode	User byte (X,N,Z,V,C bits)	Operands	Format	Length
reset	$ 4E70	P|P|P|P|P		F14	2

Receiving a string.   The algorithm for receiving a string parallels that of receiving a character. The principal difference lies in the *handler*. First, in terms of declarations we define a new variable `char_num` that is used to record the number of characters in the string that we receive.

As before, our program terminates whenever the `flag` is set. Our program sets it whenever all characters are received. Notice that according to our assumptions, whenever we are interrupted, a character has been received and the `handler` is invoked. As soon as enter the handler, we receive the character. Then, the `control_register` is reloaded; this step is required because after a character is read from the receive register, the ACIA automatically clears the interrupt request bit. Therefore, we must reset it so we will get interrupted whenever the next character arrives. Then we add 1 to the number of elements received so far. Finally, if the character just previously received character is not a CR, we return from the handler and wait for the next character to arrive. Otherwise, we set the flag to 1 to indicate that the entire string has been received; and, our program terminates upon return from the handler. It is worth noting that no interrupt of the same nature can occur while our handler executes (why?); therefore, no characters can be lost.

---

[23] ACIA requires *software* reset.

TABLE 10.12 Receiving string via interrupt-driven I/O

```
acia            equ         $10040
acia_status     equ         $0
acia_control    equ         $0
acia_receive    equ         $2
acia_reset      equ         $3
acia_mode       equ         $C5
int_mask        equ         $2000

handle          equ         $3000
vector_adres    org         $74
                dc.l        handle

                org         $6000
string          ds.b        200
char_num        dc.b        0
flag            dc.b        0

                org         $1000

                movea.l     #acia,a0
                move.b      #acia_reset,acia_control(a0)
                move.b      #acia_mode,acia_control(a0)

                movea.w     #string,a1
                move.w      #char_num,a2
                move.w      #int_mask,sr

wait            tst.b       flag
                beq.s       wait

                rts                                     ; all done

                org         handle

handler         move.b      acia_receive(a0),(a1)+
                move.b      #acia_mode,acia_control(a0)
                addq.b      #1,(a2)
                cmpi.b      #$0d,-1(a1)
                bne.s       done
                move.b      #1,flag
done            rte

                end
```

10.5.3 Principal Components of PI/T

The **MC68230 Parallel Interface/Timer** (**PI/T**) is a multifunction device designed to comple-ment the MC68000 series.[24] The PI/T provides the user with two double buffered 8-bit par-

---

[24] As distinct from the MC6850 ACIA, which was designed for the 8-bit MC6800 series.

allel ports (ports A and B), which may be combined to form a single 16-bit port; another
control port (port C); and a 24-bit programmable interrupt timer. The device permits both
vectored and autovectored interrupts, and provides a DMA request line for connection to a
DMA controller. As one might expect with such functionality, the MC68230 contains a
number of programmable registers and is complex to use.

The distinction between serial communications as provided by the ACIA and parallel communications as provided by the PI/T requires some comment. Recall that ACIA stands for
Asynchronous communications interface adaptor, that is, that each byte is sent asynchronously and without an explicit acknowledgment.[25] Thus without additional logic there
is no way for the sender to determine when the data has been received by the receiver.
Clearly using a bidirectional serial link it would be possible to have the receiver acknowledge each byte sent, by sending an explicit acknowledgment byte. This arrangement represents the first step towards forming a *protocol*, that is, a set of rules between two or more
devices to permit the transfer of information.[26] Using an entire byte simply to acknowledge
receipt of another byte seems wasteful, and it is. Another approach is to send all eight bits
together, that is in *parallel* and use a single acknowledgement signal to indicate that the
data was received. Clearly this will require additional wires (eight instead of one) but will
permit the transfer of data more quickly. We now have a problem, however, because there
is no start bit, how does the receiver know that data has been placed on the lines? The
answer is that we use another wire to indicate valid data on the output lines. Thus we have
a simple *handshaking* protocol using two control wires and eight data wires as shown in
Figure 10.32.

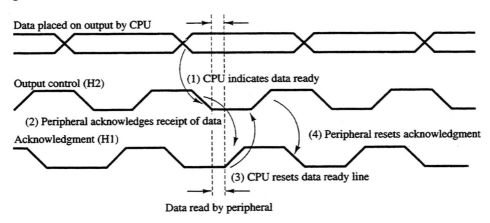

Figure 10.32   PI/T output handshaking using parallel interface with two control
lines H1 and H2.

The handshaking protocol works as follows. We assume that the output control (H2) starts
off negated (high) and the input control (H1) starts off asserted (low). The program initiates
the data transfer by writing data to the output data register, and asserting H2 as shown
in Figure 10.32 (1). The peripheral reads the data and acknowledges receipt by negating

---

[25] Notice, however, that within a byte, after the start bit has been transmitted, there is a requirement for each
bit to follow within strict time constraints as determined by the data rate.

[26] A detailed discussion of communication protocols is provided in Chapter 11.

H1 as shown in Figure 10.32 (2). Once the PI/T detects that H1 has been negated it prepares to write another byte by negating H2 as shown in Figure 10.32 (3). The peripheral completes the sequence by asserting H1. We are now in position to transmit the next byte. Notice that the PI/T buffers the output data for the data transfer and is responsible for controlling the handshaking lines, the programmer is not required to explicitly assert/negate the control lines. Notice also that the data transfer is now *synchronous* in the sense that both the sending and receiving units are synchronized together.

To provide improved performance ports A and B may be *double buffered*, that is, they have an *initial output buffer*, which corresponds the data register as seen by the programmer and a *final output buffer*, which corresponds to the output as seen on the lines. This double buffering permits the PI/T to accept data from the CPU into the initial output buffer while simultaneously transmitting the previous byte from the final output buffer. Data is latched from the initial output buffer to the final output buffer automatically. The reader is invited to establish the analogous handshaking sequence for input (*Hint:* the peripheral initiates the sequence.) Thus the PI/T offers a synchronous double buffered parallel data transfer mechanism.

In the ECB discussed earlier the MC68230 has been wired up to support a single parallel printer using both ports A and B, and a two-wire audio tape interface using port C. These wiring details are shown in Figure 10.33. and were made by the designers of the ECB so that one can connect both a printer, and a cassette tape (sequential storage medium) to the board.

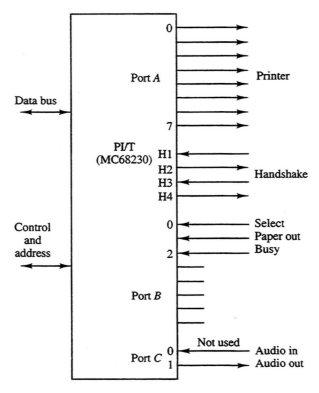

Figure 10.33 PI/T interface functional schematic diagram. Notice that both ports A and B are used to control the parallel printer, and that port C is used for audio I/O.

Components of the Parallel Interface   Control of the parallel interface portion of the PI/T is composed of 14 registers which are memory mapped in accordance with Figure 10.34. Notice that the addresses provided in the figure represent only one of several possible address sets due to the partial decoding of the address lines. In the ECB port A is wired as eight buffered output lines under the control of two handshake lines (H1 and H2), whereas port B is wired as eight unbuffered bidirectional lines under the control of two other handshake lines (H3 and H4). Thus the physical wiring and buffering is compatible with a Centronics-type printer interface. Of the eight lines in port B only three are actually required (bits 0 to 2). These are used by the printer to indicate printer status information. Of the eight lines in port C, only two are available (bits 0 and 1), and these are connected to audio encode/decode logic.

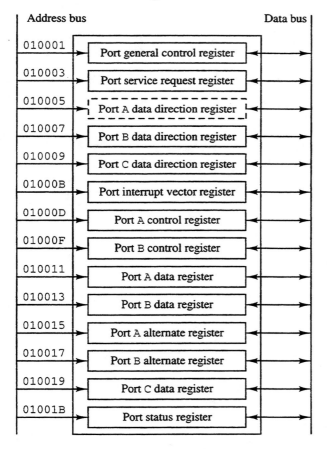

Figure 10.34   Principal components of PI/T parallel ports.

As mentioned earlier, the PI/T is a complex device and may be programmed in one of several modes. Therefore, in the following sections we will introduce the function of each register and, when necessary, (e.g. with the Port x Control Register) will discuss the way in which the PI/T should be used.

Port General Control Register (PGCR).   The PGCR controls in which of the many modes the PI/T is to be configured. Figure 10.35 shows the control fields.

Bits 7 and 6 indicate the port mode that corresponds to one of four major modes (0, 1, 2, 3). These modes have in addition, submodes determined by the two most significant bits of the individual port control registers. The submodes affect field assignments within the port control register, therefore we consider each mode and briefly discuss the functions of port control register fields appropriate for the mode in question.

Bits 5 and 4 enable the handshaking for the H3/H4 and H1/H2 pairs respectively (0 = disable, 1 = enable). These bit should be enabled last to prevent interrupts from occuring before final configuration of the PI/T. Bits 3 through 0 select the assertion sense for the handshaking wires H4 to H1 respectively (0 = assertion level low, 1 = assertion level high). The assertion level indicates which voltage level (0 or 1) the PI/T should consider assert.

MODE 0 (unidirectional 8-bit mode).   This mode contains three submodes (00, 01, and 1X) which are distinguished by bits 6 and 7 of the appropriate $PxCR$. Ports A and B behave similarly and may operate independently. Each port is double buffered (as was discussed earlier) for input. Control of the handshaking lines is determined according to Figure 10.36.

In submode 00 input is the primary mode of operation, thus double buffered input is provided. Output from the PI/T is single buffered. Bits 5 thorough 3 specify how H2 is controlled (Table 10.13). Bit 2 indicates if H2 should generate interrupts (0 = disabled, 1 = enabled). Bit 1 indicates if DMA should be used (0 = disabled, 1 = enabled). In any event the H2S status bit will be set if data are available. Note that H2 may be selected to be either under direct program control by asserting and clearing it, interlocked hand-

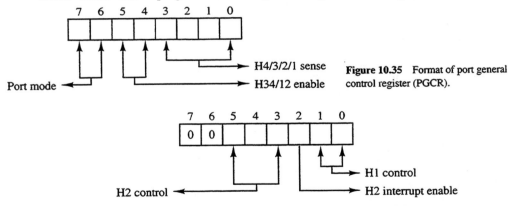

Figure 10.35 Format of port general control register (PGCR).

Figure 10.36 Format of port A control register (PACR) for different modes. (Note: interpretation of fields depends on mode and submode selected).

shaking, or pulsed handshaking. In the latter two modes H2 will be automatically asserted/negated as data is read from or written to the register, thus for output, the user need only write to the data register to have the handshaking protocol start. With pulsed mode H2 is negated automatically after 4 clock cycles regardless of whether the destination has latched the data.

In submode 01 output is the primary mode of operation, thus double buffered output is provided. Input from the PI/T is nonlatched (i.e., the input register reflects the instantaneous value of the lines). Bits 5 thorough 1 have the same interpretation as in mode 0 submode 0. If bit 0 is a 0 then H2S indicates that either the initial or final output buffers are empty, if bit 0 is a 1 then H2S indicates that both buffers are empty. (See the PSR for a description of H2S).

TABLE 10.13 H2 Control Field of PACR mode 0, submode 00

Bit number			H2 control	
5	4	3		
0	x	x	H2 is an edge-sensitive input	H2S is set on asserted edge
1	0	0	H2 output is negated	H2S always clear
1	0	1	H2 output is asserted	H2S always clear
1	1	0	H2 output interlocked handshake	H2S always clear
1	1	1	H2 output pulsed handshake	H2S always clear

In submode 1X only simple I/O is provided in both directions, that is, data read from the input is nonlatched, while data written to the output is single buffered. Double-buffering is not available in either direction. Notice that the handshaking lines are not used for handshaking although H1/3 may be used as input bits and H2/4 may be used for output bits.

MODE 1 (unidirectional 16-bit mode).   The two 8-bit ports are combined to form a single 16-bit port. The port is unidirectional with its direction and mode of operation is defined by PxDDR and PBCR (thus the handshaking pins used are H3/4). PACR and H1/2 are used to provide additional functionality for the 16-bit port. Notice that even though a 16-bit mode is supported the PI/T provides only an 8-bit interface to the bus. Therefore, for compatability with the `movep` instruction (which is discussed in Section 10.5.4), port A should be read/written before port B and should contain the MSB of the 16-bit word.

In submode X0 input is again the primary mode of operation, thus double buffered input is provided. Output is single buffered. Port A behaves exactly as in mode 0 submode 1X and may therefore be used to control the H1/2 handshaking lines for any user programmable purpose. Port B behaves exactly as though it were in mode 0 submode 00, however, the H3/4 handshake lines are used to control transfer for the entire 16-bit word.

In submode X1 output is the primary mode of operation, thus double buffered output is provided. Input is non-latched. Port A behaves exactly as in mode 0 submode 1X and may therefore be used to control the H1/2 handshaking lines for any user programmable purpose. Port B behaves exactly as though it were in mode 0 submode 01, again the H3/4 handshake lines are used to control transfer for the entire 16-bit word.

Mode 2 (bidirectional 8-bit mode).   There are no submodes for mode 2, therefore bits 7 and 6 in PxCR may be any value. Port B is used to provide true double-buffered bidirectional I/O. The handshaking pins H1/2 are used to control output transfers while pins H3/4 are used to control input transfers. Instantaneous data direction is indicated by pin H1, thus, all lines operate in the same direction. Note that since H1 is an input line this implies that the *external device* controls the transfer direction. PBDDR has no use in mode 2. The output buffers are enabled while H1 is negated and are disabled while H1 is asserted. Double buffered output transfers may be accomplished by programming the H1 status bit to be set when either of the output buffers are empty or when both output buffers are empty (PACR bit 0) while H2 may be programmed to operate in either interlocked handshake mode or pulsed handshake mode (PACR bit 3). PxCR bits 5 and 4 are not used in modes 2 and 3. Double buffered input operates in an analogous fashion with data latched into the input when H3 is asserted setting the H3S status bit (this is reset when a read is performed to the register). H4 may operate in either interlocked handshaking mode or pulsed handshaking mode (PBCR bit 3). Interrupts may be programmed using PxCR bit 2 as before.

Port A may be used for simple single buffered output or non-latched input, however, it may not use the handshake lines.

Mode 3 (bidirectional 16-bit mode). The final mode provided by the PI/T offers 16-bit bidirectional double buffered I/O. The method of operation is exactly analogous to that of mode 2 with the observation that data is transferred into both ports A and B. As with mode 1 port A should be read/written first (which is best accomplished using the `movep` instruction) and should be the MSB.

This concludes a brief introduction of the operating modes of the PI/T, we now continue discussing the PI/T registers.

Port Service Request Register (PSRR). The PSRR determines the way in which the PI/T may request service. In essence this register specifies whether interrupts will be supported, how they will be supported, and at what priority each of the different handshake lines (which will indicate successful reception/transmission of data) will operate relative to one another. Figure 10.37 indicates the format of the PSRR, whereas Tables 10.14, 10.15 and 10.16 indicate the details of individual fields.

Bit 7 is not used. Bits 6 and 5 specify whether the PI/T generates an interrupt or uses DMA when H1 (port A) or H3 (port B) are asserted. Note that DMA implies that port C is used in its alternate mode, which prevents some lines from being used. Bits 4 and 3 select how the PI/T is to respond to a service request. Note again that selecting vectored or autovectored interrupts implies that port C is used in its alternate mode and that some bits will be unavailable. Bits 2 through 0 indicate the order in which multiple outstanding interrupts will be handled.

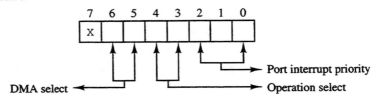

Figure 10.37   Format of port service request register.

TABLE 10.14   SVQR Select Field

Bit number		Function
6	5	
0	0	No DMA (PC4 available)
0	1	as above
1	0	DMA requests supported via DMAREQ* and associated with double buffered transfers controlled by H1 (port A)
1	1	DMA requests supported via DMAREQ* and associated with double buffered transfers controlled by H3 (port B)

TABLE 10.15   Operation Select Field

Bit number		Function
4	3	
0	0	No interrupt support (PC5/6 available)
0	1	Autovectored interrupts supported (PC6 not available)
1	0	Nothing (PC5 not available)
1	1	Vectored interrupts supported (PC5/6 not available)

TABLE 10.16   Port Interrupt Priority

Bit number			Priority Order			
2	1	0	highest			lowest
0	0	0	H1S	H2S	H3S	H4S
0	0	1	H2S	H1S	H3S	H4S
0	1	0	H1S	H2S	H4S	H3S
0	1	1	H2S	H1S	H4S	H3S
1	0	0	H3S	H4S	H1S	H2S
1	0	1	H3S	H4S	H2S	H1S
1	1	0	H4S	H3S	H1S	H2S
1	1	1	H4S	H3S	H2S	H1S

Port x Data Direction Register (PxDDR)   The PxDDR controls the direction in data will be transferred for each line of the register, as shown in Figure 10.38.

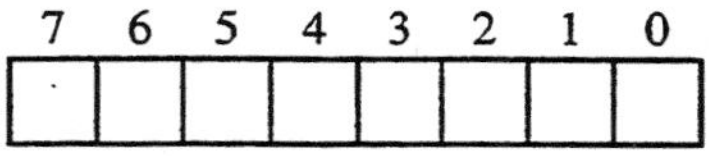

Figure 10.38   Format of port data direction register.

The direction of each data line may be specified (0 = input/1 = output). In the case of the printer we would expect port A to be ouput ($FF) and port B to be input ($00).

Port Interrupt Vector Register (PIVR).   The PIVR is used to communicate the interrupt vector number of the port generating the interrupt (H1 to H4) to the CPU during an interrupt acknowledge cycle. The PIVR contains the most significant 6 bits (i.e., bits 7 to 2) of the four port interrupt vectors. The lower two bits are automatically set according to the port generating the interrupt (H1 = 00, H2 = 01, H3 = 10, H4 = 11). This saves hardware registers by generating four consecutive interrupt vector numbers using only one register. Thus, if PIVR is loaded with the value $84 (%10000100) an interrupt initiated by H2 would result in an interrupt vector number of $85 (%10000101). After a reset the PIVR is initialized to $0F, which is the uninitialized interrupt vector number.

Port x Data Register (PxDR).   The PxDR registers are the read/write registers used to transfer the data. The data direction will depend on configuration of the data direction registers and operation will depend on the mode selected. In particular, in "normal" operation a write to an output port configured for automatic (interlocked) handshaking will cause the byte to be written. Conversely, a read from an input port will enable the PI/T to start fetching the next data byte immediately.

Note that port C behaves differently from ports A and B. Bits 7 through 2 of port C may be configured as either general purpose I/O lines or as timer control lines. This selection is made according to the configuration of the timer control register. Bits 1 and 0 are always I/O lines (these are the two lines used for the audio I/O). Using the port C lines in its alternate mode is required when either DMA or autovectored interrupts are required. In this case bits 6 to 4 will be unavailable for program use.

Port x Alternate Register (PxAR).   The PxAR are read only registers for ports A and B, which indicate the instantaneous values on the lines. Writing to these registers will initiate a DTACK* handshake sequence, but no data will be latched into the data registers. These registers operates independently of the mode selected. Note that there is no PCAR.

Port Status Register (PSR).   The port status register is a read only register that contains status information on the instantaneous and sense values for H1 to H4. Bits 7 to 4 contain the instantaneous values of H4 to H1 respectively while bits 3 to 0 contain the sense of H4 to H1 respectively (i.e. active/inactive).

I/O programming with parallel ports.   We now discuss programming the PI/T as it is wired for the ECB. In particular we will show how to send a string of characters to the printer under direct program control. The example in Table 10.17 that follows provides only a hint of programming the PI/T, additional details on using the more advanced modes may be found in the MC68230 data sheets. The wiring of the ECB prevents from making use of either DMA transfers or autovectored interrupts. Thus we will have to be satisfied with single buffered explicit programmer control. Referring to the original operation modes this corresponds to mode 0 submode.

The first characteristic to notice with this program is the liberal use of equates and comments. These make the task of understanding the code much easier. The program starts by initializing the PIT parallel port. Recall from Figure 10.33 that port A is used as the output port to the printer while port B is used to indicate printer status. We therefore reset ($00) the following registers: PCGR, PSRR, PACR and PBCR. Port A is an output register, so PADR is set ($FF) while port B is an input register, so PBDDR is reset ($00). We are now ready to begin.

The PIT is started by setting bit 4 of the PCGR so that handshaking pairs H1/H2 are enabled and pulsing bit 3 high then low to indicate that we are using *direct program control*. The parallel port will driven under direct program control by reading the PSR and writing to the PACR. The main routine in the program starts at label `loop1` and consists of writing characters to the port until a CR is encountered. This routine calls `put_char` to write the character.

TABLE 10.17 Sending string to printer

```
; This program demonstrates how to initialize and use one of parallel
; ports available on the 68230 PI/T. In this example a string
; is written to the centronics printer, assumed to be attached
; to the parallel ports.

PIT             equ     $1001           ; PIT address

                                        ; displacements
PGCR            equ     $0              ; general control
PSRR            equ     $2              ; service request
PADDR           equ     $4              ; port A direction
PBDDR           equ     $6              ; port B direction
PACR            equ     $C              ; port A control
PBCR            equ     $E              ; port B control
PADR            equ     $10             ; port A data
PBDR            equ     $12             ; port B data
PSR             equ     $1A             ; port status

; Miscellaneous bit offsets
PSR_H1_status   equ     $04             ; H1 status bit
PACR_H2_asrt    equ     $03             ; H2 control bit
PBCR_H4_asrt    equ     $03             ; H4 control bit
PBDR_select     equ     $00             ; Printer selected
PBDR_paperout   equ     $01             ; Printer out of paper
PBDR_busy       equ     $02             ; Printer busy

;Register settings
reset           equ     $00             ; reset the PIT
PGCR_go         equ     $10             ; start PIT handshaking
PADDR_dir       equ     $FF             ; port A direction
                                        ; (write)
PBDDR_dir       equ     $00             ; port B direction
                                        ; (read)
PACR_init       equ     $20             ; port A initialize
PBCR_init       equ     $20             ; port B initialize

; Return status
OK              equ     0               ; return OK
PAPOUT          equ     -1              ; printer out of paper
NOTSEL          equ     -2              ; printer off line

string          org     $6000           ; prepare string
                dc.b    'This is a string',$0d


initialize      org     $1000                    ; initialize the PIT
                movea   #PIT,a0                  ; set address of PIT
                lea     string,a1                ; set address of string
                move.b  #reset,PGCR(a0)          ;
                move.b  #reset,PSRR(a0)          ;
                move.b  #reset,PACR(a0)          ;
                move.b  #PADDR_dir,PADDR(a0)     ; set port A direction
                move.b  #PBDDR_dir,PBDDR(a0)     ; set port B direction
                move.b  #PGCR_go,PGCR(a0)        ; start PIA running
                bset.b  #PBCR_H4_asrt,PBCR(a0)   ; pulse INPUT PRIME*
                                                 ; high
                bclr.b  #PBCR_H4_asrt,PBCR(a0)   ; then low

; Finally we get to do the work

loop1           jsr     put_char                 ; call subroutine
                cmpl.b  #$0d,(a1)+               ; if CR we are finished
                bne.s   loop1                    ; get next char
                move.l  #OK,D0
                rts

put_char        btst.b  #PBDR_select,PBDR(a0)    ; check if selected
                beq     not_selected
                btst.b  #PBDR_paperout,PBDR(a0)  ; check if paper
                beq     paper_out
                btst.b  #PBDR_busy,PBDR(a0)      ; check if busy
                beq     put_char
loop2           btst.b  #PSR_H1_status,PSR(a0)   ; check H1 for ready
                beq.s   loop2                    ; if not, wait
                bclr.b  #PACR_H2_asrt,PACR(a0)   ; reset H2
                move.b  (a1),PADR(a0)            ; set data in register
                bset.b  #PACR_H2_asrt,PACR(a0)   ; set H2 - indicate
                                                 ; ready
                rts

not_selected    move.l  #NOTSEL,D0               ; cannot continue
                rts                              ; exit routine

paper_out       move.l  #PAPOUT,D0               ; cannot continue
                rts                              ; exit routine

                end
```

In `put_char` we first check to see that that printer is selected (i.e. on-line), has paper, and is not busy. These tests are accomplished by examining the status bits as indicated in port B. If the printer is ready to accept a character we enter `loop2`. It is here that we perform the handshaking. We first wait for H1 to be set (by the printer), we then reset H2 and move the character into the output buffer, finally we set H2 to indicate the character is ready. The subroutine then returns having completed the transfer of a single character.

The reader is invited to consider how the program would differ if interlocked handshaking were to be used, or if auotvectored interrupts were to be supported instead.

10.5.4 Timer

Timer's components.   Recall from Chapter 1 that one of the three principal components of the kernel of a multiprogramming operating system was the dispatcher. Its principal function is to perform context switching when a quantum of time has expired. In addition, we indicated that the dispatcher is dispatched via an interrupt that is generated by a hardware clock. This is one of the uses of a 24-bit, general purpose timer that is provided. Furthermore, this timer can be used for various other activities such as measuring time delays and various frequencies. The clock source can be the 4-MHz system clock or an external clock; its principal components from the programmer's point of view are presented in Figure 10.39.

Even though one can see eleven registers in Figure 10.39, in reality the timer consists of nine registers, whereas from the point of view in terms of functionality one can distinguish five registers: the `control register`, `interrupt register`, `counter preload register`, `counter register`, and `status register`. Each of these is briefly discussed subsequently.

Timer's Counter Register.   The operation of the timer from the software point of view is simple. The **counter register** a 24-bit, read-only register consisting of a group of three, 8-bit registers that are memory-mapped at locations $01002F, $010031, and $010033, respectively. The first register holds the high order byte, the second the middle order byte, and the third the low-order byte of the count. The contents of this register, are automatically decremented by 1 at fixed intervals of time. These intervals depend on the external clock source, as will be explained shortly; however, in the ECB, it has been set so that it decrements the count every $(1/125,000)th$ of a second. If we associate each decrement with a "tick" of this internal timer, we can say that this timer ticks 125,000 times per second. With this in mind, we can set the timer so that it keeps track of a predetermined amount of real time. For example, if we desire to count two seconds, we should load the integer $2*125,000 = 250,000$ into the timer register; if a time of 0.2 seconds is desired, then the value loaded must be $125,000*.2 = 25,000$. Notice that the binary integer stored in this register is assumed to be unsigned; therefore, the largest that the count can be is $2^{24} - 1$.

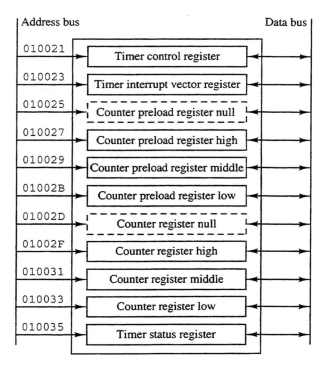

Address bus		Data bus
010021	Timer control register	
010023	Timer interrupt vector register	
010025	Counter preload register null	
010027	Counter preload register high	
010029	Counter preload register middle	
01002B	Counter preload register low	
01002D	Counter register null	
01002F	Counter register high	
010031	Counter register middle	
010033	Counter register low	
010035	Timer status register	

Figure 10.39   Principal components of PI/T timer.

Timer's Counter Preload Register   As was discussed earlier, the counter register is read-only. So to load a value into the counter register, it should be loaded into the counter preload register. When we desire, to start counting time then as we will see we can instruct the timer's logic to internally transfer the contents of the counter preload register into the counter register and then start counting time. Observe, that this way, we as soon as the indicated period has expired, then we can initiate a new counting process by just *reloading* the contents of the preload register into the counter register.

You should have noticed that the three registers that comprise the counter preload register reside in alternate locations in memory. Hence, optimally, with the instructions that we have studied so far, one would have to issue three separate move.b instructions to load the count into these registers. The designers of the MC68000 provides us with one instruction the move peripheral data (movep) instruction that is presented in Table 10.18 and can accomplish this move in a more elegant fashion as well as in a shorter amount of time.

The instruction permits the transfer of a *longword* or a *word*. As an example consider the initial situation as illustrated in Figure 10.40.

Execution of the instruction movep.l d3,6(a0) will cause the high-order byte of d3, AA, to be moved to location $00006+$010101 = $10107; the "next" byte, $BB to location $010107 + $2 = $10109, and so on. The final result as illustrated in Figure 10.40(a).

In addition, if the instruction was movep.w d3,6(a0), then the low order word of data register d0 will be moved, one byte at a time, with the result as shown in Figure 10.40(b).

On the other hand, if the register was the destination of the instruction, alternate bytes of memory, four or two, depending on the data size will be moved from alternate locations in memory. The reader is encouraged to verify the result of execution of each of the two instructions in Figure 10.41.

TABLE 10.18 movep instruction

Move peripheral data					
Action					
Contents (word/longword) of specified data register are moved 1 byte at a time in alternate byte memory locations. Conversely, contents of alternate memory locations (two/four) are moved one at a time into specified data register.					
Mnemonic	Opcode	User byte (X,N,Z,V,C bits)	Operands	Format	Length
Data register to memory					
movep.w	01_7$	P P P P P	dn,disp$_{16}$(an)	F20	2
movep.l	s01$_7$	P P P P P	dn,disp$_{16}$(an)	F20	2
From memory to data register					
movep.w	s01$_7$	P P P P P	disp$_{16}$(an),dn	F20	2
movep.l	s01$_7$	P P P P P	disp$_{16}$(an),dn	F20	2

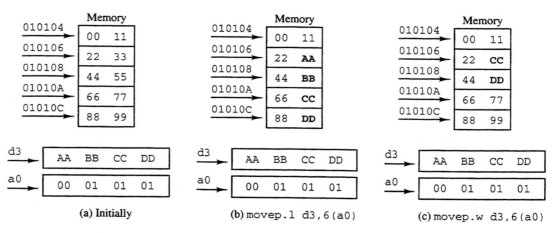

Figure 10.40 Assuming initial situation in (a), result of executing of the instruction movep.l d3,6(a0) is shown in (b), whereas that of instruction movep.w d3,6(a0) is shown in (c).

Returning to the counter preload register, we can see in Figure 10.38 the register labeled with *counter preload register null*. As its name suggests, this memory byte location is not tied up to any register.[27] Instead this memory location is used to facilitate the loading of the counter preload register with a single movep instruction. You should be aware that when a longword is moved to the register the actual count is the unsigned integer represented by the low order 24-bits of the longword.

Timer's Control Register. The bit assignments of this 8-bit register are illustrated in Figure 10.42.

---

[27] A read from the counter preload register will result to reading the number 0, whereas this register is never written to.

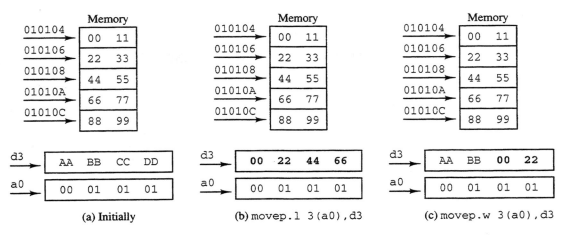

(a) Initially   (b) `movep.l  3(a0),d3`   (c) `movep.w  3(a0),d3`

Figure 10.41 Assuming initial situation in (a), result of executing of the instruction `movep.l` `3(a0),d3` is shown in (b), whereas that of instruction `movep.w  3(a0),d3` is shown in (c).

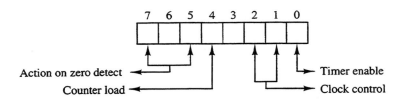

Figure 10.42 Timer's control register bit assignments.

The first field, bits 7 through 5, the *action on zero detect* field, is employed to indicate the action that must be taken when time runs out. Several different actions are illustrated in Table 10.19.

TABLE 10.19 Action on zero detect field settings
and their meanings

Bit number			Function
7	6	5	
1	0	0	No vectored interrupt is to be generated on a count of 0
1	0	1	Vectored interrupt is to be generated on a count of 0
1	1	0	No autovectored interrupt is to be generated on a count of 0
1	1	1	Autovectored interrupt is to be generated on a count of 0

The *counter load field* is used to indicate to the timer what value it should be stored into the counter register. If the value of this bit is 0, the contents of the counter preload register are loaded into the counter register; otherwise, the counter register is set to its highest possible value or as it is said it is "rolled-over." This is illustrated in Table 10.20.

The clock frequency is controlled via the *clock control* field that is presented in Table 10.21. In particular, different settings are used to determine the number of ticks per second. A setting of the code to %00 will cause the number of the ticks per second to be equal to 1/32 of the external clock's (that feeds the PI/T) frequency.

TABLE 10.20 Counter load field settings and their meanings

Bit value	Function
0	Set counter register from preload register
1	Roll over (move $FFFFFFFF)

TABLE 10.21 Clock control field settings and their meanings

Bit number		Function
2	1	
0	0	(Clock frequency DIV 32) ticks/s

As an example in the ECB, the clock runs at 4MHz. Hence, the frequency of the timer is equal to $4,000,000/32 = 125,000$ ticks/s.

Finally, a programmer can start the timer by setting the *timer enable* bit or stop the timer by resetting it (Table 10.22).

TABLE 10.22 Timer enable field settings and their meanings

Bit value	Function
0	Stop the clock
1	Start the clock

Timer's Status Register.   Whether or not time has elapsed can be detected by examining bit number 0 of the status register (Figure 10.43). In particular, the PI/T logic sets this bit when time has expired; otherwise, the value of this bit is zero[28] (Table 10.23).

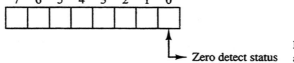

Zero detect status

Figure 10.43 Timer status register bit assignments.

TABLE 10.23 Zero Detect Status field settings and their meanings

Bit value	Function
0	The count has not reached zero.
1	The count has reached zero.

---

[28] Its value at initialization time is 1.

Timer's Interrupt Vector Register.   As was explained earlier the timer can be programmed in such a way so that it may generate a level 2 vectored interrupt. The timer's interrupt vector register can be used by the user to generate a vector of his/hers choice.

Programming with the timer.   This section will present two examples that illustrate the aid a timer can provide to the application programmer.

Timer's interrupts.   The program in Table 10.24 is written so that it interrupts the CPU at intervals of 0.5 s. In particular whenever a timer interrupt occurs, the program outputs to the terminal the character B; the process is repeated ten times before it returns to the caller. The code, which the reader is encouraged to study, uses (among several others that were discussed earlier) three specific constants: Timer_Mode, Vect_address and Quantum, as well as a subroutine output_char that are discussed briefly below.

Timer_Mode: We would like for the timer to generate a vectored interrupt, the timer counter register to be reloaded from the preload register, the format select to reflect "clock div 32," and finally the timer to be enabled. Hence, in conjunction with our previous discussions, the timer control register setting must be $A1.

Vect_Address: The timer generates a vectored interrupt of level 2. We will use exception vector number 64 to store our handler's address; therefore, this vector number is promptly stored in the timer's interrupt vector register.

Quantum: According to our assumptions the timer must interrupt the CPU at 0.5 seconds intervals. Given the ECB settings, the timer ticks 125,000 times per second; and, in view of the format select setting, the counter register must be set to $FFF0.

Finally, the output_char subroutine is the one that writes the character (through an ACIA) to a device and that was presented in a previous section.

Multitasking.   The following exemplifies how one can use the timer in order to perform multitasking. In our example, we show two tasks that alternately run for 0.5 seconds each. The first task outputs a sequence of B's, whereas the second outputs a sequence of C's. Before the code is presented several data structures that are employed are discussed.

For each task, a record is maintained whose structure is illustrated in Figure 10.44.

Current pc	Current sr	Current usp	Other data

Figure 10.44   Structure of task's context record

The first field, current PC, contains the address of the instruction that must be executed next. Initially, the value of this field is the loading origin of this task. Whenever the quantum expires, then what is saved in that field is the address of the instruction that *would* be executed next. When this task is restarted, the instruction that would be executed next is the one whose address had been saved in this field. Similarly, the next two fields, current SR and current USP, are used to record the values of the status register and the user stack pointer at the moment when the task is switched out. Finally, the *other data* field is used to record intermediate results that must be saved and restored at the appropriate times.

Initially, all records of the tasks that are to be run are stored in a table, the *task table*, whose structure is presented in Figure 10.45.

TABLE 10.24 Timer interrupts

```
; This program demonstrates how to initialize the timer to perform
; periodic interrupts.  In this example, a "B" is written every
; time the interrupt occurs.  The process is repeated 10 times.


Handler          equ      $2000               ; handler's address
                                              ; addresses
Timer_Status     equ      $10035              ; status register
Timer_Control    equ      $10021              ; control register
Timer_interrupt  equ      $10023              ; interrupt vector
Timer_Preload    equ      $10025              ; preload null register
Timer_Counter    equ      $1002d              ; counter register
Timer_Mode       equ      $A1                 ; control mode
Quantum          equ      $FFF0               ; time slice
Vect_address     equ      $64                 ; vector number

                 org      256                 ; establish handler
                 dc.l     Handler


                 org      $1000

timer_interrupt  move.b   #Vect_address, Timer_interrupt
                                              ; device returns
                                              ; vector 64

                 move.l   #Timer_Preload,a5   ; a5 gets preloads
                                              ; address
                 move.l   #Quantum,d5         ; put quantum in d5
                 movep.l  d5,(a5)             ; load the preload
                                              ; register
                 move.b   #Timer_Mode, Timer_Control
                                              ; start the timer
                 move.l   #0,d1

wait             cmpi.b   #10,d1              ; 10 timer interrupts?
                 bne      wait                ; if not, wait

                 rts                          ; all done

Handler          move     #'B',d0
                 jsr      output_char         ; use programmed I/O
                 addq.b   #1,d1               ; number of characters
                                              ; written
                 bset     #0,Timer_Control    ; reset the timer

                 rte

                 end
```

Current pc	Current sr	Current usp	Other data
Current pc	Current sr	Current usp	Other data
Current task			
Number of tasks			

Figure 10.45 Structure of task table.

Notice that there a number of records equal to the number of tasks (two in our example), a *current task* field that at each instant contains the offset off the beginning of the task table of the record of the task that is executing, and the last field, the *number of tasks* field that contains the number of tasks that remain to be executed.[29]

The code that is required is presented in Table 10.25. The program consists of five principal "parts." First, the subroutine init_timer is used to start (and restart the timer). The function of the dispatcher is to prepare the very first job for execution, to start the timer (via the call to init_timer), and to start execution of the first job (via the rte). The code for the two tasks is given in Task1 and Task2, respectively. Notice, that neither of these tasks ever terminates (because of the way that those two tasks are written) but they are "switched" out when the quantum expires by the task_switcher. This handler, saves the context of the job that is switched out, calculates which is the next task to be started, it restarts the timer, and starts the new task. The reader is encouraged to trace that example.

TABLE 10.25 Task switcher

```
;This program will allow two tasks to run under a primitive
;multi-tasking environment

Timer_Status      equ      $10035
Timer_Control     equ      $10021
Timer_interrupt   equ      $10023
Timer_Preload     equ      $10025
Timer_Counter     equ      $1002d
Timer_Mode        equ      $A1
Quantum           equ      $FFF0
acia_mode         equ      $55                          ; set for 8N1
                                                        ; receive/trans.


                  org      256
                  dc.l     task_switcher

; set the timer in such a way so that it generates an interrupt
; after 0.5 seconds.
                  org      $C00
```

---

[29] In a real-world environment, it is the responsibility of the task to remove its record from the task table when its done. We do not do this in our example; we simply alternate between the two tasks.

TABLE 10.25 (*Continued*) Task switcher

```
init_timer        move.b    #$64,Timer_interrupt
                  move.l    #Timer_Preload,a5
                  move.l    #Quantum,d5
                  movep.l   d5,0(a5)
                  move.b    #Timer_Mode,Timer_Control
                  move.l    #0,d0
                  rts

; set up the task table
Task_Table        dc.l      Task1                       ; PC for Task1
                  dc.w      $2000                       ; SR for Task1
                  dc.l      $7800                       ; USP for Task 1
                  ds.b      126                         ; data for Task

                  dc.l      Task2                       ; PC for Task2
                  dc.w      $2000                       ; SR for Task2
                  dc.l      $5800                       ; USP for Task2
                  ds.b      126                         ; data for Task

Cur_Task          dc.l      0                           ; offset in tas
                                                        ; table for
                                                        ; current task

Numb_tasks        dc.l      ((Cur_Task-Task_Table)/136) ; how many task

; the dispatcher
                  org       $1000

dispatcher        or.w      #$2700,SR                   ; set up SR

                  move.l    #Task_Table,a4              ; a4 gets
                                                        ; address of
                                                        ; Task_table
                  move.l    0(a4),-(SP)                 ; push PC of
                                                        ; first task
                                                        ; into stack
                  move.w    4(a4),-(SP)                 ; push SR of
                                                        ; first task
                                                        ; into stack
                  move.l    6(a4),USP                   ; set USP to
                                                        ; its proper
                                                        ; value

                  jsr       init_timer                  ; start clock
                                                        ; for task
                                                        ; switching

                  rte                                   ; start
                                                        ; executing
                                                        ; first task
```

TABLE 10.25   (*Continued*) Task switcher

```
; The first task; it sends a sequence of 'B's to an external device
; (programmed I/O is employed)
Task1           move     #'B',d0
                move.l   #acia,a0
Wait1           btst     #0,acia_status(a0)
                beq.s    Wait1
                move.b   d0,acia_register(a0)
                move.b   #acia_mode,acia_control(a0)
                bra      Task1

; The second task; it sends a sequence of 'C's to an external device
; (programmed I/O is employed)
Task2           move     #'C',d0
                move.l   #acia,a0
Wait2           btst     #0,acia_status(a0)
                beq.s    Wait2
                move.b   d0,acia_register(a0)
                move.b   #acia_mode,acia_control(a0)
                bra      Task2

; this exception handler performs the task switching
task_switcher   movem.l  a4/d0-d1,Save            ; save a4,d0,d1

                move.l   Cur_Task,d0              ; get number of
                                                 ; the task just
                                                 ; switched out
                move.l   #Task_Table,a4           ; get address
                                                 ; of Task_Table

; save PC, SR, and USP of the task that are to be switched out into
; the task's record
                move.w   (sp)+,4(a4,d0.1)         ; save SR
                move.l   (sp)+,0(a4,d0.1)         ; save PC
                move.l   USP,6(a4,d0.1)           ; save USP

; start a new task
                add.l    #128,d0                  ; add new task's
                                                 ; address
                move.l   Numb_tasks,d1            ; d1 has number
                                                 ; of tasks

                asl.l    #7,d1                    ;
                cmp.l    d1,d0                    ; end of table
                                                 ; reached?

                ble      get_new_task             ;
                moveq.l  #0,d0                    ; if yes,
                                                 ; offset 0;

get_new_task    move.l   0(a4,d0.1),-(SP)         ; put new values
                                                 ; on stack

                move.w   4(a4,d0.1),-(SP)         ;
                move.l   6(a4,d0.1),USP           ;

                move.l   d0,Cur_Task              ; get the task
                                                 ; number
```

TABLE 10.25 (*Continued*) Task switcher

```
           bset    #0,Timer_Control        ; restart the
                                           ; timer
           movem.l Save,a4/d0-d1           ; restore a4,
                                           ; d0,d1

           rte                             ; start the new
                                           ; task
Save       ds.l    3                       ; storage area
           end
```

10.6 EXERCISES

1. What does the term ACIA stand for? Why is the device called *asynchronous*?

2. Explain the term *memory mapped I/O*. What is the other principle method used to communicate with I/O devices.

3. Briefly explain how interrupt-driven I/O relieves the processor of work. Include the assembly program stub typical for an I/O interrupt handler.

4. Discuss the two methods used to select which of the many different devices that may interrupt the processor should be handled next.

5. How many interrupt levels has the MC68000 processor? How does an interrupt handler "know" which device has caused the interrupt?

6. What does the term DMA stand for? How does DMA relieve the processor of work?

7. Write a short program that will send the string "Hi there" to the serial port. Assume that the serial port is connected to a 300-baud terminal, 8 data bits, one stop bit, no parity.

8. The text discusses the sequence of handshaking events required to support the transfer of data from the CPU to an external device using the parallel port. Show a similar sequence for the case that the device initiates the transfer.

9. Define the term *double-buffered* and explain what the advantages of double buffering are over single buffering.

10. Rewrite question 7 to make use of interrupt driven I/O so that another program may also run while the string is being sent.

11. Explain why an interrupt timer is essential in a multitasking operating system. Could we perform multitasking without the use of such a timer? If so how, if not why?

12. Write a short program using the interrupt timer that sends successive letters in the alphabet (*A B C ... Z A ...*) to the terminal with a delay of one second between each character.

13. Explain why the designers of the MC68000 decided to implement the movep instruction. Is this instruction necessary or could one program memory mapped devices without it?

14. Newer communications controllers (e.g., the Ethernet controller) provide considerable support for the programmer in terms of automatically chaining through a list of requests, sequencing incoming requests to optimize device performance, and checking data for correct structure. Using material from Chapter 11 and 12 discuss what activities an Ethernet controller might be required to perform.

ADDITIONAL READING

CLEMENTS, A. *Microprocessor Systems Design: 68000 Hardware, Software, and Interfacing*. Boston: PWS Computer Science, 1987.

MOTOROLA. *M68000 Family Reference*, 2nd ed. Englewood Cliffs, N.J.: Prentice Hall, 1989.

11

Computer Networking

In this, the final chapter of the the text, we introduce some of the issues associated with connecting two or more computer systems together so they may communicate with one another. Such an arrangement is known as a **computer network**.

Nowadays we see computer networks in all walks of life. The office environment has been completely changed by the advent of the personal computer. Step into an average office and you will typically find the secretaries preparing letters using a word processing package or sending electronic mail to a colleague. Financial analysis and modeling is now performed directly by middle management using spreadsheet packages. The data for these spreadsheets are readily available through a corporate network. Small businesses are now in a position to prepare professional quality publications using desktop publishing packages and shared printing resources. Neither is the network revolution restricted to the office. University campuses are equipped with computer networks to provide both faculty and students with a wide variety of resources for education and research. In addition, worldwide networks allow members of these disparate communities to communicate with one another. Electronic bulletin boards are regularly used as forums for interest groups drawn from an increasing computer literate public. Interest by the common carrier (i.e., telephone companies) is moving global data networks from concept to implementation. This will result in a transformation in the way that home computers are used. In short, computer networks will soon become an integral component of the average household.

11.1 HISTORICAL PERSPECTIVE ON COMPUTING

As may be seen from the following paragraphs, from a historical perspective mainframe computing may be thought of as moving from the experimental period of the 1950s to becoming predominant in the 1960s. Since then, improvements in manufacturing design and computer aided design tools have seen computers decrease in size while increasing in performance. If mainframe computers marked the 1960s then it was minicomputers in the 1970s, personal computers in the 1980s, and networked workstations in the 1990s. During this period computer networks have become increasingly important. Originally, networks were used to connect only mainframe computers. Then as personal computers became more powerful they too were incorporated. As we shall see, networks have grown from supporting a couple of hosts to supporting tens of thousands over a period of thirty years.

When first used commercially, computers and their attached devices were physically large, required specialized air-conditioned environments, and represented a significant investment to the company. For these reasons the computer system was housed in a **computer center** as shown in Figure 11.1.

This lead naturally to the notion of a **centralized** computer system. The users would be required to either send their work to the center, use an off-site **remote job entry** system, or perhaps connect to the center using terminals. In any event, the peripherals would be located at a few sites and would be shared by many. In the early days, programs and data were encoded using **punched cards**, a 3½ * 7¾-in sheet of card with eighty columns. Each column corresponds to a single **byte** (or **octet**[1]) of information, the value of which is recorded by punching a sequence of holes vertically on the card corresponding to the binary representation of the octet. A deck of cards representing a program and its data would be placed in the hopper of a card reader. Under operating system control the card reader then scanned each card and the resulting program was loaded into memory. The program would then be executed and the output written to a printer. As time progressed the I/O devices

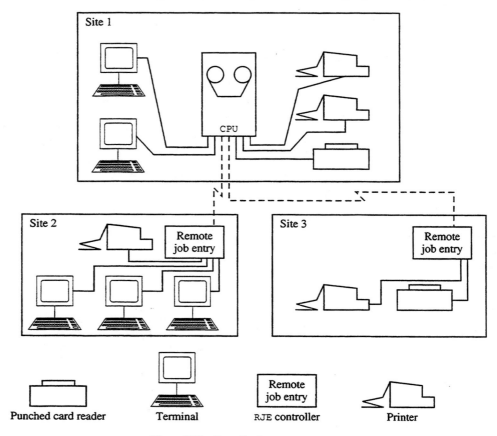

Figure 11.1 Centralized computer system.

---

[1] We shall use the term byte and octet interchangably.

became more sophisticated with card readers replaced first by teletypes and then computer terminals. As demand increased users requiring additional computing power encouraged computer vendor's to develop mainframe-to-mainframe communications facilities. In this way a user at one site could work productively on machines (or hosts) at other sites. An example communications facility would be IBM's **systems network architecture (SNA)**, which links together multiple IBM hosts allowing resources to be shared. As mainframes and terminals became less expensive and operating systems included multiuser/multitasking support the emphasis on a single site moved to that of a small number of mainframe systems connected by leased phone lines and the vendor's networking software.

As manufacturing technologies improved and circuits reduced in size, it became possible to incorporate all of the components necessary for a complete computer into progressively less expensive units. This quickly resulted in inexpensive mainframes and minicomputers. The minicomputers were championed in the late 1970s by the Digital Equipment Corporation (DEC) PDP 11 series which enjoyed great popularity due to its low cost and orthogonal instruction set. About the same time, research at AT&T Bell Labs was being conducted into a lightweight multiuser/multitasking operating system known as Unix. Unix was originally written by Ken Thompson and Dennis Richie and is significant in that for the first time much of the operating system was written in a high level language (C) and an early version was donated to the University of California, Berkeley and thus became vendor independent. While Berkeley worked on Unix for the academic environment AT&T continued to develop Unix internally, then known as AT&T System III.

As production techniques improved still further and costs continued to fall, it became possible to place an entire microprocessor on a single chip (the Intel 8008 was the first such processor, an 8-bit microprocessor based on the Intel 4004 a CRT controller!) These microprocessor chips enabled entrepereneurs such as Steve Wozinich (founder of Apple Computers Inc.) to develop inexpensive personal computers. Perhaps the first such successful commercial product was the Apple-II microcomputer using the Mostech 6502 8-bit processor. With the introduction of the IBM personal computer in 1982 using the Intel 8088 8/16 bit processor and the DOS (Disk Operating System) single user/single task operating system, the personal computer moved from a novelty to useful tool for the work place. The capabilities of early PC's were limited by today's standards with only 64K maximum memory and an Intel 8088 processor running at 4.77MHz. Compared with the cost of mainframe connections and the confusing job control languages still used on those mainframes at the time, however, the PC was an attractive alternative. Because the PC was a single-user system, the software had to be affordable to the individual pocket. In addition, the wide customer base encouraged the development of many innovative software packages. From these a number of professional products became dominant, Wordstar and Wordperfect in the word processing arena, DBASE for database applications, Lotus 123 for spreadsheet applications, and Crosstalk and Procomm for simple communications. Another important development in personal computing was the effective use of bit-mapped displays and a mouse to provide a user friendly interface to computers. The Apple corporation could be considered the champion of these **graphical user interfaces** with the Apple MacIntosh, although much of the original development in user friendly interfaces was performed by the Xerox Corporation.

The net result of this activity was that by the middle of the 1980s the personal computer had become an important component in the business field. Personal computers in businesses, however, present organizational difficulties. Whereas in the central site, all members had the potential to access any data stored, in a personal computer environment each user has only the data on his or her disk. One aspect of this is that data in one location is unavailable to others in another location. Another is that duplicates of a file may not be consistently updated, leading to erroneous files. Distributing data to multiple PC users was originally solved by using modems and communications programs that permit the copying of files between machines. Examples of these products are Crosstalk and Procomm. However this method is unwieldy, time consuming, and does not alleviate duplicate file problems. A typical company in the late 1970s might have a number of sites with personal computers either unconnected or loosely connected to the central site, as shown in Figure 11.2.

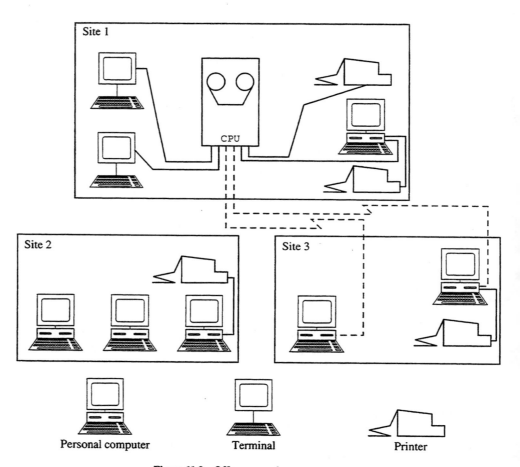

Figure 11.2   Office personal computer system.

The central site would still provide a data processing center which would typically handle large scale applications such as payroll and corporate invoicing. The solution to the personal computing data/resource problem was the integration of the ad hoc collection of personal computers and computing sites into a coherent network.

While this activity was occurring in the personal computer market, the Unix operating system, by virtue of being vendor independent, had become popular in the research community, particularly in university computer science departments. In addition, networking software for a wide area network developed in the early 1970's by the Department of Defense Advanced Research Projects Agency (DARPA) in conjunction with a few universities and corporations was included in Berkeley Standard Distribution (BSD) Unix to encourage the development of computer networks. This software permitted a variety of network functions between nodes connected together via a local area network (LAN—see Section 11.6.1) and between separate sites using leased lines. This software defines a set of protocols to permit file transfer, remote login, and mail services to be provided between all hosts on the network. The key component to this in the context of computer networks was the movement of essential networking software from vendor dependence to vendor independence. Today the version of Unix to include this networking code is Berkeley 4.3 BSD. During the same period of time AT&T had also been developing its version of Unix (similar but not the same!), which had reached version AT&T System V.

During the late 1980s offices that had supported a number of unconnected personal computers were transformed into a network of PCs in which LAN operations became an integral component of the vendor's operating system. Thus the user was now able to directly access (using the standard operating system commands such as **copy**) data on other similar machines on the same network.

At about the same time networked computers were gaining popularity in the academic community. Several companies, notably Sun Microsystems Inc., had adopted an open philosophy to computer systems by combining the latest microprocessors, bit-mapped displays, networking hardware, the powerful vendor independent multiuser/multitasking Unix operating system, and a mouse driven graphical user interface (e.g., Sunview for Sun Microsystems Inc.) into a single desktop unit. These units were called **workstations** to distinguish them from the single user PC systems. The overall effect of this was to provide a powerful user system designed specifically to operate in a networked environment. The Unix operating system far exceeded the capabilities of the single-user PC system and encouraged the development of vendor independent software (written for Unix platforms in the C programming language), while the network encouraged the exchange of user software and provided a forum for new ideas. One important result of this was the development of a vendor independent (or open) windowing environment developed by a consortium including MIT, IBM, DEC, and Cornell University known as the X windowing system. Thus, by the start of the 1990s, we see the rapid growth of the personal workstation closely coupled to a worldwide network. Figure 11.3 shows typical distributed computer environment of workstations attached to a number of LANs. The workstation are able to share resources (disk spaces, printers, etc.) and able to run applications on one another using the client/server programming model and a common windowing environment.

In many respects we consider the workstation as the critical mass for a distributed computer environment. Workstations have become become successively more powerful with the latest using full 32-bit CPU architectures, executing anywhere from 10 to 100 MIPs, equipped with several megabytes of memory, hundreds of megabytes of disk space, network controllers, and high-resolution bit-mapped displays. The operating environment has become highly portable with networking software almost seamless between different machines. This is partly due to vendor independent operating systems like Unix and the networking contribution of DARPA (originally called the ARPANET, now called the Internet) and partly due to a common network communications model known as the ISO/OSI model, to be discussed in Section 11.4. Finally, distributed computing is becoming easier to use due to the vendor independent X windowing system.

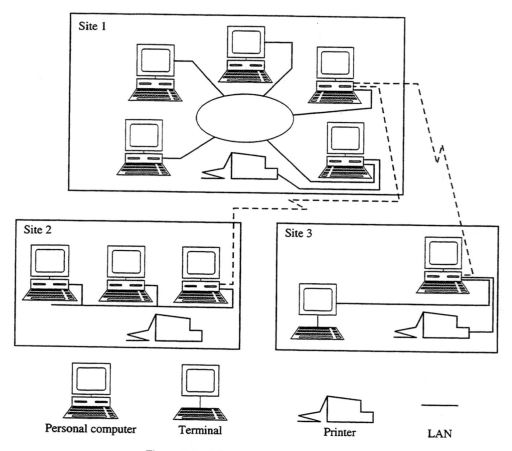

Figure 11.3   Office-distributed computing system.

11.2 ADVANTAGES AND DISADVANTAGES OF COMPUTER NETWORKS

The first question one might ask regarding the current popularity in networking is: Why network? To answer this question we need to establish the benefits and costs associated with networking. Some benefits involved with networking are obvious and were mentioned in the last section.

1. *Shared resources.* As we have already seen, the most obvious advantage in networking is the sharing of resources. In an office with five PCs it clearly makes little sense to provide five printers when a printer is only used for an average of a few minutes per day by each user. A similar argument applies to other peripherals such as plotters, tape backup units, and specialized attached devices (frame grabbers, etc.). Another important resource which may be shared is disk space. Clearly in a shared system the ability to permit many users to view and modify the same files and directories is useful. Apart from the savings from requiring only one copy of a software package instead of many, the users are now able to ensure that shared files remain consistent. A single database shared by many users will ensure that only one "version" of the file exists rather than many, as might occur with multiple users maintaining separate copies, possibly leading to inconsistencies between the users. Additionally, disk space may be more efficiently used if the combined disk space of the system is available to all users rather than a portion available to each individual. Note that an important characteristic of disk sharing is that the user's view of the file system should be consistent. Users should not be required to understand how the logical file system is mapped to the disk space available. Other obvious candidates to become shared resources are large or expensive items. Examples of the these would be supercomputers or array processors which offer very high computational performance.

2. *Improved reliability.* Another important benefit from networking is improved system reliability for each user. The failure of a shared peripheral such as a printer can be absorbed by sending those files to be printed to another networked printer. Conversely the failure of a single workstation may not effect the remaining users (although clearly devices attached to failed workstation will be unavailable).

3. *Lower costs.* The performance of workstations per dollar far exceeds those of mainframe computers. Thus, provided that the applications themselves do not explicitly require mainframes, it is more cost effective to provide each user with a workstation connected together via a network. For those applications that require mainframe access, for example, a particular vendor's product, it is usually possible to have that product attached to the network and have the user connect to it across the network.

4. *Improved capability.* There is some overlap between this category and shared resources. It is often the case that no single department can justify the expense of a particular resource (e.g., a supercomputer); however, with a network in place, either purchasing or leasing the resource may be justified based at a corporate level.

In addition to these there is another, less obvious benefit.

5. *Incremental cost update.* Because a single computer system has been replaced by many workstations, the upgrade costs will become incremental rather than a single upgrade. This permits the flexibility of selectively upgrading only those users that require a new workstation. An additional advantage is that the older workstations may now be distributed to others who previously had none.

Contrasting with these advantages we should also be wary of the disadvantages.

1. *Organizational mess.* Perhaps the most serious problem with a heterogeneous network is organizational. Recall that different workstations may have different capabilities, and may require different software tools on them. The task of keeping track of the correct versions of software for each unit or type of platform can become overwhelming. Fortunately although network organization is complex, a well-informed network administrator with the aid of currently available software/hardware tools is able to keep abreast.

2. *Network backups.* A problem related occurs with software maintenance. Consider the case of software backup. Incrementally saving the files of a single disk drive is quite simple. Keeping track of incremental backups on perhaps fifty low capacity disk drives, however, is more difficult and far more time consuming.

3. *Creeping costs.* Just as incremental upgrade costs may be considered a benefit, they may also be considered a problem. The problem occurs because new equipment requests now tend to come from individual departments rather than through central planning. This makes it far more difficult to identify real computing costs. Additionally the company may find it difficult to obtain large discounts while purchases are small but frequent. Finally, many software products are on a per machine basis; thus the cost of the package to the company may be very high.

5. *Software licensing.* With a single host, the issue of software licensing is relatively simple. The vendor is free to build into the product checks to ensure that a some maximum number of simultaneous users may access it. The problem is more complicated in a networked environment. If no protection is used by the vendor, then users are encouraged to illegally copy the software. Conversely, if each copy of the product is keyed to a particular machine then either the product is only available on particular machines or the user is forced to purchase an unnecessary number of copies. To complicate the matter, some vendors have sued companies for permitting the illegal distribution of software. By the mid-1980s the problem had become so complex that the Department of Defense would only purchase network software on the understanding that the vendors themselves would be responsible for protecting their software. Fortunately the problem has been partially alleviated by development of floating registration servers. These servers are located on a workstation and act as authenticating agents. Whenever a particular application is started, it first locates the appropriate authenticating server and requests permission to run. The server records this request and grants permission. When the application is terminated it informs the server prior to exiting.

6. *Reliance on centralized resources.* Although a network permits users to perform many tasks independently from centralized resources, this is not always the case. For example a popular networking model nowadays is to have "dataless" workstations which have only the operating system software on local disks. The remaining software and user's file space is maintained on a file server. Clearly if the file server fails, the users are stranded without their files even if their workstations are functioning. Of course this situation is not worse than that of a central site failing!

11.3 NETWORK TERMINOLOGY AND CONFIGURATIONS

Before discussing computer networks in more detail we will first provide some terminology used to describe computer networks. It is unfortunate that networking terminology often seems cyclical; thus, you should not be concerned if you are not completely clear on some definitions after this section. It is likely that the terms will be used in context again later.

We define a **network** as a collection of autonomous computers that is to communicate with one another on a peer basis. This definition precludes for example a laboratory of terminals connected to a computer or personal computers connected to one another via enhanced terminal emulator programs as mentioned earlier. It is convenient to separate the computer hardware and software actually associated with networking from the host computers which may use them. This provides the notion of a communications **subnet** and a number of **host** computers communicating with one another, as shown in Figure 11.4.

A **node** is either a computer on the network, or a dedicated **interface message processor** (IMP) and are represented as circles in the figure. Nodes may be connected to one another by **links**, which are shown as lines in the figure. A **path** between a source and destination node is a sequence of nodes such that there is a link between all adjacent pairs of nodes in the sequence. One term that we will make frequent reference to is the the notion of a **hop**,

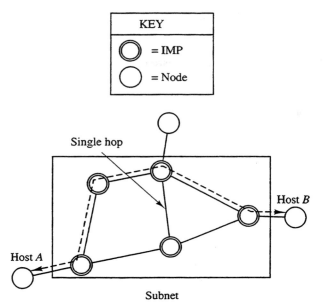

Figure 11.4 Two hosts connected through the subnet.

which is defined as the transfer between two nodes over a single communication channel. As we shall see later, we may use the **hop count** (i.e., the number of hops between the source and destination), as a measure of "distance" between nodes in a network. There are of course other measures that we may use to represent distance between nodes, for example physical distance, channel capacity, or line cost. However, hop count is a good approximation and is often used. In computer networking we are interested in those techniques whereby the source and destination are separated by several hops.

We define a **message** to be a sequence of octets that has some identifiable interpretation on its own. Thus an electronic letter, a file, a program, and so on might all be considered messages. Messages are not constrained to a particular length and may be thought of as objects to be sent between users. Contrasting with this, a **packet** is a sequence of octets that is bounded by characteristics associated with the computer network. Packets are typically of fixed maximum length and are sent between pairs of nodes in the network. Finally we define a **frame** as a sequence of octets bounded by characteristics associated with adjacent pairs of nodes in the network. Like packets, frames are of fixed maximum length and are typically smaller than packets. A message, then, is **encapsulated** in one or more packets while is it sent across the network. If the message will not fit in one packet we will send it in two or more. Similarly, a packet is encapsulated in one or more frames while it is sent between two adjacent nodes. Notice that from the programmer's perspective we are interested only in messages. It is the network that uses packets and frames. This is discussed in more detail in Section 11.4.1.

There are three basic methods in which a message may be transferred from a source node to a destination node, **circuit switched**, **message switched**, and **packet switched**. A circuit in this context implies a dedicated path through the subnet and may be considered "wire like". In a circuit switched network, a physical circuit is established between the source and destination. While this circuit exists, either end may send data. The most common example of a circuit switched network is the telephone system. Once the user places a call, a circuit between the source and destination is established. This circuit is dedicated to the users for the duration of the call. However, once a circuit is opened the communication path is "tied up" even though there may be no data flowing. Notice that when you place a phone call you are charged by the minute, not by how much you say! One alternative to circuit switching is message switching. In this, each message is passed from one node to another through the subnet. Starting from the source, the complete message is passed to the next node in path to the destination. This node then passes the message to the following node and removes its local copy. This continues until the message is delivered to the destination. The advantage of message switching over circuit switching is that the lines between the subnet IMP's are used only when a message is transferred from one IMP to the next. Thus the source to destination connection uses no resources when there is nothing to communicate. This improves network throughput and contrasts with circuit switching in which the lines are allocated at the start of the session and remain dedicated until the session is terminated. The most serious problem with message switching is that the entire message (recall a message may be a long file for example) must be stored (or **buffered**) at each node in the subnet while it is passed to the next. This places large storage requirements on the subnet IMP's. Another problem is that should the last node in the subnet fail just as it receives the message, the entire message will require resending. Both of these criticisms are solved by the final technique, packet switching. In packet switching the original message is subdivided into a number of packets. Packets are restricted to some maximum size; for example 64K octets, and contain sufficient information to ensure their delivery from the source to the destination. Each packet is transmitted from the source, through a number of intermediate nodes, to the destination, where the packets are reassembled to form the original message. Packets progress from the source to the destination on a per hop basis. In packet switching the buffer requirements are significantly less than message switching and should a node fail while it possesses a packet destined for another node, only that packet need be resent, not the entire message.

There are two basic service classifications that may be provided between a pair of nodes wishing to communicate across a network. The first is "wire like" and may be considered analogous to the telephone system. By wire like we mean that data sent by the source arrives in order and uncorrupted at the destination. Such a service is called a **connection-oriented service** and is how most communications occur. For example, this service would be used to send files, mail, and so on, between nodes. In a connection oriented service, the source node requests a connection (*dials the number*), the connection is accepted by the destination (*destination answers*) and therefore established. Data may then be transferred between the two nodes until such time either node terminates the connection (*hangsup*). The other service is designed for applications in which messages are to be delivered, but they may arrive out of order, and some may be lost, corrupted or duplicated. Such a service would be acceptable for one of two reasons: (1) the data is time critical and will not be of use if it is re-sent; or (2) each message is a self-contained unit which is not dependent on others; therefore, the order of arrival is unimportant. This service is known as **connectionless**. With a connectionless service each packet must contain the full destination address since, each packet may take a different path through the subnet to the destination.

Support for connection oriented services may be provided by any of the mechanisms described earlier. In the case of packet switched networks, two broad approaches may be used: **virtual circuits** and **datagrams**. A virtual circuit implies that a single route is selected through the subnet that all packets for the connection in question will follow. An advantage of this approach is that each virtual circuit may be separately tagged, and this tag used in the packet header instead of the rather long source and destination addresses. Other advantages are that each IMP along the path may preallocate a number of buffers for the connection. This eliminates problems associated with network congestion and deadlock (i.e., where two or more nodes become locked forever, each waiting for a response from one of the others) in the subnet. In the case of datagrams, each packet includes in its header the source and destination addresses. These are used by the subnet routing algorithms at each node to deliver the packet to the destination. Each packet may take a separate route through the subnet independently of other packets. Many different routing algorithms exist; in fact, we will explore a couple later in this section. Datagrams offer more flexibility over virtual circuits; however, there are many problems such as congestion and deadlock that require attention. Whichever method is used, it is incumbent on the communication software to ensure that a message sent by the source reaches the destination without error. In the case that a connectionless service is used, clearly a datagram subnet makes the most sense; however, any of the others may be used.

When dealing with computer networks, it is important to appreciate the characteristics of the most commonly used network configurations. The following paragraphs provide such a taxonomy. Typical measures to be considered for network configurations are maximum, minimum, and average number of hops between source/destination pairs; the channel cost to add additional nodes to the network; the geographic nature of the configuration; and the reliability of the network. We now consider the characteristics of each configuration in turn. Figure 11.5 shows four general classes of network, the **bus**, the **star**, the **ring**, and the **directed graph**. Although many additional taxonomies exist; this provides sufficient granularity for this text.

1. *Bus.* The principal characteristic of the bus (Figure 11.5[a]) is that all nodes are connected to a common communication channel.[2] In such an arrangement, each node may transmit data to all other nodes, that is, it may **broadcast** the data on the channel so that all other stations receive it. We may also use this model to represent radio broadcast systems if we consider the air as the communications channel, with all nodes "attached" to it. Clearly all nodes on a bus are only one hop from one another. The cost to increase the network is low; another node is added to the network simply by connecting it to the bus. Because a single line is required to which all nodes must attach, the bus is well suited to local area distances (less than 1 km). Network reliability is high in the context of node failure, since a failed node will not effect others; however, in the context of the channel, a single failure will partition the network. With the broadcast channel, which is a passive device (a length of cable for example), failure is rather unlikely; hence, the bus is regarded as a reliable network configuration. Example bus architectures include the Ethernet and Token Bus, both of which will be discussed later.

2. *Star.* The star (Figure 11.5[b]) configuration is composed of a single central node, or **hub**, and many attached nodes. Each of the nodes is connected to the hub by a direct point-to-point link. Communication between two nodes is through the central node; thus, all nodes are two hops from one another. Nodes communicating with the hub itself are only one hop away. Thus, the maximum hop distance is two, the minimum is one, and the mean will be depend on the relative frequency of node to node communications. The cost

---

[2] No relation to the I/O channel used in IBM architectures.

of adding another node is low. Only a single channel need be added between the node and the hub. The star is well suited to large geographic areas, particularly when common carrier (i.e., the telephone company) leased lines are used. The reliability of the star is considered low because of the reliance on a hub (a single point of failure) for network operation.

3. *Ring.* The ring (Figure 11.5[c]) configuration is composed of nodes connected as a sequence of point-to-point links with each node connected to precisely two others. Data flow around the ring in one direction only. Nodes are attached to the ring by intelligent connectors that are able to monitor the ring, collecting data that is destined for them and sending data when requested to do so. For reliability, the connectors are also able to isolate the ring from a node when the node is non-operational or fails. Note also that for rings, the node responsible for placing data on the ring is also made responsible for removing it. This permits the source to detect when the data have been corrupted and take the appropriate action. The minimum number of hops for the data is one, the maximum is $N - 1$, and the mean is $N/2$. The cost of adding another node to a ring is low; only one new line is required. Rings, like buses, are well suited to local areas and have similar reliability characteristics.

4. *Directed graph.* The final configuration is the general directed graph (Figure 11.5[d]). There is no assumed underlying structure. The number of hops between a source destination pair will clearly depend on the particular network configuration in question and route taken. The cost of adding another node varies depending on the number of nodes to which it is to be connected. Such a cost is considered medium-low, however. Because there are several possible routes between a pair of nodes, typically a **routing algorithm** is used. This algorithm selects on which outgoing link a particular incoming packet should be placed. Routing algorithms play a role in both establishing a connection (e.g., establishing a physical or virtual circuit through the subnet) and data transfer (for example in a datagram subnet each packet may be routed separately).

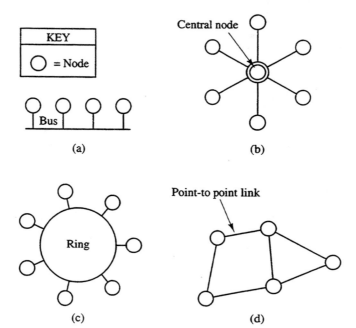

Figure 11.5 Network configurations.

11.4 ISO/OSI REFERENCE MODEL

Now that we have examined network configurations, we consider how the software used to support networks is organized. To do this, we must first identify precisely what is required. The basic service to be provided is the reliable transfer of data between any source and destination host on the network. To be completely general, we assume that the network is an undirected (i.e., all links are bidirectional) graph with multiple hops between the source and destination. Note that the host in our network could be a variety of platforms including PCs, workstations, mainframes, and so on. From this requirement we notice that an important aspect of networking is *correct operation within a heterogeneous environment*. This in turn suggests the requirement for precise specifications of the services to be provided and the way in which these **service providers** will communicate with other service providers. Typical services might be **representation transformation, data compression, session management, end-to-end data transfer**, and finally **data transfer between adjacent nodes**. Some of these services need only take place on the source and destination machine (e.g., data compression), while others will take place on every machine between the source and destination through which the data passes (e.g., adjacent node data transfer). From this discussion we see that an essential component in networking software is **layering**. The reason for this is clear; communications software is so complex, involves so many transformations to the data being sent, and is spread across so many nodes, that it is impossible to develop without decomposing it into subproblems. This characteristic was recognized many years ago by the networking community and in the interests of promoting international data communications, the International Standards Organization (ISO) developed a model in 1973 called the **ISO/OSI** (Open Systems Interconnection) **Reference Model** (see suggested reading 2) usually called the ISO/OSI model for short. The ISO/OSI model was developed based on the experience of many operational networks of the time (e.g., the Internet, IBM's SNA, and DEC's Decnet). It also attempted to anticipate some of the functions that would be required by the networking community in the future. The important characteristic of this model was to specify the number and general function of each layer, the services to be provided, where they should be placed, and how they should communicate with one another. The ISO/OSI model is composed of seven layers with the selection of these layers based on the following observations:

- A new layer is provided whenever a new level of abstraction is required.
- Each layer should perform a well-defined function.
- The layer boundaries should be selected to minimize the flow of information across them.
- There should be sufficient layers to accommodate all the required services, but there should not be more layers than necessary to do the job.

Using these guidelines, the ISO/OSI model for open communications is shown in Figure 11.6 with a textual description of its operation and layers in the following sections.

11.4.1 ISO/OSI Model Introduction

Two concepts that are important to all layers of the ISO model are **data encapsulation** and the **communications model**; these are therefore introduced before discussing the ISO layers themselves. We start with the following definitions: an **entity** is a process or task that actu-

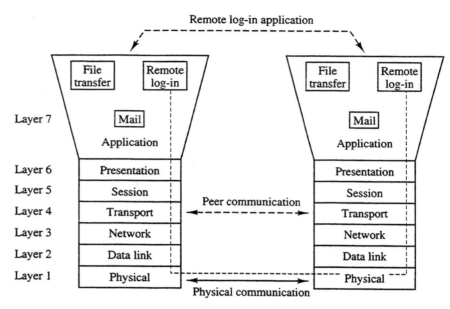

Figure 11.6 ISO/OSI reference model for communications.

ally performs work; **peer entities** are entities in the same layer (either on the same or different machines); and a **protocol** is an agreement between two entities on how to communicate. We will see that entities communicate *directly* with only the entities above and below
them on the same machine. Peer entities on different machines, however, may communicate *indirectly* with one another by passing information using an agreed protocol. This is
an important concept and will be explained further shortly.

From the preceding discussion, we see that an item of data to be communicated
between applications on different machines will pass through successive layers of the OSI
model. Each layer will perform some assigned tasks, the higher layers dealing with information representation and dialogue management, possibly modifying the data field; the
lower layers dealing with the reliable communication of data from the source to the destination. At each layer, n, the service entity will accept data from the layer above (layer $n + 1$);
the data, termed a **protocol data unit** (PDU), along with **interface control information** (ICI) is
used to coordinate activities between adjacent layers. The PDU is then modified according
to the layer in question and *encapsulated* with header and trailer information appropriate to
that layer. Finally the new PDU (a layer n PDU) is passed to the layer below (i.e., layer
$n - 1$). This implies that as the original information is passed down through successive layers, it is encased in protocol control information as shown in Figure 11.7. Thus, the path
that the data traverses from the source to the destination is down through successive layers
on the source across to the destination and then up through the same layers on the
destination.[3]

The other important concept to appreciate is the peer entity communication model
(see Figure 11.9). Although the transfer of PDU's occurs from layer n to layer $n - 1$ (or

---

[3] In fact it may go up and down through the layered model as it passes through intermediate routers and gateways.

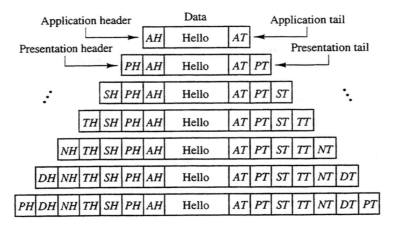

Figure 11.7 Data encapsulation through successive layers.

layer $n + 1$) on the same machine, a communication dialogue occurs between *peer entities* on different machines. This dialogue may be either driven by the data passed to the layer n entity (e.g., a request to send this data using secure links), or it might be independent of the higher layers (e.g., negotiation of the data compression algorithm to be used during connection setup). This dialogue occurs between peer entities and is defined by the communication protocol between them.

We see, therefore, that each layer offers an number of *services* to the layer above it, communicates with it's *peer entities*, and makes use of the services provided by the layer below it. The services may, therefore, be thought of as subroutine calls available to the layer above. Conversely, if the layer below has data to pass up, it interrupts the entity to pass it the data. This mechanism is formalized in OSI by four types of service primitive. **service.REQUEST, service.INDICATION, service.RESPONSE,** and **service.CONFIRMATION.** For a **confirmed** service, the requesting user invokes a service.REQUEST from the layer below, this *appears* as a service.INDICATION to the accepting user. The accepting user replies with a service.RESPONSE, which *appears* as a service.CONFIRMATION to the requesting user. This relationship between service primitives in shown in Figure 11.8. We note also that a service may be unconfirmed, in which case the response and confirmation are not used.

The actual services to be provided at each layer will depend on the layer in question; example services would be CONNECT, to open a connection; DATA, to send data (after a connection has been established); EXPEDITED-DATA, to send priority data; and CLOSE, to

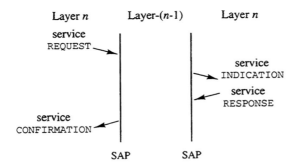

Figure 11.8 Using service primitives for a confirmed service.

close a connection. There are, of course, many others. Services at each layer start with the first letter of the layer; thus, link layer services start with L-, network layer services start with N-, session layer services start with S-, and so on. To see the relationship between peer entities and adjacent layers, consider an example using Figure 11.9, a confirmed service such as N-CONNECT.REQUEST issued by the transport layer will be received by the network layer entity (1). This is a request for the network layer entity to establish a connection with the destination; thus, it will issue an L-CONNECT.REQUEST to the link layer (2). Eventually the destination network entity will receive an L-CONNECT.INDICATION (4), which appears to have come directly from the source peer entity. It understands this request and reponds by issuing a N-CONNECT.INDICATION. If all goes well, the destination Transport layer will respond by issuing a N-CONNECT.RESPONSE (5) and so on.

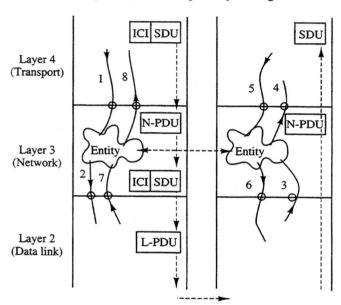

Figure 11.9 Communication between peers in OSI model.

We conclude this discussion of the ISO/OSI model by noting that there is still much activity in its functional specification. In particular, many applications are still being defined in terms of the ISO/OSI model using a variety of formal protocol specification languages. In fact it is even the case that the formal specification languages themselves have yet be to finalized. Despite this, the number of networked utilities is increasing rapidly.

11.4.2 Layer 1—Physical Layer

The physical layer is the lowest layer of the ISO/OSI model and is responsible for the specification of the electrical and mechanical characteristics of the communication equipment and lines. This includes specification of the signal waveforms used to represent a bit (e.g., the voltage levels for a logic level 1 and 0, the duration of the pulse, the frequency of data modulation, the type of modulation, etc.) Included in this level would be the specification of the line that is used (the type of wire, it's frequency response characteristics, etc.) the type of connector used to plug a wire into the communications device (e.g., size and shape of the connector, the number of pins on the connector, what signal each pin corresponds to, etc.) If the communication uses a broadcast mechanism to transmit the data, the specification would include the characteristic impedance of the line, the type of cable used, and how the nodes are to be connected to the cable. Clearly the ISO model is not responsible for actually developing these standards, partly because many of these are already standards approved either by ISO or by another standards organization, and partly because these "standards" are largely derived by the development of new products and thus vendor driven. Looking at the physical layer we see that there are many different techniques one may use to convey data between two nodes; however, these may be divided into two classifications, **point-to-point** and **broadcast**. In either case, we notice that maximum data rate that a particular communication channel is able to support is defined by the **bandwidth** and the **attenuation** of the channel (how much the signal dissipates as it travels along the channel). We will see from the examples that the data rates of a point-to-point channel vary from about 1200 bps to 100 Mbps depending on the technology used.

- *Point-to-point*. As its name suggests, a point-to-point communication link is characterized by the connection of a single source to a single destination and may be thought of as "wirelike." Examples of point-to-point communications are the well-known RS232 standard for low speed asynchronous communications (see section 10.3), which uses simple twisted pair wiring and supports data rates of up to 19.2 Kbps over distances less than a few hundred feet including the popular 1200 bps and 9600 bps. The newer RS422 and RS423 serial communication standards that again use twisted pair cables and are designed to replace RS232, offer data rates up to 1 Mbps over distances less than a few hundred feet. Another medium that may be used in point-to-point communications are **fiber optics**. A fiber optic cable is thin flexible glass cylinder drawn to a diameter such that light waves over a particular frequency-band experience total internal reflection when they enter from one end. The result of this is that they appear at the other end with only a slight loss in signal strength. By assigning light-off as a zero and light-on as a one, we are able to transmit digital data from one end to the other at very high data rates. Fiber optics are still a new technology and hence expensive; however, they are rapidly gaining popularity because of the high data rates they support, up to 1 Gbps. Although point-to-point is wirelike, the communication medium need not be a "wire." Examples of this are microwave relay stations as used by the telephone company and satellite communication links. In the former case, the signal is transmitted through the air by a highly directional microwave transmitter (the same waves used in microwave ovens!) to be received at the destination by a wave-guide receiver. The advantage of such a system is that for the common carriers the cost of building a transmitter/receiver pair is low compared with the cost of digging a trench to lay down a trunk cable consisting of many wires. Typically the data rate for microwave links is about 250–500 Mbps. In the case of satellite communications a satellite is placed in a stationary orbit (the satellite remains fixed in the sky relative to the Earth). A number of ground stations use microwave transmissions to send data from the station to the satellite; these are received by the satellite and broadcast back to the earth (at a different frequency to avoid interference) so that the destination ground stations receives the signal. Typically satellites provide a total of about 250M bps some fraction of which is allocated to users according to their demand.

- *Broadcast communications*. Contrasting with point-to-point, the characteristic of a broadcast system is that the data transmitted by one user is received by all the others. This feature has desirable properties when used in networking. One of the goals of a network is to permit any user to communicate with any other. This is easily accomplished if all the users are located on the same broadcast medium. One problem that exists in broadcast systems that is not present in point-to-point channels is **medium access**. Although the channel is shared, it is not possible to have more than one user transmitting data at a time. Thus there is a problem of contention when two or more nodes wish to transmit. There are two basic solution approaches: **contention** and **noncontention**-based protocols. Contention protocols permit multiple nodes to attempt to transmit simultaneously. In the event that more than one node transmits, the signals will interfere with one another, causing the data to be lost. The protocol is then responsible for ensuring that the nodes retransmit the data at some later period. In a noncontention based system, the protocol ensures that only one node will transmit at a time; thus, collisions will never occur. Typically this is accomplished using either reservation system in which nodes reserve the channel for future use or a token based system in which a token is passed between the nodes, and only the node currently possessing the token is permitted to use the channel.

Examples of broadcast systems are the LAN's such as ethernet, token bus, and token ring which are members of the IEEE Standard 802 (also ANSI standard 8802). This standard specifies the family and includes the specification for the data link layer. These standards are discussed in greater detail in the next section. As with point-to-point links, the broadcast medium may also make use of radio broadcast. Although the air-waves are already filled with transmissions from radio stations and broadcast television, there are still frequency bands available for digital transmission. An important milestone in packet radio communications was performed by the Aloha Network at the University of Hawaii in 1973. A network was required to connect together the main campus (on one island) with smaller sites on adjacent islands using radio transceivers. The method adopted was a simple collision detection system. Each island was provided with a small transceiver which could receive data from the central site and transmit to the central site. The central site would then broadcast all incoming data so that all the other sites could receive it. The system made no use of carrier sensing. However, collisions could be detected by the sending station listening to the signal broadcast by the central site. The erroneous frame would then be detected and original frame retransmitted.

One problem that occurs at the physical layer is data corruption during transmission. Corruption may come from noise on the line which may be caused by some external event (such as a generator starting), crosstalk with some other line (similar to the faint portions of other people's telephone conversations that you occasionally hear from a handset), atmospheric interference or one of any number of causes. These errors will typically cause a 0 to be recognized by the receiver as a 1, or vice versa. Such errors are measured in terms of **bit error rate** (or ber) which describes the number of bit errors per bit transferred and is always less than 1. Typical values range from 10^{-3} to 10^{-9} depending on the technology used. Although the physical layer may often be able to detect that a bit error has occurred; it is not responsible for its correction. This task is left for the data link layer.

11.4.3 Layer 2—Data Link Layer

The data link layer is responsible for reliable data communications between adjacent nodes in the network. This feat is accomplished by ensuring that the data stream passed from the network layer to the data link layer on the source IMP is successfully received by the network layer of the destination IMP from its data link layer. The problem to be overcome is that data transmitted by the physical layer may be corrupted prior to reaching the destination; however, without some specific format, the receiver has no way of recognizing that the data is erroneous. The solution to this is a technique called **framing**. A frame is a sequence of bits which includes control information and the user's data. A frame is composed from a **frame header**, the user's data, and a **frame trailer**. The idea behind framing is quite simple—a particular sequence of bits is transmitted to identify the start of a new frame; control information regarding the frame is then sent, followed by the user's data. Finally, additional information and an end of frame bit pattern are sent. The entire sequence is a single frame of data. The frame is either received by the destination IMP without error or is rejected. The format of a frame is designed to include data validation checks or **checksums** so that the receiver may detect errors. If the frame is rejected by the receiver, it must be retransmitted. A detailed description of a typical frame is shown in Figure 11.10.

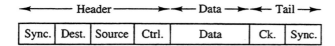

Sync.	Dest.	Source	Ctrl.	Data	Ck.	Sync.

Figure 11.10 Typical frame format.

A typical frame is composed of a number of fields as shown in Figure 11.10. Each field is an integer number of octets. The **sync** bits are usually one or more octet of a preamble pattern (%10101010 in Ethernet) followed by a start of frame octet (%01111110 in token ring). The sync is important because it allows the receiver to recognize an incoming frame. Random errors on the line will be ignored until the receiver locks on to a new start of frame. The next two fields are the destination address and source address. In the Ethernet these are each either 2 or 6 octets. The next field is a control field (3 octets) which specifies how the remaining frame is to be interpreted. The simplest case is when the frame is a user data frame. In this event the length of the user data (in octets) is also provided. The control field may also specify a control mode in which case the data field contain the information. Typical control formats might be ring status and maintenance in a ring and so on. After the data field is a checksum field, which encodes the result of some function applied to the data field. The sender applies the function to the data to generate the checksum, while the receiver applies the same function to the data and compares the result to the received checksum. If the values coincide, the data is assumed to have been received uncorrupted; if they differ, an error has occurred. A typical checksum might be to add the binary value of each octet of the data field modulo 2^{16}. This 2-octet value is used as the checksum. Another technique favored by the IEEE LANs is a **cyclic redundancy check** (CRC). In this the bits in the data field are treated as coefficients of a polynomial. This is divided by a generator polynomial, the remainder being the checksum. The final field is an end of frame marker (again %01111110 token ring). The importance of framing is that the receiver is now able to resynchronize with the sender in the event that a frame is corrupted. It simply waits for the next set of sync octets followed by a start of frame marker.

The reader might have noticed two flaws in the discussion of data transfer so far: (1) What happens if the user wishes to send the bit pattern corresponding to the end of frame marker (i.e., %01111110 in the token ring)? (2) How does the sender know when to resend frames (i.e., how does it know that a frame was not received properly)? There are basically two methods to solve the first problem: one uses out-of-band control, and the other uses in-band control. Out-of-band control implies that at the physical layer we use signaling levels that are neither a 1 nor a 0. Using these, we effectively prevent the user from sending control formats. This technique is used in the token-ring and token-bus protocols to indicate the frame start and frame end delimiters. In-band control is a rather older technique and implies that the control information is embedded in the data. There are two different approaches: **byte-oriented** and **bit-oriented** protocols. In a byte-oriented protocol, the unit of transmission is the octet (we use the term octet unless byte is more appropriate from an historical perspective). The problem then is to distinguish a control octet from a user data octet of the same value. The method employed is escaping, or character-stuffing, the user's data stream. We select a number of character codes that will identify control functions; one of these control codes has the function of a data-link escape (DLE) character. During data transmission, whenever the user data is one of the control characters, the octet is preceded by the DLE character. The receiver, on receiving a DLE, knows that the next character is a data character rather than a control character. Character sets such as ASCII and EBCDIC both define control codes with a suggestion of how they should be used. We include some of the ASCII control codes: Start of Header (SOH) = 001, Start of Text (STX) = 002, End of Text (ETX), End of Tape (EOT) = 004, Data Link Escape (DLE) = 017. As may be seen from the names, these were suggested when magnetic tapes played an important role. To see how character stuffing would be used consider transmission of the following text "A˜*DLE*" from node 5 to node 20, where *DLE* indicates the DLE octet. We assume that the source and destination fields are both two octets, the control field is a single octet (0 = regular data), and that the frame check sequence is modular 256 addition of the data. Table 11.1 shows the data as it is represented at the data-link layer.

TABLE 11.1   Octet encoding of the string A˜DLE. Where DLE is the Data Link Escape character

	Data		Checksum
A	˜	(DLE)	
%01000001	%01111110	%01000001	%00000001

as sent on the line:

FS	Dst	Src	Ctrl	Data			
SOH	20	5	0	A	*DLE*	˜	*DLE*
%01111110	20	5	0	%01000001	%00010100	%01111110	%00010100
					char stuffed		

	Checksum	FE
DLE		
%00010100	%00000001	%01111110
char stuffed		

Although byte-oriented protocols using character stuffing are still used, particularly at higher layers, the preferred method for data-link protocols is now bit oriented. In this the data stream is considered a sequence of bits. Again, we use a technique called bit-stuffing to escape a particular pattern, usually six consecutive 1's. In essence we ensure that when

data are transmitted on the line the user data is never permitted to contain six consecutive
1's. In the event that the frame transmission hardware detects five 1's in a row, it automatically inserts a 0 into the bit stream. Conversely, whenever the receiver detects five 1's followed by a 0; it deletes the zero. If the receiver detects six 1's; it must be from a frame
delimiter sequence. Again, to see how bit-stuffing would be used, consider transmission of
the previous text "A~*DLE*" from node 5 to node 20, where *DLE* indicates the DLE octet.
Again, Table 11.2 shows the data as it is represented at the data-link layer.

TABLE 11.2   Bit encoding of the string A~*DLE*. Where *DLE* is the
Data Link Escape character

	Data		Checksum	
A	~	(DLE)		
%01000001	%01111110	%01000001	%00000001	

as sent on the line:

FS	Dst	Src	Ctrl	Data			
SOH	20	5	0	A	*DLE*	~	*DLE*
%01111110	20	5	0	%01000001	%00010100	%011111010	%00010100
						bit stuffed	

Checksum		FE
%00000001		%01111110

As may be observed from the preceding example, bit-stuffing is slightly more efficient than character stuffing and may be performed under hardware control.

The second problem we noticed regarding the data link layer is verifying that a frame
sent was correctly received. The technique used is *frame retransmission*. When a frame is
transmitted, the transmitting node keeps the frame in a buffer until the destination IMP indicates that it has received the frame. This indication is termed an **acknowledgment** (ACK)
and must be sent as a frame from the receiving IMP back to the sending IMP. Thus when
the sending IMP receives the acknowledgment it may go ahead and safely delete the frame
because it knows that the frame was successfully delivered. Such a protocol is called a **positive acknowledgment** protocol and belongs to a class of **automatic repeat request** (ARQ) protocols. So far we have discussed only the successful delivery of a frame. The question
arises "What happens in the event of an error?" As we have mentioned in ARQ protocols a
frame is only deleted from the sending IMP's buffer when it has been delivered. To allow
the protocol to operate effectively with bit errors, we require that both the sender and
receiver use frame sequence numbers and timers as follows. Each frame has identified with
it a sequence number (as part of the control field). We will assume that both the sender and
receiver start with sequence number 0. This sequence number will be used to identify successive data frames (DATA-x) and their corresponding acknowledgment frames (ACK-x).
First, the sender sends frame DATA-0 and the receiver expects frame DATA-0. If a frame
does not reach the destination, the receiver will not acknowledge it. Thus, after some
agreed on time, the sender **times-out** and retransmits DATA-0. This process is repeated until
the receiver obtains a valid frame. Because the frame received corresponds to the frame

expected by the receiver, it acknowledges it with an ACK-0 frame and passes DATA-0 up to the network layer. The receiver now expects a frame with the next sequence number DATA-1 It may also be the case that although the receiver actually receives the frame, the *acknowledgment frame is corrupted.* In this case, the sender will eventually time-out and send DATA-0 again. Because the sequence number will not correspond to the expected sequence number, the receiver knows that its acknowledgment was lost. It therefore retransmits the acknowledgment with the appropriate sequence (ACK-0). Again the receiver will repeat this process until it receives DATA-1 from the sender indicating that it has received ACK-0. We are now back to the original situation with the sequence number advanced by one on both ends (i.e., having received ACK-0 the sender is sending DATA-1 and the receiver expects DATA-1). We see that this protocol guarantees that each frame will be delivered to the destination without loss or duplication, and will be passed up to the network layer in order. Clearly the sequence number is bounded; however, by using modulo arithmetic, we can "increase" the sequence number indefinitely. In fact looking at the protocol above, we notice that the sequence number need only take on the values 0 or 1. This is known as the **alternating bit protocol** (ABP) and is well known as a simple and reliable protocol.

There are several improvements to the ABP that may be made. First the performance of ABP is rather poor. Consider, that after every frame is sent the sender is then required to wait for an explicit acknowledgment before the next frame may be sent. If the propagation delay is d seconds, this implies that the sender is idle for $2d$ seconds for every frame sent. One simple improvement is **piggybacking**. Recognizing that data frames will be flowing bidirectionally we can piggyback the acknowledgment sequence for a recently arrived frame with an outgoing normal data frame. Thus the ACK information becomes an item in the control field. Additional inefficiency may be overcome by permitting multiple frames to remain unacknowledged. This is accomplished by allowing a "window" of sequence numbers to be transmitted. When the limit of the window is reached, a new frame may be sent only when the oldest (i.e., the "lowest" sequence number) frame has been received and acknowledged. Protocols using this are called **sliding window** protocols and are the primary data link control protocols used today.

Other considerations at the data link layer are **flow control** and processing **expedited data**. Flow control is a mechanism whereby a high speed source IMP is prevented from sending data too quickly to a slower destination IMP. Many methods exit to permit flow control. The most popular is for the destination to send a **choke** packet to the source informing it to stop sending data for some period. Expedited data is data that is considered of high priority. In general expedited data is placed at the front of the transmit buffer queue (see the Section 11.6.1 for other mechanisms).

11.4.4 Layer 3—Network Layer

While the data link layer is concerned with the reliable transfer of information between two adjacent IMP's, the network layer is responsible for the transfer of data between any two IMP's in the network. Addresses are specified by using a NSAP address format. Recall that while the data link layer uses frames, the network layer uses packets, with a field identifying a source/destination pair in it's header. The primary task of the network layer then, is in routing packets from the source IMP to a destination IMP. As we mentioned earlier, the typical network will be organized as a general undirected graph. Each IMP will possess a **routing algorithm**, which is used to determine how packets are to be treated. In the case of a virtual circuit, the routing algorithm is used to establish a route from the source host to the destination host. During this **connection establishment phase** an entry is made in each IMP along the selected path from the source to the destination by a control packet. The entry allocates buffer space for the particular virtual circuit and specifies the next IMP in the path. Once established, each data packet is conveyed through the subnet along the same route. At the termination of a virtual circuit another control packet is used to deallocate the buffers in each IMP along the path. In the case of a (connectionless) datagram service, each packet is free to navigate a different route from the source to the destination. Thus the routing algorithm is applied to each packet. In either case, the routing is an essential component to correct operation of the subnet.

When the packet is received by an IMP, the IMP first checks to see if it is the destination. If so, the routing is complete and the destination has been reached. If not, the IMP must select one of its adjacent nodes and forward the packet to it. Tables that indicate the next hop for a packet are called **routing tables**. Thus a packet "hops" through the subnet one IMP at a time towards the destination.

Most of the problems to be solved in the network layer center on two observations: (1) that the network configuration changes over time and (2) that network traffic changes over time. The difficulty with a changing network configuration is that as the configuration changes so do the routes between IMP pairs. This implies that the routing tables require modifying periodically. Notice, however, that the only way to inform an IMP of new routes is by sending control packets to the IMP. Thus, we must ensure that the control packets do not fall foul of changes in network configuration otherwise it will be impossible to update IMP routing tables to reflect these changes! There are many different routing algorithms. These may, however, be divided into two classes: **nonadaptive** and **adaptive**.

A nonadaptive algorithm operates without regard to changes in the network configuration, with the routing information computed in advance. The advantages of nonadaptive algorithms are of course their simplicity and the ability to compute globally optimal routes for each source/destination pair in the subnet. The disadvantage is that the network is unable to automatically adapt to changes in network configuration; for this reason alone nonadaptive routing algorithms are rarely used. An exception to this is flooding algorithms. With flooding, whenever an IMP receives a packet it immediately sends it to all its neighbors with the exception of the IMP from which it was received. This algorithm guarantees that the packet is transmitted to *all* IMP's assuming that the graph is connected and is therefore considered extremely reliable. Additionally it guarantees that the shortest path from the source to the destination will be used (since every link is used!) The disadvantages of course is the large number of unnecessary packets that are also generated. To see how flooding might be used in a virtual circuit, consider the case of a control packet that is flooded from the source host. As control packet(s) pass through an IMP, we append the IMP ID to a list of IMP's seen. When a control packet reaches the destination, we are able to use the accumulated path (in reverse) to directly specify a path back to the source. A return control packet would then be routed back using this path and would responsible for requesting buffer allocation in each IMP. The technique of specifying a complete source to destination route within a packet is known as **source routing**.

The second class are adaptive and may be subdivided into three categories: **centralized control, distributed control**, and **local control**. In the case of centralized control, a single IMP is responsible for computing the routing tables used by each IMP. Each IMP periodically sends the control IMP information regarding its own connections and any other pertinent data (e.g., traffic flow through it, propagation delays to neighbors, etc.) Using this combined data, the control IMP computes the best routes between all source destination pairs. It then generates the routing table for each IMP and sends it to the IMP. By keeping the update period small, the IMP's respond quickly to changes in the network. The disadvantage of this method is that the status information from the IMP's to the control node is large and, because it converges on a single node, tends to swamp a portion of the subnet. An alternate to centralized control is distributed control. With this each IMP attempts to maintain a reasonable "map" of the state of the network by exchanging control packets with its neighbors. Using this map, an IMP is able to direct incoming packets towards the destination. One popular technique is reverse path forwarding. In this we append to each packet the number of hops that it has so far traveled. As a packet is received by an IMP it notes the incoming line and the recorded number of hops to the source. If this recorded value is lower than its current minimum *toward that node* it changes it's routing table information to reflect this new destination information. Thus we use source information to update our destination routes! Another popular technique is to have each node record which nodes are connected to it. It assembles this information into a control packet and sends it to all its neighbors which then use this information to update their own maps of the network, append the information they know, and send this to their neighbors. The information is used to maintain distance matrices (the number of hops between all source destination pairs) and the routing tables. Once the network is quiescent control packets are generated only when the state of the network changes (i.e., a link fails or a link is re-established). This will cause a brief period of activity until a new network configuration is recognized. Problems with distributed adaptive algorithms are that the network is quick to respond to bad news but slow to respond to good news, and oscillations may occur between two or more stable states. The distributed adaptive algorithms are the most popular for both virtual circuits and datagrams.

The last class of routing algorithm is local information. In this, the IMP makes no attempt to maintain a map of the network. Instead it makes use of limited information regarding IMP's in close proximity. One such algorithm is the hot-potato algorithm in which the outgoing link is selected as the one with the minimum number of queued packets. Another is to send an incoming packet to a designated gateway node if the current IMP is unaware of the destination. The gateway IMP's might then broadcast the packet to all other gateway IMP's hoping that one of them will know the destination. This last suggestion indicates that we may divide the network into a hierarchy of subnetworks.

Apart from responding to changes in the network configuration, a good routing algorithm should also respond to traffic flow. Consider the case in which a shortest path metric is used (i.e., routes selected are the shortest between the source/destination) in the subnet as shown in Figure 11.11. Notice that *all* routes will pass through IMPs 3 and 4 even though other routes exist. Such a situation will cause **local congestion**, resulting in long queues of packets in IMPs 3 and 4. This will reduce the throughput of the network and increase delay. Also as the IMPs become blocked, flow control algorithms will begin to block adjacent IMPs exacerbating the problem. Finally as packets are not delivered in a timely manner, protocols at higher layers will assume that the packet was lost and retransmit it—making the situation still worse! Thus, in the same way that the data-link layer is concerned with flow control, the network layer is concerned with **congestion control**. Congestion control (as the name suggests) is an attempt by the subnet to prevent the subnet from becoming congested with packets. Congestion control occurs in two contexts, **local congestion control** in which we prevent individual IMPs from becoming swamped with more packets than they

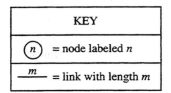

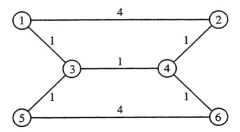

Figure 11.11 Example subnet with shortest path routing.

are able to effectively handle, and **global congestion control** in which we prevent the hosts from collectively sending more packets into the subnet than the subnet can handle. Algorithms for congestion control are beyond the scope of the text, however, we mention that local congestion is usually achieved by incorporating IMP load into the routing metric, whereas global congestion control is achieved by slowing (or **choking**) the rate at which a host submits packets to the subnet.

The other task that requires attention by the network layer is the naming function. Clearly, layers above the network layer will be required to specify a destination host. Although this task sounds simple, it is in fact quite complex. As a first attempt we might give each host a unique address (much like a phone number). The problem now becomes how do the users discover the address of another host that they wish to communicate with. One possible solution is an electronic version of the telephone book; however, humans would soon become lost if they had to keep books for all the telephone districts in the United States, never mind the rest of the world. The solution, of course, is to provide a hierarchical directory service much like the common carriers provide (local assistance, long distance assistance, international assistance, etc.). In the context of computer networks these services are offered by **name servers**, which map "user-friendly" logical names to network addresses. Like the common carriers these are hierarchically organized; however, they are designed to permit computers to communicate with one another.

11.4.5 Layer 4—Transport Layer

The function of the transport layer is the reliable delivery of data from one process (or entity) to another. Addresses are specified using a TSAP address format. Thus the destination entity is uniquely defined by a TSAP, NSAP pair. This is the first layer at which we have true end-user to end-user communication. If the delivery service is to be connectionless, then the transport layer has little to do. In fact all it does when invoked from the layer above (the session layer), is to call the services provided by the layer below (the network layer), and pass the data to them. In the case of a connection oriented service the transport layer is responsible for providing a **bit pipe** between the two ends. That is, whatever data is passed into the pipe at one end arrives at the destination, *regardless of the underlying subnet*. In a sense, then, the transport layer and data-link layer are much alike. They both are point-to-point connections, and they are both charged with the delivery of data in sequence. In fact, the methods used by the data-link layer are similar to the transport layers. Packet checksums are appended to ensure that the data arrives uncorrupted, sequence numbers are used to prevent duplicate and lost packets, and end-to-end acknowledgments to permit packet retransmission. It was recognized, however, that there are differences. In particular there are many different types of subnet; some are highly reliable (a virtual circuit subnet for example) while others are not. It is clearly a duplication of effort if both the network layer *and* the transport layer use reliable end-to-end protocols. With this in mind, the ISO/OSI standard defines five classes of transport service TP0 to TP4. These classes make differing assumptions regarding the reliability of the underlying service. TP0, for example, assumes that the underlying service is completely reliable and therefore does nothing. TP4 on the other hand assumes a datagram subnet and includes all the packet delivery control discussed earlier. In any event the remaining layers of the ISO/OSI standard assume that a connection-oriented service is a bit pipe.

The other functions performed by the transport layer are (1) end-user flow control which, like its partner at the data-link layer, is responsible for preventing a high speed sender from swamping a low speed receiver; (2) expedited data; and (3) multiplexing multiple connections onto a single circuit. We conclude with the observation that the transport layer is the last layer at which we are concerned with the transmission of "data." Layer 5 and above are concerned with the transmission of "information."

11.4.6 Layer 5 — Session Layer

The session layer is responsible for organizing and managing a logical session between two end users. A **session** in this context refers to a single logical activity. Depending on the circumstances, a session might span several transport layer connections, or a connection might involve several sessions. For example, an airline reservation system might consider an employee's work on a booking terminal a single session even though connection is occasionally broken, conversely a transfer protocol might open a connection and consider each file that is transferred a separate session. Sessions are delineated by a start of session primitive and an end of session primitive. Within a session, the user may use primitives to specify **synchronization points**. These points may be used as reference points in the case that the dialogue requires resynchronizing. Notice that these service primitives do not effect the data. They are simply a mechanism to enable the higher layers to insert control information out of band. Thus, in the case of a file transfer, we might send a sync point after each page. In the event of some communication difficulty, it would then be possible to resynchronize at the the start of the last page.

Other services offered by the session layer are **half-duplex control** and **token management**. In the case of half-duplex control, we notice that many distributed applications operate in a client/server mode. In this mode the dialogueue is strictly half-duplex. One side communicates information while the other quietly listens, then the roles are reversed. Half-duplex control ensures that applications using this model have no doubt when they should be transmitting or receiving. A **token** is maintained by the session layer (it is actually represented as state information at both ends). This may be requested, and voluntarily passed between the two ends using session layer primitives; however, only the holder of the token may actually transmit data. The session layer is responsible for ensuring that the token is properly passed between the ends, without corruption. In fact the user may specify any number of tokens and organize the communications semantics (how different collections of tokens are to be interpreted) according to their requirements.

11.4.7 Layer 6—Presentation Layer

The presentation layer is concerned with the representation of data. By representation we mean a formal syntax notation for defining data structures on a wide variety of machines so that a data structure defined on host A may be passed to host B and correctly interpreted. In addition, the presentation layer is responsible for compressing the data before sending it and also for encrypting it. We now discuss these tasks in greater detail.

Data representation.   The need for an abstract syntax notation arises because different vendors use different methods to represent primitive and compound data types. A primitive data type is one that is manipulated directly in most hardware implementations. Primitives data types include integer, string, boolean, and floating point. Compound types are aggregates of primitive types: typical structures are records, arrays, sets and structure unions (sometimes called variant records). Consider the simple case of the lowly integer. Signed integers may be described in a variety of ways: in this text we have introduced signed magnitude, 1's complement and 2's complement. Thus the bit representation for the value -1 will be different in each case (for 16 bit integers with LSB leftmost we have %1000000000000001, %1111111111111110, and %1111111111111111). Also the ordering of octets in memory for a particular data type may be different for different vendors, even if the representation is the same. For example Motorola Corp. stores the most significant octet first (low address), while Intel Corp. stores the least significant octet first. Thus, even though both the Motorola and Intel architectures use 2's complement their representation of 1 would be quite different as shown in Table 11.3.

TABLE 11.3   Representation of 1 in 2's complement using little and big endian

Address	Little endian	Big endian
0003	00	01
0002	00	00
0001	00	00
0000	01	00

As may be seen from the previous discussion, there are numerous problems in the transmission of even a simple integer. Consider the complexities that are required for other simple types: strings, booleans, enumerated types, floating point types, and so on. Additionally, we have yet to consider compound data structures. We would expect there to be major differences between the internal representation of arrays, records, and so on. To see the importance of consistent representation of structured information, consider the simple case of a connection request between peer Network Layer entities:

```
CONNECT.request(destination,source,....)
```

Clearly the parameters of this request form a record structure that must be conveyed to the destination network entity. Thus the source network entity will use a data structure such as

```
struct connect_request_params {
        char destination[20];
        char source[20];
        int  priority;
}
A typical value for this structure might be

        121.204.15.3
        134.219.11.4
        2
```

This structure must be passed to the destination, which might be a different machine with the network software written in a different language (e.g., Ada). How then can we insure that it is correctly interpreted?

The answer to this dilemma is the use of a canonical representation for data structures. By canonical representation we mean a single language that is used by all communications software. The representation should ideally include a **data structure specification language** independent of the programming language, a **data value specification language**, and a **transmission line encoding**. The first item is used to describe the data structures. Each vendor is then responsible for ensuring that a compiler exists that will generate an appropriate data structure for the language used on the machine. The second item is used to allow humans to describe a particular value set for a data structure. Although this seems unnecessary, it is useful in testing, particularly when one has a compiler which takes a text representation of a data value and the corresponding data structure and generates the line encoding. The last item is of course essential; it specifies precisely how a particular data value is to be sent along a communications line. Having a canonical line encoding ensures that all machines may communicate with one another. The ISO/OSI recognized this need early on and defined an **abstract syntax notation** (ASN.1), which may be used to describe data structures, values, and line encoding.

A detailed discussion of ASN.1 is outside the scope of this text; however, we briefly mention the pertinent features. ASN.1 provides three specifications: the data structure definition, the data value representation, and the line encoding. Data structures are composed of basic and compound types. Basic types are BOOLEAN, INTEGER, BIT STRING, OCTET STRING, and NULL. Compound types are SEQUENCE, SEQUENCE OF, SET, SET OF, CHOICE, and ANY. In addition there is an object identifier type used to specify the source location of predefined types. This permits ISO and individual companies to define standard structures. Example structures are standard representations for time (UniversalTime), character set specifications (International Alphabet 5, i.e., ASCII), and network service specifications (X.400). An idea central to ASN.1 is the notion of tagging data items. Each data item has an associated tag which is a non-negative integer used to identify the type. Four classes of tag are defined: Universal, Application, Private, and Context-specific. The idea behind tagging is to allow individual data items to be self identifying. Thus a data item sent with its tag contains sufficient information for the destination to identify the *type* of the data as well as its value. Universal tags are defined by the ISO/CCITT standards bodies and include all the types mentioned earlier. For example,

```
UNIVERSAL 1              Boolean type
UNIVERSAL 2              Integer type
UNIVERSAL 3              Bitstring type
UNIVERSAL 4              Octetstring type
UNIVERSAL 5              Null type
UNIVERSAL 6              Objector identifier type
UNIVERSAL 7              Objector descriptor type
...
```

Each compound type that the user defines is explicitly given a new tag value which may be either Application (local to that application), Private (tag defined by company), or Context-specific (tag depends on context). The usefulness of tagging is seen when we consider line encoding. Data values sent along the communication lines in ASN.1 are **self-identifying** and are composed of a tag, a length, and a value. (known as TLV encoding) The tag field is one or more octets and identified the tag number as shown subsequently.

```
ccpiiiii [1ttttttt 1ttttttt ... 0ttttttt]
Octet 1  Octet 2  ....
```

where:
```
    cc = class (00=Universal, 01=Application, 10=Private,
         11=Context-specific)
    p  = primitive/constructed (0 = primitive, 1 = constructed)
    iiiii = tag number, or
    11111 = indicates that it is defined in the following octets,
            with each octet containing a 1 followed by 7 tag bits,
            except for the last octet which contains a 0 followed
            by 7 tag bits.
```

Thus for example the type [Application 2] would be encoded as %01000010, while [Universal 255] would be encoded as %00011111 %10000001 %01111111.

The length (in octets) of the value is also encoded and takes on one of two forms, the definite form and the indefinite form. The definite form specifies the length as shown subsequently.

```
0nnnnnnn (short form)
Octet 1
```

where:
```
    nnnnnnn = number of octets in value field.
```

or

```
11111111 [nnnnnnnn nnnnnnnn ... nnnnnnnn] (Long form)
Octet1    Octet2    Octet 3 ...
```

where:
```
    1111111 = number of octets in the length field.
    nnnnnnnn = octets indicating length of value field
```

Thus, for example, if the value field was five octets the length field could be encoded as either %00000101 (short form) or %10000001 %00000101 (long form). The indefinite format of the length field is used when the length of the structure is not know in advance. In this case a special octet indicating the end of data value is used instead of a length. The indefinite form is indicated by a "length" of %10000000 which would normally be the short form, length 0.

The final field is the data value itself. In the case of simple types, the data is encoded according to rules described in the ASN.1 specification for each data type. The specifications include the octet ordering for multioctet fields and conventions to be used in each type. For example, the type boolean is sent as a single octet, with 0 for false and 1 for true; integers are sent low octet first in two's complement representation using as many octets as are necessary to represent the value; bit strings are sent as an integer number of octets with the first octet indicating how many bits of the last octet are valid (0 to 7). In the case of constructed types, the data is a concatenation of the tagged data used in each field. Of course, since each field will be either a constructed or simple type, each field will have its own TLV. We conclude the discussion of ASN.1 with an annotated example using the above connection request parameter list, along with a sample data value and it's line encoding, all defined in ASN.1.

```
description of structure:

Connect_request_params ::= [APPLICATION 0] SEQUENCE OF {
    destination Visible_String,     -- Length 20
    source      Visible_String,     -- Length 20
    priority    Integer,
}


example record:

{
    destination "cis.ufl.edu",
    source      "eng.auburn.edu",
    priority    123,
}


Line encoding (in binary and ascii):

%01000000 %00100000
    %00011010 %00001011  "cis.ufl.edu"
    %00011010 %00001110  "eng.auburn.edu"
    %00000010 %00000001   %10110100
```

Data compression. Another function provided by the presentation layer is data compression. As the name suggests, the goal of data compression is to reduce the number of bits required to represent the information sent. Notice that data compression will always improve the performance of the network. It is independent of channel bandwidth. If a line has a capacity of x bps, and we send a message S_1 of length $4x$ bits, then it will take 4 s. If we are able to compress that message so that only $2x$ bits are required, then we are able to send the same message in half the time! Data compression is an activity that would typically be decided during the peer entity exchange that precedes data transfer. In this case, a negotiated parameter would be the data compression algorithm to be used. In the following paragraphs we define a measure for encoding efficiency known as *entropy*, introduce the two main techniques for data compression **online** and **offline**, and discuss a popular data compression algorithm known as **Huffman encoding**.

The topic of data compression is a field within information theory. We start with some assumptions and definitions. We allow our transmitted characters s_i to be drawn from an alphabet of n distinct characters $\Sigma = \{s_1, \ldots, s_i, \ldots, s_n\}$ in which each character is sent with probability p_i. We assume that the probabilities are independent of one another (called the first order assumption). The basic premise is this: The information content of a message is defined in terms of the likelihood of receiving the message. The more likely a message, the less information it conveys and vice versa. Consider for example the case of sending the same character s_i from an alphabet all the time. Clearly the probability of sending that character (p_i) is 1 and for all others $(p_j, i \neq j)$ is 0. Thus the receiver learns nothing from this exchange, that is, the information content is low. Notice also that we need 0 bits to send it! Conversely, suppose that each character is sent with probability $p_i = 1/n$. Then reception of this character provides the maximum amount of information that may be obtained from a single character; thus, the information content is high. Because every character is equally likely, we require at least $k = \lceil \log_2(n) \rceil$ bits to send it. Thus the information content of the ith character in the alphabet is given by

$$I_i = \log_2\left(\frac{1}{p_i}\right) \quad \text{measured in bits} \tag{12.1}$$

This measure of information content was formalized in the 1940s by C. E. Shannon as follows. If we average the information content of a particular message S_1 then we have what he defined as the **entropy** of the message. The entropy of a (binary) message S using characters from Σ is given by

$$H(S) = \sum_{i=1}^{n} p_i \log_2(1/p_i) \tag{12.2}$$

Because the information content of a character is proportional to the probability of sending it, we realize that the most frequent characters should be coded using the least number of bits. Note that for the two examples above we see that the entropy (average information content) is $H(S) = 0$ when we receive no useful information and is $H(S) = 1 + \log_2(n - 1)/2$ when each character is equally likely.

To see how data compression works, consider a message from our alphabet. As we have seen, in a purely random string the probability of the next character being s_i is $1/n$. Because each character must be encoded using a sequence of 0's and 1's we could use k bits to represent each symbol (e.g., Section 3.1.9—the 128 symbols of the ASCII character set are encoded using seven bits) because there is no reason to expect any symbol to occur more often than any other. Thus for a random string, we are unable to improve on this coding scheme. Consider, however, a typical text message; the frequency with which each character appears is far from equal. We now see how data compression might be achieved. We wish to encode each character according to the probability that it will occur, with fewer bits for the most likely character, and so on. The reader might wonder if one could improve the coding efficiency still further by examining sequences of characters together and assigning bit patterns to *sequences* rather than individual characters. The answer is yes! These are called *higher-order* codes and while similar in principle are much more complex to implement. For these reason they will not be discussed further.

There are two classes of data compression algorithm available, online encoding and offline encoding. The easiest of these is offline encoding. Assuming that we have a finite message S_1 to send from a source to a destination with offline encoding we transmit an optimal encoding for the message (i.e., minimize the average bit length of the message) using our knowledge of the *entire* message. This implies that the message is scanned prior to sending any data. The second class of compression algorithm is online. With this class then we scan the source message one character at a time, and send a sequence of bits dependent on what has been sent so far and the character in question. Thus, online encoders do not have access to the entire message. As one might expect, for finite messages, offline encoding is superior. For infinite strings, we must modify the notion of offline to permit blocks of the message to be examined. Regardless of the scheme used, we must ensure that the receiver is able to decipher the bit patterns sent and reconstruct the original message (i.e., the encoding scheme must be **uniquely decipherable**).

As an example of a compression algorithm, we briefly describe **Huffman encoding**. The Huffman encoding scheme is an offline encoding algorithm that generates **optimal** codes. That is, for a given string there is no algorithm that will provide a lower average bit length than that found by Huffman encoding. To see how this works, consider the following alphabet (Σ) and sample message (S_1) using characters from that alphabet:

$$\Sigma = \{ a, b, c, d, e, f \}$$

$$S_1 = ababfcfcdeabde$$

We see clearly that the characters in S_1 are not evenly distributed. Therefore, we are able to compress the data: notice incidentally the close relationship between compressibility and randomness. The Huffman code for each distinct character in the above message is obtained by construction of a tree as shown in Table 11.4.

TABLE 11.4 Huffman code algorithm

---

[1]. Compute the probabilities for each character.

[2]. Place these probabilities in ascending order (leaf nodes of the tree).

[3]. At each level of the tree combine the lowest two probabilities, placing the the higher probability subtree to the left. Continue this this until all probabilities have been combined. Ties are resolved using some previously agreed upon procedure.

[4]. Working back down the tree from the root, assign a 0 to the left side of the tree and 1 to the right side at each branch.

[5]. Read the code word for each of the characters by starting from the root of the tree and tracing to the leaves.

This procedure is clearly demonstrated using the example message as shown in Figure 11.12. Notice that we compute the probabilities for each character using the frequency obtained from the message. As expected, the most probable characters are encoded using the least number of bits. Once the destination is equipped with the Huffman code, the incoming message may be decoded immediately from the coding tree.

Message S_1 = ababfcfcdeabde

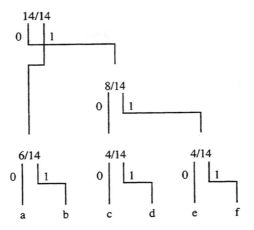

Symbol probability	3/14	3/14	2/14	2/14	2/14	2/14

Decreasing probability

Code generated	10	11	000	001	010	011

Figure 11.12   Demonstration of the Huffman code.

The reader might wonder what the efficiency of this method is. We are able to computer this as follows. For the preceding message the average code length is given by

$$\textbf{Average code length} = 2 * \frac{3}{14} + 2 * \frac{3}{14} + 3 * \frac{2}{14} + 3 * \frac{2}{14} + 3 * \frac{2}{14} + 3 * \frac{2}{14}$$

$$= \frac{36}{14}$$

$$= 2.5714$$

while the entropy (which represents the actual average information content of the message) $H(S_1)$ is given by

$$\textbf{Entropy,}\ H(S_1) = 2\left(\frac{3}{14} * \log_2\left(\frac{14}{3}\right)\right) + 4\left(\frac{2}{14} * \log_2\left(\frac{14}{2}\right)\right)$$

$$= 2(0.2143 * 2.2222) + 4(0.1429 * 2.8074)$$

$$= 2.5566$$

This yields a very reasonable coding efficiently of 99.4 %.

We conclude data compression by mentioning one interesting form of static character encoding, the **Morse code**. In a typical English message the most common character is the letter "*e*"; thus, for *English text* we could use the least number of bits to represent this character, at the expense of a longer encoding of less frequently used characters. In Morse code each character is assigned a different bit pattern (dot and dash). The shortest bit sequences given to the most frequently occurring characters. We show the first few in Table 11.5.

TABLE 11.5 Data
compression using
Morse code

Sample Morse codes	
Symbol	Morse code
e	. (or 0)
t	- (or 1)
c	-.- (or 101)

Using only this, the number of bits required to send a text message may be substantially reduced. While Morse code offers some improvement with text it is far form optimal and fails in many cases. For example, if we are sending a Pascal program the most common symbol might be "*" (Pascal programs often have an abundance of *******'s in comment blocks!). It is usual, then, to invoke more sophisticated compression schemes.

Encryption.   The final major function provided by the presentation layer is data encryption. In fact security, like network management, is a function that occurs at many levels throughout the ISO/OSI model. In the context of the presentation layer, data encryption is a mechanism to prevent an assailant from reading or modifying an intercepted message. In the following paragraphs we will introduce some terminology used in data encryption and discuss two important data encryption algorithms, the **data encryption standard** (DES), and the **public key encryption algorithm.**

We define the unencoded message as **plaintext** and the encrypted message as **ciphertext**. The translation from plaintext to ciphertext is achieved with an **encryption algorithm**, and **key**. The encryption algorithm takes as input a plaintext string and a key, and generates as output the corresponding ciphertext. The reverse process is achieved using a **decryption algorithm**, which may be considered an image of the encryption algorithm. We may consider encryption as a game in which the assailant has obtained a copy of our ciphertext message, our encoding/decoding algorithms, and a plaintext and corresponding ciphertext sample message using the same key. The only item of information the assailant is lacking is the key. The object of the game is for the assailant to decode the ciphertext message. An example of a simple encryption algorithm applied to ASCII text might be to rotate the characters through the ASCII sequence by a constant amount: thus, with a rotation of 13, A→N, B→M, or in general if x is the ASCII value of the plaintext, $G(x) = (x + 13)$ modulo 128 is the value of the ciphertext. Clearly this encryption algorithm is not very secure! In fact it has many deficiencies: for example the frequency of occurrence of the encoded symbols is identical to it's plaintext equivalents and identical plaintext words yield identical ciphertext words; thus, interword spacing is identical. Like data compression, cryptology is within the field of information theory and is a subject on which many books have been written. It is sufficient for this introduction to mention that two encryption algorithms are of particular interest. The first is the **data encryption standard** (DES), which until recently was the Department of Defense's recommended encryption algorithm for nonmilitary data. The second algorithm is the public key encryption algorithm which is particularly interesting because of some unusual characteristics.

The DES algorithm uses a 56-bit key and operates in either stream mode (a continuous stream of plaintext bits are encrypted to a stream of ciphertext bits) or block mode (a message is a padded to a fixed size block (64 bits); the block is then encrypted and resulting ciphertext block is sent). The algorithm uses a sequence of **permutation cells** and **substitution cells** to effectively jumble the input based on the key. A permutation cell has n input lines and n output lines with the output a permutation of the input (i.e., the number of 1's at the output is the same as on the input). A substitution cell also has n input lines and n output lines with the input mapped to the output according to some function. Using the block mode as an example, the following procedure is repeated several times. First the key is rotated and combined with the half the data; this output is then passed through the permutation and substitution cells; finally this result is recombined with the uneffected half by swapping the two halfs. This sequence is repeated a number of times, for the DES the number of iterations is 16. As you may see, the output from this procedure is an extremely complex function of the input, which we hope the adversary will be unable to determine.

Public key encryption algorithms use an an interesting variation on traditional encryption algorithms such as DES. We design our encryption algorithm so that the encoding and decoding keys are different and that given the decoding key it is extremely hard to find the encoding key. We also require that text encoded by either key may be decoded by the other, but not by itself. These properties are satisfied by particular prime factors of certain very large integers. We define these keys as a **public key** (the encoding key) and a **private key** (the decoding key). The public key we make known to all. The private key remains a secret of the owner.

The interesting feature of public key encryption is that it may be used to provide electronic signatures. Consider that user A wishes to send a message to user B. The problem is how does user B know that it was user A that sent the message, and not some assailant user C masquerading as user A? One solution, using the public key encryption algorithm, is as follows. User A encrypts a short signature (such as "This is user A") using user A's own private key. This signature is appended to the plaintext message and the resulting text is encrypted using user B's public key as usual. The resulting ciphertext is sent through the network to user B. User B may then decrypt the message using user B's own private key and establish the authenticity of the text using user A's public key to decrypt the signature. We assume of course that the keys are inverses on one another, that is, either key may be used to encode or decode a message.

11.4.8 Layer 7—Application Layer

The application layer is the final layer of the ISO/OSI model and is different from the others in the following ways: (1) Services provided by this layer are designed for use by the end-user rather than another communication layer, and (2) there are a vast number of services available in this layer. As the name suggests, the application layer is a repository for any application that the user might wish. Its function therefore, is to provide a mechanism for the formal definition of the services provided by the application, and the protocol by which peer applications communicate. Thus an application, when implemented according to the ISO service and protocol specifications, should be able to communicate across the network with another implementation without difficulty. Notice that by the time we have reached this layer, we no longer need worry about connection management, session management, and data representation. Provided we use the services defined by the presentation layer all this is taken care of for us. Although there are an unlimited number of potential applications, there are several that require explicit mention. These services are **file transfer, remote**

log-in, electronic mail, network news, and **remote job entry.** In addition to these, typical applications might be **network time synchronization, network weather information, network directory information, graphical image transfer,** and so on. We now discuss the first five services in more detail.

File transfer, as the name suggests, permits the transfer of files across the network. Although connection establishment and maintenance is straight forward there are still sticky problems to be resolved. These include transfer control, property mapping, and special routing information. Transfer control permits the user to specify which files are to be transferred, where they are to go on the destination file system, and so on. Typically, files have associated with them a number of properties including: file type, creation date, modification date, permissions, security classification, version control information, size, and so forth. A particular vendor's file system will support either some or all of these; however, the exact representation will of course vary from system to system. The file transfer protocol must permit these parameters to be exchanged prior to the transfer of data. It may be that some of the parameters require intelligent mapping from the source to the destination, for example, access permissions. It may also be that different file types must be treated differently, for example, a binary image file would be transferred without modification, whereas a text file might require that the newline sequence be changed for different destinations. The approach used to resolve these conflicts is similar to the presentation layer philosophy. The service specification attempts to accommodate all different forms, with a canonical representation for structured files which is encoded by the source and interpreted by the destination. Finally, it may be necessary for the user to specify general routing information for security reasons.

Another important service is remote login. This permits a user on host A to *log-in* to another host B across the network. Again, this apparently simple activity poses several difficult problems. Each host supports several different terminal types; these different terminals use a variety of distinct control sequences to perform terminal operations (e.g., clear the screen, move the cursor, highlight a region on text, set function key macros etc). While there are ANSI standards (for example the ANSI terminal mode), many are vendor defined industry standards (for example the IBM 3270 or the DEC VT100), and all handle similar properties differently. Clearly we require that a user should be able to use any one of these terminals and communicate effectively with any remote application. One possible method is again based on the canonical representation philosophy. We define a terminal independent **virtual terminal protocol.** The protocol defines a set of high level functions in which the applications are written. For screen control, each function is realized as a sequence of terminal-dependent control actions, similarly each key (or sequence of keys) is mapped to a high level function. These mappings are associated with the appropriate terminal type. When the service is started, the terminal type is passed as a parameter and used to configure the terminal server. From then on, a short dialogue occurs between the protocol entities to establish each others characteristics, the completion of which provides the users with a virtual terminal. This virtual terminal may then communicate effectively with any application written using the virtual terminal model. As with other layers, there may be more than one virtual terminal protocol, and more than one version of the same protocol. These issues are resolved by the peer entities.

Another important service is mail. In electronic mail the sender sends a text file to one or more recipients. Problems in the mail utility are (1) how does the sender establish the recipients mailing address, and (2) should delivery of mail be confirmed? The mailing address problem is similar to the host name service problem encountered in the network and transport layers. The difference is that the directory information will be significantly larger, which makes consistency a problem. We also have to deal with problems caused by a user having access to possibly many hosts. This might result in multiple mailing addresses. Despite these problems, the essential mechanism will remain as with the host name server, that is, the directory information will be distributed to domain servers; these will communicate with one another to establish a user's mail address based on information supplied. The problem of mail confirmation is one of user privacy. We have a dilemma in that when a mail message is sent, the sender would like to know that it was received; however, from the receiver's perspective releasing this information could be considered an intrusion. Although this problem is not a technical one, it again demonstrates the the breadth of issues that require consideration. An electronic mail facility is usually organized in two separate components, the user interface and the mail transfer server. There may be many user interfaces, ranging from a simple teletype interface to a window based tool that provides many additional features. In either event the function is essentially the same. The user interface permits the user to read the mail he or she has received (along with filing, printing, etc.) which is stored in a spool area, and compose letters to other users which, once completed, are placed in an outgoing spool area. The second component of the mail facility is the mail transfer entity. This communicates indirectly with the user interface through the spool areas. The transfer utility is responsible for sending the outgoing mail to the appropriate destination by establishing a dialogue with the destination server, and conversely, receives mail from other servers placing it in the local spool area. The separation of the user interface from the network component is important. It permits the underlying mail transfer protocol to be changed without affecting the user interfaces, and vice versa.

Another service that we encounter on a daily basis and has a place in computer networks is news. Electronic news, like the newspaper, is a mechanism whereby individuals may subscribe to particular news feeds and read the news on their workstation. Unlike the newspapers, electronic news presents a forum by which anyone may submit an article to a particular group for the interest of others. This potential for instantaneous feedback is a characteristic of electronic news that makes it ideal for members of special interest groups to engage in exchanges that add a conversational flavor to the proceedings. Electronic news has much in common with electronic mail; in both cases we are concerned with moving short files between servers. As with mail, the news utilities are composed of two distinct components: (1) user interface and (2) news server. The user interface permits users to browse the numerous news groups available and read articles. There may be literally hundreds of different news groups spanning all areas of interest, from technical forums in specialist topics to news groups of broad interest. Each of these groups may have many articles posted daily. The number of articles that the user is required to process may, therefore, easily be in the thousands! To assist in processing this information, the user interface will typically screen out all but a few selected news groups. Within these, the user interface may again provide user defined filters to further prune the number of articles that are presented to be read. The other function of the user interface is to permit the user to submit articles to be read. The articles, once submitted and screened, are posted to the appropriate news group for the enjoyment of others. The news server communicates with other servers to exchange news articles. Each server maintains a database of all the articles in all the newsgroups for a certain period of time past. Whenever a user wishes to read a news group the user interface opens a connection to the server. Each user maintains information regarding those news groups they subscribe to and those articles that have been read. The user interface interprets this information to request only those articles that the user is interested in. These are transferred from the database to the user's workstation. Whenever a user submits a news article the user interface "passes" it to the server. The server adds this into it's database and then sends it to other news servers. In this way, the article is "broadcast" throughout the network. Periodically the news database is purged of all articles older than some time period, but even with this house cleaning the database may grow to hundreds of megabytes.

The final service that we mention is remote job entry (RJE). Although the concept of a job is rather outdated it is still an important notion for mainframe computer operations. A **job** in computer terms represents a program and the data files for that particular invocation. Thus RJE amounts to the transfer of all pertinent data from the source to the destination host, along with command procedures for execution of the job on that host. Once completed, the results are returned to the source host. Activities that are required by RJE include some method of monitoring the status of the remote job and perhaps rudimentary control of the job (premature termination for instance). These facilities are easily accommodated by providing the user with process information on destination machine and remote command execution.

As we mentioned earlier, there are literally hundreds of deserving services that might be available to the user. The five above are found in almost all networked environments and represent the bare minimum.

11.5 DESIGN CONSIDERATIONS

Now that we have defined the organization of networking functions we consider some of the issues that must be addressed in network design. Components to consider include **subnet design** which includes specifying the location and connection of backbone nodes and how secondary nodes are to be connected to these.

11.5.1 Subnet Design

A **wide area network** (WAN) is typically composed of a backbone of IMPs connected together by high-speed point-to-point links. These links might be either a pair of microwave towers, high-speed telephones lines leased from the common carriers, or if the network is a corporate network, the lines might actually be owned by the company. The number of backbone nodes would be rather small, usually between five and ten. Because of the high data rates involved, anywhere from 1 Mbps to 100 Mbps, the IMPs will be dedicated to the task of switching packets and will not constitute a general purpose computing facility. Figure 11.13 shows how such a backbone might be organized. Each of the backbone nodes serves as the network connection point for a geographical region. Within this region gateway nodes will be connected to the backbone, usually by leased lines, at a somewhat lower data rate. These nodes will be either small dedicated units or may be mainframe/server type machines which also provide general computing facilities. These servers or gateways will finally be connected to a LAN to which user's workstations are connected. Notice that although this discussion suggests a tree structure, this need not be the case. It may be that a secondary LAN is connected to other peer gateways that are in turn connected to the other nodes in the backbone. This is in fact desirable from the perspective of reliability and traffic flow as we shall see shortly.

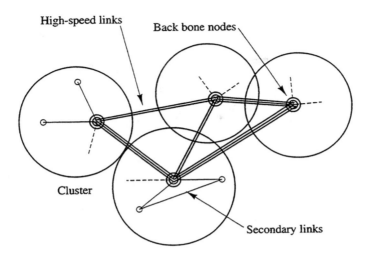

Figure 11.13   Network backbone.

When deciding which links to include in a network configuration and what data rates to select, we make several assumptions regarding network use. In particular, assume that the network has reached a steady state that is defined by a traffic matrix specifying the volume of traffic between all source/destination pairs and that this matrix is invariant. We also assume that packet sizes do not vary greatly in size and are small compared to the capacity of the network, and that packets do not influence the generation of others. Although these assumptions are violated in a real network, the effects are negligible. In terms of design considerations we are confronted with a large set of variables and constraints. The total network cost includes the following considerations:

Line costs. These are dependent on the location of the backbone nodes and the data rates required. These costs are highly nonlinear with different tariffs, peak and off peak rates, and different charges for the few select data rates (e.g., 9.6 Kbps, 56 Kbps, and 1.44 Mbps). Services and rates may also vary with geographical location.

Equipment costs. These will depend on the vendor selected and the data rates to be switched. An important characteristic of modern computer networks is open systems interconnection as discussed earlier. Using these open systems, the communications processors may differ from the computers used at the sites.

Software costs. These are generally dependent on the hardware vendor selected and may even come either hardcoded or packaged with the operating system software.

The network will presumably offer some level of performance in terms of the data rate that it may accommodate. This is usually measured by the following metrics:

Throughput. This measures the number of bits (or packets) of user data passing through the network per unit time. Clearly the offered load to the network must be less than the network's maximum throughput. Even with this constraint satisfied, the performance of the network may be unsatisfactory due to localized congestion within the subnet.

Delay. This measures the time taken for data to traverse the network. In many applications there are response time constraints which must be satisfied for the performance to be acceptable. For example in an ATM system the maximum acceptable delay per transaction may be one second.

Utilization. This measures the sum of the user and control data as, a percentage of the network capacity. Capacity is defined as the maximum number of bits that may be handled by the network. Throughput and delay are of often of interest to the users, whereas network utilization is of interest to the network managers.

Notice that by satisfying one constraint, a design may adversely affect another. In particular, a network is cost effective when it is busy, that is, high use; however, under these conditions the delays may be large. In addition if the utilization becomes too high, the network may become congested resulting in either rejected connection attempts or reduced throughput for the active users.

Network performance metric.   Before the design of a network it is necessary to develop a metric to measure the relative merits of a particular design. With the conflicting constraints described above, this is not easy. We start by assuming that the network has some cost function that is to be optimized. This cost function will be related to the traffic flowing on the network, which is described by the traffic flow on each link in the network. We define F_{ij} as the link flow from node i to node j in the network, measured in either bits/s or frames/s. We also define C_{ij} as the capacity of the same line, measured in the same units. Assuming that each link has a separate cost function (related to the flow) we, therefore, define $Q_{ij}(F_{ij})$ as the cost for that link, where Q is a monotonically increasing function. Thus the total cost of the network may be defined as

$$\sum_{(i,j)} Q_{ij}(F_{ij})$$

(1)

A popular formula for Q_{ij} is

$$Q_{ij}(F_{ij}) = \frac{F_{ij}}{C_{ij} - F_{ij}} + q_{ij}F_{ij}$$

(2)

where q is the link propagation delay and processing overhead. Notice that when the link flow is low, the first term is approximately F_{ij}/C_{ij} which is the link use. As F_{ij} approachs C_{ij} the first term tends to infinity reflecting this undesirable situation. The second term represents the linear dependence between the flow on the link and the "real" cost in using it.

Other cost functions exist. Another popular cost function may defined as the maximum link utilization in the network. Again, the rational is based on the observation that in a well designed network the traffic is proportionally distributed according to the capacity of each link: Therefore, an overall cost may be ascertained by considering the highest link use.

Design methodology.   Given the location of the nodes in the backbone, the routing algorithm to be used, and the input traffic matrix (the individual flows of all source/destination pairs), the task in subnet design is to assign capacities to each of the links in the fully connected graph so as to satisfy a number of constraints while minimizing costs. The constraints in question are typically delay and reliability (e.g., ensuring that there are at least two paths between all source/destination node pairs). The complex nature of the problem demands that for any real network a heuristic approach be used. The heuristic may be considered as cyclic sequence of steps as shown below, starting with a proposed network configuration.

1. Using the current link capacities, assign flows to each link based on the routing algorithm to be used. This step will require that the network be simulated and the steady state flows recorded or that some routing model be used. In either event the exercise is computationally expensive.

2. Evaluate the estimated delay for the network using the delay function Q given in equation 1. Check to see if Q is below some threshold. If it is, go to step 3; otherwise, go to step 5.

3. Evaluate the reliability of the network. If the network is considered reliable, go to step 4; otherwise, go to step 5. Measures of reliability involve computing the network connectivity to establish the number of node and link disjoint paths that exist between all source/destination pairs. Algorithms to accomplish this are well known although computationally expensive.

4. Evaluate the cost of the network and determine if it is lower than the cost of the previous configuration. If it is, then replace the old network with the new one; otherwise, keep the original. The cost function will be determined by the line tariffs, distances, and data rates selected for the each link.

5. If you still have resources to spend, generate a new network and goto step 1; otherwise, we are finished.

The final step requires a special mention. Clearly the more "intelligent" the capacity assignment, the quicker an acceptable solution will be reached. There are several heuristics that work well. One is to reduce the capacity (or eliminate altogether) those links that are underused. Another is to increase the capacity of the those links that are highly used. Finally a combination of these may be used. Another consideration is the generation of the initial network configuration. An intelligent first selection may significantly reduce the number of iterations required. In network design, experience is essential.

11.5.2 LAN Design

The characteristics of LAN design make the procedure rather easier than WAN design. Recall that LANs cover only short distances and that all devices are attached to the common medium. Thus all devices are close to one another regardless of the configuration. The issues that require addressing are, therefore, where to place the LAN cabling and when to use **bridges** or **routers**. The first issue is dependent on local site considerations. We will use as an example the Ethernet (discussed in Section 11.6.1) noting that others LANs have are similar requirements. The original design intentions of Ethernet were to use one segment (single coaxial cable) for each floor of a building. These segments are then connected together by bridging to another segment running vertically through the building. This allows the entire building to be viewed as a single Ethernet segment, that is, a single LAN. In the event that multiple buildings are to be connected together, we require that either another segment be used or that we connect the buildings as separate networks. If another segment is used, then again the LAN grows in size. As one might expect, the advantages of a single large LAN network lie in its simplicity. One must be careful, however, to satisfy the maximum distance requirements of Ethernet (about 2.5 km between the most separated nodes). Additional disadvantages are that the network traffic for all users is now higher, since all nodes are competing for the same channel and that individual corporate entities (e.g., departments) cannot restrict the propagation of data outside their environment which may cause security hazards.

The alternate to bridging LANs is to use **routers**. As with bridges, a router connects together two LANs; however, the data transfer is now viewed at the higher level of network addressing. Thus routers detect packets that are destined for another network and pass them between networks. By moving the task of data transfer from the data link level to the network level, routers are able to perform two services: They may use network addressing to prevent data from leaving/entering a particular LAN, and they permit LANs using different protocols to be connected to one another.

11.6 EXAMPLE NETWORK PROTOCOLS—INTERNET

As an example of how several differing protocols may be combined to provide end-user services across a network, we discuss the Internet protocols (or simply the Internet). We mention at the outset that the Internet predates the ISO/OSI model and in fact played a major role in shaping the layers and specification mechanisms used in the OSI. A side effect of this situation is that the Internet differs in several respects from the OSI. In particular the Internet is something of an adhoc collection of protocols (albeit layered) which, however, has become remarkably popular. The Internet protocols are monitored by a governing board (the Internet Activities Board [IAB]), which regularly produces a manual specifying the components of the Internet. When originally conceived, the Internet was designed to connect together a small number of IMPs using leased telephone lines. Because of this, the physical layer characteristics were defined by the common carriers. The essential protocol on the Internet was the **internet protocol** (IP) itself and the **transmission control protocol** (TCP). Finally a number of useful applications were defined to be used on top of TCP/IP, namely **ftp** (file transfer protocol) **telnet** (remote log-in), and **sendmail** (mail transfer protocols). With time, the Internet expanded to incorporate LAN interfaces including the Ethernet standard (IEEE 802.3) and new applications. Thus the Internet may now be regarded as a collection of communication protocols and applications using it. This network structure is described in Figure 11.14.

Notice that even some of the OSI layers now considered essential for the networked communication are missing. In particular, the concepts of standardized session management and data representation were not fully appreciated, although the Internet does specify a network octet order for data. We may wonder why the Internet has been selected for discussion. The reason for this is that the Internet is by far the largest networking protocol in use today, and it is also currently going through a period of unprecedented growth. Finally, we have selected the Internet because of its close affiliation with the Ethernet (ISO 8802.3) standard, an important standard in the context of the distributed workstation environment.

11.6.1 LAN Standards

The IEEE 802 standards describe the physical and data link layers for LANs and MANs (as discussed in Section 3.2.2). The standards are defined by six specifications: a general overview (802.1); a data-link layer interface description known as the logical link control (LLC, 802.2); the ethernet specifications (802.3); the token bus specifications (802.4); the token ring specifications (802.5); and finally DQDB (802.6). We now consider each of the LAN standards in more detail.

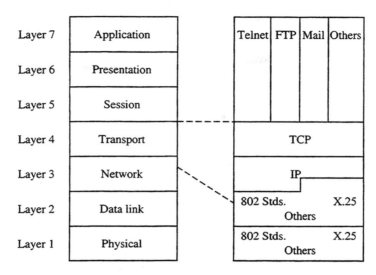

Figure 11.14   ISO/OSI model versus Internet.

The general overview (802.1) provides the framework for the remaining documents. It was recognized that because of the divergent goals, no single LAN/MAN standard would suffice. Thus a common set of link level service access points was established in document 802.2 and a number of **sublayers** were defined that provided the additional information pertinent to each of the protocols.

The **logical link control** (LLC, 802.2) provides a common service specification for data transfer and media access control for the different sublayers. Using this ensures a high degree of compatibility between them. Although the particulars of the frame format is different for each sublayer, they are all similar to the one given in Secion 11.4.3.

The first media access sublayer is **ethernet** (IEEE 802.3), which is a contention-based protocol developed by the Xerox Corp. in 1973 (Figure 11.15). The original specification used a special coaxial cable with a thick core that allowed nodes to be connected simply by screwing a **vampire tap** (a shielded pin that penetrates the outer cable and makes contact with the core) into the cable at a chosen point (see Figure 11.15). The ethernet provides a 10 Mbps communication rate under ideal conditions. The protocol used is **carrier sensed multiple access** with **collision detection** (CSMA/CD). In this protocol, each node listens to the channel prior to transmitting. If the channel is available the node goes ahead; if it is busy, it waits (that is the **carrier sense** component). Even with this, a collision may still occur. For example, consider the case in which two stations are waiting for the channel to be free and then both start to transmit. In the event of a collision, each node will recognize that its own transmission was corrupted and attempt to retransmit latter. Ethernet has enjoyed great popularity over the past few years and since the original thick-wire Ethernet (10BASE5 in IEEE standard terms) there have been several extensions to the standard including a broadband ethernet (10BROAD36), a cheap thin wire Ethernet (10BASE2), and a new twisted pair Ethernet (10BASET). The latter is significant because the wiring may use the same conduit as the phone wires, allowing digital data into every office with a phone.

Another popular broadcast system is the token ring (IEEE 802.5), as shown in Figure 11.16, pioneered by IBM. Although the token ring is a broadcast system, it is actually a sequence of unidirectional point-to-point lines arrange in a loop. Each node in the ring is

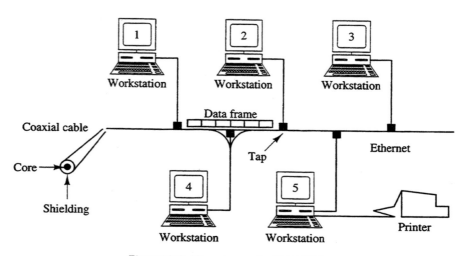

Figure 11.15 Ethernet network—IEEE 802.3.

responsible for receiving data in its incoming line, examining it, and transmitting it on its outgoing line. The protocol makes use of a token (a special frame format) which circulates the ring. Whenever a node wishes to transmit, it waits for the the token to come around, takes it off the ring, and replaces it with a data frame. The data frame will traverse the ring enabling the appropriate destination to read it. When the frame arrives back at the source node, the source removes the data frame and places the token back on the ring. This basic algorithm is augmented by the following features:

- The ring supports a number of different priority levels. Each level is allocated a certain percentage of the channel bandwidth thus permitting high priority data to be passed preferentially while preventing starvation of the lower priority levels.

- The ring has a complex procedure for ring management. Tasks to be performed are node insertion and deletion, token management, and token timeout management functions.

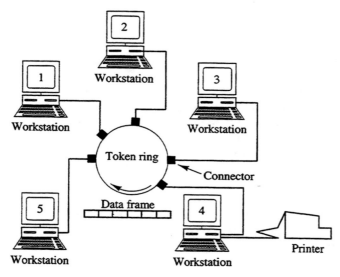

Figure 11.16 Token ring network—IEEE 802.5.

The other LAN standard in the IEEE 802 series is the token bus (IEEE 802.4) designed by General Motors Corp. Like the Ethernet, the token bus is a "real" broadcast system that uses a coaxial cable as a common bus. Unlike Ethernet, the token bus is a noncontention protocol. Like the token ring, a token "circulates" around a logical ring, connecting all the nodes together. In fact, of course, the token is transmitted from a particular source node (the current token holder) to a destination node (its successor in the logical ring) by broadcaasting it; as is shown in Figure 11.17. For example in Figure 11.17 we assume that node four is the current token holder. While node four holds the token, it may transmit data to any node it wishes. When it is finished (i.e., it has no more data to send or its allotted time is used up), it will pass the token on to node one, which is its successor. If node one has data to send, it takes the token; otherwise, the token is passed to the next node in the ring (node two). In this way, each node receives its fair share of the channel.

As with the token ring, the token bus permits multiple priority levels and requires a sophisticated ring management protocol to allow the addition and deletion of nodes and the management of the token.

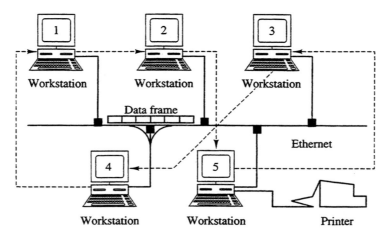

Figure 11.17   Token bus network—IEEE 802.4.

It is interesting to compare the token ring and token bus because of their similarities. Both make use of a token system to provide fair access to the channel, prevent starvation, and offer guaranteed maximum waiting time. Also, both support several levels of priority. Looking at the design backgrounds of these two systems, we see that the goals are very different. The token ring was designed for an office environment with no particular requirements regarding vulnerability. The token bus however was designed to be used in the manufacturing environment. Typical applications might include realtime control of robots in an automobile assembly plant. Clearly the provisions for guaranteed maximum delay are critical in such applications.

11.6.2 MAN Standards

One Metropolitan Area Network (MAN) which has become popular is FDDI. Based on the same protocol as 802.5 (token ring), FDDI makes use of optical communications to achieve data rates in the order of 100 Mbps. We note without further mention that there are currently two standards for FDDI, original FDDI and FDDI-II, the latter addressing some shortcomings in the original specification. Recall that although we call 802.5 a ring, it is in actual fact a series of point-to-point communication links. In FDDI, each node is composed of a photodiode transmitter for transmitting to the next station in the ring, and a photodetector to receive the signal from the previous station. The communication medium used is fiber optic cable, a thin glass strand protected by a plastic sheath. The physical communication uses single mode baseband signaling, that is, a zero is represented by no light and a one is represented by a single frequency. The media access control is similar to that of the token ring. In addition to the characteristics found in 802.5, FDDI possess the following features.

1. The FDDI ring may be configured as a double, counter rotating ring system. In this configuration under normal operation the ring pair will support twice the single ring data rate with data transferred in both directions simultaneously. In the event of line or node failure the appropriate segment may be switched out by joining the two rings together either side of the failure. In this case the data rate falls to that of a single ring, with a length equal to approximately twice that of the original pair.

2. The FDDI-II ring system is also designed to support both **synchronous** and **asynchronous** data. The requirement for synchronous data becomes obvious when viewed in the context of telecommunications. By supporting synchronous data at different rates (particularly at one slot every 125 μs) an FDDI ring may be used to convey telecommunications data to/from the 1.544 Mbps trunk lines (T1 lines) to send voice traffic. This greatly increases the general utility of FDDI. Notice that the asynchronous and synchronous modes run concurrently. That is, nodes may request one service or the other; asynchronous packets are inserted between the synchronous slots so as to not interrupt synchronization.

The most recent addition to the MAN arena is **Distributed-Queue Dual-Bus** (**DQDB**) which is also IEEE 802.6. This uses two fiber optical cables to provide a dual bus structure. Again, datarates exceed 100 Mbps and both synchronous and asynchronous data are supported.

11.6.3 TCP/IP Internetworking

As we have already said, the Internet was designed to connect different *networks* together. Recall that from Section 11.4, the subnet (in this context the Internet) may provide different levels of service, from reliable/connection oriented to unreliable/datagram. The designers of the Internet decided that since the Internet would make use of a wide variety of different connection mediums (including leased phone lines, LANs, and direct connections) and would use unreliable host computers, it would be easier to assume that the subnet was unreliable and have the transport layer take care of lost/duplicated packets. Thus, in the Internet, the internet sublayer IP, is a connectionless unreliable/datagram service. To provide a reliable connection oriented service for stream based applications, the transport layer provides TCP that uses the IP service to provide its communication needs. Prior to discussing the IP and TCP protocols, we first introduce the addressing mechanism that is employed on the Internet.

Internet addressing. Because the Internet is primarily concerned with joining together networks it naturally follows that to specify a host address on the internet two fields are used, a **network number** and a **host number** within that network. Thus each network (LAN) is assigned a unique IP address. Within a particular network, each machine is assigned a unique IP host identifier. Notice that two or more hosts may have the same host ID provided they are on different networks. Notice also that the IP host ID need not be the same as the ID of that host on its LAN. The host ID and the data link layer (e.g., the Ethernet source and destination fields mentioned earlier) are completely separate from the network layer addresses, although of course there must be a translation from one to the other at some point. In fact, Internet addresses are defined as a single 32 bit address. There are four different forms of the address as shown in Figure 11.18.

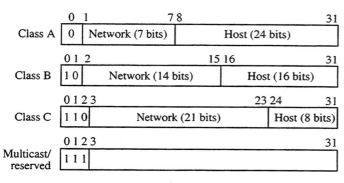

Figure 11.18 Internet addressing: (a) class A: few hosts, many users/network; (b) class B: medium hosts, medium users/host; (c) class C: many hosts, few users/host; and (d) control format.

When the addressing scheme was first conceived, no one expected that the Internet would grow to the level it is today. In retrospect, the Internet addressing scheme (with only 32-bit addresses) is rather restrictive. Notice that according to the current scheme, the number of networks supported is 64 large networks, 16K medium networks and 4M small networks. Although this is large, it is insufficient in the context of global network addresses.

The Internet specifies a standard method for specifying the address known as **dotted decimal notation (ddn)**. In this, each octet of the Internet address is described by an unsigned decimal number. The four octets are separated by single periods. For example the IP address 128.200.200.0 would correspond to %10000000 %11001000 %11001000 %00000000. Notice that all class A addresses are less than 128.$x.x.x$, while those in class B are in the range 129.$x.x.x$ to 190.$x.x.x$ and those in class C are in the range 192.$x.x.x$ to 222.$x.x.x$. We also note that certain Internet address values have special meanings. In particular the number 127.0.0.1 is always a local loopback; a host ID of zero corresponds to the associated network itself (rather than a node *on* it); a host ID of all ones corresponds to a broadcast to *all* nodes on the associated network; and the network ID all zeros is illegal for each class. These restrictions prevent the assignment of certain network numbers.

In addition to a network address, which is understood by the Internet routing algorithms and is used in IP packets for the source and destination address fields, each host on the Internet also has an Internet name. The naming convention is used for human interfaces, recognizing that humans are poor in remembering twelve digit numbers! The naming convention also has the flexibility that it's structure need not be identical to the Internet numbering system. This is because the translation from Internet names to addresses is performed by a utility known as a **name server**, which, when given the name, "looks up" the address. With this in mind, we see that Internet names could be any structure. In fact the system used is an hierarchical system called the domain name system. A host name is defined as a series of names separated by periods specifying successive (sub) domains within the enclosing domain. Arranged as follows:

```
...subsubdomain.subdomain.domain
```

There are at present some one hundred top-level (rightmost) domains, including a country code for each country, with the exception of the United States, which is otherwise implied. The other top level domains are .com, .mil, .edu, .gov, .arpa and .net, which are all assumed to be within the United States (privilege of developing the Internet!) and correspond to commercial, military, educational, governmental, arpanet, and network administration. Under these domains a user may register a subdomain, and then within the subdomain he or she may create subsubdomains etc. To see this more clearly, a list of popular host names and their Internet addresses is provided in Table 11.6.

TABLE 11.6   Internet host/gateway names and addresses

IP address	IP hostname
4.0.0.0	satnet.arpa
8.7.0.2	labs-b.bbn.com
10.1.0.5	cronus-gw.bbn.com # gateway
10.6.0.5	bbn-pr-gw.arpa # gateway
10.3.0.96	cu-arpa.cs.cornell.edu cornell.arpa cu-arpa.arpa
31.4.0.10	lilac.berkeley.edu
128.18.10.3	unix.sri.com sri-unix.arpa sri-unix.sri.com
128.210.2.2	j.cc.purdue.edu
128.103.51.4	porgy.harvard.edu
128.112.20.4	hania.princeton.edu
131.204.19.4	banana.cse.eng.auburn.edu

Another aspect of addressing that requires some discussion at this point is the connection to a particular process running on the destination host. Clearly there will be more than one networked application running on a network; thus, when a connection is established to the destination host, it is necessary to distinguished between different processes. In the Internet each machine has a number of **ports** to which an application may be attached, the port number is a 16-bit unsigned integer and separate set of ports are provided for different services. Thus when a TCP connection is opened to a destination, the TCP port number must be specified. The reader may be wondering how a particular application is able to determine the port numbers of applications on a given destination. This a accomplished in two ways, the most popular applications (e.g., telnet, ftp etc.) are registered with the IAB and use predefined port numbers which are the same on all hosts; the other applications use a **portmapper**, which, like telnet and ftp, is registered and sits on a well defined port number. The portmapper plays the role of a directory service for the host in question. An application connects to the portmapper and inquires as to the port number of the application it wishes to use; it then connects to this port number. This mechanism permits an application to use whatever ports are available when the connection request is made.

Internet protocol (IP). It is assumed that all hosts within a particular network are able to recognize packets that are destined for them once the packet is placed on the LAN to which they are attached. Thus we see that the task of IP is to route packets from the source *network* to the destination *network*. The Internet, therefore, is composed of networks connected together by gateways as shown in Figure 11.19. For a packet to traverse an internet, it will, therefore, have to pass through one or more gateways before reaching the destination network. As we have seen from our discussion of the network layer, there are a number of different routing algorithms that could be used. Recall that the Internet provides a datagram service; therefore, packets between a source/destination pair could take different routes. Specifically, when a gateway receives a packet, it must make decision on where to route the packet based on its understanding of the network.

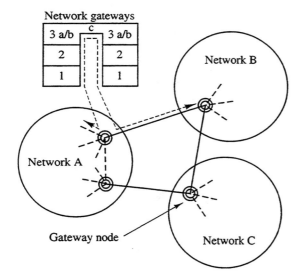

Figure 11.19 Internetworking using subnet enhancement concepts of the OSI model.

In particular the Internet protocol uses the heuristic for processing a received packet as shown subsequently.

```
IF (this gateway attached to destination network) THEN
    Send over network to destination
ELSE IF (Packet has Source Route field) THEN
    Send to gateway specified in source route
ELSE IF (Destination mentioned in Routing Table) THEN
    Send to gateway specified in Routing Table
ELSE IF (Default Route specified) THEN
    Send to Default Gateway
ELSE
    Unable to Send, toss it.
```

We first test see if we are **directly connected** to the destination network (i.e., we are the terminal gateway). If so, the gateway need only look up the data link layer address for the host, encapsulate the Internet packet in a data link layer frame, and send it directly to the destination on the appropriate network.

If we are not the terminal gateway, then there a number of choices which are selected in order. If the packet uses **source routing** then the IP datagram contains a field which specifies *exactly* the route, hop-by-hop, through the internet. This route must be computed by the source and may differ greatly from the optimal route. In fact source routing is used primarily for debugging and maintenance of the network, since we know in advance where the packet will be going. Notice that is it unsuited for general routing since the network is dynamic and source routes are inflexible to these changes. Notice also that to be generally useful each gateway would have to know source routes to every other network in the internet, a most undesirable situation. If source routing is not used, the gateway uses a **routing table** to select the next hop for the packet to be sent. These routing tables include (1) a list of all the networks that this gateway knows how to reach (both directly and through other gateways); (2) the gateway to forward the packet; and (3) the number of hops that the destination is from this gateway. This list may be incomplete in terms of knowing where to send datagrams for every destination network, but as we shall see, this is not a problem. If the routing table makes no explicit mention of the network in question then we rely on **default routing**. A default routing table entry is just that, a default gateway to send all datagrams that are not covered in the routing table. An example routing table for a typical network is shown in Figure 11.20 below.

```
# Internet routing table - format used:
# <net|gateway> <host> gateway <host2>  metric <count> <active|passive>
#
# <net|gateway> indicates the destination type.
# <host 1> is the destination net or gateway.
# <host 2> is where to send packets destined for <host 1>.
# <count>  is the number of hops to the destination.
# <active|passive> indicates whether this information is to be
#          forwarded to other routers.

#
net 128.223.200 gateway 128.223.128.15 metric 1 active
net 128.224.300 gateway 128.223.128.15 metric 2 active
```

Figure 11.20 Typical routing table for a node on the Internet.

In the event that all else fails, the Gateway simply throws the datagram away, since this is, after all, an unreliable service! The reader may be wondering how the routing tables are maintained. Originally these files were maintained by the system's administrator; soon, however, it became obvious that this procedure would become unmanageable. Therefore, the notion of dynamic routing tables developed. Particular gateways run routing utilities that communicate with one another. These **routers** exchange information regarding the current connectivity of the network and compute routes for the different destination networks. The result is a network which remains adaptive in the sense that dynamic routing tables are kept up to date regarding where a gateway should forward a datagram.

We now discuss briefly the frame format of the Internet protocol. Recall that the the IP sublayer is a datagram service. Therefore, each packet contains complete source/destination routing information. IP packets have a maximum total size of 65536 octets, including the header field. The format of the header is shown in Figure 11.21.

The interpretation of the fields is as follows:

Version. The version number of the protocol. This permits new versions of the IP sublayer to be installed while the network is running. An important consideration when

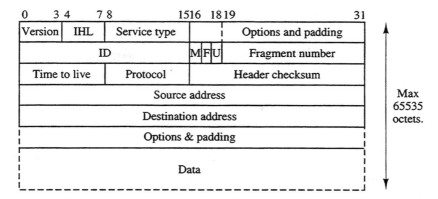

Figure 11.21 Internet Protocol frame format.

one realizes that it would be impossible to "shutdown" the current Internet of many thousands of nodes.

IHL (internet header length). The header may vary in length; however, it's size in octets must always be a multiple of 4 (i.e., an integer number of long words). The IHL specifies the number of long words contained in the header.

Type of service. Allows the sender to request quality of service parameters. For example, reliability, priority, delay, and throughput. The IP gateways are under no obligation to actually honor these requests.

Total length. The length of the IP datagram including header information, in octets.

Identification. When taken with the source, destination, and protocol fields this is used to uniquely identify this datagram. Thus no two packets on the network will have duplicates of all three of these fields.

M (more). This flag indicates that this datagram has been fragmented (broken into smaller chunks) for transmission along a single link and that more is to follow.

F (do not fragment). This flag indicates that this datagram is not to be fragmented.

U (unused). Not used at present.

Fragment offset. Indicates where in the original datagram this fragment came from. The field must be a multiple of 8 octets.

Time to live. Indicates the time measured in second increments that this packet has to live. This value is decremented by the gateways until 0 is reached. At which point the datagram is discarded. This prevents stray packets living indefinitely.

Protocol. Indicates the next higher level protocol to receive this datagram.

Header checksum. A separate checksum is used to ensure that the header was not corrupted during transmission. The algorithm is a simple ones-complement addition of all the octets into the 16-bit field. Notice that this changes every hop as the header changes.

Source address. A 32-bit Internet address as explained in the previous section.

Destination address. A 32-bit Internet address as explained in the previous section.

Options and padding. There are many different control formats that IP packets may use. These are defined in the options field. Formats that do not terminate as a multiple of 4 octets are padded appropriately.

Data. The data field which may be variable in length. Note that the entire IP packet (including header) is constrained to 65535 octets.

In addition to IP the Internet specifies a protocol for providing control and feedback to the gateways. This protocol is known as the Internet Control Message Protocol (ICMP). ICMP uses IP; thus, IP control messages are sent between gateways using the normal IP datagram service. Gateways recognize ICMP packets by the service field. The particular format of the ICMP packet will depend on the control function. Notice, however, that this information is considered part of the data field of the IP datagram. There are nine types of ICMP packet currently defined: **destination unreachable**, sent by a gateway to the originator of a packet that could not be delivered; **time exceeded**, sent to the originator of a packet that has expired; **parameter problem**, erroneous IP header; **source quench**, provides primitive flow control as a request to the sender to slow down its packet transmission rate; **redirect**, allows a gateway to suggest better routes to an originator; **echo**, used to check reachability; **echo reply**, a response to receipt of an echo ICMP; **timestamp**, allows a gateway to measure the time between itself and another gateway; and **timestamp reply**, a response to receipt of a timestamp ICMP.

Transmission control protocol (TCP). As mentioned earlier, TCP corresponds to the Transport Layer of the ISO/OSI model. The primary function of TCP is to provide a reliable connection oriented service to the higher layers. In the case of the Internet these are the applications themselves, because there are no session and presentation layers. Because the TCP layer provides connections between processes while the IP layer only provides a host to host service, it is clear that an additional piece of addressing information is required by TCP to reach the user, namely the **port number**. The combination of a port number and an Internet address is called a **socket** and is the access mechanism employed by processes on the Internet. That is, we say that we "open a socket" to a destination port when we open a TCP connection to that port. The basic services provided by TCP are outlined below:

Multiplexing. In TCP a server process may accept multiple connections on a particular port simultaneously. This facility is known as multiplexing. Consider for example a simple news database. The database contains a list of news articles which may be read by news readers. One or more news reader process may establish a connection (i.e., open a socket) to the news database. Each sends requests to the database to read particular articles. The news database receives these requests along with information as to who sent them (the source port/Internet address fields). The news database is then able to reply on the appropriate socket by sending back the requested news article from its database.

Connection management. The primary function of TCP is connection management. TCP offers services which may be divided into two classes, requests (to TCP) and responses (from TCP) corresponding approximately to *X*.request and *X*.response in ISO/OSI terminology. Parameters that may be associated with each request are local connection name, source port, destination port, destination address, timeout, timeout action, precedence, and security. The TCP requests permit the following actions: **unspecified passive open**, listen on a particular port for a connection attempt by anyone; **specified passive open**, listen on a particular port for a connection attempt by a particular destination port/Internet address; **active open**, attempt to connect to a port on another host; **active open with data**, attempt to connect to a port on another host and send some data with the request; **send**, send data on an already opened socket; **allocate**, allocate buffer space for expected incoming data; **close**, to neatly close a socket; **status**, to request information regarding a socket; and **abort**, to terminate a connection immediately. The responses provide the following information to the user: **open** indicates the status of a pending connection; **deliver**, indicates newly arrived data; **closing**, indicates that the connection is closing and that all data on the socket has been received; **terminate** indicates that a socket has terminated; **status response** indicates connection status; and **error** indicates either an error in a request or an internal error.

Data control. TCP offers bidirectional data flow between the source and destination. The data is delivered reliably (no lost, erroneous, or duplicate data), in sequence and in a timely fashion. TCP manages the data flow between the two ends to prevent one end from swamping the other.

Special services. TCP provides mechanisms for forcing the immediate transmission of buffered data, and for sending expedited data (i.e., data that must "jump the queue"). The latter is useful to send control commands outside the normal data stream.

The TCP protocol itself, like the IP protocol, sends data from one port to another by encapsulating the data with a header. Since TCP is stream oriented, the data may be any integer number of octets. It is the responsibility of the IP layer to break it into small packets to send through the network. Figure 11.22 shows the frame format of the TCP header.

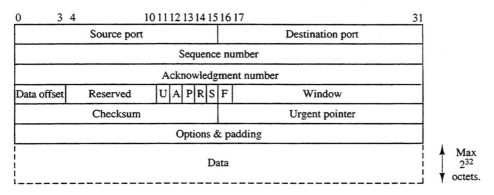

Figure 11.22 Packet format for TCP.

The TCP protocol attaches a header to the user's data. This header is composed of a number of fields as shown in Figure 11.22. Recall that TCP is intended as an end-to-end protocol; therefore, the destination network information that is passed to it in the TCP service primitives will be used not in the TCP header, but in the IP packet header. We now briefly discuss the interpretation of each of the fields. ·

Source port. Identifies the source port number.

Destination port. Identifies the destination port number.

Sequence number. Each octet in a TCP stream is assigned a sequence number. Successive octets are assigned successive sequence numbers, modulo 2^{32}. In general the sequence number field indicates the sequence number of the first octet in this TCP packet.

The only exception to this is at the start of a connection or during resynchronization (both of which are indicated by setting the S bit). In this case the sequence number field indicates the initial sequence number (ISN) for the stream; thus, the first octet in the stream will be ISN+1.

Acknowledgment number. Only used if the *A* bit is set. This is an acknowledgment field for data received so far. The field contains the sequence number of the next octet expected by this TCP entity. The data in this field represents piggybacked data in the sense that periodic acknowledgments would be sent in a separate packet if they could not share one. Thus we are piggybacking this acknowledgment on an outgoing data packet.

Data offset. The number of 32-bit words in the header.

Reserved. Unused at present.

U. Indicates that the urgent pointer field is valid, that is, that urgent data has arrived.

A. Indicates that the acknowledgment field is valid, that is, that an acknowledgment is piggybacked with the data.

P. Specifies that the received data is to be passed immediately to the user (i.e., the **push** function).

R. Specifies that the connection is to be reset.

S. Indicates that the sequence numbers are to synchronized.

F. Indicates there is no further data from sender.

Window. Specifies the new window limit in octets. The limit is relative to the sequence number in the acknowledge field. Thus a limit of one indicates that the TCP entity will only accept the octet with the sequence number given in the acknowledgment field, and so on. This field may be used for flow control by changing the window accept limit.

Checksum. A checksum for the packet. The routine used is the one's complement of the sum (modulo $2^{16} - 1$) of all 16-bit words in the packet along with a 96-bit pseudoheader which includes the following: source and destination IP addresses, protocol used, and TCP segment length. This pseudoheader is not actually sent, but is used by the checksum to ensure that IP does not misdeliver a packet to the wrong destination and have it accepted by TCP.

Urgent pointer. Points to the octet following the urgent data that placed at the front of the regular data stream.

Options and padding. Allows additional options to be defined.

Routing in the Internet.   Interestingly enough routing in the Internet is not handled by any single algorithm, but instead is achieved by the coordinated efforts of several different protocols. The primary members of this *ensemble* are EGP, and GTP, in addition at the network level there are also the protocols **routed** and **gated**.

11.6.4 Sample Applications: Telnet, ftp, smtp, and nntp

We conclude the section on the Internet with description of the major applications available on it. In particular the applications to be discussed are **Telnet**, the remote login utility; **ftp** (file transfer protocol) for sending/receiving files; **smtp** (simple mail transfer protocol) for sending/receiving electronic mail; and **nntp** (network news transfer protocol) for sending/receiving electronic news. As we have already mentioned, the ARPANET was originally designed specifically to support the first two of the applications and was designed prior to the ISO/OSI layered model. This becomes evident in the protocols as is noted later.

Telnet.   One of the original motivations for the ARPANET was to support a remote login (i.e., terminal access) capability from one machine on a network to another. This capability is offered by Telnet and is fully described in the Defense Communications Agency, Military Standard MIL-STD-1782, 1984. The Telnet utility is an application that may be thought of as a pair of closely coupled processes, a user telnet process and a server telnet process as shown in Figure 11.23. In the figure the relevant processes are indicated by circles, I1 is a terminal interconnect, and I2 is a network interconnect. The user telnet process is invoked by the user and allows the user to specify a number of options regarding the terminal services to be provided. It is also responsible for opening a connection to the specified destination server telnet process. Also, it permits the data to be passed to/from the destination with any appropriate modification required and exchanges control information with the server telnet process. Finally, it closes the connection when the user is finished. The server telnet process is a demon that waits on a well-known port (SAP in ISO/OSI phraseology) and provides a terminal service to the local machine. When the server telnet process receives a connection request, it establishes the correct terminal connection options and then opens a connection to one of the operating systems logical terminal ports. During the remainder of connection the server telnet process monitors the data stream and responds to control requests from the either the user telnet process or the operating system. Notice from Figure 11.23 that telnet processes communicate with one another using the TCP transport services.

From the preceding discussion it should be clear that the telnet protocol does considerably more than simply pass user data from one machine to another. In particular there are

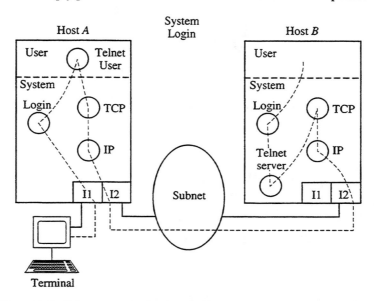

Figure 11.23   Telnet communications between user's host (A) and destination host (B).

two components to consider, the issue of terminal support, and the issue of transfer protocol. Different hosts support a variety of different terminal types. The task of supporting all of these is overwhelmingly complex. Instead, telnet is designed to provide general bidirectional character oriented communications between terminal devices and terminal oriented processes. The approach used in telnet is to provide a basic service with a lowest common denominator terminal type, and to permit option negotiation between the user and server telnet processes so that more sophisticated terminal types and transfer protocols may be used. When option negotiations are concluded the characteristics of the connection will be appropriate to both the user and the server.

The basic telnet virtual terminal is called the **network virtual terminal** (NVT). It is a bidirectional character oriented device with input (keyboard) and output (simple printer). NVT supports only the 7-bit ASCII codes. From the keyboard the user may also send a few simple control signals, for example, **are you there?** and **erase character**. The printer is assumed to be a simple line printer with unlimited width lines and page length which can print the 96 printable ASCII characters along with the usual carriage control codes, NUL, LF, CR, BEL, BS, HT, VT, and FF. A newline is always sent the pair <CR LF>. To pass data between the two telnet processes (i.e., the transfer protocol) a bidirectional communication channel based supplied by TCP is assumed (i.e., error-free octet stream) which is used in half-duplex mode. The data stream is a sequence of octets (although using the basic NVT only the 128 ASCII codes may be used). In addition to the user data, the telnet processes communicate with one another using command codes. These are preceded by characters from the extended ASCII (high bit set to 1) set. The telnet command codes are embedded in the user data stream and may be multioctet. Table 11.7 shows the telnet command codes.

A command is always started by the symbol IAC with regular telnet commands of size two octets. For example, the user telnet process may send <IAC BRK> to send a break. Negotiations are initiated using the SB code followed by an option number (e.g., <IAC SB 0>) and terminated with the SE code (i.e., <IAC SE>). The details of negotiations depend

TABLE 11.7 Telnet command codes

Code	Title	Symbol
240	End of subnegotiation	SE
241	No operation	NOP
242	Data mark	DM
243	Break	BRK
244	Interrupt process	IP
245	Abort Output	AO
246	Are you there	AYT
247	Erase character	EC
248	Erase line	EL
249	Go ahead	GA
250	Begin subnegotiation	SB
251	(Request set option)	WILL
252	(Request unset option)	WONT
253	(Agree to request)	DO
254	(Refuse request)	DON'T
255	Interpret as command	IAC

on the option selected. Example options are 0 for binary data negotiations, 1 for remote echo, 2 for reconnection, 17 for extended ASCII, and 255 for extended options list. All negotiations are confirmed and are arranged so that either side may initiate them.

The protocol specification for telnet was originally designed to be very flexible. It's success may be measured by noting that it is still a very popular utility. Its flexibility permits new options to be included as applications demand them. A good example of this is the X windowing system which uses the telnet protocol for transferring data in large networks. An aspect of telnet that we have not discussed is the user interface. This is largely unspecified from the telnet perspective. In the Unix environment, the telnet user interface is quite plain as the demonstration in Figure 11.24 shows. Notice that annotation is indicated by using the "--" indicator.

```
Host_A>                              System prompt.
Host_A> telnet Host_B               -- either a hostname or an internet number
Trying <internet number> ...
Connected to Host_B.ufl.edu.
Escape character is ' ]'.

4.3 BSD Unix (Host_B)               -- Connection established to login process.

login: myname                       -- Users account name.
Password:                           -- Password is not echoed.
Last login:....                     -- usual login information.
                    .
                    .
Host_B>                             -- system prompt on destination host.
                    .               -- user performs work on Host_B.
                    .
Host_B> logout                      -- finished working.
Connection closed by foreign host.
Host_A>                             -- back to original host.
```

Figure 11.24   Example telnet session.

After the user types telnet the telnet user process will attempt to open a telnet session on the remote machine. If this is successful, the user will then receive the standard Unix login prompt and may begin typing. During the session the user may break back and communicate with the local user telnet process by sending a telnet escape (a control left bracket) followed by a command, "help" for example! The remote login session is terminated either by the user terminating the remote session or by sending the telnet close command, as shown earlier.

FTP.   Another of the primary motivations in the ARPANET project was the transfer of files from one host to another. That is, a user sitting on Host *A* should be able to either send/receive files to/from Host *B*. Clearly this implies that the user must have access to an account on Host *B* as well as Host *A*. This function is satisfied by the FTP utility and is described in the Defense Communications Agency Military Standard MIL-STD-1780, 1984. As with telnet, this apparently simple task quickly becomes complex on closer inspection. The problems in file transfer arise by noting that between different systems there is little commonality regarding what actually constitutes a file. In particular files often possess some structure, may have attributes, and may require some translation. One possible method managing file transfer would be to specify a **network virtual file** in a similar vein to the network virtual terminal of telnet. This is the long term goal of the ISO/OSI file transfer package (FTAM); however, at the time FTP was under consideration, an abstract syntax notation was unavailable greatly compounding the problem. The designers, therefore, decided to keep the file transfer mechanism as simple as possible, while again providing great flexibility. This was achieved by permitting the two communicating hosts three services to negotiate when establishing a common ground. The three services are **file type, data type,** and **transmission mode.**

FTP starts by using a mechanism similar to telnet with a user FTP process and a server FTP process. The user FTP process is command driven, the server FTP process runs as a demon. When the user invokes FTP, the user FTP process is executed. As with telnet the actual user interface is not precisely specified; it is the communication *between* the FTP processes that is important. The user FTP process interacts with the user and responds to an **open** request by establishing a connection with the destination server FTP process as shown in Figure 11.25.

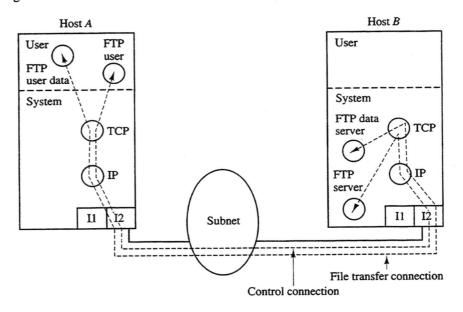

Figure 11.25   File transfer using FTP.

Once this connection is established, the two processes may exchange control information until a common communication ground is agreed upon. In particular the user FTP process sends an account name and password which is used for access on the remote machine. The user is now connected to the destination machine and is in fact logged in, but is restricted to a limited set of commands associated with file transfer. The user may now specify a file transfer operation; this request is relayed by the user FTP process to the server FTP process at the destination. Both the user and server processes now initiate *new* processes (user data process and server data process) and a connection is established from the latter to the former. The data transfer now takes place between these data processes, with the user and server FTP processes acting as supervisors. This method allows control information to pass along a separate connection from the data connection. Once the data transfer is complete the source data process issues a **CLOSE** request to TCP connection and then terminates. The destination receives the close indication and also terminates. In this manner the data processes terminate leaving the original user and server FTP processes connected. This process is repeated for each file transferred. When the user has finally completed file transfers, he or she informs the user FTP server to close the connection to the destination server. Thus the connection is closed, the user FTP process terminated, and the server FTP process awaits another connection request.

We now look at three option classes that may be changed by the user. Recall that these option classes represent a negotiation phase between the user and server FTP processes. As with telnet, precise structure of the codes used in this dialogue is unimportant for this discussion but may be found in the FTP specification for the interested reader. Recall that the three option classes are file type, data type, and transmission mode.

File type. FTP supports three different structures: **file structure, record structure,** and **page structure**. File structure is most commonly used. In this mode a file is simply considered a sequence of octets terminated by an end-of-file marker. In some situations it is more convenient to consider a file a sequence of records where each record is terminated by an end-of-record marker. This is provided by the record mode. This mode may offer advantages when the record size is closely aligned with hardware device characteristics, such as the disk drive block size. Of course the advantages in such alignments may be lost during data encapsulation in either the TCP or IP layers. Finally (for historic reasons) there is also a page structure. In this a file is considered as a nonconsecutive sequence of pages, where each page is a fixed sized. A page table is used to indicate the order of pages in the file. This mode was designed for compatibility with the DEC TOPS-20 operating system and is now obsolete.

Data type. FTP supports four different data types: **ascii, ebcdic, image,** and **logical octet size**. Text files are intended as human readable documents (i.e., contain alphanumerics, punctuation and simple printer control information) and are supported by the first two modes. In addition there are options to permit the user to specify how the carriage control information is to be processed. For text data the Internet transmission standard is ASCII. In general there is no provision in FTP to perform file translation between different character formats, usually FTP on EBCDIC machines will translate an EBCDIC file into its ASCII equivalent. In the event that EBCDIC mode is specified FTP will assume that both source and destination are EBCDIC and will turn off character conversion resulting in improved performance. The nontext types are supported using image and logical octet size. In image mode the file is copied exactly as is without modification of any type. Thus first bit in the source is the first in the destination and so on. Image mode is used extensively for transferring executables between similar architectures and so on. The final mode is logical octet size. In this mode the user specifies the size, in bits, of the logical octets to be transferred. Successive logical octets on the source are copied to successive logical octets on the destination. This mode is useful when passing files between machines with different word lengths.

Transmission mode. This is used to increase the performance of the file transfer by improving the subnet communications. FTP offers three transmission modes: **stream mode, block mode,** and **compressed mode**. Again the most common mode used is stream mode. In this mode, the data to be transferred are viewed as a stream of octets. The special file type markers used to identify end-of-record and end-of-file in record structure are encoded using escaped codes much like the telnet embedded control characters are. Recall that all data is sent between the user data FTP process and server data FTP process. The second mode that may be selected is block mode. With this the source sends the data as a sequence of blocks, each block individually identified. The user and server processes may therefore use this information to restart a file transfer after failure. Recalling that the TCP service is presumed reliable this feature is rarely used, in fact the FTP standard does not describe checkpoint and restart procedures. The final mode offered is the compressed mode. This mechanism provides a simple algorithm to compress text files using a repetition count for replicated data. As with other aspects of TCP, it was later recognized that this is an inappropriate point at which to perform compression. It is more efficient to compress a file as a function of the presentation layer than to integrate the service directly into file transfer utility.

We mention a couple of additional features before leaving FTP. The control codes and dialogue between the user FTP process and the server FTP process are all encoded as NVT-ASCII strings of maximum length four. Responses to the commands are always a 3-digit NVT-ASCII reply along with an optional, human readable, text string. This text string is used only for debugging purposes and is not interpreted by the FTP processes. The use of NVT-ASCII coded strings greatly simplifies network debugging since it is now possible for a human user to connect directly to a server FTP process and test it. An example showing this is (assuming the connection has been made to the destination) given in Figure 11.26.

```
User pel                         --send user command.
   331 User OK                   --receive response.
PASS testpass                    --send password.
   231 User Logged In            --receive response.
TYPE binary                      --select binary.
   200 Command OK                --OK.
MODE stream                      --select mode.
   200 Command OK                --OK.
STOR filei                       --file transfer.
   {data process are created, transfer file, and quit}
   226 Action completed.         --OK.
```

Figure 11.26   ASCII dialogue with FTP server process.

Another point that requires consideration regards file protections. The destination file requires some file protection value. The precise details of this are dependent on the operating system and are therefore system dependent. Finally, as we have mentioned earlier, the FTP standard does not specify any particular user interface; however, a typical dialogue using FTP is given is given in Figure 11.27. As before, comments are given by the "--" indication.

SMTP.   The final primary service that was considered essential for computer networks was an easy transfer of electronic mail. Host computers usually already have a mail system that operates on the local mail. The networking protocol is concerned with the transfer of mail between *different* hosts. This network protocol is called SMTP (Simple Mail Transfer Protocol) and is described in the Defense Communications Agency Military Standard MIL-STD-1781, 1984. Electronic mail is not a new concept. Almost since the day computers supported multiple users, there have been packages that allow one to compose a text message and **e-mail** it to others. E-mail when properly implemented combines the best characteristics of telephone and regular mail. Consider the number of times that you have played "telephone tag" with another. You call to discuss an issue with person X; X is not there, so you leave a message to contact you; later while you are out, X returns your call leaving you a message to call back and so on. With electronic mail you are able to

```
Host_A>                                                    -- system prompt.
Host_A>ftp Host_B.ufl.edu                                 -- invoke FTP utility.
220 Host_B.ufl.edu FTP server (Version..) ready.
Name (Host_B ID>:myname): anonymous                       -- we use anonymous account
331 Guest login OK, Send ident as password                -- no password required.
Password:                                                 -- password not echoed.
230 Guest login OK, access restrictions apply.            -- we are now logged in.
FTP> cd /pub/gnu                                          -- FTP allows change directory.
250 CWD Command successful.
FTP> get README                                           -- copy README from Host_B to Host_A.
200 PORT Command successful.                              -- request accepted
150 OPENing data connection for README                    -- start FTP data processes
    (<Host_B ID>, <port number>) (1000 bytes)
220 Transfer complete.
   local: README    remote: README
   1000 bytes received in 0.1 seconds (10 Kbytes/s)
FTP>                                                      -- transfer finished, still connected.
FTP> close                                                -- close connection.
221 CLOSe
FTP> quit                                                 -- exit ftp.
Host_A>                                                   -- system prompt.
```

Figure 11.27 User interaction with FTP to get the file README.

compose the message and have it delivered immediately to the destination. If the recipient is in his or her office he or she will receive it immediately (assuming a workstation environment), otherwise he or she will see it when he or she returns. His or her reply is made easy by the mail's automatic reply facilities and the tag cycle is averted. We see from this discussion several aspects of e-mail utilities: (1) a mail message is comprised of two parts, a body which represents the text of the message, and an envelope which contains the addressing, routing, and date information (in this context the envelope is simply a formatted header attached to the body); (2) each user has an e-mail address which corresponds to an account on a particular machine, note that the e-mail address and accounts are not necessarily related; (3) for each user there will exist a queue of mail messages that are unread; this queue may be a file in the user's local directory or it may be in a system area, in any event the user must be able to access it via a mail interface. A typical e-mail scenario is given in Figure 11.28.

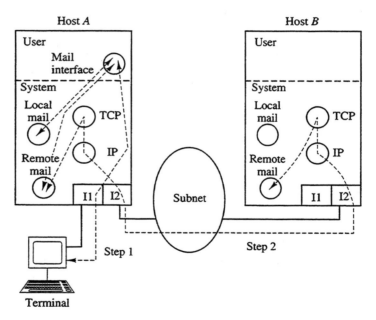

Figure 11.28   Mail transfer using SMTP.

As with the other utilities there are two issues in question, mail composition and retrieval (i.e., the user interface) and mail transport (i.e., sending electronic mail). Even on non-networked mail systems this distinction is sensible, a mail user interface will change as different terminal capabilities become available and user needs grow. The process of taking a composed mail message and delivering it, however, remains largely unaffected. For this reason we consider a mail facility to be composed of one or more user interfaces that are invoked by the user, and a mail transfer demon that is able to communicate with other hosts on the network. The relationship between the e-mail user interface and the mail demons is shown in Figure 11.28. The user interface passes a complete composed message to the mail transfer process. This process then checks to see if the mail is local or remote; if local, it places it in the appropriate local mailbox; if remote, it must pass it to the mail transfer process on that remote host. This may be achieved either by the mail transfer process itself or it may be delegated to a dedicated process depending on the mail utility. From the perspective of networking then we note that SMTP is the transfer protocol for sending a composed mail message between two mail transfer processes across the network. It is not concerned with how that mail was composed or how it is delivered at the destination, only that it was received. To achieve this goal SMTP reads (and modifies) the envelope of the mail message passed to it. SMTP is unconcerned with the actual contents of the mail message itself.

The mail transfer mechanism requires the description of several related but disjoint concepts. We, therefore, discuss each of them separately in the following paragraphs.

Header specification. Clearly the mail utility must be able to distinguish the "envelope" from the letter within. In addition there are many fields associated with the envelope that must be processed by the mailer. The precise syntax of header fields is essential if SMTP mailers are to understand one another. With SMTP, header fields precede the message and are defined as keywords followed by a colon followed by the pertinent information on a single line. Essential fields are **To:** and **From:**; there are many other optional fields, for example **Subject:, CC:, Message-ID:, Posted-Date:, Return-Path:,** and **Received:.** Some of these are used by the mailer; others are for the receiver's information only. After the headers the message follows (identified as such by virtue of a blank line) which is a text file terminated by the three character sequence <CR.CR>.

Mailbox specification. All users of mail are required to have a mailbox. This mailbox is an account name within a mail domain. Mail domains are closely coupled to Internet domains although in principle this need not be the case. The account name is character string and is usually the same as the user's account name. This is separated from the domain by the @ character. Thus, example mailboxes would be joe@art.auburn.edu or aardvark@ufl.edu. The mailbox domain system allows the user (for example aardvark) to have a mailbox in ufl.edu without the need to know on which particular machine ardvark's mail resides.

Routing information. Remote mail transfer is performed by the source SMTP server opening a TCP connection to the remote SMTP server as given by the destinations mail address. If there are multiple addresses then the server will open a connection to each one in turn. There are also occasions when a mail path must be specified, particularly if the mail is to leave the Internet. In this case the mail path is identified by a sequence of `@domains` separated by comma's with a colon preceding the final `username@domain`. For example, a path might be `@cornell.edu,@mit.edu:aardvark@ufl.edu`.

Mail transfer dialogue. As you might expect, the heart of SMTP is the mail transfer protocol, a dialogue between the source and destination mail servers consisting of keyword requests and numeric replies. Example commands used by SMTP are given below in Figure 11.29. As with the other protocols the replies are a three digit number indicating the status of the request, optionally followed by a comment. Notice that when a message is passed

```
Hello <SP> domain> <CR LF>
MAIL <SP> FROM: <reverse-path> <CR LF>
RCPT <SP> TO: <forward-path> <CR LF>
DATA <CR LF>
RSET <CR LF>
QUIT <CR LF>
TURN <CR LF>
```

Figure 11.29   Sample SMTP command formats.

from one server to another it may have its header fields modified to reflect reverse path information and so on.

As with the previous utilities we conclude with an example of how the mail system might be used. First the user would compose the mail using either a general purpose word processing utility or a specialized mail interface. At the point that the mail message is ready to be sent it might look as shown in Figure 11.30.

```
To: joe@eng.auburn.edu
CC: aardvark@ufl.edu
Subject: Report on monarch migration sightings
You will be pleased to note that monarch butterflies have
been sighted in north Florida again this year. As we
thought, the cold weather has little effect on their migratory
pattern.

Chris Beaver :-)
```

Figure 11.30   Mail message as typed by user.

This mail message will be passed to the local mail handler which will establish the action to be taken for each of the recipients. Assuming that the recipient is on a different host the SMPT sender first opens a TCP connection to the SMTP receiver at the appropriate destination, the receiver identifies itself and the state of the SMTP service, the sender responds by identifying itself, and finally the receiver acknowledges the identification. This sequence is shown in Figure 11.31.

```
                -- Connection to destination established
     220 mailbox.eng.auburn.edu Sendmail service ready
HELLO sea.cis.ufl.edu
     250 sea.cis.ufl.edu Hello mailbox,eng.auburn.edu, pleased to meet you
                -- The SMPT connection is now established
                -- and mail transfer may take place, as shown below:
MAIL from: <beaver@sea.cis.ufl.edu>
     250 <beaver@sea.cis.ufl,edu> ... Sender OK
RCPT to: <joe@eng.auburn.edu>
     251 <joe@eng.auburn.edu> User not local:
                           will forward to <joe@hamming.eng,auburn,edu>
DATA
     354 Enter mail, end with "." on a line by itself
Date 1 Jan 91 12:01:00
From: beaver@ufl.edu
To: joe@eng.auburn.edu
CC: aardvark@ufl.edu
Subject: Report on monarch migration sightings
You will be pleased to note that monarch butterflies have
been sighted in north Florida again this year. As we thought,
the cold weather has little effect on their migratory
pattern.

Chris Beaver :-)
     250 Mail accepted
QUIT
     221 mailbox.eng.auburn..edu delivering mail
```

Figure 11.31   SMTP connection dialogue.

The destination mail transfer process would then fulfill its obligation and send the mail on the next hop of its journey. Eventually the mail message would reach its destination and would be placed in the user's incoming mail queue awaiting his or her inspection. The next time the user invoked the mail interface he or she would be presented with the mail message.

NNTP.   Another utility that is rapidly increasing in popularity is that of network news (also called bulletin boards). Within the Internet community a popular network news system is News. The news utility permits users to post electronic mail that may be read by any number of subscribers. Thus news may be thought of a form of broadcast mail. Because different users have particular interests, a news article is posted to a particular newsgroup rather than the entire community. Therefore, each user will have a list of news groups to which they subscribe (i.e., read) and will be able to post articles to these or other newsgroups. As with mail, the service is divided into two activities: the user interface which responsible for presenting the news to the user, and the nets transfer process which is responsible for passing posted articles from one host to another. The NNTP (Network News Transfer Protocol) (NNTP) specifies the protocol by which this dialogue takes place. As you might expect, the system works in much the same way as mail operates. Whenever a user posts an article, it is appended to the appropriate newsgroup file and passed to the news transfer process which simply informs each of the news hosts from which it receives a news feed of the new posting. These in turn pass the posting to others until all hosts have received the article. Without going into the same detail of the previous services it should be clear that a dialogue sequence similar to that of SMTP is required and that many of the issues are the same.

11.7 ISDN AND WAN

A discussion of modern computer networks would scarcely be complete without some mention of the **Integrated Services Digital Network** (ISDN). As we have seen, many organizations now make use of computer networks to manage their business. At the moment it is the responsibility of the organization to design and install this network. While this is reasonable for larger organizations it is often difficult for smaller organizations who are uninterested in supporting such a task. A similar case may be made for the home computer user (although the wide spread use of modems diminishes this comment). Additionally many home users are finding that they may use only the phone or the modem, but not both together! The common element in these requirements is the need for digital data access into the home/office just as the plain old telephone system (POTS) provides for voice. It is this goal, with much embellishment, that ISDN attempts to provide. Specifically ISDN was planned in the 1970s by the common carriers as an international concept of how telecommunications in the future should evolve. It was recognized that an essential component would be the integration of voice and digital data. CCITT, the standards body for international telecommunications and responsible for WAN standardization defined ISDN as: A network evolved from the telephone **Integrated Digital Network** (IDN) that provides end-to-end digital connectivity to support a wide range of services, including voice and nonvoice services, to which users have access by a limited set of standard, multipurpose, user-network interfaces.

It is important to recognize that ISDN is planned as an evolution from the present telephone system with a gradual transition from analog communications to digital services;

thus, while a POTS telephone uses analog signalling to the local exchange an ISDN telephone will supply digital data to the network. To see the ISDN picture we first consider the user interface. The principle concept in ISDN is that the user (or customer site) has access to a "bit pipe" of a certain data rate. The data rate will vary according to customer needs and will be constrained to particular values reflecting the underlying communication mechanism. ISDN will use an addressing scheme (again evolved from the current international phone number scheme CCITT recommendation E.163) that will permit a user to establish a connection with another user, just as the user is currently able. It was anticipated that residential requirements would be at least two data channels (one telephone, and one personal computer type) with an additional channel used for channel control and low data date functions (signalling). Commercial requirements, on the other hand, might include higher speed links into LAN's or gateways. Using such a system would enable businesses to simply "buy" the appropriate bit pipes for their data needs. Networking then becomes a matter of connecting to the destination using the ISDN services. From the customer's perspective issues regarding network backbones and routing become obsolete. Notice that to be effective the charges for using the network should be based on the amount of data and the distance it is sent rather than the connection. Otherwise the user ends up paying for unused bandwidth and is little better off than using leased lines.

11.7.1 ISDN Services

We now consider in more detail the features (or *integrated services*) under consideration in ISDN. The services may be classed in four categories, telephony, data, text, and image. We now consider each of these separately.

Telephony. Obviously one of the most important services that will be supported under ISDN will be voice traffic. Recall that ISDN is evolutionary, the current voice grade line (4 KHz bandwidth) is encoded using 56 Kbps in the United States. The analog signal to/from the local exchange is converted to digital data using **time division multiplexing** (TDM). In TDM the signal is sampled periodically and for each sample the signal amplitude quantized into a digital number. For voice traffic in North America the sample rate is 8000 samples/s with the data quantized into one of 256 levels, that is, 8 bits, for a data rate of 64 Kbps. This basic rate (64 Kbps) and multiples of it are employed in all the trunk/international lines. For example the North American DS1 trunk line at 1.544 Mbps (the TDM version of the T1 communication line) is composed of 24 voice grade lines while the CCITT level 1 communications line at 2.048 Mbps is composed of 30 such lines. Thus the basic building block of ISDN is a 64 Kbps channel, which is sufficient to support a voice grade line. Other voice related services in ISDN would be leased circuits, voice controlled information retrieval, and music (notice this would require more than a single 64 Kbps line).

Data. ISDN data services would include virtual circuits using either packet switching or circuit switching and may include datagram services. While voice services will always remain important, the data services that ISDN provides will offer major growth for the common carriers. In addition to the data services ISDN may include information retrieval, mailbox facilities, signalling facilities (e.g., alarms) and, of course, computer communications.

Text. ISDN text services would include a number of disparate services already available such as telex and teletex and incorporate some new services such as videotex along with some of those mentioned under Data.

Image. As with text services, ISDN image services would include services already in use such as facsimile and would provide new services based on information retrieval and, in conjunction with Broadband ISDN (B-ISDN), could provide video phone, teleconferencing, and a close coupling between video and information retrieval services.

In addition to these services there will be a number of supplemental services which are associated with channel control. Examples of these are **call forwarding**, in which calls are automatically rerouted to another ISDN address; **group communications**, in which self contained groups are recognized; **call waiting**, which notifies the user of additional incoming calls; **automatic call back**, in which a previously busy number is automatically retried when it becomes available; and **third-party charging**, which permits the call to be billed to another number.

11.7.2 Channel Access and Reference Points

From the above discussion, you will not be surprised to find that the channel access and reference points in ISDN are already well defined. Access links are composed of different combinations of channel types. The three channel types are the D channel (always a control channel) at 16 Kbps or 64 Kbps; the B channel at 64 Kbps; and H channels at 384 Kbps for H0, 1536 Kbps for H11 and 1920 Kbps for H12. The H channel types are for high data rate requirements. The channel access specifications correspond to channel type packages that the user may select and are defined by two main interface structures, the **basic** structure and the **primary** structure. The basic structure is designed for residential use and is composed of 2B + 1D channels. The D channel is 16 Kbps and is used to control the other two channels. This represents a total data rate of 144 Kbps which is attainable using the current telephones wiring (an important consideration considering the 200 million users in the United States alone!). Clearly this configuration permits simultaneous use of an ISDN telephone and a ISDN linked home computer. The other structure is the primary structure and is intended for businesses. It is composed of 23B + 1D (in North America) or 30B + 1D (in Europe) channels. Before leaving the discussion of channel access, we note that technology has already forced some changes. Due to improved encoding techniques, it is now possible to send voice grade signals using considerably less than 64 Kbps. Because of this a single B channel may be configured as several sub-channels, for example, 4 * 16 Kbps. For compatibility with original ISDN planning, for example, all these sub-channels must originate and terminate at the same ISDN number.

The ISDN reference points are a set of points defined within the ISDN hardware communications model to ensure that different ISDN products will be compatible. In particular, ISDN recommendations specify different classes of user equipment and to which reference points they are connected. Looking at Figure 11.32, we see that the equipment may be divided into two broad groups, equipment on the customer's premises and exchange equipment. Notice that not all of the equipment on the customers premises will necessarily be owned by the customer. In particular the NT1/2 equipment (to be explained shortly) may be owned by the carrier. We now describe interpretations of each class and reference point.

Equipment classes:

Terminal equipment 1 (TE1). ISDN-compatible customer-owned equipment. This equipment will plug directly into an ISDN jack with a communication interface as specified by reference point S. Examples of TE1 equipment would be ISDN telephones, ISDN per-

R,S,T,U,V = ISDN Reference points
TE1 = ISDN terminal equipment
TE2 = Non-ISDN terminal adapter
TA = Non-ISDN to ISDN terminal adapter
NT = Network termination
LT = Line terminal
ET = Exchange terminal

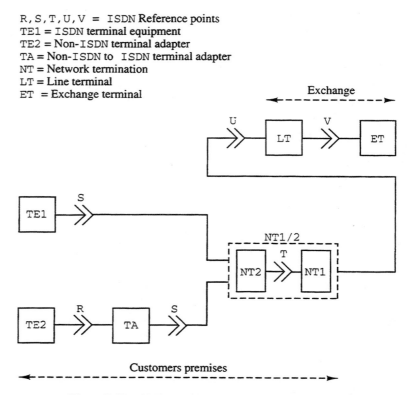

Figure 11.32   ISDN equipment classes and reference points.

sonal computers (most likely this would be a personal computer with an ISDN communications card installed), and ISDN fascimilie machines.

Terminal equipment 2 (TE2). Non-ISDN customer-owned equipment. This equipment class represents whatever is currently in use today. These units have a variety of different interfaces (e.g., RS 232C) which are incompatible with the ISDN reference point S.

Terminal adapter (TA). Adapter unit that will permit non-ISDN terminal equipment to be connected to the network. Clearly there will be many TA units corresponding to the different TE2 interfaces.

Network termination (NT1, NT2, NT12). Represents the equipment between the customer's ISDN products and the ISDN network itself. NT1 represents the termination of the physical layer services as provided by the carriers (know as ISDN providers). This includes hardware for loopback tests to the exchange and line monitoring. NT2 represents the higher layers (the data link and network layers) associated with terminating the network. In the case of a company this equipment would be the modern private branch exchanges (PBXs) and may be either owned by the company or supplied by the carrier. Recognizing that NT1 and NT2 always coexist there is also an NT12 class for when they are an integrated unit. This is particularly useful in the case when the common carriers are state controlled, limiting the types of NT2 units available.

Line terminal (LT). Carrier equipment associated with providing ISDN services to one or more ISDN numbers. This equipment forms the local exchange equipment.

Exchange terminal (ET). Carrier equipment associated with providing ISDN services between ISDN exchanges.

Reference Points

R. Could be any one of a number of existing standards (e.g., RS-232C).

S. 4-wire, 144 Kbps (2B + 1D) or 192 Kbps (2B + 1D + overhead).

T. For basic access, same as S. For primary access this would be 4-wire, 1.544 Mbps (23B + 1D + overhead).

U. For basic access, 2-wire with echo suppressor. For primary access this would be 4-wire common carrier transmission system.

V. Common carrier transmission system.

11.7.3 Numbers and Addressing

Equipment developed for use in the ISDN environment will use an addressing scheme which is an extension of the telephone numbering system used today. In ISDN a distinction is made between a **number** and an **address**. An ISDN number corresponds to the T reference point and may be thought of as a number for the user's equipment which interfaces to the network. This might be the NT2 equipment for a residential user or any be a complete PBX for a company, depending on the service type. An ISDN address on the other hand corresponds to an S reference point and as such contains an ISDN number as a prefix. Thus for a residential service each attachment (ISDN phone, ISDN terminal, etc.) will have its own address. For compatibility purposes ISDN, addressing uses only digits and is an extension of the current dialing convention, CCITT E.163. An ISDN address may be up to 55 (!) digits composed of a country code, a national destination code, an ISDN subscriber number, and an ISDN subaddress. The first three fields correspond to the ISDN number and are limited to 15 digits. From this it should be obvious that there is plenty of scope in the ISDN subaddress field to accommodate new ISDN service information and access codes (e.g., extensions). We close this section by noting that some subscriber and subaddress information may be transparent to the user. Thus an easy transition exists from the plain old telephone system to ISDN in the sense that users will not be expected to dial long numeric sequences for the simple phone service.

11.7.4 Standards and ISDN

It is impossible to discuss ISDN without at least some mention of the standards bodies responsible for its design, just as it is impossible to talk about layered networks without mentioning the ISO/OSI model. ISDN is an international standard with input from many sources, the most important of which is of course CCITT, the international standards body for the common carriers. CCITT conducts its work through a number of study groups, each of which is responsible for activities in a particular area. The study group mainly responsible for ISDN is Study Group XVII (Digital Networks) but there is also input from others. Within S.G. XVII, a number of subgroups are responsible for answering particular questions; these subgroups make recommendations to the CCITT plenary assembly which meets every four years. The first set of recommendations was reviewed in 1984 and is know by its color, the Red Book series. The last set, is the Blue Book series. An introduction to ISDN is to be found in Blue Book III (1991) as the I-series recommendations. These are organized as follows:

I.100 series: Is a general introduction to the ISDN concept including structure and terminology. Included in these reports are the principles, historical perspective, and anticipated direction for ISDN. This series may be regarded as an overview to the remaining reports.

I.200 series. Describes the service capabilities provided to the users (i.e., customers). This includes the lower level service specifications related to the teleservices to be available (e.g., call forward, etc.), and the higher level specifications of precisely what services are to be offered (e.g., fascimile, teletext, etc.) In addition this series covers compatibility requirements for ISDN terminals. An important aspect of ISDN is ensuring that the specifications will ensure service compatibility at the *global* level. Thus a user in country X will be able to open a connection to a user in country Y without the worry of terminal/protocol incompatibilities.

I.300 series. Describes how the network capabilities are to be provided. This includes specification of the communication protocols used to connected telephone networks together. The ISDN network specification is modeled closely on the ISO/OSI seven layer model discussed earlier. Included in this series are ISDN addressing issues and service types, both mentioned earlier.

I.400 series. Describes the user/network interface. This series include a specification of the ISDN equipment classes, reference points and channel services (the 2B + 1D, etc.) This series also provides the protocol specification for the channels as they are seen at different points in the customers premises.

I.500 series. Describes internetwork issues. In addition to the ISDN reference points described earlier there are many others. In particular this series defines the reference points and protocols required to connected ISDN-to-ISDN and ISDN-to-non_ISDN networks. This includes mapping addresses, mapping control signals, defining chargeback mechanisms etc.

I.600 series. Describes the maintenance considerations required to support ISDN. This includes network support for channel control, equipment diagnosis, switch failure identification and correction, and billing.

11.7.5 Summary

To see how a typical residential customer will benefit from ISDN consider Figure 11.33. The customer will have an ISDN network interface (NT12) to which he or she may connect one or more pieces of ISDN terminal equipment (TE1 or TE2 via a TA); typically these will include a telephone, a personal workstation, and perhaps a personal fax machine. In addition to these there may be one or more D channel signal controlled units. For example intelligent ranges, microwave ovens, video cassette recorders, etc. may be controlled remotely by "connecting to them" by specifying the appropriate ISDN address. Automatic services based on the intelligent controllers in the residence will also be possible; for example an ISDN fire detection unit in the house may use the D channel to alert the fire services in the event of a fire. Although many of these features are already available in the regular phone system, they are currently separate entities. It is expected that ISDN will provide a common framework with which to tie these and many other, as yet unthought of, products into a coherent body.

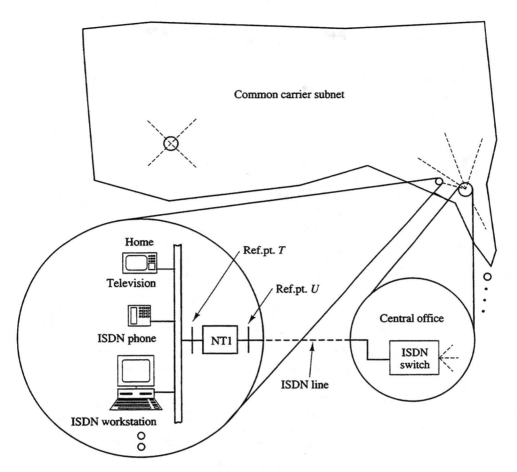

Figure 11.33 Using ISDN in a residential situation.

Although ISDN appears to be gaining support, there is one point of caution that should be noted when considering its future. ISDN has been designed by the common carriers (the service providers) rather than the service users. Such arrangements often fail due to the providers failing to respond quickly enough to new user demands. These demands are supported by other companies who are quicker to recognize the ever changing user needs. There are already those who say that ISDN is obsolete!

11.8 NETWORKING SUMMARY

In this chapter we have looked at the necessary framework for connecting together computers so that users may communicate with one another easily. As you should now be aware, open communications is a complex task which has evolved from the connection of terminals to a host computer to a heterogeneous *ensemble* of personal workstations and computers providing a distributed computing environment. Although the goal of a completely seamless computing environment has yet to be realized, each year brings it closer. We would expect that the trend towards multiprocessing, open systems, and an ISDN will contribute to permit an environment in which the requirement to work "at the office" will be removed. This may eventually lead to a paperless society.

11.9 EXERCISES

1. Explain the difference between a personal computer and a workstation.
2. How high would a deck of cards have to be to store a 500,000 byte program if the average punched card is 0.01 in thick?
3. Briefly, what are the principal advantages of using a computer network? What are the disadvantages?
4. Why are software licenses a problem in networked environments? Explain one way in which they might be solved.
5. What does ISO/OSI stand for? Name the seven layers of the ISO/OSI reference model.
6. Which of the layers appears to do the most work? Which appears to do the least work? Could the ISO/OSI model have ommited any of the layers, if so, where would those services go?
7. Do SPDUs encapsulate TPDUs or the otherway around?
8. Which layer would issue a N-CONNECT.request? Which layer would receive an N-CONNECT.indication?
9. Explain the functions of the network and transport layers. Which of these provided end-user to end-user service?
10. Compare octet stuffing with bit stuffing. Which is more efficient? For the string "This is ⁓ a test (*DLE*)", where (*DLE*) indicates the DLE character, show the data send on the line.
11. Why is ASN.1 necessary?
12. Consider the following alphabet, $\Sigma = \{ a , c, b, d \}$ and the following strings $S_0 = aabbcaad$, $S_1 = bbccca$. Write a Huffman code for S_0 and S_1. What is the coding efficiency for each string. If you knew that both strings were to be transmitted what would happen to your codes?
13. What is entropy?"
14. What advantages does public key encryption offer over regular encryption?
15. Name four applications that make use of network communications.
16. What do **ftp, smtp,** and **tcp** stand for?
17. What costs need to be considered when designing a network? Name two performance metrics that you might use when designing a network.
18. In terms of functions provided at different layers, how does the Internet compare with the ISO/OSI model?
19. Which of the following layers is not supported explicitly in the Internet: Transport, Network, Session, Application.
20. The Ethernet is defined as a CSMA/CD system using collision detection. Another possibility is collision avoidance. How might this work?
21. What possible token ring management problems might take place in a token ring system?
22. What are the following Internet addresses in binary: `127.4.16.23`, `192.13.204.17`, `10.1.0.5`, `128.204.34.12`?
23. What class are the following Internet numbers: `123.12.34.8`, `127.0.0.1`, `128.0.0.1`, `63.17.12.34`, `132.1.2.13`?
24. How may a single host have more than one Internet address?

25. What is the relationship between an Internet name and an Internet address?
26. In establishing a telnet connection, are the user ID and password fields in the IP header?
27. What is the difference between an Internet port and an Internet address? Name three Internet applications that have dedicated ports, what are they, and what are the port numbers.
28. Explain the function of telnet. How does **telnet** accommodate different terminal types?
29. Explain the function of TCP. Why is a transmission control protocol required?
30. In FTP, what is the difference between stream mode and block mode?
31. What is SMTP used for? Explain briefly how it works.
32. What does ISDN stand for? Who are the primary instigators of ISDN.
33. What are the anticipated benefits in using ISDN?

ADDITIONAL READING

BERTSEKAS, D., and GALLAGER, R. *Data Networks*. Englewood Cliffs, N.J.: Prentice Hall, 1987.

COMER, D. *Internetworking and TCP/IP*, 2nd ed. Englewood Cliffs, N.J.: Prentice Hall, 1991.

DAY, J., and ZIMMERMAN, H. *The OSI Reference Model*. Proceedings of the IEEE, December 1983.

DEPARTMENT OF DEFENSE. *Military Standard Internet Protocol*. MIL-STD 1777, August 12, 1983.

DEPARTMENT OF DEFENSE. *Military Standard Transmission Control Protocol*. MIL-STD 1778, August 12, 1983.

DECINA, M. "CCITT Recommendations on the ISDN: A Review." *IEEE Journal on Selected Areas in Communications*, May 1986.

ELLIS, R. *Designing Data Networks*. Englewood Cliffs, N.J.: Prentice Hall, 1986.

HALSALL, F., *Data Communications, Computer Networks and Open Systems*, 3rd ed. New York, N.Y.: Addison-Wesley, 1992

MAINE, A. *Linked Local Area Networks*, 2nd ed. New York: John Wiley, 1986.

ROSE, M. T. *The Open Book: A Practical Perspective on OSI*. Englewood Cliffs, N.J.: Prentice Hall, 1990.

SCHWARTZ, M. *Telecommunication Networks, Protocols, Modeling, and Analysis*. Reading, Mass.: Addison-Wesley, 1987.

STALLINGS, W. *Data and Computer Communications*, 2nd ed. New York: MacMillan, 1988.

STALLINGS, W. *Handbook of Computer Communications Standards*, vol. 3. Department of Defense Protocol Standards. New York: MacMillan, 1988.

STALLINGS, W. *ISDN An Introduction*. New York: MacMillan, 1989.

TANEMBAUM, A. *Computer Networks*, 2nd ed. Englewood Cliffs, N.J.: Prentice Hall, 1989.

Appendix A

Software for the Text

The following software packages are available without cost. Executables are provided on a 5 1/4-in diskette shipped with the instructors manual or may be obtained via the Internet using the file transfer protocol ftp from ftp.cis.ufl.edu (login anonymous). The file to be retrieved is /cis/pel/*arch*/mc68k.tar.Z and contains all the software required.[1] Currently they have been ported for the IBM and Amiga personal computers, and Sun Microsystems Sun-3, and Sparc workstations.

SIM68: A simulator for SIM68, the MC68000 subset model computer. The simulator provides a friendly, easy to use interface. Students are presented with a visual model for programming.

ASM68: An assembler for ASM68, the SIM68 assembly language. The output generated by the assembler is a list file and an S-record object code file.

SIM68K: A simulator for the MC68000 based on Motorola's Educational Computer Board (ECB). SIM68 supports the complete MC68000 instruction set; provides an interface compatible with TUTOR, the ECB interface; and supports the more useful tutor functions and traps.

XSIM68K: A graphical user interface to SIM68K for use on SUN platforms supporting the X Windows System.

ASM68K: A full MC68000 assembler with macro capability. The output generated by the assembler is a list file and an S-record object code file. This assembler is well tested and compiles code very quickly. Using ASM68K and SIM68K one may teach the entire introductory MC68000 assembly programming course on any of the platforms mentioned earlier.

TEXTTOS: A utility to convert text files to S-record files. This permits users to upload data files etc. to SIM68 or SIM68K.

STOTEXT: A utility to convert S-records files to text files. This permits users to translate output data files which have been downloaded from SIM68 or SIM68K.

MKLOAD: A utility to convert textual versions of machine language files (using ASCII zeros and ones along with comments) into S-record format. This permits users to "write" machine language programs directly. It is intended for use with SIM68.

SAMPLES: Source code for the samples provided in Appendix F.

---

[1] Users of the Internet are expected to be familiar with the ftp and tar utilities.

640

Appendix B

SIM68 and ASM68: The MC68000 Subset Simulator and Assembler

SIM68 is a simulator for a small subset of the MC68000 instruction set. That is, it will "run" machine code generated either from textual machine language files using mkload or from assembler files using ASM68. The simulator is visually oriented and easy to use. This manual is designed only to tutor you on the use of SIM68, and does not provide information regarding the SIM68 machine language itself which may be found in Chapter 4.

B.1 LOAD FILES FROM TEXTUAL MACHINE LANGUAGE FILES

To run a textual version of a SIM68 machine language program you should first create a source file using a text editor. Please adhere to the following file naming conventions.

- Machine language source: use the extension ".sim"
- Load files (created by mkload): use the extension ".s"
- Text files: use the extension ".txt"

Within the editor type in your program using the format **location, code, comment** (no commas) for each line. The field **location** must start in the first column and be six (hexadecimal) characters long. The instruction following the address may contain only the characters 0, 1, and the space. Be sure to have a space between the address and the start of the first instruction. You may break instructions across lines provided the breaks occur at word boundaries. Comments are started by a semi-colon (;), may be composed of any characters, and terminate at the end of the line. A semi-colon at the beginning of a line specifies that the entire line is a comment. Blank lines are ignored. A sample program appears in Table B.1.

TABLE B.1 Sample SIM68 Program

```
;  Name:    Johnny Perfect
;  Std id:  666-66-6666
;  Class:   CDA3101, Fall '92
;  Assn:    Sim68 program #1
;
```

TABLE B.1   (*Continued*) Sample SIM68 Program

```
;   Description:
;
;   This program is used to demonstrate the syntax and mechanics of
;   your SIM68 program source file to be turned in.  It must execute
;   properly (no errors) and produce the desired result and output.
;   Also it must be commented thoroughly, and accompanied by a
;   flowchart.
;
;
;location                 code              comment
;
000000          0110 0000 0000 1000   ;
000002          0000 0000 0000 0011   ;
000004          0000 0000 0000 0100   ;
000006          0000 0000 0000 0000   ;
000008          0000 0000 0000 0000   ;
00000A          0011 0000 0010 1000   ;  Get Data 1 into D0
00000C          0000 0000 0000 0010
00000E          0011 0000 0110 1000   ;  Get Data2 into A0
000010          0000 0000 0000 0100
000012          0011 0001 0110 1000   ;  Store A0 to memory
000014          1111 1111 1111 1110
000016          0000 0000 0000 0010
000018          1011 0010 0100 0000   ;  Compare D0 with D1
00001A          0110 0111 1110 1110   ;  If equal, goto BEGIN
00001C          0100 1000 0100 0000   ;  SWAP high/low of D0
00001E          0100 1000 0100 0000   ;  SWAP high/low of D0
000020          1101 0010 0100 0000   ;  D1 = D1+D0
000022          1001 0010 0100 0011   ;  D1 = D1-D3
000024          0011 0100 0000 0001   ;  Copy D1 into D2
000026          1100 0101 1100 0001   ;  D2 = D2*D1
000028          1000 0101 1100 0001   ;  D2 = D2/D1
;
;
;   STANDARD EXIT   (these are required to be the last six instructions
                     of your program:  you MUST have a DUMP followed
                     by an EXIT)
;
;
00002A          1001 0000 0100 0000   ;  SUB D0 from D0
00002C          0011 0000 0100 0000   ;  MOVE D0 into A0
00002E          0100 1110 0100 0000   ;  TRAP (dump regs. and memory)
000030          0011 0000 0010 1000   ;  MOVE from memory to DO
000032          0010 0000 0000 0000   ;  Displacement = $2000
000034          0100 1110 0100 0000   ;  TRAP (stop simulator)
;
;   CONSTANT (needed for standard exit)
;
002000          0000 0000 0000 0011   ;  3 - values for trap stop
```

After you have edited your source program, you must now convert your program into a form that can be loaded by the simulator. You may do this using the utility `makeload`. To run `makeload`, type the following:

```
makeload <filename>
```

If `makeload` detects an error, it will print the line with the error and an error message to the screen. It will then proceed to the next line. If more than six errors are detected, `makeload` will terminate. Do not run the simulator until *all* errors that `makeload` has detected have been corrected. Otherwise, unpredictable results may occur.

Assuming all has gone well, `makeload` will create a file with the extension ".ld". (For example, if your source file was called `prog1.sim`, `makeload` will create a load file called `prog1.s`.)

B.2 LOADING FILES FROM ASM68, THE SIM68 ASSEMBLER

You may also write assembly language programs for SIM68 using ASM68. ASM68 is a subset of `ASM68K` and details of its syntax are provided in Chapter 5. The command syntax for invoking the ASM68 assembler is:

```
asm68 <filename.asm> [-l]
```

where:

- `<filename.asm>` is the name of the source file you want assembled. Notice the extension ".asm" is required.
- **-l** is an optional "switch" that tells the assembler to produce a listing file. The listing file will contain your source file and the corresponding list of the code the assembler produced. It will also show all errors (if any) in your source. The file will have the extension ".lst".

The assembler will produce a load file with the extension ".s". If any assembly time errors are detected, the errors will be displayed on your screen. Note: Do not run the simulator until ALL errors have been corrected. Unpredictable results may occur.

Examples:

1. To assemble the file `hello.asm` type the following:

```
asm68 hello.asm
```

   The file `hello.s` will be created.
2. To assemble the file `test.asm` and produce a listing file, type the following:

```
asm68 test.asm -l
```

   Two files will be created: `test.s` and `test.lst`

When all the assembler errors have been removed, you may load the SIM68 load file (the ".s" file) by invoking the SIM68 simulator as shown next.

B.3 LOADING YOUR LOAD FILE INTO SIMULATOR

Once you have created a loadable file, you will want to run it. In order to run your program, you must invoke the SIM68 simulator. To do this, you must type the following (notice the ".s" extension, the simulator will only load files with this extension):

```
sim68 filename.s
```

This will put you in the simulator while your machine language program has been loaded into SIM68's memory. Next you will wish to run your program, step by step, to make sure each individual instruction works as you intended it to work.

B.4 USING SIM68

B.4.1 Setting the Program Counter

Before running your program, you must initialize the program counter to the address of first instruction you want executed (i.e., the loading origin). The way to do this is by typing

```
.PC <contents>      Display/Modify Program Counter
```

where [<contents>] are the hexadecimal contents with which to replace the PC. If this field is left blank, the indicated register will just be displayed, not changed.
Examples:

```
SIM68 > .PC       {Program counter is displayed}

SIM68 > .PC 1000  {PC is set to $1000}

SIM68 > .PC       {PC is displayed again}
```

B.4.2 Running Your Program

Next you want to execute the program. To do this you must use the GO command. The program will run until either a run time error occur or it hits the exit code. If at any time you would like to suspend execution type control-c.

B.4.3 Trace

This command is one of the most useful for debugging that SIM68 provides. It allows you to see the exact results of execution of any instruction you trace. This command will execute one (and only one) instruction and automatically displays the contents of the internal registers after that instruction is executed. Since the instruction is actually executed, (remember this consists of a fetch and execute cycle) the program counter is automatically incremented by the size of the instruction so that it is ready to fetch the next instruction. The syntax is:

TR

Note that the register display which results after the instruction is executed includes the disassembled output of the NEXT instruction to be executed.

Examples: Notice, the : provided in the prompt SIM68 :>. This indicates that SIM68 is in trace mode. Therefore, by depressing the return key the next instruction will be traced. Entering any other command will get you out of this mode.

B.4.4 Register Modify

Register Modify will allow you to change or display any of the internal registers of the SIM68 processor.

The syntax is:

```
.<register> [<contents>]
```

These commands allow the user to display/modify individual registers.

```
.A0 - .A3    Display/Modify Address Register
.D0 - .D3    Display/Modify Data Register
.PC          Display/Modify Program Counter
.SR          Display/Modify Status Register
```

[<contents>] are the hexadecimal contents with which to replace the register. If this field is left blank, the indicated register will just be displayed, not changed.
Examples:

```
SIM68 > .D2        {the contents of D2 is displayed}
D2 = 00002500

SIM68 > .D2 1000   {D2 is set to $1000}

SIM68 > .D2        {D2 is displayed again}
D2 = 00001000
```

B.4.5 Viewing the Effects of Your Program

You may view the contents of the memory or the registers by using the MD and DF commands, respectively. The syntax for the memory dump command is

```
MD <address> [<count>] [;<option>]
```

where <address> is the hex address of the location in memory you wish to view. <count> is a decimal count of the number of bytes you wish to view. Three modes of display are available; the memory can be displayed in hexadecimal form, binary form, or in disassembled form. If no [;<option>] is specified, the memory will be displayed in hexadecimal. If the option [;BI] is specified, the memory will be shown in a binary format and if the option [;DI] is specified, the memory will be disassembled.
Examples:

```
SIM68 > MD 0
00000000    9040 3040 3428 002C 3228 002E 3628 0030
```

```
SIM68 > MD 0 ;BI
00000000     1001 0000 0100 0000      0011 0000 0100 0000

SIM68 > MD 4 ;DI
00000004     3428 002C          move           $002C(a0),d2
```

The number of bytes displayed for a hexadecimal dump will be a multiple of sixteen and the number of bytes displayed for a binary dump will be a multiple of eight. If no other command is issued after a MD command and the return key is pressed, the next ten lines of memory will be displayed[1]. The syntax for a register dump is:

$$DF$$

This command will display all registers, including the program counter and the status register. It also shows the disassembled output of the next instruction to be executed along with its machine code in hexadecimal. The next instruction to be exectued is the instruction which begins at the location pointed to by the program counter. Display formatted will not change any registers, or memory locations and no commands will be executed.
Example:

```
SIM68 > DF

PC=00000002 SR=0004=..Z..
DO=00000FA0 D1=00000000   D2=00000110 D3=0F000B10
AO=000000D0 A1=00000000   A2=00000100 A3=0000A00A
-------------------00000002     3040          movea     d0,a0
SIM68 >
```

B.4.6 Help and Exit

To display the list of the available SIM68 commands enter help. To exit from the simulator simply enter the command exit.

---

[1] This will be 160 bytes in the case of a hexadecimal dump, 80 bytes in the case of a binary dump, and ten instructions in the case of a disassembly.

Appendix C

SIM68K and XSIM68K: The MC68000 Simulators

SIM68K is a simulator for the MC68000 instruction set. That is, it will "run" machine code generated for the MC68000 processor. Thus SIM68K can be used as a stand-alone debugging tool, providing an environment to test, modify and display registers and memory. The interface to SIM68K mimics TUTOR, the firmware package written by Motorola to complement the Education Computer Board (ECB) printed circuit board which includes an actual MC68000 microprocessor. This guide is intended to provide instruction on how to use each command provided by SIM68K and explains the subtle differences found in certain instances. These rare variations are either necessary or intended to help you and will be explained where a difference can be expected between SIM68K and TUTOR.

C.1 The SIM68K ENVIRONMENT

Throughout this guide, as well as most of the texts you will encounter, syntax conventions will be as follows:

Mandatory commands will be presented without punctuation if they are to be entered *as is*.
Commands will be presented with delimiting <> punctuation marks if their contents are variable.
Optional commands will be presented with [] punctuation marks and their contents may or may not be variable.
For example, the syntax for the memory dump command is

```
MD <address> [<number>] [;DI]
```

which means that all of the following are valid commands:

```
MD 1000
MD 2000 20
MD 2000 20 ;DI
MD 3000 ;DI
```

SIM68K will also remember the last instruction. If there is just a carriage return entered on the prompt line, SIM68K will attempt to execute the same instruction again. SIM68K only recognizes capital letters in the commands. In other words, "GO" and "go" are not equal. Exit should always be used to leave SIM68K, because this instruction will free the memory used by SIM68K. Then normal mode of operation for using SIM68K is to:

1. Load your program into the simulator. (LO filename.s)
2. Set the status register to $0700. (.SR 0700)
3. Set the user stack to $7800. (.US 7800)
4. Then trace or run the program.

C.1.1 Viewing commands

C.1.1.1 Display formatted. The syntax is

```
DF
```

This command will display all registers, including the program counter and the status register. It also shows the disassembled output of the next instruction to be executed along with its machine code in hexadecimal. The next instruction to be executed is the instruction which begins at the location pointed to by the program counter. Display formatted will not change any registers, or memory locations and no commands will be executed.
Example:

```
PROGRAM TERMINATED PROPERLY
PC=???????? SR=????=???????? US=???????? SS=????????
D0=???????? D1=???????? D2=???????? D3=????????
D4=???????? D5=???????? D6=???????? D7=????????
A0=???????? A1=???????? A2=???????? A3=????????
A4=???????? A5=???????? A6=???????? A7=????????
--------------------008232    46FC2700              MOVE.W #9984,SR
```

C.1.1.2 Memory Dump. The syntax is

```
MD <address> [<count>] [;DI]
```

<address> is the hex address of the location in memory you wish to view. <count> is a decimal count of the number of bytes you wish to view. [;DI] is a flag indicating whether you want the disassembled interpretation or (if you leave this field blank) the ASCII interpretation. Two modes of display are available.

1. Hexadecimal data and its equivalent ASCII representation.
   Example:

   ```
   TUTOR 1.X > MD 1000
   001000 FF 00 FF 00 FF 00 FF 00  FF 00 FF 00 FF 31 32 33 .....123
   ```

   Note: The number of bytes displayed will always be in groups of 16.
2. Disassembled format.
   Example:

   ```
   TUTOR 1.X > MD 1000 ;DI
   001000  2248              MOVE.L  A0,A1
   ```

   Note: All opcodes contained in the byte count will be displayed.

The default depends on the mode of memory dump you are executing. If you wish a disassembled interpretation of the data, the default is one instruction. If you call MD again, by pressing return at the `SIM68K 2.0 >` prompt, the default is sixteen instructions. If you wish an ASCII interpretation of the data, then default is 16 bytes the first time, and 16 rows of 16 bytes the second time.

C.1.2 Modify Commands

C.1.2.1 Memory modify.   The syntax is

`MM <address> [;<option>]`

`<address>` is the hex address of memory you wish to modify (or view). `<option>` is either W for word-sized, L for longword-sized, or left blank for byte-sized operations. This command will allow you to modify or display memory until you want to stop. Stopping is indicated by a special control character. If any numbers are entered, the location displayed is changed to that value of data in hexadecimal. When entering data, the format can be:

`<data>`—location is changed to this value (hex) address is automatically incremented by size of data.

`<data> <control>`—location is changed to this value (hex) then control is executed.

`<control>`—no memory is changed, control is executed.

`<carriage return>`—no memory is changed, address is automatically incremented by size of data.

The various `<control>` options follow. If no control option is selected, the address will automatically be incremented to the next memory location. By themselves, these controls never modify any data.

^ Will decrement the address to the next lower memory location.

= Will re-open the same memory address.

. Will quit memory modify.

Example:

```
SIM68K 2.0 > MM 1000;W
001000   FFFF  ?0000
001002   1111  ?2222
001004   F5F5  ?.
```

C.1.3 Register Modify

Register Modify will allow you to change or display any of the internal registers of the MC68000 processor.
The syntax is

`.<register> [<contents>]`

These commands allow the user to display/modify individual registers.

```
.A0 - .A7    Display/Modify Address Register
.D0 - .D7    Display/Modify Data Register
.PC          Display/Modify Program Counter
.SR          Display/Modify Status Register
```

```
.SS          Display/Modify Supervisor Stack Pointer
.US          Display/Modify User Stack Pointer
```

<contents> are the hexadecimal contents with which to replace the register. If this field is left blank, the indicated register will just be displayed, not changed.
Examples:

```
SIM68K 2.0 > .PC          {Program counter is displayed}

SIM68K 2.0 > .PC 1000  {PC is set to $1000}

SIM68K 2.0 > .PC          {PC is displayed again}
```

C.1.4 Block Fill

Block Fill is a useful command for debugging. You can initialize large blocks of data to any value you choose, so you can tell exactly what memory locations are affected by the execution or loading of your program.
The syntax is

```
BF <address1> <address2> <data>
```

<address1> is the hexadecimal address to start the block fill. <address2> is the hexadecimal address to end the block fill. Address2 must be greater than address1 for this instruction to have any effect and both must be word aligned. <data> is the hexadecimal word sized contents with which to fill the block.
Example:

```
SIM68K 2.0 > BF 1000 2000 0000
PHYSICAL ADDRESS=00001000 00002000
```

Note: This command "zeros out" memory from location $1000 to $2000.

C.1.5 Program Control

C.1.5.1 Go.

This instruction will execute instruction after instruction without stopping unless there is an error, or the program has completed.
The syntax is

```
GO [<address>]
G [<address>]
```

<address> is the hexadecimal contents with which to initialize the program counter before running the program. If this field is blank, the program will begin execution with whatever value the previous program counter held. .
Example:

```
SIM68K 2.0 > GO 1000          Start execution at location $1000
```

Note that GO 1000 is identical in function to .PC 1000 followed by GO. As with all simulators, SIM68K is much slower than TUTOR. GO is the only command where this difference will be readily evident. SIM68K executes an average of 800 instructions per second—so some patience is required to run large programs with SIM68K.

C.1.5.2 Trace.

This command is one of the most useful for debugging that SIM68K provides. It allows you to see the exact results of execution of any instruction you trace. This command will execute one (and only one) instruction and automatically displays the contents of the internal registers after that instruction is executed. Because the instruction is actually executed, (remember this consists of a fetch and execute cycle) the program counter is automatically incremented by the size of the instruction so that it is ready to fetch the next instruction. The syntax is[1]

```
TR [<address>]
T [<address>]
```

<address> is the hexadecimal value with which to initialize the program counter before any instructions are executed. If this field is left blank, then trace will execute the instruction that is found at the previous value of the program counter. Note that the register display which results after the instruction is executed includes the disassembled output of the NEXT instruction to be executed.
Examples:

```
SIM68K 2.0 > TR            Trace a single instruction

SIM68K 2.0 :>              Pressing the <Return> key here will trace
                           the next instruction.
```

C.1.5.3 Breakpoints.

A breakpoint is a helpful tool that is very popular when debugging. The idea behind breakpoints is simple. Suppose you have a large program that contains a bug and you know the approximate location. Ideally, you would like to trace only particular instructions to determine exactly which instruction contains the bug. Breakpoints allow you to execute code at full speed, stopping only at particular locations. When the program has stopped, you can trace, display registers, display memory, or look at the instructions. Unless you modify the program counter, you can type go again, and SIM68K will then continue from where it left off.
There is a maximum of eight breakpoints that can be set at any one time. Any attempt to set more than eight, or to set a duplicate breakpoint will be ignored.
The syntax is

```
BR [<address>]      - set/display breakpoints
NOBR [<address>]    - clear breakpoints
```

<address> is the hexadecimal address of the location either to set a breakpoint if BR is used, or to clear the breakpoint at address if NOBR is used. If this field is blank and BR is used, then the breakpoints are displayed and none are set or changed. If this field is left blank while NOBR is used, then all breakpoints will be cleared.

---

[1] TR [address] is not supported in TUTOR. For example, the command .TR 1000 must be replaced by the commands .PC 1000 followed by TR.

A common mistake is to set a breakpoint in the middle of an instruction. This will cause an error. There are two simple ways to prevent this from happening. One way is to obtain a current list file from the ASM68K assembler. The second way is to have SIM68K show you the disassembled output of your program using MD.
Example:

```
SIM68K 2.0 > MD 1000 ;DI

001000    2076 00001200        MOVE.L #$1200,A0
001006
```

This tells you that you can either set a breakpoint at $1000 (before the move instruction is executed) or at $1006 (immediately after the move is executed and before the next instruction is executed). A breakpoint cannot be set at $1001, $1002, $1003, $1004, $1005 because these are all in the middle of the instruction. It should also be obvious that a breakpoint can never be set at an odd address, because all instructions require an even number of bytes.

C.1.6 Load/Store

These commands allow you to input and output your program to SIM68K.
The syntax is[2]

```
LO <filename>
ST <filename> <address> <count>
```

<filename> is the exact name of the external file in the current directory. SIM68K, like TUTOR always expects an S-record input file, assembled by an appropriate MC68000 assembler. <address> is the hexadecimal address to start output from. <count> is the decimal number of bytes to write.
Example:

```
SIM68K 2.0 > LO TEST.S
SIM68K 2.0 > ST OUT.S 1000 10
```

Because you are giving SIM68K the filename, you must specify it exactly.

C.1.7 EXIT

This command will exit SIM68K and return control to the native operating system.
The syntax is

```
                              EX
```

You should always use exit to leave SIM68K, because this command will free all memory requested by the simulator.

---

[2] Loading a file in SIM68K is much simpler than in TUTOR. SIM68K will automatically read the specified file into memory. TUTOR loading is a two-step process. LO will put TUTOR in a receive state for a specified period, where it will simply wait for a program to be given to it. You must then manually send your program from an external source to TUTOR via the serial port. Additionally, TUTOR offers you the option of ;x, which will echo the S-record back to the terminal screen as it is being read into memory. Tutor has no ST command.

C.2 USING SIM68K

SIM68K is invoked by typing "SIM68K" (without the quotes) in the directory where the file SIM68K.EXE (on the IBM) or SIM68K (on the Suns) is stored. You may then load your S-Record file into SIM68K when you get the "SIM68K 2.0 >" prompt. (See the load instruction for the correct syntax).

C.3 TRAP #14 I/O FUNCTIONS

Several functions are provided to permit simple I/O to the screen. These functions can be accessed by placing the appropriate vector number in the low-order byte of register d7 and then executing the instruction trap #14 in your program. The sequence is therefore

```
move.b #<function number>,d7
trap   #14
```

<function number> is the number of the vector of the corresponding function you want your program to perform as shown subsequently. Note all vector numbers are indicated by their decimal equivalents.

C.3.1 #241 (PORTIN1)

Description: Allows the program to read in a string.
Initial Registers: Register a6 contains the location to start storing the ASCII representation of each character read. Register a5 contains the start of the buffer. The string will be read only if Register a6 is less than or equal to Register a5.
Final Registers: Register a6 will point 1 byte past the last character read and stored in memory after this trap is finished. The cursor will also be given a carriage return and line feed after the string is entered.

C.3.2 #224 (PORTIN1N)

Description: Allows the program to read in a string.
The only difference between PORTIN1N and PORTIN1 is what happens after the string is entered. This trap expects a carriage return but not a linefeed.

C.3.3 #247 (INCHE)

Description: Allows the program to read in a single character.
Initial Registers: None needed.
Final Registers: The low-order byte of register d0 contains the ASCII value of the character read.
Other: Register d1 is destroyed, Register a1 is destroyed. The character is not echoed onto the screen when it is typed.

C.3.4 #243 (OUTPUT)

Description: Allows the program to output a string from memory to the screen.
Initial Registers: Register a6 contains one plus the location of the last byte of the string in memory. Register a5 contains the address of the first byte of the string in memory.

Final Registers: Register a5 contains the location of the last byte of the string plus one. There is no linefeed or carriage return automatically given when the string is displayed, unless they are included with the string in memory.

C.3.5 #227 (OUT1CR)

The only difference between OUT1CR and OUTPUT is that a carriage return and linefeed are automatically printed to the screen after the string is printed.
Other: Registers a0, d0, d1 are destroyed.

C.3.6 #248 (OUTCH)

Description: Allows the program to output a single character.
Initial Registers: The low-order byte of register d0 contains the ASCII value of the character to be printed.
Other: Registers a0, d0, d1 are destroyed.

C.3.7 #228 (EXIT)

Description: Normal termination sequence for a program written to run on SIM68K. SIM68K prints out the message PROGRAM TERMINATED PROPERLY if the supervisor bit is reset.[3] If the supervisor bit is set, SIM68K will not give a message. However, this may cause other errors if not used carefully. You should run your programs in user state, that is, with a reset supervisor bit.

C.4 XSIM68K

XSIM68K is a graphical user interface (GUI) to SIM68K written for the X Window System. Unlike SIM68K which is designed to provide a command line interface, XSIM68K makes use of the high resolution displays available on workstations. As may be seen from Figure C.1 the user interface contains a number of regions. One displays the current values of all the registers in the CPU, a second contains the appropriate portion of main memory, a third contains the users list file, a fourth contains the users Input/Output display and the fifth contains the execution command buttons. The user may load a file by clicking on the "load file" button and specifying the filename to a popup window that is displayed. The popup contains a complete directory searching facility for the target system. Other options include the ability to inspect the registers in either Binary, Decimal or Hex; step through a program while seeing the active memory region updated instantaneously; modify portions of main memory; set and reset breakpoints; and save regions of memory to a file. The interface supports all the Trap #14 Input/Output functions provided in SIM68K and displays the input and output in the I/O window. Figure C.2 shows XSIM68K adorned with a number of popup windows. The interface is designed to be completely compatable with SIM68K, comes with extensive online help, and is extremely easy to use.

---

[3] On TUTOR, vector #228 (exit) causes a PRIV TRAP ERROR which is normal but sometimes causes confusion.

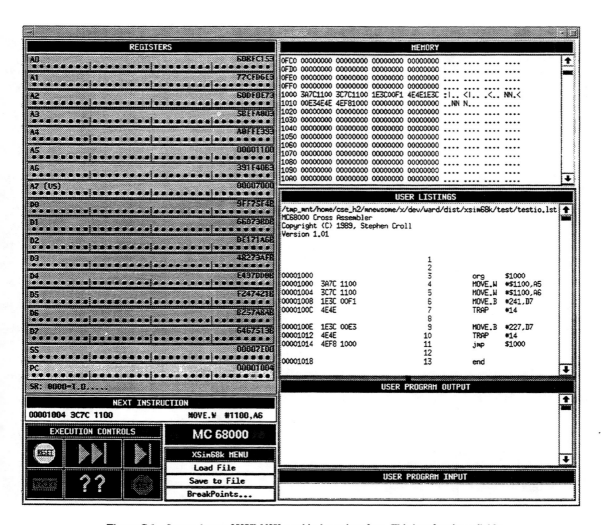

Figure C.1   Screen dump of XSIM68K graphical user interface. This interface is available only for Unix based workstations that support release 4 or greater of the X Window System.

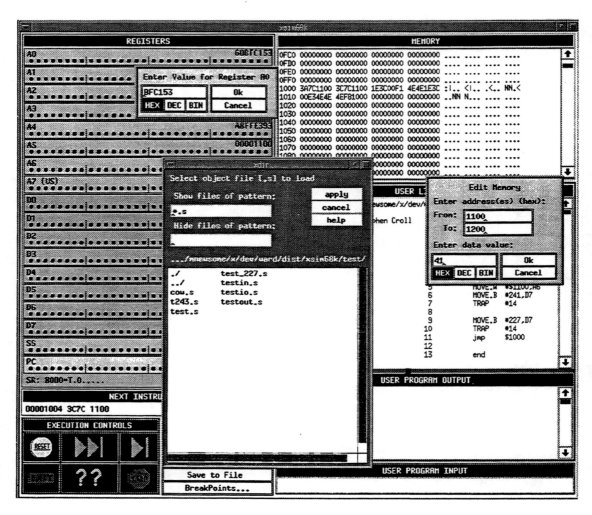

Figure C.2 Screen dump of XSIM68K adorned with popup windows. Notice that registers and memory may be viewed in binary, decimal, or hex.

C.5 Explanation of Terms Used

Source Code: Form of the program that you type. It is a text file, human readable, but not readable by `SIM68K`. The filenames containing source code are appended with `.asm`.

Machine Code: Form of your program when in binary code. This form of your program is understandable by `SIM68K` but is not human readable.

Object Module: Machine code along with information regarding where and how it should be loaded into memory.

Simulator: In this context, a program that acts like a hardware system. Simulators are slower than the hardware, but are less expensive and are portable.

SIM68K: Name of the simulator that simulates a subset of the ECB hardware and TUTOR software.

Assembler: Program that takes as input source code and generates object code for the machine it is running on.

Cross-assembler: Program that will take source code and translate it into object code for a different machine.

Disassembler: Program that has the opposite effect of an assembler. It takes machine code and translates into source code. The disassembler in `SIM68K` will only allow you to view the source code, not change it directly.

S-record Format: Name of the object code format produced by the `ASM68K` cross-assembler for `SIM68K` and the ECB. This format is composed of the machine code along with location information and byte count checks. Files containing this format are appended with `.s`.

Appendix D

ASM68K: The MC68000 Assembler

D.1 INVOKING ASSEMBLER

The command line format for invoking the assembler is as follows:

```
asm68k <filename> [-l[x]] [-r]
```

where

-l This causes the assembler to produce a listing file. This file contains for each line of source the following: a list of all errors found on the line (if any), the location counter with the code/data produced, and the original assembly source line. The listing file will have the extension ".lst". If an "x" is specified immediately following the "-l", then a cross-reference table will be appended to the listing file.

The code produced by the assembler will be in Motorola S-record format. The file produced will have the extension ".s".

-r This causes the assembler to produce relocatable code. The file produced will have the extension ".o".

Examples:

1. `asm68k test.asm`
   This will assemble the file test.asm and will create the code file test.s.
2. `asm68k parse.asm -l`
   This will assemble the file parse.asm and will create two files: the code file parse.s and the listing file parse.lst.
3. `asm68k sort.asm -lx`
   This will assemble the file sort.asm and will create two files: the code file sort.s and the listing file sort.lst. A cross-reference table will be appended to the listing file.
4. `asm68k sort.asm -r`
   This will assemble the file sort.asm and will create the relocatable code file sort.o.

D.2 FIELDS

General format of an assembly language statement:

```
[<label>]   <opcode>   [<operand>[,<operand>]...   [<comment>]
```

Each field must be separated by one or more *space* or *tab* characters. Symbols are treated by the assembler as being case-sensitive. Everything else (instructions, directives, registers etc) are treated as case insensitive. The maximum line length recognized by this assembler is 128 characters. Any characters beyond this limit are ignored.

D.2.1 Comments

This assembler supports the following "methods" of commenting:

- A semicolon (;) anywhere (except immediately following a field—see Section D.3) on a line denotes that the rest of the line is a comment.

Examples:

```
; This line is a comment.
      ; This line is also a comment.
Loop     move.w  d0,d1 ; A comment at the end of a line.
```

- An asterisk (*) in the first column of a line specifies that the entire line is a comment. This method of commenting is included for compatibility with other assemblers.

Example:

```
* This line is a comment.
```

- Comment text can follow any complete instruction or directive as long as at least one space separates the instruction/directive and the comment.

Example:

```
Loop     move.w  d0,d1   This is a comment.
```

- Blank lines are considered comments.

D.2.2 Label Field

A label is a symbol (see Section 4.3) that (if present) starts in the first column. A label can be followed by any instruction, most directives, or can stand alone on a line. A label can also be immediately followed by a colon (:). The colon is ignored, but this feature is included for compatibility with other assemblers. Labels can be local or nonlocal.

Nonlocal labels. A valid symbol must start with one of the following characters:

- An alphabetic character (a-z, A-Z).
- An underscore (_).
- A period (.).

Any subsequent character can be an alphanumeric character, an underscore, or a period. The maximum symbol length is 128 characters (the maximum line length). As stated earlier, symbols are case sensitive.

Local labels.   Local labels are only valid between any two (nonlocal) labels. They take the form nnn$ and can be reused (in different scopes) throughout the program source. Examples:

```
proc     move.w   LoopCount,d1
         bra      2$
         clr.w    d0
1$       addq.w   #2,d0
2$       dbra     d1,1$

exit     cmp.w    #$20,d0
         beq      1$
         clr.w    d0
1$       rts
```

D.2.3 Opcode Field

The opcode field can contain one of the following: an instruction opcode, an assembler directive, or a macro expansion "call." Up to 32 operands are recognized by this assembler (up to nine in the case of macro calls --see Section D.6). An optional extension may be included on instructions that allow variable-size operations. The following extensions are recognized:

.b Byte-sized data or short branch (8-bits).

.w Word-sized data or word branch (16-bits).

.l Longword-sized data (32-bits).

.s Short branch (8-bits).

The default extension (when applicable) is word-sized (.w).

D.2.4 Operand Field

This field contains zero or more operands for an instruction, a directive, or a macro call. If more than one operand is present, they must be separated by commas (,). Do not use a space when separating operands, the assembler will interpret this as the operand field terminator. This also means that expressions contained in the operator field can not contain spaces (unless contained within single quotes).

Expressions.   Expressions consist of combinations of algebraic operators, symbols, and numeric constants.

Numeric Constants.

The following numeric constants are supported:

```
Type                Example
----------------------
Decimal             1234
Hexadecimal         $EF01
Octal               @765
Binary              %101
Character           'ABCD'
```

To include a single quote in a character constant, use two quotes (example: 'Joe"s').
Numeric constants are always right justified and padded with null bytes if necessary.
(Example: `move.l #$FF,d0` is interpreted as: `move.l #$000000FF,d0`). Overflows on hex, binary, and character constants are detected by the assembler and a warning
is issued. Overflows are left truncated on the hexadecimal level. This means that the (hex)
constant $123 that is "used" as a byte will be truncated to $23. The (decimal) constant
300 that is "used" as a byte will be truncated to $2C.

Operators.

The following operators are supported (in order of preference):

```
Unary minus (-), Logical NOT (~)
Left shift ( << ), Right shift ( >> )
Logical AND (&), Logical OR (!) or (|), Logical XOR (^)
Multiply (*), Divide (/), Modulo ( %% )
Add (+), Subtract (-)
```

Operators of equal precedence are evaluated left to right. Parentheses can be used to override operator precedence.

Operations on absolute and relative expressions.
The operators '*', '/',
'%%', '&', '!', '|', '^', '<<', '>>', unary minus, and '~' accept only absolute operand(s).
The other combinations and their results:

```
Absolute + Absolute = Absolute        Absolute - Absolute = Absolute
Relative + Relative = Illegal         Relative - Relative = Absolute
Absolute + Relative = Relative        Absolute - Relative = Illegal
Relative + Absolute = Relative        Relative - Absolute = Relative
```

Numeric constants are always absolute. A symbol is absolute if SET or EQUated to an
absolute value and are relative if SET or equated to a relative value or used as a label.

Special symbols.
The following special symbols are recognized by the assembler and are case insensitive:

```
*       Current value of the program counter.
pc      Program counter.
sp      Stack pointer (equivalent to register a7).
ccr     Condition code register.
```

sr   Status register.
usp   User stack pointer.
narg   Special symbol for use with macros (see Section 6.6).

D.2.5 Comment Field

See Section D.2.1.

Addressing modes. The MC68000 effective addressing modes are supported as
follows:

Addressing Modes	Assembler Syntax
Data Register Direct...........................	Dn
Address Register Direct.......................	An
Address Register Indirect.....................	(An)
Address Register w/Postincrement..............	(An)+
Address Register w/Predecrement...............	-(An)
Address Register Indirect w/Displacement......	disp_16(An)
Address Register with Index (long)...........	disp_8(An,Xn.L)
(default)...........	disp_8(An,Xn)
Address Register with Index (word)...........	disp_8(An,Xn.W)
Absolute Short...............................	(xxx).W
Absolute Long................................	(xxx).L
Program Counter Indirect w/Displacement.......	disp_16(PC)
Program Counter Indirect with Index (long)....	disp_8(PC,Xn.L)
(default)...........	disp_8(PC,Xn)
Program Counter Indirect with Index (long)....	disp_8(PC,Xn.W)
Immediate....................................	#<data>

Defaults and Conversions

- Address register indirect with displacement mode will accept either an absolute
  expression or a relative expression as its displacement. If the expression is relative,
  the assembler will assume a *short* address is to be used as the displacement. An error
  will occur if the address cannot fit into a *short*.

- Notice the defaults for "address register with index (long)" and "program counter
  indirect with index (long)" earlier.

- If an absolute addressing mode is used and the size is not specified, the assembler
  will use *absolute short* if the size can be determined on pass 1, otherwise the assembler will default to *absolute long*.

- For the pc-relative addressing modes, the displacement will be calculated the following way: If the operand is specified via an absolute expression then the displacement
  is set to the value of the operand otherwise the displacement is set to (value of the
  operand pc).

- Branch instructions will be converted to *short* if the assembler can determine on pass
  1 that a *short* is possible. To force a *short* branch, use the extension .s or .b.

- Instructions that allow variable-size "attributes" will default to word (.w) extensions.
- add, cmp, sub, and move to an address register will be converted to adda, cmpa, suba, and movea respectively.
- addi, cmpi, and subi to an address register will be converted to adda, cmpa, and suba, respectively.
- add, and, cmp, eor, or, and sub will be converted to addi, andi, cmpi, eori, ori, and subi, respectively, if the source operand's addressing mode is immediate.
- cmp will be converted to cmpm if both operands use postincrement mode.

D.3 DIRECTIVES

In the following sections, the symbol <abs_exp> represents an absolute expression and the symbol <exp> represents an expression that can be either absolute or relative.

D.3.1 Assembly Control Directives

Format

```
[<label>]    org          <abs_exp>
```

The org directive changes the program counter to the value specified in the <abs_exp>. If an org directive is not specified, the assembler will start assembling instructions at location $000000.

Format

```
[<label>]    end
```

The end directive tells the assembler that the end of the program source has been reached. Anything after the end directive is ignored. A warning is issued if an end directive is not found in the program source.

D.3.2 Symbol Definition Directives

Format

```
<label>  equ          <exp>
```

The equ directive assigns a permanent value to the label specified. You cannot make a forward reference with an equ directive.

Format

```
<label>  set          <exp>
```

The set directive assigns a temporary value to the label specified. You cannot make a forward reference with a set directive.

D.3.3 Data Definition Directives

Format

```
[<label>]    dc[.<size>]        <exp>[,<exp>]...
```

The dc directive defines constant values in memory. The size specifier may be .b, .w, or .l. If no extension is specified, the default is .w. If the data is word, or longword sized, the assembler will insure the data is on a word boundary. The dc.b form handles character constants in a special way. The character string is converted byte by byte to its corresponding ASCII code. To use a single quote in a string, use two single quotes (see Section D.4.3).

Example: The following will define the string Hello World with a terminating null byte.

```
dc.b      'Hello World',0
```

Format

```
[<label>]    ds[.<size>]        <abs_exp>
```

The ds directive allocates uninitialize storage of the size given in the <abs_exp>. The expression cannot contain forward references. The size specifier is the same as the dc directive earlier. If the size specifier is word or long, the space is aligned at a word boundary. If the size specifier is word or long and the <abs_exp> is evaluated to zero, the directive will force a word boundary alignment without allocating space (example: ds.w 0).

D.3.4 Listing Control Directives

Format:

```
list
```

The list directive tells the assembler to turn on the production of the listing file. This directive is only valid if a listing file was specified to be produced when the assembler was invoked.

Format:

```
nolist
```

The nolist directive tells the assembler to turn off the production of the listing file. This directive is only valid if a listing file was specified to be produced when the assembler was invoked.

Format:

```
fail
```

The fail directive produces an error message. This is useful for situations involving conditional assembly and/or macros.

D.3.5 Conditional Assembly Directives

Format:

```
[<label>]    cnop      <abs_exp>,<abs_exp>
```

The cnop directive allows code to be aligned on any boundary. The second expression represents the boundary to be aligned on (evenly divisible by the expression) and the first expression represents an offset that is added to the boundary address calculated.

Example: The following will align code/data on a word boundary:

```
cnop    0,2
```

Format:

```
ifxx    <abs_exp>
ifc     <string>,<string>
ifnc    <string>,<string>
ifd     <symbol>
ifnd    <symbol>
```

The ifxx directives disable assembly if the conditions are not satisfied. A matching endc will re-enable assembly if disabled. These directives may be nested provided a matching endc exists. The <string> operands consist of a series of characters. Each such directive together with its meaning is indicated in the following table.

Conditional directives		
Mnemonic	Arguments	Condition
ifeq	<exp>	Assemble if (exp ≡ 0)
ifne	<exp>	Assemble if (exp ≠ 0)
ifgt	<exp>	Assemble if (exp > 0)
ifge	<exp>	Assemble if (exp ≥ 0)
iflt	<exp>	Assemble if (exp < 0)
ifle	<exp>	Assemble if (exp ≤ 0)
ifc	<string>,<string>	Assemble if character strings are identical
ifnc	<string>,<string>	Assemble if character strings are not identical
ifd	<symbol>	Assemble if symbol has been defined
ifnd	<symbol>	Assemble if symbol has not been defined

Format:

```
endc
```

The endc directive terminates the most recent conditional ifxx directive.

D.3.6 Macro Directives

Format:

```
<label>     macro
```

The macro directive informs the assembler that the following code is a macro definition. The assembler "builds" up the macro until a matching endm is found. Macro definition nesting is not allowed. To use a macro, type the name of the macro in the opcode field followed by a list of operands (if any). Macro calls may be nested up to 16 levels. Recursive macro calls are supported (within the 16-level maximum). Note that forward referencing a macro definition is illegal.

Arguments for a macro call (expansion) follow the same rules as "normal" operands. If an argument contains a spaces not within quotes, enclose the argument with the characters '<' and '>'.

The backslash (\) has a special meaning in a macro definition. Following a backslash with a number "n" causes the assembler to insert the nth operand into the macro expansion. The number "n" can be in the range [1–9]. If the backslash is followed by an "@", the text ".nnn" is inserted into the macro expansion. This ".nnn" represents the number of times the \@ has been used (used is counted as only once per macro expansion).

The character "+" will be appended to the source line in the listing file for each line of the macro expansion.

Example: The following is a macro definition:

```
WasteTime    macro

             ifne    narg-1      ; macro needs exactly one argument
             fail                ; notify programmer of error
             mexit               ; an exit the expansion
             endc

             move.l  d0,-(a7)    ; save d0
wt\@         move.w  #\1,d0      ; move count into d0
             dbra    d0,wt\@     ; spin
             move.l  (a7)+,d0    ; restore d0

             endm
```

If the macro was encountered for the *third* time, the expansion will look like this (code produced was omitted for this example):

```
+                 WasteTime    2000    ; macro called here
+
+    WasteTime    macro
+
+                 ifne    narg-1      ; macro needs exactly one argument
+                 fail                ; notify programmer of error
+                 mexit               ; an exit the expansion
+                 endc
+
+                 move.l  d0,-(a7)    ; save d0
+    wt.003       move.w  #2000,d0    ; move count into d0
+                 dbra    d0,wt.003   ; spin
+                 move.l  (a7)+d0     ; restore d0
```

Format:

```
            narg
```

The special symbol narg contains the count of the arguments supplied in a macro call. If referenced while not in a macro expansion, it has the value 0.

Format:

```
            endm
```

The endm directive ends the macro definition

Format:

```
          mexit
```

The `mexit` directive aborts the expansion of a macro. This directive is usually used with the conditional `ifxx` directives earlier.

D.3.7 General Directives

Format:

```
          include   '<file name>'
          include   "<file name>"
```

The `include` directive allows an external file to be "included" with the source program. The file is inserted at the point where the `include` directive is located. `includes` can be nested up to three times. An error message is issued if this nesting depth is exceeded.

D.4 RELOCATABLE ASSEMBLER

The assembler creates an object code file that in addition to containing code, contains information for internal relocation and external definitions and references. This file will have the extension ".o". A linker (described subsequently) is required to produce a loadable (S-record format) file.

Whenever our assembler is to be invoked with the the relocatable switch (`-r`) the programmer should be aware of the following restrictions.

- The assembler and linker only support 32-bit relocatable references.
- PC-relative addressing modes can only be used to access memory locations within the same section.
- Branches via the `bcc,dbcc` and `bsr` instructions can only be made to addresses within the same section. To span sections, one should use either a `jmp` or a `jsr`.
- The displacement in both modes, the address indirect with the displacement and address indirect with the displacement and index must be defined only via absolute expressions.
- Absolute word addressing may only be used with an argument of type `<abs_exp>`.

D.4.1 Additional Directives

The syntax

```
          section      <name>,<type>
```

The `section` directive defines a relocatable section of code or data. The `<type>` field can be one of three types:

code Tells the assembler the following section contains code. Both external definitions and references may be made within a `code` section.

data Tells the assembler the following section contains (usually) initialized data. Both external definitions and references may be made within a `data` section.

bss   Tells the assembler the following section contains uninitialized data. Only external
definitions may be made within a bss section.

The <name> field is passed to the linker to produce a map file. This is useful for determining where sections (and their associated code/data) will ultimately reside in memory. It is prudent but not necessary to uniquely name sections. If multiple sections exist within a single source file, the ASSEMBLER will not allow sections to have the same name.
A section is terminated by another section directive or by the end directive.

Format:

```
xdef    <symbol>[,<symbol>]...
```

The xdef directive externally defines a symbol for use outside the current section. The symbol may be absolute or relative. The assembler "knows" by usage the type (absolute or relative) of the symbol and passes this information to the linker.

Format:

```
xref    <symbol>[,<symbol>]...
```

The xref directive allows the current program section to reference symbols located outside the current section. The referenced symbol may be absolute or relative and may be of size byte, word, or longword. These references are resolved at link time. It is the responsibility of the programmer to ensure correct size usage of external definitions; the linker will *not* report such (possible) misuse.

D.4.2 Linker

The command line format:

```
link <loading_origin> [-s <filename> ] [-m] filelist
```

where filename.s is the name of a file that the linker will build by *linking* n object modules

```
object_1.o object2.o object_3.o .. object_n.o
```

denoted by filelist. If the -s switch is omitted, the linker will use name of the first file in the filelist (and add the extension .s) as the file the linker will build. The linker will link the modules so that the object codes are sequential in memory: in the order in which they appeared in filelist with the loading origin loading_origin being the one specified in the link command. Invocation of the linker with the switch -m will force the linker to create a map file with the name <filename> and the extension ".map".
Because files are added in order of appearance specified in the command line, the only "preknown" address (without looking at a map file) is the base address. The first instruction to be executed (usually) therefore must be located at the base. An easy way of handling this situation is to create an object file that is always linked first and "calls" some predetermined subroutine name. For example the following file could be (assembled) and linked like this:

```
          link  1000 -s trees.s startup.o main.o library.o
startup.asm:

          section Startup,code

          xref    _main

          jsr     _main
          move    #228,d0
          trap    #14

          end
```

A map file is useful for determining "where" your sections and externally defined routines will be ultimately located in memory. An example map file is shown below.

Section	Type	Address
Startup	CODE	$00001000
main	CODE	$0000100C
main_data	DATA	$00001812
main_bss	BSS	$000019F2
library	CODE	$00001A00
library_data	DATA	$00001CA4
library_bss	BSS	$00001D08
*** end of program ***		$00002D0C

External symbol	Section	Value	Type
_main	main	$0000100C	REL
Count	main_data	$00001854	REL
ExitMsg	main_data	$00001840	REL
HelloMsg	main_data	$00001812	REL
Index	main_bss	$000019F2	REL
Malloc	library	$00001A60	REL
MAX_DYNAMIC_MEM	library	$00001000	ABS
memory_pool	library_bss	$00001D0C	REL
memory_ptr	library_data	$00001CA4	REL
mem_table	library_data	$00001CA8	REL
table	main_bss	$000019F6	REL
WriteEOL	library	$00001A40	REL
WriteString	library	$00001A00	REL

Relocation   Internal (section local) relocation is performed only on 32-bit references. PC-relative (16-bit and 8-bit) relocation is handled (automatically) by the assembler. External definitions may be absolute or relative. External references to external definitions are resolved as indicated in the following table:

Reference (size)	Absolute	Relocatable
32 bits	32 bits	32 bits
16 bits	16 bits	PC relative
8 bits	8 bits	PC relative

Appendix E

ASCII Codes

The 128 ASCII codes are listed in Table E.1. This set of codes can be divided into a group of 33 *control* characters (decimal codes 0-31, and 127) and a group of the remaining 95 *printable* characters. The primary difference between these two groups is that the latter group consists of characters that are printable (on an ordinary printer), whereas the characters in the former group are used to define communications protocols as well as special operations on peripheral devices. For example, from Table E.1 we can see that the ASCII decimal code 13 defines the control character **Carriage Return** (CR) that is used to move the cursor to the beginning of the current line. As several additional examples we will mention that the control character BEL is used to ring the bell on a terminal, the control character HT moves the cursor to the next tab stop, whereas the control characters **Back Space** (BS), **Line Feed** (LF), and **Form Feed** (FF) cause the cursor to backspace, advance to the beginning of the next line, and advance to the beginning of the next page, respectively.

TABLE E.1   ASCII Codes

ASCII Codes											
Dec	Hex	Char	Dec	Hex	Char	Dec	Hex	Char	Dec	Hex	Char
0	00	NUL	32	20	SP	64	40	@	96	60	`
1	01	SOH	33	21	!	65	41	A	97	61	a
2	02	STX	34	22	"	66	42	B	98	62	b
3	03	ETX	35	23	#	67	43	C	99	63	c
4	04	EOT	36	24	$	68	44	D	100	64	d
5	05	ENQ	37	25	%	69	45	E	101	65	e
6	06	ACK	38	26	&	70	46	F	102	66	f
7	07	BEL	39	27	'	71	47	G	103	67	g
8	08	BS	40	28	(	72	48	H	104	68	h
9	09	HT	41	29	)	73	49	I	105	69	i
10	0A	LF	42	2A	*	74	4A	J	106	6A	j
11	0B	VT	43	2B	+	75	4B	K	107	6B	k
12	0C	FF	44	2C	,	76	4C	L	108	6C	l
13	0D	CR	45	2D	-	77	4D	M	109	6D	m
14	0E	SO	46	2E	.	78	4E	N	110	6E	n
15	0F	SI	47	2F	/	79	4F	O	111	6F	o
16	10	DLE	48	30	0	80	50	P	112	70	p
17	11	DC1	49	31	1	81	51	Q	113	71	q
18	12	DC2	50	32	2	82	52	R	114	72	r
19	13	DC3	51	33	3	83	53	S	115	73	s
20	14	DC4	52	34	4	84	54	T	116	74	t
21	15	NAK	53	35	5	85	55	U	117	75	u
22	16	SYN	54	36	6	86	56	V	118	76	v
23	17	ETB	55	37	7	87	57	W	119	77	w
24	18	CAN	56	38	8	88	58	X	120	78	x
25	19	EM	57	39	9	89	59	Y	121	79	y
26	1A	SUB	58	3A	:	90	5A	Z	122	7A	z
27	1B	ESC	59	3B	;	91	5B	[	123	7B	{
28	1C	FS	60	3C	<	92	5C	\	124	7C		
29	1D	GS	61	3D	=	93	5D	]	125	7D	}
30	1E	RS	62	3E	>	94	5E	^	126	7E	~
31	1F	US	63	3F	?	95	5F	_	127	7F	DEL

Appendix F

SAMPLE ROUTINES

F.1 INTRODUCTION AND ASSEMBLER EQUATES

In this appendix we introduce some sample code segments to assist the reader when writing assembler programs. In addition to demonstrating how assembler programs are written, they provide a starting point for a "programmers library" of useful SIM68K routines. Notice that all internal loops and so forth are written using local labels.

```
;====================================================================
;
; Equates for various routines
;
INCHE          equ      247
OUTCH          equ      248
```

F.1.1 Read a Character

```
;====================================================================
;
; ReadChar — Will read in a character from the keyboard and put
; it in the low-byte of d0.  This routine will not return until a
; character has been entered.
;               Out Parameters:
;                   d0.b—character read from keyboard.
;

ReadChar
               move.l   d7,-(sp)             ; save d7
               move     #INCHE,d7
               trap     #14
               move.l   (sp)+,d7             ; restore d7
               rts
```

F.1.2 Read a String

```
;====================================================================
;
; ReadString — Will read in a string from the keyboard and put it
; in memory pointed to by a0.  This routine will not return until a
```

```
; carriage return has been entered.  A null byte will be moved to
; the end of your string.
;                  Out parameters:
;                     a0.1 — string read in.
;

ReadString
            move.l   d7,-(sp)              ; save d7
            movea.l  a0,a1
            move     #INCHE,d7
2$          trap     #14

            jsr WriteChar                  ; echo the character

            cmp.b    #13,d0
            beq 1$
            move.b   d0,(a1)+
            bra 2$
1$          move.b   #0,(a1)+              ; move the null to memory
            move.l   (sp)+,d7              ; restore d7
            rts
```

F.1.3 Wait on Space Bar

```
;====================================================================
;
; WaitSpaceBar — will print a message to the screen asking the user
; to hit the space bar to continue;  this routine will return only
; when the user presses the space bar.

WaitSpaceBar
            movem.l  a2/d7,-(sp)     ; save d7
            lea      3$,a2           ; get the start address of the
                                     ; string
1$          move.b   (a2)+,d0        ; get a character
            beq      2$              ; branch if null
            move     #OUTCH,d7       ; print the character
            trap     #14
            bra      1$              ; goto 1$

2$          move     #INCHE,d7
            trap     #14             ; read a character
            cmp.b    #' ',d0         ; is the char a space?
            bne      2$              ; branch if not space
            movem.l  (sp)+,a2/d7     ; restore d7
            rts

3$          dc.b     '<Space bar to continue>',0

            cnop     0,2             ; force a word alignment if
                                     ; necessary
```

F.1.4 Write a Character

```
;===================================================================
; WriteChar — will write a single character contained in the low byte
; of d0 to the screen
;               In parameters:
;                   d0.b—character to print.
;

WriteChar
          move.l    d7,-(sp)          ;save d7
          move      #OUTCH,d7
          trap      #14
          move.l    (sp)+,d7          ;restore d7
          rts
```

F.1.5 Write End-of-line Character

```
;===================================================================
; WriteEOL — This character writes an EOL to the screen
;

WriteEOL
          move.l d7,-(sp)
          move #OUTCH,d7
          move #13,d0
          trap #14
          move #10,d0
          trap #14
          move.l (sp)+,d7
          rts
```

F.1.6 Write a String

```
;===================================================================
;
; WriteString — given the starting address of a string in a0, this
; routine will write the string to the screen.  The string must be
; terminated by a null byte ($00).
;               In parameters:
;                   a0.l — start of string
;

WriteString
          move.l    d7,-(sp)          ; save d7
          move.l    a0,a1             ; a0 is overwritten when OUTCH is
                                      ; called so keep track of location
                                      ; within the string using a1
          move      #OUTCH,d7
```

```
1$              move.b  (a1)+,d0        ; get a byte
                tst.b   d0              ; check for null
                beq     2$
                trap    #14             ; print it
                bra     1$
2$              move.l  (sp)+,d7        ; restore d7
                rts
```

F.1.7 Clear Screen

```
;====================================================================
;
; ClearScreen - clears the screen!
;

ClearScreen
                move.b    #$1A,d0
                jsr WriteChar
                rts
```

F.1.8 Skip to End of Line

```
;====================================================================
;
; SkipToEOL - This subroutine uses a0 as the pointer into a text
; file.  This subroutine modifies a0 to point to the byte immediately
; following an end of line.  The end of a line is signified by a
; carriage return/line feed pair, which has the ASCII values of
; $0D and $0A, respectively.
;               InOut parameters:
;                   a0.1—start of string.
;
SkipToEOL
1$              cmpi.b  #$0D,(a0)+          ;check for value $0D
                beq     2$                 ;value = $0D  -->branch out
                bra     1$                 ;value <> $0D -->branch up
2$              cmpi.b  #$0A,(a0)+          ;check for value $0A
                beq     3$                 ;value = $0A  -->exit
                bra     1$                 ;value <> $0A -->branch up
3$              rts                        ;exit subroutine
```

F.1.9 Convert to Lower Case

```
;====================================================================
;
; ConvertLC - This subroutine will convert a string to its lowercase
; equivalent. The string will be pointed to by a0 and will terminate
; with a null byte (ASCII value $00).  The result will be stored
```

```
; over the original.  The user must determine if the string is valid
; before calling this subroutine. The value of a0 will be corrupted
; when using this subroutine.
;              InOut parameters:
;                  a0.1 — start of string to be converted.
;

ConvertLC
            cmpi.b  #0,(a0)             ;compare to 00
            beq     3$                  ;char = 00 -->exit
            cmpi.b  #'A',(a0)           ;compare to 'A'
            blt     1$                  ;char < 'A'-->not a capital
            cmpi.b  #'Z',(a0)           ;compare to 'Z'
            ble     2$                  ;char <= 'Z'-->is a capital
            bra     1$                  ;char > 'Z'-->not a capital
1$          adda    #1,a0               ;increment pointer to
                                        ;string
            bra     ConvertLC           ;branch for comparisons
2$          addi.b  #32,(a0)+           ;convert to lower case
            bra     ConvertLC           ;branch for comparisons
3$          rts                         ;exit
```

F.1.10 Convert to Upper Case

```
;======================================================================
;
; ConvertUC — This subroutine will convert a string to its uppercase
; equivalent. The string will be pointed to by a0 and will terminate
; with a null byte (ASCII value $00).  The result will be stored over
; the original.  The user must determine if the string is valid
; before calling this subroutine. The value of a0 will be corrupted
; when using this subroutine.
;              InOut parameters:
;                  a0—string to be converted.
;
ConvertUC
            cmpi.b  #0,(a0)             ;compare to 00
            beq     3$                  ;char = 00 -->exit
            cmpi.b  #'a',(a0)           ;compare to 'a'
            blt     1$                  ;char < 'a'-->not a lower
            cmpi.b  #'z',(a0)           ;compare to 'z'
            ble     2$                  ;char <= 'z'-->is a lower
            bra     1$                  ;char > 'z'-->not a lower
1$          adda    #1,a0               ;increment pointer to
                                        ;string
            bra     ConvertUC           ;branch for comparisons
2$          subi.b  #32,(a0)+           ;convert to upper case
            bra     ConvertUC           ;branch for comparisons
3$          rts                         ;exit
```

F.1.11 Convert Ascii Hex to Integer

```
;=================================================================
; CAHtoInteger — Converts a string of ASCII characters to a 16-bit
; signed integer.  Call with a0 pointing to the first character of
; the ASCII string.  This routine will 'stop conversion' when a
; non-hex character is found. On return, d0 will equal zero if the
; conversion is successful, else it will hold a non-zero value (1).
; Register d1 will hold the integer (if the conversion was
; successful).
;                In parameters:
;                   a0.l — start of string.
;                Out parameters:
;                   d0.w — status (0=success, 1=error).
;                   d1.l — 16 bit integer result.
;
;

CAHtoInteger
              move.l   d3,-(sp)        ; save d3 on stack
              move.l   d2,-(sp)        ; save d2 on stack
              moveq    #0,d1           ; clear d1—the resulting integer
              moveq    #0,d2           ; clear d2—negative flag
              moveq    #4,d3           ; max number of 4 bit
                                       ; digits that can be shifted
                                       ; into d1

              cmp.b    #'-',(a0)       ; test for a negative sign
              bne      1$              ; branch if no sign
              moveq    #1,d2           ; set a negative flag
              addq     #1,a0           ; increment a0 to point to next
                                       ; byte
1$            move.b   (a0)+,d0        ; get a byte

              cmp.b    #'0',d0         ; check if digit is in range
                                       ; '0'-'9'
              blt      6$              ; if less than '0', exit
              cmp.b    #'9',d0
              bgt      2$              ; if greater than '9', check next
                                       ; range
              and.b    #$0F,d0         ; isolate four bits and 'shift'
                                       ; them in
              bra      4$

2$            cmp.b    #'A',d0         ; check if digit is in range
                                       ; 'A'-'F'
              blt      6$              ; if less than 'A', exit
              cmp.b    #'F',d0
              bgt      3$              ; if greater than 'F', check
                                       ; next range
              sub.b    #'A'-$0A,d0     ; calculate four-bit digit
              bra      4$              ; and 'shift' in
```

```
3$              cmp.b   #'a',d0                 ; check if digit is in range
                                                ; 'a'-'f'
                blt     6$                      ; if less than 'a', exit
                cmp.b   #'f',d0
                bgt     6$                      ; if greater than 'f', exit
                sub.b   #'a'-$0A,d0             ; calculate four-bit digit
                bra     4$                      ; and 'shift' in


4$              lsl.w   #4,d1                   ; shift the contents of d1
                or.b    d0,d1                   ; insert next four bits
                dbra    d3,1$                   ; branch only if number of 4-bit
                                                ; digits
                                                ; has not exceeded 4

5$              moveq   #1,d0                   ; set error flag and exit
                bra     7$

6$              cmp     #4,d3                   ; check if some digits have been
                beq     5$                      ; converted, error if not --
                                                ; branch

                moveq   #0,d0                   ; no error
                tst     d2                      ; return if no sign
                beq     7$
                neg     d1                      ; sign set, so negate the number

7$              move.l  (sp)+,d2                ; restore d2
                move.l  (sp)+,d3                ; restore d3
                rts
```

F.1.12 Convert Integer to Ascii Hex

```
;=====================================================================
; CItoAHex — Converts a 16-bit integer into its corresponding (hex)
; ASCII representation. The result is four bytes long and is stored
; starting at the location pointed to by a0.  Call with the low-word
; of d0 holding the integer to be converted and a0 holding the address
; of where the 'result' is to be stored.  For this routine, a0 will
; hold the address of the first memory location after the 'result'.
;               In parameters:
;                   d0.w — integer to be converted.
;               Out parameters:
;                   a0.1 — start of result string.
;

CItoAHex
                move.l  d2,-(sp)                ; save register
                moveq   #0,d1
                lea     2$,a1                   ; get address of character
                                                ; table
                moveq   #3,d2                   ; set to loop four times
```

```
1$          rol.w    #4,d0                ; locate next 'digit'
            move.b   d0,d1
            and.b    #$F,d1               ; isolate the low four bits

            move.b   $0(a1,d1),(a0)+      ; move corresponding digit
                                          ; from the character table
                                          ; to desired memory location
            dbra     d2,1$                ; loop four times

            move.l   (sp)+,d2             ; save register
            rts

2$          dc.b     '0123456789ABCDEF'   ; character table
            cnop     0,2                  ; make sure the assemblers
                                          ; pc is word aligned
```

F.1.13 Convert Integer to Ascii Binary

```
;====================================================================
; CItoABinary — Converts a 16-bit integer into its corresponding
; (binary) ASCII representation.  The result is 16 bytes long and is
; stored starting at the location pointed to by a0.  Call with the
; low-word of d0 holding the integer to be converted and a0 holding
; the address of where the 'result' is to be stored.  For this
; routine, a0 will hold the address of the first memory location
; after the 'result'.
;               In parameters:
;                   d0.w — integer to be converted.
;               Out parameters:
;                   a0.l — start of result string.
;

CItoABinary
            move.l   d2,-(sp)             ; save register
            moveq    #15,d2               ; set up to loop 16 times
1$          rol.w    #1,d0                ; locate next bit
            move.w   d0,d1                ; isolate the bit
            and.b    #$1,d1
            or.b     #$30,d1              ; turn it into an ASCII digit
            move.b   d1,(a0)+             ; store it
            dbra     d2,1$                ; loop 16 times

            move.l   (sp)+,d2             ; save register
            rts
```

F.1.14 Convert Integer to ASCII Decimal

```
;====================================================================
; CItoADecimal — Convert an integer (word-size) to its equivalent
; ASCII (decimal) representation.  Call this routine with a0 holding
; the start address of the buffer, the low-word of d1 holding the
```

```
; length of the buffer, and the low-word of d0 holding the integer
; to be converted.
;                        In parameters:
;                            d0.w — integer to be converted.
;                            d1.w — length of integer (in words).
;                        Out parameters:
;                            a0.1 — start of result string.
;

CItoADecimal
; First, fill the buffer with spaces and terminate it with a NULL
; byte

            subq     #2,d1              ; set for use of dbra
1$          move.b   #' ',(a0)+         ; set all bytes in string
                                        ; to spaces
            dbra     d1,1$              ; (except for the NULL byte)
            move.b   #0,(a0)            ; set NULL byte

; Check to see if the number is negative or zero and handle it

            moveq    #0,d1              ; this is the negative
                                        ; flag (cleared)

            tst      d0                 ; do the test
            bgt      3$                 ; if the number is positive,
                                        ; handle normally
            beq      2$                 ; if the number is zero, do
                                        ; special case

            ; if we are here, the number is negative

            moveq    #1,d1              ; set the negative flag
            neg      d0                 ; "make" the number positive
            bra      3$

2$          move.b   #'0',-(a0)         ; put a zero in the buffer
            bra      5$


3$          cmp      #0,d0              ; branch if low-word=0
            beq      4$
            divu     #10,d0             ; divide by 10
            swap     d0                 ; remainder in low word
            ori      #$30,d0            ; make an ASCII digit
            move.b   d0,-(a0)           ; put in buffer
            move     #0,d0              ; clear low word
            swap     d0
            bra      3$

; Get ready to exit
```

```
4$              tst     d1              ; check the negative flag
                beq     5$
                move.b  #'-',-(a0)      ; put a minus sign in the
                                        ; buffer


5$              rts
```

F.1.15 Convert Binary to Text

```
;===================================================================
; BinaryToText — This subroutine converts the bits of a binary number
; (may be multi-byte length) to their ASCII byte equiv alents, which
; makes a null terminated ASCII text string ('1's and '0's) in the
; buffer based on the contents of address a0.  The high order bits
; to low order bits of ; each byte will be printed consecutively in the
; buffer starting at a1.
;                   In parameters:
;                       a0.l — points to the binary number.
;                       d0.w — contains the number of bytes whose bits
;                               will be converted to an ASCII text string.
;                   Out parameters:
;                       a1.l — start of result string.
;

BinaryToText
                sub     #1,d0           ; number of bytes decremented by one
                                        ; for dbra
1$              move    #7,d1           ; number of bits in byte
2$              cmp     #-1,d1          ; check to see if past last bit
                beq     4$              ; then nextbyte
                btst.b  d1,(a0)         ; test bit
                beq     3$              ; if its a zero, process as such
                move.b  #'1',(a1)+      ; move '1' to buffer
                dbra    d1,2$           ; next

                bra     4$              ; exit

3$              move.b  #'0',(a1)+      ; move '0' to buffer
                dbra    d1,2$           ; next

4$              adda    #1,a0
                dbra    d0,1$
                move.b  #0,(a1)         ; put nullbyte on end of buffer
                rts
```

F.1.16 Convert Decimal to Integer

```
;===================================================================
; DecimalToInteger — Converts a string of ASCII characters to a 16-bit
; signed integer.  Call with a0 pointing to the first character of the
; ASCII string.  This routine will 'stop conversion' when a non-hex
```

```
; character is found. On return, d0 will equal zero if the conversion
; is successful, else it will hold a nonzero value (1).  Register d1
; will hold the integer (if the conversion was successful).
;                        In parameters:
;                            a0.l — start of decimal string.
;                        Out parameters:
;                            d0.w — status (0=success, 1=error).
;                            d1.w — integer result.
;

DecimalToInteger

          movem.l  d2/d3,-(sp)        ; save d3 on stack
          move.l   #0,d0
          move.l   #0,d1              ; clear d1—the resulting integer
          move.l   #0,d2              ; clear d2—negative flag
          moveq    #4,d3              ; max number of 4 bit digits
                                      ; that can be shifted into d1
          cmp.b    #'-',(a0)          ; test for a negative sign
          bne      1$                 ; branch if no sign
          moveq    #1,d2              ; set a negative flag
          addq     #1,a0              ; increment a0 to point to next
                                      ; byte
1$        move.b   (a0)+,d0           ; get a byte

          cmp.b    #'0',d0            ; check if digit is in range
                                      ; '0'-'9'
          blt      6$                 ; if less than '0', exit
          cmp.b    #'9',d0
          bgt      2$                 ; if greater than '9', check next
                                      ; range
          and.b    #$0F,d0            ; isolate four bits and 'shift'
                                      ; them in
          bra      4$

2$        cmp.b    #'A',d0            ; check if digit is in range
                                      ; 'A'-'F'
          blt      6$                 ; if less than 'A', exit
          cmp.b    #'F',d0
          bgt      3$                 ; if greater than 'F', check
                                      ; next range
          sub.b    #'A'-$0A,d0        ; calculate four-bit digit
          bra      4$                 ; and 'shift' in

3$        cmp.b    #'a',d0            ; check if digit is in range
                                      ; 'a'-'f'
          blt      6$                 ; if less than 'a', exit
          cmp.b    #'f',d0
          bgt      6$                 ; if greater than 'f', exit
          sub.b    #'a'-$0A,d0        ; calculate four-bit digit
          bra      4$                 ; and 'shift' in
```

```
4$          muls     #10,d1
            add.w    d0,d1          ; shift the contents of d1
            dbra     d3,1$          ; branch only if number of
                                    ; 4-bit digits
                                    ; has not exceeded 4

5$          moveq    #1,d0          ; set error flag and exit
            bra      7$

6$          cmp      #4,d3          ; check if some digits have been
            beq      5$             ; converted, error if not—branch

            moveq    #0,d0          ; no error
            tst      d2             ; return if no sign
            beq      7$
            neg      d1             ; sign set, so negate the number

7$          movem.l  (sp)+,d2/d3    ; restore d2 and d3
            rts
```

F.1.17 Convert Integer to Decimal

```
;====================================================================
; IntegerToDecimal — Converts an integer (word-size) to its equivalent
; ASCII (decimal) representation.  Call this routine with a0 holding
; the start address of the buffer, the low-word of d1 holding the
; length of the buffer, and the low-word of d0 holding the integer
; to be converted.
;                      In parameters:
;                          d0.w — integer.
;                          d1.w — length of buffer in bytes.
;                      Out parameters:
;                          a0.l — start of decimal string.
;

IntegerToDecimal

; First, fill the buffer with spaces and terminate it with a NULL byte

            subq     #2,d1          ; set for use of dbra
1$          move.b   #' ',(a0)+     ; set all bytes in string to
                                    ; spaces
            dbra     d1,1$          ; (except for the NULL byte)
            move.b   #0,(a0)        ; set NULL byte

; Check to see if the number is negative or zero and handle it

            moveq    #0,d1          ; this is the negative flag
                                    ; (cleared)

            tst      d0             ; do the test
```

```
        bgt     3$                  ; if the number is positive,
                                    ; handle normally
        beq     2$                  ; if the number is zero, do
                                    ; special case

        ; if we are here, the number is negative

        moveq   #1,d1               ; set the negative flag
        neg     d0                  ; "make" the number positive
        bra     3$

2$      move.b  #'0',-(a0)          ; put a zero in the buffer
        bra     5$


3$      cmp     #0,d0               ; branch if low-word=0
        beq     4$
        divu    #10,d0              ; divide by 10
        swap    d0                  ; remainder in low word
        ori     #$30,d0             ; make an ASCII digit
        move.b  d0,-(a0)            ; put in buffer
        move    #0,d0               ; clear low word
        swap    d0
        bra     3$

; Get ready to exit

4$      tst     d1                  ; check the negative flag
        beq     5$
        move.b  #'-',-(a0)          ; put a minus sign in the
                                    ; buffer

5$      rts
```

F.1.18 Memory Allocate

```
;==================================================================
; Malloc — (short for Memory ALLOCate) call with register d0 (long)
; holding the size of the memory block requested.  A pointer to a
; block of memory will be returned in register a0.  The start address
; of the memory block will always be on a word boundary.  The memory
; 'heap' that Malloc uses is from $5000 to $5FFF.  If Malloc cannot
; handle a request (lack of available memory), it will print an
; error message and terminate the process.  This routine is useful
; for programs which require additional storage during execution.
;          In parameters:
;              d0.l—size of requested memory block.
;          Out parameters:
;              a0.l—start of block allocated.
;
```

```
malloc
              move.l   1$,a0                ; address of the top of the
                                            ; 'heap'
              move.l   a0,d1
              add.l    d0,d1                ; add req. size to top
              btst     #0,d1                ; check if result is odd
              beq.s    2$
              addq     #1,d1                ; make new top an even address
2$            cmp.l    #$6000,d1
              bgt.s    3$                   ; abort if top > $6000
              move.l   d1,1$                ; save new top
              rts

; abort

3$            lea      4$,a0
              jsr      WriteString
              move     #228,d7
              trap     #14


1$            dc.l     $5000                ; address of the top of the
                                            ; heap

4$            dc.b     13,10,'NO MEMORY AVAILABLE FOR MALLOC',13,10,0
              cnop     0,2
```

F.1.19 Print Elements in a Linked List

```
;================================================================
; PrintList — This routine demonstrates traversing a linked list
; forwards and then backwards.  Each element in the list is a structure
; containing three fields, a next pointer (longword), the data (word
; — assumed to be an unsigned integer), and a previous pointer
; (longword).  The routine expects the address of the head of the list
; in a0, which it leaves unchanged.  This subroutine makes use of the
; subroutines WriteString, IntegerToDecimal, and WriteEOL.
;               In parameters:
;                   a0.l — start of list.
;

NEXT    set     6
INFO    set     4
PREV    set     0
NULL    set     $00000000

PrintList

; printf("forward\n");
```

```
        movem.l  a0-a1,-(a7)        ; save register
        lea      For(pc),a0         ; first, print the list forward
        jsr      WriteString
        movem.l  (a7)+,a0-a1
        move.l   a0,a1

; while (ptr != NULL)

2$      move.l  a0,d0
        beq     1$

;       printf("%d0,ptr->info);

        movem.l  a0-a1,-(a7)
        move.w   INFO(a0),d0
        moveq    #6,d1
        lea      buffer(pc),a0
        jsr      IntegerToDecimal
        lea      buffer(pc),a0
        jsr      WriteString
        jsr      WriteEOL
        movem.l  (a7)+,a0-a1

;       tmp = ptr;

        move.l  a0,a1

;       ptr = ptr->next;

        move.l  NEXT(a0),a0
        bra     2$
; }

;       ptr = tmp
1$      move.l a1,a0

; printf("backward\n");

1$      movem.l  a0-a1,-(a7)
        lea      Bac(pc),a0         ; second, print the list backward
        jsr      WriteString
        movem.l  (a7)+,a0-a1

; while (ptr != NULL) {

4$      move.l  a0,d0
        beq     3$

;       printf("%d0,ptr->info);
```

```
        movem.l  a0-a1,-(a7)
        move.w   INFO(a0),d0
        moveq    #6,d1
        lea      buffer(pc),a0
        jsr      IntegerToDecimal
        lea      buffer(pc),a0
        jsr      WriteString
        jsr      WriteEOL
        movem.l  (a7)+,a0-a1

;     ptr = ptr->prev;

        move.l   PREV(a0),a0
        bra      4$
; }

3$      rts

For     dc.b     'Forward',13,10,0
Bac     dc.b     'Backward',13,10,0
buffer  ds.b     6

        cnop     0,2
```

Index

Absolute (memory direct) addressing, 295–96, 330
Abstract data types, 21
Access time, 122
Accumulator architecture, 121–22
ACIA, *See* Asynchronous communication interface adapters (ACIA)
Activation record, 454–55
Adders, 13, 90–93, 211
Addition:
  of binary numbers, 34–35, 146–48, 343–50
  of decimal integers, 33–34, 417–18
  of hexadecimal numbers, 35–36
  two's complement representation, 46
Address, 107
Address bus, 108
Address bus errors, 497, 501–4
Address field, 231, 235
Addressing modes, 292–303
  categories of, 333–34
  immediate addressing schemes, 293–94
  memory addressing schemes, 295–301
    absolute (memory direct) addressing, 295–96
    deferred (double-indexed) addressing, 300–301
    indirect addressing with displacement, 297
    indirect addressing with index, 297
    program counter relative addressing, 299–300
    register indirect addressing, 296
    register indirect addressing with postincrement, 298
    register indirect addressing with predecrement, 298–99

    scaled indirect addressing with index, 297–98
  purpose of, 302–3
  register addressing schemes, 294–95
  use of, 301–2
Address register direct addressing, 326
Address register indirect addressing, 327
  with displacement, 328–29
    with index and displacement, 329
  with postincrement, 327–28
  with predecrement, 328
Address registers, 118, 142, 144, 304–5
Address space, 108
Algorithms, 2
  decryption algorithm, 600
  distributed adaptive algorithms, 589–90
  hot-potato algorithm, 590
  public key encryption algorithms, 600–601
  routing algorithms, 578, 588–90
Alignment, words, 111–12
Alphabet, machine language, 6
Alternating bit protocol (ABP), 588
ALU, *See* Arithmetic logic unit (ALU)
AND function block, 214–15
Application administration view, 19–20
Application programs, 14, 15
Architecture, 8–12, 238–39
  cache, 239
  function unit, 238
  Harvard architecture, 238
  IBM 360/370 system, 8–10
  illustrative examples, 286–89
  MC68000 system, 11–12
  MC68010, 505
  MC68020/MC68030, 286–87

  MC68040, 287
  MC88100, 287–89
  pipelining, 238–39
  Von Neumann architecture, 238
Arithmetic logic unit (ALU), 13, 210, 211–20, 239
  AND function block, 214–15
  conceptual circuit realization, 215–17
  MINUS function block, 215
  NEG function block, 214
  OR function block, 215
  PLUS function block, 215
  status lines, 217–20
    C bit, 220
    N bit, 220
    V bit, 218, 219
    X bit, 220
    Z bit, 217
  XFR function block, 213–14
Arithmetic region, CPU, 262–64
Arithmetic shifts, 399–403
ARPANET, 571, 579, 621, 623
ASCII (American Standard Code for Information Interchange), 113, 600, 625, 670–71
ASM68, 180–93, 643
  comments, 183–85
  constants, 184–85
  directives, 188–92
  expressions, 184–85
  instructions, 186–88
  invocation of, 643
  mode specification/operand notation, 183
  name field, 182
  opcode field, 183
  symbols, 182
ASM68K, 658–69
  directives, 335–39, 471, 663–67
    assembly control directives, 337, 663
    conditional assembly directives, 338, 477, 479, 664–65

ASM68K (*cont.*)
data definition directives, 335–36, 664
external directives, 463, 668
general directives, 338, 667
listing control directives, 338, 664
macro directives, 471, 665–67
section directive, 462, 667–68
symbol definition directives, 336, 663
fields, 319–39, 659–63
comment field, 339, 662–63
comments, 339, 659
label field, 320, 659–60
name field, 320
opcode field, 320, 660
operand field, 321, 660–62
invoking, 658–59
linker, 463–67, 668–69
manual, 618–59
register notation, 325
relocatable switch, 667
symbols, 320
Assemblers, 14, 15, 180
source module, 180–86
See also ASM68; ASM68K
Assembly language, 180–93, 319–436
position-dependent vs. position-independent code, 339–42
Associative operators, 48
Asynchronous communication interface adapters (ACIA), 533–46
control register, 537–38
to device communication, 535–40
I/O programming, 540–46
interrupt-driven I/O, 542–46
programmed I/O, 540–42
pin assignments, 535–36
principal components of, 534–35
registers, 536–40
status register, 538–40
Asynchronous communications controller, 131–32
Asynchronous serial communications, 511–12
Automatic repeat request (ARQ), 587

Backplane, 11
Barrel shifter, 210, 220
Baud rate generator, 512
Binary coded decimal (BCD), 415
Binary integer arithmetic, 343–67
addition, 34–35, 146–48, 343–50
condition code, 343–44
extended operations, 348–49

immediate and quick operations, 346–48
multiprecision arithmetic, 349–50
regular operations, 345–46
data:
clearing of, 365
comparison of, 361–63
division, 40, 152–54, 357–59
exchanging contents of two registers, 365–66
extending data in data register, 367
immediate operations, 363
multiplication, 38–39, 150–52, 355–57
negation of binary integers, 359–61
extended operations, 360–61
regular operations, 359–60
sign of a binary integer, testing, 364
subtraction, 37, 149–50, 350–55
condition code, 351
extended operations, 354–55
immediate and quick operations, 352–53
regular operations, 351–52
swapping words of data register, 366
Binary number system, 26
unsigned integer representation, 27–28
Binary operations, 4
Binary operators, 48
Bipolar technology, 75–80
diode transistor logic (DTL), 75, 77–78
emitter coupled logic (ECL), 75, 80
input injection logic (IIL), 75, 79–80
resistor transistor logic (RTL), 75, 77–78
transistor transistor logic (TTL), 75, 78–79
Bit pipe, 591–92
Bits, testing/setting, 412–15
Bit-stuffing, 586–87
Block addressable devices, 128
Block multiplexor channel, 10
Boolean algebra, 49–57
axioms and theorem construction, 53–57
operator interpretation, 49–52
Boolean logic, 48–74
boolean algebra, 49–57
boolean functions/circuits, 57–58
boolean representations/operator precedence, 60–62

definitions, 48–49
Karnaugh maps, 65–73
normal forms for expressions/minimization, 62–65
truth tables, 58–60
Booting, 498
Bottom-up programming, 24
Boundaries, words, 110
Branching, 164–70, 382–87
conditional branches, 166–68
unconditional branches, 164–66
Branch instructions, 383–84
Bridges, local area networks (LANs), 607–8
Broadcast communications, 583–84
Bus, width of, 108
Bus errors, 497, 501–4
Bus master, 11
Bus slaves, 11
Byte, 106, 568
Byte addressable memory, 106
Byte multiplexor channel, 10

Cache memory, 8, 9
Caches, 239, 523–25
Carrier sensed multiple access with collision detection (CSMA/CD), 609
Carry bit, 147, 150, 153, 155, 157, 158
Cascade adder, 92–93, 211
Cathode ray tube (CRT), 112
CD-ROM, 126, 129
Centralized computer system, 568–69
Centralized control, 589–90
Central Processing Unit (CPU), 8, 115–22
accumulator architecture, 121–22
control design, 220–37
clocked sequence implementation, 222–31
microprogramming implementation, 231–37
state table logic design, 220–22
design, 239–86
general-purpose register designs, 242–45
multiple-register designs, 241–42
single-register designs, 240–41
general-register architecture, 115–21
MC68000 system, 304–7
principal components of, 119
SIM68 computer, 141–43, 245–49
cycles, 247–48
design, 249–77
t-states, 248–49
Channels, 8–9, 519–20

Character strings, 113
Ciphertext, 600
Circuit symbols, 52
CISCs, 243
   architectures, 238–39
Clocked sequence implementation,
   222–31
   register transfer languages,
      223–26
   sequence control, 226–31
Clocked SR flip-flop, 95
Clocks/timing cycles, 86–89
   clocks to regulate circuit activities,
      88–89
   digital circuits, delays in, 86–88
Closed subroutines, *See* Subroutines
CMOS (complementary metal-oxide
   semiconductor), 81–83
Color table, 132
Combinational circuits, 86, 89–93
   eight-bit parallel cascade adder,
      92
   four-bit parallel cascade adder,
      92–93
   full adder, 91–92
   half adder, 90–91
Command register, 521
Commutative operators, 48
Compilers, 14
Compression, *See* Data compression
Computation unit, 210–37
   arithmetic logic unit (ALU), 13,
      210, 211–20, 239
   barrel shifter, 210, 220
   CPU control design, 220–37
Computer communications, 133–37
   multiprocessng, 135–37
   networks, 134–35
Computer networking, *See* Networks
Computer programs, 2–3
Computer systems, 4–20
   Central Processing Unit (CPU),
      115–22
   computer communications,
      133–37
   hardware layer, 5–13
   I/O device interaction, 130–33
   main memory organization,
      106–15
   principal components of, 106–39
   secondary storage, 122–30
   software layer, 13–19
   user layer, 19–20
   See also specific topics
Computing, historical perspective
   on, 567–72
Conditional assembly, 477–81
Conditional branches, 166–68
Condition field, 231
Congestion control, 590–91

Conjunctive normal form (CNF), 64,
   74
Constants, 335–37
   assembly-time constants, 336–37
   run-time constants, 335–36
Controller, 7–8, 10
Control lines, 202–3
Control points, 203
Control register:
   ACIA, 537–38
   timer, 558–60
Control store, 231–32
Control word, 231, 236–37
Conversion, 29–33, 421–24
   from base *r* to decimal, 29
   from decimal to base *r*, 29–31
   from/to hexadecimal to/from
      binary, 31–33
Counter preload register, timer,
   557–58
Counter register, timer, 554–56
CPU, *See* Central Processing Unit
   (CPU)

Daisy chain, 517
DASD, *See* Direct-access storage
   devices (DASD)
Data, 4
Data bus, 108–9
Data compression, 596–600
   entropy, 596, 599
   Huffman encoding, 596, 598–99
   online encoding/offline encoding,
      596, 597–98
Data cycle, 227
Data encryption standard (DES),
   600–601
Data register direct addressing, 326
Data registers, 118, 141, 144, 156–57
   extending data in, 367
   MC68000 system, 304
   swapping words of, 366
Data structure specification lan-
   guage, 594
Data transfer acknowledge (DTACK)
   signal, 499, 500
Data value specification language,
   594
Decimal arithmetic, 33–37, 415–20
   addition, 33–34, 417–18
   negation of decimal integer, 420
   subtraction, 36–37, 418–20
Decoders, 200–202, 208, 257,
   260–61
Decryption algorithm, 600
Dedicated view, 19
Default routing, 616
Deferred (double-indexed) address-
   ing, 300–301
Definition block, 223–24

Delay, networks, 606
Demultiplexers, 204
Device control block (DCB), 520
Diminished radix-complement,
   41–42
Diodes, 75–76
Diode transistor logic (DTL), 75,
   77–78
Direct-access storage devices
   (DASD), 126–30
   disk architecture, 128
   disk capacity, 127
   fixed vs. fixed head disks, 128
   floppy disks, 129
   general characteristics of, 126–27
   optical disks, 129–30
   seek and latency time, 127–28
Directives:
   ASM68, 188–92, 335, 337–39
   ASM68K, 663–67
Direct memory access (DMA), 121,
   510–12
   channels, 519–20
   NS32490C Ethernet controller,
      520–22
Disjunctive normal form (DNF), 62,
   74
Disk-drive controllers, 130–31
Dispatcher, 17–18
Distributed adaptive algorithms,
   589–90
Divide by zero exception, 489–91
Division, of binary numbers, 40,
   152–54, 357–59
DMA, *See* Direct memory access
   (DMA)
DTACK, *See* Data transfer acknowl-
   edge (DTACK) signal
DTL, *See* Diode transistor logic
   (DTL)
D-type flip-flop, 96–97
Dual Inline Package (DIP), 84
Dumping memory, 169–70

**EBCDIC (extended binary coded
   decimal interchange code),
   112–13, 625**
ECL, *See* Emitter coupled logic
   (ECL)
Editors, 14
Educational Computer Board (ECB),
   533–66
   asynchronous communication
      interface adapters (ACIA),
      533–46
   control register, 537–38
   to device communication,
      535–40
   I/O programming, 540–46
   pin assignments, 535–36

Educational Computer Board (*cont.*)
principal components of,
534–35
registers, 536–40
status register, 538–40
parallel interface/timer (PI/T),
533–54
parallel interface portion of,
549–54
principal components of,
546–54
timer, 554–66
components, 554
control register, 558–60
counter preload register,
557–58
counter register, 554–56
interrupt vector register, 561
programming with, 561–66
status register, 560–61
Effective address, 144, 160–62
Effective address region, CPU,
253–56
Effective procedure, 2
Eight-bit parallel cascade adder, 92
Electrically alterable programmable
read-only memory
(EAPROM), 115
Electrically erasable programmable
read-only memory (EEP-
ROM), 115
Electronic signatures, public key
encryption and, 601
Electro-optical disks, 126, 129
Emitter coupled logic (ECL), 75,
80
Enable line, 99
Encapsulated messages, 575
Encoders, 199–202
See also Decoders
Encryption, 600–601
Entity, 579–80
Equipment costs, networks, 605
Erasable programmable read-only
memory (EPROM), 115
Ethernet, 132, 609
NS32490C Ethernet controller,
520–22
See also Networks
Exception handler, 484
Exceptions, 483–503
classification of, 483
exception processing:
in MC68010, 505
in MC68020, 505–6
in MC68030, 506
exception vector table, 487
external exceptions, 497–504
high-level view of, 484
internal exceptions, 489–97

nested exceptions, 504
RTE instruction, 488
See also External exceptions;
Internal exceptions
Exception vector number, 484
Exception vector table, 485, 486
Execution, 2–3, 7, 14
Execution cycle, 222, 228, 240,
272–75
Expedited data, 588
Extend bit, 147, 150, 153, 155
External exceptions, 497–504
bus error, 501–4
interrupts, 498–501
reset exception, 497–98
See also Exceptions; Internal
exceptions

**Fetch cycle, 117, 222, 227, 240, 269,
270**
Fiber Distributed Data Interface
(FDDI), 611–12
Field-effect transistors (FETs), 80
Fields, ASM68K, 659–63
Files, 7
File support, operating system,
18–19
First-level interrupt handler, 17
Fixed-head disks, 128
Fixed-point numbers, 26
Fixed-point register, 118
Flip-flops, 93–99
D-type flip-flop, 96–97
JK flip-flop, 98–99
SR flip-flop, 93–96
T-type flip-flop, 97–98
Floating-point numbers, 26
Floating-point register, 118
Floppy disks, 7, 129
Flow control, 588
Four-bit parallel cascade adder,
92–93
Frame format, 616–18
Internet protocol (IP), 616
Transmission control protocol
(TCP), 618
Frame pointer register, 454
Frames, 454–55, 527, 585
Frame transmission technique,
587–88
Ftp (file transfer protocol), 608,
623–26
data type, 624, 625
file protection, 626
file type, 624, 625
transmission mode, 624, 625–26
Full adder, 91–92
Function encoding, 237
Function fields, 231, 235–36
Function unit, 238

Gallium arsenide technology, 83
Gate propagation delay, 87
Gates, 13, 52
bipolar technology, 75–80
circuit characteristics, 75
gallium arsenide technology, 83
integrated circuits and IC packag-
ing, 83–85
unipolar technology, 80–83
General-purpose register designs,
242–45
CISCs, 243
RISCs, 243–45
General-register architecture,
115–21
Global congestion control, 591
Graphical user interfaces (GUIs),
569
Graphics controller, 132
Gray scales, 132

Half adder, 90–91
Half-duplex control, 592
Hardware, 1, 5–13, 74
Central Processing Unit (CPU), 8
computer architecture, 8–12
controller, 7–8
inner layers of, 12–13
I/O devices, 6
primary storage, 5–6
secondary storage, 6–7
See also Software
Harvard architecture, 238
Hexadecimal numbers:
addition of, 35–36
multiplication of, 39
subtraction of, 38
Hexadecimal number system, 26
unsigned integer representation,
28–29
High-order bit, 106–7, 110
HMOS, 80–81
Hop, 134
Horizontal microprogramming,
236–37
Hosts, 134
Hot-potato algorithm, 590

IBM 360/370 system, 8–10
cache memory, 9
channel, 8–10
ICI, *See* Interface control informa-
tion (ICI)
ICMP, *See* Internet Control Message
Protocol (ICMP)
IDN, *See* Integrated Digital Network
(IDN)
IIL, *See* Input injection logic (IIL)
Illegal instruction exceptions,
493–95

To Debra and Kathleen

Computer Organization and the MC68000

Panos E. Livadas
University of Florida

Christopher Ward
Auburn University

PRENTICE HALL, Englewood Cliffs, NJ 07632

Library of Congress Cataloging-in-Publication Data

Livadas, Panos E.
  Computer organization and the MC68000 / Panos E. Livadas,
Christopher Ward.
    p. cm.
  Includes index.
   1. Computer organization. 2. Assembler language (Computer
program language) 3. Motorola 68000 (Microprocessor)--Programming.
I. Ward, Christopher, II. Title
QA76.9.C643L58 1993
004.165--dc20
                 92-24684
                 CIP

Acquisitions editor: **WILLIAM ZOBRIST**
Editorial/production supervision and
 interior design: **RICHARD DeLORENZO**
Copy editor: **ANDREA HAMMER**
Cover design: **KAREN MARSILIO**
Prepress buyer: **LINDA BEHRENS**
Manufacturing buyer: **DAVID DICKEY**
Editorial assistant: **DANIELLE ROBINSON**
Supplements editor: **ALICE DWORKIN**

The author and publisher of this book have used their best efforts in preparing this book. These efforts include the development, research, and testing of the theories and programs to determine their effectiveness. The author and publisher make no warranty of any kind, expressed or implied, with regard to these programs or the documentation contained in this book. The author and publisher shall not be liable in any event for incidental or consequential damages in connection with, or arising out of, the furnishing, performance, or use of these programs.

Printed in the United States of America

10 9 8 7 6 5 4 3 2 1

ISBN 0-13-158940-7

Prentice-Hall International (UK) Limited, London
Prentice-Hall of Australia Pty. Limited, Sydney
Prentice-Hall Canada Inc., Toronto
Prentice-Hall Hispanoamericana, S.A., Mexico
Prentice-Hall of India Private Limited, New Delhi
Prentice-Hall of Japan, Inc., Tokyo
Simon & Schuster Asia Pte. Ltd., Singapore
Editora Prentice-Hall do Brasil, Ltda., Rio de Janeiro

SIM68K, 647–54
  .An, .Dn, .PC, .SSR, .USR,
    649–50
  BF (block fill) command, 650
  breakpoints, 651–52
  BR command, 651
  DF (display formatted) command,
    648
  environment, 647–48
  EX (exit) command, 652
  GO command, 650–51
  LO (load) command, 652
  MD (memory dump) command,
    648–49
  MM (memory modify) command,
    649
  NDBR command, 651
  Register Modify command,
    649–50
  ST (store) command, 652
  TRAP #14 I/O functions, 653–54
  TR (trace) command, 651
  using, 653
Single bus architecture, 11
SMTP (Simple Mail Transfer Proto-
    col), 628–31
  header specification, 629
  mailbox specification, 629
  mail composition/retrieval, 628–29
  mail transfer dialog, 629–30
  routing information, 629
Software, 4, 13–19
  costs, networks, 605
  operating system, 14–16
  layers of, 15–19
  See also Hardware
Software for the text, 640
Source routing, 589, 616
Space interval, 88
Spurious interrupts, 497, 500
SR flip-flop, 93–96
  clocked, 95
  master-slave, 95–96
Stack/stack pointer, 440–41
State dependent circuits, 86
Statement block, 223–24
State table logic design, 220–22
Static RAM, 208
Status lines, ALU, 217–20
Status register, 118, 142–43, 239
  ACIA, 538–40
  MC68000 system, 305–6
  timer, 560–61
Stop, 169
Storage cells, 206
Subnets, 134
  design, 604–7
    design methodology, 606–7
    network performance metric,
      606

Subroutines, 437–70
  calling, 441–43
  external subroutines, 461–67
  in high-level language environ-
    ment, 454–60
    concept of a frame, 454–55
    using LINK/UNLK instruc-
      tions, 456–60
  internal subroutines, 461
  passing parameters, 446–49
    using parameter blocks, 448–49
    using registers, 447
    using stacks, 449
  recursive routines, 449–53
  returning from, 443–46
  stack, 440–41
  standard parameter convention,
    468
  subroutine libraries, 468–70
    input-output, 469
    language support, 468
    operating system support, 469
    special applications, 469
    static vs. dynamically linked
      libraries, 469–70
Substitution cells, 601
Subtraction:
  of binary numbers, 37, 149–50,
    350–55
  of decimal integers, 36–37,
    418–20
  of hexadecimal numbers, 38
  two's complement representation,
    46–47
Supervisor mode, MC68000, 307
Swapping, 156–58
Symbols, 320
  ASM68, 320
Synchronization points, 592
Synchronous data transfer, 511
System administrators, 15
System clock, 88
System component implementation,
  199–291
Systems administration view, 19, 20
Systems network architecture (SNA),
  569
System stack pointer (SSP), 305
System utilities, 15

Tasks, 15
TCP/IP internetworking, 608,
  612–31
  Internet addressing, 613–14
  Internet protocol (IP), 615–18
  transmission control protocol
    (TCP), 618–20
Telnet (remote log-in), 608, 620,
  621–23
Test and set/clear operations, 412–15

Three-operand instructions, 302
Throughput, networks, 605
Timer, 554–66
  components, 554
  control register, 558–60
  counter preload register, 557–58
  counter register, 554–56
  interrupt vector register, 561
  programming with, 561–66
    interrupts, 561, 562
    multitasking, 561–66
  status register, 560–61
Timing and control region, CPU,
  264–68
Timing cycles, See Clocks/timing
  cycles
Token Bus, 586, 611
Token management, 592–93
Token Ring, 132, 586, 609–10
Top-down programming, 21–24
Trace exception, 489
Transistors, 12, 74, 76–77
Transistor transistor logic (TTL), 75,
  78–79
Transmission control protocol
  (TCP), 608, 618–20
Transmission line encoding, 594
Trap exceptions, 495–96
Tristate buffers, 205–6
Truth tables, 50, 58–60
  don't-care conditions, 60
t-state, 89, 248–49
TTL, See Transistor transistor logic
  (TTL)
T-type flip-flop, 97–98
Two-operand instructions, 302
Two's complement representation,
  44, 45–47
  addition, 46
  multiplication, 47
  subtraction, 46–47

Unary operations, 4
Unary operators, 48
Unconditional branches, 164–66
Unimplemented instruction exceptions, 491–93
Unipolar technology, 80–83
Unpacked decimal representation,
  415
Unsigned integer arithmetic, 33–40
  addition, 33–36
  division, 40
  multiplication, 38–39
  subtraction, 36–38
Unsigned integer representation,
  27–29
  binary number system, 27–28
  hexadecimal number system,
    28–29

Index

Unsigned integers, 26–27
User layer, 19–20
User (problem) mode, MC68000, 307
User programs, 14, 15
User stack pointer (USP), 305
Utilization, networks, 606

Valid peripheral address (VPA), 499
Vampire tap, 609
Variables, 48
VAX 11/780 instruction set, 243
Vector processing, 137
Versa module europe (VME) bus, 11

Vertical microprogramming, 237
Virtual machine, 15–16
Virtual memory, 525–31
  paging, 527–31
    segmentated paging, 530–31
  segmentation, 525–27
Volatile memory, 6
Von Neumann architecture, 238

Wide area network (WANs), 604
Word boundaries, 110
Words, 109–15, 310, 344, 557
  alignment, 111–12
  character representation, 112–15
    ASCII, 113

    collating sequence, 113–15
    EBCDIC, 112–13
  longwords, 111, 310, 344, 557
Working registers, 118
Workstations, 571
WORM (write once read many) devices, 126, 129
Writable control store, 231

XFR function block, 213–14
XSIM68K, 654–56

Zero bit, 147, 150, 153, 155, 157, 158
Zero-operand instruction, 302

Mode specification (MS), 144
Modular programming, 21
Modules, 21–22
Morse code, 599–600
MOSFET technology, 80–82
Most significant bit, 106–7, 110
Movable-head disks, 128
Moving data, 367–82
    CCR/SR operations, 373, 374
    immediate operations, 371–72
    pushing/loading of an EA,
        377–82
    quick operations, 373
    regular operations, 369–70
    saving/restoring contents of set of
        registers, 375–77
    USP operations, 373, 374
Multiple application view, 19
Multiplexers/demultiplexers, 202–5
Multiplication:
    of binary numbers, 38–39,
        150–52, 355–57
    of hexadecimal numbers, 39
    two's complement representation,
        47
Multiprocessing, 135–37
Multiprocessor systems:
    design considerations, 532–33
    TAS instruction, 533
Mutual exclusion, 18

Name servers, 591, 613
Negation of binary integers,
    359–61
    extended operations, 360–61
    regular operations, 359–60
Negation of decimal integers, 420
Negative bit, 147, 150, 153, 155,
    157, 158
NEG function block, 214
Nested exceptions, 504
Network controller, 132–33
Networks, 134–35, 567–639
    advantages/disadvantages of,
        572–74
    circuit switched networks,
        575–76
    classes of:
        bus, 577
        directed graph, 577, 578
        ring, 577, 578
        star, 577–78
    connectionless services, 576
    connection-oriented service,
        576–77
        datagrams, 576–77
        virtual circuits, 576–77
    definition of, 574
    design, 604–8
        LAN design, 607–8
        subnet design, 604–7

Internet protocols, 608–31
ISDN, 631–37
ISO/OSI reference model,
    579–604
message switched networks,
    575–76
packet switched networks,
    575–76
service providers, 579
terminology/configurations,
    574–78
    hop, 574–75
    message, 575
    node, 574
    packet, 575
    path, 574
    subnet, 574
    See also Ethernet; Internet;
    Internet protocols; ISO/OSI
    reference model; Subnets;
    TCP/IP internetworking
Network virtual file, 623–24
Network virtual terminal (NVT),
    622
NMOS, 80–81
NNTP (Network News Transfer Pro-
    tocol), 631
Nonvolatile memory, 6
NS32490C Network Interface Con-
    troller, 520–22
Number systems, 26–47
    conversion from one base to
        another, 29–33
    signed integer representation,
        40–44
    two's complement representation,
        45–47
    unsigned integer arithmetic,
        33–40
    unsigned integer representation,
        27–29

Octet, 568
Offset, 165
One-operand instructions, 302
One's complement representation,
    43
Opcodes, 4, 210, 320–21, 471
Open subroutines, See Macros
Operand addressing, 143–44
Operating system, 14–16
    functions, 16
    interface to, 17
    layers of, 15–19
Operating system library, 469
Operation mode field, 310
Operator precedence, boolean opera-
    tors, 60–62
Operators, 21
Optical disks, 129–30
OR function block, 215

Overflow, 46
Overflow bit, 147, 150, 153, 155,
    157, 158

Packed decimal, 415
Page start/page stop registers, 521
Paging, 527–31
    address translation for, 529
    segmented paging, 530–31
    address translation using, 531
Parallel interface/timer (PI/T),
    533–54
    I/O programming with parallel
        ports, 554
    parallel interface portion of,
        549–54
        port general control register
            (PGCR), 549–52
        port interrupt vector register
            (PIVR), 553
        port service request register
            (PSRR), 552–53
        port status register (PSR), 554
        port x alternate register (PxAR),
            554
        port x data register (PxDR),
            553–54
    principal components of, 546–54
Parallel load registers, 99, 101–2,
    220
PC memory indirect
    postindexed/preindexed, 316
PC-relative addressing:
    with displacement, 330–32
    with index and displacement, 332
Peer entities, 580
Permutation cells, 601
Piggybacking, 588
Pipelining, 238–39
PI/T, See Parallel interface/timer
    (PI/T)
Pixels, 132
Plaintext, 600
PLUS function block, 215
PMOS, 80–81
Point-to-point communication link,
    583
Polling, 500, 517
Portmapper, 614
Positional number systems, 27
Positive acknowledgment protocol,
    587
Prefix notation, 4
Primary storage, 5–6
    See also Secondary storage
Principle of duality, 63
Privileged instruction exception,
    491
Program counter register, 118, 142,
    239
    MC68000 system, 305

Index

Program counter relative addressing, 299–300
Program (location) counter, 117
Programmable read-only memory (PROM), 115
Programmed I/O, 515
Programming design techniques, 20–24
   bottom-up programming, 24
   middle-out programming, 24
   top-down programming, 21–24
Protocol data unit (PDU), 580
Protocols, 580
Pseudocode, 2
Public key encryption algorithms, 600–601

Radix-complement, 42–43
Random access memory (RAM), 115, 208–10
Read write memory (RWM), 115
Real number arithmetic, 420–32
   converting from one base to another, 421–24
   internal representation of real numbers, 424–32
      binary arithmetic, 424–25
      decimal arithmetic, 425–26
      floating-point arithmetic, 426–32
Re-entry point, 438
Register access region, CPU, 256–62
Register address, 144
Register addressing schemes, 294–95
Register dumps, 169–70
Register indirect addressing, 296
   with postincrement, 298
   with predecrement, 298–99
Register notation, ASM68, 324–25
Registers, 99–102, 116–18
   ACIA, 536–40
   parallel load registers, 99, 101–2
   serial shift registers, 99–102
Register-to-memory transfers, 160–62
Register-to-register transfers, 159–60
Register transfer languages, 223–26
Relocatable loader, 342
Reset exception, 497–98
Resistor transistor logic (RTL), 75, 77–78
Resources, 15
Return address, 438
Reverse path forwarding, 590
RISCs, 243–45
   addressing modes, 316–17
   architectures, 238–39
Rotations, 406–12
   extended rotations, 410–12
   simple rotations, 407–10

Routers, local area networks (LANs), 608
Routing algorithms, 578, 588–90
   adaptive, 589–90
   local information, 590
   nonadaptive, 589
Routing tables, 589, 616
RTL, *See* Resistor transistor logic (RTL)

Sample routines, 672–87
SASD, *See* Sequential access storage devices (SASD)
Scaled indirect addressing with index, 297–98
Secondary storage, 6–7, 122–30
   direct-access storage devices, 126–30
   sequential access storage devices, 123–25
   See also Primary storage
Sector addressable devices, 128
Segmentated paging, 530–31
Segmentation, 525–27
Selector channel, 10
Semaphore mechanism, 17–18
Semiconductors, 74–75
Sendmail (mail transfer protocols), 608
Sequence control, 226–31
Sequence control fields, 231
Sequencer, 231
Sequential access storage devices (SASD), 123–25
   density/capacity/use, 124–25
   general characteristics, 123
   magnetic tape,
      advantages/disadvantages of, 125
   vertical and longitudinal parity check, 124
Sequential circuits, 86, 93–102
   flip-flops, 93–99
   registers, 99–102
Serial asynchronous communications, 511–12
Serial shift registers, 99–102
Shared memory systems, 136
Shift registers, 13
Shifts, 399–406
   arithmetic shifts, 399–403
   logical shifts, 403–6
Short branch, 165
Signed integer representation, 40–44
   one's complement representation, 43
   sign-magnitude representation, 40–43
   two's complement representation, 44

Signed integers, 26–27
SIM68, 140–98, 641–46
   assembly language, 180–93
   Central Processing Unit (CPU), 141–43
      address registers, 142
      data registers, 141
      program counter register, 142
      status register, 142–43
   coding/executing machine language programs, 170–79
   CPU design, 245–77
      arithmetic region, 262–64
      effective address region, 253–56
      microinstruction sequencing, 268–77
      register access region, 256–62
      timing and control region, 264–68
   DF (display formatted) command, 645–46
   EXIT command, 648
   HELP command, 648
   instruction set, 212
   invoking, 644
   machine language, 143–70
      branching, 164–70
      instructions, 145–56
      moving data around, 158–64
      operand addressing, 143–44
      swapping, 156–58
   main memory organization, 140–41
   MD (memory dump) command, 645–46
   microprogrammed implementation, 277–95
   object records, 177
   program counter, setting, 644
   register and memory dumps, 169–70
   Register Modify, 645
   running, 644
      textual version, 641–43
   sample program, 641–42
   system component implementation, 199–291
      architecture terminology, 238–39
      computation unit, 210–37
      CPU design, 239–86
      encoders/decoders, 199–202
      illustrative architectures, 286–89
      main memory, 206–10
      multiplexers/demultiplexers, 202–5
      tristate buffers, 205–6
   TR (trace) command, 644–45

Immediate addressing mode, 293–94, 313–14
  immediate data instructions, 313
  MC68000, 332–33
  quick data instructions, 314
IMPs, *See* Interface message processors (IMPs)
Indirect addressing:
  with displacement, 297
  with index, 297
Indirect cycle, 227
Indirect destination cycle, 248, 271–72
Indirect source cycle, 248, 269, 270
Infix notation, 4
Input injection logic (IIL), 75, 79–80
Instruction execution cycle, 120–21
Instruction execution rate, 89
Instruction fields, 231–32, 235
Instruction interpreter, 117
Instruction register, 117, 239
Instruction sequencer, 13
Integers, classes of, 26–27
Integrated circuits, 13
  and IC packaging, 83–85
Integrated Digital Network (IDN), 631
Integrated Services Digital Network, 631–37
  channel access/reference points, 633–35
  numbers/addressing, 635
  services, 632–33
  standards and, 635–36
Interface control information (ICI), 580
Interface message processors (IMPs), 134, 588–89
Internal exceptions, 489–97
  address error, 497
  CHK instruction, 496
  divide by zero exception, 489–91
  illegal instruction exceptions, 493–95
  privileged instruction exception, 491
  trace exception, 489
  trap exceptions, 495–96
  unimplemented instruction exceptions, 491–93
  See also Exceptions; External exceptions
Internal fragmentation, 528
Internal subroutines, 461
Internet:
  routing in, 620
  sample applications, 620–31
    FTP, 623–26
    NNTP, 631
    SMTP, 628–31

Telnet, 608, 620, 621–23
  See also Networks
Internet Control Message Protocol (ICMP), 618
Internet protocols, 608–31
  Fiber Distributed Data Interface (FDDI), 611–12
  IEEE 802 LAN standards, 608–11
    Ethernet, 609
    general overview, 609
    logical link control, 609
    TCP/IP internetworking, 608, 612–31
    token bus, 611
    token ring, 609–10
Interrupt acknowledge cycle, 499
Interrupt driven I/O, 515–17
  bus arbitration, 517
  daisy chain, 517
  identification/priorities, 516–17
  polling, 517
Interrupt handler, 499
Interrupt mask, 308, 499
Interrupts, 497, 498–501
Interrupt vector register, timer, 561
I/O channels, 519–20
I/O commands, 8
I/O devices, 6
  device controller, 130–33
  device drivers, 133
I/O modules, 509–15
  external interface, 510–12
  internal interface, 510, 512–15
    direct memory access (DMA), 518–22
    isolated I/O, 514–15
    memory-mapped I/O, 512–14
    interrupt driven I/O, 515–17
    programmed I/O, 515
I/O program, 7–8
I/O routines, 18
ISDN *See* Integrated Services Digital Network
Isolated I/O, 514–15
ISO/OSI Reference Model, 579–60
  application layer (layer 7), 601–4
    electronic mail, 602–3
    file transfer, 601, 602
    network news, 602, 603–4
    remote job entry, 604
    remote log-in, 601, 602
  communications model, 580–82
  data encapsulation, 579–81
  data link layer (layer 2), 584–88
    alternating bit protocol (ABP), 588
    bit-stuffing, 586–87
    flow control, 588
    frame transmission technique, 587–88

    framing, 585
    out-of-band control/in-band control, 585–86
    piggybacking, 588
    processing expedited data, 588
    token-ring/token-bus protocols, 586
  network layer (layer 3), 588–91
    function of, 588
    naming function, 591
    problems to be solved in, 589
    routing algorithms, 588–91
    routing tables, 589
  physical layer (layer 1), 582–84
    broadcast communications, 583–84
    point-to-point communication link, 583
  presentation layer (layer 6), 593–601
    data compression, 596–600
    data representation, 593–96
    encryption, 600–601
  session layer (layer 5), 592–93
  transport layer (layer 4), 591–92

JK flip-flop, 98–99
Jump instruction, 382–83

Karnaugh maps, 65–73, 74
  don't-care conditions, 72–73
  five-/six-variable maps, 71–72
  four-variable maps, 69–71
  three-variable maps, 67–69
  two-variable maps, 65–67
  using to represent maxterms, 72
Kernel, 17, 18
Keyboard, 6
k high-order/low-order bits, 110–11

LANs, *See* Local area networks (LANs)
Least significant bit, 107, 110
Lexicographical ordering, 113–14
Library monitor routine, 470
Line costs, networks, 605
Linker, 342, 463–66
Linking loader, 342
Loaders, 14
Local area networks (LANs), 520
  bridges, 607–8
  routers, 608
Local congestion/local congestion control, 590–91
Local control, 589–90
Location field, 235
Logical and bit operations, 387–415
  and operator, 392–94
    condition code, 393–94
    immediate operations, 392–93

Logical and bit operations (*cont.*)
  regular operations, 392
  eor operation, 396–98
  not operator, 398
  or operator, 394–96
    immediate operations, 395–96
    regular operations, 394–95
Logical shifts, 403–6
Logic circuits, 86–102
  clocks/timing cycles, 86–89
  combinational circuits, 89–93
  sequential circuits, 93–102
Logic gates, 13
Long branch, 165
Longword boundary, 111
Longwords, 111, 310, 344, 557
Looping, 382–87
  See also Branching
Loop instructions, 384–87
Low-order bit, 107, 110

Machine language, 6
  MC68000 system, 308–14
  SIM68 computer, 143–70
Machine language instructions
      (machine code), 3, 14,
      115–16, 145–56
  coding, 310–14
Macroinstructions, 89, 222
Macros, 437, 470–76
  body, 471
  expansion of, 472–73
  header, 471
  local macro labels, 475–76
  parameters, 473–75
  trailer, 471
Magnetic disks, 7, 122, 126
Magnetic drums, 122
Magnetic tape, 7, 122, 123
  advantages/disadvantages of, 125
  density/capacity/use, 124–25
  vertical parity bit, 123
  vertical parity check, 124
Magneto-optical (MO) disks, 7, 122,
      129–30
Main memory organization, 106–15,
      206–10
  address space and bus, 108
  data bus, 108–9
  dynamic RAM, 208–10
  MC68000 system, 304
  memory capacity, 108
  memory types, 115
  smallest addressable unit, 106–7
  static RAM, 208
  unit of storage, 106
  words, 109–15
    alignment, 111–12
    character representation,
        112–15
    longwords, 111

Main storage (memory), *See* Primary
      storage; Main memory orga-
      nization
Mark interval, 88
Mark-space ratio, 88–89
Master-slave SR flip-flop, 95–96
Maxterm expansion, 63–64
MC68000 system, 11–12, 286
  addressing modes, 292–303,
      308–10
    immediate addressing schemes,
        293–94
    memory addressing schemes,
        295–301
    purpose of, 302–3
    register addressing schemes,
        294–95
    use of, 301–2
  architecture, 286
  CPU, 304–7
    address registers, 304–5
    data registers, 304
    program counter register,
        305
    status register, 305–6
  instructions, 342–432
    binary integer arithmetic,
        343–67
    branching/looping, 382–87
    decimal arithmetic, 415–20
    logical and bit operations,
        387–415
    moving data, 367–82
    real number arithmetic,
        420–32
  machine language, 308–14
    addressing modes, 308–10
    coding instructions, 310–14
    instructions, 308
  main memory organization, 304
  operating modes, 306
  supervisor mode, 307
  user (problem) mode, 307
MC68010, exception processing in,
      505
MC68020/MC68030:
  addressing modes, 314–16
  architectures, 286–87
  exception processing in, 505–6
MC68040:
  addressing modes, 314–16
  architecture, 287
MC88100 architecture, 287–89
Memory addressing schemes,
      295–301
  absolute (memory direct) address-
      ing, 295–96
  deferred (double-indexed)
      addressing, 300–301
  indirect addressing with displace-
      ment, 297

  indirect addressing with index,
      297
  program counter relative address-
      ing, 299–300
  register indirect addressing, 296
    with postincrement, 298
    with predecrement, 298–99
  scaled indirect addressing with
      index, 297–98
Memory address register, 118
Memory address register (MAR),
      118
Memory buffer register, 118
Memory capacity, 108
Memory chips, 206–8
Memory dumps, 169–70
Memory hierarchy, 523–31
  caches, 523–25
  virtual memory, 525–31
  See also Main memory organiza-
      tion
Memory indirect addressing post-
      indexed, 315–16
Memory indirect addressing pre-
      indexed, 316
Memory management processes,
      operating system, 18
Memory-mapped I/O, 512–14
Memory space, 14
Memory-to-memory transfers,
      163–64
Memory-to-register transfers,
      162–63
Memory types, 115
MESFETs, 83
Message passing, 136
Metal-oxide semiconductor (MOS)
      technology, 80
Microinstruction register, 232
Microinstructions, 89, 210, 222
Microinstruction sequencing, 268–77
  execution cycle, 272–75
  fetch cycle, 269, 270
  indirect destination cycle, 271–72
  indirect source cycle, 269, 270
  realization of MC68, 275–77
Microprocessors, 13
Microprogram counter, 232
Microprogrammable devices, 13
Microprogrammed implementation,
      277–95
Microprogramming, 231–37, 242
  control store, 231–32
  horizontal, 236–37
  sequencer, 231
  vertical, 237
Middle-out programming, 24
Minterm expansion, 62–64
MINUS function block, 215
MIPS (million instructions per sec-
      ond), 8